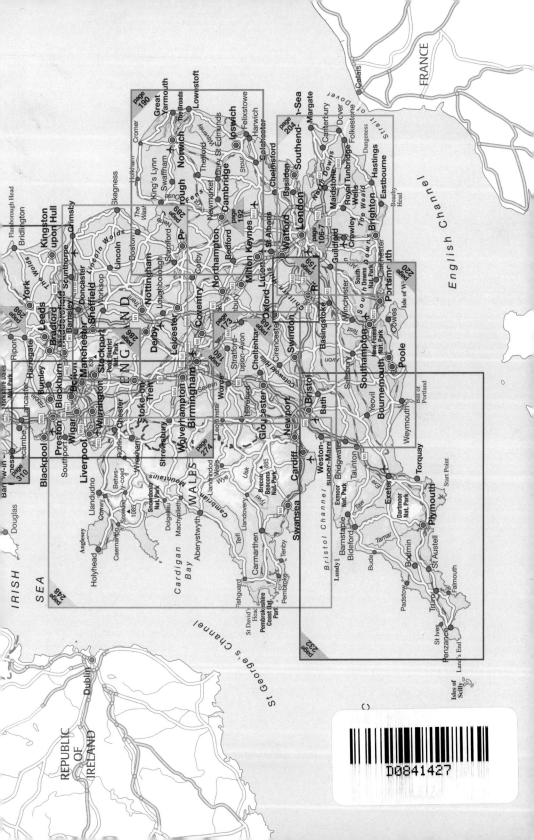

INSIGHT GUIDES
GREAT BRITAIN

APA PUBLICATIONS L
Part of the Langenscheidt Publishing Group

✖ INSIGHT GUIDE
GREAT BRITAIN

Editorial

Series Manager
Rachel Lawrence
Publishing Manager
Rachel Fox
Art Director
Steven Lawrence
Senior Picture Researcher
Tom Smyth

Distribution

UK & Ireland
**Dorling Kindersley Ltd, a Penguin
Group company**
80 Strand, London, WC2R 0RL
customerservices@dk.com

United States
Ingram Publisher Services
1 Ingram Boulevard, PO Box 3006,
La Vergne, TN 37086-1986
customer.service@ingrampublisher
services.com

Australia
Universal Publishers
PO Box 307
St Leonards NSW 1590
sales@universalpublishers.com.au

Worldwide
**Apa Publications GmbH & Co.
Verlag KG (Singapore branch)**
7030 Ang Mo Kio Avenue 5
08-65 Northstar @ AMK
Singapore 569880
apasin@singnet.com.sg

Printing

CTPS-China

©2012 Apa Publications UK Ltd
All Rights Reserved

First Edition 1984
Ninth Edition 2012

ABOUT THIS BOOK

A region with such a rich history and culture as Great Britain lends itself especially well to the approach taken by the award-winning Insight series.

The first Insight Guide pioneered the use of creative full-colour photography in travel guides in 1970. Since then, we have expanded our range to cater for our readers' need not only for reliable information about their chosen destination but also for a real understanding of that destination.

Now, when the internet can supply inexhaustible – but not always reliable – facts, our books marry text and pictures to provide that much more elusive quality: knowledge. To achieve this, they rely heavily on the authority of local writers and photographers.

How to use this book

The book is carefully structured to convey an understanding of Great Britain and its culture and to guide readers through its sights and attractions:

◆ The Features section, which has a red colour bar, covers the region's history and culture in lively, authoritative essays written by specialists.

◆ The Places section, with a blue bar, provides full details of all the sights and areas worth seeing. The chief places of interest are coordinated by number with specially drawn and cross-referenced maps. There are recommendations for restaurants and bars at the end of each chapter.

◆ The Travel Tips section, with a yellow bar, at the back of the book, offers a point of reference for information on travel, accommodations, restaurants and other practical aspects of the region. Information may be located quickly using the index printed on the back cover flap, which also serves as a bookmark.

LEFT: enjoying the beach at Wells-next-the-Sea, Norfolk.

into a manageable size? The task fell to Insight regular **Pam Barrett**, who has a history degree from London University.

Such is the density of sites and attractions in Britain that each area of the country is worth a book in its own right – and indeed many have been covered fully in Insight Guide's *Great Breaks* series, which includes titles on *Cornwall, Cotswolds, Edinburgh, Glasgow, Oxford, York* and *Bath and Surroundings*, as well as popular national park titles such as *Devon and Exmoor, Lake District* and *Snowdonia.*

Insight Guide Great Britain concentrates on must-see sights and events, with a generous sprinkling of lesser-known but rewarding destinations. The current Places chapters build on the work of previous contributors, including **Marcus Brooke**. **Roland Collins, Iain Crawford, Alyse Dar, Catherine Dreghorn, Andrew Eames, Rebecca Ford, Alexia Georgiou, Rachel Lawrence, Darroch MacKay, Paula Soper, Dorothy Stannard** and **Roger Williams**.

The stunning images that illustrate this book were taken by a host of talented photographers, including **Lydia Evans, Ming Tang Evans, Tony Halliday, William Shaw** and **Corrie Wingate**.

This edition was copy-edited by **Naomi Peck**, proof-read by **John King** and indexed by **Helen Peters**.

The contributors

This fully revised and updated edition was commissioned by series editor **Rachel Lawrence**. The principal updater was **Michael Macaroon**, a writer specializing in travel and the arts. Having lived in various parts of Britain, he is now based in London. While he enjoys the hubbub of the big city, his favourite place remains the North Norfolk coast, where he goes for bucket-and-spade holidays with his 2-year-old son.

The current history and features chapters build on the work of contributors to previous editions, including **Brian Bell, Alan Hamilton, Richard Johnson, Daniela Soave**, **Angela Wilkes** and **Roger Williams**.

It's impossible to understand modern-day Great Britain without some knowledge of its turbulent past, but how do you squeeze several thousand years of British history

Map Legend

- – – – National Boundary
- – – – County Boundary
- – ▪ – National Park
- – – – Ferry Route
- ⊖ Underground
- ✈ ✈ Airport: International/Regional
- 🚌 Bus Station
- ⓘ Tourist Information
- ✝ † ⸸ Church/Ruins
- † Monastery
- ∴ Archaeological Site
- 🏠 Mansion/Stately home
- 🏰 Castle/Ruins
- ☾ Mosque
- ✡ Synagogue
- ∩ Cave
- ⚊ Statue/Monument
- ★ Place of Interest

The main places of interest in the Places section are coordinated by number with a full-colour map (eg ❶), and a symbol at the top of every right-hand page tells you where to find the map.

Contents

LEFT: view of Somerset from Glastonbury Tor.

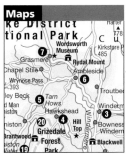

Maps

Inside front cover: Great Britain. Inside back cover: Central London.

The Best of Great Britain: Top Attractions

Packed into this compact island are hundreds of things worth seeing and doing. Those shown here give a taste of the rich and varied fare on offer

△ **The Tower of London** is one of the capital's great icons – dating back to 1078 and housing the Crown Jewels. *See page 131.*

▽ **The Cotswolds** hills are dotted with picture-postcard villages. *See pages 173.*

△ **Bath**, one of the country's finest Regency towns, has stunning architecture and was home to one of England's sharpest writers, the novelist Jane Austen. *See page 233.*

◁ **The Edinburgh Festival** is the world's largest arts festival, filling the Scottish capital with music, comedy, drama and eccentricity every August. *See page 372.*

△ **Chatsworth House** is one of Britain's finest aristocratic estates, with a fine house and gardens. *See page 288.*

△ **Stratford-upon-Avon** is Shakespeare's birthplace, shown above, and is a good base from which to explore the beautiful and historic Warwickshire countryside. *See page 181.*

△ **The Scottish Highlands** are as wild as Britain gets: deer roam the hills, salmon leap in the rivers and eagles soar overhead. *See page 339.*

▷ **Oxford**'s dreaming spires have represented one of Europe's most renowned places of learning since the 12th century. *See page 167.*

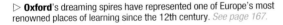

△ **Snowdonia**'s mountainous magnificence is the high spot in Wales. Its highest peak is Snowdon, at 3,560ft (1,085 metres). *See page 265.*

▷ **Durham Cathedral** is indisputably the finest Norman building in the country, dramatically perched above the River Wear. *See page 303.*

THE BEST OF GREAT BRITAIN: EDITOR'S CHOICE

Setting priorities, the sights worth seeing, best pubs and pageants, unique attractions… here, at a glance, are our recommendations, plus tips even the locals may not know

TOP ATTRACTIONS FOR FAMILIES

● **Alton Towers, Warwickshire**
Britain's best-known theme park has wild white-knuckle rides and other thrills. Not cheap. *See page 286.*

● **New Forest, Hampshire**
From the forest's free-roaming wild ponies to Peppa Pig World, a theme park based on the popular cartoon character. *See page 225.*

● **Ironbridge Gorge Museums, Telford**
Award-winning string of museums on the River Severn celebrating the "birthplace of industry". *See page 275.*

● **Natural History Museum, London**
One of the world's finest collections of dinosaur bones and an animatronic T-Rex. *See page 143.*

● **Legoland, Windsor**
Rides, shows and multiple attractions. *See page 159.*

● **Longleat Safari Park**
The first safari park outside Africa, in the grounds of a stately home. *See page 235.*

● **National Maritime Museum, Greenwich**
Recalling when Britain ruled the waves. *See page 148.*

● **Museum of Childhood, Edinburgh**
Toys, games and nurseries add up to "the noisiest museum in the world". *See page 325.*

● **SS *Great Britain*, Bristol**
A brilliant re-enactment of life on the world's first iron-hulled ship with a screw propeller. *See page 233.*

BEST FESTIVALS AND PAGEANTS

● **Chinese New Year**
London's Chinatown explodes with fire-crackers and dancing dragons. *See page 119.*

● **Edinburgh Military Tattoo**
The largest event of its kind in the atmospheric castle. *See page 324.*

● **Mela Festival**
Asian festival celebrating Bangla New Year in various cities, including Bradford and London. *See page 295.*

● **Royal National Eisteddfod of Wales**
This annual celebration of Welsh culture dates from the 12th century. *See page 372.*

● **Notting Hill Carnival**
Exuberant August parade, with West Indian bands and floats, is Europe's largest street festival. *See page 146.*

● **Trooping the Colour**
Britain honours the Queen's birthday in Horse Guards Parade, London. *See page 112.*

● **Hay-on-Wye Literary Festival**
Events for bookworms take over this literary border town each May. *See page 251.*

● **BBC Proms**
From July to September, (mostly) classical music concerts in the Royal Albert Hall. *See page 144.*

ABOVE: the Queen rides out in Trooping the Colour.
LEFT: the magnificent SS Great Britain in Bristol.

THE TOP ROYAL HOMES

● **Balmoral Castle**
The royals' Scottish home since 1848. *See page 341.*

● **Buckingham Palace**
Their London base, with Changing of the Guard. *See page 113.*

● **Caernarfon Castle**
The fortress where Charles became Prince of Wales. *See page 263.*

● **Edinburgh Castle**
This one-time Scottish royal residence is still keeper of the nation's crown. *See page 324.*

● **Hampton Court Palace, Surrey**
Henry VIII's magnificent Surrey palace has equally magnificent gardens. *See page 153.*

● **Kensington Palace**
Birthplace of Queen Victoria, and future home of Prince William and the Duchess of Cambridge. *See page 145.*

● **Palace of Holyroodhouse, Edinburgh**
The Queen's Scottish residence in early summer. *See page 325.*

● **Sandringham House**
Norfolk base for the royals at Christmas. *See page 194.*

● **Windsor Castle**
England's most famous castle is a daytrip from London. *See page 158.*

THE BEST GARDENS

● **Eden Project, Cornwall**
Futuristic glass domes are the hothouses in this award-winning, eco-friendly extravaganza. *See page 241.*

● **Powis Castle**
Tuscany comes to Wales in fine Italianate gardens. *See page 268.*

● **RHS Gardens, Wisley**
The Royal Horticultural Society's showcase. *See page 206.*

● **Royal Botanic Gardens, Kew**
Fine day out from central London to legendary gardens first planted in 1759. *See page 151.*

● **Sissinghurst Castle, Kent**
Vita Sackville-West's charming garden. *See page 209.*

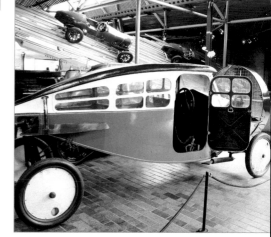

ABOVE: the National Motor Museum at Beaulieu Abbey.
BELOW: the futuristic Eden Project in Cornwall.

MOST ENTHRALLING MUSEUMS

● **Ashmolean, Oxford**
A peerless museum of art and archaeology collected by scholars from around the world. *See page 171.*

● **British Empire and Commonwealth Museum, Bristol**
Recalls the ships and traders that built the Empire. *See page 233.*

● **British Museum, London**
Embraces no less than the history of civilisation. *See page 121.*

● **Merseyside Maritime Museum**
Slavery and emigration are the abiding themes in this evocative museum in Liverpool. *See page 277.*

● **National Museum of Scotland, Edinburgh**
Attached to the Royal Museum, this new building gives a detailed history of the nation. *See page 325.*

● **National History Museum, Cardiff**
Welsh culture is celebrated in this museum of social history. *See page 254.*

● **National Media Museum, Bradford**
Covers history of film, television and photography. *See page 295.*

● **National Motor Museum, Hampshire**
Beaulieu Abbey, home of the aristocratic Montagu family, puts veteran cars on show. *See page 226.*

● **V&A, London**
The Victoria and Albert Museum houses one of the world's finest collections of decorative arts. *See page 143.*

RIGHT: the futuristic Eden Project in Cornwall.

ABOVE: Blenheim Palace's imposing facade.

TOP TRADITIONAL PUBS

- **George Inn**
Borough High Street, Southwark. London's only remaining galleried coaching inn dates from 1676 and was a haunt of Charles Dickens. *See page 139.*
- **Globe Inn**
High Street, Dumfries. "...the Globe Tavern here, which these many years has been my Howff [haunt]", wrote the Scottish bard, Robert Burns, whose memorabilia fills this 17th-century pub.
- **Ye Olde Gate Inn**
Well Street, Brassington. This Derbyshire pub has been described as the "cosiest pub in Britain". One for cold winter evenings.
- **Philharmonic**
Hope Street, Liverpool. One of the city's many Victorian glories (and John Lennon's favourite); ladies are invited to inspect the elaborate tilework in the gents if there is nobody using it. *See page 283.*
- **Pot Still**
Hope Street, Glasgow. This famous whisky pub has more than 500 different labels in store.
- **Tan Hill Inn**
Richmond, Swaledale. In the Yorkshire Dales National Park, this is the highest pub in Britain, and full of pets, from ducks to ponies.
- **Ye Olde Trip to Jerusalem**
Brewhouse Yard, Nottingham. Built into the town's castle walls, this is reputed to be England's oldest pub, dating from the 12th century when ale was healthier than most drinking water. *See page 291.*

FINEST STATELY HOMES

- **Alnwick Castle**
Home of the Dukes of Northumberland; Harry Potter flew around here in the films. *See page 305.*
- **Blenheim Palace, Oxfordshire**
This vast, English baroque pile is the family home of the Dukes of Marlborough; Winston Churchill was born here. *See page 172.*
- **Chatsworth House, Derbyshire**
Seat of the Dukes of Devonshire. *See page 288.*
- **Castle Howard, Yorkshire**
The location for adaptations of *Brideshead Revisited*. *See page 301.*
- **Hopetoun House**
Echoing the style of Versailles, the Scottish house was built for the forebears of the current resident, the Marquess of Lithgow. *See page 328.*
- **Inveraray Castle**
Scottish home of the Duke of Argyll, chief of the Clan Campbell. *See page 345.*
- **Woburn Abbey, Bedfordshire**
Home of the Dukes of Bedford, who installed a safari park to attract visitors. *See page 94.*

MOST SPECTACULAR BRITISH LANDSCAPES

- **Ben Nevis**
In the Scottish Grampians, this is the highest mountain in the British Isles. *See page 343.*
- **The Lake District**
Characterised by fells, lakes and valleys, this is an area of such natural beauty that it inspired some of the country's finest poets, including William Wordsworth. *See page 311.*
- **The West Country**
Typified by rolling hills, sleepy villages and medieval churches. *See page 231.*
- **Norfolk Beaches**
Most notably the broad, sandy expanse of Holkham Beach. *See page 197.*
- **Cornish beaches**
For Atlantic rollers, dizzying cliffs and pristine sands. *See page 236.*

LEFT: Liverpool's famous Philarmonic Dining Rooms.

LEADING ART GALLERIES

● **Baltic Centre for Contemporary Art**
The largest contemporary arts venue outside London. *See page 304.*

● **Barbara Hepworth Museum, St Ives**
The sculptor's home in an attractive Cornish fishing town. *See page 238.*

● **David Hockney Gallery, Saltaire**
Britain's most famous living artist has a permanent gallery in this splendid old mill in his native Bradford. *See page 295.*

● **National Gallery, London**
Treasures from the Renaissance to the Impressionists. *See page 109.*

● **National Gallery of Scotland, Edinburgh**
World-class display of European art. *See page 326.*

● **Tate Modern, London**
Wildly popular gallery in a former power station. *See page 134.*

● **The Lowry Centre, Manchester**
Great collection of Victorian and Pre-Raphaelite paintings. *See page 279.*

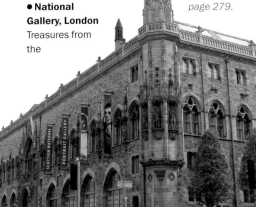

ABOVE: the Scottish National Portrait Gallery is one of several world class galleries in Edinburgh.

ABOVE: Orkney's Ring of Brodgar, dating from 2300 BC.

IMPORTANT ANCIENT SITES

● **Cerne Abbas Giant, Dorset**
The massive naked figure carved into a hillside is thought to be a pagan fertility symbol. *See page 172.*

● **Chester, Cheshire**
Roman highlights in this attractive northwestern town include the largest amphitheatre in Britain. *See page 275.*

● **Hadrian's Wall**
One of the country's most important Roman monuments, which is popular with walkers. *See page 304.*

● **Fishbourne Roman Palace, Sussex**
This archaeological site includes magnificent floor mosaics. *See page 206.*

● **Orkney**
There is evidence on the island of Neolithic farmers, dating from around 3000 BC. *See page 347.*

● **Stonehenge, Wiltshire**
Nobody is certain how or why this dramatic stone circle was erected. *See page 220.*

● **Sutton Hoo, Suffolk**
Burial site of Anglo-Saxon kings. *See page 198.*

MONEY-SAVING TIPS

● **Travel** Rail travel in Britain is expensive. You could make a saving with a GB Flexi Pass, which allows travel throughout Britain over a certain number of days in a 1-month period. There are various fare options and passes are cheaper in low season (1 Nov–28 Feb). Much cheaper but more time-consuming are buses, which cover the country. Most are run by National Express and Megabus. *See page 355.*

● **London Transport** The cheapest and easiest way to travel around is by using an Oyster card, which can be bought in advance from abroad *(see page 355)*. Children under 11 and wheelchair users travel free.

● **Eating out** Take advantage of set lunch menus, which are generally cheaper than evening menus. Some restaurants also offer what they call pre- or post-theatre meals, where you dine early or late with a (usually restricted) set menu. When eating out, ask for a jug of tap water rather than paying for bottled water. In cafés, there may be an option to take food out (takeaway): usually a cheaper option than "eating in".

● **Museums** One of the best things about visiting Britain is its many free museums. Some have late evening openings once or twice a week. City churches in London and elsewhere often put on free lunchtime concerts.

PAST AND PRESENT

Britain combines the riches of what were once three distinct nations – England, Scotland and Wales – and the three entities are still substantially defined by the legacies of their separate pasts

Britain's past reaches back to prehistory and the Bronze Age mysteries of standing stones, burial mounds and the Scottish broch. This is a land that, since 1066, has never been invaded, a land that can trace a line of descent through 62 monarchs to the current queen, Elizabeth II. And this land is the birthplace of democracy, whose citizens, since the signing of the Magna Carta in 1215, have built on that foundation for individual freedom.

Britain's history made its impact felt around the world. The circumnavigation of the globe by Francis Drake in 1577 inaugurated a great tradition of cultural exchange, of expansion and of widening objectives. Britain's is the history of an Empire whose influence once extended to all corners of the globe, and whose legacy is seen in its culturally rich, multi-racial society. Britain still plays a leading role in the Commonwealth of nations, with the Queen the head of state of 15 Commonwealth realms in addition to the UK.

British culture, whether it be the anonymous lines of the Anglo-Saxon poets, the plays of William Shakespeare, the realist novels of Charles Dickens or Thomas Hardy, or the masterpieces of the painters John Constable, Thomas Gainsborough or J.M.W. Turner, has entered into the imagination of many throughout the world. Modern British culture continues to exercise a worldwide influence; added to the historic creative legacy are the globally acclaimed magical worlds of the writers J.R.R. Tolkien and J.K. Rowling, the lyrics of the Beatles and a plethora of internationally successful bands since them, the talents of actors including Dame Judi Dench, Keira Knightley, Daniel Day-Lewis and Colin Firth, and the high-fashion creations of designers from Mary Quant to Alexander McQueen. An ever-evolving architectural, political, cultural and social landscape, and the hosting of world-class events such as the 2012 Olympics, are sure to keep Britain firmly on the global map. ❏

PRECEDING PAGES: Guardsmen at the Trooping the Colour ceremony, London; racegoers in full regalia at Royal Ascot. **LEFT:** the past on sale at Lavenham, Suffolk. **ABOVE LEFT:** Doc Marten discovers patriotism. **ABOVE RIGHT:** timber-framed house.

THE BRITISH CHARACTER

If the English are ambiguous, the Welsh loquacious and the Scots cantankerous, how do they all manage to get along on the same overcrowded island?

Millions of people in Britain, wrote George Orwell in 1947, "willingly accept as their national emblem the bulldog, an animal noted for its obstinacy, ugliness, and impenetrable stupidity." A foreigner, he went on, would find the salient characteristics of the common people to be "artistic insensibility, gentleness, respect for legality, suspicion of foreigners, sentimentality about animals, hypocrisy, exaggerated class distinctions, and an obsession with sport."

The Welsh and the Scots would point out that Orwell was thinking primarily of the English, who, to the fury of the Welsh and Scots, persistently equate the terms "British" and "English".

The contradictory English

But then the English have a gift for ambiguity. As a character in Alan Bennett's play *The Old Country* put it: "When we say we don't mean what we say, only then are we entirely serious." If

> To understand Great Britain, the British say, will take many visits. This, bearing in mind their inability to say exactly what they mean, translates as: "Although we regard tourism as terribly vulgar, we do rather need the repeat business."

that seems contradictory, there's more to come. The British continue to embrace marriage, yet their divorce rate is one of the highest in

LEFT: London mayor Boris Johnson aboard a new-model Routemaster, now used on only two routes.
RIGHT: Napoleon called the English "a nation of shop-keepers" – and shopping remains popular.

Europe. They laud family life, yet the traditional practice of the upper classes is to pack their children off to boarding school as soon as possible, and many feel they have no choice but to park their aged parents in old people's homes. They pride themselves on their solidarity in war, yet cling to a divisive class system in peacetime.

They are also famed for their tolerance and sense of humour, yet, as the writer Paul Gallico observed: "No one can be as calculatedly rude as the British, which amazes Americans, who do not understand studied insult and can only offer abuse as a substitute." Britain's nearest neighbours can be just as amazed as Americans. André Maurois advised his fellow countrymen:

"In France it is rude to let a conversation drop; in England it is rash to keep it up. No one there will blame you for silence. When you have not opened your mouth for three years, they will think, "This Frenchman is a nice quiet fellow." But, if Maurois had been in Liverpool, Glasgow or Cardiff, though, he might not have got a word in. The Englishman who has "all the qualities of a poker except its occasional warmth" probably lives in the overcrowded southeast, where standoffishness is a way of protecting precious privacy.

However, certain generalisations can be made. Because Britain is an island its people have retained their bachelor outlook despite

English history to the influence of Wales." The Welsh, for their part, have had to work hard, like many minority nations, to protect their self-esteem and culture from a strong neighbour, but have been wary of independence.

Within Wales itself, the people seem anything but homogeneous. Many in North Wales, where Welsh is still widely spoken, look down on peo-

> The gift of the gab was nourished in the 19th century, when Wales was fertile ground for preachers and trade union leaders.

marrying into the European Union. Because it has not been successfully invaded for nearly 1,000 years, Britain remains deeply individualistic. On the one hand, its people perhaps overvalue tradition – a substitute for thought, critics say; on the other hand, they tend not to kill one another in civil conflict, and they have absorbed, with relatively little civic pain, large numbers of their former imperial subjects.

The voluble Welsh

To the English, the Welsh seem ebullient, warmhearted and emotional but also rather garrulous. A certain amount of antipathy exists. Evelyn Waugh, for instance, claimed in his novel *Decline and Fall*: "We can trace almost all the disasters of

ple from South Wales whose blood is much more mixed and whose habits are thought too anglicised. Naturally, South Walians return the compliment by regarding North Walians as less progressive and less sociable.

Whether their preferred tongue is English or Welsh, however, most of the Welsh are extremely voluble. As the poet Dannie Abse commented: "The English are happy with few words and like to keep strangers at a comfortable distance from themselves. And in a train leaving England for Wales, who knows who is not English? Only when the train had passed through the Severn Tunnel, only when the passengers felt themselves to be safely in Wales, only then would the carriage suddenly hum with conversation."

The uncompromising Scots

In contrast, the Scots are seen by the English as "dour", though they'd be hard put to justify the claim in a noisy Glasgow pub. English literature is peppered with anti-Scots aphorisms, such as P.G. Wodehouse's observation that "it is never difficult to distinguish between a Scotsman with a grievance and a ray of sunshine."

The Scots' principal grievance is that the London-based parliament treats them as second-class citizens, especially when implementing its economic policies. This is far from being a new complaint, having been echoed long before the two nations united in 1707 in what

avoided Norman centralisation after the Conquest in 1066. Their religious experience also set them apart: while England absorbed the Reformation with a series of cunning compromises, Scotland underwent a revolution, replacing the panoply of Roman Catholicism with an austere Presbyterianism designed to put the people directly in touch with their God.

In many ways, the Scots character baffles the English. It combines sourness and humour, stinginess and generosity, arrogance and tolerance, cantankerousness and chivalry, sentimentality and hard-headedness. That's a potent broth.

most Scots still regard as a shotgun marriage. Indeed, when the future Pope Pius II visited the country in the 15th century, he concluded: "Nothing pleases the Scots more than abuse of the English."

That's not to say that the Scots can't cooperate with the English when it suits them: the work ethic and ingenuity of Scots played a major role in creating the British Empire. But the differences in character are long established. Unlike the English and Welsh, the Scots were never conquered by the Romans, and they also

LEFT: crab fishing off the Welsh coast; the Welsh national flag. **ABOVE:** Sir Sean Connery became a firm supporter of the Scottish National Party.

In 1997 the Scots voted to set up their own parliament in Edinburgh, and in 2011 the Scottish National Party (SNP) won a majority government for the first time ever. The SNP leader, Alex Salmond, has already promised the Scots a referendum on independence from the UK, making divorce from the English increasingly likely.

So the bonds that once tied these three distinct nations together are loosening, which raises the question of how this will affect the British, English, Welsh and Scottish characters. Traditional British stoicism (the famed stiff upper lip, so often portrayed in films), ultra-politeness and insistence on doing things fairly and behaving decently should see these islanders through however bumpy the ride to the future may be. ❏

DECISIVE DATES

PREHISTORY
5000 BC
Britain is separated from Europe by rising tides and becomes an island.

3000 BC
Stone Age people arrive.

2300 BC
Stonehenge is built.

700 BC
Celts arrive from Europe.

ROMAN OCCUPATION
55 BC
Julius Caesar heads the first Roman invasion.

AD 61
Rebellion of Boudicca, Queen of Iceini in East Anglia, is crushed.

AD 119
Romans build Hadrian's Wall to keep back Picts and Scots.

ANGLO-SAXONS AND DANES
449–550
Arrival of Jutes from Jutland, Angles from Denmark and Saxons from Germany.

563
St Columba establishes a monastery on the island of Iona, Scotland.

597
St Augustine comes as a missionary and ends up first Archbishop of Canterbury.

779
King Offa builds a dyke to keep out the Welsh.

897
Danish Vikings are defeated at sea by Alfred the Great, generally regarded as having founded the British navy.

980–1016
Viking invasions renewed.

1017
Canute, first Danish king, chosen by Witan (council).

THE NORMANS
1066
William, Duke of Normandy, conquers England; Norman barons given power and land.

1080–1100
Great monastery and cathedral building begins.

1086
The Domesday Book, a complete inventory of property in Britain, is completed.

1124
David I succeeds to the Scottish throne.

THE PLANTAGENETS
1154
Henry II, descendant of Geoffrey of Anjou, becomes the first Angevin king of England.

1170
Archbishop Thomas Becket, having defied Henry II, is killed in Canterbury Cathedral.

1215
Barons force King John to sign Magna Carta guaranteeing freedoms.

1265
First House of Commons meets at Westminster Hall.

1277–88
English conquer Wales, killing the last prince, Llewellyn ab Gruffydd.

1306
Robert Bruce is crowned King of the Scots.

1348–49
The Black Death plague kills nearly half the population.

1337–1453
Hundred Years War with France drags on.

1381
Peasants' Revolt marks the erosion of serfdom.

1387
Chaucer's *Canterbury Tales* is published.

HOUSES OF LANCASTER AND YORK

1415
Owain Glyndwr, the Welsh hero, dies.

1455–85
Wars of the Roses between the Houses of York and Lancaster.

1476
William Caxton sets up Britain's first printing press.

THE TUDORS

1485
Henry VII, grandson of the Welsh Owain Tudor, crowned.

1509
Henry VIII begins his reign at the age of 17.

1534
Henry abolishes Papal authority in England.

1535
Henry becomes Supreme Head of Church of England.

1536–39
Henry VIII dissolves 560 monasteries and religious houses.

FAR LEFT TOP: a Pict as subsequently imagined. ABOVE: London's mayor and aldermen. RIGHT: The Peasants' Revolt in 1381 saw the serfs revolt against authority.

1536
Act of Union joins England and Wales.

1558
Elizabeth I begins her 45-year reign.

1577–80
Sir Francis Drake voyages around the world.

1585
William Shakespeare begins his career in London.

1587
Mary, Queen of Scots and sister of Elizabeth I, is executed.

1588
Spanish Armada is defeated.

THE STUARTS

1603
James VI of Scotland is crowned James I of England, uniting the kingdoms.

1605
Guy Fawkes attempts to blow up parliament.

1620
Pilgrim Fathers set sail for America.

1642–49
Civil War between Royalists and Roundheads. Charles I is beheaded and the country effectively becomes a republic.

1660
Monarchy is reinstated with Charles II.

1665
The Great Plague of London.

1666
The Great Fire of London.

THE HOUSE OF HANOVER

1714
George I of Hanover, Germany, is invited to take the throne. He speaks no English and shows very little interest in his new subjects.

1721
Sir Robert Walpole becomes Britain's first prime minister, a new British concept.

1739
Wesley begins to preach Methodism.

1746
Battle of Culloden is final defeat for Stuart dynasty.

1775
James Watt builds the first steam engine.

1805
Admiral Lord Nelson is killed at Battle of Trafalgar.

1807
Abolition of the slave trade.

1815
Duke of Wellington defeats Napoleon at Waterloo.

1830
A railway is opened from Liverpool to Manchester.

THE VICTORIAN AGE
1837
Victoria becomes Queen, aged 18. She marries Albert of Saxe-Coburg in 1840.

1851
The Empire-boosting Great Exhibition is held in London.

1876
The Queen becomes Empress of India.

1890–96
Cecil Rhodes, founder of Rhodesia, becomes prime minister of Cape Colony, South Africa.

1898–1902
British fight Dutch in Boer War to settle South Africa.

THE EDWARDIAN ERA
1909
Chancellor David Lloyd George introduces old-age pensions.

1914–18
World War I. Over 1 million British and Allied soldiers die.

HOUSE OF WINDSOR (SO NAMED FROM 1917)
1918
Universal suffrage (except for women under 30).

1926
General strike by workers paralyses the nation.

1936
Edward VIII abdicates so that he can marry a divorcée, Mrs Wallis Simpson. His younger brother, Albert ("Bertie"), succeeds him as George VI.

1939–45
World War II. Fewer military casualties than in World War I, but many civilians die in heavy bombing.

1946
Labour government sets up National Health Service.

1947
Edinburgh Festival is begun, and the Welsh Eisteddfod re-established. India and Pakistan gain independence.

1951
Festival of Britain lifts spirits after postwar austerity.

1953
Queen Elizabeth II is crowned at the age of 27.

1961
Commonwealth ejects South Africa for its apartheid policy.

1962
The Beatles have their first hit, Love Me Do.

1965
Capital punishment ends.

1969
Troops sent to Northern Ireland to tackle Unionist/Nationalist sectarian strife.

1972
Northern Ireland government replaced with direct rule from Westminster.

1973
Britain joins the European Community.

1979
Margaret Thatcher is UK's first woman prime minister.

1981
Prince of Wales marries Lady Diana Spencer.

1982
Argentinian troops defeated off the Crown Colony of the Falkland Islands.

1984
IRA bomb targeting the Conservative government at its conference at Brighton kills five people.

1990
Tory party votes Margaret Thatcher out of office.

1994
First trains run through the Channel Tunnel.

1996
Shakespeare's Globe, a replica of the 16th-century theatre, opens in London.

1997
Labour wins its first general election since 1974. Diana, Princess of Wales, dies in a car crash in Paris.

1998
Northern Ireland peace accord signed.

1999
Scottish and Welsh assemblies begin to exercise a limited degree of devolution.

2003
A congestion charge is levied on cars entering central London on weekdays. Britain joins the US in going to war with Iraq.

2005
London is chosen to stage 2012 Olympic Games. On 7 July bombs explode on three Tube trains and a bus, killing more than 50 people.

2007
The new Wembley Stadium opens four years late and more than £470 million over budget. In November the new Eurostar terminal opens at St Pancras.

2008
The long boom in the stock market and house prices comes to an abrupt end.

2009
Recession officially sets in in January.

2010
The May General Elections result in a hung parliament. David Cameron's Conservatives, who win the most seats, eventually form a coalition government with Nick Clegg's Liberal Democrats.

2011
Prince William marries Catherine Middleton at Westminster Abbey.

2012
London hosts the Olympic Games.

FAR LEFT TOP: The Great Fire of London, 1666. LEFT: James I of England. RIGHT: British Olympic hopeful Tom Daley dives in at London's new aquatic centre.

BEGINNINGS

One wave of immigrants followed another, creating
a truly mongrel breed. Then came the conquerors:
the Romans, Saxons, Angles and Normans

Whence French and British construction workers met beneath the English Channel in 1990, Britain became linked to Continental Europe for the first time in 7,000 years. For it was then, when the last Ice Age ended, that melting ice flooded the low-lying lands, creating the English Channel and the North Sea, and turning Britain into an island. This fact of being "set apart" from Europe was one of two seemingly contradictory factors that would affect every aspect of the country's subsequent history. The other was a genius for absorbing every invader and immigrant, creating a mongrel breed whose energies would establish an empire incorporating a quarter of the population of the planet.

Early settlers

A race of nomadic hunter-gatherers were the earliest inhabitants. By about 3000 BC tribes of Neolithic people had crossed the water from

> The Celtic tribes are ancestors of the Highland Scots, the Irish and the Welsh, and their languages are the basis of both modern Welsh and Gaelic.

Europe, probably from the Iberian peninsula, now Spain. They were farming folk who kept animals and grew crops. The barrows which can still be found, mostly in the chalky lands of Wiltshire and Dorset, were their huge communal burial mounds.

More dramatic monuments were the henges, the most important of which was Stonehenge in Wiltshire, constructed before 2000 BC. Exactly why it was built is unknown, but it must have had religious and political significance; the massive undertaking involved in bringing bluestones all the way from Wales for part of its construction suggests that its builders had a substantial power base.

The next wave of immigrants were the Celts. They began to arrive about 700 BC and kept coming until the arrival of the Romans. They may have come from eastern and central Europe and they probably became dominant because, being ironworkers, their weapons were superior.

The Romans

British recorded history begins with the Roman invasion. Julius Caesar first crossed the English

Channel and arrived in Britain in 55 BC but, meeting resistance and bad weather, he returned to Gaul. A successful invasion did not take place until nearly a century later, in AD 43, headed by the Emperor Claudius. This time, the land they knew by its Greco-Roman name, Pretani, was subdued with relative ease, apart from the country in the far north they called Caledonia (now Scotland). To repel persistent raids by the warlike Picts, or "painted ones", the Emperor Hadrian had a wall built right across the north of England.

When the Romans left, nearly 400 years later, to defend Rome against the barbarians, they left behind a network of towns, mostly walled,

were confined to Kent, and the Angles settled in East Anglia, Mercia (the Midlands and the Welsh borders) and Northumbria, which reached to the Scottish border. In Scotland, the Picts and Scots were eventually united under King Kenneth MacAlpin.

In the mid-9th century the Danes or Norsemen, popularly known as Vikings, who had been raiding the country for almost a century and taking their booty home, decided it was time to settle. Of the local leaders, Alfred of Wessex (AD 871–901) was the only one strong enough to defeat them and come to a relatively amicable agreement. The Danes, who

many on the sites of Celtic settlements or their own military camps, and a good road network. Yet their influence faded surprisingly fast. Buildings crumbled through lack of repair and language, literacy and religion soon disappeared.

Anglo-Saxon assault

The new waves of invaders from central Europe, Saxons, Angles and Jutes, gradually pushed the native Celts westward into Wales and north into Scotland. The Saxons established their kingdoms in Essex, Sussex and Wessex (which covered most of the West Country), the Jutes

LEFT: Pict warrior. **ABOVE:** Roman mosaic found in Dorset.

established a large settlement in York, were to control the north and east of the country ("the Danelaw"), while Alfred would rule the rest. Alfred is known as "the father of the British navy" as he founded a strong fleet which first beat the Danes at sea, then protected the coasts and encouraged trade.

Alfred, said to have taught himself Latin at the age of 40, translated Bede's work into English. A learned man himself, he encouraged learning in others, established schools and formulated a legal system, and built up the army and navy, earning his title "Alfred the Great".

After the great king's death, trouble broke out again. His successors reconquered the Danelaw, but in 980 Viking invasions recommenced.

King Ethelred tried paying them to stay away by imposing a tax, called the *danegeld*, on his people. But Ethelred, whose title "The Unready" was as well earned as Alfred's, was a poor psychologist. The Danes merely grew more predatory while he grew more confused.

When his death left no strong Saxon successor, the Witan chose Canute, the Danish leader, as king. Canute proved to be a wise ruler. He divided power between Danes and Saxons and, to protect his northern border, compelled Malcolm II, king of the Scots, to recognise him as overlord. Had Canute's sons, Harold and Hardicanute, not died within a few years of him, the whole

the council advising the king chose Harold, son of Godwin, as monarch.

Harold's reign lasted less than a year. In October 1066 William of Normandy came to claim the throne. He landed at Pevensey on the Sussex coast and defeated Harold in battle on Senlac Field, near Hastings. William was crowned king in Westminster Abbey on Christmas Day and set out to consolidate his kingdom. Many Saxon nobles had died in battle while others fled to Scotland. William filled the vacuum with Norman barons and strengthened and formalised the feudal system that had begun before his arrival.

history of Britain might have been very different. As it was, the succession passed to Edward, son of Ethelred, who had spent most of his life in Normandy, the part of France settled by the Vikings.

The Norman Conquest

Edward (1042–66), known as the Confessor, was a pious man who built Westminster Abbey to the glory of God. He was also far more Norman than Saxon and soon upset his father-in-law, Earl Godwin, by filling his court with "foreign" favourites and appointing a Norman priest Archbishop of Canterbury. He is also said to have promised the English throne to William, Duke of Normandy. But, when Edward died,

THE DOMESDAY BOOK

William needed to know exactly who owned what in his new kingdom, the amount of produce he could expect and the taxes he could demand. So he sent out his clerks to compile a meticulous property record. From archbishop to ploughman: nobody was to escape the great reckoning. The massive survey, called the Domesday Book because it seemed to the English not unlike the Book of Doom to be used by the greatest feudal lord of all on Judgment Day, was completed in 1086. Today, it is kept in a specially made chest at the National Archives in Kew, London, and is a fascinating document of early social history. An online version is available (www.domesdaybook.co.uk).

His barons received their land in return for a promise of military service and a proportion of the land's produce. The barons then parcelled out land to the lesser nobles, knights and freemen, also in return for goods and services. At the bottom of the heap were the villeins or serfs, unfree peasants who were virtually slaves.

William's influence was strongest in the south. Faced with combined Saxon–Danish rebellion in the north, he took swift and brutal action, devastating the countryside and destroying much of the Roman city of York. He then built a string of defensive castles, and appointed a Great Council, which consisted of his new tenants-in-chief and met three times a year in the southern cities of Winchester, Westminster and Gloucester.

The early Norman kings had trouble keeping peace on their borders. William's son, Henry I, tried a pacific approach to Scotland: he married King Malcolm III's daughter, Matilda. He died in 1135, leaving no male heir. His daughter, also called Matilda, had married Henry Plantagenet, Count of Anjou, and became embroiled in a civil war against the followers of her cousin, Stephen. This war ended in 1153 with Stephen in control of the Crown but forced to accept Matilda's son, Henry, as joint ruler. When Stephen died the following year, Henry, founder of the Angevin dynasty (the dynasty of Anjou), usually known as the Plantagenet dynasty, became king and went on to rule for 35 years.

The great monasteries

While battles raged and kings connived, there was another side to life in this period, which has been described as "the flowering of Norman culture on English soil". The monasteries, both Benedictine and Cistercian, formed the new cultural centres; Canterbury, Westminster and Winchester were among the most active in the south, as were Fountains Abbey and Rievaulx in the north and Strata Florida in mid-Wales.

In Scotland the great monasteries at Melrose, Dryburgh, Jedburgh and Kelso were all built in the reign of Malcolm III's son, David I (1124–53), who also established a capital at Edinburgh. These great houses produced erudite historians and scholars, some of whom went in search of other branches of learning in European monas-

teries, but they made no attempt to educate those outside the Orders. Benedictine monasteries were a vital part of the feudal system, some gradually becoming almost indistinguishable from the great landed estates. Their abbots lived very well indeed, eating and drinking with great abandon.

King Arthur and Albion

But Chaucer's knight shows another side of medieval life: the courtly tradition and the code of chivalry. The highly exaggerated, romantic ideals of knights first gained popularity in the 12th century at the time of the Crusades. From this tradition sprang the Arthurian myth.

Arthur was possibly a Celtic king of the 6th or 7th century, but it was the 12th-century historian, Geoffrey of Monmouth, who invented the Arthurian legends such as the sword, Excalibur, and the wizard Merlin. Tintagel Castle in Cornwall, supposedly Arthur's birthplace, was not built until the 12th century. As more people learned to read, curiosity about the history of Britain grew, and writers were tempted to embellish and romanticise; William Caxton (1422–92), the printing pioneer, blended historical fact, myth and legend in a fascinating account called *The Description of Britain*. A century later, Raphael Holinshed compiled his *Chronicles* featuring the story of King Lear, later dramatised by Shakespeare, who relied heavily on Holinshed's work for several plays. ❏

LEFT: a panel from the Bayeux Tapestry shows William the Conqueror setting sail for England in 1066.
RIGHT: pilgrims on their way to Canterbury.

PREHISTORIC TIMES

Of all Britain's historic places, it is the prehistoric sites that are the most evocative – the legacy of ancient and mysterious cultures

It is impossible to travel far in Britain without seeing some evidence of the peoples who settled the land in the far-off centuries before history was recorded. These sites are not always immediately apparent – only a grassy bank between two fields may remain, perhaps, or a series of ridges around the summit of a prominent hill. These ridges were the banks and ditches that defended the hilltop forts of Iron Age tribes, who could watch over the lower ground from behind the encircling wooden palisades. Maiden Castle in Dorset is a particularly fine example of an Iron Age hill fort, and another, Cadbury Castle, just south off the busy A303 in Somerset, has been linked to Arthurian legend as the possible site of Camelot.

Circles of stone

While the hill-forts were obviously places of habitation, the enigmatic stone circles that loom on many a remote hillside still lack a definitive explanation. Were they temples of ancient religions, places for sacrificial rituals, meeting places, monuments celebrating some wonder of nature...?

Stonehenge *(see page 220)* is the most famous site, and remains a remarkable place even at the height of the season, when it is overrun by visitors. Many maintain that Castlerigg Stone Circle, high up on remote moorland near Keswick in the Lake District, has the most picturesque setting, while the standing stones and ancient burial cairns of Orkney have a very special atmosphere. Cornwall and Wales, last strongholds of the Celtic tribes of Britain, are littered with cairns and standing stones.

ABOVE: Britain's most famous prehistoric monument is Stonehenge in Wiltshire. It was assembled between 3000 and 2300 BC – but how, why and by whom is unknown. The axis of Stonehenge is aligned with the sunrise on 21 June, the longest day of the year, so some believe it may have been used to calculate the passing of time.

BELOW: the neolithic village of Skara Brae, on the Orkney islands, Scotland, was inhabited between 3200 and 2200 BC. There are ei houses, linked together by low alleyways.

BELOW: a dolmen at Lanyon Quoit in Cornwall known as "the Giant's Table."

THE MAGIC OF THE DRUIDS

The original Druids, spiritual leaders of the Celts, were a far cry from the present-day variety, who don flowing robes and gather at Stonehenge to celebrate dawn on midsummer's day. Now largely based in Wales, these Druids appear principally to be a society for promoting Celtic culture.

Druidism was a pre-Christian religion that formed the cornerstone of Celtic society, and its priesthood held tremendous power and influence. The Celts were volatile and warlike, but they were also hospitable, extremely artistic and very spiritual. They worshipped gods who controlled nature and the seasons, having a direct bearing on their day-to-day lives, and the Druids were the fount of all knowledge.

Well versed in magic, the Druids revered the oak tree and mistletoe, and held their rituals in oak forests. They probably used dolmens (stone monuments) as temples and altars, though Stonehenge itself predates them by many centuries.

The Druids, who acted not only as priests but also as religious teachers and judges, maintained their power by creating an aura of mystery. They committed their knowledge to memory. Thus it was literacy as much as the conversion of many Druids to Christianity that ultimately eroded their influence in the 2nd to 4th centuries AD.

ABOVE: the Callanish Stones, on the Isle of Lewis in Scotland's Outer Hebrides, form a spectacular megalithic monument, built around 2000 BC. There are 13 primary stones.

BELOW: the cairn at Dyffryn Ardudwy, Gywnedd, Wales, dates from around 4000 BC. It contains two burial chambers, and sits amidst a cluster of tombs around the small village.

RIGHT: Maiden Castle in Dorchester, Dorset, is the largest and most complex Iron Age hill fort in Britain. The castle was first laid out in 600 BC over the remains of a Neolithic settlement. Several hundred people lived here from 800 BC until AD 43, after which the site was occupied by the Roman army. The ramparts, English Heritage estimates, enclose a total area equivalent to 50 football pitches.

SHAKESPEARE'S KINGS

**Threatened at home by powerful barons and abroad
by fragile alliances and the power of the Pope,
England's monarchs were a dramatist's dream**

For his historical plays ("Histories"), William Shakespeare drew on the lives of the Plantagenet and Tudor kings who ruled from 1154 to 1547, and his stirring dramas colour our view of them today. These were the King Henrys, the Richards and King John, around whom he wove fanciful plots, bloody deeds and heroic tales.

Henry II and Richard the Lionheart

Shakespeare did not, however, tackle the first of the Plantagenet kings, Henry II: that was left for the 20th-century poet and playwright T.S. Eliot, who made a classic drama out of the king and his archbishop in *Murder in the Cathedral*. Henry cemented the Anglo-Norman state: through his mother's line he was the rightful king of England and through his father he inherited the title Count of Anjou. With his marriage to Eleanor of Aquitaine he also gained control of her lands, which stretched to the Pyrenees. But Scotland, Ireland and Wales formed no part of his kingdom.

Relations between Church and State became increasingly strained during Henry's reign. He tried to end the Church's monopoly of jurisdiction over members of the clergy who committed secular crimes, and to bring clerics under the law of the land. Thomas Becket, his strong-willed Archbishop and erstwhile friend, resisted this and was berated by the king. In 1170, four knights of the royal household took literally Henry's wish that someone would "rid me of this meddlesome priest" and murdered Becket on the altar steps of Canterbury Cathedral.

When Henry II died in 1189, his son Richard came to the throne. Richard has always been one of England's most popular kings, even though – or maybe because – he spent most of his time in the Holy Land fighting Crusades against the Infidel. Known as Coeur de Lion (Lionheart) for his bravery, he was deeply mourned when killed in France, despite the domestic mess into which his prolonged absence and expensive exploits had plunged the country. It was the injustice at home, presided over in part by Richard's brother and successor John, that produced the legendary Nottingham outlaw, Robin Hood, who, with his Merry Men, is imagined to have preyed on the rich to give to the poor.

King John and the Magna Carta

King John scores poorly among English monarchs. He quarrelled with the Pope over his practice of siphoning off the revenues of ecclesiastical estates and over the Papal appointment of Stephen Langton as Archbishop of Canterbury. This resulted in John's excommunication.

He also caused increasing resentment among the barons, chiefly because he failed to protect their Norman lands from the advances of the

To consolidate his power, Henry II made administrative reforms and instigated the system of common law that operates today, distinguishing English from Continental and Scottish legal systems.

terms, the Church was given back its former rights. The Charter also limited royal power over arrests and imprisonments and prevented the king from expropriating fines. For the barons the main interest was to stop him encroaching on their feudal rights and privileges.

Although history sees the charter as a milestone and the document on which British freedoms are based, it brought no immediate solution. The Pope condemned it, and John defied it and his barons; as soon as he could, he raised troops and ravaged the north. The barons retaliated by turning to Louis of France for help, but John died in 1216 before he could cause any more trouble.

French king, Philip Augustus. Another important grievance was that John had imposed high taxes, undermined the power of the feudal courts and taken for himself the fines of offenders which had previously been part of the barons' income.

Angered by the king's contempt of them, the barons threatened to take up arms against John unless he agreed to a series of demands on behalf of the people. These became the basis of the Magna Carta (Great Charter), signed at Runnymede near Windsor in 1215. Under its

LEFT: King John stirred the barons to revolt.
ABOVE: a romanticised 19th-century view of Robin Hood and his Merry Men, the mythical Nottingham outlaws who took from the rich and gave to the poor.

Henry III

John's son, who became Henry III, proved little better. His most senior advisors were foreign favourites who flocked to England after his marriage to Eleanor of Provence, and, in 1242, he embarked on a disastrous war with France that ended with the loss of the valuable lands of Poitou. The barons, under Simon de Montfort, rebelled, and the king was defeated at the Battle of Lewes (now the county town of East Sussex). In 1265 de Montfort summoned a parliament, which represented the chief towns and boroughs (which has since been called the first House of Commons, although anything like a fair system of representation was still centuries away), but de Montfort's lust for power soon lost him the support of the barons. In 1266 Henry was restored to the throne where he reigned peacefully, if not very well, until his death in 1272.

The Edwards

Under Edward I, Henry's son, Wales was conquered. Llewellyn, Prince of Wales, was killed in the Battle of Builth on the River Wye, and his brother David was captured and executed. The Statute of Wales in 1284 placed the country under English law and Edward presented his newborn son to the Welsh as Prince of Wales, a title held by the heir to the throne ever since.

In England, the reign of Edward II had little

to commend it. His defeat by Robert the Bruce (King of Scotland 1306–29) paved the way for a Scottish invasion of Ireland. He lost Gascony and upset his own barons by appointing unsuitable friends to high office. Even his wife deserted him and joined his enemy, Roger Mortimer. The pair assumed power, and in 1327 Edward was deposed by Parliament, who named his young son king. Edward was later brutally murdered, unmourned, in Berkeley Castle in Gloucestershire.

> At the Battle of Crécy more than 30,000 French troops were killed and the Massacre of Limoges, led by England's Black Prince, left 3,000 dead.

As soon as he was old enough, young Edward III, showing little filial loyalty, had his mother incarcerated for life in Castle Rising, Norfolk, and Mortimer executed. Much of his long reign was spent fighting the Hundred Years War with France, which actually lasted from 1337 to 1453 with several periods of peace. These protracted hostilities began when Edward, whose maternal grandfather was Philip IV of France, claimed the French throne. The fortunes of war shifted from one side to the other. But by 1371 the English had lost most of their French possessions.

On the domestic front, times were also hard in the 14th century. The Black Death, which reached England in 1348, killed nearly half the population. Followed by lesser epidemics during the next 50 years, it had reduced Britain's population from 4 million to 2 million by the

THE STRUGGLE WITH SCOTLAND

Scotland became a united country in the 12th century – apart from the islands, which were still controlled by the Danes. Gaelic was still the language of the Highlands, but elsewhere most people spoke English, and trade links with England had been established. But this didn't mean that the Scots had to like the English.

When Alexander II died in 1286, rivals claimed the throne. The first, John Balliol, son of the founder of Balliol College, Oxford, was persuaded to accept the throne as England's vassal. But he resented owing allegiance to England and made a treaty with Edward I's enemy, the king of France, then crossed the border and ravaged Cumberland. Edward fought back, Balliol was captured and imprisoned

and the sacred kingmaking Stone of Scone was taken to Westminster Abbey.

The struggle against English domination was later renewed by Robert the Bruce (1274–1329), one of Scotland's greatest heroes. Through his aristocratic father he was distantly related to the Scottish royal family, and his mother had strong Gaelic antecedents.

Defeated by the Earl of Pembroke, Bruce became a fugitive but re-emerged to be crowned at Scone, and in 1314 defeated the English at Bannockburn in Stirlingshire. Scottish independence was recognised. Robert's daughter Margery married Walter Stewart, and their son Robert II came to the throne in 1371, the first Stuart King.

end of the century. This had far-reaching effects. By leaving so much land untended and making labour scarce, it gave surviving peasants, and those who came after them, a better bargaining position. But it also meant that some landlords, unable or unwilling to pay higher wages, tried to force peasants back into serfdom. The more affluent peasants of Kent and East Anglia began to flex their economic muscles, and, when a Poll Tax was introduced in 1381, they rose in rebellion, both against the tax and against the landlords' oppressive treatment.

Wat Tyler and Jack Straw were the most prominent leaders of the Peasants' Revolt, which gained

created a whole new class of yeomen farmers. The name originally meant simply "young men", presumably those with the energy to scratch a living from the often poor pieces of land and gradually convert them into valuable smallholdings.

Henrys IV, V and VI

In 1399 the Lancastrian Revolution overthrew Richard II and put Henry IV, Duke of Lancaster, on the throne. It was during his reign that the first English heretic was burned at the stake. He was William Sawtrey, Rector of Lynn, in Dorset, and his heresy was preaching the Lollard Doctrines. Lollards were the followers of John

the support of the urban poor and briefly took control of London. The rebellion was quickly and brutally suppressed, and Richard II reneged on his promise to abolish serfdom. But this manifestation of the power of the people had made their lords and masters nervous, and landlords became more wary about enforcing villeinage. Gradually the feudal system withered until it died. After the plagues, landlords found it more profitable to rent out much of their land rather than pay labourers to tend it and in so doing they

Wycliffe, who rejected the Pope's authority and had the Bible translated into English, so that any literate person could understand it. The persecution of the Lollards continued into the next reign when the movement, not organised enough to withstand the pressure, went underground. The demands for change and reform in the Church would resurface successfully 100 years later, when they suited the purposes of the king.

These were turbulent times. Foreign wars were fought to gain or retain land and glory, while at home periodic attacks on the throne by rival contenders were equally bloody. Henry IV had to deal with the Rebellions of the Percys, a powerful Northumberland family, and the guerrilla warfare conducted by Owain Glyndwr (Owen Glen-

LEFT: a trial takes place in Westminster Hall.
ABOVE: Wat Tyler was beheaded by the Lord Mayor of London after the Peasants' Revolt, watched by King Richard II (seen on the right inspecting his troops).

dower, 1354–1416), a self-declared prince who was pressing hard for independence for Wales.

Henry IV's son, Henry V (1413–22), was immortalised by Shakespeare as the heroic Prince Hal. With miraculously few English casualties – although rather more than Shakespeare claimed – Henry defeated the French at Agincourt, starved Rouen into submission 4 years later, and made a strategic marriage to a French princess. By the time of his death in 1422 he controlled all of northern France.

Henry V was succeeded by Henry VI, but in 1455, after the latter had gone insane and the government was put into the hands of a Protec-tor, rivalries between the powerful Dukes of York and Somerset led to the Wars of the Roses. This name was, in fact, coined by the 19th-century novelist Sir Walter Scott, but it is a convenient shorthand for these battles between the great House of York, symbolised by the white rose, and that of Lancaster, symbolised by the red.

> *In Oxford, a memorial on St Giles commemorates the martyrs Latimer, Ridley and Cranmer. A cross on Broad Street marks the spot where they were burned at the stake.*

The House of York

Edward IV (1461–83) reigned for most of the duration of these wars, which were particularly nasty because of the number of people who were executed, with or without a trial, off the field of battle. Perhaps the best known of these murders was that of the young princes, Edward and Richard, said to have been smothered while imprisoned in the Tower of London in 1483. The guilt of their uncle, Shakespeare's hunch-backed Richard III, has never been proven, and there is today a society dedicated to proving his innocence. Certainly, he's unlikely to have been as black as he was painted by Shakespeare – who, after all, was writing a melodrama cal-culated both to entertain and to conform diplo-matically to the prejudices of his own time.

The circumstances of Richard's own death are also well known. He was killed during the Battle of Bosworth, in Leicestershire, where Shakespeare had him offering his kingdom for a horse.

ENGLISH MONARCHS SINCE THE NORMAN CONQUEST

Norman
William I 1066–87
William II 1087–1100
Henry I 1100–35
Stephen 1135–54

Plantagenet
Henry II 1154–89
Richard I 1189–99
John 1199–1216
Henry III 1216–72
Edward I 1272–1307
Edward II 1307–27
Edward III 1327–77
Richard II 1377–99

Lancaster
Henry IV 1399–1413

Henry V 1413–22
Henry VI 1422–61

York
Edward IV 1461–83
Edward V 1483
Richard III 1483–85

Tudor
Henry VII 1485–1509
Henry VIII 1509–47
Edward VI 1547–53
Mary 1553–58
Elizabeth I 1558–1603

Stuart
James I 1603–25
Charles I 1625–49

[Commonwealth 1649–53,
Protectorate 1653–60]
Charles II 1660–85
James II 1685–89
William and Mary
1689–1702
Anne 1702–1714

Hanover
George I 1714–27
George II 1727–60
George III 1760–1820
George IV 1820–30
William IV 1830–37

Saxe-Coburg-Gotha
Victoria 1837–1901
Edward VII 1901–10

Windsor
(so called from 1917)
George V 1910–36
Edward VIII 1936
George VI 1936–52
Elizabeth II from 1952

Tudor rule: Henry VIII

The wars ended with the marriage of Henry VII (1485–1509) to Elizabeth of York. This united the opposing factions and put the country under the rule of the Tudors. Henry was something of a financial wizard and, determined to enrich a throne impoverished by years of war, proceeded to extort money wherever possible. Through loans, subsidies, property levies and fines he refilled the royal coffers but, regrettably, most of the money was squandered by his son, Henry VIII, on a series of French wars. These renewed hostilities gave the Scots an opportunity to ally themselves with the French and invade England. But they were terribly defeated at the Battle of Flodden Field, where James IV and 10,000 of his men were slaughtered.

Henry VIII is the most famous of British kings. He was the hugely fat, gluttonous and licentious ruler who married six times, divorced twice and beheaded two of his wives. He is also famous as the man who brought about the Reformation, which made England a Protestant rather than a Catholic country, because the Pope refused to annul his marriage to Catherine of Aragon, who could not oblige him by producing a male heir.

There are other well-known characters in this drama: one is Thomas Wolsey, Archbishop and Lord Chancellor, who had Hampton Court Palace built as an exhibition of his wealth and who was later charged with high treason for not giving sufficient support to his King. Another is Sir Thomas More, beheaded for refusing to recognise Henry as Supreme Head of the Church of England; and a third is Thomas Cromwell, who carried out the King's drastic wish to destroy the country's monasteries. But he made the mistake of taking Protestantism too far for Henry's liking and was rewarded with decapitation on Tower Hill in 1540, while all the monastery lands and riches went to his ungrateful monarch.

The causes of the English Reformation were not, of course, quite so simple. Papal dispensation for the divorce was only withheld because Pope Clement VII feared Charles of Spain, the Holy Roman Emperor and Europe's most powerful monarch – and Catherine's nephew. A desire for Church reform had been growing for many years and now, encouraged by the success

of Martin Luther (1483–1546), the great German reformer, many believed its time had come.

Tudor rule: "Bloody Mary"

Under Henry, Wales was joined with England in the 1536 Act of Union, which gave it representation in parliament. When he died in 1547, Henry was succeeded by his only male heir, Edward, a sickly 10-year-old who died six years later. His half-sister Mary then came to the throne and won herself the nickname "Bloody Mary", proving that a woman could be just as ruthless as a man when the occasion demanded. A devout Catholic, she restored the Old Religion and raised fears that

her marriage to Philip II of Spain would lead to undue Spanish interefence and the introduction of the dreaded Inquisition. Her Marian Persecution, as it was called, saw at least 300 Protestants burned as heretics, including Archbishop Cranmer, who died at Oxford after first thrusting into the flames "the unworthy hand" which had earlier signed a recantation.

Mary is also remembered as the monarch who lost the French port of Calais, the "brightest jewel in the English crown" and the last British possession on the Continent, during a renewed war with France. More remorseful about the loss of land than the loss of so many lives, she declared that when she died the word "Calais" would be found engraved on her heart. ❏

FAR LEFT: Henry V, Shakespeare's most heroic king.
LEFT: Henry VIII as Holbein's paintings portray him.
RIGHT: beheading was the punishment for traitors.

THE GOLDEN AGE

Under Elizabeth I, Britain ruled the waves and
produced great literature. But then power began
to shift from the monarch to the politicians

The Elizabethan Age has a swashbuckling
ring to it: the Virgin Queen and her dash-
ing courtiers, the defeat of the Spanish
Armada, and the exploits of the "sea dogs", Fro-
bisher and Hawkins. Sir Walter Raleigh brought
tobacco back from Virginia; Sir Francis Drake
circumnavigated the world.

In this age of the renaissance man, even the
great poets Sir Philip Sidney and John Donne
spent time before the mast – although William
Shakespeare, born six years after Elizabeth had
been crowned queen, stayed at home, entertaining the crowds at the Globe Theatre in London's
Southwark. Poetry, plays and pageants were the
thing, and they accompanied the Queen on her
tours of the country.

Conspiracies against the Queen

Elizabeth I, Henry VIII's daughter by Anne
Boleyn whom he beheaded, may have had an
interesting life at court but in fact she spent

*Defeating the Spanish Armada gave England
naval supremacy, which laid the foundations
for a future of flourishing trade, expansionism
and colonisation.*

nearly 20 years of her long reign (1558–1603)
resisting Catholic attempts to either dethrone
or assassinate her. She had re-established Protestantism but was constantly challenged by those
who wished to put Mary Stuart, Queen of Scots,
on the throne and return to the Old Religion.

Mary had a colourful background. Sent to
France as a child, she returned a young widow
and in 1565 married her cousin, Lord Darnley.

But she became far too friendly with her secretary, Rizzio, who was stabbed to death by her
jealous husband at the Palace of Holyroodhouse
in Edinburgh (tour guides point out the exact
spot where it happened – some can even discern
traces of faded bloodstains). Shortly afterwards
Darnley himself was killed and, as Mary rather
swiftly married Lord Bothwell, suspicions were
aroused, a rebellion mounted, and Mary had to
abdicate in favour of her son, James.

On fleeing to England, however, she was
promptly incarcerated by Elizabeth and lan-
guished in prison while plots were fomented,
mostly involving the assistance of Spain. The
trial and execution of Mary in 1587 removed the
conspirators' focal point, and the defeat of the

Spanish Armada the following year put an end to Catholic conspiracies against Elizabeth.

When Elizabeth died without an heir, she was succeeded by Mary's son, James. He was James VI of Scotland, but James I in England, where he was the first of the Stuarts to take the throne. His succession brought a temporary union of the two countries but his reign, too, was bedevilled by religious controversy. The Puritans became prominent, believing that the Reformation had not gone far enough and calling for a purer form of worship. And the Catholics engineered a number of plots, one of which resulted in Sir Walter Raleigh's 13-year imprisonment in

however sceptical of politicians, burn effigies of Fawkes on the night of 5 November, and set off thousands of pounds worth of fireworks.

The Puritan protests were more peaceful, but James had little sympathy with their demands. A new translation of the Bible into English (the "Authorised" or "King James" Version) was a rare concession. James said he would make them conform or "harry them from the land". Some left voluntarily. Going first to Holland, a small group who became known as the Pilgrim Fathers set sail in the *Mayflower* in 1620 and founded New Plymouth in North America, Britain's first toehold in the New World.

the Tower of London (his well-appointed rooms can be visited). Ironically, Raleigh was released by James, who was short of money, and sent in search of gold in Guiana. The expedition failed and Raleigh, accused of treason, was executed.

The Gunpowder Plot

The most famous of the Catholic conspiracies was the Gunpowder Plot of 1605, when Guy Fawkes attempted to blow up the Houses of Parliament. The immediate result was the execution of Fawkes and his fellow conspirators and the imposition of severe anti-Catholic laws. Curiously, people today,

LEFT: Elizabeth I, the "Virgin Queen".
ABOVE: the defeat of the Spanish Armada in 1588.

Meanwhile, in Ireland, events were taking place that would leave a long and bloody legacy. The lands of northern Irish lords had been seized in Elizabeth's reign after a series of rebellions had been brutally suppressed. Now they were redistributed among English and Scottish settlers. The county of Derry was divided up among 12 London merchant guilds and renamed Londonderry. Ulster became England's first important colony.

The Stuart period was one of conflict between Crown and Parliament. James I, a staunch believer in the Divine Right of Kings, a belief held by most European rulers of the time, would have preferred no Parliament at all and actually did without one for 7 years. But, once recalled in

1621, the House of Commons renewed its insistence on political power in return for the taxes it was constantly asked to raise.

The Civil War

Under Charles I, relations with Parliament went from bad to dreadful. In 1628 he reluctantly accepted the Petition of Right, one of the most important documents in British history, which forbade arbitrary arrest and imprisonment and deemed that taxes should be raised only by an act of Parliament. But a year later he dissolved Parliament and initiated 11 years of absolute rule.

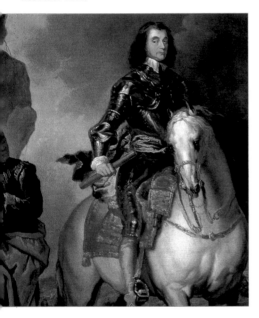

Surprisingly, he managed very well and might have continued indefinitely had it not been for the over-zealous attempts of William Laud, the anti-Puritan Archbishop of Canterbury, to impose the English Book of Common Prayer on the ferociously independent Scottish Church, or Kirk.

Influenced by the great French theologian, John Calvin (1509–64), the Scottish Church had embraced Puritan values, and was referred to as Presbyterian because its elders were known as Presbyters, not Bishops. Laud's intransigence provoked a massive popular rebellion. The Covenanters, so-called because they had signed a National Covenant "to resist Popery", formed an army and invaded England.

> *The English Civil War of 1642–51 has become romanticised, and today a society flourishes which re-enacts the principal battles for fun.*

Short of money and trained men, Charles was unable to cope. He had to summon a Parliament, but King and Commons were constantly at each other's throats and in 1641 discontented Irish Catholics took advantage of their disarray to attack the settlers who had taken their land. Thousands were massacred and the outcry in England was heightened by a belief that Charles had backed the Irish Catholic side. This belief, together with Charles's attempt to arrest the five members of Parliament most openly opposed to him, precipitated the Civil War.

Charles gained the support of the north and west of the country and Wales. Oliver Cromwell, Member of Parliament for Huntingdon, then for Cambridge, and a stout defender of the Puritan cause, became leader of the Ironsides, backed by London and the southern counties and later joined by Scottish troops. Enormous damage was done to castles, churches and fortified houses during the war and when it was over many were "slighted" – either destroyed completely or made indefensible. Today the King and his Cavaliers are shown more sympathy than Cromwell and his Roundheads – so called because of their short haircuts.

Cromwell's republic

King Charles's execution in 1649, on a scaffold erected outside Inigo Jones's new Banqueting House in Whitehall, has also become the stuff of which legends are made. He reputedly wore two shirts, so that he would not shiver in the January cold and cause people to think he was afraid. The poet Andrew Marvell, deeply moved by the event, wrote: "He nothing common did or mean/Upon that memorable scene."

As so often in politics, making a martyr of the enemy proved a big mistake. There was public outrage at home, while at Scone, in Scotland, Charles's son and namesake was crowned king. Young Charles, however, was not happy with the Presbyterian religion he was pledged to uphold. He marched into England, where he was defeated at Worcester, was pursued south and, after many adventures, finally escaped to France.

Meanwhile, Cromwell and "the Rump" – the Parliamentary members who had voted for Charles's execution – declared England a Commonwealth. One of Cromwell's first acts was to exact reprisals for the massacres in Ireland by killing all the inhabitants of the towns of Drogheda and Wexford. Another was the suppression of the Levellers, a group within his own army who did not believe that his democratisation had gone far enough. In 1653 Cromwell dissolved Parliament, formed a Protectorate with himself as Lord Protector and ruled alone until his death in 1658. Without him, republicanism faltered, and, in 1660, Charles II (1660–85) was declared king.

Britain prospered under Charles, who, it was said, "never said a foolish thing nor ever did a wise one". True or not, one unwise thing Parliament was afraid he would do was become a Catholic. They therefore passed the Test Act, which excluded all Catholics from public office of any kind. In 1678 Titus Oates (whose house can still be seen in the narrow high street in Hastings in Sussex) disclosed a bogus "Popish Plot" to assassinate the king. In the resultant hysteria, thousands of Catholics were imprisoned, and no Catholic was allowed to sit in the House of Commons – a law that was not repealed for nearly 200 years.

Whigs and Tories

Fear of the monarchy ever again becoming too powerful led to the emergence of the first political parties. Both were known by nicknames: Whigs was a derogatory name for cattle drivers, Tories an Irish word meaning brigand or outlaw. Loosely speaking, the Whigs opposed absolute monarchy and supported the right to religious freedom for Nonconformists, while Tories were the upholders of Church and Crown, the natural successors of Charles I's Royalists. The Whigs were to form a coalition with dissident Tories in the mid-19th century and become the Liberal Party. The Tories were the forerunners of the Conservative Party, which retains the nickname.

In 1685 Charles was succeeded by his brother. The reign of James II (1685–89) was not a success. Within a year he had imposed

illegal taxation and tried to bring back absolute monarchy and the Catholic religion. Rebellions were savagely put down, with hundreds being hanged and many more sold into slavery to the West Indies.

In desperation, Whigs and Tories swallowed their differences, and in 1688 offered the crown to James's daughter, Mary, and her husband, the Dutch prince William of Orange. This became known as the Glorious Revolution, and, although bloodless, was a revolution nonetheless. By choosing the new monarch, Parliament had proved itself more powerful than the Crown. This power was spelled out in

SIR CHRISTOPHER WREN

Although Wren (1632–1723) was renowned in his day as an astronomer, it is his architectural achievements that have gained him immortality. He designed 51 new London churches and replaced many other prominent buildings after the devastating Great Fire in 1666, influencing generations of architects. St Paul's Cathedral, which took 36 years to build, remains his greatest achievement – a plaque in the crypt displays the words: "Reader, if you seek his memorial – look around you."

LEFT: Oliver Cromwell, who ruled Britain as Lord Protector from 1653 to his death in 1658; after the Restoration, his corpse was dug up and hanged.
RIGHT: the monarchy restored, Charles II walks out on Horseguards Parade.

a Bill of Rights, which limited the monarch's freedom of action and ushered in a new era, in which Divine Right and Absolute Monarchy had no place.

But James II had not yet given up hope. Backed by the French, he landed in Ireland in 1689, believing that the disaffected Irish Catholics would support him. This they did, but with disastrous results for both sides. At Londonderry 30,000 pro-William Protestants survived a siege lasting 15 weeks, but were finally defeated. Their Loyalist descendants still call themselves "Orangemen", and "No Surrender" is the Protestant rallying cry heard in Ulster's streets today.

The next year, William's troops defeated James at the Battle of the Boyne. James fled to France (dying in 1701), the south of Ireland was subdued, and Protestant victory complete.

War with France dragged on through the reign of William and Mary (1689–1702) and that of Mary's cousin, Queen Anne (1702–14), who followed, since William and Mary died childless. During Anne's reign, it became the War of the Spanish Succession, its aim being to put Charles, Archduke of Austria, on the Spanish throne. John Churchill, Duke of Marlborough, won a famous victory at Blenheim in 1704, for which he was rewarded with Blenheim

WILLIAM OF ORANGE

William the Conqueror's 1066 invasion of England was a hostile one, but William of Orange's 1688 invasion was by invitation. England's Protestant establishment saw the Dutch ruler as being the best means of overthrowing the Catholic James II, whose daughter, Mary, William had married. As a child, William (1650–1702) had been taught by Calvinist preachers and he gained his military experience in wars against France. Though he ruled England tolerantly, his heart remained in the Netherlands.

Palace in Oxfordshire. In the same year Gibraltar was taken. Still in British hands, this remains a source of dispute with Spain today. The Treaty of Utrecht ended the war in 1713, and the Queen died without an heir the next year.

The birth of Great Britain

It was during Anne's reign that the name Great Britain came into being, when, in 1707, the Act of Union united England and Scotland, largely for economic reasons. Under the Act the two countries were to share the same monarch and

ABOVE: Scotland's Catholic clansmen face defeat at Culloden in 1746. **RIGHT:** William Hogarth's painting *Gin Lane* depicts the squalor of slums in London.

parliament, while trade and customs laws were to be standardised, though Scotland was to retain its own Church and legislature. The Act did not, however, bring about instant friendliness and accord between the two nations, and it was largely the cause of the Jacobite Rebellions a few years later.

On Anne's death, a reliable Protestant monarch was needed in a hurry, and George of Hanover, great-grandson of James I on his mother's side, but a Hanoverian through his father's line and German in language, upbringing and outlook, was invited to Britain. Throughout his 13-year reign he never learned to speak English fluently, nor did he have any great liking for his subjects.

Hanoverian Britain

The Hanoverian dynasty, under the four Georges (I: 1714–27; II: 1727–60; III: 1760–1820; IV: 1820–30), spanned a period of nearly 115 years. It was a time of wars with France and Spain, of expanding empire, industrialisation and growing demands for political reform. It also saw the last violent attempts to overthrow a British monarch, in the shape of the two Jacobite Rebellions in support of the "Pretenders", descendants of James II.

The first rebellion, in 1715, in support of his son James, the "Old Pretender", was defeated near Stirling, and its leaders fled to France. Thirty years later English war with France encouraged the Jacobites to try again. Charles, the "Young Pretender", popularly known as Bonnie Prince Charlie, raised a huge army and marched into England. Find-

ing little support from English Jacobites, he returned north of the border, where in 1746 his Highland troops were savagely defeated at the Battle of Culloden. The power of the clan chiefs was destroyed.

No more "Pretenders" arose. From then on power struggles would be political ones, for it was with politicians and Parliament that real power lay. Monarchs were gradually becoming titular figures. Historians may talk about the reign of George III, but it was the policies of William Pitt or Lord Liverpool that mattered. Similarly, the Victorian Age was really the age of Peel and Palmerston, Gladstone and Disraeli. ❏

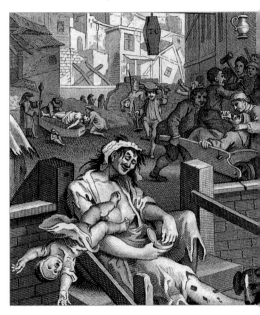

THE GROWTH OF LONDON

London was partially rebuilt after the Great Fire of 1666, which started in a baker's shop in Pudding Lane and destroyed two-thirds of the cramped, timber-built city. But the subsequent elegant buildings of Sir Christopher Wren (1632–1723), such as St Paul's Cathedral, were a far cry from the overcrowded and insanitary slums in which most people lived. In the more affluent areas, some streets were widened to allow carriages to pass, and rudimentary street lighting was introduced in the mid-18th century.

London was then, as now, the country's leading commercial centre, and fortunes were made in colonial trade that stimulated banking, insurance and share dealing. A flourishing trade and financial sector also created work for craftsmen and artisans, to furnish homes, build carriages and make clothes. At the same time it brought in service industries to cater for the habitués of the theatres, concert halls and newly fashionable coffee houses.

London was also the centre of court life and the seat of political power. The royal families spent their time at Buckingham House, Kensington Palace and Hampton Court. George III was the first monarch to live in Buckingham House and George IV had it redesigned by John Nash into a Palace from around 1826. A system of patronage flourished around Parliament, which met at Westminster, although not in the present building, which was built after a serious fire destroyed its predecessor in 1834.

BRITANNIA RULES

Trade boomed, cities burgeoned, railways spread, the Empire swelled. It was a great time to be British – unless, that is, you were poor

The treaty signed at the end of the Seven Years' War with France in 1763 allowed Britain to keep all its overseas colonies, making it the leading world power. The empire had been growing since 1607, when Virginia, the first British colony in America, had been established. In 1620 English Puritans had settled in Massachusetts, and other settlements were made later in the century. By 1700 most were governed by a Crown official and incorporated into Britain's Atlantic Empire.

Throughout the 17th century the demand for goods – furs, rice, silk, tobacco, sugar – led to a series of wars with the Dutch and the French, from which Britain emerged in control of much of West Africa, Newfoundland and Nova Scotia and some of the Caribbean islands. The French and English battled for supremacy in Canada and India during the 18th century. By 1760 England had proved the clear winner: General James Wolfe's capture of Quebec ended French power in Canada, and Robert Clive had beaten both Indians and French for control of the Indian subcontinent, a victory which made the East India Company a private colonial power.

Convicts and slaves

Britain's loss of its American colonies in 1783 was eased by the opening up of the Pacific. Captain Cook reached Tahiti in 1768 and then went on to New Zealand and Australia, where he landed at Botany Bay. When American Independence deprived Britain of a place to send its convicts, the harsh, undeveloped lands of Australia were the obvious alternative.

Colonial trade, unfortunately, went hand in hand with slavery. European traders bought slaves in West Africa, shipped them to the

Americas under appalling conditions and sold them to plantation owners, often in exchange for produce, which they took back home. The raw materials would then be converted into finished products and exported to other parts of the Empire. It was a neat trade triangle, which meant high profits for some, and misery and degradation for others. It was not until 1807 that the tireless efforts of William Wilberforce made the trade illegal and another 27 years before slavery itself was finally abolished in all British colonies.

The agricultural revolution

Radical changes took place in the English countryside in the late 18th century. Since Saxon times, large areas of land had been cultivated in narrow strips by tenant farmers, and common land had been used for grazing. Little was known about crop rotation or fertilisation, and land would be worked until it was exhausted.

During the late 18th and early 19th centuries this system ended when the Enclosure

The paintings of Suffolk by John Constable (1776–1837) depict a landscape that was the product of the Enclosure Acts; in some parts of the country little has changed to this day.

their lands by the enclosures and the labourers thrown out of work by mechanisation, it was a disaster. Riots erupted in many areas, but they could not prevent the march of progress. Many dispossessed peasant farmers had to leave their homes and look for work in the towns, which became hopelessly overcrowded. In Ireland and the Scottish Highlands the agricultural revolution led to mass emigration, particularly to America, and to lasting resentment.

Those who had done well out of new farming methods began to look for ways to invest their capital. They soon joined flourishing city bankers and merchants who had been made

Acts empowered wealthier landowners to seize land to which tenants could prove no legal title and to divide it into enclosed fields. This explains the patchwork quality of much of Britain's countryside.

A system of crop rotation meant land could be exploited to the full, while the cultivation of fodder crops enabled livestock to be kept through the winter months. Artificial fertilizer and new agricultural machinery, such as the seed drill invented by the agriculturalist Jethro Tull, also made arable farming more efficient and more profitable. But for the tenants evicted from

prosperous by international trade, to finance what we now call the Industrial Revolution.

This surfeit of capital was one reason why Britain was the first country to industrialise, but it was also helped by relative political stability, and by the security that came from being an island, from natural resources and from good trade arrangements. These fortunate circumstances combined to produce a genuine revolution, so rapid and complete were the changes it made.

The Industrial Revolution

The first steam engine was devised at the end of the 17th century but it was only when the Scottish inventor James Watt (1736–1819) modified and improved the design in the 1770s

LEFT: Bristol traded profitably with the New World.
ABOVE: coal mines stoked the Industrial Revolution.

that steam became an efficient source of energy, which would power trains and ships as well as factory machinery and make many later developments possible. The new steam pumps, for example, allowed speculators to drain deep coal mines, which vastly increased coal production, an important factor when opencast and shallow mines were nearly exhausted.

> Attempts to wreck the hated power looms were made by "Luddites", named after Ned Ludd of Leicestershire. But the rebels lost the fight.

Textiles had long been a vital part of Britain's economy, and the invention of the Spinning Jenny and the power loom in the 1770s and 1780s opened the way to mass production. As in agriculture, mechanisation destroyed the livelihoods of those who could not invest in it. Handloom weavers, many of them women and children, were obliged to leave their homes and work in these "dark satanic mills", as the poet William Blake described them in *Milton a Poem* (famously set to music in 1916 by Sir Hubert Parry as the hymn *Jerusalem*).

Perhaps the most important element in speeding industrialisation was the breakthrough made by Abraham Darby of Coalbrookdale, Shropshire, who succeeded in smelting iron with coke, instead of charcoal. This hugely increased the production of iron, which was used for machinery, railways and shipping. Here, in 1776, the world's first cast-iron bridge was built and can still be seen. Cast steel was first produced in the mid-18th century, but it was another 100 years before the Bessemer process made possible the cheap mass production of steel.

It was, of course, pointless to produce goods or materials unless they could reach a market, so improved transportation ran parallel with production. The 18th century saw massive outlay on canal building. By 1830 all the main industrial areas were linked by waterways, and Scotland was sliced in two by the Caledonian Canal. Unfortunately, most of these would fall into disuse when the new railways proved faster and more efficient, but today, cleared out and cleaned up, they provide thousands of miles of leisure boating. There are more miles of canal in Birmingham than there are in Venice.

New roads were built. A process involving crushed stones and a layer of tar was named after its inventor, the blind Scot John Macadam, and gave us the road surface called "tarmac". By the early 19th century, engineers such as Macadam and Thomas Telford, whose masterpiece is the magnificent Menai Strait Bridge in North Wales, had created a road network totalling some 125,000 miles (200,000km).

The Railway Age

But above all this was the age of the railways, when iron and steam combined to change the face of the country, and were romanticised in such vivid paintings as *Rain, Steam and Speed* by J.M.W. Turner (1775–1851). Isambard Kingdom Brunel (1806–59), who also designed the elegant Clifton Suspension Bridge across the Avon Gorge, laid down the Great Western Railway, consolidating a reputation that led him to being voted the second greatest Briton (after Winston Churchill) in a 2002 historical poll by the BBC (see page 65). The Stockton and Darlington line, designed by George Stephenson, inventor of the *Rocket*, was the first steam line to open, in 1825, followed 5 years later by the first inter-city line, from Liverpool to Manchester. This historic occasion was marred when William Huskisson, the President of the Board of Trade, was accidentally killed while officiating at the opening.

In the 18th and 19th centuries a whole new class of industrialists and entrepreneurs made fortunes to rival those of the aristocracy, who in turn looked down on them as *nouveaux riches*, with no breeding. But what about the workers? The new factories and mines certainly provided employment, but working conditions were dreadful. Fatalities in the new deep-cast mines were high, and those workers who survived sudden death often had their lives shortened by pneumoconiosis. Children as young as 4 were employed underground, and women worked alongside the men. In factories, too, employees of all ages were treated abominably, working 15-hour days in poor light and deafening noise.

It was not until 1833 that the first Factory Act made it illegal to employ children under 9 and for women and under-18s to work more than 12 hours a day. Sixty years were to pass before another act dealt with health and safety at work, and then in a very minor way.

These early industrial reforms were the initiatives of enlightened, liberal-minded men, acting on behalf of the underprivileged, often arousing great opposition from members of their own class for their "interference". It would be some time before working people would be able to achieve benefits on their own behalf.

The Combination Acts of 1824 allowed workers to "combine" together to improve wages, but nothing else. The case of the Tolpuddle Martyrs, six Dorset men sentenced to deportation for their attempts to organise a more comprehensive union, demonstrated the need for workers to protect themselves against exploitation, but it was not until 1868 that the first Trades Union Congress met. Unions then went from strength to strength, although for a long time they largely benefited the so-called "Triple Alliance" of miners, railwaymen and transport workers, and did little for workers in other areas.

The fear of revolution

The two events that most alarmed the British ruling classes in the closing decades of the 18th century were the American War of Independence (1775–83) and the French Revolution of 1789. In the former, people proved themselves willing to fight and die for equality, national identity and political representation. In the latter, they were prepared to cut off the heads of the aristocracy and anyone else who denied them liberty, equality and fraternity.

The fear of revolution was exacerbated by wars with France and Spain and the dissatisfaction provoked by the heavy taxes and loss of trade they caused. Known as the Napoleonic Wars, these hostilities began with the threatened French invasion of Belgium and Holland in 1793 and rumbled on, with only 3 years' break, until 1815.

These were wars that gave Britain two of its greatest heroes, Admiral Lord Nelson (1758–1805) and the Duke of Wellington (1769–1852),

LEFT: the coaches of the 1830s were soon to be made redundant by the railways. ABOVE: labouring on London's Bankside, as trade continued to expand.

RADICAL THINKERS

Radical thinkers such as Edmund Burke (1729–97) and Tom Paine (1737–1809) enthused over the American people's struggle. Paine also supported the ideals of the French Revolution, although he later became sickened by its excesses. *The Rights of Man*, which he published in 1791, defended the people's right to reform what was corrupt. It seriously worried the government. Freedom of the press was suppressed and many radical leaders imprisoned, and Paine escaped to France.

and some of its most famous victories. There was the Battle of the Nile in 1798, when Nelson annihilated the French fleet; the Battle of Trafalgar, where he himself was killed after reminding his men that "England expects that every man will do his duty"; Sir John Moore's inspired strike at Corunna; and Wellington's victory at Waterloo, which ended Napoleon's career in 1815.

But political change in England was to come not through revolution but through gradual reform. Between 1832 and 1884 three Reform Bills were passed. The first abolished "rotten boroughs", places that returned members to Parliament but had few or no inhabitants, and redistributed parliamentary seats more fairly among the growing towns. It also gave the vote to many householders and tenants, but the right was based on the value of their property. Only in 1918 was universal suffrage granted and, even then, it was not quite universal: women under 30 were excluded and had to wait another 10 years. It is likely that women would not have been enfranchised until much later had it not been for the determined and sometimes violent efforts of the suffragettes, led by Emmeline Pankhurst, and the role women had played in the workforce during World War I.

TRAFALGAR'S HERO

Remembered for his stirring words before the 1805 Battle of Trafalgar, in which he died – "England expects that every man will do his duty" – Vice-Admiral Horatio Nelson is credited from saving Britain from an invasion by Napoleon. Born at Burnham Thorpe, in Norfolk, in 1758, he joined the navy at the age of 12 and was a captain by 20. Later, as head of the navy, he was known as an inspiring leader. History also remembers him for his long and romantic affair with Emma, Lady Hamilton, an ambassador's wife.

The 1829 Emancipation Act, which allowed Catholics to sit in Parliament, was another measure that frightened many of the old school, who feared it might pave the way for Popish plots and undermine both Church and State. And the controversial Repeal of the Corn Laws – the heavy taxes on imported corn, which were crippling trade and starving the poor – split the ruling Conservative Party. The "Peelite" faction, followers of the pro-repeal Prime Minister Sir Robert Peel (1788–1850), joined with Whigs to form the embryonic Liberal Party. This new grouping was committed to free trade, religious tolerance and a growing conviction that Ireland should be granted Home Rule.

The trouble with Ireland

The "Irish Question" was one to which no satisfactory answer could be found. The resentment of centuries bubbled to the surface after the potato famine of 1848, when about 20 percent of Ireland's population died of hunger and more than a million people emigrated to escape a similar fate. Hostility to Britain and all things British manifested itself in sporadic outbreaks of violence over the next decades. In 1885, after the extension of the franchise, 86 members of the Irish Party were elected to Parliament.

Lead by Charles Parnell, the "Uncrowned King of Ireland", and with the backing of Prime Minister Gladstone and many of his Liberal Party, it seemed that their demands for Home Rule would be met. But Gladstone's bills were defeated and Parnell brought down by a personal scandal. It was not until 1914 that Britain agreed to establish an Irish parliament. But World War I intervened, delaying action, and Irish nationalists, tired of waiting, decided to fight.

At Easter 1916 a group of nationalists staged a rebellion. It was savagely repressed, and the ringleaders executed. The severity of the reprisals swung Irish public opinion firmly behind the rebels, who established their own parliament, the Dail, and fought a guerrilla campaign against the British. This prompted a compromise: in 1921 Ireland was partitioned. The Irish Free State in the south was given Dominion status, not full independence, and obliged to accept the loss of six counties in the north, which remained under British rule as Northern Ireland. Partition led to civil war in Ireland. In 1932, a new party, Fianna Fáil, won the election, and 5 years later the Prime Minister, Eamon de Valera, declared southern Ireland a Republic.

The age of Dickens

In 1848, as famine raged in Ireland, revolution broke out all over Europe. In Britain, once fear of the Chartists was quashed, the country entered a period of self-confidence and relative domestic harmony, despite the polarisation of rich and poor, which Benjamin Disraeli, a later Conservative prime minister, called "the two nations" in his mid-century novel, *Sybil*. Poverty was nowhere more evident than in London, for

many of whose citizens the squalor and crime which Charles Dickens (1812–70) portrayed so evocatively in his novels – which were first written for serialisation in popular newspapers – were all too real.

Dickens was not the only one who saw a need for improvement. Change, although slow, was on the way. The idea that public health was a public responsibility was gradually taking hold. After a cholera epidemic in 1832 claimed thousands of lives, health officials were appointed and measures taken to provide drainage and clean water.

The police force that Sir Robert Peel had established in 1829, and which took the nick-

Jeremy Bentham founded University College, London, and his body, fully clothed, still sits in a glass case in the entrance hall (the head is wax).

name "bobbies" from him, was helping combat crime in London and other large towns. At the same time, Peel had abolished the death penalty for many petty crimes, such as pocket-picking, influenced perhaps by the ideas of Jeremy Bentham, the utilitarian philosopher and jurist who believed there should be a balance between reward and punishment.

A new class of clerks, tradespeople and artisans were adopting the values of thrift, sobriety

---

LEFT: an election meeting in Blackburn, Lancashire.
RIGHT: a *chiffonier*, or rag gatherer, portrayed in Charles Dickens's novels.

and self-improvement which Samuel Smiles exhorted in his famous work, *Self-Help*. The Co-Operative Movement, which began in 1844, was run on self-help lines, providing cheap goods and sharing profits with its members. Methodism, founded by John Wesley (1703–91), who established the first Methodist chapel in Bristol, had become the religion of the working class. It is often said that the British Labour Party owes more to Methodism than to Marxism.

The working class

It is certainly true that working-class people, on the whole, were not attracted by revolutionary struggle and preferred to pursue their aims through trade-union organisation and representation in Parliament. The first working-class member of Parliament in 1892 was John Keir Hardie, the Scottish miners' leader, and 14 years later the British Labour Party won its first parliamentary seats. Although Karl Marx (1818–83) lived and worked in London for much of his life – his tomb can be seen in London's Highgate Cemetery – his ideas were known and shared only by a relatively small group of middle-class intellectuals.

Also largely ignored by the working man for whom he hoped to speak was John Ruskin (1819–1900), one of the founders of the Pre-

THE COMPLACENCY OF THE VICTORIAN MIDDLE CLASSES

Funded largely by the wealth of the Empire, middle-class life had become comfortable and pleasant. Improved transport – including the world's first underground railway, opened in London in 1863 – enabled people to work in towns but live in leafy suburbs. Most of their new homes had bathrooms, and the majority employed a maid.

Art and drama flourished. Aubrey Beardsley's fluid, sensual drawings were creating a stir. The Art Nouveau movement influenced the work of Charles Rennie Mackintosh (1868–1928), who founded the Glasgow School.

At the theatre, audiences were being entertained by the plays of two Anglo-Irish writers: George Bernard Shaw, who believed in combining education with entertainment and introduced radical politics into his work, and Oscar Wilde, who poked sophisticated fun at London's high society in plays such as *The Importance of Being Earnest* but who ended his glittering career in a prison cell on charges of homosexuality.

Married women were finally allowed to control their own property in 1882 and were soon permitted to vote in a few local elections. Social reformers were making some progress in alleviating poverty. All in all, Britain was feeling quite pleased with itself by the end of the century.

Raphaelite Brotherhood of painters and writers which flourished in the late 19th century. Another member, William Morris (1834–96), devoted himself to the revival of medieval arts and crafts, and shared Ruskin's anger at the social deprivation caused by capitalism. Fellow Pre-Raphaelites were Edward Burne-Jones, John Millais and Dante Gabriel Rossetti, artists who were perhaps less concerned with the social ills of the 19th century but equally convinced of the need to return to pre-Renaissance art forms. They eventually became establishment figures, and their work is spread through galleries in London and other major cities across the country.

with Scotland, which had had state education since 1696.

Working-class life improved considerably during the last quarter of the 19th century. Many homes had gas lighting, and streets were cleaned by newly created municipal councils. The music hall provided inexpensive entertainment in towns. Bicycles became a common method of transport, and day trips by train to seaside resorts were the highlight of the summer, even if most excursionists could not afford the bathing machines that allowed more affluent visitors to get into the water without any great loss of modesty.

Ruskin and Morris were among a growing number of those who believed that the lot of working people would only be improved through education. Despite fears in some quarters that education for the masses was a dangerous thing, two Education Acts were passed towards the end of the century that made schooling free and compulsory up to the age of 13. The educational provision may have been rudimentary, but at least it was there – which put England on a more equal footing

LEFT: a painting by Phoebus Leven shows Covent Garden market in 1864. **ABOVE:** the princess who became the long-reigning Queen Victoria. **RIGHT:** the Crystal Palace, built for the Great Exhibition of 1851.

Celebrating the empire

Queen Victoria's Diamond Jubilee in 1897 celebrated 60 years on the throne for the woman who had spent much of her reign as a black-clad widow and who ruled over the biggest empire in the world. Atlases of the time showed vast areas coloured red, signifying that they were British colonies. The Punjab and much of Southern Africa had been added to earlier possessions. Egypt and the Sudan had become colonies – in practice if not in name – after Britain invaded in 1882 to protect its shipping routes to India through the newly built Suez Canal. Britannia did indeed rule the waves. Like most empires at their peak, Britain's seemed unassailable. Then came the 20th century… ❑

MODERN TIMES

The British won their wars but lost their empire and then faced the big question: did they really and truly want to join a United States of Europe?

All good things must come to an end. The (Second) Boer War of 1899–1902 ended in victory for Britain in South Africa but damaged its international reputation. France, Germany and America were competing for world markets. The newly united German state was the biggest threat, its education system putting it far ahead of Britain in scientific and technological developments. Germany had good reserves of coal and iron and was becoming the world's biggest producer of steel, which it was using to build battleships to rival those of the British navy.

Fear of Germany's growing strength forced Britain and France into an alliance. This, together with an earlier treaty that promised to guarantee Belgium's neutrality, plus the fear that Germany would overrun Europe and gain control of parts of the Empire, brought Britain into World War I in 1914. The Edwardian era, sandwiched between the turn of the century

The scale of the carnage on the French battlefields in World War I shocked even such patriots as the writer Rudyard Kipling, who had been firmly committed to the aims of the war.

and the outbreak of war, is remembered as the zenith of prosperous stability, but its foundations had been rocky for some time.

The Roaring Twenties

World War I claimed over a million British casualties, most of them under the age of 25. But had the sacrifice been worth it? Men who had fought in France and been promised a "land fit for heroes" were disillusioned when they found unemployment and poor housing awaited them at the war's end in 1918. Women who had worked in factories while the men were away were not prepared to give up any of their independence. There were strikes on the railways and in the mines, and political unrest led to four general elections in just over five years, including one which brought the Labour Party to power for the first time. In 1926 a general strike paralysed the country, but the unions' demands were not met, and the men returned to work, much disgruntled and worse off than before.

There was another side to life, of course. For some, unaffected by gloomy financial reality, these were the Roaring Twenties. Women with cropped hair and short dresses drank cocktails and danced to the new music, jazz, which had crossed the ocean from America. Silent films, another US import, were the wonder of the age. Writers such as Virginia Woolf and D.H. Lawrence were opening new horizons for the curious and daring – although it would be another 30 years before Lawrence's *Lady Chatterley's Lover* could be published in Britain, so shocking was the affair between its eponymous upper-class heroine and Mellors, her working-class gardener.

The New York Stock Market crash of 1929 looked as if it would bring the party to an end. The effects soon spread throughout Europe,

electrical and light engineering industries. The bold, geometric designs of Art Deco (first showcased at the International Exhibition in Paris in 1925), could soon be seen adorning the new factories that lined the main roads that in turn were increasingly filling with small family cars.

World War II

With memories of the "war to end all wars" still fresh in people's minds, there was great reluctance to enter another conflict. But by 1939 the policy of appeasement of German aggression was no longer tenable. Although Britain's island status saved it from invasion, the war involved civilians

and by 1931 Britain was entering the Great Depression. Many fortunes were ruined, but the principal victims of the recession were in the industrial areas of northern England, south Wales, and Clydeside in Scotland. Three million people lost their jobs and suffered real misery with only the "dole" (from "doling out" money), a limited state benefit, to keep them from starvation and homelessness. British cinema thrived, as people sought an escape from reality.

In the south of England and the Midlands, the depression hit less hard, and recovery was faster, mainly due to the rapid growth of the motor,

LEFT: bathing belles in the 1920s. **ABOVE:** London's Underground stations became bomb shelters in 1940.

THE ABDICATION

In 1936, the country was rocked by an unprecedented crisis. Edward VIII succeeded his father Geroge V but was obliged to abdicate, when family, Church and Government united in their refusal to let him marry a twice-divorced American, Mrs Wallis Simpson. The British public was kept in the dark about the matter. The couple married in France and remained in permanent exile as the Duke and Duchess of Windsor.

Edward's brother came to the throne, and, as George VI, became a popular monarch, not least for the solidarity which he and his Queen, Elizabeth, later the Queen Mother, showed with their subjects during the Blitz, as the German bombing raids were called.

in an unprecedented way. German bombing raids tore the heart out of many cities – in the Battle of Britain, from July to September 1940, the Germans tried to gain air superiority over the British air force. They failed, creating a turning point for the war and contributing to the Germans' ultimate downfall, but the cost was high. Coventry was particularly badly hit; its present cathedral, with its renowned John Piper windows, was built to replace the one that was lost. Ports and shipyards around the country were battered by repeated raids. Much of the modern building in British towns, not always blending too harmoniously, has been erected on former bomb sites.

Many London families spent their nights in the Underground stations, the safest places during an attack, and a lot of people from cities and industrial areas were evacuated to the countryside during the worst of the Blitz. For children, sent to live with strangers while their parents remained behind, it was both a time of great loneliness and the first glimpse many of them had ever had of green fields and woodlands. For some of the country families on whom they were billeted, it may have been their first glimpse of the effects of urban deprivation.

Sir Winston Churchill had received massive popular support as an inspirational war leader, and is still regarded by many people as Britain's greatest prime minister. But when hostilities ended in 1945 the electorate, to his surprise and dismay, declined to re-elect him and voted overwhelmingly for a Labour government: the war effort had fostered egalitarianism, and many returning servicemen felt that electing a Conservative government again would simply resuscitate the old class differences.

The problems of the war-torn country proved intractable, but the Labour government laboured to keep its promises. The basis of the welfare state was laid, providing free medical care for everyone and financial help for the old, the sick and the unemployed. The Bank of England, coal mines, railways and steelworks were nationalised. These were hard and joyless years, however, and wartime rationing of food, clothing and fuel continued into the early 1950s.

The end of empire

One of the most far-reaching consequences of the war was that it hastened the end of Britain's empire. Starting with India's independence in 1947, the colonies one after another achieved autonomy during the next two decades. Jamaica and Trinidad did not gain independence until 1962, but they were two islands whose people were among the first black immigrants to Britain in the early 1950s, when work was plentiful and immigrants were welcomed to fill the labour gap. Newcomers from the Caribbean settled mainly in London at first, while later immigrants from the Indian subcontinent made their homes in the Midlands, where textiles and the motor industry offered employment.

The post-war years were ones of uneasy peace. Britain joined the war against North Korea in

> *Britain's departure from the Indian subcontient and the consequent creation of the states of India and Pakistan along religious lines led to the displacement of 10–14 million people, and the death of up to 1 million.*

1950, and its troops, still a conscripted army, fought there for four years. In 1956, following Egyptian nationalisation of the Suez Canal, British and French forces conspired to attack Egypt, pleading bogus provocation. The action was widely condemned both at home and particularly in the United States, and it represented an ignominious end to Britain's imperial ambitions.

These were also the years of the Cold War between the Soviet Union and the West, which prompted Britain to become a nuclear power. The first British hydrogen bomb was tested in 1958, three years after the world's first nuclear power station had opened in Cumberland (now Cumbria). The Campaign for Nuclear Disarmament was born in response and organised large protest marches.

A new Elizabethan Age

All was not gloom and doom. In 1947 Edinburgh staged a highly successful festival of music and drama, which has gone from

minster Abbey. Britain's Television Age began in earnest on that day, too, as millions watched the coronation live on tiny flickering screens.

By the latter half of the decade things were definitely looking up. Harold Macmillan, the Conservative prime minister, declared in a famous speech that people had "never had it so

> Princess Elizabeth was in Kenya when she learnt on 6 February 1952 that her father George VI had died and she had acceded to the throne. She was crowned on 2 June 1953.

strength to strength. At the same time the first annual International Music Eisteddfod was held in Llangollen in Wales. Four years later the Festival of Britain was held in the newly built Royal Festival Hall on London's South Bank – the National Theatre was added to the concrete complex in 1964.

The Festival was designed to commemorate the Great Exhibition 100 years earlier and strongly signalled the beginning of the end of postwar austerity. In 1953, a new Elizabethan Age began, as Elizabeth II was crowned in West-

LEFT: Churchill appeals to the electorate in 1945.
ABOVE: the climax of *If…*, Lindsay Anderson's 1968 allegorical film pitting youth against the establishment.

good": unemployment was low, average living standards were rising. New universities were built, with the aim of making higher education a possibility for more than just the privileged elite. Most people had two weeks' paid holiday a year, and, alongside the traditional seaside resorts, holiday camps blossomed, offering cheap family vacations.

Social attitudes were changing too, reflected in the rise of a group of writers known as "angry young men", including John Osborne and Arnold Wesker, whose plays challenged conventional values. Their popularity marked the beginning of a move away from middle-class and American dominance in literature and popular culture.

The swinging '60s

The 1960s saw an explosion of new talent, much of it from the north of England. Alan Sillitoe and Stan Barstow wrote about working-class life in a way no one had done before. Actors such as Albert Finney and Tom Courteney achieved huge success, and film directors Lindsay Anderson and Karel Reisz (best known for *If...* and *Saturday Night and Sunday Morning*, based on Sillitoe's novel of that name) made British films box-office hits. Pop music, as it was now called, underwent a revolution when a group from Liverpool, the Beatles, became world celebrities and turned their home town into a place of pilgrimage.

oil prices pushed up the cost of living, high inflation took its toll, and unemployment soared. Oil was discovered in the North Sea, but despite the building of oil rigs providing jobs, the oil revenues were largely soaked up in payments to the jobless. There was no economic miracle.

To deepen the gloom, English cities were again bombed. This time the perpetrators were the IRA, who were fighting to end British rule in Northern Ireland. The province spent most of the 1970s and '80s in a state akin to civil war, as a dispute over the unfair allocation of public housing spiralled into a bitter struggle over national identity.

The introduction of the contraceptive pill prompted a revolution in sexual attitudes, and the laws relating to abortion, homosexuality and censorship were liberalised. It was a decade of optimism, and national self-confidence was infectious: in 1966 England's footballers even beat Germany to win the World Cup.

The subdued '70s

It was during the winter of 1973, when an oil embargo and a miners' strike provoked a State of Emergency and brought down Edward Heath's Conservative government, that the self-confidence collapsed. In the same year, with mixed feelings, Britain finally became a full member of the Common Market (now the European Union). Rising

The 1970s also saw nationalism flourish in Wales and Scotland. Plaid Cymru (pronounced "plyed cumree") became a political force in Wales, where TV and radio channels in Welsh were launched. In Scotland, support grew for the Scottish National Party (*see panel, opposite*).

The Thatcher years

By 1979, unemployment had reached 3½ million and a wave of strikes plunged the country into what was called "the winter of discontent". The country lost confidence in its Labour government, and an election returned the Conservatives to office under their new leader, a grocer's daughter from Grantham, Lincolnshire, Margaret Thatcher.

The impact of the West's first woman prime minister was enormous, but her personal popularity soon began to fade, as the economy remained weak. However, her political stock was dramatically strengthened in 1982 by the Falklands War, when an invading Argentinian force was beaten off these South Atlantic islands, remnants of the empire.

For many, the 1980s meant increased prosperity. The most ambitious development was the renewal of London's derelict docklands area into a new industrial site, with its own small airport and light railway system and prestige housing for young urban professionals. Docklands' Canary Wharf development was proclaimed to be the future city of London. For many people, however, the dream of living in London faded, as the strong economy pushed up the capital's house prices and rents.

The nervous '90s

As the 1990s began, the economy was no longer riding so high. A long, acrimonious miners' strike in 1984 had weakened the unions, and coal mines, including most of those in the closely knit mining communities of South Wales, were subsequently closed. Most of Britain's nationalised industries were privatised, a move that a former Conservative prime minister, Harold Macmillan, likened to "selling the family silver".

After 11 years of Thatcherite rule, people began to tire of the Iron Lady's uncompromising style, and she was finally voted out in November 1990 – not by the electorate, but by her own party. The Conservatives believed she had lost touch with the country, particularly over its role within the European Union, and that they might therefore lose the next election. She was replaced by a less combative leader, John Major.

Britain's technical status as an island was removed in 1994, when the first fare-paying passengers travelled by rail to Paris and Brussels through the long-awaited Channel Tunnel. But the big question remained: did Britain really feel European enough to be part of a full monetary union – perhaps even, one day, a political union?

That *fin-de-siècle* feeling

Two events in 1997 shook the nation out of its wary complacency. In a general election the Conservative Party was swept from power after 17 years, as the Labour Party roared in with an unassailable overall majority of 179 seats in the House of Commons. The Conservatives were left without a single seat in either Scotland or Wales, both of which voted in subsequent referenda for a greater degree of self-rule; this limited devolution took effect in 1999 with the setting up of new assemblies in Edinburgh and Cardiff.

But Tony Blair's new government, dubbed "New Labour", soon disappointed many by

SCOTLAND'S FUTURE

Scotland has been an integral part of the UK since the 1707 Treaty of Union, yet talk of independence is ongoing. Many Scots were incensed that, when oil was discovered in the North Sea in the 1970s, the proceeds flowed into the national coffers in London. The English, on the other hand, feel resentful that while there are now prescription charges and university fees in their country, Britain's taxes go towards giving the Scots the free prescriptions and fee-free higher education voted for by the Scottish Parliament. With Alex Salmond's Scottish National Party (SNP) firmly ensconced as the dominant party in Scotland a referendum on independence has been promised.

LEFT: as prime minister, Margaret Thatcher inspired great loyalty and great antagonism. **RIGHT:** outpouring of grief for Diana, Princess of Wales.

abandoning its socialist roots, promoting unexpectedly conservative economic policies with evangelical fervour.

The second defining event in 1997 was the death of Diana, Princess of Wales, in a car crash in Paris. The wave of grief that swept the country took everyone by surprise. Some attacked the royal family for failing to display sufficient anguish – a predicament dramatised in a 2006 film, when actress Helen Mirren portrayed the Queen. A third notable event in 1997 was the handover of sovereignty of Hong Kong to the Chinese – a move that signalled yet another reduction in Britain's role on the world stage.

To mark the new century, a huge Millennium Dome was built at Greenwich in London, but the pedagogic exhibition it contained failed to catch the public imagination, and the venture lost a fortune. (It has since been bought by a telecommunications giant and hosts large-scale exhibitions and events.) The London Eye, a giant revolving wheel on the south bank of the Thames in London, was a far greater success and became a permanent fixture. In June 2001 the Labour Party won another landslide election victory, despite a great deal of voter apathy. The crucial question of whether Britain should embrace the single European currency, the euro, totally divided public opinion, and effectively the issue was put on the back burner.

The American connection

Europe remains an issue that can still destroy governments because it forces people to confront questions of identity and loyalties. For centuries Britain had warred with Spain, France and Germany, and, although Britons

> The 2010 general election resulted in the first British hung parliament – where no one party has a majority – since 1974, when Labour under Harold Wilson eventually formed a short-lived minority government.

today are happy to holiday in a *gîte* in Normandy or a resort on the Costa del Sol, most still regard Europe as "foreign". Because of ancestral links and a shared language, many feel more comfortable with the United States, even though its values and attitudes are often far more different than those of, say, Germany or Italy.

Tony Blair argued that Britain was ideally placed to be a bridge between America and the European Union, but European politicians regularly accused Britain of being a less-than-faithful partner, as it professed eternal love for its fellow Europeans but remained reluctant to learn their languages, wouldn't accept the euro as national currency, and continued to cast come-hither glances towards its muscular friend across the Atlantic.

This conflict came to a head when George W. Bush's administration determined to invade Iraq. While much of Europe opposed the war, Tony Blair went against public opinion by making Britain a full coalition partner; more than 1 million people marched in protest. The failure to find the much-touted weapons of mass destruction in Iraq severely dented Blair's reputation for trustworthiness, and, although Britain's economy had remained more robust than most European economies, criticism mounted that Labour had failed to deliver adequate public services and had no answers to chronic problems such as traffic congestion and threats to the environment.

Yet Labour's hold on power remained secure, because not only had the Conservative Party failed to heal the splits (especially over Europe) that had forced Margaret Thatcher from power, but the acrid arguments between the Thatcherite sympathisers and their opponents made them look unfit to govern.

London is targeted

In July 2005, London surprised itself by winning its bid to host the 2012 Olympic Games. The building programme needed to accommodate the games would, it was promised, rejuvenate run-down areas of East London, notably around Stratford.

On the very next day, the jubilation ceased, when suicide bombers killed 52 people and injured more than 700 on three Underground trains and a bus. Two weeks later, other bombers failed to detonate four more devices on the city's transport network. These attacks raised the question of how to make such a sprawling cosmopolitan city more secure, particularly since the bombers were not foreign terrorists who had evaded the country's border checks but British-born Muslims.

An insecure society

Confidence within the country was becoming increasingly shaken, not only with respect to security, but also regarding the economy. Following the "credit crunch" of 2008, Britain's economy went on to crash into recession – a state officially declared in January 2009. As banks that had been believed to be infallible went into liquidation, some of Great Britain's troubled economic institutions were nationalised, in the worst financial crisis in the West since the 1929 Wall Street crash and the subsequent Great Depression of the 1930s.

Britain's booming housing bubble well and truly burst, with stagnation in the market way outlasting all initial predictions. And there was trouble in Parliament, too: in 2009 the extent of expenses claimed by MPs – everything from the cost of cleaning their moats and installing a "duck island" to new toilet seats, facecloths and lawnmower repairs – threatened to undermine Parliament itself, when the scandal was revealed by a national newspaper.

In the UK general election of May 2010, the public decided that enough was enough, at least as far as Labour rule was concerned. The election resulted in a hung parliament, with David

Cameron's Conservatives, who won the most seats, forming a Coalition government with Nick Clegg's Liberal Democrats. The focus of Cameron/Clegg government has been to reduce the country's massive financial deficit, with tough economic measures quickly introduced – measures its critics have condemned as slash-and-burn tactics. For now, the public remains anxious, not only as to whether these "austerity measures" will really set the country's economy back on track, but also because their full impact has yet to be felt, despite unemployment, inflation, tax rates (including VAT, now set at 20 percent) and the cost of living all rising.

In 2011 the grey mood across the country, was somewhat relieved by the long-anticipated wedding of Prince William to Catherine Middleton (now the Duchess of Cambridge) with much attendant interest from the world's press.

Optimists hope that two further feel-good events – the London 2012 Olympics (which has resulted in a huge regeneration project in East London) and the Queen's Jubilee in the same year – will further improve morale, as well as boosting the economy through tourism. And in troubled times, it is perhaps reassuring – and very typically British – to feel that age-old traditions, such as these historic sporting and monarchical ones, might be just what is needed to propel us into a better future. ❑

LEFT: flowers laid outside Kensington Palace following the death of Princess Diana. **ABOVE:** protest outside the Bank of England during the banking crisis.

AN A TO Z OF BRITISH CULTURE

Like an iceberg, the British psyche is mostly hidden
from view. In a series of penetrating essays,
we reveal what lies beneath the surface

The stereotype of the British is that they take a masochistic delight in hearing how bleak their outlook is. As Sir Winston Churchill put it, they "are the only people who like to be told how bad things are – they like to be told the worst." And it's certainly a conspicuous characteristic. Noël Coward lampooned it in the song "There are bad times just around the corner" – which, of course, became immensely popular. Reactions to this self-deprecation, which is probably more real than romanticised, vary among visitors, from intrigue to finding it aloof.

Yet beyond this conventional view of its inhabitants, this astonishing island – a place that is very much the algebraic sum of its three parts of England, Scotland, Wales – offers a wealth of historic and cultural riches to entice and delight the visitor.

The A to Z of the nation and its foibles on the following pages looks at the ruling establishment of government, knights, lords and monarchy, and the role of such British institutions as the BBC (the country's original and still most influential television corporation). It examines the country's preoccupation with the weather and considers its hang-ups about accents, class and sex. This chapter extols its games, its theatre and its pubs. It explains the particular peculiarities of tea-drinking and forming queues. And the section finishes by trying to analyse the peculiar

PRECEDING PAGES: exuberant audience at the Last Night of the Proms, the annual musical festival staged by the BBC at London's Royal Albert Hall.
LEFT: accompanying the Changing the Guard ceremony at Buckingham Palace. RIGHT: examining the art at London's Tate Modern.

zeitgeist that has gripped post-imperial Britain – this "soggy little island huffing and puffing to keep up with Western Europe", as the American novelist John Updike once characterised it.

This alphabetical analysis does not explain everything that goes on either in public or behind closed doors between John O'Groats and Land's End, but it may shed light on the shadier areas of a society renowned for curious customs, mild eccentricities and confusion as to whether or not it's European.

ACCENTS

When, in his play *Pygmalion* (later to be reborn as the film, then stage show, *My Fair Lady*),

George Bernard Shaw set Professor Henry Higgins the task of passing off Eliza Doolittle, a common Cockney flower-seller, as a duchess at an ambassador's dinner party, there was no question about Higgins's first priority: he had to change her accent. Then, as now, a person's origins, class as well as locality, could be identified by the way he or she speaks. Shaw cynically observed: "it is impossible for an Englishman to open his mouth without making another Englishman despise or hate him."

Although such snobbery is most associated with the English, the Welsh and Scots are not immune. The linguistically alert can detect a

range of class differences between the North Welsh and the South Welsh, for instance, and the ambassador might well prefer a dinner party guest who greeted him in the soft-spoken tones of middle-class Edinburgh than in the harsh-sounding vernacular of working-class Glasgow.

It is remarkable – given these social pressures, the small size of Britain and the smoothing influence of television – that a vast variety of regional accents continues to flourish. Yet they do, so much so that at times even someone from within the country itself has to listen carefully to a strong accent, such as one from the West Country or the extremes of Scotland.

With Asian, African and West Indian immigrants having added to the variety of speech patterns in Britain, consensus about what constitutes "proper English speech" remains as elusive as ever. Television presenters often embrace a neutralised, accent-free English – something of a downmarket turn from the plummy Queen's English that was typical of mid-20th-century BBC broadcasting. And it's increasingly fashionable nowadays to use presenters with accents, such as the Brummie (Birmingham) or Geordie (Newcastle) ones. In Scotland and Wales, too, it is standard to have a stronger focus on the local accent.

ART

Centuries of aristocratic and royal collectors have ensured that Britain is rich in artistic treasures. Wealthy patrons have long displayed their trophies in their private, country-house galleries. The first public museums in Britain were based on antiquarian collections of curiosities, prints, drawings and books. Oxford's Ashmolean Museum opened in 1683, London's British Museum in 1759. Both subsequently acquired large art and archaeological collections, and moved into sprawling neoclassical buildings in the first half of the 19th century. The first purpose-built art gallery, however, was South London's Dulwich Picture Gallery, completed in 1817 to designs by Sir John Soane.

The 19th century also brought museums founded on the entrepreneurial wealth born of the Industrial Revolution. Most notable was Henry Tate, who made his fortune from sugar lumps and gave his name to the museum of British art now known as Tate Britain. The Tate foundation subsequently established galleries in Liverpool, St Ives and on London's South

ALLOTMENTS

Around 250,000 people rent allotments, small parcels of land on which to grow vegetables and fruit. They also provide opportunities to exchange tips with other gardeners. Allotments, which are grouped together and average 300 sq yards (250 sq metres) – based on an ancient measurement of 10 rods – are generally owned by local town or parish councils. Their popularity peaked during World War II, though the practice can be traced back a thousand years to when Saxons would clear a piece of woodland and allocate portions to local citizens. In the 19th century, the government made it obligatory for local authorities to provide allotments when there was a demand for them.

Bank (Tate Modern). The Victoria and Albert Museum in South Kensington was also founded on Britain's industrial prosperity. It was originally devoted to the applied arts and science, but the collection has evolved to encompass decorative art and design.

Art historians have long held that Britain has never given birth to an avant-garde art movement. This is often attributed to the conservatism of the British nation, and the stability and relative prosperity that have characterised its history. However, the 1990s brought the closest thing yet to a home-grown avant garde. The Young British Artists (or YBAs) – Damian

(tel: 01908 676 900; www.mkgallery.org) in Milton Keynes; the Ikon Gallery (tel: 0121 248 0708; www.ikon-gallery.co.uk) in Birmingham; and Newcastle's Baltic Centre for Contemporary Art (tel: 0191 478 1810; www.balticmill.com).

The centre of the European art market, London, is home to more than 200 commercial galleries, as well as the British headquarters of major auction houses including Sotheby's and Christie's. The capital's Mayfair district is the location of many of Britain's high-end galleries, while its grittier East End is home to many of Britain's younger generation of artists. The best-known gallery here is White Cube, on Hoxton Square.

Hirst, Tracey Emin, Sarah Lucas and Gary Hume, among others – were graduates of the same art school and exhibited together after leaving. Their work, which is varied in form and content, can be seen in galleries including Tate Modern and the Saatchi Gallery. Each year, the Tate hosts the Turner Prize, Britain's most prestigious competition for contemporary artists. Works by those who are shortlisted are usually displayed at Tate Britain. Important exhibitions of contemporary art are also held at London's Whitechapel, Hayward and Serpentine galleries; the MK Gallery

Scotland has a distinguished art history too, with museums including Edinburgh's National Museum of Scotland and Scottish National Gallery. It is particularly rich, however, in museums for more recent art. Since its industrial heyday in the 19th century, Glasgow has been a major centre for artists, from the anti-academic Glasgow Boys to the artist and designer Charles Rennie Mackintosh. In Edinburgh, the Scottish National Gallery of Modern Art presents a good survey of the art movements of the last century.

BBC

Depending on your viewpoint, the BBC (British Broadcasting Corporation) is either the world's biggest and best broadcasting organisation, or a

LEFT: he loves boating and is bound to have an Oxford accent. **ABOVE:** filming one of the BBC's celebrated costume dramas, Charles Dickens's *Little Dorrit*.

power-crazed and profligate monster that's out of control. Since it is a public-service organisation funded through an annual licence fee that must be paid by everyone who owns a TV set – whether they watch BBC channels or not – public opinion cannot be ignored. (Anyone can, of course, access the BBC website free of charge.)

The corporation is certainly big. It runs eight advertising-free TV channels in the UK, including two children's channels and a politics channel, a similar number of ad-free national radio channels, a host of local radio channels, several choirs and orchestras, and Europe's biggest website. It also publishes books and magazines.

In addition, it runs commercial operations overseas, such as BBC America, and is paid by the government to promote Britain's image and values by broadcasting BBC World Service radio around the world in 32 languages. Its costume dramas and high-profile entertainment shows such as *Strictly Come Dancing* are not only popular at home but make a lot of money in export sales. Crucially, it nourishes emerging talent – actors, writers, directors and executives – who often go on to form the creative backbone of many of its commercial rivals.

The BBC's powers and obligations are vested in a trust of 12 worthy and theoretically inde-

THE CHANNEL ISLANDS

Victor Hugo called the Channel Islands "pieces of France which fell into the sea and were gathered up by England". Best known as tax havens, the two main bank-rich islands are Jersey (45 sq miles/117 sq km) and Guernsey (24 sq miles/62 sq km). The 2-sq-mile (5-sq-km) island of Sark is a feudal remnant, ruled over by a hereditary seigneur.

The islands lie just off the French coast and constitutionally are not part of the United Kingdom, yet their ambience is resolutely British. English holidaymakers tend to like the combination of the islands' slightly French ambience and the familiar English language.

pendent people appointed by the Queen on government recommendation. These powers are exercised through a permanent staff headed by a director-general and a board of management. The government confines itself to insisting that the BBC, which was established in 1927, must be impartial and free from political interference and must stay within its budget.

That's the theory. In practice, the political parties tot up the number of minutes' reporting of each side of an issue, looking for bias – and usually claim to find it. When in 2003 a reporter seemed to allege on an early-morning radio news programme that Tony Blair's government, in order to justify going to war with Iraq, had exaggerated the threat from Saddam Hussein, all hell broke loose, and both the BBC chairman and its director-general eventually resigned.

Unconcerned with pleasing advertisers, the BBC could ration its audience to what is excellent and edifying rather than what people necessarily want to watch, but audience ratings matter. If the BBC appeals to too few people, the universal annual licence fee could no longer be justified. But if it dumbs down too much in pursuit of ratings, its commercial rivals – and in particular Rupert Murdoch, who controls Sky TV's satellite channels – would say it is no longer fulfilling its public-service purpose. In an age of proliferating digital channels, the licence fee is increasingly under attack, and the Corporation is constantly looking at ways of financing its output, from index-linked licences to pay-as-you-view TV.

CLASS

A newspaper cartoon cunningly caught the British confusion over its social attitudes. "I don't believe in class differences," its well-heeled gentleman was explaining, "but luckily my butler disagrees with me." The implication is that the lower classes, far from being revolutionaries, are as keen as anyone to maintain the status quo.

At the top end of the scale, the monarchy cements the social hierarchy; fringe aristocrats define their social standing in relation to their closeness to royalty, and the elaborate honours system transforms achievement into a (usually) much sought-after feudal rank because the titles (even though generally decided by politicians) are bestowed in person by the monarch.

From time to time, the class rigidities seem set to crumble, but the promise is never quite fulfilled, mainly because the British have a genius for absorbing dissenters into "the system". The 1960s promoted a new egalitarianism; but it wasn't long before such former rebels as Rolling Stones frontman Mick Jagger were consorting with the royal family – "Sir Mick" is not the only one of his formerly rebellious peers to be knighted. In the 1980s, the consensus among classes seemed again to be threatened, this time by Thatcherism, whose economic policies created stark inequalities between the

regions and swelled the ranks of the disgruntled unemployed; worried about their election prospects, the Conservative Party replaced Mrs Thatcher in mid-term with the more emollient John Major.

Mr Major's humble origins suggested that any working-class boy who applied himself diligently could become prime minister – surely a threat to the power of the upper classes? And what about the supposedly left-wing traditions that nurtured Tony Blair and Gordon Brown? If the current prime minister and his cabinet (his ministers) are anything to go by, the old school tie has as durable a knot as ever. In 2010

David Cameron became the 19th Prime Minister to have attended the country's most exclusive school, Eton College. To add fire to the flames of the class/power/elitism debate, for his first cabinet Cameron gave 20 of the 29 posts to Oxbridge graduates, two of whom had also attended Eton and three of whom, including the deputy Prime Minister, Liberal Democrat leader Nick Clegg, had attended Westminster, a public school almost as elite. And with only four women in ministerial posts, this is the poshest, most male-dominated cabinet for decades. In late 2010 *The Times* listed Home Secretary Theresa May as the most important woman in politics, with Samantha Cameron (a Baronet's daughter) at No. 2 – it's telling that

LEFT: local boys look on with curiosity and amusement at two Harrow schoolboys in their formal uniform at an Eton vs Harrow cricket match, at Lord's cricket ground in the 1930s. **RIGHT:** John and Norma Major.

the second-most influential woman in politics is there by merit of her husband. Although in popular culture it seems as though anyone – regardless of class – can aspire to be rich and famous, among the ruling classes it still helps to have come through traditional channels after all.

CRICKET

It's playing the game that counts, as the old saying (or excuse) goes, not the winning. That's certainly true of cricket, which has been described as "a game which the British, not being a spiritual people, had to invent in order to have some concept of eternity." The main purpose is simple: a bowler hurls a leather-covered ball at three wooden stumps in order to dislodge two strips of wood (bails) resting on top of them, and the batsman tries to deflect the ball with a paddle-shaped piece of willow.

But the byzantine rules, first laid down by London's Marylebone Cricket Club in 1788, are best captured by a satirical definition: "You have two sides, one out in the field and one in. Each man that's in the side that's in, goes out and when he's out he comes in and the next man goes in until he's out. When they're all out, the side that's out comes in and the side that's been in goes out and tries to get those coming in out.

Sometimes you get men still in and not out. When both sides have been in and out, including the not-outs, that's the end of the game."

Not surprisingly, an international match can take from 3 to 5 days to complete.

CRIME

The incidence of most kinds of crime, including pickpocketing, car crime and violence, is falling in Britain, according to government statistics for 2010. Not that you'd know it from the press, certain elements of which thrive on scare-mongering, with dramatic reporting of high-profile crimes. And reporting of this kind does make an impact. A spate of teenage knifings in 2008, for example, gave the impression

ECCENTRICS

In *English Eccentrics*, Edith Sitwell (1887–1964) stated that English eccentricity was born of "that peculiar... knowledge of infallibility that is the hallmark and the birthright of the British nation." The aristocracy has provided many such characters, such as the 8th Earl of Bridgewater, who organised banquets for dogs, or the 5th Earl of Portland, who liked to live underground. Today's eccentrics are often less oddball and more charming than their predecessors, such as the comedian/actor Russell Brand, who fashions himself as a silver-tongued English fop, and the Mayor of London, Boris Johnson, whose bumbling boyishness seems to get him out of numerous scrapes.

that such crime was out of control. Yet when London police conducted a 6-week shakedown of youths, only 500 of the 27,000 people frisked were carrying knives – less than 2 percent. And an analysis of hospital admissions found that the vast majority of violent crimes occur in Britain's most impoverished areas, with men aged 18–30 the most-likely victims.

The unsurprising moral: it's best not to wander through a deprived inner-city area late at night looking like an affluent tourist.

DRAMA

In spite of its reputation, the West End of London is not always the place to find the country's dramatic cultural pearls. Here the tradition is as much of the theatre as of performances. This is where velvet-and-gilt Victorian playhouses were designed so that most of the audience would peer down over the cast, where "the gods" (the seats high at the back) bring on vertigo and a concern that, had the buildings been conceived today, fire regulations would have ensured they never left the architects' drawing boards.

Nevertheless, the West End is still a theatrical magnet, because that is where the money is. Catering for audiences by the coachload, impresarios look to musical spectacles, revivals and plays that will please the widest range of tastes. As a result, such middle-of-the-road creatives as composer Andrew Lloyd Webber (now Lord Lloyd-Webber) have become both famous and exceedingly rich.

Traditionalists claimed that the mania for musicals squeezes out new drama productions. Yet a glance at the theatre listings doesn't entirely bear out this claim. Classics continue to be staged at the National Theatre, the Old Vic and the Young Vic (the latter also puts on international work), new writing features strongly at the Royal Court, and experimental work and alternative comedy are mounted at fringe venues such as the Islington Almeida, Hackney's Arcola, Notting Hill's Gate Theatre, London Bridge's Menier Chocolate Factory and the Battersea Arts Centre.

As well as locally grown stars such as Michael Gambon, Ian McKellan, Maggie Smith, Diana Rigg and Judi Dench, and their younger coun-

LEFT: Jeff Goldblum and Kevin Spacey in *Speed the Plow* at London's Old Vic. **RIGHT:** 10 Downing Street, the address every British politician would like to have.

terparts such as Keira Knightley, Sienna Miller, James McAvoy and Daniel Radcliffe, American actors have never been strangers to the West End. Kathleen Turner, Jerry Hall and Amanda Donohoe took turns to disrobe as Mrs Robinson in a stage version of *The Graduate*, while Nicole Kidman was described as "theatrical Viagra" when she briefly appeared naked in David Hare's *The Blue Room*; more recently, Jeff Goldblum starred in Neil Simon's *The Prisoner of Second* Avenue and *Mad Men's* Elisabeth Moss appeared in Lillian Hellman's *The Children's Hour*. And after Kevin Spacey scored a hit in *The Iceman Cometh* at the Old Vic, he accepted the

job of artistic director of the venerable theatre, helping to raise funds to repair its leaky roof and cracked walls and promising to act as well as direct there.

Shakespeare is certainly alive and well. The replica of Shakespeare's Globe on London's South Bank has been a triumph of culture over commercialism, with audiences paying to savour the 16th-century ambience by standing for hours in front of the stage or sitting on rock-hard benches. The Royal Shakespeare Company, based in Stratford-upon-Avon, takes much of its repertoire to London and several regional cities, and the National Theatre, which has three auditoria on the South Bank, regularly features the Bard. The National's current director, Nicholas Hytner, has produced more innovation (he brought in the outrageous *Jerry Springer – The Opera*) and, with the help of business sponsorship, made many seats available for just £10. Other leading theatre directors include Peter Hall, Michael Boyd (Artistic Director of the RSC), Dominic Cooke (Artistic Director of London's Royal Court Theatre), Vicky Featherstone (Artistic Director of the National Theatre of Scotland) and Thea Sharrock (the director of *Equus*, and widely tipped to be Hytner's successor at the National when his tenure there finishes).

In the provinces, most large cities have at least one mainstream theatre which hosts touring

productions, as well as a smattering of fringe theatres. The Cambridge Arts Theatre, the playhouses in Oxford and Nottingham, the Old Vic theatres in Bristol and Stoke, the Leeds Grand, the Sheffield Crucible, Manchester's Royal Exchange, Glasgow Citizens' and Edinburgh Traverse, to name but a few, all have good reputations, and the Fringe Festival in Edinburgh every August is where myriad actors and comedians clamour to show their earliest promise.

ENVIRONMENTAL ISSUES

The British have traditionally lagged somewhat behind their European cousins in terms of environmental awareness, but things are changing, and there is increased general concern with

respect to climate change and preserving the environment for future generations. Recycling is now common both in the home and in public spaces, for example, and green, organic products are a desirable, up-market option.

Apart from gardening, one of the nation's most popular leisure activities is walking – or rambling, as it is often known. During the Industrial Revolution, workers in the polluted northern mill towns fought for the right to roam the countryside on their days off. Rights of way from time immemorial were legally enshrined as public footpaths – which is just as well, as even in 1908 a member of the Commons and Footpaths Preservation Society complained in *The Times* that the motorcar had made walking on narrow country roads too dangerous to contemplate. Nowadays, every local tourist authority can supply information on attractive walks in its vicinity (both urban and rural), which generally happen to pass conveniently close to a good pub.

Cyclists, too, are increasingly well catered for with a network of cross-country cycle routes – a combination of traffic-free paths and quiet roads, sometimes even along disused, paved-over railway lines.

Since 1951 Britain has created national parks – areas of countryside that are protected for their beauty, wildlife or cultural heritage – of which there are now 15 (The Broads, Dartmoor, Exmoor, Lake District, New Forest, Northumberland, North York Moors, Peak District, South Downs and Yorkshire Dales in England; the Cairngorms and Loch Lomond and the Trossachs in Scotland; and the Brecon Beacons, Pembrokeshire

> *The charity Sustrans (www.sustrans.org.uk), which promotes sustainable, safe transport, can advise on both walking and cycling routes all over Great Britain.*

Coast and Snowdonia in Wales). The parks, each of which is run by its own authority, are popular with walkers and cyclists. Other environmental agencies include the Wildlife Trust, which maintains a network of nature reserves around the country, and the RSPB (Royal Society for the Protection of Birds), which promotes bird conservation and has 200 reserves that are home to 80 percent of the UK's rarest species.

FILM

Historically, Britain has played a major role in the development of modern cinema. The British film industry's heyday was the 1940s, when studios led by J. Arthur Rank and Alexander Korda made such classics as Powell and Pressburger's *A Matter of Life and Death* and Laurence Olivier's *Henry V*. Britain has also produced many great directors – Alfred Hitchcock, Carol Reed, David Lean, Mike Leigh and Danny Boyle (whose 2008 romantic drama *Slumdog Millionaire* won eight Academy Awards at the 2009 Oscars) – and numerous iconic film stars, including Charlie Chaplin, David Niven, Peter Sellers and Sean Connery.

In recent decades, however, the British film industry has been largely subsumed into the international (largely American) film industry. While films such as Woody Allen's *Match Point* (2005) were made in London using mainly English actors and technicians, they are not generally regarded as British. Even the James Bond and Harry Potter movies, despite their English backgrounds and origins, have the flavour of international productions. On the other hand, Hugh Grant's caricature Englishness stamps films such as *Four Weddings and a Funeral* (1994) and *Notting Hill* (1999) as British, even though his American co-stars (Andie MacDowell and Julia Roberts) signal a desire for international appeal; likewise the casting of Keira Knightly, with her clipped vowels, injects the box-office-boosting combination of archetypal English Rose and Hollywood star into a movie. Period drama-style films, such as *Atonement* (2007) and *The Duchess* (2008), both starring Knightley, put out the romantic and stereotypical view of the Brits as sexually repressed, exquisitely dressed toffs. And the British film industry's 2010 success, *The King's Speech*, flies the flag for the stereotypical British stiff upper lip.

FOOD

Few people contemplating a first visit to Britain would cite the cuisine as a major attraction. They may have heard disconcerting reports of soggy vegetables, unidentifiable "gravy" and stodgy, unsophisticated puddings, but, in reality, Britain has a fine culinary tradition going

LEFT: Colin Firth as King George VI in *The King's Speech*, which won four Academy Awards.
ABOVE: celebrity chef Jamie Oliver.

back to the days of the grand Victorian country houses, and even earlier. In the Brighton Pavilion, visitors today can not only see the enormous kitchen and its elaborate implements and fine copper serving dishes, but can read the menu, for a banquet given in in 1817. More than 100 dishes feature, from delicate soups to every kind of meat or game, including quail and wood pigeon.

Victorian culinary knowledge was codified by a Mrs Beeton, who published her renowned *Book of Household Management* in 1861. She provided expert advice on everything from how to dry herbs to judging the age of a partridge, and

her book, having been updated many times over the years, is still in print.

How, then, did the country acquire its reputation as a culinary wasteland? In Victorian times, most middle-class families employed servants, including a cook. But in the years leading up to World War II, changing social conditions led most people to give up their servants. Then came the wartime rationing of meat, eggs and butter. By the time these basic items were available once again, many traditional ways of cooking had been forgotten or, without servants, were no longer practical.

In their place came an emphasis on convenience, with time-saving appliances and the modern supermarket with its rows of tinned and frozen foods. The neighbourhood grocer, butcher and fishmonger began to disappear – and with them, the attention to freshness and understanding of ingredients that had been taken for granted.

But the supermarkets had their advantages. Thanks to modern modes of transport, they could bring produce from sunnier parts of the world to the British masses, and at a reasonable price. Oranges, avocados and olive oil were once luxury items, and could now be afforded by all. Gradually, British chefs – and humble dinner-party hosts – have learned how to incorporate the full flavours of the Mediterranean and Asia

into the wholesome staples of the British diet. An army of foodies has goaded the supermarkets into providing fresh herbs year round, bread baked on the premises, and a rapidly expanding selection of organic produce and meats.

Today, from Cornwall to Caithness, you will find upmarket restaurants and "gastropubs" offering "Modern British" dishes such as roast cod with basil mash, roast rack of lamb with Provençale herbs, and lightly prepared classic steamed puddings for dessert. Chefs such as Gordon Ramsay, Jamie Oliver, Heston Blumenthal and Hugh Fearnley-Whittingstall have become ubiquitous television celebrities; recently, they've been joined by flush of amateur celebrity cooks, such as ex-models Sophie

Dahl and Lorraine Pascale, who are adding a dash of glamour to the male-dominated world of TV chefs.

Britain's multiracial society is reflected in its cuisine too: in towns and villages across the country there are Indian restaurants, and

> *Fried fish is thought to have been introduced to Britain by 17th-century Jewish immigrants who coated the fish in batter as part of the cooking process; the batter was not intended to be eaten.*

chicken tikka masala is often cited as the nation's favourite dish. The influence of the influx of Eastern European and Afro-Caribbean migrants can also be seen both in restaurants and in supermarkets, many of which (particularly in London) cater well for ethnicities other than White British. Major cities, most notably of course the vast melting-pot that is London, are impressive for the variety of cuisines offered by their restaurants – a broader range, for example, than one might expect to find in countries such as France or Italy, which focus much more exclusively on their own food; that said, the more remote regions will likely be more conservative in the types of food they offer.

And if you don't fancy a seared tuna steak drizzed with a sun-dried tomato coulis, a home-baked wheat-free organic muffin or even that chicken tikka masala, you can still find the classic fish-and-chip shops that are a British culinary icon the world over.

FOOTBALL

Britain's most popular sport fields three national teams: one for England, one for Scotland, and one for Wales. England pioneered "the beautiful game" – the first known written reference to "football" dates to 1409, and the rules of the modern game were codified in London in 1863 – and has more clubs than anywhere else in the world, including amateur teams and youth leagues as well as internationally known clubs.

Unlike the national teams, whose players must have been born in the country, the Premier League teams can shop for talented players from around the world. This has turned the major clubs into wealthy corporations glamorous enough to attract rich patrons, with the result that half the Premier League teams, especially the top clubs (notably excepting Arsenal), are now foreign-owned. US sports tycoon Malcolm Glazer paid £790 million in 2005 to take control of Manchester United. Manchester City was bought by Thailand's former prime minister, Thaksin Shinawatra, who then sold it on to a group of Arab billionaires led by Abu Dhabi's Sheikh Mansour bin Zayed al Nahyan. Since 2003 Chelsea has been the plaything of Russia's Roman Abramovich.

It helps to be wealthy if you're a fan, too. Ticket prices for top games are on a par with

international players, bought for millions of pounds, and expensive sponsorship deals, the football teams of today may feel very different from those of yesteryear, but the English football fan's greatest dream most likely remains the same: to bring the World Cup, which was last won in 1966, back to England.

GOLF

The Scots lay claim to inventing the game in the 14th or 15th century, and the Royal and Ancient Golf Club of St Andrew's remains one of the golf world's governing bodies: indeed, an ambition of many golfers is to

those for West End musicals, and the souvenir market is a money-spinner. Manchester United, for example, has an online megastore offering a vast range of branded items, from pyjamas and earrings to inflatable chairs and baby clothes.

The injection of capital vastly improved facilities at major football grounds and halted the fall in attendances caused by endemic hooliganisim in the 1980s. But it has also polarised the game, with smaller clubs seeing potential revenues siphoned off by the big-name clubs.

With their super-stadia, glamorous celebrity

LEFT: England's capture of the World Cup in 1966 was marked by a commemorative stamp. **ABOVE:** heritage replaces heavy industry in Ironbridge in Shropshire.

play the Old Course at St Andrew's, where rounds are allocated by daily ballot as well as by being requested in advance.

The Scottish Parliament banned the game (along with football) in 1457 on the grounds that it was distracting youth from archery practice. Mary, Queen of Scots took the game to France, where her attendants were known as cadets, hence "caddies". The links (golf course) on which she played, at Musselburgh, are still in operation – the world's oldest.

Today the UK has more than 7,500 golf courses. A concentration of courses between Liverpool and Blackpool – the "Golf Coast" – includes three famous Royal links courses: Birkdale, Liverpool and Lytham & St Annes.

HUMOUR

For a slightly objective view of something so intensely subjective as humour, one could do worse than seek the opinion of George Mikes, a Hungarian who moved to England, where he became a humorous writer. "Britain is the only country in the world which is inordinately proud of its sense of humour," he said. "In other countries, if they find you inadequate or they hate you, they will call you stupid, ill-mannered, a horse-thief or hyena. In England, they will say that you have no sense of humour. That is the final condemnation, the total dismissal."

national life. Also, given the rigidity and conservatism of most national habits and institutions, it's easier to joke about them than to change them. Political pamphleteering nourished that habit, which continued in such TV programmes as *Yes, Prime Minister*. The great visual tradition of vicious caricature, which reached its peak in the 18th and 19th centuries with James Gillray, George Cruikshank and William Hogarth, was continued in the 1980s/90s TV puppet show *Spitting Image*. *Have I Got News for You* is a popular, long-running satirical quiz show, in which regular panellists Ian Hislop and Paul Merton dissect and mock

Yet no monolithic British sense of humour exists. There are many varieties, of which five are most common:

• **Irony.** To justify their view of themselves as good losers, to whom playing the game is more important than winning it – fortunately, given their usual performance – the British have developed a sophisticated self-mockery. It is a virtue to be able to laugh at oneself. Losers loom large in British television sitcoms, from the rag-and-bone men of *Steptoe and Son* (translated to the US as *Sanford and Son*) to Ricky Gervais's cringe-inducing *The Office* (which also spawned a US version).

• **Satire.** The satirist, who laughs at others, is nourished by the prevalence of hypocrisy in

> *"Mark my words," warned playwright Alan Bennett, "when a society has to resort to the lavatory for its humour, the writing is on the wall."*

the actions of those in the current news with the help of guest comedians, politicians, journalists and other well-known figures.

• **Smut.** Farces remain popular theatre, and stand-up comics often rely on lewdness. Because the British are stereotypically repressed about sex, dirty jokes abound, and TV hits such as *Little Britain* seem obsessed with bodily functions.

• **Absurdity.** Perhaps as a palliative against the national failings of formality and pomposity, surreal humour is highly developed. Lewis Carroll is the greatest literary exemplar, and there is a long tradition of nonsense verse. Modern examples are the radio *Goon Shows* of the 1950s (in which Peter Sellers made his name) and the *Monty Python's Flying Circus* TV comedies of the 1970s. More recent devotees to surreal humour include Eddie Izzard, Miranda Hart and The Mighty Boosh.

• **Wit.** Shakespeare is full of it, and Dr Johnson is still endlessly quoted ("A second marriage is the triumph of hope over experience"). The richness of the English language, with its wealth of homonyms and synonyms, encouraged ver-

ISLANDS

Great Britain is the largest of the British Isles, an archipelago made up of around 2,000 islands. It is distinguished from the United Kingdom (of Great Britain and Northern Ireland) by the specific exclusion of any part of Ireland, and from the British Isles by the exclusion of the self-governing Isle of Man and Channel Islands.

The Isle of Man, in the Irish Sea midway between England and Ireland and 16 miles (25 km) from the Scottish coast, has a population of some 50,000. Its parliament, the House of Keys, is said to be the world's oldest. The Manx language, from the same root as Gaelic, was spoken by half

bal acrobats such as Oscar Wilde ("He hasn't a single redeeming vice.") and George Bernard Shaw ("An Englishman thinks he is moral when he is only uncomfortable."), and continues today with comedians including Jimmy Carr and likeable Northern lad Peter Kaye. But there's also ready wit to be found in most areas of national life, even in Parliament. In one famous exchange, Lady Astor spat at Sir Winston Churchill, "If the Rt. Hon. Gentleman were my husband, I'd put poison in his tea," to which Churchill replied, "If the Hon. Lady were my wife, I would drink it."

the inhabitants at the end of the 19th century, but it has now died out. The island is famous for the tail-less Manx cat, and for its relaxed tax regime.

The idea of being a king of an island is clearly attractive, and whole islands do occasionally come up for sale. The reclusive Barclay brothers, owners of *The Daily Telegraph* newspaper, bought Brecqhou, one of the Channel Islands. But the most marketable islands are on the western side of Britain, from the Isles of Scilly off Land's End in Cornwall, past Anglesea in Wales to the more prolific Western Isles of Scotland. In the far northwest are the Hebrides; flying off the northeast are Orkney and the Shetland islands, where Britain's most northerly island (uninhabited) is Out Stack.

LEFT: Winkle Street cottages in Calbourne, Isle of Wight. **ABOVE LEFT:** comedian Jimmy Carr. **ABOVE RIGHT:** Oscar Wilde.

One word of caution: when a new owner has taken possession of an island, he is only the lord of all he can see when the tide is high; when the tide is low, he is surrounded by the Crown, because the monarch owns the foreshore.

KNIGHTS ETC

Twice a year, at New Year and on the Queen's official birthday in June, British newspapers carry two pages of tiny type: the Honours List of medals given out to the good, the worthy, the dedicated, the long-serving and the self-important. Most simply receive medals (Order of the British Empire or Commander of the British Empire), a

The Queen turns the winners of the Honours system into knights (or dames) by dubbing them (tapping lightly) on each shoulder with a ceremonial sword.

few are made lords, others will be made knights, to be called, for ever after, Sir or Dame.

This is what is left of the system of patronage and chivalry upon which wars were fought, taxes levied and monarchs, however mad or bad, could guarantee a faithful following. In the Middle Ages there were two kinds of knight: religious and secular. By the 14th century, however, knights had become merely wealthy landowners, and anyone holding property worth more than £20 a year could buy a title.

Today, the Honours List is compiled by the civil service for the government of the day, although the public can also nominate worthy recipients in their communities. The recipients are for the most part unknown beavers, busybodies and bureaucrats. Headlines focus on the sprinkling of knighthoods for people in the arts and sport, since the public might at least have heard of them. There are 10 different orders of knighthood, and membership is for life only, unless, as in the case of the odd businessman, they are jailed ("detained at Her Majesty's pleasure" is the euphemism), in which case Her Majesty can show her displeasure by demanding the title back.

LITERATURE

A whistle-stop tour of Britain's rich literary heritage starts with Geoffrey Chaucer (c.1343–1400), whose Middle English *Canterbury Tales* is collection of fables told by pilgrims en route from London to the shrine of St Thomas of Becket. Next is Stratford-upon-Avon's most grandiloquent son, William Shakespeare (c.1564–1616), Britain's greatest playwright, whose works are still widely studied and performed. The 17th and 18th centuries were notable for the work of the Metaphysical poets, including John Donne (1572–1631) and George Herbert (1593–1633), and the epic poem *Paradise Lost* by John Milton (1608–74). In the 18th century, the Scottish poet Robert Burns wrote *Auld Lang Syne*, traditionally sung as the clock strikes midnight to bring in the New Year, while in England, Daniel Defoe published *Robinson Crusoe*, often regarded as the first English novel.

In the 19th century, poets such as William Wordsworth (1770–1850) and his Lake District contemporaries (the Lakeland Poets) wrote some of the finest lyrical works of the Romantic movement. But the 1800s are perhaps best known as the century of the novel. Bath's Jane Austen (1775–1817), famed for her caustic wit, wrote on society and its outdated class and gender structures in novels such as *Pride and Prejudice*, while Haworth's Brontë sisters, Charlotte (1816–55), Emily (1818–48) and Anne (1820–49), considered romantic torment, the struggle of the individual, fate, and society, class and women in poetic, imaginative works of which the most acclaimed are *Jane Eyre* (Charlotte) and *Wuthering Heights* (Emily). Also writing at this time was

Charles Dickens (1812–70), whose books (often set in London) are full of detailed descriptions, providing a panorama of Victorian England. Another 19th-century literary behemoth to have vividly evoked a sense of place is Thomas Hardy (1840–1928). Fate, the industrial revolution, the

> *Most of the locations and landmarks featured in Thomas Hardy's novels, including* Far from the Madding Crowd *and* Jude the Obscure, *can be identified in his home county of Dorset – or "Wessex", as he preferred to call it.*

decline of the peasantry, and class and gender struggles are themes that dominate his output. On a lighter note, the Scot Sir Arthur Conan Doyle (1859–1930) was popularising crime fiction, with his astute detective Sherlock Holmes.

In the 20th century, writers included the intellectuals of the Bloomsbury Group (Virginia Woolfe, 1882–1941, and Lytton Strachey, 1880–1932, among others) and the World War I poets Wilfred Owen (1893–1918) and Siegfried Sassoon (1886–1967). In the interwar period, the literary scene was hit by the scandal caused by the publication of the sexually controversial *Lady Chatterley's Lover* (1928) by D.H. Lawrence (1885–1930). Other notable novels of this time include E.M. Forster's (1879–1970) 1924 novel *A Passage to India*, which deals with the demise of colonial rule. Equally topical were 1945's *Brideshead Revisited* by Evelyn Waugh (1903–66), on social disintegration, and the dystopian novel *Nineteen Eighty-Four* (1949), in which George Orwell (1903–50) considers the future of society.

Speeding through the rest of the century, seminal works include the novels of Graham Greene (1904–91) and the poetry of the American-born, English-based T.S. Eliot (1888–1965), and the works of the stylistically accomplished Anglo-American W.H. Auden (1907–73) and the Welshman Dylan Thomas (1914–53). Martin Amis (b.1949), Ian McEwan (b.1948) and the Indian-British novelist Salman Rushdie (b.1947) are key literary figures from the later part of the century, while in the 21st century, the novels of Zadie Smith (b.1975), Monica Ali (b.1967) and

LEFT: Sir Elton John is a knight of the realm.
RIGHT: entrepreneur and media personality Alan Sugar was given a peerage in 2009.

Andrea Levy reflect Britain's growing multiculturalism. Mention should be made, too, of J.K. Rowling, who on the back of the success of her *Harry Potter* novels is now the one of the richest women in Britain. Literary festivals such as the annual Hay-on-Wye festival (www.haye-on-wye. co.uk), held in the Welsh/English border town in late spring, offer the opportunity to hear contemporary authors talk about their work.

LORDS

Some Britons are born lords (by heredity), some achieve their lordships (by doing something remarkable), and some have theirs thrust upon

them (by passing their sell-by date as a member of parliament and being shoved into the House of Lords by the prime minister). The pecking order of the nation's nobility, at last count, goes like this: royal dukes, ordinary dukes, marquesses, earls, viscounts and barons. In general, English lords take precedence over Scottish lords.

With few exceptions titles pass through the male side of the family. The heirs to a large chunk of Britain will undoubtedly attend a top public school, but may or may not go to university, with many preferring instead officer training at the Royal Military Academy, Sandhurst, after which they would hope to join one of the army's prestigious Guards regiments. Until 1999, all were entitled to sit in the House of Lords, where they were able to review government legislation and, if they wished, block it. But the Labour government, deeming this process to be inegalitarian, removed the right of most hereditary peers to sit in the House of Lords, where their role is to improve the legislation sent to them from the more turbulent House of Commons.

Some democrats argue for the popular election of Life Peers, but others say that the public would tend to vote for celebrities rather than wise legislators. However, since the government elevated the maestro of the West End musical to become Lord Lloyd-Webber, that precedent has already been set.

whistle-stop tour of Britain's major palaces to realise that she is the world's richest woman and is the custodian of the world's largest private collection of art. Conscious of certain criticism, in the 1990s she began to pay tax on her private earnings, and many "lesser" royals were removed from the Civil List, which provides public money towards their expenses.

Sometimes, there is an outcry, if lesser royals are seen to be living off the fat without putting in time on what can be an arduous stream of official engagements. But the British still regard the monarchy as a useful and desirable institution. By its very age it is a potent symbol of

MONARCHY

"Her majesty's speech delivered upon the reassembling of parliament was, as usual, insipid and uninstructive. Its preferred topic was her majesty's approaching marriage, a matter of little importance or interest to the country, except as it may thereby be burdened with additional and unnecessary expense." That curt dismissal of Queen Victoria was written by a correspondent of *The Times* 150 years ago. Since then the tribes of Britain have become noticeably more democratic, more pluralistic, more educated, more informed and far more reverential to the family whose historic role they continue to acknowledge.

Her Majesty Queen Elizabeth II earns around £1.8 million a day. It takes only the briefest

The Queen is a descendent of both King Egbert of Wessex (827–39) and King McAlpin of Scotland (1057–93), and is related to all of the half-dozen remaining monarchs of Europe.

national identity; by being above party politics and not subject to election, it provides the State with a sense of last-bastion hope against the incompetence of often uninspiring politicians; and not least it is a darned good show.

Unlike Queen Victoria, who tried to interfere with her democratically elected prime ministers and became so disenchanted with the whole business of politics that she seriously considered packing her bags and ruling the Empire from Australia, her descendents who have reigned this century as the House of Windsor have been adept at keeping clear of the political arena.

The Queen passed retiring age in 1986, but it seems increasingly unlikely that she will break the solemn promise "that my whole life, whether it be long or short, shall be devoted to your service and the service of our great imperial family", which she made on her 21st birthday. In 2007 she became the oldest monarch to have sat on the English throne (beating George III, who died aged 81 years, 7 months and 24 days), and she is ever closer to beating Queen

his consort, Camilla, Duchess of Cornwall, who previously had been portrayed as the third person in the marriage of Charles and Diana, Princess of Wales.

There are still occasional calls that Charles should stand aside in favour of his more paparazzi-friendly eldest son, Prince William – the image of his much-adored late mother – but they are less fervent than in the past.

Following Diana's tragic death, there has been perhaps more sympathy with regard to the royals' possible infallibility. Nobody wants them to return to being the remote figureheads they were until the 1960s; Diana's overwhelming

Victoria's record-breaking reign – something she will achieve if she stays in office until 9 September 2015. The opinion polls show, too, that she retains broad support. Her son and heir, Charles III (as he would be), is far less popular and often seems ill at ease in public, although he has successfully carved out a role for himself (like his sister Princess Anne) in promoting charitable causes and supporting ethical and cultural values. And the opinion polls show too that the public is warming to

popularity certainly stemmed from her rejection of formal protocol and willingness to express her emotions as well as from her glamour. Her eldest son William continues in the same vein: his recent wedding to Catherine Middleton, now Duchess of Cambridge, has helped to boost the royal family's popularity, and his understated approach, coupled with the Duchess's "commoner" background, helps to show that the young generation of royals is more in touch with the public than the critics might like to argue.

MUSIC

LEFT: the Queen and Prince Philip at the annual Braemar Highland Gathering in Scotland. **ABOVE LEFT AND RIGHT:** from The Beatles to Jessie J, Britain has a rich musical heritage.

Britain has an active and varied music scene, with much to cater to every musical taste. Over the last 50 years, the country has made a major contribution to popular music, from the ground-breaking sounds of The Beatles, The Rolling Stones and The Kinks (great for English nostalgia) in the 1960s through the hard-edged, anti-establishment punk rock and the showmanship of artists such as David Bowie in the 1970s and '80s. In the 1990s the charts were dominated by the catchy, lyrical Brit Pop sounds of Mancunian Oasis and rival rockers Blur, who hail from London, while the 21st century has been marked by the music of super-groups from Coldplay, The Streets, The Arctic Monkeys and Scottish band Biffy Clyro to singers including the late Amy Winehouse, Adele and Jessie J.

The jazz scene features club stalwarts such as Ronnie Scott's in London's Soho, probably Britain's best-known jazz venue, which showcases top international artists. Over the years, famous UK stars to have performed here include multi-instrumentalist Tubby Hayes and "godfather of British jazz" Stan Tracey (who was the house pianist until 1967).

Classical music enthusiasts will find that many British cities have their own professional orchestras and promote seasons of concerts. These include the Royal Liverpool Philharmonic, The Hallé in Manchester and the City of Birmingham Symphony Orchestra. The spectacular ultra-modern St David's Hall in Cardiff hosts the annual Welsh proms. There are numerous professional orchestras in London; perhaps the best at the moment is the London Symphony Orchestra, which usually performs at the Barbican Arts Centre. In the summer the Scottish National Orchestra (SNO) presents a short Promenade season in Glasgow, while in London the BBC sponsors the Proms festival of around 100 concerts at the Royal Albert Hall. The BBC also funds several of its own orchestras, the BBC Symphony Orchestra and the BBC Scottish Symphony Orchestra. Also on offer on summer evenings is a programme of open-air concerts at the Kenwood Lakeside Theatre, Kenwood House, Hampstead.

For opera buffs, the Royal Opera and the English National Opera perform regular seasons in London at Covent Garden Opera House and the Coliseum, respectively, where British opera singers from Sir Thomas Allen and Dame Janet Baker to Ian Bostridge, Sir Geraint Evans, Simon Keenlyside, Sir Peter Pears (close associate of the English composer Benjamin Britten) and Bryn Terfel have made their mark. Elsewhere in the country, Welsh National Opera performs at the Wales Millennium Centre in Cardiff Bay, and Scottish Opera is based at the Theatre Royal in Glasgow. Opera North is based in Leeds at the Grand Theatre, but tours various venues in the

> *Ever since an ex-schoolmaster inherited a mansion located off the beaten track in Sussex, and built an opera house there, Glyndebourne has become one of the world's leading opera venues.*

north of England. The Derbyshire spa town of Buxton hosts a major opera, theatre and music festival for three weeks in July each year. Perhaps the most glittering event in the opera calendar is Glyndebourne (*see page 155*).

NEWSPAPERS

After listening to a journalist passionately defending the importance of a politically free and unfettered press in a modern democracy such as Britain, a character in Tom Stoppard's play *Night and Day* replied: "I'm with you on the free press. It's the newspapers I can't stand."

Many share that ambivalence because, while Britain has some of the world's best newspapers, it also has some of the worst. By "worst", one means that objective news is consistently subordinated to highly imaginative stories about the sex lives of TV personalities, pop stars, footballers and the royal family, and that the few columns of genuine news are grotesquely sensationalised.

The saving grace is the diversity of Britain's papers. Ten national dailies and eight Sundays are distributed nationwide, augmented by a host of regional dailies, local weeklies and urban freesheets. Circulations have shrunk alarmingly, as readers and advertising migrate to the internet – mostly still free, although Rupert Murdoch now charges for subscriptions to any papers in his stable – and most papers have tried

Sunday scandal-sheet after the phone- and email-hacking scandal it was itself embroiled with, Rupert Murdoch still owns three national bestsellers: *The Sun*, the top daily tabloid; *The Times*, the moderately centre-right daily quality paper; and its chunky sister paper, *The Sunday Times*, the best-selling of the quality Sunday papers. If Murdoch decides to throw his weight behind one political party, the influence is significant – Murdoch backed New Labour for much of Tony Blair's time in office, but in the last election, he shifted his papers' bias to the Conservatives, for example. Other papers of note include *The Independent*, which is owned by Alexander Lebedev

to broaden their appeal. But the wide choice still makes possible the facile characterisation of people according to what they read. Thus *Guardian* types are held to be arrogant, soft-centred liberals who value rehabilitation of wrongdoers above punishment. *Daily Mail* types are flag-waving patriots who would crack down on immigration and bring back the death penalty, while *Telegraph* readers are characterised as stuffy, well-heeled, ageing Tory voters.

One worry is concentration of ownership: while he was forced to close the *News of the World*

and takes a liberal, centre-left stance, and *The Observer*, the Sunday version of *The Guardian*.

NORTH-SOUTH DIVIDE

The Scots and Welsh have their distinctive cultures and a degree of self-government. But the English are remarkably heterogeneous and, as in many European countries, there is a tendency to differentiate broadly – and controversially – between northerners and southerners.

The stereotype portrays northerners as being more outgoing, forthright and gregarious; southerners as being more wary, noncommittal and reserved. Join a bus queue in London, it's said, and you'll stand in silence; join one in Liverpool and you'll soon strike up a conversation. Even

LEFT: newspapers announce Prince William's engagement to Kate Middleton. **ABOVE:** Murdoch's News International Ltd hit the headlines in 2011.

allowing for wide individual differences, the usefulness of that broad distinction is undermined in areas with large numbers of immigrants, who have added a touch of their own cultures to the mix. In addition, there is debate about whether the Midlands, the area centred on Birmingham, belongs to "the North" or "the South".

Danny Dorling, professor of human geography at the University of Sheffield, cut through this confusion by drawing a diagonal line from the Bristol Channel in the west to the fishing port of Grimsby in the east. "The South has a few pockets of poverty in a sea of affluence," he said, "whereas the North has a few pockets

of affluence in a sea of poverty." The decline in manufacturing, weighted towards the north since the Industrial Revolution, has emphasised the gap, as has the sky-high cost of housing in the crowded southeast.

Health statistics bring little cheer to people living in northern England and Scotland – they are more likely than southerners to smoke and drink to excess, their mental health is poorer, and their life expectancy is on average up to 4 years less and at worst up to 13 years less. Life expectancy rates overall in England are higher than those in Scotland by 2 to 3 years. Wales sits somewhere in the middle.

Such news, of course, emanates from London, where government and the national media are based, as are most of the big cultural institutions. If a northern city is flooded, said one cynic, it's a weather story; if Chelsea or Westminster were to flood, it would be a national emergency.

PARTY POLITICS

There are three significant parliamentary political parties in Britain: the Conservatives (familiarly known as the Tories), Labour and the Liberal Democrats. Plaid Cymru (Welsh nationalists), the Scottish National Party (SNP) and the Greens trail a long way behind them. There is also a handful of fringe parties, most of whom make more of a splash in the headlines than anywhere else; the most famous of these over recent decades has been the Official Monster Raving Loony Party, whose candidates would reliably add a touch of humour to the proceedings on election night.

The general election of 2010 put an end to some degree to the two-party, ding-dong fight between the Conservatives and Labour that had dominated British politics for decades. The Tories had held power from 1979 until 1997, when Labour won a landslide election and kept a fairly tenacious grip on power until 2010. The old stereotypes of the Tories as "the toffs' party" and Labour as "the working-class party" have eroded to some degree, as both increasingly sought the middle ground. The Liberal Democrats, meanwhile, had traditionally always been viewed as the mild-mannered mediators in the middle.

The 2010 election changed this two-horse race, however, resulting in the first hung parliament in Britain since 1974. This stalemate necessitated the formation of a coalition government, in this case between the right-wing Tories, led by David Cameron, and the middle-ground Liberal Democrats, under Nick Clegg. The "Lib Dems" may no longer be purely the butt of everyone's political jokes, but they do seem to be bearing the brunt of the reaction to Tory-led austerity measures.

The House of Commons, Parliament's lower house, is furnished with green seats, which distinguishes it from the red seats of the Lords in the upper house (where some peers are hereditary and others are appointed, not elected). The Commons can just about hold all 648 MPs (Members of Parliament), though the amount of committee work means there are often no more than a handful of members in the chamber at any one time. Like most British institutions, parliament is male-dominated, and the frequently raucous behaviour is reminiscent of an elite public school and generally fairly offputting to women.

Unpardonable sins include accusing fellow MPs of lying (though they can be mendacious or "economical with the truth"). As recompense, they are free to libel members of the public without fear of prosecution – so long as they don't repeat the libel outside the House. The ministers are answerable to the House, and the prime minister, relying on quick wit and practised evasiveness, answers questions in person on Wednesdays at Prime Minister's Question Time.

any time within that period, giving 6 weeks' notice. A prime minster who hangs on until the last possible moment has probably got good reason to feel insecure, and most premiers pick an opportune moment after about 4 years. The voting system used is "first past the post", as opposed to proportional representation, which was given the absolute thumbs-down by around 70 percent of those who bothered to vote in a 2011 referendum. The prime minister is not chosen by the people: after an election, the leader of the party with the most elected MPs is invited by the Queen to form a government and so becomes PM.

Parliament has no written constitution. It relies on statutes and acts which have been passed over the centuries. The monarch has a right of veto, but, wisely, it has not been used since the 18th century. The Queen is not allowed to set foot in the chamber unless she is invited, which she is at the start of each session in November, when she reads a speech prepared by ministers and civil servants outlining her government's plans for the nation's future.

A government may be in office for 5 years and the prime minister can call an election at

In 2007, the Scottish National Party, often accused of being anti-English, won control of the Scottish Parliament, which runs domestic affairs in Scotland; 4 years later, the SNP won a historic victory by gaining the first majority government since the opening of the Scottish Parliament – a move that surely points the way towards independence. In Wales, Plaid Cymru is a significant force in the country's devolved National Assembly.

Both Scotland and Wales also elect MPs to the Westminster parliament, where they are allowed to vote not only on national and international questions but also, anomalously, on the domestic affairs of England, which does not have a separate regional parliament.

LEFT: multiracial Britain waves the flag.
ABOVE: voting at a general election becomes a pleasure when a pub doubles as a polling station.

Elections for the European Parliament stir fewer passions than domestic polls, and a surprising number of voters are unable even to say who their member for Europe is.

PUBS

There are around 52,000 pubs in Britain – though dozens close every week, hit by a fatal combination of cut-price competition from supermarket alcohol, drink-driving laws and rising costs. Some of the survivors are a great deal closer to perfection than others. Perfection is in the eye of the beholder, of course, and just as many "Irish pubs" round the world bear only

the faintest resemblance to a traditional Gaelic boozer, many an "old-worlde" English pub may not be true to pub traditions.

What, then, makes a good traditional pub? There are certain well-defined ground rules. In an old edition of the English beer-drinker's bible, the annual (still running) *Good Beer Guide*, the late author, journalist Michael Jackson, wrote: "In a good pub, the greatest attention is given to the drink, and in particular to the beer. Sociability, on both sides of the bar, comes a close second. A good pub encourages social intercourse, and is not dominated by cliques. A good pub has a caring, responsive landlord, not an uninterested time-server or an arrogant buffoon. In a good pub, whatever

further services are offered, there is always one bar (and preferably two) to accommodate those people who simply want to drink and chat without the distraction or inhibition induced by overbearing decor, noisy entertainment, or intrusive dining."

Many very traditional pubs have at least two bars: the "public bar", which is the basic drinking shop; and the "lounge bar". There may be a difference of a few pence in the drink prices; all pubs are required by law to put their price lists prominently on display. Some would say that the public bar is for serious, usually male, drinkers, traditionally labourers in dirty work boots and clothes. It would traditionally have had a bare floor and a dartboard, or a pool table. Conventionally, the more comfortable (possibly carpeted) lounge bar was intended for sitting down, for entertaining women, for an evening out.

The word "pub" is merely a shortened form of "public house", an indication that the earliest ale houses were simply private homes where the occupant brewed beer and sold it at the front door or across a table in the living room. To indicate that the house sold ale, the owner would put a pole topped with a bough of evergreen outside.

There is no shortage of claimants to be the Oldest Pub in Britain, but one with a stronger case than most is the Ye Olde Trip to Jerusalem, hacked into the rock beneath the walls of Nottingham Castle, and certainly in business at the time of the 13th-century Crusades, hence its name. Like so much else in British life, the pub reached its zenith in Victorian times; the

> *Traditional pub names were often derived from symbols of the heraldic badges of royalty or local nobility, so displaying local allegiances. The pub sign was largely pictorial as much of the pub-going population was illiterate.*

country is still immensely rich in opulent pub interiors from that period, despite all the efforts of philistine pub-owning corporations to rip them out in the name of "modernisation".

Pubs have changed a lot over the past few decades, however. More and more sell good, inexpensive food and some ("gastropubs") are competing strongly with restaurants. Tea and coffee are often on offer, and children and women drinkers – even solo ones – are being made more welcome

The legal age for purchasing alcoholic drinks in Britain is 18. Those younger than this can usually go into a pub, but they must be accompanied by an adult. Most pubs – particularly gastropubs – welcome families, particularly during the daytime; some have special rooms for children, and where there are gardens they are almost always welcome. It is, in the end, up to the absolute discretion of the landlord, and how strictly the local police chief applies the law. In bigger cities, some pubs have a predominantly gay clientele.

A radical change came about with laws passed around the turn of the millennium that allowed pubs to open not just at lunch time and in the evening, but largely to set their own opening hours, depending on the habits of their customers. Twenty minutes' "drinking up" time is still allowed after the closing time.

QUEUES

"A man in a queue is as much the image of a true Briton as a man in a bull-ring is the image of a Spaniard or a man with a two-foot cigar of an American," wrote humorist George Mikes. "An Englishman, even if he is alone, forms an orderly queue of one."

Queue-jumping incurs severe social disapproval. This can be a torrent of abuse, though usually it takes no more serious form than tut-tutting and loud remarks such as: "I say, don't they know there's a queue?" The easiest response is to pretend one is a foreigner; the affronted queuers will then sigh, knowing that you know no better, poor soul, having been deprived of their cultural conditioning.

Some think that the orderly behaviour of most crowds is the only rational option when one lives in a small, overpopulated island. Others see such conspicuous respect for order as the Germanic trait never far below the surface in the British character. Ralf Dahrendorf, a German who became head of the London School of Economics, may have got to the heart of the matter when he said: "I have a feeling that this island is uninhabitable, and therefore people have tried to make it habitable by being reasonable with one another." Don't all rush to agree: there's a queue!

LEFT: Britain's pubs are still a focal point for communities. **ABOVE:** an orderly bus queue.

RACE

Britons have the blood of many people coursing through their veins. Even before history was written, tribes arrived from Iberia, central Europe and the Indian subcontinent. Romans were followed by waves of northern Europeans, Scandinavians and Normans (originally Scandinavian Norsemen). What Prince Llewellyn was fighting for in Wales was not the original Celtic heritage, but the last bastion of a tribe driven up from Iberia and finally stopped by the Irish Sea. Robert the Bruce, champion of the Scots, was descended from Robert de Bruis, a French Norman knight who arrived with William the Conqueror.

Trade, persecution and war brought Flemish weavers, French Huguenots, Chinese sailors, White Russians, Poles and German Jews. Hunger brought, among others, the Irish. In the 1950s Commonwealth citizens were enticed to Britain with job offers, but when they arrived, mostly from the West Indies, they found a welcome not quite as warm as they had been led to expect.

Asians came, too, from Africa and the Indian subcontinent, heading for the manufacturing cities of Birmingham, Bradford and Leicester. In 1972 Asians thrown out of Uganda were reluctantly allowed into Britain: increasingly, Her Majesty's Principal Secretary of State for Foreign and Commonwealth Affairs did not want to allow its Commonwealth citizens the right of abode – as many Hong Kong Chinese discovered when the colony reverted to China in 1997 – and the word "immigrant" became a euphemism for ethnic minorities.

Many Ugandan Asians were professional businessmen and, though they had to start their lives again from scratch, some were able to build up highly successful companies. On a smaller scale, newsagents and local grocers' shops with long opening hours are often Asian-run.

At the time of the last available government census in 2001, there were more than 1 million Indians in England and Wales (the census excludes Scotland), 747,000 Pakistanis, 283,000 Bangladeshis, 1.1 million people of Afro-Caribbean origin and 247,000 Chinese. The results of the 2011 census will no doubt show that the percentage of the population that is not "White British" will have risen in that decade, reflecting the increasing multi-ethnicity.

> The 2001 census figures showed that the number of all non-white residents in England and Wales made up less than 8 percent of the 59.6 million combined population of the two countries.

Racial intolerance is not endemic, but some nasty incidents are reported and paranoia about terrorism has caused concern in Muslim communities, particularly since the bombing of the World Trade Centre on 11 September 2001 and the London bombs in July 2005. This magnified when it emerged that three of the four suicide-bombers who targeted London's transport system in 2005 had been born in Britain.

Many surveys suggest that race is seen as a diminishing social problem, but the financial benefits provided to immigrants remains a hotly debated political topic.

RELIGION

"What a pity it is that we have no amusements but vice and religion," said Sydney Smith. As a journalist as well as a clergyman, Smith, who was born in Essex in 1771, knew both the failings and the predelictions of the British. And, nearly two centuries after his death, the vicar

THE GREAT BIG BRITISH MELTING POT

The population of Britain is estimated at some 60 million people, around 52 million of whom live in England, 3 million in Wales and 5 million in Scotland. Not only is the population rapidly growing, with a huge increase in immigration – citizens of any EU country can settle in Britain, and recent years have seen an influx of Eastern Europeans – over the last couple of decades, but it is also ageing. According to the Office of National Statistics (whose figures do not include Scotland), the number of people in the UK aged 85 and over was 1.4 million in mid-2009, comprising around 2.2 percent of the total population and double the percentage in that age bracket in 1981. Both the nation's growth and its ageing population presented challenges to its creaking transport infrastructure, strained healthcare system and already stretched pension pot even before the swingeing cuts of recent years.

According to figures for 2009 compiled by the Office for National Statistics, 83.35 percent of the population of England and Wales is White British (unchanged since 2001), with the non-white population increasing from 6.6 million in 2001 to 9.1 million in 2009. The ethnic breakdown is as follows: 1.8 percent of the English/Welsh population is of mixed race, 5.87 percent is Asian or Asian British, 2.81 percent is Black or Black British, 0.82 percent is Chinese, and the rest White Irish and White Other. In London, the population is heavily multicultural, with just 59.5 percent in the White British ethnic category.

is still portrayed as an object of affectionate ridicule and the stuff that farces are made of.

In reality, the clergyman who pops in for afternoon tea and lives in a large grace-and-favour vicarage is a disappearing breed, and Britain is no longer a nation of churchgoers. The Church is, however, a microcosm of society. Mosques, synagogues and temples co-exist beside cathedrals, churches and chapels. But it is the Church of England, with the Queen as its head, that is the official backbone of Britain's moral society. The sovereign's role, established by Henry VIII, gives her power to appoint (these days to approve) the two archbishops, of Canterbury

instead of digging in their heels when women donned dog collars, most of those who objected walked out and became Roman Catholic. The question of gay clergy provoked another heated controversy, particularly from affiliated churches in Africa and the Caribbean, and some believed the Church of England might split in two. For now, at least, stability reigns.

The Church's Welsh and Scots counterparts are less flexible. The Scots Presbyterian Church is a stern church, Calvinist in its beliefs. Worshippers in the remoter parts of the country still regard cooking, washing up or reading a newspaper on Sundays as a cardinal sin. Scots Catholics, too,

and York, who are in turn responsible for their bishoprics and for the church's ruling body, the General Synod, which regulates church matters subject to parliament and royal assent.

On the whole, the Church of England, though rather stuck with a typically British misogynous establishment, is pretty easy-going. It has a liberal, ecumenical approach and prefers compassion to fire and brimstone. The ordination of women was one important issue on which some establishment figures could not yield – but

LEFT: the Archbishop of Canterbury, Dr Rowan Williams, meets Prince Charles, in line to head England's established church. **ABOVE:** Rugby Union scrum.

are typically far stricter than English ones. In Wales, the utilitarian Methodist chapels are well attended; the Methodist movement was founded by the 18th-century evangelist John Wesley, and promoted thrift and hard work. It appealed to the working class especially, notably in the northeast of England, parts of Cornwall and, particularly, Wales, where, linked with the Welsh language, Calvinistic Methodism evolved.

RUGBY

Rugby, it has been said, is a thug's game played by gentlemen, while soccer is a gentleman's game played by thugs. Rugby Union (largely an amateur sport) and Rugby League (the professional variant) are both played with an oval ball and supposedly originated in England's Rugby School in 1823, when a pupil playing football picked up the ball and ran with it. Rugby's rules are relatively simple, but it involves a lot of body contact.

In England, though not in Wales, Rugby Union was historically a participatory sport rather than a spectator sport. The Six Nations Championships each year involve teams from England, France, Ireland, Italy, Scotland and Wales.

SEX

Stereotypically prudish, repressed Brits are said to prefer their sex to be a bit of a naughty joke

The reality is that in the 21st century sex is just as in blatant in Britain as in most other countries in the world, and the Brits aren't anywhere near as shy of it as the stereotype likes to make out – this is arguably borne out in the fact that the UK ranks as having one of the highest rates of teenage pregnancy in Western Europe. The increasingly invasive tabloid press and a huge range of gossip magazines make millions on the back of sex-scandal stories and no-holds-barred reports of celebrities' sex lives. Just as this most basic of recreational pursuits ended the career of the Secretary of State for War in the Profumo Scandal of 1963, so the reputations

rather than a dangerous affair. A classic example was the wheeze dreamed up by a group of Yorkshire women, members of the normally staid Women's Institute, who posed for a nude calendar to raise money for cancer research. The idea so caught the imagination that it was made into a film, *Calendar Girls*, in 2003 and subsequently became a stage play, which is still a smash hit.

The old joke goes that there is a distinct parallel between Britain's attitudes to sex and to cooking: performed when needs dictate, with minimum flair. The country's defenders might like to point out that British cuisine has improved almost beyond recognition over the last 10 years, and any tie-ins with sexual prowess might similarly need to be reassessed…

of today's society giants are threatened by its magnetism. In 2011, a Premiership footballer's attempt to keep his extramarital affair with a reality-TV star quiet through a court superinjunction saw tabloid copies fly off the shelves, TV debate shows fuelled, a legion of social networkers tweeting across the globe, and even the Prime Minister voicing his opinions. The idea of *No Sex Please, We're British* (the title of a long-running West End play) seems somewhat out of date.

SURVEILLANCE

In 1948 the English author George Orwell (1903–50) wrote the ultimate critique of a surveillance society, his seminal dystopian novel

Nineteen Eighty-Four, about a totalitarian society in which the super-state monitors every move of its repressed citizens. It might well have Orwell turning in his grave to know that more than 60 years on the warning bells about the surveillance state are ringing louder than ever,

> Some CCTV cameras also have speakers, so that remote operators can instruct pedestrians to pick up litter they have just been spotted dropping; the disembodied voice is felt to embody authority.

with no democracy in the world turning more surveillance cameras on its citizens than Britain. CCTV cameras, government databases containing vast amounts of personal data, and the massive increase of personal data-sharing that has gone hand in hand with the mobile-phone and internet explosion add to the mix; the government may have dropped the idea of bringing in ID cards, but there's still reason enough for anyone wishing to keep private as much as possible to be concerned.

In 2006 the country's information commissioner, who monitors such dangers on behalf of parliament, warned that the country was "sleepwalking into a surveillance society"; in 2010 his successor, Christopher Graham, admitted that monitoring techniques are growing at such a rate that regulators are struggling to keep up. There are estimated to be between 4 and 5 million CCTV cameras in Britain, in department stores, tiny corner shops, airports, railway stations, car parks and housing estates. They track your progress in city streets and along the nation's motorways. London's congestion zone alone has 197 camera sites to record the number plates of every vehicle that enters, triggering fines for those that don't pay the charge. Some taxis have installed cameras to deter passengers from assaulting the driver. Some "lollipop ladies" – the women who carry signs on poles to shepherd children across roads near schools – had cameras fitted to their headgear to record uncooperative drivers.

Critics draw parallels with the repressive society imagined by Orwell, and attack traf-

fic cameras as nothing but revenue-producing devices. Yet across the country citizens' groups have enthusiastically lobbied their local councils to install cameras in town centres to help curb vandalism and violence. The police point to their usefulness in tracking criminals, including terrorists, and in finding lost children.

It is also becoming increasingly standard for younger internet and mobile-phone users to happily reveal vast amounts of valuable personal information, something that much of the older generation is wary of. And in the workplace, employer contracts increasingly state nowadays that workers' email and internet may

be monitored, to check for fair use, but this too is held up by many as a personal invasion too far.

Orwell was again invoked when government ministers, citing the need to counter terrorism, proposed a massive database detailing all telephone calls and emails sent in the UK. Given the state's traditional inability to set up computer systems that worked properly, this was felt to be a rash proposal.

The law-abiding, argued the government, have surely nothing to worry about. Nigel Shadbolt, a computer scientist at the University of Southampton, responded: "If you keep within the law, and the government keeps within the law, and its employees keep within the law, and the computer holding the database doesn't screw

---

LEFT: police monitor surveillance cameras in London.
RIGHT: an olde-worlde tearoom in East Anglia.

up, and the system is carefully designed according to well-understood software engineering principles and maintained properly, and the government doesn't scrimp on the outlay, and all the data are entered carefully, and the police are adequately trained to use the system, and the system isn't hacked into, and your identity isn't stolen, and the local hardware functions… well, you have nothing to fear."

TEA

On average, Britons drink five cups of tea a day, consuming about one-third of the total tea export market every year. The "real" cup of tea

is, however, not always easy to find. Places to go looking are posh hotels that cater for the better-off tourist, low-budget cafés of the fish-and-chip variety that thrive in seaside towns, and British homes that have not gone over to teabags.

The finest tea is made from the bud and first two leaves of the tea bush. They should be steeped in boiled water for between 3 and 5 minutes. Traditionally, very strong Indian tea, rigid with tannin and probably jaw-clenchingly sweet, is favoured by burly men who work with their hands, while women, children and wimpy males like their cuppa watery-weak and China. But an occasional macho workman called out to fix something in a British home has reportedly voiced approval of delicately scented, pale Earl Grey.

There are as many ways of making a cup of tea properly as there are British residents, and all methods involve mysterious and magical warmings and stirrings of the pot, exact timings and individual blends. Up North, they tend to put the tea in first, then add milk; down South they do the reverse and both halves of the country swear blind that theirs is the only way to make tea. Anyone with Far or Near East connections may well add a sneaky pinch of cardamom.

Diarist Samuel Pepys found his first cup of China tea such a novelty in 1660 that he gave it a special entry. In its early days, it was so expensive that it was locked away in metal caddies to stop the servants helping themselves. Adding to the price was the cost of transportation from the Far East on such speedy clippers as the *Cutty Sark*, now in dry dock at Greenwich, in London.

A cup of tea, without sugar or milk, contains only about 4 calories. Its stimulating effect is due to caffeine (weight for weight, tea leaves contain more than twice the caffeine of coffee beans). Its astringency and colour come from the tannin content, which determines its flavour from volatile oils.

The habit of taking afternoon tea with cakes was started around 1840 by the Duchess of Bedford. The West Country's rich cream teas, with scones, jam, clotted cream and cakes to accompany the pot of tea, is delicious in a sickly way and packed with cholesterol. For a traditional afternoon tea, try a big hotel such as the London Ritz or The Savoy; it will cost around £40 per person for a seemingly endless supply of delicate sandwiches, cakes, scones and tea (or coffee, if you really must), though you have to book. To work one off, find a Tea Dance where you can do the foxtrot to such nostalgic interwar orchestral numbers as *Blue Moon* and *Smoke Gets In Your Eyes*. Such dances were once highly fashionable and are still popular with older people, the occasional member of parliament, the retro younger crowd and anyone else with a little free time in the afternoon.

UNION JACK

The flag of Great Britain is the same as that of the United Kingdom, which includes Northern Ireland. The Union flag is a bit lopsided

nal cross on a blue background (saltire argent in a field azure). In 1801, the red diagonal cross (saltire gules in a field argent) of Ireland's St Patrick was added. No room is left for Wales's St Dewi, or David, whose emblem is a dove.

> The constituent parts of the UK have animals and plants for their own flags and heraldic devices: lions for England and Scotland, a dragon for Wales, a rose for England, a thistle for Scotland and a leek for Wales.

and may only be flown one way up. If hoisted incorrectly, particularly at sea, where mariners are well informed in these matters, it may be taken for a distress signal. The flag of any country hoisted on the jackstaff of a ship's bow is called the Jack, hence the flag's popular name of Union Jack.

The Union flag was designed after the union between England and Scotland in 1606, combining the red cross of St George (heraldically speaking, cross gules in a field argent) with Scotland's cross of St Andrew, a white diago-

LEFT: the nation's flag keeps off the nation's rain at Tunbridge Wells. **ABOVE:** when your home is flooded, what you need is a nice cup of tea.

V-SIGN

In World War II, that master of morale-boosting, Winston Churchill, signalled eventual victory by raising two fingers with the palm facing outwards. A more familiar modern gesture is to raise two fingers with the back of the hand facing outward; this is an uncompromising expression of abuse and often provokes a fracas. Care is needed here.

WEATHER

"When two Englishmen meet, their first talk is of the weather," wrote Dr Samuel Johnson. Nearly three centuries later, this relatively harmless national obsession is still going strong, and no weather-related phrase is considered too banal or boring to merit use as a conversational opening gambit between strangers. A 2011 study of over 2,000 people for Walkers Crisps showed that a quarter of the population use the weather as an opening gambit, that over half of Brits talk about the weather at least once every 6 hours, and that around 70 percent (and over 80 percent of over-55s) check the weather forecast at least once a day.

But why should the British be so interested in the vagaries of their climate? In addition to it being a fail-safe ice-breaker – useful for stereotypically reserved Brits – the key lies in its unpredictability. Its swings of mood don't bear out its

WINE

Climate change may give a boost to home-grown wine, but there are already around 400 vineyards, producing 2 million bottles a year. Many are tiny affairs, often run as a hobby. The biggest is Denbies (www.denbies.co.uk), about 20 miles (32km) south of London. Chapel Down (www.englishwinesgroup. com), near Tenterden, is also very highly rated – it was reportedly served to guests at Prince William and Catherine Middleton's wedding reception.

Today's vineyards are dominated by the German vines planted in the 1950s and '60s. Around 90 percent of production is white wine, described as having a floral bouquet, a fresh taste and an acidic finish.

dull reputation at all. Far from always having the drizzly, mediocre summers and mild, wet winters, British weather can switch rapidly from drought to flood, damp cold to oppressive heat.

In August 2003, in Faversham, Kent, temperatures reached the highest ever recorded in Britain: 100.6°F (38.1°C); the record in Scotland was 91.2°F (32.9°C), during that same month. Hurricanes in 1987 (called The Great Storm) and 1990 caused several deaths and uprooted thousands of trees; Western film-style dust "devils" blew through the lanes of Surrey, and waves higher than a double-decker bus submerged a seaside town in Wales.

Such violent extremes are made all the harder to bear because national habits, buildings and clothing are simply not designed to cope with them. Air-conditioning is much more common in shops and offices nowadays than in the past (though rare in homes). In winter, heating and insulation systems work at half-cock, while road and rail networks inevitably come to a standstill in anything more than an inch of snow (one railway company, brought to a halt by one light snowfall, asserted – to general hilarity – it was the "wrong kind" of snow). Unwary motorists, villagers and livestock disappear under mounds of drifting snow in a manner that puzzles Continentals, especially Northern Europeans and particularly Scandinavians, who are used to handling such seasonal hazards.

Global warming may change British weather forever; in recent years heavy rain has been a feature of at least part of the summer, which tends to come early, leave early but then return – for a few days at least – in the form of a September "Indian summer". Scientists say that global warming could bring us hot, dry summers: the writer Virginia Woolf thought that such weather might turn us all into outgoing Mediterraneans. But relentless, reliable sunshine is far more likely to provoke consternation, as we debate whether or not the temperature is actually too hot. And although the British have always dreamed of an empire upon which the sun never sets, dependable good weather spoils their "just-in-case" philosophy. Umbrellas, extra woollens and fold-up plastic raincoats are much-loved accessories. British women might have been considered as chic as Parisiennes were it not for their just-in-case cardigans flung inelegantly over summer dresses. In the days before golfing, umbrellas were big, and country people waxed their coats, ugly folding plastic macs used to make rainswept holidaymakers look like film-wrapped, self-basting chickens. The small plastic rainhat, furled down to the size of a condom and secreted in the handbag, is still favoured today by older ladies with tightly permed, snowy hair, as well as a more trendy crowd, whose tastes are distinctly retro.

Britons traditionally kept a keen weather eye on their climate by frequently tuning in to radio and television forecasts; today, there is also a plethora of weather-dedicated websites and apps – something that should ensure that this endearing habit is maintained for years to come.

of damp climate and soft water flowing through the peat cannot be replicated elsewhere. These days there are two kinds of Scotch whisky: *malt*, made from malted barley only; and *grain*, made from malted barley together with unmalted barley, maize or other cereals. Most popular brands are blends of both types of whisky – typically 60 percent grain to 40 percent malt.

> Only the very brave should think about sampling Bruichladdich X4 whisky; with 92 percent alcohol it is the world's strongest.

A single malt, the product of one distillery, has become an increasingly popular drink, thanks largely to the aggressive marketing by William Grant & Sons of their Glenfiddich brand. But sales of single malts still account for only around one bottle in 20 sold around the world, and most of the production of single-malt distilleries is used to add flavour to a blended whisky.

The Scots themselves tend to favour the relatively light whisky Glenfiddich (around 43 percent alcohol), which in 2010 took the top spot from long-time favourite Glenmorangie; The Glenlivet is currently the best-selling malt whisky in the United States. To work out which is your favourite, take one of the many distillery tours on the Scotch Malt Whisky Trail (www.maltwhiskytrail.com) or enjoy the annual Speyside Whisky Festival (every May). Because whisky "breathes" while maturing in its casks, up to 4 million gallons (20 million litres) evaporate into the air each year. All you have to do is inhale.

WHISKY

The first reference to whisky was in 1494 when Scottish Exchequer Rolls record that Friar John Cor purchased a quantity of malt "to make aquavitae". It's not a hard drink to make, and by 1777 Excise officers estimated that Edinburgh had eight licensed stills and 400 illegal ones. Today more than 2,500 brands of Scotch whisky, one of Britain's top export items, are sold globally.

Yet something as easy to make cannot be made authentically outside Scotland. Many have tried, and the Japanese have thrown the most modern technology at the problem; but the combination

ZEITGEIST

The second decade of the 21st century has brought tough economic times, with more hardship likely to come, as the current government's austerity measures kick in. However, if there's one thing to be said about the Brits, it is that they are resilient in times of trouble – their Blitz spirit and ability to "make do and mend".

Britain may have lost an Empire and is no longer a superpower, but her prime minister is still insistent that the country's relationship with the United States is "essential" (if not special) and that she is still an influential member of the European Union. Time will tell how well the country repositions herself long-term in the global village. ❑

LEFT: Britain is known for its changeable weather.
ABOVE: single malt, Scotland's most famous export.

STATELY HOMES

They reflect more than privileged lives. They also illustrate centuries of social history, and of great artistic and architectural achievement

England's stately homes have a fascination that attracts visitors in their millions every year. Many have embraced tourism enthusiastically, with such added incentives as safari parks, transport museums, historical re-enactments and adventure playgrounds, but at the heart of them all lies a house with a story. It may tell of great achievement in a palatial mansion crammed with priceless works of art; it may reflect centuries at the heart of a close-knit country community in the form of a rambling old manor house, crammed with centuries of acquisitions; it may even show how the servants and estate workers would go about their daily duties.

Changing times

A house that may appear to be pure 18th-century neo-classical may well be hiding a medieval core and perhaps a Tudor fireplace where Elizabeth I once warmed her toes. Victorian high-flyers often confused the issue by building convincingly fanciful medieval-style castles, complete with every convenience that Industrial Revolution technology provided.

The short Edwardian era saw both the carefree hey-day of the country house party and the onset of World War I, which marked the demise of stately homes in their traditional role. Maintaining them was costly, and an ingenious solution was provided in 1953 when the 13th Duke of Bedford, faced with huge death duties when he succeeded his father, was faced with the prospect of donating Woburn Abbey in Bedfordshire to the National Trust. Instead, he opened it to the public, charging them to view the 12th-century building and its contents. He later added a safari park to its grounds. A golf club and antiques centre, plus wedding and conference facilities, were later added to the menu. Initially, many fellow aristocrats condemned the Duke's ideas as crass commercialism, but soon many followed his example.

ABOVE: Blenheim Palace is Britain's largest private house. The exterior of the palace is an orgy of the baroque style, with Doric and Corinthian columns. Inside is a maze of magnificent state apartments.

BELOW: Lyme Park in Cheshire, used in the BBC's 1995 version of Jane Austen's *Pride and Prejudice*, has Tudor origins, but was transformed in the 18th century.

LEFT: the statues, figurines, iron benches and sundials that grace the gardens of stately homes have not escaped the attention of professional thieves, who have been known to peruse *Country Life* magazine to identify opportunities.

THE POWER OF THE PAST

The National Trust, founded in 1895, is a registered charity that initially protected open spaces and threatened buildings in England, Wales and Northern Ireland, but soon began also to preserve places of historic interest or natural beauty for the enjoyment of future generations.

It now cares for ancient monuments, historic houses and gardens, industrial sites, coastline and countryside. Many country houses and gardens were donated to it by their owners who could no longer afford to maintain them or to pay death duties. Broadening its heritage ambitions, it even acquired the childhood homes of John Lennon and Paul McCartney. The Trust is funded entirely by membership subscriptions and donations from its 3½ million members, by legacies and by admission charges.

Another organisation, English Heritage, a quasi-governmental body, cares for historic buildings and monuments such as Stonehenge. It also advises on the preservation of the historic environment, and also offers a membership scheme.

ABOVE: Knole in Kent, birthplace of the writer Vita Sackville-West, was built by an Archbishop of Canterbury in 1456–86 and is surrounded by a 1,000-acre (400-hectare) deer park.

BELOW: the maze at Chatsworth House now stands where Joseph Paxton's Great Conservatory once stood.

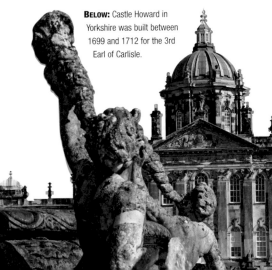

BELOW: Castle Howard in Yorkshire was built between 1699 and 1712 for the 3rd Earl of Carlisle.

PLACES

A detailed guide to the entire country,
with principal sites clearly cross-referenced
by number to the accompanying maps

In the early 1960s, Dr Barbara Moore began a brief craze of walking the length of the country, 874 miles (1,408km) from John O'Groats in the northeast of Scotland to Land's End in Cornwall. (Even in this land of eccentrics she was thought rather crazy.) Though it took several weeks, it made the island seem small. Today a motorist could make the trip in not much more than a day, and it seems to have shrunk still further. But within that short distance there is an extraordinary variety of landscape, of peoples and places to see.

Apart from in winter, getting around the country is very easy, particularly by car, and minor roads are generally good. Britain is, however, a crowded island: traffic can be bumper to bumper on motorways, while in London the average speed of traffic is ironically the same as it was in the days of horse-drawn carriages.

Britain has its own favourite holiday haunts: the Lake District in the northwest, the Broads in East Anglia, the Peak District in the Midlands, Devon and Cornwall in the West Country, the Pembroke Coast in South Wales. The

traditional coastal resorts of Brighton (in the southeast) Scarborough, Whitby and Blackpool (in the north of England) and Llandudno in Wales offer all the ingredients for a typical British seaside holiday of sun, sea and sand. Spectacular historic buildings, ancient monuments and verdant gardens, and places of literary and artistic interest, also attract visitors from Britain and abroad. While this book gives all the necessary information about these important and popular spots, it also suggests a host of other places to visit, places often missed but which give just as much insight into the life and culture of Britain. The chapters have been divided geographically, with suggestions that will help you gain an insight into Britain both on and off the beaten track. ❏

PRECEDING PAGES: the picturesque village of Bilbury in the Cotswolds; Eilean Donan in the Scottish Highlands; Tower Bridge, London. **LEFT:** Canterbury Cathedral. **ABOVE:** traditional town crier; country pub in Warwickshire.

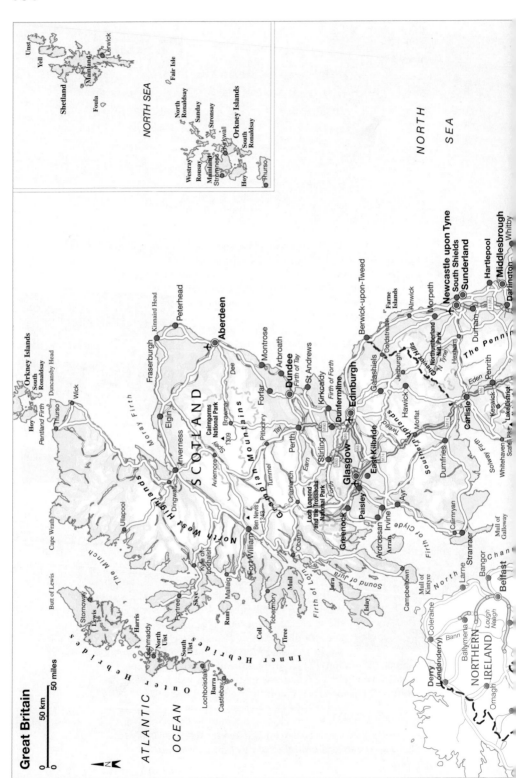

Great Britain

0   50 km
0   50 miles

ATLANTIC OCEAN

Orkney Islands
Hoy
South Ronaldsay
Duncansby Head
Pentland Firth
Thurso
Wick

Cape Wrath

Butt of Lewis
Stornoway
Lewis
Harris
Outer Hebrides
Lochmaddy
North Uist
South Uist
Barra
Castlebay
Lochboisdale

The Minch

Ullapool
Dingwall
Inverness
North West Highlands

Skye
Kyle of Lochalsh
Portree
Mallaig
Rum
Coll
Tiree
Tobermory
Mull
Oban
Fort William
Ben Nevis 1344
Jura

Inner Hebrides

Sound of Jura
Islay
Firth of Lorn
Crianlarich
Loch Lomond and the Trossachs National Park
Campbeltown
Mull of Kintyre

North Channel

Moray Firth

Elgin
Spey
Aviemore
Cairngorms National Park
1309
Braemar
Grampian Mountains
Dee
Tay
Pitlochry
Tummel
Earn
Perth
Crieff
Stirling
Forth
Glasgow
Paisley
Greenock
East Kilbride
Ardrossan
Irvine
Ayr
Arran
Firth of Clyde

SCOTLAND

Fraserburgh
Kinnaird Head
Peterhead
Aberdeen
Montrose
Arbroath
Forfar
Dundee
Firth of Tay
St Andrews
Kirkcaldy
Firth of Forth
Dunfermline
Edinburgh
Galashiels
Hawick
Jedburgh
Moffat
Dumfries
Cairnryan
Stranraer
Larne
Bangor
Belfast
Mull of Galloway

Berwick-upon-Tweed
Coldstream
Cheviot Hills
N. Tyne
Hexham
Nt. Northumberland Nat. Park
Alnwick
Morpeth
Farne Islands
Newcastle upon Tyne
South Shields
Sunderland
Durham
Hartlepool
Middlesbrough
Darlington
Whitby

The Pennines
Eden
Penrith
Keswick
Carlisle
Scafell Pike
Lake District
Whitehaven
Solway Firth

Southern Uplands
Tweed
Teviotdale

Coleraine
Derry (Londonderry)
Ballymena
Bann
Lough Neagh
Ballymena
NORTHERN IRELAND
Omagh

NORTH SEA

Inset map (top):

Unst
Yell
Lerwick
Mainland
Shetland
Foula
Fair Isle

NORTH SEA

North Ronaldsay
Sanday
Stronsay
Westray
Rousay
Mainland
Stromness
Kirkwall
Orkney Islands
Hoy
South Ronaldsay
Thurso

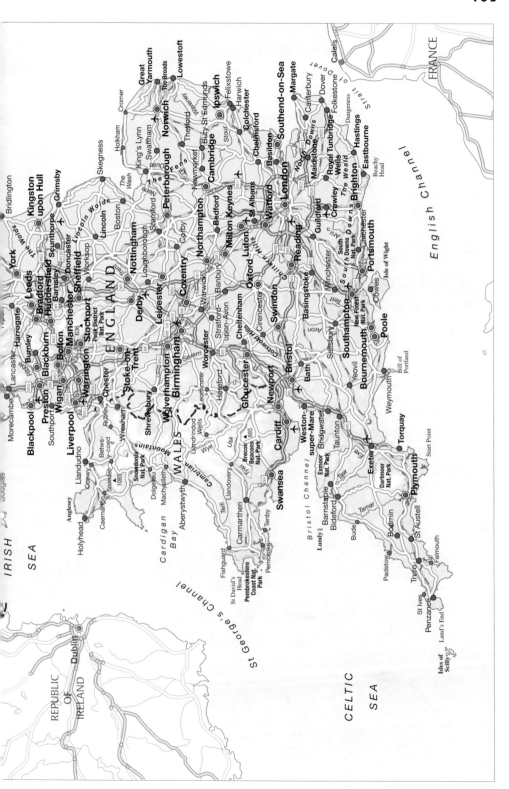

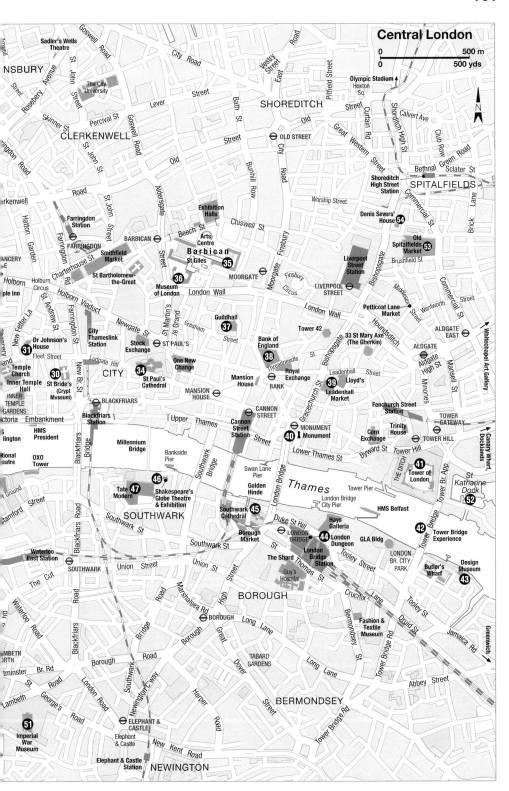

Central London

0	500 m
0	500 yds

NSBURY

Sadler's Wells Theatre

Goswell Road

City Road

SHOREDITCH

St John Street

Rosebery Avenue

The City University

Lever Street

Bath St

Vestry Street

Pitfield Street

Hoxton Sq

Olympic Stadium

Curtain Rd

Calvert Ave

Shoreditch High St

Club Row

Green Road

Skinner St

Percival St

Goswell Road

CLERKENWELL

St John St

Old Street

City Road

OLD STREET

Old Street

Great Western Street

Bethnal Green Road

Sclater St

Shoreditch High Street Station

SPITALFIELDS

rkenwell Road

Hatton Garden

St John Street

Aldersgate

Bunhill Row

Worship Street

Commercial St

Brick Lane

Farringdon Street

Charterhouse Rd

Exhibition Halls

Chiswell St

Finsbury

Denis Severs' House **54**

Farringdon Station

FARRINGDON

Smithfield Market

BARBICAN

Beech St

Arts Centre

Barbican

St Giles **35**

Old Spitalfields Market **53**

Brushfield St

NCERY

St Bartholomew-the-Great

Museum of London

36

London Wall

MOORGATE

Moorgate

Finsbury Circus

Liverpool Street Station

Bishopsgate

Holborn

Holburn Circus

Farringdon St

City Thameslink Station

St Martin's le Grand

Gresham

Guildhall **37**

London Wall

Tower 42

LIVERPOOL STREET

Petticoat Lane Market

Wentworth Street

Commercial St

ALDGATE EAST

ple Inn

New Fetter La

St Andrew's St

Dr Johnson's House **31**

Fleet Street

Newgate St

ST PAUL'S

Stock Exchange

Ludgate Hill

One New Change

Street

Bank of England **38**

Threadneedle

Royal Exchange

Houndsditch

33 St Mary Axe (The Gherkin)

Leadenhall Street

Lloyd's

ALDGATE

Aldgate High St

Minories

Mansell St

Whitechapel Art Gallery

and

Temple Church

Inner Temple Hall

30

St Bride's (Crypt Museum)

CITY

34

St Paul's Cathedral

MANSION HOUSE

Mansion House

BANK

Gracechurch St

Leadenhall Market **39**

Fenchurch Street Station

Trinity House

TOWER GATEWAY

INNER TEMPLE GARDENS

BLACKFRIARS

Upper Thames

CANNON STREET

Cannon Street Station

MONUMENT

Corn Exchange

Byward St

TOWER HILL

Canary Wharf, Docklands

ictoria Embankment

HMS President

Blackfriars Station

Blackfriars Bridge

Millennium Bridge

Bankside Pier

Southwark Bridge

London Bridge

Monument **40**

Lower Thames St

Tower Hill

41

Tower of London

St Katharine Dock

52

lington

tional eatre

OXO Tower

Swan Lane Pier

Thames

Tower Pier

HMS Belfast

Tower Bridge

r Ground

tamford Street

46

Tate Modern **47**

Shakespeare's Globe Theatre & Exhibition

Golden Hinde

London Bridge City Pier

SOUTHWARK

Southwark Cathedral **45**

Hays Galleria

GLA Bldg

42

Tower Bridge Experience

Butler's Wharf

Design Museum **43**

Southwark St

Borough Market

Duke St Hill

LONDON BRIDGE

44

London Dungeon

LONDON BR. CITY PARK

Tooley Street

Waterloo East Station

SOUTHWARK

Union Street

The Cut

Blackfriars Road

Southwark St

Union St

Marshalsea Rd

High Street

The Shard

London Bridge Station

Guy's Hospital

Crucifix Lane

Bermondsey St

Tooley St

Druid St

Jamaica Rd

Greenwich

Waterloo Road

BH.

s

Borough Road

Long Lane

BOROUGH

Great Dover Street

Long Lane

BERMONDSEY

Tower Bridge Rd

Fashion & Textile Museum

Abbey Street

MBETH RTH

tminster

Br. Rd

Lambeth

St George's Road

London Road

Southwark Bridge Road

BOROUGH

TABARD GARDENS

Harper Street

51

Imperial War Museum

ELEPHANT & CASTLE

Elephant & Castle

New Kent Road

Elephant & Castle Station

NEWINGTON

CENTRAL LONDON

Each year London attracts millions of visitors, who are enticed by this multi-faceted metropolis, where you never know what you'll find round the next corner

N o one has captured in words the excitement of London as well as Samuel Johnson, the doctor who had a literary cure for just about everything: "When a man is tired of London he is tired of life, for there is in London all that life can afford." Today, over 250 years later, Johnson's words still ring true. London's variety is inexhaustible.

A good starting point is **Trafalgar Square ❶**. One of the most impressive public squares in the world, it was laid out in the 1830s and '40s by Sir Charles Barry and dedicated to the memory of Admiral Lord Nelson and his decisive victory over Napoleon's fleet off Cape Trafalgar in 1805. The square is a paragon of the Classical style, enclosed by graceful white facades and dominated by the 162ft (50-metre) **Nelson's Column** and four sculpted bronze lions. This is the strategic centre of London: the statue of **Charles I** occupies the spot from where all distances to/from London are measured. The financial wizards of the City of London work to the east; the main shopping centres are to the west; the entertainment empire of the West End lies directly to the north; and the government palaces of Whitehall and Westminster stretch to the south along the River Thames.

The square has long been the site of public gatherings, political demonstrations and New Year celebrations. Every Christmas a 70ft (20-metre) Norwegian spruce is erected in the square, a gift from the city of Oslo in recognition of the protection given by Britain to members of the Norwegian royal family in World War II.

The National Gallery

Running along the north flank of Trafalgar Square is the **National Gallery ❷** (www.nationalgallery.org.uk; daily 10am–6pm, Fri until 9pm; charge for some exhibitions). Founded in 1824, the gallery has grown into one of the

Main attractions
TRAFALGAR SQUARE
COVENT GARDEN
BUCKINGHAM PALACE
HOUSES OF PARLIAMENT AND
  BIG BEN
REGENT'S PARK
PICCADILLY
SOHO
BRITISH MUSEUM
HAMPSTEAD

LEFT: Piccadilly Circus. **RIGHT:** Trafalgar Square and the National Gallery.

The Hay Wain, *John Constable's classic 1821 painting of Flatford Mill, is on show in the National Gallery.*

most outstanding and comprehensive collections in the world, with a list of masters ranging from Leonardo and Rembrandt to El Greco and Van Gogh. The collection is arranged chronologically, from the 13th century to the end of the 19th century. The modern Sainsbury Wing, designed by Robert Venturi, houses the rich Renaissance collection.

Around the corner, established in 1856, is the **National Portrait Gallery** (www.npg.org.uk; daily 10am–6pm, Thur–Fri until 9pm; charge for some exhibitions). Presenting an illustrated who's-who of British history, it contains the faces of the nation's illustrious men and women by the nation's illustrious artists and photographers. Only a fraction of the collection's paintings, drawings, sculptures and photographs is on display at any given time.

To the right of the National Gallery is the church of **St Martin-in-the-Fields** (www.stmartin-in-the-fields.org; daily 8am–7pm; free), the oldest surviving structure on Trafalgar Square, built along simple but elegant lines by James Gibbs in 1722–6. The church became well known during World War II, when its crypt was a refuge from the Blitz. St Martin's is still the parish church for Buckingham Palace, with royal boxes at the east end.

Covent Garden

Northeast of Trafalgar Square begins the maze of narrow streets and tiny alleys called **Covent Garden ❸**. There has been some type of market on this spot for more than 300 years, but the name actually derives from the convent garden that occupied the area until Henry VIII's Dissolution. At the centre of Covent Garden lies a cobblestone piazza, designed by Inigo Jones, and superb steel-and-glass market pavilions constructed in the 1830s to house flower, fruit and vegetable stalls. The market was moved to new quarters south of the river at Nine Elms in 1974, and in the early 1980s Covent Garden was refurbished into an area of restaurants, shops and cafés. It's also a favourite venue for street entertainers.

The market and boutique-lined streets are popular for shopping, especially cobbled **Neal Street**, which is mostly shoes and fashion. Off Earlham Street is **Neal's Yard**, with an apothecary, bakery and natural food shops surrounding a tiny square full of potted trees. The covered **Jubilee Market** (what most Londoners think of simply as Covent Garden Market) shelters an appealing medley of fashion boutiques, gift stores, arts and crafts stalls, restaurants, the occasional puppet show and, on Mondays, an antiques market. Nearby is **Stanford's** at 12–14 Long Acre (off Covent Garden, to the north of the piazza), a specialist map and travel book shop.

Covent Garden is also busy in the evenings, offering a plethora of places to drink and eat, many of which offer pre- and post-theatre menus. Those

BELOW: Covent Garden Market.

with a taste for English tradition might imbibe at one of the many ancient pubs in the area such as the **Lamb and Flag** (on Rose Street, off Floral Street), a 17th-century pub once frequented by prizefighters and known as the "Bucket of Blood".

Used as a backdrop for the movie *My Fair Lady* in 1964, Covent Garden is also synonymous with British theatre. Dominating the west end of the piazza, **St Paul's Church** (1633), by Inigo Jones, is known locally as the "actor's church". On the second Sunday in May a service commemorates the Punch and Judy puppet tradition, first noted here in 1662 by diarist Samuel Pepys. There's a brass-band procession of Mr Punches around the area at 10.30am and puppetry performances in the afternoon.

The **Theatre Royal** was established on Drury Lane in 1663 and is still a showcase for musicals. In 1733, another theatre was built nearby, on the site now occupied by the majestic **Royal Opera House ❹** (box office tel: 020-7304 4000; www.royaloperahouse.org), home of both the Royal Opera and the Royal Ballet. Inside, the magnificent Floral Hall houses a bar and restaurant.

The old flower market, in the southeastern corner of the square, is now home to the impressive **London Transport Museum,** which has a big collection of horse-drawn coaches, buses, trams, trains, rail carriages and some working displays (www.ltmuseum. co.uk; daily 10am–6pm; charge). It effectively traces the social history of modern London, whose growth was powered by transport, and deals intelligently with issues such as congestion and pollution. Facilities for children are good: there are extensive play areas, simulators to allow them to "drive" a Tube train, and a picnic area where you can eat your own packed lunch.

Charing Cross Road

Bibliophiles usually make haste for **Charing Cross Road**, which is dotted with bookshops, though there are far fewer here than was once the case. Most notable is **Foyle's**, said to be the largest bookstore in London.

Charing Cross Road is on the east side of **Leicester Square ❺**, where the city's main multiplex cinemas stage

Every Christmas since 1947, the Norwegian government has presented a Norway Spruce to the people of London in gratitude for Britain's support during World War II. In the autumn, the Lord Mayor of Westminster visits Oslo to participate in the felling of the tree.

BELOW LEFT: human statue in Covent Garden.
BELOW RIGHT: London Transport Museum.

Charlie Chaplin statue in Leicester Square. The comic was born in Walworth, south London, in 1889.

celebrity-filled film premieres. Look out, too, for the statue of London-born Charlie Chaplin as *The Little Tramp*, a Shakespeare fountain and the half-price tickets booth *(see page 373)*.

Somerset House

To the south of Covent Garden lies the Strand, a broad thoroughfare that links Trafalgar Square with the City of London in the east. Here, by Waterloo Bridge, is the neoclassical **Somerset House ❻** (www.somersethouse.org.uk), built in 1770–1835. It now houses the **Courtauld Institute of Art** (www.courtauld.ac.uk; daily 10am–6pm; charge), which is particularly noted for its collection of paintings by Van Gogh, Gauguin and Cézanne. In the winter, the courtyard of Somerset House is the setting for a temporary ice rink; in summer, rows of fountains play out here, and in the evenings there are sometimes outdoor film screenings. At the rear of the building (to the south) is the splendid River Terrace, which in summer has outdoor seating for the café with great river views and, sometimes, showcases artworks.

BELOW: St James's Palace.

St James's Palace

A much different atmosphere is found in **Pall Mall ❼**, which runs through the heart of the St James's district on the west side of Trafalgar Square. This is London's "Club Land" – the grand buildings lining the road are the exclusive gathering places of the Great and Good. The street takes its name from *paille maille*, a French lawn game imported to England in the 17th century and played by Charles I on a long green which once occupied this site.

Wedged between the wood-panelled halls of Pall Mall and the leafy landscape of Green Park are a number of stately homes. The most impressive of these, built by Henry VIII in the 1530s, is **St James's Palace ❽**, now occupied by royal offices. Nearby is **Clarence House** (tel: 020-7766 7303; www.royalcollection.org.uk; Mon–Fri 10am–4pm, Sat–Sun 10am–5.30pm; charge), the London residence of Prince Charles. Guided tours of some of the rooms are offered daily during August and September.

The Mall

The Mall is London's impressive ceremonial way, a broad avenue that runs from Buckingham Palace to Admiralty Arch, by Trafalgar Square. The spectacular Trooping the Colour takes place on the Mall each June, as Queen Elizabeth II rides sedately down the avenue in a horse-drawn carriage with an escort of Household Cavalry as part of a 300-year-old ceremony to mark the official birthday of the monarch. The legions mass on **Horse Guards Parade**, a huge open space behind Whitehall, where a royal unit troop their regimental flags to the tune of marching music and thundering drums.

The Household Cavalry participate in the **Changing the Guard** ceremony, which takes place outside Horse Guards Parade on alternate days (see www.changing-the-guard.com for details); you can also catch the soldiers making their way from Buckingham Palace via The Mall and Whitehall during Changing the Guard.

On the Mall is the **Institute of Contemporary Arts** ❾ (www.ica.org.uk; daily noon–9.30pm; charge), offering a programme of cutting-edge modern painting, sculpture and performing arts as well as arthouse movies and documentaries.

Buckingham Palace

Londoners have a love-hate relationship with **Buckingham Palace** ❿. To some, the Queen's home is one of the ugliest buildings in the capital, but it's also held in esteem as the symbol of Britain's royalty. The palace arose within a mulberry grove in the early 18th century as a mansion for the powerful Duke of Buckingham. It was purchased in 1762 by George III (who preferred to live in St James's Palace). However, it wasn't grand enough for George IV (the Prince Regent), and soon after the building came under his control in 1820, he commissioned his favourite architect, John Nash, to rebuild it on a more magnificent scale. Despite costly alterations, the palace wasn't occupied until Victoria became queen in 1837 and made it the official royal residence in London. (She famously complained that it had too few bedrooms, and had another wing built.) If the flag is flying above the palace, it means that the Queen is in residence. Visitors today can see the **State Rooms** (www.royalcollection.org.uk; late July–Sept daily 9.30am–6.30pm; charge), which are open when the Queen is in residence at Balmoral in Scotland. Other areas that can be visited include the **Royal Mews** (Apr–Oct daily 10am–5pm, Nov–Dec Mon–Sat 10am–4pm; charge), which contain royal vehicles from horse-drawn coaches to Rolls Royces, and the **Queen's Gallery** (daily 10am–5.30pm; charge), which displays artworks from the Royal Collection.

In front of the palace, the **Queen Victoria Memorial**, built in 1901 (the year of Victoria's death), encompasses symbolic figures glorifying the achievements of the British Empire and its builders.

Bounding Buckingham Palace on the north and east are two of London's renowned green spaces – the arboreal tracts of St James's Park and Green Park. **St James's** ⓫ in particular has lush vegetation and a tranquil lake.

The gates of Buckingham Palace were made by the Bromsgrove Guild, a group of artists and designers associated with the Arts and Craft Movement.

BELOW: the Mall and Buckingham Palace.

The Grand Staircase of Buckingham Palace.

BELOW:
Westminster Abbey.

Indeed, the park provides a haven for a multitude of water birds, office workers on their lunch breaks and pram-pushing mums. The wooden footbridge across the lake gives a superb view of Buckingham Palace.

The more rugged **Green Park** ⓬ is where Charles II used to take his daily stroll in the 17th century, and has deck chairs for hire in the summer months.

Westminster Abbey

A short walk from the southeast corner of St James's Park is **Westminster**, the seat of English government for some 750 years. Westminster is also a holy place – the burial ground of English monarchs, the site of one of the greatest monasteries of the Middle Ages and a showcase for some of the most inspiring Gothic architecture in London. The area was a marshy wasteland inhabited by lepers until the 11th-century reign of Edward the Confessor, who built both a great church and a palace upon the reclaimed land.

Westminster Abbey ⓭ (www.westminster-abbey.org; Mon–Fri 9.30am– 4.30pm, Wed until 7pm, Sat 9.30am– 2.30pm; charge) was founded by Edward the Confessor, who is buried in front of the high altar. In December 1066, the ill-fated Harold (soon to lose his throne to William the Conqueror) was crowned as the new king in the Abbey. Since that day, all but two English monarchs have been crowned here.

Little remains of Edward's Saxon abbey; it was completely rebuilt under the Normans and then redesigned in flamboyant French-Gothic style 200 years later. The **Henry VII Chapel** is a 16th-century masterpiece of fan-vaulted stone ceilings, decked out in colourful medieval banners. **Poets' Corner** contains the graves of Chaucer, Tennyson and Dryden, plus monuments to Shakespeare, Milton, Keats, Wilde and many others. The abbey also houses the **English Coronation Chair**, built in 1300 for Edward I and still used for the installation of new monarchs.

The Houses of Parliament

On the river side of Westminster Abbey rise the **Houses of Parliament** ⓮, an elaborate Gothic structure designed in

the 1830s by Charles Barry and August Pugin to replace the old Westminster Palace built by Edward the Confessor. The building is one of the triumphs of Victorian England: 940ft (280 metres) long with 2 miles (3km) of passages and more than 1,000 rooms.

At the south end is **Victoria Tower**, from which a Union flag flies whenever Parliament is in session, while on the north flank rises the Clock Tower, commonly known as **Big Ben** after the massive bell, cast in 1858, that strikes the hours. Facing Big Ben is **Portcullis House**, a modern office block for members of parliament.

Within Parliament convene the two governing bodies of Great Britain, the House of Commons and the House of Lords, which moved into the old Palace of Westminster after Henry VIII vacated the premises in the 16th century. The Commons, comprised of the elected representatives of various political parties, is the scene of lively debate. You can watch proceedings from the safety of the **Visitors' Gallery**; see website for details (www.parliament.uk).

One of the few relics of the old Westminster Palace to withstand a devastating fire in 1834 is **Westminster Hall**, a 240ft (72-metre) -long room built in 1099 with a hammer-beam roof of ancient oak. The hall has seen some of English history's most dramatic moments, from the trial of Sir Thomas More in 1535 to the investiture of Oliver Cromwell as Lord Protector in 1653.

Whitehall is the avenue that runs north from the Houses of Parliament to Trafalgar Square. It is the location of numerous government ministries, as well as the Prime Minister's residence at **No. 10 Downing Street**, just off Whitehall and blocked by security gates.

At the end of King Charles Street, down Clive Steps, a small wall of sandbags identifies the **Cabinet War Rooms and Churchill Museum** ⓯ (www.cwr.iwm.org.uk; daily 9.30am–6pm; charge), the underground nerve-centre from which Winston Churchill directed Britain's war effort. Using old photographs for reference, the rooms have been meticulously restored to their 1940s appearance.

On the other side of Whitehall is **Banqueting House** (Mon–Sat 10am–5pm; charge), a remnant of the old Whitehall Palace and a masterpiece of the English Baroque. Inigo Jones built the hall in 1622 at the request of James I. A decade later Peter Paul Rubens added the allegorical ceiling.

Surprising modernity

The rather unspiring **Victoria Street**, peppered with chain stores and lunch stops that serve the office workers in the modern blocks that dominate this traffic-logged road, runs southwest from Parliament Square. Set back from the street is the terracotta **Westminster Cathedral** ⓰, England's most important Roman Catholic church, built in the 1890s in a bizarre Italo-Byzantine style, with a lavish interior of multicoloured marble and an exterior in alternating red and white bricks. The **Campanile Tower** (Mon–Fri 9.30am–5pm, Sat 9.30am–6pm; free) offers superb views.

TIP

The name Big Ben, commonly used for the clock tower of the Houses of Parliament, properly refers only to the 13-ton bell. If you want to climb the 393 steps to see it, and enjoy a fantastic view, you will need to be a UK resident and contact your MP to arrange a tour. Children under the age of 11 are not admitted. Tours last around 1 hour.

BELOW: Richard the Lionheart, King of England from 1189 to 1199, inspires the Houses of Parliament.

Millbank follows the gentle curve of the Thames to the south of Parliament Square, first passing the **Victoria Tower Gardens** (home of Rodin's *The Burghers of Calais*) before sweeping round to the neoclassical home of **Tate Britain** ⓱ (www.tate.org.uk; daily 10am–6pm, until 10pm on the first Fri of the month; free except for special exhibitions), in an area of London called Pimlico. The Tate, founded in 1897 by Henry Tate, of the Tate & Lyle sugar empire, holds the national collection of British art (and has a sister venue on the south bank, the Tate Modern, *see page 134*). Among the outstanding British paintings are portraits by Thomas Gainsborough (1727–88), evocative views of the English countryside by John Constable (1776–1837), and dramatic and impressionistic seascapes and landscapes by the prolific J.M.W. Turner (1775–1851) which are housed in the Clore Gallery. These are the paintings Turner bequeathed to the nation on his death, with the stipulation that they should all be hung in one place, and should be available for the public to see, without charge.

Oxford Street

Just three stops on the tube from Pimlico station is Oxford Circus and London's busiest shopping street, **Oxford Street** ⓲, which marks the boundary between Marylebone and the exclusive district of Mayfair. The western half of Oxford Street contains most of London's top department stores, including the capacious and stylish **Selfridge's** and beloved stalwart John Lewis; the eastern end is less upmarket and accommodates a mixture of souvenir shops and chain stores, especially as you get towards **Tottenham Court Road**, a centre for electronics stores, a 10-minute walk east from the major crossroads at Oxford Circus.

Marylebone

To the north of Oxford Street is the district of **Marylebone** (pronounced *marly-bun*), which continues up to the southern edge of Regent's Park. The area's cultural highlight is the **Wallace Collection** ⓳ (www.wallacecollection.org; daily 10am–5pm; free), in Manchester Square. This treasure trove of 17th- and 18th-century fine and decorative

BELOW: Marylebone High Street.

Liberty & Co

On Regent Street, this elegant department store, founded in 1875 by Arthur Lasenby Liberty, has always been strongly associated with good design, especially the Arts and Crafts and Art Nouveau movements. It continues to showcase new designers, whether it is cutting-edge fashion by Christopher Kane, furniture by Vitra, or accessories such as bags and bracelets. The basement has a beautifully laid-out men's wear department; the ground floor has beauty accessories and jewellery and the sumptuous haven of the scarf hall where you can find traditional Liberty prints such as the famous ostrich-feather pattern alongside pieces by up-and-coming talents. Upstairs, in the wood-panelled rooms, you can find Liberty's very eclectic selection of high-fashion women's wear, linens and homewares.

arts includes Sèvres porcelain, French furniture and works by Titian, Rubens and Holbein.

Infamous in the 18th century for its taverns, boxing matches and cock-fights, Marylebone is now best known for its high street, which is lined with chic boutiques and excellent cafés and restaurants. The renaissance in this part of town started with the opening of a branch of the Conran Shop here – the store, housed in a former stables, is at the top (northern) end of the street.

On the northern edge of Marylebone is the very popular tourist attraction, **Madame Tussauds** ⓴ (www.madame-tussauds.co.uk; daily 9.30am–5.30pm with exceptions such as longer hours in summer; charge). It was first established in 1802 by Marie Tussaud, who learned her craft in post-Revolution Paris, making wax effigies of the heads of guillotine victims. Today's waxworks are of celebrities, from pop stars to sports heroes – though anyone who fades from the headlines is soon melted down.

On Baker Street itself, at No. 221b, is the **Sherlock Holmes Museum** (www.sherlock-holmes.co.uk; daily 9.30am– 6.30pm; charge), which celebrates Arthur Conan Doyle's fictitious detective, who supposedly lived here. The museum recreates Victorian rooms and has waxwork tableaux.

Regent's Park

Regent's Park ⓶ is a vast green space with a long and chequered history. Henry VIII established a royal hunting ground here on land seized from the Abbess of Barking. Later, in the early 19th century, the park became part of the Prince Regent's (later George IV) great scheme for a huge processional thoroughfare and palace complex to stretch from Pall Mall to Primrose Hill. The Prince commissioned John Nash to design and develop the scheme, but the dream got only as far as the famed Regency terraces on the southern fringe of the park, which represent Nash at his best.

London Zoo (www.zsl.org; daily Apr–Sept 10am–5.30pm, Oct–Mar until 4pm; charge) was founded in Regent's Park in 1826 by Sir Stamford Raffles, who also founded Singapore. Among the zoo's features are an avi-

Selfridge's imposing frontage.

BELOW: David Hockney with a massive canvas he donated to Tate Britain, *Bigger Trees Near Warter*, a scene from his native Yorkshire.

TIP

Shepherd Market

Off Piccadilly, down White Horse Street, is this pretty square with a clutch of good pubs, and places for alfresco dining. This used to be the scene of the annual May Fair (after which the district is named), held here from 1686 until 1764, when it was banned in this location because of riotous behaviour.

ary designed by Lord Snowdon, a glass pavilion housing the ecologically oriented Web of Life Exhibition, and Penguin Beach, the spacious home (replacing the iconic but sadly penguin-unfriendly old Art Deco area) for one of the zoo's ever-popular aquatic birds, which opened in 2010.

Mayfair and Piccadilly

Exclusive **Mayfair** is home to many of Britain's wealthiest residents. By the mid-18th century, the powerful Grosvenor family had purchased the land here and developed Mayfair into an elegant Georgian housing estate. This enticed the wealthy of dreary inner London to move out and settle in one of the city's first suburbs.

Today, the area is known for its expensive designer shops; the main thoroughfare, **Bond Street** ㉒, is lined with names such as Chanel, Gucci, Bulgari, Calvin Klein, Prada and many others. Mayfair is also renowned as a centre of the European art market. It is home to all of the country's top antiques dealers as well as numerous private art galleries, around Cork

Street, and the top auction houses, including Sotheby's (New Bond Street) and Christie's (King Street). It's worth looking out, too, for **Savile Row**, the traditional home of bespoke tailoring.

Among all these upmarket retail opportunities is the **Handel House Museum** (25 Brook Street; Tue–Sat 10am–6pm, Thur until 8pm, Sun noon–6pm; charge), located in the former home (from 1723 to 1759) of the composer of the *Messiah*.

Piccadilly is the bustling road that runs due west from Piccadilly Circus towards Hyde Park Corner. Along it are many smart shops, such as high-class grocer Fortnum and Mason and several attractive Victorian arcades – covered shopping streets of which **Burlington Arcade** with its uniformed doormen is the most famous. Just south of Piccadilly is Jermyn Street, which is dotted with traditional men's outfitters.

A few doors from Burlington Arcade is the prestigious **Royal Academy of Arts** ㉓ (www.royalacademy.org.uk; daily 10am–6pm, Fri until 10pm; charge), which stages blockbuster exhibitions of major artists.

BELOW: Madame Tussaud's waxwork collection.

At the eastern end of Piccadilly is **Piccadilly Circus** ㉔, a busy junction crowded with black cabs, red buses and awestruck tourists. At its centre stands what is known as the Statue of Eros: this is, though, a misnomer as it is, strictly, a fountain and was originally entitled *The Angel of Christian Charity* in honor of the philanthropist Lord Shaftesbury.

Nearby in Holland Street is the **Trocadero Centre**, a complex of shops, restaurants and cinemas.

Running northwest from Piccadilly Circus, and dividing Mayfair from Soho, is John Nash's curving **Regent Street**, home to classy shops from Aquascutum and Liberty's to Hamleys and an Apple Store, as well as a scattering of more standard chain stores. The Britain and London Visitor Centre is at No. 1 Regent Street, and is the central source of tourist information.

Soho

The district of **Soho** was long known for its low-life bars and sex clubs, but the sleazy side has largely gone, with only a few strip shows remaining. Instead, the area is now a fashionable quarter for restaurants, bars and media companies, and popular with the trendy London gay crowd. Just off Regent Street is the pedestrianised Carnaby Street, famous in the 1960s as a centre for avant-garde fashions; nowadays, its fashion stores are distinctly less ground-breaking. The southern part of the district – to the south of Shaftesbury Avenue, around Gerrard Street and Lisle Street – is known as **Chinatown**, and is packed with Chinese (and some Japanese and Vietnamese) restaurants.

In the heart of Soho is **Berwick Street**, the site of a fruit-and-vegetable market. Karl Marx lived around the corner on **Dean Street** in the building now inhabited by the Quo Vadis restaurant.

Bloomsbury

A short stroll away but a complete change of scene is **Bloomsbury**, the intellectual and scholastic heart of the city. Many University of London colleges have buildings in this area, including the **School of Oriental and African Studies**, and **University College** in Gower Street. Bloomsbury was the address of such intellectual figures

The upmarket Burlington Arcade was Britain's first shopping arcade when it opened in 1819.

BELOW: Frith Street in Soho.

Posh Pampering

Most of London's swisher hotels *(see page 360)*, such as Claridges and St Martin's Lane, have in-room massage, and a lot of them, such as the W Hotel, the Sanderson, the Berkeley and Browns, have spas where you can get lost on a cloud of fragrance and steam. Or just give your feet a treat and walk them to the pedicure room at the upmarket grocers Fortnum & Mason *(see opposite)*, on Piccadilly, to be soothed and beautified. The Sanctuary Spa in Covent Garden is exclusively for women, while The Porchester, in Queensway, West London, offers men-only sessions.

For organic beauty products, soothing therapies and remedies in a relaxed, hippyish atmosphere, go to Neal's Yard *(see page 110)*. More luxurious is Spa NK, at 40 Hans Crescent, Knightsbridge, just round the corner from Harrods *(see page 142)*.

A Night on the Town

The West End is synonymous with evening entertainment, but London's other areas have much to offer too

Soho is one of the most fashionable areas, and is the sex centre of London, although smut is on the retreat. Some of the best food and popular clubs are here, including Ronnie Scott's jazz club in Frith Street and, for clubbers with a sense of fun, Madame Jo Jo's on Brewer Street. Soho entertains a real cross section of Londoners, from the casually-dressed lager drinkers packing out the more traditional pubs, to the city boys swilling champagne in their private-members' bar.

Old Compton Street is the centre of the gay scene, with pubs such as the Admiral Duncan and Comptons drawing big crowds. Around the corner on Wardour Street, Village Soho is another popular gay venue with unthreatening clientele and a sprinkling of glam. Other fashionable hotspots in Soho include The Box, favoured by celebrities and young royals.

Thanks to the late-licensing laws, many bars stay open until at least 3am, which has removed much of the 11pm rush towards neighbourhood clubs.

Some bars can be difficult to get into, but this tends to be because of capacity rather than any particular dress code. Many of the cafés, such as Bar Italia opposite Ronnie Scott's, also stay open into the small hours and do a roaring trade in de rigueur post-bar/club coffee and snacks.

Further afield

However, Soho is not the only place to go at night in the West End; Covent Garden and Leicester Square are popular for promenaders simply taking in the atmosphere on a fine summer's evening, as is the South Bank (see page 135), across the pedestrian Hungerford Bridge from Embankment. Trendy hangouts include the bars of swanky hotels such as the W Hotel, on Wardour Street, and the Light Bar at the St Martin's Lane Hotel, opposite the National Portrait Gallery.

Other areas, too, especially in the East End, are on the up. The redevelopment in the east of London resulting from the 2012 Olympics has put the spotlight on the area, though trendy clubbers have been heading east for years. The pubs and bars of Shoreditch attract a young, trendy crowd, as do the bars and restaurants on and around Brick Lane and clubs, such as Fabric in Farringdon. Cabaret-influenced nights are popular in several East London venues.

The club scene has also headed south of the river, with Brixton venues increasing in popularity. Perenially hip Notting Hill, youth-obsessed Camden and trendy Islington also get busy in the evening. Nighttime haunts in South Kensington (such as Boujis) and around Chelsea's King's Road also attract a well-heeled young crowd. For old-fashioned glamour, however, you still can't go wrong with Mayfair and St James's, where discreet restaurants attract an older crowd who don't have to ask the price, as do local sedate pubs, bars and jazz clubs. ❑

ABOVE: pouring a drink at Wardour Street's Freedom Café-Bar, a popular venue with the gay crowd.
LEFT: Old Compton Street in Soho.

as John Maynard Keynes (1883–1946) and Virginia Woolf (1882–1941).

The novelist Charles Dickens was another Bloomsbury resident. He lived with his family at 47 Doughty Street in the late 1830s, during which time he wrote parts of *Oliver Twist* and *Pickwick Papers*. His home, now the **Charles Dickens Museum ㉕** (www.dickens museum.com; daily 10am–5pm; charge), is filled with his portraits, letters, furniture and other personal effects.

Bloomsbury's main visitor attraction, however, is the **British Museum ㉖** (www.britishmuseum.org; daily 10am–5.30pm; charge for special exhibitions), one of the world's greatest collections of art and archaeology. Its Great Court, a large indoor plaza containing the majestic Lion of Knidos and an Easter Island statue, is worth a visit in itself. Don't expect to see everything in a day; a month wouldn't be time enough. It's best to try to see just a few highlights or a specialist area. *See page 126.*

At 35 Little Russell Street, which runs off Museum Street, the **Cartoon Museum** (Tue–Sat 10.30am–5.30pm, Sun noon–5.30pm; charge) highlights the work of top British cartoonists, past and present.

Northeast of Russell Square, at 40 Brunswick Square, is the **Foundling Museum ㉗** (Tue–Sat 10am–5pm, Sun 11am–5pm; charge), home of a fine art collection built up by a philanthropic sea captain who started a hospital and school for foundlings and encouraged artists, including William Hogarth, to donate works to raise funds. Other artists featured include Gainsborough and Reynolds and there is a collection of artefacts relating to the composer George Frideric Handel. Adjacent are **Coram's Fields**, a children's playground where adults may enter only if accompanied by a youngster.

Holborn

To the south of Bloomsbury is **Holborn**, which centres on the busy street and tube station of the same name. This is London's legal district, where you can find the historic Inns of Court. **Staple Inn ㉘**, a timber-framed Elizabethan structure that once served as a hostel for wool merchants, survived the Great Fire of London. It shows how

The Brewster Memorial Gates in Lincoln's Inn Fields were made in 1872. They were designed to commerate Lt. Col. W. B. Brewster, first commanding officer of the Inns of Court Volunteer Rifle Corps.

BELOW: the Great Court at the British Museum.

The spire of Wren's St Bride's Church in Fleet Street is said to have inspired the first tiered wedding cake.

BELOW: Sir John Soane's Museum.

much of the city must have looked before the 1666 fire devastated it. There were originally 12 inns, founded in the 14th century for the lodging and education of lawyers on "neutral" ground between the merchants of the City and the monarchs of Westminster. Today only four remain and barristers in England and Wales must belong to one of them in order to practise.

Gray's Inn has a garden designed by Francis Bacon in 1606 – a haven of plane trees and smooth lawns that provides a tranquil lunch-time retreat. **Lincoln's Inn**, north of Fleet Street, is perhaps the most impressive inn, with a medieval hall and a 17th-century chapel by Inigo Jones. Outside is the leafy expanse called **Lincoln's Inn Fields**, once a notorious venue for duels and executions, but nowadays a magnet for summer picnickers and sunbathers.

On the north side of the park square, is the **Sir John Soane's Museum** (13 Lincoln's Inn Fields; www.soane. org; Tue–Sat 10am–5pm; charge), an eccentric town house that is a sort of British Museum in miniature. Soane, a celebrated 19th-century architect,

lived here and built up a remarkable collection of antiquities and paintings, which all remain *in situ* for visitors to enjoy. A highlight of its art gallery is Hogarth's satirical *Rake's Progress*. On the first Tuesday of the month the museum stays open late and is lit by candlelight, which makes for a wonderfully atmospheric visit.

The most fascinating of the inns is the twin complex of the **Inner** and **Middle Temples** ㉙. The name derives from the Knights Templar, a medieval religious fraternity that occupied this site until the early 14th century. The temple has changed little: it is still a precinct of vaulted chambers, hammerbeam roofs and lush wood panelling. In the 16th-century Middle Temple Hall, Shakespeare's own company once performed *Twelfth Night* for the Elizabethan court.

The 12th-century **Temple Church** is one of only four "round churches" left in England. It contains a number of knights' tombs and a tiny punishment cell.

Fleet Street

In **Fleet Street**, centre of the national newspaper industry until the 1980s, **St Bride's** ㉚ is still the parish church of journalists. It is an impressive 17th-century church by Sir Christopher Wren, and its crypt contains remnants of Roman and Saxon London. At 17 Fleet Street, **Prince Henry's Room** (see www.cityoflondon.gov.uk for details of opening after renovations) contains artefacts relating to the diarist Samuel Pepys (1633–1703).

Just north of Fleet Street at 17 Gough Square is the **Dr Johnson's House** ㉛ (Mon–Sat 11am–5.30pm; charge), where the great man of letters and compiler of the first English dictionary, Samuel Johnson, lived from 1748 to 1759.

North London

Full of pretty houses on leafy groves, **Hampstead** ㉜ seems the quintessence of an English village. In reality, it is not

so much rural idyll as exclusive suburb, but a haven in a hectic city nevertheless. Until not so long ago, Hampstead was the home of artists, writers and anyone with a liberal disposition. At the last count, the suburb had over 90 blue plaques commemorating such famous residents as John Constable, George Orwell, Florence Nightingale and Sigmund Freud. Now, you only need to have deep pockets to live here: its pretty alleys, leafy streets and expansive heath make this suburb a desirable address.

On Keats Grove is **Keats House** (www.keatshouse.cityoflondon.gov.uk; May–Oct Tue–Sun 1–5pm, Nov–Mar Fri–Sun only 1–5pm; charge), the Regency villa where the consumptive poet lodged before departing for Rome, where he died a year later, in 1821, aged just 25. Under a plum tree in the garden he penned one of his best-loved poems, *Ode to a Nightingale*.

Sigmund Freud briefly lived here too, after fleeing the Nazis in 1938; the **Freud Museum** preserves his house at 20 Maresfield Gardens much as he and his daughter Anna left it (www.freud.org. uk; Wed–Sun noon–5pm; charge).

Despite the encroachment of suburbia, the area retains a village atmosphere, aided by the proximity of 790-acre (310-hectare) **Hampstead Heath**. An 18th-century decree forbade building on the Heath, thus preserving a rambling tract of dark woods and lush meadows where the only large structure is **Kenwood House** (daily 11am–4pm; free). This mansion houses the art collection of brewing magnate Edward Guinness, and includes some well-known works by Rembrandt, Vermeer and Turner. There are also fine Robert Adam interiors.

Haverstock Hill runs from Hampstead into Camden Town, where weekend crowds flock to markets. Since 1972, **Camden Lock Market** ❸ has featured antiques, crafts, old clothes – and talented buskers. The Dingwalls music venue and Jongleurs comedy club are sited here, and a traditional canal boat runs trips from the West Yard area along the Regent's Canal to Little Venice (www.londonwaterbus.com). Meanwhile, Camden High Street is full of bars, pubs and small-scale music venues such as the Dublin Castle and the Jazz Café.   ❏

Temple Church, within the Inner and Middle Temple complex, near Fleet Street, is famous for its round structure and its effigy tombs.

BELOW LEFT: Clifford's Inn on Fleet Street. **BELOW RIGHT:** Hampstead Heath.

RESTAURANTS, PUBS AND BARS

Restaurants

Soho

Andrew Edmunds
46 Lexington Street, W1
Tel: 020-7437 5708 **£££**
A lack of signage gives an anonymous, secretive feel to this romantic hideaway. Soft candlelight and wood panelling make it cosy and intimate. Dishes are simple but varied, ranging from beef to well-presented pasta. Friendly, relaxed staff.

Arbutus
63-4 Frith Street, W1
Tel: 020-7734 4545
www.arbutusrestaurant.co.uk
£–£££
Anthony Demetre and Will Smith's unpretentious, minimalist restaurant opened in 2006 and has won many accolades since, including a Michelin star for its modern European food. Everything on the wine list can be ordered by the 250ml carafe for perfect meal–wine pairings. Superb-value three-course pre-theatre menu includes a glass of champagne. The same team runs Wild Honey (12 St George Street) in Mayfair and Les Deux Salons (40–42 William IV Street) in Covent Garden.

Bar du Marché
19 Berwick Street, W1
Tel: 020-7734 4606
http://bardumarche.co.uk **£**
Tucked behind Berwick Street Market, this is a surprisingly unpretentious Soho hangout. Serves a mix of French brasserie-style food, salads and seafood.

Haozhan
8 Gerrard Street, W1
Tel: 020-7434 3838
www.haozhan.co.uk **££–£££**
It's hard to differentiate between the plethora of Chinese restaurants around Lisle Street, but those in the know head here. The food is upmarket, modern Oriental fare, mixing Chinese, Japanese and Malay dishes, and the presentation is refined. Excellent dumplings.

Randall & Aubin
16 Brewer Street, W1
Tel: 020-7287 4447
www.randallandaubin.com
££–£££
Named after the old deli that stood here for over 90 years, Randall & Aubin has inherited an atmosphere of pleasant retail bustle. Piles of lobsters, crabs and oysters greet you as you enter and the place is filled with diners eagerly consuming them.

Spuntino
61 Rupert Street, W1
No tel (no reservations)
http://spuntino.co.uk
££–££££
With minimalist signage outside and trendy industrial decor inside, this cool, supremely urban spot is one of the capital's currently hippest eateries. Its little plates – styled like those of a Venetian *bacaro* – include mini burgers and pizzettas and deep-fried anchovies, all cooked to perfection. Good wines by the carafe and part-carafe. In the same group are Polpetto, the restaurant above the French House on Dean Street, and Polpo, on Beak Street.

Covent Garden

J. Sheekey
28–32 St Martin's Court, WC2
Tel: 020-7240 2565
www.j-sheekey.co.uk
£££–££££
Dishes at this chic establishment might include chargrilled squid with gorgonzola polenta, Cornish fish stew, or New England baby lobster, followed by rhubarb pie or the famed Scandinavian iced berries with white-chocolate sauce. Booking is essential.

Rules
35 Maiden Lane, WC2
Tel: 020-7836 5314
www.rules.co.uk **£££–££££**
Established in 1798, this is Covent Garden's oldest restaurant, and the decor, notably the wonderful Art Nouveau stained-glass ceiling and the wood panelling, reflects its heritage. The robust food is very

English, with beef, lamb and game from Rules' own estate in the Pennines.

Mayfair and Piccadilly

Benares
12a Berkeley Square House, Berkeley Square, W1
Tel: 020-7629 8886
www.benaresrestaurant.com
£££–££££
This is one of the few Indian restaurants in Europe to win a Michelin star. Dishes include Goan-style lobster Masala in coconut, clove and cinnamon sauce.

Le Gavroche
43 Upper Brook Street, W1
Tel: 020-7408 0881
www.le-gavroche.co.uk **££££**
Chef Michel Roux Jr offers haute cuisine in the grand style at his three-Michelin-starred restaurant. The three-course set lunch, including half a bottle of wine per person, coffee and water, is a bargain. Undoubtedly one of London's best restaurants. Booking essential.

Marylebone

La Fromagerie
2–4 Moxon Street, W1
Tel: 020-7935 0341
www.lafromagerie.co.uk **££**
The café at the back of this upmarket cheese shop does inventive seasonal salads, wholesome soups and, unsurprisingly, fine cheese plates.

Prices for a three-course dinner per person with a half-bottle of house wine:
£ = under £25
££ = £25–50
£££ = £50–100
££££ = over £100

Orrery

55 Marylebone High St, W1
Tel: 020-7616 8000
www.orrery-restaurant.co.uk
£££–££££
Dinner in this Conran restaurant set in a former stables is a romantic gastronomic experience. Barbary duck with *pain d'épice*, foie gras *tarte tartin* and *banyuls* jus are typical dishes.

Quiet Revolution

28–9 Marylebone High Street, W1
Tel: 020-7487 5683 **£–££**
At the back of the Aveda shop is this laid-back organic café serving healthy food. Trestle tables add to the friendly atmosphere.

Bloomsbury

London Review Cake Shop

14 Bury Place, WC1
Tel: 020-7269 9030
www.lrbshop.co.uk/cake shop **£** (no alcohol)
The café of this independent high-brow bookshop is convenient for the British Museum, which is just around the corner; the crowds for refreshments in the museum's Great Court can be offputting. Does excellent homemade cakes and good coffee; just look for the passage in the history section of the bookshop.

Westminster

Grumbles

35 Churton Street, Pimlico
Tel: 020-7834 0149
www.grumblesrestaurant.co.uk **££–£££**
A cosy neighbourhood bistro, conveniently located for Tate Britain, that offers homely cooking and good-value set-price menus.

Portrait Restaurant

Third Floor, National Portrait Gallery, W1
Tel: 020-7312 2490
www.npg.org.uk **££**
The fashionable, airy restaurant and bar at the top of the National Portrait Gallery has decent modern British cuisine but it is the fabulous views over Trafalgar Square and Whitehall that is the big attraction here.

North London

The Horseshoe

28 Heath Street, Hampstead
Tel: 020-7431 7206 **££**
For real ales (the pub has its own microbrewery) and classic British food, this gastropub is a good option. Feast on lamb or beef, then tuck into traditional puddings such as trifle or fruit crumble and custard.

Pubs

For those who like their ale from a barrel and not a bottle, Soho has plenty of classic Victorian pubs, including the **Coach and Horses** (29 Greek Street) and the **Dog and Duck** (18 Bateman Street).

Historic pubs around Covent Garden include the **Lamb and Flag** (33 Rose Street), tucked away down the tiniest of alleyways, and **The Punch and Judy**, on the upper level of the Market itself.

In Mayfair, the area's second-oldest pub, built in the 1730s, is **The Punch Bowl** (41 Farm Street). It is now part-owned by film director Guy Ritchie, so people are much more interested in its celebrity-spotting potential than its history. Also in Mayfair are the historic pubs in Shepherd

Market, notably **Ye Grapes**, at No. 16.

In Fitzrovia, the chic, low-profile area north of Oxford Street, they still display George Orwell's journalists' union card at the **Fitzroy Tavern** (16 Charlotte Street), while the **Newman Arms** (23 Rathbone Street) is famed for its pies.

Around Fleet Street, **Ye Olde Cheshire Cheese** (145 Fleet Street) was frequented by both Dickens and Samuel Johnson. The **Black Friar** (174 Queen Victoria Street), by Blackfriars, is worth seeing for its Arts and Crafts interior, but it also has a good choice of ales.

Bars

If you're in search of a hip hang-out, head for Soho and **Mark's Bar** (66 Brewer Street), a basement bar (beneath the British restaurant, **Hix Soho**), with Chesterfield sofas and a clubby feel, or **Milk and Honey** (61

Poland Street; access to non-members before 11pm and by reservation only; tel: 020-7065 6840).

In the West End, the bar of the **W Hotel** (Wardour Street) is a celebrity favourite hangout and popular for fashionable events, as is the bar at the **St Martin's Lane Hotel**, on the street of the same name.

Mayfair has grand hotel bars aplenty. Sip in style at the designer **Coburg Bar at the Connaught** (Carlos Place), the mirrored piano **Dorchester Bar** (53 Park Lane), the fashionable Art Deco **Claridges' Bar** (49 Brook St) or the **Rivoli Bar** at The Ritz (150 Piccadilly).

In Westminster, on Villiers Street near Embankment tube station, is **Gordon's Wine Bar**, where drinkers sit under the arches on chilly nights and out on the terrace in summer. Sherry and port are the specialities here.

LEFT: Ye Olde Cheshire Cheese, Fleet Street.
RIGHT: Soho bars provide the latest mix of cocktails.

THE BRITISH MUSEUM

Founded in 1753 and eventually housed in a Greek Revival building designed by Sir Robert Smirke, this world-class institution contains some 8 million objects

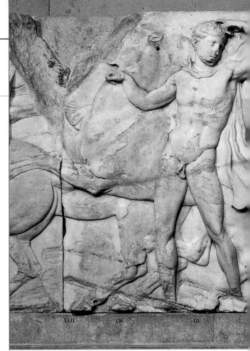

Devote just one minute to each object owned by the British Museum and you'd be there, without sleep or meal breaks, for more than 15 years. Even though only a fraction of the collection is on display at any given time, this is not a place to "do" in a couple of hours – if possible, try and make several visits (the museum's free entry makes this a practical option, at least). It is best to concentrate initially on what interests you most. A tour of the highlights is a very good start (see right-hand column, join one of the organised tours or check out www.britishmuseum.org for recommendations of what to see in one- and three-hour visits).

The British Museum is the most traditional of institutions, with most objects in glass cases in its 100 or so galleries and few buttons and levers for children to manipulate (although there are children's trails and handling sessions); it is, however, rarely boring. The best time to visit is soon after opening at 10am, before the crowds arrive (the museum opens daily until 5.30pm). This is also an ideal time to appreciate the Great Court, a dramatic glassed-over space in the heart of the complex, added for the millennium, and the round Reading Room, where Marx and Lenin once studied and which is now an information and research centre.

LEFT: assistant to the Judge of Hell, a 16th-century stone figure from China's Ming Dynasty. The bunch of scrolls he is holding record the sins of the dead.

ABOVE: the British Museum's Great Court was roofed over in time for the millennium. Designed by Sir Norman Foster, the roof is made of 3,312 panes of glass, no two of which are the same.

ABOVE: a section from the north freize of the Parthenon. Often known as the Elgin Marbles, these 5th-century sculptures, whose muscular detail and fluidity of movement transcend their origins as blocks of marble, were removed from Athens to decorate his Scottish mansion by Lord Elgin (1766–1841). The Greek government has long demanded their return.

ABOVE: the so-called Portland Vase is a Roman glass masterpiece and was made in about 20 BC.

BELOW: double-headed wooden serpent from Mexico, with a mosaic n turquoise – a symbol of fertility to the Aztecs.

THE TOP 10 HIGHLIGHTS

The Egyptian mummies
The museum has one of the richest collections of Egyptian funerary art outside Egypt.

The Sculptures of the Parthenon
Commonly known as the Elgin Marbles, these 5th-century BC sculptures have a wondrous muscular detail.

The Rosetta Stone
This granite tablet from the 2nd century BC provided the elusive key to deciphering Ancient Egypt's hieroglyphics.

The Nereid Monument
The imposing facade of a 4th-century monument from Turkey.

The Mausoleum of Halikarnassos
A giant tomb (c.351 BC) from Turkey, one of the seven wonders of the Ancient World.

The Sutton Hoo Burial Treasure
The richest hoard ever dug from British soil. The early 7th-century longboat was probably the burial chamber of an East Anglian king.

The Lewis Chessmen
Some 82 elaborately carved 12th-century chess pieces, found in the Outer Hebrides, off the Scottish coast.

The Benin Bronzes
Extraordinarily detailed brass plaques found in Benin City, Nigeria, in 1897.

The Oxus Treasure
A superb collection of 4th- and 5th-century BC Persian gold and silver.

The Flood Tablet
Mesopotamia's famed cuneiform tablet, whose story is similar to the Old Testament's Noah's Ark.

TOP: horse's head from the Parthenon Gallery (Room 18).
ABOVE: the gilded wooden inner coffin of Henutmehyt, a Theban princess (c.1290 BC).

LONDON: THE CITY AND SOUTHWARK

The City is the oldest part of London, where Britain's financial institutions are tightly packed. Across the river, Southwark has revived its ancient role as an entertainments centre

Main attractions
ST PAUL'S CATHEDRAL
THE BARBICAN
THE TOWER OF LONDON
BOROUGH MARKET
SHAKESPEARE'S GLOBE
TATE MODERN
SOUTH BANK CENTRE
THE LONDON EYE
SPITALFIELDS MARKET

Fleet Street sweeps from London's theatreland into Ludgate Hill and the **City of London**, a history-packed square mile that sits atop the remains of both Roman and medieval towns. "The City", as it is generally known, was for centuries the domain of merchants and craftsmen, a powerful coalition of men who helped force democracy upon the English monarchy and then built the world's largest mercantile empire.

Despite the encroachment of modern office blocks, the area retains something of its medieval ways: the square mile is still governed separately from the rest of London, by the ancient City Corporation and its Court of Common Council – relics of the medieval trade and craft guilds. Outside the jurisdiction of London's popularly elected mayor, it has its own separately elected Lord Mayor, who rides through the City each November in a golden coach.

Wren's masterpiece

Sitting at the top of Ludgate Hill and dominating the skyline is **St Paul's Cathedral ③④** (www.stpauls.co.uk; Mon–Sat 8.30am–4pm; charge), its massive dome punching upward through the forest of highrises that has come to surround it since World War II. For the first time in 12 years, the cathedral became free of scaffolding in June 2011, after a massive renovation project, and its exterior and interior both now dazzle.

After the Norman St Paul's was destroyed in the Great Fire of 1666, Charles II asked the architect Christopher Wren to design a new cathedral to befit the status of London. Wren's first plan was rejected as too radical, but he responded with a blend of Italian baroque and classical influences – a huge cruciform building, whose stone cupola takes it to a height of 365ft (111 metres), second only to that of St Peter's in Rome.

LEFT: St Paul's Cathedral.

St Paul's arose in 1675–1710 as the first cathedral built and dedicated to the Protestant faith. It played host to Queen Victoria's Diamond Jubilee ceremonies in 1897, Winston Churchill's funeral in 1965 and the wedding of Prince Charles and Lady Diana Spencer in 1981. The cathedral miraculously survived the Blitz, though the neighbourhood around it was destroyed by German bombs and missiles.

St Paul's is a notable burial place; among those entombed within are Wellington, Nelson, Reynolds, Turner and Wren himself. Its interior displays the work of the finest artists and craftsmen of the late 17th century: iron grillework of Tijou, wooden choir stalls by Grinling Gibbons and the murals inside the dome by Sir James Thornhill.

The cathedral's appearance is deceptive. The famous dome viewed from afar would look overly large if seen from inside the building. The dome you look up at from within is in fact a much smaller dome, on top of which is built a brick cone. The cone's purpose is to support the massive weight of the

external Portland stone dome, which weighs more than 50,000 tons.

Around the inside of the dome stretches the **Whispering Gallery**, so called because you can easily comprehend the voices of anyone standing on the opposite side of the void. A winding stairway leads to the outside of the dome, where there are panoramic views of London.

A chapel behind the High Altar, damaged during the Blitz, was restored as the American Chapel, with a book of remembrance paying tribute to the 28,000 American citizens based in the UK who died in World War II.

The acoustics of St Paul's Whispering Gallery mean that a faint whisper can be heard across the gallery, 107ft (33 metres) away.

BELOW: George William Joy's 1895 oil painting *The Bayswater Omnibus*, from the Museum of London.

Each November, the Lord Mayor's Show sets off from the Guildhall, as the newly elected mayor rides through the City in a golden coach. Thousands of spectators line the route to watch the colourful procession.

The Barbican

To the north of St Paul's is the **Barbican Centre ③⑤** (www.barbican.org.uk), its 1960s Brutalist architecture contrasting starkly with the stately form of the cathedral. This urban renewal project arose from the rubble of an old neighbourhood that had been destroyed in the 1940–41 Blitz. Within the complex is the Barbican Arts Centre, accommodating an art gallery, a theatre, a cinema and a concert hall; the complex also houses a large number of apartments and a library, and is home to the London Symphony Orchestra.

Nearby, on London Wall, is the fascinating **Museum of London ③⑥** (www.museumoflondon.org.uk; daily 10am–6pm), which charts the history of the city. There are models of old buildings, reconstructed shop fronts, interactive exhibits, special exhibitions (such as on town criers and street photography), a reference library, antique vehicles and a number of historic artefacts such as the Lord Mayor's state coach.

Also in this neighbourhood is **St Bartholomew-the-Great**, a Norman church that has also served as a stable, factory, wine cellar, coal store and even as Benjamin Franklin's London printworks during its 1,000-year history.

The Guildhall

In the shadows of the Barbican's skyscrapers is the **Guildhall ③⑦** (Gresham Street; tel: 020-7606 3030; www.cityoflondon.gov.uk; opening times vary; free), one of the few buildings to survive the Great Fire and now the home of the City government. This ornate Gothic structure was built in 1411 with funds donated by various livery companies, the medieval trade and craft guilds that held sway over the City. Inside the Guildhall is the **Great Hall**, decorated with the colourful banners of the 12 livery companies and the shields of all 92 guilds.

The Lord Mayor's Show *(see margin, left)* sets off from the Guildhall and ends at **Mansion House**, the official residence of the Lord Mayor since the mid-18th century.

Britain's financial heartland

A short walk east along Gresham Street brings you to a bustling intersection dominated by the bulk of the

BELOW: the Barbican Centre.

neoclassical **Bank of England** ㊳. The Bank still prints and mints all British money, administers to the national debt and also now sets interest rates.

Around the corner on Bartholomew Lane is the entrance to the **Bank of England Museum** (www.bankofengland.co.uk; Mon–Fri 10am–5pm; free), where visitors are even allowed to pick up a gold bar.

Nearby stands the old London **Stock Exchange**, founded in 1773. The trading floor is no longer used, as shares are now traded electronically. This computerisation brought demands for office buildings purpose-built for modern communications. One of the first, and most dramatic, is the 1986 **Lloyd's of London** building in Lime Street, designed for the insurance group by Richard Rogers. Another impressive piece of architecture is **30 St Mary Axe**, a 40-storey tapering glass tower designed by Lord Foster and known affectionately as "The Gherkin". The slightly taller **Tower 42** (25 Old Broad Street), named after the number of floors, also soars up at this point – the bulk of the building is given over to offices, but those with a head for heights can enjoy drinks at **Vertigo 42**. Visitors go through airport-style security checks on the ground floor before being allowed up to this sky-high champagne bar. And there are only 70 seats so you have to book ahead (tel: 020-7877 7842; www.vertigo42.co.uk). Ask for the seats nearest the lift to ensure the best view.

Just south of this modern icon of architecture, down Gracechurch Street, is **Leadenhall Market** ㊴. Once the wholesale market for poultry and game, the magnificent Victorian structure has been converted into a handsome commercial centre, with a collection of restaurants, cafés, fashion boutiques and book and gift shops that attract City workers at breakfast and lunchtime.

The City of London's other steel-and-glass Victorian constructions – the railway stations – were also given facelifts during the 1980s building boom. **Liverpool Street** was overhauled and Fenchurch Street acquired a 1930s Manhattan-style office block, **1 America Square**, over its railway lines. **Broadgate**, a complex of 13 office blocks around three squares, includes an ice rink and a voluptuous sculpture, Fernando Botero's *Broadgate Venus*.

Gracechurch Street leads further south to London Bridge and the Thames. Just before you reach the river, a huge fluted column peers over the helter-skelter of rooftops: the 202ft (60-metre) **Monument** ㊵ (www.themonument.info; daily 9.30am–5.30pm; charge). This is Sir Christopher Wren's memorial to the Great Fire of 1666, which destroyed more than 13,000 houses. You can climb 311 steps to a small platform, from which there is an impressive view.

The Tower of London

Lower Thames Street traces the medieval banks of the river past the old Billingsgate Fish Market and the elegant Custom House. A medieval fortress commands this southeast corner of the City: the **Tower of London** ㊶

The innovative design of the Lloyd's Building on Lime Street places functional features, such as lifts, staircases and water pipes, on the outside.

BELOW: the West Wing entrance of the Guildhall.

The Imperial State Crown, with 2,868 diamonds, was made in 1937 and is on display in the Tower of London.

BELOW: attired in Tudor uniforms, Yeoman Warders (Beefeaters) have been guarding the Tower of London for around 500 years.

(www.hrp.org.uk; Tue–Sat 9am–5.30pm, Sun–Mon 10am–5.30pm; charge). The Tower has served, over the centuries, as fortress, palace, prison and museum, as well as arsenal, archive, menagerie and treasury. William the Conqueror built the inner keep (the **White Tower**) as both a military stronghold and a means of impressing his new subjects in England. Constructed between 1078 and 1098, it was the largest building in Britain and soon symbolised royal domination. It remained a royal residence until the 16th century, when the court moved to more comfortable quarters in Westminster. The Tower then became the storehouse for the Crown Jewels and the most infamous prison and execution ground in London. After 1747 it became the Royal Mint, Archive and Menagerie. German spies were executed here in both world wars.

The White Tower houses the diminutive **St John's Chapel**, built in 1080 and now the oldest church in London. Beneath Waterloo Barracks is a vault containing the **Crown Jewels**, including the Imperial State Crown, which sparkles with 3,000 stones, and the

Royal Sceptre, which centres around a 530-carat diamond called the Star of Africa. A moving walkway ensures that visitors cannot linger long over the principal exhibits.

Also worth seeing are the **Crowns and Diamonds** exhibition in the Martin Tower, and the permanent display of weapons from the mid-17th to mid-19th centuries in the **Royal Fusiliers Museum**.

The Tower is protected by the Yeomen Warders or Beefeaters, so called not because of their carnivorous habits but because they were founded in the 16th century as the *buffetiers* or guardians of the king's buffet.

Outside again, there are magnificent views of **Tower Bridge ㊷**, London's most famous river crossing. This striking Gothic structure looks deceptively old – in actual fact, it opened in 1894. Its bascules still rise frequently – four or five times on some days – to let tall vessels through. The **Tower Bridge Experience** (www.towerbridge.org.uk; daily Apr–Sept 10am–6.30pm, Oct–Mar 9.30am–6pm; charge) offers a tour of the inside of the bridge, as well as superb views.

Bankside

On the south side of Tower Bridge is the restaurant-lined **Butler's Wharf** and the **Design Museum ㊸** (www. designmuseum.org; daily 10am–5.45pm; charge), which presents exhibitions related to architecture and graphic and product design.

The riverside walk between Tower Bridge and London Bridge passes by the World War II battleship **HMS *Belfast*** (http://hmsbelfast.iwm.org.uk; May–Oct 10am–6pm, Nov–Feb 10am–5pm; charge). A tour takes you round the cramped accommodation endured by its 950-man crew.

Continuing past more renovated warehouses towards London Bridge, cut through **Hay's Galleria**, a small shopping mall carved out of a former tea wharf, to reach Tooley Street. Here, the **London Dungeon ㊹** (www.thedungeons.

com; daily 10am–5.30pm with exceptions; charge) provides a gruesome, actor-led account of London's history, including the Black Death, the Great Fire and the grisly deeds of Sweeney Todd and Jack the Ripper – children love it, but be prepared for long queues and steep entrance charges.

To its left is **Winston Churchill's Britain at War Experience** (www.britainatwar.co.uk; Apr–Oct 10am–5pm, Nov–Mar 10am–4.30pm; charge), which includes a simulation of a World War II bombing raid and lots of 1940s memorabilia.

Nearby, at 83 Bermondsey Street, is the unmissably pink-and-orange **Fashion and Textile Museum** (www.ftmlondon.org; Tue–Sat 11am–6pm during exhibitions only; charge), created by Zandra Rhodes to honour 1950s British designers and to teach students.

At the other end of the street, on Friday morning only, is Bermondsey Square Antiques Market, which has successfully shed its bad reputation. Arrive early if you are after a bargain and for the best choice, as the hundreds of traders start gathering at 4am.

London Bridge and Southwark Cathedral

Looking up from London Bridge, you can't miss the newest addition to the area: **The Shard** (http://the-shard.com), which, when completed in May 2012, will be the tallest building in Western Europe, at 1,016ft (310 metres) high, housing offices, a hotel, restaurants and apartments. Just to the south of London Bridge, the imposing **Southwark Cathedral** ⑤ (http://cathedral.southwark.anglican.org), where Shakespeare was a parishioner. Augustinian canons erected the original church in the 13th century, but the cathedral

The cruiser HMS Belfast, which served in World War II and the Korean War, is Britain's only surviving example of the big-gun armoured warships built during the first half of the 20th century.

BELOW LEFT: Tower Bridge. **BELOW RIGHT:** Southwark Cathedral.

The nave of Southwark Cathedral was rebuilt in 1895 to the design of Sir Arthur Blomfield. The stained glass window at the west end shows scenes of the Creation.

BELOW:
Shakespeare's
Globe theatre.
RIGHT: gallery in
Tate Modern.

has been much altered since then, and now has a sensitively designed refectory, library, conference centre and shop. It holds free organ recitals on Mondays at 1pm and free classical concerts on Tuesdays (3.15–4pm).

Adjacent is **Borough Market**, a wholesale fruit-and-vegetable market whose history dates back 1,000 years. On Thursdays, Fridays and Saturdays crowds flock to a retail market here offering a wide range of gourmet and organic products, in addition to fruit and veg.

Beyond the cathedral, by the Thames in the St Mary Overie Dock, is a full-size copy of Sir Francis Drake's galleon, the **Golden Hinde** (www. goldenhinde.com; daily 10am–5.30pm; charge). The original circumnavigated the globe in 1577.

Just to the west, the **Clink Prison Museum** features old armour and torture instruments. Beyond it, **Vinopolis** runs audio tours of vaults portraying the world's wine-producing regions,

and the **Anchor Inn** is an historic pub, rebuilt in 1676 and gradually added to over the years.

Shakespeare's Globe

Continue westwards along the river to reach a replica of the 1599 **Shakespeare's Globe** 🐵 (tel: 020-7401 9919; www.shakespearesglobe.com). This open-roofed theatre-in-the-round stages the Bard's plays close to where they were first performed (performances in summer only; guided tours every half-hour 9.15am–12.15pm). **Shakespeare's Globe Exhibition** is well worth a visit – there are traditional displays, but it's the touch-screens and hands-on exhibits that are fun, enabling you to speak some of the playwright's greatest lines in response to the recorded voices of great actors and then listen to the result.

Tate Modern

Next door to the Globe is a towering brick chimney that identifies **Tate Modern** 🐵 (www.tate,org.uk; Sun–Thur 10am–6pm, Fri–Sat 10am–10pm; charge for special exhibitions). This

iconic former power station houses the national collection of international modern and contemporary art (Tate Britain houses British art; *see page 116*). The massive turbine hall gives temporary, large-scale installations room to breathe. Displays in the gallery's main rooms are arranged thematically rather than chronologically, mixing the work of artists including Picasso, Bacon, Pollock, Rothko and Warhol.

Tate Modern is linked to St Paul's across the river by the **Millennium Bridge**, a slender footbridge designed by Sir Norman Foster.

The South Bank

Further west along the river is the **National Theatre** (www.nationaltheatre.org.uk) – actually three theatres under one roof. For a peek behind the scenes, you can book a backstage tour (tel: 020-7452 3400). Adjacent is the **Southbank Centre ㊽** (tel: 020-7960 4200; www.southbankcentre.co.uk), London's largest arts complex. The **Royal Festival Hall** plays host to orchestral concerts, while next door are the **Queen Elizabeth Hall** and the **Purcell Room**, used for smaller-scale events, from chamber music to poetry readings. There are often free performances at lunch time and in summer.

On the upper level of the complex is the **Hayward Gallery**, which has changing exhibitions of contemporary art. **BFI Southbank**, in the shadow of Waterloo Bridge, presents a repertory of vintage and foreign-language films as well as the London Film Festival each November. The British Film Institute also runs **London IMAX Cinema**, which rises like a behemoth from the roundabout at the south end of Waterloo Bridge.

The London Eye

Continuing westwards, you come to the 450ft (135-metre) -high **London Eye ㊾** (tel: 0870-5000 600; www.london eye.com; daily, Jan–Mar and Sept–Dec 10am–8.30pm, Apr–Jun until 9pm, Jul–Aug until 9.30pm; charge), an observation wheel erected for the millennium. The 32 enclosed capsules take 30 minutes to make a full revolution, and on a clear day, you can see for 25 miles (40km).

Next to it is the majestic **County Hall**, built between 1909 and 1933 and until 1986 the seat of the Greater London Council. It now contains two hotels, as well as the **London Sea Life Aquarium** (www.visitsealife.com; Mon–Thur 10am–6pm, Fri–Sun until 7pm; charge), which accommodates underwater species from sharks to stingrays. Also in the complex are several restaurants, a hotel and **Namco Station**, a games and entertainments centre.

Upriver from the South Bank complex, beyond Westminster Bridge, is **Lambeth Palace ㊿**, which has been the London residence of the Archbishop of Canterbury for nearly 800 years. It is seldom open to the public. The garden and deconsecrated church of St Mary nearby are home to the lovely **Garden Museum** (www.garden

The London IMAX cinema to the south of Waterloo Bridge.

BELOW: the London Eye.

The 2012 Olympic Effect

Whether for good or for bad, one thing's for sure; London's East End will never look the same again...

The 2012 Olympic Games (www.london2012.com) will take place from 27 July to 12 August, with the focus of attention on the Olympic Park in Stratford, East London. There are in addition numerous other venues across the capital and across the country – from football at Old Trafford in Manchester to rowing at Eton Dorney. After the Games, most of the venues will remain in use as part of the Olympics' legacy, and can still be visited, whether for sports or other activities or just to view the spectacular architecture and design.

The Olympic Park itself is a vast site accommodating nine sporting venues: the Olympic Stadium, Aquatics Centre, Water Polo Arena, Basketball Arena, Handball Arena, Velodrome, BMX Track, Hockey Centre and Eton Manor (wheelchair tennis). Visitors can travel there from central London by public transport, with Stratford Station on the east side of the park and West Ham Station to the south. Overground trains will run from London Liverpool Street, tube trains on the Jubilee and Central lines,

and Docklands Light Railway (DLR) trains from Tower Gateway. The high-speed Javelin shuttle service will ferry visitors between St Pancras and Ebbsfleet International, via Stratford International.

The centrepiece is the 80,000-capacity Olympic Stadium in the south of the Olympic Park, where the main track events will be staged. Sweeping away from the stadium are gardens that celebrate the tradition of British horticulture. In the park's southeast corner is the Aquatics Centre, designed by the architect Zaha Hadid, and already an iconic building. Another architectural feat is the Velodrome at the northern end of the site; this eco-friendly structure is clad in wood, and is 100 percent naturally ventilated.

Other London Olympic venues

In Docklands, the ExCeL exhibition centre will accommodate arenas for boxing, fencing, judo, table tennis, weightlifting and wrestling, while across the river the equestrian events benefit from the setting of Greenwich Park. Not far away, the O2 Arena, formerly known as the Millennium Dome, is hosting gymnastics.

In central London, there will be beach volleyball on Horse Guards Parade in Westminster, and, nearby, the marathons and cycling road races will start and finish in grand style on The Mall in front of Buckingham Palace. Fifteen minutes' walk to the north in Hyde Park, spectators can watch the triathlon. West of Hyde Park Corner, volleyball will take place in the exhibition centre at Earls Court.

The iconic Lord's Cricket Ground in leafy St John's Wood is where the archery tournament is to be held, while, further north, Wembley Arena will host the badminton and rhythmic gymnastics events. Next door, the 120,000-seat Wembley Stadium will stage the gold medal matches in the football competition. ❑

ABOVE: computer-generated image of the main Stadium. **LEFT:** the velodrome and the BMX track.

museum.org.uk; Sun–Fri 10.30am–5pm, Sat 10.30am–4pm, closed 1st Mon of the month; charge).

The Imperial War Museum

Another landmark south of the river is the **Imperial War Museum** ⑤ (http://london.iwm.org.uk; daily 10am–6pm; charge for special exhibitions), situated on Lambeth Road. Perhaps it is no accident that the grand structure in which it is housed was once Bethlem, a hospital (opened in 1815) for the care of the insane (from which the word "bedlam" comes), for the Imperial War Museum does a marvellous job of conveying the madness of war. Busy with parties of enthusiastic school children during term time, the Imperial War Museum has dedicated itself to living history rather than dusty cases of artefacts. So you don't just see photographs of bombed-out London streets; you can go and sit in a replica of a bomb shelter and listen to the neighbours argue. There are also changing exhibitions covering different aspects of war from the slightly glamorous espionage to the more mundane – food and rationing.

The East End

Back on the north bank of the river, downstream from Tower Bridge lie **St Katharine's Docks** ⑤. Built in 1828 as a shipment point for wool and wine, the docks were renovated in the early 1980s and have become a posh residential and commercial district. The complex contains a shopping arcade, a yacht harbour, pub, a hotel and several old warehouses (such as the Ivory House) now converted into modern offices and flats. It is the most successful of the docklands developments which extend east from here to the Isle of Dogs, home to the cluster of

The Large Exhibits Gallery at the Imperial War Museum is home to vehicles and weapons from both world wars.

BELOW: clothes shopping at Spitalfields Market.

At Dennis Severs' House, the visitor is transported back in time, seemingly interrupting a family of Huguenot silk-weavers who appear to always be just out of sight.

BELOW: St John restaurant, near Smithfield's Market.

skyscrapers known as Canary Wharf. The development is testimony to the continuing ambition of the City's financiers. A branch of the Museum of London, the **Museum of Docklands** (West India Quay; http://www.museum oflondon.org.uk/Docklands; daily 10am–6pm; free), documents the city's history as a port and hosts excellent events for young children. The skyscraper generally referred to as "Canary Wharf", unmissable for its pointy hat and visable from across London, is actually **One Canada Square**. It was long the UK's tallest building, although the Shard at London Bridge has overtaken it. Below it is a shopping centre, with fashion and food stores.

Northeast of the Tower is the warren of narrow streets that marks the start of the **East End**, traditionally London's working-class district. For centuries, the East End has been the place where newly arrived immigrants have settled. Huguenots, Jews, Bangladeshis and Somalis have all made their mark on the area, and it is one of the most culturally exciting parts of the capital.

On Commercial Road is **Old Spitalfields Market** ❸, (www.oldspitalfields market.com) a former wholesale fruit-and-vegetable market that now has antiques, clothes and crafts stalls (depending on the day). A contender for London's best market (busiest on Sunday), it is also surrounded by interesting boutiques, including along Hanbury Street, the northern part of Brick Lane and (to the west) Commercial Street.

Two streets beyond Spitalfields Market, at 18 Folgate Street, is the 18th-century time warp of **Dennis Severs' House** ❹ (www.dennissevershouse.co.uk; Sun noon–4pm and other times, check website; charge). In 1967, Severs moved from his native California and bought this former silk weaver's house. Living with no electricity or modern appliances, he re-created its 18th-century state. It is now as if the original family have just left the room, leaving a half-eaten scone and a smouldering fire (note: no children allowed).

A short walk south, around Middlesex and Wentworth streets, is **Petticoat Lane Market** (Sundays) a chromatic jumble of clothes, antiques and food.❏

East London's Art Scene

The East End is home to some of the capital's best contemporary art galleries, both public and commercial. The major public art space here is the **Whitechapel Art Gallery** (tel: 020-7522 7888; www. whitechapel.org; Tue–Sun 11am–6pm, Thur until 9pm; charge), founded by a local vicar and his wife in 1897 as part of their aim to combat spiritual and economic poverty in the East End. The building, designed by the Arts and Crafts architect Charles Harrison Townsend, today hosts important exhibitions of contemporary art. Also of note is **Rivington Place** (Rivington Street; www.rivingtonplace.org; Tue–Thur 11am–6pm, Thur until 9pm, Sat noon–6pm), one of London's newest public galleries, devoted to cultural diversity, with both art exhibitions and film screenings. Its latticed facade was inspired by a Sowei tribal mask.

Close to Rivington Street is Hoxton Square, a contemporary art hub and home to superdealer Jay Jopling's flagship **White Cube** (www.whitecube. com; Tue–Sat 10am–6pm), the gallery that sells the work of "Young British Artists" Damien Hirst, Tracey Emin and the Chapman brothers. Other notable commercial galleries in the East End include **Victoria Miro** (16 Wharf Road, N1), while smaller galleries can be found along Hackney's **Broadway Market** and **Vyner Street** – the latter is lined with less-established galleries run on tiny budgets in old shops and post-industrial buildings.

RESTAURANTS AND PUBS

Restaurants

Prices for a three-course dinner per person with a half-bottle of house wine:
£ = under £25
££ = £25–50
£££ = £50–100
££££ = over £100

The City

The Eagle
159 Farringdon Road, EC1
Tel: 020-7837 1353 £–££
This was the place that launched a thousand gastropubs with its pioneering menu of inventive dishes, although some say the quality has gone down a little since its heyday. The food has a Mediterranean bias, and there's a good choice of European beers.

Hix Oyster and Chop House
36–37 Greenhill Rents, off Cowcross Street, EC1
Tel: 020-7017 1930
www.hixoysterandchophouse.co.uk £££
Chef Mark Hix showcases his modern British cooking. Dishes, which vary with the seasons, might include beef and oyster pie, Porterhouse steaks and grilled fish.

St John
26 St John Street, EC1
Tel: 020-7251 0848
www.stjohnrestaurant.com
£££–££££
Close to Smithfield Market, this Clerkenwell favourite has a cult following who appreciate its "nose-to-tail" approach to the food. It offers simple but unusual ingredients such as lamb tongues,

pigeon, ox cheek and rabbit.

Sweetings
39 Queen Victoria Street, EC4
Tel: 020-7248 3062 ££
First-rate fish restaurant with bags of traditional City atmosphere, and well-prepared dishes such as grilled skate, turbot in mustard sauce and dressed crab, and old-fashioned puddings such as treacle tart.

Tayyabs
83 Fieldgate Street, E1
Tel: 020-7247 9543
www.tayyabs.co.uk £–££
This Pakistani restaurant is chaotic and often has long queues, but it does offer good food and low prices; the seekh kebabs (spicy meat patties) are delicious. Bring your own alcohol (no corkage).

Vinoteca
7 St John Street, EC1
Tel: 020-7253 8786
www.vinoteca.co.uk ££
Located on a side street, opposite Smithfield Market, this wine bar and wine shop does great-value, delicious modern European food, together with wines by the glass from a 200-strong list (also sold in the shop).

The South Bank and Southwark

The Anchor and Hope
36 The Cut, SE1
Tel: 020-7928 9898 ££
Meat and offal feature strongly on the gastropub menu. Reasonable prices, hefty portions and friendly staff. The no-booking policy can mean long queues.

Delfina
50 Bermondsey Street, SE1
Tel: 020-7564 2400
www.thedelfina.org.uk ££
Lunch-time creatives flock to this light, airy restaurant in a former chocolate factory for well-prepared modern British dishes using seasonal, often organic, produce, and for the calm atmosphere.

Meson Don Felipe
53 The Cut, SE1
Tel: 020-7928 3237
www.mesondonfelipe.com ££
Londoners in the know flock to this excellent tapas bar. Tables fill up fast, but there's sometimes room at the bar. The juicy fresh anchovies are great.

Le Pont de la Tour
Butlers Wharf Building, 36d Shad Thames, SE1
Tel: 020-7403 8403
www.lepontdelatour.co.uk
££££
Prime ministers and presidents have enjoyed the splendid view of Tower Bridge from this up-market Conran restaurant, where the stress is on seafood. Impeccable but very expensive.

Roast
Floral Hall, Stoney Street, SE1
Tel: 020-7940 1300
www.roast-restaurant.com
££–£££
Spectacularly set on the upper floor of Borough Market, with gorgeous views through vast windows. Sourced from the market, the excellent food is resolutely British. Good-value breakfasts and brunches.

Tas
33 The Cut, SE1
Tel: 020-7928 2111
www.tasrestaurant.com £–££
It's easy to go overboard on the meze at this Turkish restaurant, so save room for the equally tasty mains. Good for vegetarians.

Pubs

In the City, the **Jerusalem Tavern** (55 Britton Street) is an intimate little pub dating from 1720, with cubicles, Georgian-style furniture and a selection of real ales and fruit beers. The **Counting House** (50 Cornhill) is a bank-turned-pub, which still has its high ceilings and chandeliers. On Carey Street (No. 53) is **The Seven Stars** – built in 1602, it survived the Great Fire, and, thanks to proprietor Roxy Beaujolais, remains unspoilt to this day. Does good beer and good food (oysters, herrings, meatloaf, stews).

In Southwark, the **The George Inn** (77 Borough High Street), owned by the National Trust, is London's only galleried coaching inn. **The Market Porter** (9 Stoney Street) is famous for opening 6–8.30am for Borough Market workers.

The Boot and Flogger (10–20 Redcross Way; closes 8pm) is a traditional wine bar named after a corking device. Reminiscent of a gentleman's club, it trades as a Free Vintner, meaning that it doesn't need a licence.

At 9–11 Folgate Street, **The Water Poet** has a sweet beer garden and hosts gigs and movies.

LONDON: CHELSEA AND KENSINGTON

Home to some of Britain's best and brightest – and wealthiest – Chelsea and Kensington offer the visitor fine museums, lovely streets to stroll along, and chichi shopping

In the 19th century Chelsea was an avant garde "village" just outside the sprawl of central London. Among its more famous residents were Oscar Wilde, John Singer Sargent, Thomas Carlyle, Mark Twain and T.S. Eliot. Cheyne Walk, a row of elegant Georgian terraced houses just off the river, has long been one of Chelsea's most desirable residential streets. George Eliot, Turner and Carlyle lived here in the 19th century; J. Paul Getty, Mick Jagger and Keith Richards lived here more recently. Chelsea is where England swung in the 1960s, and where punk began in the 1970s.

King's Road ❶ is Chelsea's main artery. It started life as a tranquil country lane but was later widened into a private carriage road from St James's Palace to Hampton Court on the order of King Charles II. It rose to its pinnacle of fame in the 1960s, when designers Mary Quant and Ossie Clark set up shop here, and it was in its boutiques that the miniskirt first made its revolutionary appearance. In the 1970s Vivienne Westwood and

Harrods

London's most famous department store employs over 5,000 staff across 330 departments – a far cry from its humble beginnings as a grocery store with two assistants. It famously claims to be able to source any item and then send it anywhere in the world: its motto is *Omnia Omnibus Ubique* (All Things for All People, Everywhere). Noël Coward was bought an alligator for Christmas, and former US President Ronald Reagan was given a baby elephant, although most customers are more likely to come away with teddy bears, toiletries and other items bearing the bottle-green Harrods logo. Its 15 million annual visitors are asked to dress "cleanly" and "presentably" and wear "appropriate" shoes, although there is no specific information as to what the latter entails exactly. Doormen are on hand to enforce these house rules.

Malcolm McLaren took up the avant-garde baton, dominating the punk scene with their boutique, Sex. Today the street attracts a well-heeled crowd and is far more mainstream. Among the fashion stores, a more cultural attraction is the **Saatchi Gallery** (www.saatchi-gallery.co.uk; daily 10am–6pm; free), housed in a former army barracks set back from the King's Road on Duke of York Square, and showcasing modern and contemporary art in changing exhibitions.

Soldiering on

Running parallel with King's Road, down by the river, is Royal Hospital Road, home to the **Chelsea Royal Hospital** ❷ (www.chelsea-pensioners.org.uk; Mon–Fri 10am–noon, 2–4pm (grounds), Mon–Fri 10am–5pm (museum); free), Sir Christopher Wren's masterpiece of the English baroque style, opened as a home for invalid and veteran soldiers in 1682. A few hundred army pensioners still reside here, and parade in their scarlet frockcoats on Oak Apple Day (29 May). Visitors can see the Great Hall,

the Octagon, the Chapel, the museum and Ranelagh Gardens, the site of the Chelsea Flower Show since 1862.

On Royal Hospital Road, tracing the history of the British military from the 15th century, is the **National Army Museum** (www.nam.ac.uk; daily 10am–5.30pm).

Further along the same street is the entrance to the **Chelsea Physic Garden** (www.chelseaphysicgarden.co.uk; Apr–Oct Tue–Fri noon–5pm, Sun noon–6pm; charge), a botanical laboratory founded in 1676. It's a pretty place for a stroll and afternoon tea. On the south bank of the river, opposite here, is **Battersea Park** ❸, with gardens designed as part of the Festival of Britain in 1951, and the Buddhist Peace Pagoda, commemorating the 1985 Year of Peace.

Belgravia

East of Sloane Square is the exclusive district of **Belgravia**, originally grazing land until Thomas Cubitt developed it as a town estate for aristocrats in the early 19th century. The neighbourhood retains this exclusive quality as

The Chelsea Flower Show (www.rhs.org.uk/chelsea), one of the largest of its kind in the world, is a great social event, held in the Royal Hospital's spacious gardens during 5 days (3 for public access) in May.

BELOW LEFT: King's Road. **BELOW RIGHT:** Chelsea Pensioners at a Founder's Day Parade.

The Victoria and Albert Museum's British Galleries trace the country's changing tastes from 1500 to 1900.

the home of diplomats, senior civil servants, celebrities and the occasional duke or baron. Belgravia is littered with grand Regency terraces and squares, bound by cream-coloured mansions and carefully tended gardens. Behind the grand facades lie the diminutive mews, tiny cobblestoned alleys that once served as stables.

North of Belgravia via Sloane Street is **Knightsbridge**. Another upmarket part of London, it is the home of **Harrods** *(see page 140)* ❹, the city's most famous department store, formerly owned by the flamboyant Egyptian Mohamed Al-Fayed but sold in May 2010 to the Qatari royal family. At night, its light-spangled facade resembles an enormous Victorian birthday cake. Inside, the tiled food halls are especially impressive.

Victoria and Albert Museum

At the end of the Brompton Road is the district of South Kensington, noted for its large museums (all free). The

Victoria and Albert Museum (V&A) ❺ (www.vam.ac.uk; daily 10am–5.45pm, Fri until 10pm) on Cromwell Road, is the most famous of these. Its 7 miles (11km) of galleries house more than 5 million items of fine and applied arts, with exhibits ranging from exquisite Persian miniatures to a whole room designed by Frank Lloyd Wright. One minute one can be admiring the 1515–16 Raphael cartoons drawn for the tapestries in the Sistine Chapel, and the next examining E.H. Shepard's illustrations for *Winnie-the-Pooh* or admiring a plaster cast of Michelangelo's *David*. Other highlights include an outstanding collection of Indian art in the Nehru Gallery, fashion from the 17th century to the present day in the Fashion Galleries, and the British Galleries, which trace the country's tastes from 1500 to 1900. The museum has a particularly pleasant café in the basement, as well as a smaller one in a room designed by William Morris.

Natural History Museum

If any of London's museums encapsulates the Victorians' quest for knowl-

edge and passion for cataloguing data, it's the **Natural History Museum** ❻ (Cromwell Road; tel: 020-7942 5000; http://nhm.ac.uk; daily 10am–5.50pm), just across the road from the V&A. Occupying an extravagant Gothic-Romanesque building, it has one of the best dinosaur and prehistoric lizard collections anywhere in the world. The highlight is a full-scale animatronic T-Rex that roars and twists convincingly.

The Life Galleries section of the museum also has fascinating exhibits on early man, Darwin's theory of evolution, human biology, birth and whales (including a life-size model of a blue whale). In the Earth Galleries (Geology section) you can experience a simulated earthquake, or examine a piece of the moon. The Creepy Crawlies section demonstrates how many uninvited housemates occupy an average home. In the basement, children can touch, weigh and examine specimens under a microscope.

A new addition is the eight-storey Darwin Centre, a research centre that houses a vast collection of bottled

Ancient fish skeleton in the Natural History Museum.

BELOW: the Central Hall of the Natural History Museum.

specimens and is open to the public. Over the Christmas period, the museum makes a beautiful backdrop to an outdoor ice-skating rink.

Science Museum

Adjacent to the Natural History Museum, with its entrance on Exhibition Road, is the **Science Museum** ➐ (www.sciencemuseum.org.uk; daily 10am–6pm). It has more than 10,000 exhibits, plus attractions such as an IMAX theatre and an interactive play area for children. Highlights include the world's oldest surviving steam locomotive, the Apollo 10 command module (1969), the huge Spacelab 2 X-ray telescope – the actual instrument flown on the Space Shuttle – and full-size models of the Huygens Titan probe and Beagle 2 Mars Lander. Also of note is the 1919 Vickers Vimy, in which Alcock and Brown made the first non-stop transatlantic flight, and a replica of the Wright Flyer, in which Wilbur and Orville Wright pioneered powered flight in 1903.

The Wellcome Wing, linked to the main building, concentrating on information technology, hums with hands-on displays relating to the human experience.

Royal Albert Hall

On the northern fringe of South Kensington is the **Royal Albert Hall** ➑ (tickets and tours, tel: 020-7589 8212; www.royalalberthall.com). Queen Victoria laid the foundation stone for the concert hall in 1867 in memory of her late husband, Prince Albert, a highly cultured man who was responsible for founding many South Kensington institutions. The circular 8,000-seat auditorium stages a varied programme from pop concerts to the BBC-sponsored summer Promenade Concerts – the Proms – an annual showcase of mostly classical music, although there are also some jazz and contemporary music Proms.

Across Kensington Gore sits the **Albert Memorial** ➒, an extravagant Gothic monument that rises suddenly from the plane trees of Kensington Gardens and Hyde Park. Prince Albert sits under a lavishly gilded canopy, forever reading the catalogue from the

BELOW: the
Albert Memorial.

1851 Great Exhibition. Marble figures on the lower corners of the steps depict America, Asia, Africa and Europe.

Palaces and gardens

A short walk westwards through the park brings you to **Kensington Palace** ⑩ (www.hrp.org.uk; daily 10am–6pm; charge). Christopher Wren refurbished the mansion for William and Mary in the 1690s, and for nearly 100 years it served as the principal royal residence in London. Princess Diana once lived here, and an apartment is currently being refurbished for her son, Prince William, who is to move there with his wife, the Duchess of Cambridge. Many of the first-floor State Apartments can be viewed, as well as the Royal Dress Collection, a presentation of royal, court and ceremonial dress dating from the 18th century to the present day, including some of Diana's gowns.

To the north of the palace is the **Princess Diana Memorial Playground**, where children can let off steam.

Also in Kensington Gardens is the **Serpentine Gallery** ⑪ (www.serpentine gallery.org; daily 10am–6pm during exhibitions only; charge), a small art museum that stages adventurous exhibitions of modern and contemporary art. The museum will open a new space, the Serpentine Sackler Gallery, in 2012, in a Grade II-listed building ("The Magazine") just northeast of the original gallery, to showcase "the stars of tomorrow" in the visual arts.

To the east, Kensington Gardens merges into Hyde Park. At the southeast corner is **Apsley House** (149 Piccadilly; www.english-heritage.org. uk; Apr–Oct Wed–Sun 11am–5pm; charge), which was formerly the home of the Duke of Wellington, who defeated Napoleon at Waterloo in 1815. The mansion displays a fine collection of furniture, silver, porcelain and paintings.

In the northeast corner of Hyde Park is **Speakers' Corner** ⑫, where orators and idiots passionately defend their beliefs. This tradition began when the Tyburn gallows stood here (1388–1783), and felons were allowed to make a final unexpurgated speech to the crowds before being hanged.

Leighton House

Holland Park ⑬, just west of Kensington Palace via Kensington High Street, incorporates a Japanese garden, an adventure playground and a youth hostel. In summer an open-air theatre stages opera and drama.

At 12 Holland Park Road is **Leighton House** ⑭ (Wed–Mon 10am–5.30pm; charge), the home of the Victorian artist Lord Frederic Leighton from 1866 until he died in 1896. The *pièce de résistance* is the Arab Hall, inspired by a Moorish palace in Palermo. Leighton entered the record books for having the shortest-lived peerage in history – it was issued on 24 January 1896, but he died the following day.

You can hire boats to row on The Serpentine in Hyde Park. Hardy members of the lake's swimming club are permitted to compete in the annual Peter Pan Christmas Day Race, on 25 December.

BELOW: Notting Hill Carnival, held at the end of August.

Map on page 142

Peacock Ban

When the Pre-Raphaelite artist Dante Gabriel Rossetti and the poet Algernon Charles Swinburne lived at 16 Cheyne Walk, they kept peacocks in their garden. The birds so disturbed their neighbours that every lease on the row now prohibits tenants from keeping these birds.

BELOW: the Triton Fountain in Regent's Park.

Notting Hill and Shepherd's Bush

North of Holland Park (and northwest of Kensington Gardens) is **Notting Hill**, one of London's most highly sought-after residential districts, with handsome white stucco Victorian terraces and villas. On the last Sunday and Monday of August the narrow streets explode with music and colour as the city's West Indian population stages Europe's largest street carnival here.

The district's other famous attraction is the **Portobello Road Market** (Mon–Wed and Fri–Sat 8am–6.30pm, Thur 8am–noon). By far the busiest day is Saturday, when the street becomes jammed, as people browse the antiques and bric-a-brac. There is also a more fashion-forward market, with original-designer along with second-hand clothes, jewellery and ephemera stalls underneath the Westway flyover further along Portobello, which is also open on Sunday mornings. More interesting stalls (mostly bric-a-brac) set up on the Golborne Road (Saturdays only), which intersects with the most northern stretch of Portobello Road.

Little Venice and St John's Wood

The posh residential district of **Little Venice** lies at the junction of the Grand Union, Regent's and Paddington canals and residential moorings for barges here are much sought after. Refurbished canal barges operated by the **London Waterbus Company** (www.londonwaterbus.co.uk; service information tel: 020-7482 2660; bookings tel: 020-7482 2550) run east from Little Venice to Regent's Park through another exclusive residential neighbourhood, **St John's Wood**. At its heart is **Lord's Cricket Ground**, home of the Marylebone Cricket Club (MCC), the governing body of the quintessentially English sport. The **Cricket Museum** (entrance on St John's Wood Road; www.lords.org; Mon–Fri 10am–5pm; charge) is filled with two centuries of memorabilia.

Also in St John's Wood are the Abbey Road recording studios, with the zebra crossing the Beatles made so famous, and the **London Central Mosque**, completed in 1977, incorporating an Islamic Cultural Centre. ❑

RESTAURANTS AND PUBS

Restaurants

Prices for a three-course dinner per person with a half-bottle of house wine:
£ = under £25
££ = £25–50
£££ = £50–100
££££ = over £100

Chelsea

Cadogan Arms
298 King's Road, SW3
Tel: 020-7352 6500
www.thecadoganarms chelsea.com £££
Traditional Victorian pub turned fashionable gastropub, offering real ales along with good food. Dishes might include rack of Welsh lamb or pan fried sea bass. Good selection of British cheeses.

Gordon Ramsay
68 Royal Hospital Road, SW3
Tel: 020-7352 4441
www.gordonramsay.com
££££
The celebrity chef's gastronomic offerings – such as roasted sea scallops with octopus, black pudding tempura, cauliflower purée and parmesan velouté – are well worth his three Michelin stars. The lunch-time set menu, at £45 for three courses, is a bargain.

Poissonnerie de L'Avenue
82 Sloane Avenue, SW3
Tel: 020-7589 2457
www.poissonneriedel avenue.com ££–£££
Run by the same family for over 40 years, this restaurant serves fresh fish and seafood from the adjoining fishmonger's.

Dishes are old-school French, although some come with a distinctly Italian flourish.

Royal Court Café
Royal Court Theatre, Sloane Square, SW1
Tel: 020-7565 5058
www.royalcourttheatre.com
££
The roomy ambient vaulted café of Sloane Square's Royal Court Theatre is tucked away in what was the 19th-century theatre "pit". Slouch on the sofas with a drink, graze on tapas, some procured at Borough Market, or, for more substantial fare, try the generous mains (served until 8pm), such as mackerel salad or duck confit, and the excellent chocolate fudge cake. Limited wines but try a glass of the well-priced Prosecco.

Tom's Kitchen
27 Cale Street, SW3
Tel: 020-7349 0202
www.tomskitchen.co.uk £££
Relaxed brasserie run by award-winning chef Tom Aikens. The menu changes daily, but features classic British dishes such as Cumberland sausages and mash, steak sandwiches, fish pie and macaroni cheese.

Kensington

Bibendum
Michelin House, 81 Fulham Road, SW3
Tel: 020-7581 5817
www.bibendum.co.uk ££££
Opened by Sir Terence Conran and Paul Hamlyn in 1987, Bibendum continues to thrive; there's an oyster bar on the

ground floor and a restaurant on the first floor of this individual Art Deco-style building, with its famous tiles and stained glass depicting the Michelin man, mascot of the tyre company.

Daquise
20 Thurloe Street, SW3
Tel: 020-7589 6117 £–££
Reach this Polish restaurant by taking the right-hand exit out of South Kensington tube, and turning immediately right. Daquise is at the end of the row of shops. A loyal Polish and local clientele come here for the excellent authentic food at very cheap prices (especially for this upmarket area). The decor, including the squishy banquettes, has not changed for decades.

Kensington Place
201–9 Kensington Church Street, W8
Tel: 020-7727 3184
www.kensingtonplace-restaurant.co.uk £££
A trailblazer of the Modern British food scene, it still serves simple yet inventive good food. Note that the noise levels can be high.

Racine
239 Brompton Road, SW3
Tel: 020-7584 4477
www.racine-restaurant.com
£–££
The smart glass exterior promises a sophisticated meal, and you will not be disappointed by the classic French fare, cooked with panache. The prix-fixe menu, available at lunch and dinner, offers excellent value for this

posh part of town.

The Terrace
33c Holland Street, W8
Tel: 020-7937 3224
www.theterracerestaurant. co.uk ££
On fine days you can sit outside at this small restaurant serving modern British food. The excellent mains include duck breast with spring onion mash and cabbage.

Pubs

The area's best watering holes include the **Pig's Ear** (35 Old Church Street), lacking in authenticity after a Continental-style refit, but with a fine real ale to its name; the **Cooper's Arms** (87 Flood Street), upholding the Campaign for Real Food; the **Cross Keys** (1 Lawrence Street), dating from 1765 and worth a visit for its gorgeous rooms and good food; and the **Lots Road Pub and Dining Room** (114 Lots Road), a good gastropub.

Closer to Belgravia, the **Orange Brewery** (37–9 Pimlico Road) still retains remnants of its former brewery.

This part of London is awash with gastropubs, with great food and often real ales and specialist beers. You might want to check out the **Anglesea Arms** (15 Selwood Terrace, South Kensington), the **Churchill Arms** (119 Kensington Church Street), **Windsor Castle** (114 Campden Hill Road), **The Cow** (89 Westbourne Park Road) or **The Fat Badger** (310 Portobello Road).

DAYTRIPS ALONG THE THAMES

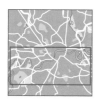

The Thames has played a central role in London's history. You can travel by boat to a variety of fascinating places along its banks, including Greenwich, Kew Gardens and Hampton Court

Main attractions
GREENWICH
HOGARTH'S HOUSE
KEW GARDENS
RICHMOND
TWICKENHAM
HAMPTON COURT PALACE

London's riverside areas can be reached by local London transport including river taxis, as well as by privately run riverboats (www.thamesriverservices.co.uk). Eastwards is elegant historic Greenwich and London's Docklands – the latter greatly developed since the 1980s but rather lacking in tourist attractions apart from a few old historic riverside pubs. To the west are the upmarket suburban areas of Kew, Richmond and Twickenham, and Hampton Court, further beyond. The western stretch of the river is very much a focus of pleasure: in summer, oarsmen and yachtsmen pit their wits against its tides and people stroll along its towpaths, laze at its bankside pubs or cruise about in their "gin palaces" (motor yachts).

Royal Greenwich

There have long been settlements at **Greenwich ❶**. In the 11th century Vikings pulled their longboats ashore, slew Archbishop St Alfege and ravaged London. In 1427 Bella Court Palace was built on the riverside and became a royal retreat. Henry VI made it his favourite residence and subsequent Tudor monarchs – Henry VIII, Elizabeth I and Mary – were all born at Greenwich. It was here that Sir Walter Raleigh is supposed to have laid his cloak over a pool of mud, so that Queen Elizabeth would not get her feet wet.

James I had the old palace demolished and commissioned Inigo Jones to build a new private residence for Queen Anne. The result was the **Queen's House**, completed in 1637, a masterpiece of the Palladian style and perhaps the finest piece of Stuart architecture in England.

Greenwich has been associated with British sea power for the past 500 years, and next door is the **National Maritime Museum** (www.nmm.ac.uk;

LEFT: the Royal Observatory and Flamsteed House.

daily 10am–5pm; charge for special exhibitions and shows), showcasing an excellent seafaring collection. Here, the 1805 Battle of Trafalgar is relived and the glory of the nation's maritime tradition unfolds, with boats, paintings, and memorabilia from heroic voyages. A short walk up the hill is the **Royal Observatory** (details as above), constructed at Greenwich by Charles II in 1675 in order to perfect the arts of navigation and astronomy. Since that time, the globe's longitude and time zones have been measured from the Greenwich Meridian, which cuts right through the middle of Flamsteed House, now a museum of astronomical instruments and timepieces (charge).

By the waterfront (on dry land) are two of England's most famous ships. The *Cutty Sark* and the tiny *Gipsy Moth IV*, the yacht in which Sir Francis Chichester sailed solo round the world in 1966. Built in 1869, the *Cutty Sark* (www.cuttysark.org.uk) was the last of the great China clippers, a speedy square-rigger that once ran tea from the Orient to Europe. The ship was preserved for the nation in 1922 and has sat by the Thames in naval Greenwich since 1954. She is being restored after being damaged by a fire in May 2007. When reopened in spring 2012, she will contain a collection of ship figureheads – her own one being the witch who pursued Tam O'Shanter in the poem by the Robert Burns *(see page 332)*, getting so close she pulled off his horse's tail. The Scottish name "cutty sark" relates to the cut-down shift that the witch is wearing.

Market mecca

The other main highlight of Greenwich is its crafts and antique markets, especially the covered one at the heart of the town centre. Full markets are held at weekends, although some stalls set up in the week as well (Wed–Fri). There are also several outdoor markets at the weekend, one by the Picturehouse Cinema opposite the railway station and the other at the foot of Croom's Hill.

From Greenwich you can take river boats further downstream. Sights en

The Painted Hall of the Royal Naval College, Greenwich.

BELOW: National Maritime Museum.

The Thames Path

Starting at the Thames Barrier in the east and ending at the river's source in the Cotswolds, 180 miles (290km) away, the Thames Path provides some of the best views of the city and beyond.

From Putney in West London the path takes on a rural aspect, passing the London Wetland Centre in Barnes (with excellent opportunities to spot all manner of birdlife), the grand riverside houses of Chiswick and the pretty cottages of Strand on the Green. After Kew Bridge, the path skirts round Kew Gardens, with Syon Park across the river. At Richmond, with Petersham Meadows on your left and a great sweep of the river ahead of you, it's hard to believe the city is within spitting distance. Along this stretch you'll see Marble Hill House and, a little further along, Ham House.

The Royal Naval College, begun by Christopher Wren in 1696, was designed as two halves to preserve the view from Queen's House to the river. It was originally a royal hospital but was given over to the training of naval officers in 1873.

route include **The O2 concert arena** ❷ (North Greenwich tube station; bookings tel: 0844-856 0202; www.theo2.co.uk), built as the Millennium Dome and now named after the mobile phone company that bought the naming rights. It is a massive entertainments centre hosting top rock concerts and sports events, with lots of eating places inside. Further down the river still is the **Thames Barrier** ❸ *(see margin, opposite)*.

Also downstream from Greenwich is the Royal Navy's **Historic Dockyard** at Chatham *(see page 211)*, which flourished under Henry VIII and Elizabeth I. In the late 17th century, Sir Christopher Wren built the **Royal Hospital for Seamen** at Greenwich, an elegant

complex in the baroque style that became the **Royal Naval College**. Its highly decorated chapel and Painted Hall, decorated in the early 18th century by Sir James Thornhill, are open to the public (www.oldroyalnavalcollege. org; daily 10am–5pm; free).

Upstream: gardens and grand houses

River boats go upriver from Charing Cross past Westminster and Lambeth to Battersea and Chelsea, followed, on the north bank, by the District tube line, and on the south bank by the overground train line from Waterloo. Opposite the Peace Pagoda in **Battersea Park** ❹, erected by Japanese Buddhists for the 1985 Year of Peace, is Sir Christopher Wren's **Chelsea Hospital** ❺ and, beyond, the upmarket development at **Chelsea Harbour** ❻. But the leafy riverbank does not really begin until **Putney** ❼, the starting point for the university boat race between Oxford and Cambridge universities each March. Putney can be reached by river boat, or by taking the District Line to Putney Bridge.

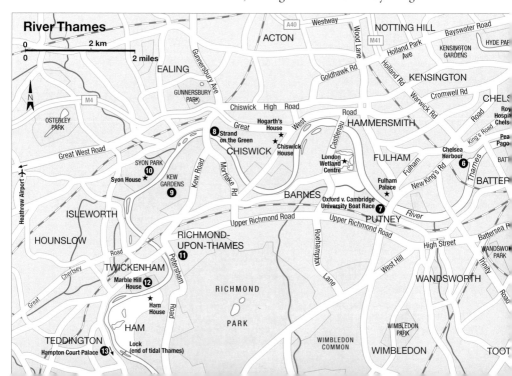

Beyond is Hammersmith Bridge. The Piccadilly and District tube lines go to Hammersmith, the starting point of a riverside walk that leads to Chiswick and has a number of popular riverside pubs, such as the Dove on Upper Mall; this historic 18th-century tavern is where the words of *Rule, Britannia* are supposed to have been written by James Thomson. **Strand on the Green ❽**, just beyond, has pretty Georgian houses and charming fishermen's cottages. After your walk, try one of the good riverside pubs, including the Bull's Head and the City Barge, both nearly 400 years old.

A further diversion at Chiswick is **Hogarth's House** (due to reopen in summer 2011; tel: 020-8994 6757; www.hounslow.info/arts/hogarthshouse), a 17th-century mansion now filled with engravings and personal relics of one of England's most famous artists. **Chiswick House**, an early 18th-century Palladian villa designed by the third Earl of Burlington, is even more delightful (overground train from Waterloo to Chiswick, or District or Piccadilly tube line to Turnham Green; Easter–Oct Wed–Sun 10am–5pm; charge).

Tropical house in Kew

Kew, a quiet suburb upstream and across the Thames from Chiswick, plays host to the Royal Botanic Gardens, generally known simply as **Kew Gardens ❾** (www.kew.org; daily 9.30am–6.30pm, winter until 4.15pm; charge), 300 acres (120 hectares) of exotic plants from around the world. The gardens were first planted in 1759 under the direction of Princess Augusta, who was then living on the site. In 1772, George III put Kew in the hands of botanist Sir Joseph Banks, who had just returned from a round-the-world expedition to collect plant specimens with Captain Cook, and the collection grew and grew. There are special areas given over to redwoods, orchids, roses, rhododendrons, and alpine and desert plants. Kew is now a Unesco World Heritage Site.

The most famous of Kew's nurseries is the **Palm House**, a vast Victorian pavilion of steel and glass that contains hundreds of tropical plants. The ecologically correct and energy-saving **Princess of Wales Conservatory**, opened in 1987, has 10 climatic zones, ranging from arid to moist tropical, under one roof.

The Thames Barrier, with The O2 arena in the background. Since 1982 the barrier, with 10 steel gates stretching 1,700ft (520 metres) across the Thames, has protected London from the danger of flooding (visitor centre at 1 Unity Way, open Apr–Sept Thur–Sun 10.30am– 5pm; charge; nearest train station is Charlton, around 20 minutes' walk away).

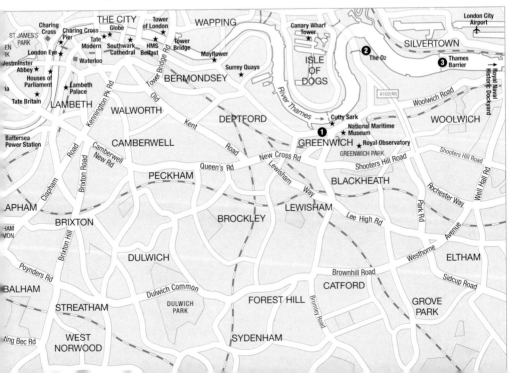

BELOW: the Palm House, Kew Gardens.

In addition to the glasshouses there are various temples and other follies dating back to the period of royal ownership of the gardens in the 18th and early 19th centuries. The **Chinese pagoda**, built in 1762, reflects the fashion for chinoiserie in English garden design in the mid-18th century. The classically-styled, Grade I-listed Orangery, dating from 1761, too dark to house citrus trees as was intended, is now a pleasant café-restaurant.

Across the Thames from Kew is another famous botanical centre, **Syon Park ⓾** (District Line to Gunnersbury, then the 237 or 267 bus to "Brentlea Gate"). The Dukes of Northumberland built a great mansion here in the 16th century, while the lush gardens were added by the great English landscape gardener, "Capability" Brown (see page 217). **Syon House** (www.syonpark. co.uk; house: Mar–Oct Wed–Thur, Sun 11am–5pm, gardens: mid-Mar–Oct 10.30am–5pm, Nov–early Mar Sat–Sun 10.30am–4pm or dusk, if earlier; charge), a neoclassical building remodelled in the 18th century by Robert Adam, has a lavish baroque interior and

vivid conservatory. In the park, there's a zoo aimed at children, with a variety of exotic species including marmosets, crocodiles and raccoons.

Richmond-upon-Thames

Reachable by train from Waterloo or via the District tube line, or on foot along the towpath from Kew, **Richmond-upon-Thames ⓫** retains its village atmosphere with its cluster of book and antiques shops, upmarket fashion boutiques, tea salons and charming riverside pubs, such as the White Cross. The Victorian-style **Richmond Theatre** sits on the edge of the green and is a showcase for productions on their way to the West End. **Richmond Park** was enclosed by Charles I as a royal hunting estate and is now the only royal park that keeps a large stock of deer. On the way to the park, a walk up Richmond Hill from the centre of town leads to a magnificent view west over the Thames.

Bus 371 from Richmond will take you to the flamboyant 17th-century **Ham House**, an annexe of the Victoria and Albert Museum (www.national

trust.org.uk; house: Apr–Oct Sat–Thur noon–4am (for tours see website), garden: Jan–mid-Feb and Nov–mid-Dec 11am–4pm, mid-Feb–Oct 11am–5pm; charge). Ham House contains a rich collection of period paintings (including Reynolds and Van Dyck), tapestries, furniture, carpets and clothing.

Richmond Bridge leads across to **Twickenham**, the home of English rugby (international games are staged in winter at the huge Twickenham Rugby Football Ground). The 18th-century **Marble Hill House** ⑫ on Richmond Road is a Palladian-style dwelling that has long provided a retreat for the secret affairs of the Crown. Both George II and George IV kept their mistresses in this mansion. Today the house contains a fine picture gallery and a lovely garden, the scene of outdoor Shakespeare productions and concerts in summer (Apr–Oct Sat 10am–2pm, Sun until 5pm; charge).

Hampton Court Palace

Above Twickenham is Teddington, the first lock that marks the end of the tidal Thames, and then **Hampton**

Court Palace ⑬ (www.hrp.org.uk; daily 10am–6pm; charge). Its two distinctive architectural styles make it both the paragon of the Tudor style and the self-proclaimed English version of Versailles. In the early 16th century, Hampton Court was built by Cardinal Wolsey as the finest and most flamboyant residence in the realm. When Wolsey fell from grace, he gave the palace to Henry VIII in a futile attempt to regain favour. The king instantly fell in love with it and moved there with Anne Boleyn. He ordered the construction of the Great Hall, the Clock Court and the Library, and enlarged the gardens. It is said that Elizabeth I used Hampton Court as an illicit love nest away from the prying eyes of Westminster. She also planted the gardens with exotic trees and flowers brought to England from the New World by Sir Francis Drake and Sir Walter Raleigh.

In the 1690s, the sumptuous **State Apartments** were designed by Wren for William and Mary, who also commissioned the Maze. Today the 1,000 rooms are filled with paintings, tapestries and furnishings from the past 450 years. ❑

The King's Staircase in the State Apartments of William III, Hampton Court Palace. The paintings are by Antonio Verrio (c.1639–1707).

RESTAURANTS

Greenwich

The Coach and Horses
13 Greenwich Market
Tel: 020-8293 0880
www.greenwich-inc.com/
coach_and_horses **££**
Located within the market, this inn's British pub classics (bangers and mash, big homemade burgers, fish and chips, Sunday roasts etc) come with a contemporary twist.

Trafalgar Tavern
6 Park Row
Tel: 020-8858 2909
www.trafalgartavern.co.uk **££**
A historic riverside pub, built in 1837, where Victorian politicians including Gladstone and Disraeli used to celebrate the end of the par-

liamentary session with fish dinners. It was also popular with writers Thackeray, Wilkie Collins and Dickens, who set the wedding breakfast scene in *Our Mutual Friend* here. Known for its baskets of whitebait, the more usual pub grub of fish and chips or sausage and mash is also reasonable.

Kew

Inn at Kew Gardens
292 Sandycombe Road
Tel: 020-8940 2220
www.kewgardenshotel.com
£–££
This award-winning gastropub serves platters of fish and charcuterie to share, alongside classics such as rib-eye steak, followed by

satisfying desserts that may include pumpkin tart with crème fraîche.

Richmond

Fishworks
13–19 The Square, Old Market
Tel: 020-8948 5965
www.fishworks.co.uk **££**
A big skylight and blue-and-white decor give Fishworks a bright, seaside feel. Lots of shellfish, salads and a good fish soup are on offer, along with standards such as skate with black butter. There are other branches in Islington, Westbourne Grove and Marylebone High Street.

Petersham Nurseries
Off Petersham Road

Tel: 020-8605 3627
www.petershamnurseries.com
£££
Gorgeous café with an excellent reputation and a Michelin star for Skye Gyngell's inventive cuisine. The produce is fresh and, as far as possible, locally sourced and organic (much from Petersham's kitchen garden). Tables are attractively set around a greenhouse. Reservations essential. Closed Mon.

Prices for a three-course dinner per person with a half-bottle of house wine:
£ = under £25
££ = £25–50
£££ = £50–100
££££ = over £100

THE ENGLISH SEASON

The Season is when high society is on display. The events are mostly sporting, but a sense of style is more important than a sense of fair play

The English Season was an invention of upper-crust Londoners as a series of midsummer amusements. This was the time when young girls "came out" at society balls, at which eligible young men would be waiting to make a suitable match. The presence of royalty is an important ingredient, and the royal family has long taken a keen interest in the sports highlighted by the Season.

The events, cynics say, are insignificant compared to their importance as social gatherings. People who care nothing for rowing attend Henley Regatta in the first week of July; philistine amateurs flock to the Royal Academy's Summer Exhibition; the musically challenged die for a ticket to Glyndebourne's opera season; and ill-informed people queueing for tickets to Wimbledon seem to think it's the only tennis tournament in the world.

ABOVE: being a tennis umpire at Wimbledon (end of June) takes nerves of steel as the players fight it out in the game's top championship.

BELOW: International Polo Day is held at the Guards Polo Club, Windsor Great Park, in July. The event's royal patronage and Cartier's sponsorship set the tone.

ABOVE AND BELOW: the Chelsea Flower Show in May has everything you need for the garden – and a few things you probably don't.

ABOVE: life's a picnic at the Henley Regatta, held in the Oxfordshire town at the beginning of July. Some people even take an occasional break to watch the rowing championships.

ABOVE: Cowes Week, held off the south coast of England in August, is the highlight of the sailing season.

THE ALTERNATIVE SEASON

Muddy fields and dripping campsites don't dampen the spirits of those attending the "alternative" Season – the annual round of music festivals. The larger ones attract the best bands from around the world and you don't have to be a hippy, crustie or a member of a youth tribe to attend. Many people take a tent to the large weekend events.

The largest such event, the Glastonbury Festival in Somerset, takes place at the end of June. More than 1,000 performances are given on 17 stages by more than 500 bands, and it attracts big names from Beyoncé to Leonard Cohen. Tickets can sell out quickly.

If you can't get to Glastonbury, try the two-day Big Chill festival which takes place in early August in the rolling Herefordshire hills. This is a family-oriented, eco-conscious event, with a wide variety of music vying with art, dance and film.

The best world music festival is WOMAD (right), held in Malmesbury, Wiltshire, in mid-July. The Reading Festival in late August attracts some of the best UK and US rock groups, and the Cambridge Folk Festival takes place in July.

BELOW: Glyndebourne, a summer opera location set on the South Downs near Brighton, is renowned as much for its lavish picnic hampers as it is for the performances of its star singers.

THE THAMES VALLEY

Winding its way across the western Home Counties of Buckinghamshire, Berkshire and Oxfordshire, the Thames crosses some of the gentlest and most quintessentially English of landscapes

The banks of this historic waterway have seen civilisations come and go. On the twin hills of Sinodun (*dun* means fort in Celtic), south of Dorchester-on-Thames, the early Britons built a major camp as early as 1500 BC. After the arrival of Caesar, the Romans did the same, and the remains of both settlements can be seen today. The Thames is a river of plenty and has made its valley a fertile farmland. In the Middle Ages the river was so thick with salmon that even the poor ate it as a staple. Great abbeys and monasteries flourished here, and kings and queens have made it their home.

Runnymede

To fly-fishermen, the Thames Valley begins at Bell Weir Lock just a mile north of **Staines**, south of the M4 beside the orbital M25. From Bell Weir north to the river's source (a muddy patch in a field near Coates in Gloucestershire), the river is bordered almost continuously by hills. On the west side of the motorway is Egham and the riverside meadow at **Runnymede ❶** where, on 15 June 1215, King John signed the Magna Carta *(see page 33)*. Tradition maintains that the barons encamped on one side of the Thames while the king's forces occupied the other. Magna Carta Island, the larger of the two river islands, was the neutral ground on which they met. Above is **Cooper's Hill**, which affords a panoramic view of Windsor Castle to the north.

At the bottom of the hill lies the Magna Carta Memorial, a domed neoclassical structure presented by the American Bar Association in recognition of the charter's influence on the American Constitution. Nearby is the John F. Kennedy Memorial, standing in the plush acre that, in 1965, the Queen gave to the United States in perpetuity.

A pleasant diversion from Runnymede follows the riverside road

Main attractions
RUNNYMEDE
WINDSOR CASTLE
ETON
MAIDENHEAD
COOKHAM
HENLEY-ON-THAMES
SONNING
DORCHESTER
ABINGDON

LEFT: Windsor Castle. **BELOW:** the Queen owns unmarked mute Thames swans.

BELOW:
Windsor Castle has extensive gardens.

from Staines to **Datchet**. This was once the Datchet Lane, mentioned in Shakespeare's comedy *The Merry Wives of Windsor*, along which Sir John Falstaff was carried in a basket of dirty linen to be ducked in the Thames.

Windsor's royal castle

England's most famous castle lies across the river from Datchet at **Windsor ❷**, (daily Mar–Oct 9.45am–5.15pm, Nov–Feb 9.45am–4.15pm, last admission year-round 1 hour 15 mins before closing, also closed for state visits; charge). The town is 30 miles (48km) west of London, 50 minutes by train from

London's Waterloo (direct) or about 30 minutes from Paddington (change at Slough from the latter).

Since the reign of Henry I in the 12th century, Windsor Castle has been the chief residence of English and British sovereigns. William the Conqueror founded the original structure, a wooden building that consisted most likely of a motte and two large baileys enclosed by palisades. The stone fortifications were built in the 12th and 13th centuries. Rising dramatically on a chalk cliff, the castle you see today incorporates additions by nearly every sovereign since. In the 19th century, George IV and Queen Victoria spent almost £1 million on additions. The late 20th century saw great restoration of the interior, in particular of **St George's Chapel** (closed Sun except for worship), the worst casualty of a disastrous fire in 1992.

Exploring the castle

Part of the Lower Ward, St George's Chapel is one of the finest examples of Perpendicular architecture in England (rivalled only by King's College

Chapel at Cambridge and the Henry VII Chapel at Westminster). Dedicated to the patron saint of the Order of the Garter, the chapel displays in the choir stalls the swords, helmets, mantles and banners of the respective knights.

In the Upper Ward are the **State Apartments**. These serve as accommodation for visiting foreign sovereigns and are occasionally closed to the public. Lavishly furnished, they include many important paintings from the royal collection, including works by Rubens, Van Dyck, Canaletto and Reynolds. There are also drawings by Holbein, Michelangelo, Leonardo and Raphael.

The Round Tower is what everyone thinks of as Windsor Castle. Climb the 220 steps for the wide valley view, but you won't be able to see the east side of the Upper Ward, which houses the Queen's private apartments. Instead, venture outside and south of the castle to the **Great Park**, more than 4,800 acres (1,920 hectares) of lush greenery. The **Savill Garden**, created in the 1930s by Sir Eric Savill, is renowned for its rhododendrons, and incorporates a landscaped garden created to mark the

Queen's Golden Jubilee and a Rose Garden by Andrew Wilson.

Legoland

Some 2 miles (3km) from Windsor town centre on the B3022 Windsor/Ascot road is **Legoland Windsor** (Winkfield Road, Windsor; tel: 0871-222 2001; www.legoland.co.uk; Apr–Oct daily 10am–5pm, with exceptions; charge), a popular theme park aimed at 3- to 12-year-olds and based around the children's building blocks – millions of them. Its 150 acres (60 hectares) of wooded landscape includes rides – such as the underwater Atlan-

The Thames between Windsor and Eton. The river, which rises in Gloucestershire and flows into the North Sea, is 215 miles (346km) long. In London, where it is tidal, the level rises at high tide by 23ft (7 metres) and the currents are strong enough to drown most people who fall in before they can be rescued.

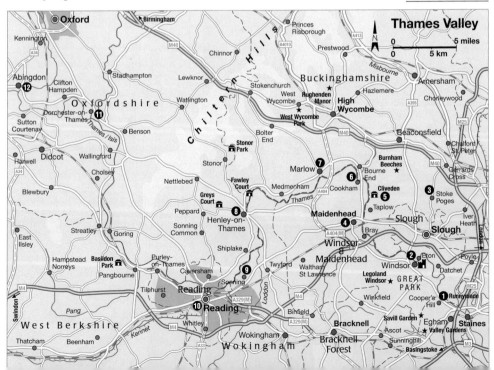

In the Middle Ages, all swans on the Thames belonged to the Crown to ensure there would always be sufficient swan meat for royal feasts. Each July, in the (now-conservational) ceremony of "Swan Upping", swans are weighed and measured, then the Queen's Swan Warden, a Professor of Ornithology at Oxford University, rings the beaks of cygnets to show ownership by the Crown, before setting the birds free again.

tis Submarine Voyage – shows and workshops. Lego is a contraction of two Danish words, *leg godt*, meaning "play well", and the park puts a worthy emphasis on learning as well as having fun. (Shuttle buses run from Windsor; Greenline buses run from London Victoria, tel: 0844-801 7261.)

Eton

Across the river from Windsor is **Eton College**, that most famous of English public schools, founded in 1440 by 18-year-old Henry VI. The original set of buildings included a collegiate church, an attached grammar school and an almshouse. It was Henry's intention that the church and school become a place of pilgrimage and devotion to the Virgin. The Wars of the Roses cut him short. He was murdered in the Tower of London, and every year on the anniversary of his death an Etonian lays a wreath of lilies in the cell in which he died.

To the visitor, Eton is a cluster of red-brick Tudor buildings with little towers and hulking chimneys. The **School Yard** (the outer quadrangle), the **Long Chamber** and the **Lower School** all

date from the 15th century. The chapel, in Perpendicular style, has 15th-century wall paintings depicting the miracles and legends of the Virgin. Most of the windows were damaged in World War II, but some of the modern installations are interesting. The cloisters dating from the 1440s are stunning; beyond them stretch the fields on which, according to the Duke of Wellington, the Battle of Waterloo was won.

Stoke Poges ❸, north of Eton and beyond the commuter town of **Slough** (damned by critics from Sir John Betjeman to Ricky Gervais), is the final resting place of the poet Thomas Gray and the inspiration for his *Elegy Written in a Country Churchyard*. The monument erected in 1799 commemorates him with a maudlin inscription, but the sheer beauty of the churchyard – its old lychgates, its rose bushes and its garden of remembrance – is what attracts visitors.

Maidenhead

Half a dozen miles (10km) upriver from Eton lies **Maidenhead ❹**, the starting point of some of the most beautiful countryside in the valley. Known in medieval times as Maydenhythe – one suggested meaning being maidens' landing place – its bridges are its most interesting feature: the 128ft (38-metre) arches of Brunel's railway bridge are thought to be the largest brick spans ever constructed.

From Maidenhead the A4130 goes 8 miles (13km) directly to Henley, but there are several picturesque villages and towns clustered on either side of the river nearby. **Bray**, nestled in a bend in the Thames just south of Maidenhead, has a lovely church that dates from 1293. The **Jesus Hospital**, founded in 1627, is also interesting, and still cares for 26 older citizens from a trust set up by its originator. A more contemporary claim to fame is as a mecca for foodies, thanks to its having two Michelin-starred restaurants: Heston Blumenthal's Fat Duck and Alain Roux's Waterside Inn.

BELOW: Cliveden, former seat of the Astors and now a luxury hotel.

Taplow is another pretty village, on the north side of the Thames opposite Maidenhead. From here, a road runs through Burnham to **Burnham Beeches**, a pastoral stretch of 375 wooded acres (150 hectares), especially attractive in autumn.

Upstream from Maidenhead is **Cliveden Reach**, another wooded tract, this one owned by the National Trust. The Italianate house, called **Cliveden ❺**, once the home of a Prince of Wales, several dukes and the Astor family, is poised dramatically above cliffs. Before World War II Nancy Astor turned it into a meeting place for politicians and celebrities, and in the 1960s it became notorious as the place where Secretary of State for War John Profumo and call-girl Christine Keeler met.

Today, Cliveden is leased out from the National Trust and run as a luxury hotel (www.clivedenhouse.co.uk). The main rooms are viewable part of the year (Apr–Oct Thur and Sun 3–5.30pm; charge). The gardens are open to the public and are decorated with Roman fountains, temples and topiary (daily mid-Feb–Oct 10am–5.30pm, Nov–Dec 10am–4pm; charge). Maps, available at the entrance, show suggested walks through the woodland, with spectacular views of the Thames.

Cookham

Cookham ❻ is yet another picturesque riverside village, though it is best known as the home of the artist Stanley Spencer (1891–1959). Spencer's painting of Cookham Bridge hangs in London's Tate Britain (*see page xx*). The Stanley Spencer Gallery, dedicated to his work, is housed in The King's Hall, on the High Street, where he attended Sunday school (http://stanleyspencer.org.uk; Easter–Oct daily 10.30am–5.30pm, Nov–Easter Sat–Sun 11am–4pm; charge).

A copy of his painting of *The Last Supper* hangs in Holy Trinity Church, parts of which date from the 12th century. The 15th-century tower is unusual; it is one of the few church towers with both a clock and a sundial.

Six miles (9km) upriver is **Marlow ❼**, the market town in which Mary Wollstonecraft wrote *Frankenstein*. In 1817 she lived in West Street ("Poets' Row") with her husband, the poet Percy Bysshe Shelley, while he was writing the poem, *The Revolt of Islam*. In Saxon times, Marlow was known as Merelaw, but what you see today is comparatively new: the suspension bridge and **All Saints Church** date from the 1830s. The rustic walks along the river below Marlow Lock are refreshing, as is **Quarry Wood**, 25,000 acres (10,000 hectares) of beechwoods on the Berkshire bank.

Henley-on-Thames

Henley-on-Thames ❽, a small market town with many old buildings, has been known for its rowing since 1839, when it hosted the world's first river regatta. The 4-day Henley Royal Regatta, usually held in the first week of July (*see page 154*), attracts rowers from all over the globe; it's also a major social event, where spectators dress for

TIP

Famous recent Etonians include the actors Hugh Laurie, Dominic West and Damian Lewis, oarsman Sir Matthew Pinsent, the art dealer Jay Jopling, Mayor of London Boris Johnson, Conservative Prime Minister David Cameron (one of 19 prime ministers to study at Eton), chef Hugh Fearnley-Whittingstall and princes William and Harry.

BELOW: Henley Royal Regatta.

BELOW: Sonning, which Jerome K. Jerome in his humorous 1889 novel *Three Men in a Boat* called "the most fairy-like little nook on the whole river."

show and overindulge in champagne. More minor regattas are held at weekends throughout the summer.

As its name implies, the **River and Rowing Museum** in Mill Meadows (daily May–Aug 10am–5.30pm, Sept–Apr 10am–5pm; charge) casts its net wider than just rowing to include a re-creation of *The Wind in the Willows*, Kenneth Grahame's much-loved children's classic, published in 1908.

There are several stately homes around Henley, but the most exquisite is the National Trust's **Greys Court** (Apr–Oct Wed–Sun 1–5pm; charge). To the west of Henley, this well-preserved Tudor house has remains of an earlier manor house dating from the 14th century. There is a crenellated tower, a huge wheel once used for drawing water using donkey-power, and a maze.

Shiplake is a sprawling village notable for its church, rebuilt in 1689, but housing lovely 15th-century stained glass from the abbey church of St-Bertin in St-Omer, France. The poet Alfred, Lord Tennyson (1809–92) was married here to Emily Sellwood in 1850.

Reading and around

Shiplake is en route to **Sonning ❾**, considered by many to be the prettiest of Thames villages. The little islands that rise here in the river make the views especially pastoral. In Saxon times, Sonning was the centre of a large diocese, with a cathedral, a bishop's palace and a deanery. Today, only parts of the deanery garden walls remain, though the present church incorporates fragments of Saxon work. The bridge is one of the oldest on the river.

Reading ❿ is the main industrial town in the lower valley: an important traffic hub and retail centre and known for its annual rock festival, but generally regarded as a somewhat uninspiring place. The playwright Oscar Wilde (1854–1900) was broken by 2 years' hard labour in the red-brick jail.

Streatley and **Goring**, 10 miles (16km) north of the A329, face each other on either side of the river. Streatley is the prettier of the two villages, situated at the foot of the Berkshire Downs. Five miles (8km) northwest is **Blewbury**, a lovely town with thatched cottages, watercress beds and winding lanes.

Located upriver about 8 miles (13km) away is **Dorchester-on-Thames** ⓫. This ancient village was, at different times, a Roman fort (Durocina) and a cathedral city. The abbey church (www.dorchester-abbey.org.uk; daily 8am–6pm, or until dusk in winter) was spared demolition at the Dissolution by a local resident who bought it from the Crown for £140. The stained glass in the nave dates from the 14th century. In the chancel is a Jesse Window in which Jesse, Christ's ancestor, lies on the sill with a fruit vine springing from his belly. The High Street, which follows the line of the Roman road to Silchester, is lined with timber-framed buildings.

Sutton Courtenay and **Clifton Hampden** are riverside villages with lush willow trees hanging low over the banks. There's good swimming here in summer. Sutton Courtenay is especially interesting, with a well-preserved Norman church and a cluster of medieval houses nearby. In the graveyard is the resting place of Eric Blair (1903–50), better known as the writer George Orwell.

Abingdon

After Sutton Courtenay the river turns north, on its way to **Abingdon** ⓬, on the doorstep of Oxford. This old town sprang up in the 7th century around a powerful Benedictine mitred abbey (St Mary's). In the 14th century the townspeople led a bloody uprising against the monks, though it was not until the Dissolution that the abbey lost its power. Most of the ecclesiastical buildings were destroyed – don't be fooled by the 19th-century artificial ruins (follies) in the abbey grounds. But there are some authentic remains, including the abbey **Gateway**, the 13th-century **Checker** (with its idiosyncratic chimney), whose name – similar to "exchequer" – is thought to reflect its former use for accounting, and the 15th–16th-century **Long Gallery**.

Dating from 1682, Abingdon's Town Hall, of the open-ground-floor type, was built by Sir Christopher Wren's mason, the same man responsible for the dome of St Paul's Cathedral in London. East Saint Helen's, with the church at the foot, is perhaps the prettiest street. ❏

Dorchester Abbey. Today's building was begun in the 12th century, replacing two earlier Saxon cathedrals, and was enhanced over the next 500 years. It is still used for worship and for concerts.

RESTAURANTS

Bray
The Fat Duck
1 High Street
Tel: 01628-580 333
www.thefatduck.co.uk **££££**
Heston Blumenthal creates complex, adventurous, scientifically approached dishes such as snail porridge and nitro-scrambled egg-and-bacon ice cream. The restaurant has three Michelin stars. Book far ahead.

The Waterside Inn
Ferry Road
Tel: 01628-620 691
www.waterside-inn.co.uk **££££**
In an idyllic riverside spot, this is one of England's most exceptional restaurants, winner of three Michelin stars for its French cuisine.

Goring
The Leatherne Bottel
On the B4009 north of Goring
Tel: 01491-872 667
www.leathernebottel.co.uk
££–£££
Expect imaginately produced British food prepared using the best ingredients at this pretty old riverside inn.

Henley
La Bodega
38 Hart Street
Tel: 01491-578 611 **££**
Spacious tapas bar and restaurant with a wide menu and good choice of Spanish wines.

Shinfield
L'Ortolan
The Old Vicarage, Church Lane

Tel: 01189-888 500
www.lortolan.com **£££**
Innovative Anglo-French cuisine is served at Reading's only Michelin-starred restaurant, in a village 5 minutes from the M4's junction 11. Offers good vegetarian options.

Sonning
The Mill at Sonning
Sonning Eye, Reading
Tel: 0118-969 8000
www.millatsonning.com **££**
The setting is the main attraction, along with concerts and plays; The Mill offers a combined price for a meal and a show. The food is more run-of-the-mill – chicken in white-wine sauce, cheesecake etc.

Windsor
Carpenters Arms
4 Market Street
Tel: 01753-863 739
www.nicholsonspubs.co.uk/the carpentersarmswindsor/ **£–££**
In a building dating from 1518, this traditional pub serves award-winning real ales and affordable classic pub grub (such as prawn cocktails, gammon and eggs, steaks, Cumberland sausage and mash, tasty Sunday roasts etc).

Prices for a three-course dinner per person with a half-bottle of house wine:
£ = under £25
££ = £25–50
£££ = £50–100
£££ = over £100

OXFORD TO BIRMINGHAM

The triangle of Britain between Oxford, Warwick and the River Severn contains history, culture and architectural style which seem to grow out of the ground. At its heart are the Cotswolds

The Cotswolds are part of a range of limestone hills that stretch from the Dorset coast northeast to Lincolnshire. What distinguishes them here is oolite. Oolite, also called egg-stone because it looks like the roe of a fish, is the fine-grained freestone that has given a special character to the houses, barns, churches and pigsties from the hills' edge above Chipping Camden to the southern full stop at Bath.

As if to reinforce the idea of a natural triangle, this area of the west Midlands is now enclosed by motorways on its three sides: the M4 from London to Bristol at its base; the M40 from London to Birmingham via Oxford and Warwick on the eastern side; the M5 from Birmingham to Bristol on the west. A good hopping-off point to the region is Oxford, which is about 1 hour's drive (60 miles/95km) from both London and Birmingham. London's Paddington station serves the region.

City of dreaming spires

However you arrive in **Oxford** you can't miss its famous dreaming spires – of Christ Church Cathedral, Tom Tower and Magdalen Tower. The city has given its name to many things from marmalade to movements, and is where undergraduates, cycling around corners, trail their gowns in the wind.

But Oxford is also the site of the first Morris Motors works, and since World War II it has been an industrial city in addition to an academic one, although this is now less marked than several decades ago. Yet despite the inevitable takeover of Cornmarket Street by the usual high-street chains, Oxford has reached the 21st century relatively unscathed.

A tour of **Oxford** ❶ is essentially a tour of the colleges, but a good starting point is **Carfax Tower** Ⓐ (daily Apr–Sept 10.30am–5.30pm, Oct

Main attractions
OXFORD
BLENHEIM PALACE
BIBURY
GLOUCESTER
CHELTENHAM
BROADWAY
BOURTON-ON-THE-WATER
STRATFORD-UPON-AVON
WARWICK

PRECEDING PAGES: Chipping Steps, Tetbury.
LEFT: Oxford's High Street.
RIGHT: Magdalen College, Oxford.

Busts such as the Emperors' Heads (or "Bearded Ones") put up in 1669 outside the Sheldonian Theatre were often used in antiquity to create boundaries.

10.30am–4.30pm, Nov–Feb 10am–3pm, Mar 10am–4pm; charge). (The name derives from the French, *Quatre Voies*, "four ways".) This is the old centre of the city, around the pedestrianised area, where the four main streets meet: Cornmarket, High Street, Queen Street and St Aldate's. The tower at the northwest corner, all that remains of St Martin's Church, dates from the 14th century, and from the top of it you take in a good view of the city. From Carfax, walk south along St Aldate's (passing the impressive, neo-Jacobite Town Hall on the left) to **Christ Church** ⓑ (Mon–Sat 9am–5.30pm, Sun 2–5.30pm; charge), the grandest and largest of the colleges.

Christ Church

Known as "The House", Christ Church was founded in 1525 by Cardinal Wolsey (his pointed hat is The House's insignia), on the site of an old priory said to have been established by the Saxon princess, St Frideswide. **Tom Tower** was built by former student Sir Christopher Wren in 1681. **Tom Quad**, the largest quadrangle in Oxford, has splendid grace and magnitude, and it was in the pool here, which is known as Mercury, that Anthony Blanche was dunked in Evelyn Waugh's influential 1945 novel, *Brideshead Revisited*.

Christ Church chapel is also the **Cathedral** (closes at 4.30pm) of Oxford. The 144ft (43-metre) spire is one of the earliest in England, dating from the 13th century. As well as the reconstructed tomb of St Frideswide, the cathedral also contains some exquisite stained glass, including works by the Pre-Raphaelite artist Edward Burne-Jones. Lining the south side of Tom Quad is the enormous **Hall** of Christ Church, with its magnificent hammerbeam ceiling and now famous for featuring in the Harry Potter movies. To the north is the neoclassical Peckwater Quad and the smaller Canterbury Quad, where the **Picture Gallery** has a fine collection of Renaissance paintings and drawings. South of the college, extending down to the confluence of the Isis and Cherwell rivers, is the glorious **Christ Church Meadow**, which runs down to the river. It's a pleasant walk along the leafy

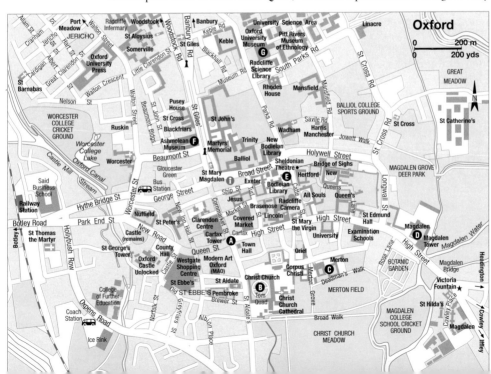

avenue here, at the bottom of which are the university and college boathouses. It's here, in Torpids in March and Eights Week at the end of May that the college rowing races take place.

College tour

From the Broad Walk, the wide path running east–west across the Meadow, there's a path cutting north to **Merton College** **C** (Mon–Fri 2–5pm, Sat–Sun 10am–5pm; charge). Founded in 1264, making it one of the university's first colleges, Merton has some of the oldest buildings in Oxford. Its library in Mob Quad (the oldest complete quadrangle in Oxford) was built in the 1370s. The library's 16th-century bookshelves make it the first Renaissance library in England, one where the books were set upright instead of being kept in presses. One of Merton's illustrious graduates was the writer and caricaturist Max Beerbohm (1872–1956), and in Mob Quad is a set of rooms decorated with a selection of his memorabilia. T.S. Eliot also studied here.

Opposite Merton are **Corpus Christi** (1.30–4.30pm) and **Oriel**

(daily 2–5pm), smaller colleges both, though no less picturesque. Oriel is famed for the sporting prowess of its students; the chapel at Corpus has an altarpiece ascribed to Rubens. Merton Street turns left at the top and into the **High Street**, where the landmark tower of **Magdalen College** **D** (pronounced *maudlin*; Oct–June 1–6pm, July–Sept noon–7pm; charge) rises to the right.

Magdalen, one of the most highly rated colleges, with alumni including Oscar Wilde, C.S. Lewis and Sir John Betjeman, was founded in 1458 by William of Waynflete. The chapel is a fine example of Perpendicular architecture and the cloisters are stunning. Behind them is the **Grove**, Magdalen's deer park, and the lovely **Water Walks**, a maze of garden and stream-side paths. Punts can be hired from the river below Magdalen Bridge. On the opposite side of High Street is the rose-rich **Botanic Garden** (daily 9am–5pm; charge).

Walking west along High Street you pass on the left the **Examination Schools**, built in 1882 in the style of a Jacobean country house with Clas-

The Cotswolds town of Chipping Campden was a prosperous wool trading centre in the Middle Ages.

BELOW: Oxford's Bridge of Sighs.

The Radcliffe Camera. It was built in 1737–49 to house the Radcliffe Science Library and was absorbed as a reading room of the Bodleian in 1860. Its subterranean storage space can cope with around 600,000 books.

BELOW: tour in progress in the Divinity School.

sical and Gothic elements, and on the right **St Edmund Hall** (entrance in Queen's Lane; daily 10am–4pm). This was incorporated as a college in 1957. Before that, it remained the sole survivor of the once numerous residential halls of the medieval university. The name of St Edmund Hall, founded in the mid-13th century, honours Edmund of Abingdon, who died in 1240 and was the first Oxford graduate to become Archbishop of Canterbury and be canonised. The chapel, decorated by William Morris and Edward Burne-Jones, is worth a look.

Further west along High Street are **University College** ("Univ") on the left (with a Shelley memorial) and, on the right, **All Souls** (Mon–Fri 2–4pm; closed Aug), which is as magnificent as it is exclusive – it doesn't accept undergraduates, only the cream of finalists, who are invited to sit its entrance exam, with only a couple being admitted for post-graduate study each year. A meandering stroll along Queen's Lane will take you to the rear of **New**

College (daily Easter–Oct 11am–5pm, Nov–Easter 2–4pm; charge), renowned for its choir. The chapel and cloisters of both are stunning, as is the garden with the remains of the medieval town wall. As Queen's Lane curves, you will reach Oxford's **Bridge of Sighs**, a 1914 copy of the Venetian original, which connects the new and old buildings of **Hertford College** (daily 2–4.30pm).

The Bodleian Library

From here there is a lovely view of the huge, circular Palladian-style **Radcliffe Camera** (*c.*1749), a university library, on the left (the name comes from the Latin, meaning "room") and Sir Christopher Wren's 1669 **Sheldonian Theatre** (www.sheldon.ox.ac.uk; Mon–Sat 10am–12.30pm, 2–4.30pm; charge), which hosts degree ceremonies as well as public concerts, straight ahead. Dominating the scene, however, with the magnificent **Old Schools Quadrangle** as its centrepiece, is the **Bodleian Library** **Ⓔ** (www.bodleian.ox.ac.uk). This is one of the world's largest libraries, founded in 1602 by Sir Thomas Bodley. Having agreed to receive a copy of every book registered

Port Meadow

If you walk northwards along Oxford's Walton Street and then turn left down Walton Well Road, you come to a bridge over the railway and canal, leading to the 400-acre (160-hectare) **Port Meadow**.

Used for grazing ever since its first mention in the Domesday Book (1087), the meadow is a rare piece of Old England, as it has never been ploughed. Dotted about with cattle and horses, it is also rich in birdlife and wildflowers. Annual winter floods bring flocks of wildfowl and waders, and the meadow is a magnet for migrating birds, notably Canada geese. In summer, you can often make out the outlines of Iron Age farming enclosures and hut circles, delineated by the buttercups that grow taller over buried features such as ditches and foundation trenches.

with Stationers' Hall in 1610 (it is one of three of this kind in England, along with Cambridge University Library and the British Library), the library now houses more than 7 million volumes, including 50,000 precious manuscripts, on almost 120 miles (193km) of shelving, much of it underground.

The Bodleian has never been a lending library; even Charles I was once refused the loan of a book. Although the library is not open to the public, tours (10.30am, 11.30am, 2pm and 3pm; charge) can be booked at the old Divinity School (beyond the main entrance of the library, with a fine vaulted ceiling) and include a brief look into the main hall and Duke Humfrey's library, which featured in the Harry Potter films and where undergraduates are not allowed to use pens, only pencils.

If you actually want to buy a book rather than just look at them, **Blackwell's** in Broad Street, which started in a small room in 1879, stocks around 200,000 titles. Its vast Norrington Room, carved out beneath Trinity College, has the largest display of books for sale in one room anywhere in the world.

Opposite **Balliol College** (daily 10am–5pm; charge), on Broad Street, a cross in the road marks the point where the Protestant Martyrs, bishops Cranmer, Latimer and Ridley, were burnt at the stake in 1555 and 1556. Around the corner at the top end of St Giles', they are further commemorated by the **Martyrs' Memorial**, erected in 1841.

City museums

The neoclassical building opposite the Martyrs' Memorial, and the oldest public museum in Britain, is the **Ashmolean Museum** Ⓕ (www.ashmolean. org; Tue–Sun 10am–6pm; free). The museum (occupying the original building and a spectacular new space designed by Rick Mather) houses a superb collection of Italian Renaissance, Dutch still-life and modern French painting. It also has an impressive collection of 16th- and 17th-century tapestries, bronzes and silver; Greek, Roman and Egyptian sculpture; a Stradivarius, ceramics and jewellery.

North along St Giles' is **St John's College**, founded in 1555. Its lovely gardens, landscaped by "Capability"

TIP

Most of Oxford's colleges open daily to visitors, but an increasing number now charge for a look around. Colleges do tend to close to visitors at exam times; some also close at the end of term, when conferences are held. Check the notice boards outside each college for opening times.

BELOW: Oxford University Museum.

Brown, rival those of Wadham and Trinity as the prettiest in Oxford (daily 1–5pm; free). Behind St John's is the **Oxford University Museum** (daily 10am–5pm; free), built in 19th-century neo-Gothic to the taste of the art critic John Ruskin (1819–1900). The family-friendly museum is a storehouse of zoological, entomological, mineralogical and geological odds and ends. Close by, on Parks Road, is **Keble College** (summer 10am–5pm, winter until 7pm), with its distinctive Gothic zebra-striped architecture by William Butterfield.

Around Oxford

There are several villages worth visiting nearby. **Iffley**, south of the city, has a well-preserved Norman church that dates from 1170 and stands gracefully and timelessly above the river. The thatched cottage is the old church school. Some 16 miles (25km) southwest is the market town of **Wantage**, birthplace of King Alfred (AD 849–99), and 3 miles (5km) further west is **Uffington**, where the 360ft (110-metre) **White Horse ❷** *(see below)* was carved

in the Iron Age at the highest point in the Berkshire Downs.

Eynsham, 8 miles (13km) west of Oxford along the A40, is a picturesque village with the remains of a once-famous abbey. Northwest via Witney is **Minster Lovell ❸**, which has a 15th-century cruciform church and the romantic moated ruins of Minster Lovell Hall. The remains of this 15th-century manor house stand above the Windrush River with a gloomy beauty. Francis, the 9th Baron Lovell, went into hiding here and starved to death in 1487.

Blenheim Palace

Eight miles (13km) north of Oxford on the A34 is **Blenheim Palace ❹** (www.blenheimpalace.com; mid-Feb–Oct daily, Nov–mid-Dec Wed–Sun, palace and gardens: 10.30am–5.30pm, park: 9am–4.45pm; charge), the destination not only of admirers of Sir Winston Churchill, who was born here, but of those who like the natural-style gardens of Britain's best-known landscape gardener, "Capability" Brown. An afternoon stroll at Blenheim, followed by tea and a stroll round the antiques

White Horses

Around two dozen white horses decorate hills around England. They have been created by removing the top layer of soil and grass to reveal the chalk underneath. Some date back to the Bronze Age (such as the White Horse of Uffington in Oxfordshire), though many are comparatively modern (19th century). There are also some human carvings, such as the Cerne Abbas giant, a naked man 180ft (55 metres) long near Dorchester in Dorset. All need to be maintained regularly to stop grass and bushes obliterating them.

What is their significance? Some may have had religious connotations, some may have represented civic pride and others had an historical connection – the Westbury White Horse, for example, may have celebrated the charger King Alfred rode when he defeated the Danes in 878.

shop in the handsome village of Wood-stock, is a quintessentially English country excursion.

Britain's largest private house, covering 7 acres (2.8 hectares) including the courtyards, the Churchills' family home is the masterpiece of the playwright and architect John Vanbrugh (1664–1726). The exterior of the palace is an orgy of the baroque style, with both Doric and Corinthian columns. Inside is a maze of magnificent state apartments and, on the ground floor, the small bedroom where Winston Churchill was born in 1874. There's also an exhibition of Churchilliana, including photographs and letters. When the house is closed, there is still the 2,500-acre (1,000-hectare) park to enjoy. Originally designed in the ornate French style by Henry Wise, the landscaping was completely redone in 1764 by Brown, who constructed a dam across the River Glyme and created the majestic lake seen today.

Cotswolds villages

Shaking off the clay of Oxford's vale, the roads west climb gradually to the

heights of the edge facing the Severn and the distant mountains of Wales. Here are the Cotswold Hills, broken by steep wooded valleys and rushing streams, Coln and Churn, Windrush, Dikler, Leach and Evenlode. Height and defensibility made their upper slopes the settlements of prehistoric man. Their pastures and rivers provided subsistence in Roman times, and wealth for medieval peoples in the production of wool and cloth. Cirencester, 40 miles (65km) west of

An Edwardian steam launch cruises along the Thames towards Lechlade.

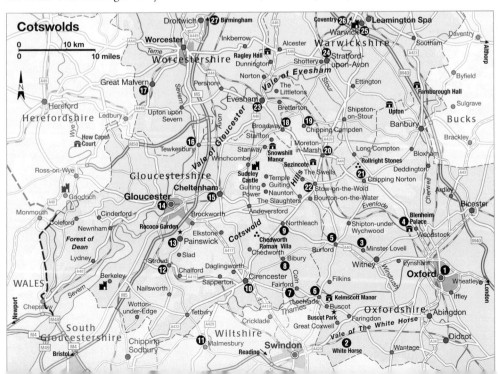

Oxford, was second only to London in size in Roman Britain, and Burford, halfway between the two, had its wool-merchants' guild before the Norman Conquest. Thus, the architecture of Cotswold villages was subsidised by the profits of the clothing industry. With its collapse, the Cotswolds went to sleep till pricked awake by the tourist.

The churchyard at the pretty town of **Burford ❺** has tombs in the shape of wool bales. Wool merchants' houses of the 14th–16th centuries can often be found hiding behind later fronts. Just south of Burford, at Filkins, is **Cotswold Woollen Weavers** (Mon–Sat 10am–6pm, Sun 2–6pm; charge), a traditional working mill where you can watch craftsmen spinning and weaving fleece using age-old skills.

A mini tour

South of Filkins, **Lechlade ❻**, 22 miles (36km) west of Oxford on the A420/A417, on the upper Thames, makes a good starting point for a circuitous tour. Below St John's Bridge cabin cruisers pass, and trout wait beside the 13th-century **Trout Inn**. No doubt

William Morris, the utopian craftsman, dropped in here from his house just downstream at **Kelmscott Manor** (Apr–Sept Wed and Sat 11am–5pm; charge). A typical Cotswold stone-built house, the manor has a roof of split stones, of which Morris said: "It gives me the same sort of pleasure in their orderly beauty as a fish's scales or a bird's feathers." Morris took the house with Dante Gabriel Rossetti, in 1871, and it became a centre for the Pre-Raphaelite movement. His body was carried from here to the churchyard in 1896.

Morris delighted in taking friends to the tithe barn at **Great Coxwell** (daily until dusk; charge). This cathedral among barns owes its importance to the 13th-century monks at Beaulieu Abbey in Hampshire. The great oak timbers that support the roof rest on pillars of stone taller than a man. The nave, aisles and transept convey the message that this is indeed a house of God.

Just across the river from Kelmscott is **Buscot Park** (Easter–Sept Wed–Fri and 2nd and 4th Sat–Sun in month 2–6pm; charge). Lord Faringdon enlarged the Adam-style house in the late 19th cen-

tury, engaging the Pre-Raphaelite artist Edward Burne-Jones to paint panels for the saloon and design the glass for the east window in the church.

Rare stained glass

In **Fairford ❼**, 5 miles (8km) west of Lechlade, a major draw is the stained glass at St Mary's Church. It is unknown where these marvels came from. Was this extraordinary stained glass the work of Henry VIII's master glass painter, the man who worked on King's College Chapel, Cambridge? Or was it a prize taken from a captured ship? Did it come, perhaps, from the Netherlands, and did Dürer have a hand in it? Was the glass made for the church, or the church built for the glass? How did it survive the Civil War? Speculation aside, the "Last Judgment" is a masterpiece, and the red and blue devils, all with spiked teeth and yellow horns, are wonderfully frightening.

Five miles (8km) north of Fairford, up the River Coln, is the beautiful village of **Bibury ❽**. William Morris is credited with having discovered it, but Bibury's beauty has been there for all to see since the 17th century. **Arlington Row's** gables and high-pitched roofs are the very essence of the Cotswolds. These stone-built cottages, beside a stream running from the mill, once housed weavers, who dried the cloth on Rack Isle, now a wildlife reserve.

Just to the west of Bibury, the Cirencester–Northleach road (A429) follows the route of the original Roman road, the Fosse Way. **Chedworth**, on the left, 5 miles (8km) north of Cirencester, has cottages scattered in terraces above the river. The woods below shelter what is probably the country's best-preserved **Roman villa** (Mar 10am–4pm, Apr–Oct 10am–5pm; charge), dating from AD 180 and covering an area of 6½ acres (2.6 hectares). The baths are especially well preserved, and the mosaics are made from two varieties of local Cotswold stone.

The church tower at **Northleach ❾**, 10 miles (16km) northeast of Cirencester, soars above the rooftops in the Perpendicular style. The wool merchants who built the church are remembered in the fine memorial brasses dating from the 15th and 16th centuries.

BELOW: Chedworth Roman villa.

*Cirencester town
centre.*

siter" and the Romans "Corinium", though locals call it "Ciren". Second only in size and importance to London under the Romans, its fortunes flourished under the wool merchants, and floundered during the 19th century. Today, the medieval character of this "capital of the Cotswolds" is remarkably preserved.

One of the best examples of Perpendicular style in the country, the porch of the parish church of St John the Baptist, once doubled as the town hall. Of the 12 bells in the tower, the ninth is called the "Pancake Bell", because it is always rung on Shrove Tuesday.

In the town centre, the museum at **Keith Harding's World of Mechanical Music** (daily 10am–5pm; charge) is concerned with the intricacies of antique musical boxes and clocks, gramophones and self-playing pianos.

The story of Roman Cirencester is compellingly told at the **Corinium Museum** (Nov–Mar Mon–Sat 10am–4pm, Sun 2–4pm, Apr–Oct until 5pm; charge) and substantial remains of the town walls are still in evidence, along with a well-preserved amphitheatre.

Ermin Street is now the A417 leaving the town to the northwest, where two village churches are not to be missed. First is **Daglingworth**, 4 miles (6km) away, with Saxon sculptures, including a crucifixion of compelling simplicity.

Cirencester

BELOW RIGHT:
beautiful stained
glass in Cirencester
Cathedral.

The Fosse Way leads south to join two other Roman roads, the Icknield Way and Ermin Street, in **Cirencester** , which some would have you say "Cis-

Cotswolds Buildings' Distinctive Look

There are several basic ingredients of almost all Cotswold architecture. Roofs are steeply pitched to carry the heavy stone tiles. These are applied in a fish-scale pattern, starting with the smallest, hand-sized tiles at the ridges and descending to table-sized ones at the eaves. The eaves overhang the walls because, with no guttering, this best carries rainwater away from the walls. Other features that look decorative but which are practical do the same job of shedding water, especially the drip moulds found around the chimneystack and above windows and doors.

The area's style of window frames are also made of stone, usually with a cross-shaped mullion (upright bar) and transom (horizontal bar) dividing the space into four, with two tall lights in the bottom half and two smaller lights above.

Then, high up, 5 miles (8km) further on, is **Elkstone's** church, with a view from its east window under low Norman arches like a limestone cave.

Malmesbury

Malmesbury ⓫, 12 miles (20km) southwest of Cirencester on the A429, is known for two distressing incidents: the killing of a woman by a tiger from a visiting menagerie and the conversion of the abbey into a factory. The woman was Hannah Twynnoy, who died in 1703. At the Dissolution a rich clothier bought the abbey in a package deal that allowed him to convert it into a weaving shed, and the parishioners to use the nave for services. Enough remains, especially a richly decorated porch, to give a good idea of the abbey's former glory.

Five miles (8km) northwest of Malmesbury, in **Tetbury**, a fine 17th-century market hall recalls the bustle of trading in wool once conducted in the pillared open space beneath it.

Golden Valley

Returning north 6 miles (10km) beyond Tetbury, the A46 arrives at Nailsworth and the start of the gorge-like valleys of Stroudwater, of wheels now still and looms long silent. There are still one or two cloth mills here, and cottages hug the terraces above the steep streets. At **Chalford**, off the A419, the descent into the **Golden Valley** begins.

Curiosities are both here and further east at **Sapperton**. One is a round house with conical roof and Gothic windows on the banks of the canal that opened in 1789 to link the Thames with the Severn. At Sapperton the canal disappears into the hillside under a triumphal arch.

From where the River Frome breaks through the western wall of the Cotswolds, **Stroud** ⓬, on its hill, looks across to the mountains of Wales. The country's cloth industry was concentrated here in the Stroudwater valley in the 16th century, and England's armies went to war in uniforms of scarlet and blue cloth from these mills.

Take to the heights to the east of the A46, and you are in a land of swift-

Gloucester Cathedral, which doubled as Hogwarts School of Witchcraft and Wizardry in the Harry Potter movies.

BELOW:
Cheltenham is a major race centre.

Sudeley Castle, a great, castellated house just south of Winchcombe, was built in the 1440s. It has been carefully restored, and displays a fascinating collection of royal relics and paintings.

BELOW: a cottage in Chipping Campden.

flowing streams and wooded ravines. **Slad**, on the B4070, is the village on which (Stroud-born) Laurie Lee based his novel, *Cider With Rosie*.

On the A46, 3 miles (5km) north of Stroud, is **Painswick** , whose traditions include weaving, tomb-carving and "clipping". The mills have closed and the masons have put down their tools, but the clipping (meaning "embracing") service is still held every September when children join hands to encircle St Mary's Church. Just north of Painswick on the B4073 is the **Rococo Garden** (Jan–Oct daily 11am–5pm; charge), restored to its former glory as depicted in a painting of 1748.

Gloucester

Nearby **Gloucester** is a cathedral city and inland port and has been a strategic centre guarding the route to Wales since Roman times. King Alfred held a parliament here in AD 896, Canute signed a treaty and William the Conqueror ordered the Domesday survey from the Chapter House. Henry I died here of eating lampreys (a kind of eel), Henry III was crowned and crook-backed Richard III reputedly ordered the murder of his nephews while in the town. Charles II took out his spite on the city for opposing his father, by having its walls demolished.

Of the Roman walls, vestiges remain; of the medieval town, very little. The old docks have been renovated and include the excellent and child-friendly **National Waterways Museum** (daily Sept–June 11am–4pm, July–Aug 10.30am–5pm; charge), which tells the story of England's waterways and offers cruises around the docks.

The **cathedral** remains the city's focal point. The nave is Norman, and the windows in the south transept are in earlier Perpendicular style. Fourteenth-century stained glass fills the largest east window in England and over the choir is a complicated cross-ribbed vault. Pilgrims once came to the richly ornamented tomb of Edward II, murdered at nearby Berkeley Castle. There is marvellous fan vaulting in the cloisters and even the Monks' Lavatory has its appeal.

In the town there is a **Folk Museum** packed with displays on local history (Tue–Sat 10am–5pm; charge). There are Turners and Gainsboroughs in the **City Museum and Art Gallery** (Tue–Sat 10am–5pm; charge), and at 9 College Court, off Westgate Street, the sweet **House of the Tailor of Gloucester** (Mon–Sat 10am–5pm, Sun noon–5pm; charge) recalls Beatrix Potter's famous story, which was based on real people and events. Gloucester is one of three bases for the acclaimed **Three Choirs Festival** (www.3choirs. org), which alternates between here, Hereford and Worcester (a city also renowned for its cathedral).

Cheltenham

Just 8 miles (13km) northeast is **Cheltenham** , an upmarket spa town that makes a good base for the Cotswolds. Lord Byron came here, as did George III. The discovery of the mineral spring in 1718 started it, but it was the visit of George III and his queen 70 years later that made the

spa fashionable as a summer resort. Like Bath, it was fortunate in its architects, J.B. Papworth and J.B. Forbes, who chose Cotswold stone or stucco, and in the lightness and gaiety of the Greek Revival style. Graceful terraces and squares form a backdrop to the **Rotunda** and the **Pittville Pump Room** (Wed–Mon 10am–4pm; charge). The elegant **Promenade** and **Montpellier** are the places to shop. Future attractions for the city include the **Cheltenham Art Gallery and Museum** (www.cheltenhamartgallery.org.uk), set to open by early 2013 in a new building on Clarence Street.

Cotswold limits

The Cotswolds's western limit is 10 miles (16km) north at **Tewkesbury** ⓰, where the Avon joins the Severn. Here stone gives way to attractive timbered cottages, many of them serving as pubs, such as the 17th-century Bell Inn. In 1473 the Battle of Bloody Meadow, the last of the Wars of the Roses, was fought here, spilling over into the **Abbey** itself. Even the monks took a hand. From the Abbey's square tower

there are views over the river valleys to the Malvern Hills and the mountains of Wales.

Twelve miles (20km) northwest of Tewkesbury is **Great Malvern** ⓱, from which there are magnificent views over 10 counties. The hills here are the source of a reputable bottled mineral water. The area is also famous for its connections to the composer Edward Elgar, who was born just outside Worcester and spent his life in the Great Malvern area. There are a number of Elgar trails and tours – for details, ask at tourist offices.

Back in the Cotswolds proper, 6 miles (10km) northeast of Cheltenham on the B4632 is **Sudeley Castle** (daily 10.30am–5pm; charge); *see margin left*.

Two villages further along this road to Broadway are **Stanway**, with scallop shells over the rather pretentious gateway to the manor, and **Stanton**. Nearly every cottage here was built during the best period of Cotswold architecture, from the mid-16th to the mid-17th century. **Snowshill Manor** (Apr–June and Sept–Oct Wed–Sun noon–5pm, July–Aug Wed–Mon 11.30am–4.30pm,

Sudeley Castle saw Tudor history pass like a pageant. Catherine Parr lived here after Henry VIII's death, and was married again to Thomas Seymour. Lady Jane Grey stayed here, and Queen Elizabeth I was a frequent visitor.

BELOW LEFT: Upper Slaughter. **BELOW RIGHT**: Painswick's bowling green, Britain's oldest, dates to 1554.

Indian influences at work at Sezincote.

garden also open Nov–mid-Dec noon–4pm; charge), an attractive Tudor mansion in a valley south of Broadway, houses an eclectic collection from musical instruments to toys.

Broadway ⑱ is the Cotswolds' show village. Houses and cottages face one another across an expanse of green on the road from London to Worcester, all in the same style and honey-coloured stone. The **Abbot's Grange** dates from the 14th century and the **Lygon Arms** from the 16th. Charles I and Cromwell stayed here, but not, of course, at the same time. The **Broadway Tower** (daily 10.30am–5pm; charge) on the escarpment above is the second-highest point in the Cotswolds and has great views.

Chipping Campden ⑲, 5 miles (8km) northeast of Broadway, has a long main street lined with fine stone houses dating from before the 17th century, when this was one of the most prosperous wool towns. Especially interesting are the almshouses and church, the town hall, and the house of William Grevel, a wool merchant, who died in 1401, and to whom there is a brass memorial in the church.

Sezincote

Turning east towards Oxford on the A44, the circuitous route reaches the town of **Moreton-in-Marsh** ⑳, which took to linen weaving when the woollen industry failed. Every Tuesday, it hosts the largest open-air market in the Cotswolds. The antiques shops along the High Street are also well regarded. Nearby is **Sezincote** (www.sezincote.co.uk; house: May–Sept Thur–Fri 2.30–5.30pm, garden: Jan–Nov Thur–Fri 2–6pm; charge), a house in the Indian style, which gave the Prince Regent his ideas for Brighton Pavilion *(see page 207)*.

Eight miles (13km) further on is **Chipping Norton** ㉑ ("Chipping" means market). Alongside many 18th-century houses is **Bliss Tweed Mill**, looking like a country mansion crowned with a factory chimney (now luxury apartments). The town is handy for an excursion 3 miles (5km) northwest to the **Rollright Stones**, a large circle of 70 Bronze Age standing stones known as the King's Men; a smaller group called the Five Whispering Knights; and a lone menhir, the King (daily dawn–dusk; www.right

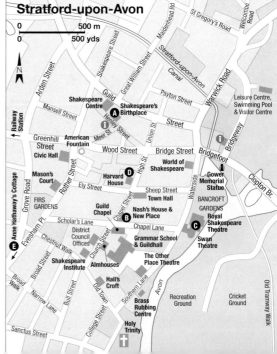

Stratford-upon-Avon

stones.co.uk; charge). Their origins are unknown, but, according to legend, a local witch turned the king and his knights to stone.

Secret valleys

The hill town of **Stow-on-the-Wold** ㉒, 4 miles (6km) south of Moreton-in-Marsh, was once the scene of great sheep fairs. Writer Daniel Defoe recorded as many as 20,000 sheep being sold on one occasion. Like sheep, 1,000 defeated Royalists were penned in the church after the last battle of the Civil War in 1646. To the west of the town are the Swells, **Upper Swell** and **Lower Swell**, pure Cotswold villages on the River Dikler.

Temple Guiting and **Guiting Power**, in thick woods on the Windrush a few miles further west, are quintessential picture-perfect Cotswold villages. Between them, the **Cotswold Farm Park** (mid-Mar–Oct daily 10.30am–5pm; charge), a rare-breeds centre, offers a chance to see local domestic animals such as Cotswold lions – sheep with fleeces like lions' manes.

Over the hill, just below the Swells, are **Upper Slaughter** and **Lower Slaughter**, with fords on the tiny Slaughterbrook, dovecotes and mills. Nearby is **Bourton-on-the-Water**, one of the best of the Cotswold stone villages. Set on the River Windrush, it has all the ingredients of fairyland: miniature footbridges over streams and under willow trees, a model railway and a model village.

Also nearby, **Birdland** (Apr–Oct 10am–6pm, Nov–Mar 10am–4pm; charge) is the home of hundreds of species of exotic birds, many of which were bred at the park and roam freely.

On their northern side, the Cotswolds merge into the **Vale of Evesham**, part of the Avon valley, where the climate is ideal for growing the fruit and vegetables that have given the town of **Evesham** ㉓ a prosperous air.

Stratford-upon-Avon

Above Evesham the A439 follows the Avon for 14 miles (22km) to **Stratford-upon-Avon** ㉔. William Shakespeare was born here in Henley Street on 23 April 1564. He was chris-

The Gower Memorial to Shakespeare in Stratford-upon-Avon.

BELOW: Mary Arden's house in Wilmcote.

Lord Leycester Hospital, Warwick.

Althorp Park (tel: 01604-770 107; www.althorp.com; July–Aug 11am– 5pm; booking advised), in Northamptonshire, is the family estate of the Earl of Spencer and the burial place of his sister Diana, Princess of Wales.

BELOW:
Warwick Castle.

tened in the local Holy Trinity Church and went to the local school; at 18 he married 26-year-old Anne Hathaway and they had three children. In 1597, after his extraordinary career as a playwright in London, he bought New Place in Chapel Street, to where he retired. He died on his 52nd birthday, in 1616, and is buried at Holy Trinity.

In spite of the numbers of tourists, the town of half-timbered buildings beside the river still manages to evoke the atmosphere of Shakespeare's times. His **birthplace** **A** (www.shakespeare. org.uk; daily Apr–May, Sept–Oct 9am– 5pm, June–Aug until 6pm, Nov–Mar 10am–4pm; charge; joint tickets available for all the main Shakespeare sights) is the starting point for a tour of the town. Adjacent is the tourist information office.

Shakespeare's granddaughter married Thomas Nash in 1626, and they lived in **Nash's House** **B** (Apr–Oct 10am–5pm, July–Aug until 6pm, Nov–Mar 11am– 4pm; charge), on Chapel Street.

The living legacy of the playwright can be found at the **Royal Shakespeare Theatre** **C** (www.rsc.org.uk), where a

remodelled auditorium includes a thrust-stage; at the smaller, galleried **Swan Theatre**; and at The Other Place.

Between Shakespeare's birthplace and Nash's House is **Harvard House** **D** (for hours tel: 01789-204 016). Built in 1596, this was the home of Katherine Rogers, whose son, John Harvard, funded the famous US university. It now houses the Museum of British Pewter.

In **Shottery**, a mile or so west of the town, is **Anne Hathaway's Cottage** **E** (daily Apr–Oct 9am–5pm, Nov–Mar 10am–4pm; charge). Anne lived in this thatched cottage during the many years Shakespeare was in London.

Three miles (5km) northwest of Stratford, in **Wilmcote**, the childhood home of Shakespeare's mother has been restored as **Mary Arden's House** (Apr–Oct daily 10am–5pm; charge) The timber-framed farmhouse has been furnished in keeping with the tastes of a wealthy Tudor family.

Warwick

Eight miles (13km) north of Stratford, just off the A46, is **Warwick** **㉕**. Despite a serious fire in 1694, many build-

ings from the Tudor period remain standing. First fortified in 914 by Ethelfleda, the daughter of Alfred the Great, **Warwick Castle** (www.warwick-castle.co.uk; daily 10am–5pm, Apr–Oct until 6pm; charge) has had a rich history. Although only a mound of earth remains of the original Saxon structure, the 14th-century towers standing today are the proud features of England's finest medieval castle. For centuries England's most powerful families lived at Warwick. A collection of paintings, including portraits by Rubens, Van Dyck and Holbein, is complemented by sets of arms and armour. The graffiti in the dungeon and torture chamber is attributed to Royalist soldiers from the Civil War. Bordering the River Avon, the castle's 60-acre (25-hectare) gardens, landscaped by "Capability" Brown, are well kept.

Lord Leycester Hospital (Tue–Sun, summer 10am–5pm, winter 10am–4.30pm; charge), by Warwick's West Gate, was founded as a guildhall in 1383. In 1571, Robert Dudley, Earl of Leicester, had the buildings renovated as almshouses. Today, the hospital is a museum and the home of ex-servicemen.

Adjacent to Warwick, **Royal Leamington Spa** is a spacious Regency and Victorian spa town that has prided itself on its amenities since it began to develop bathhouses and other amenities around its saline springs in the late 18th century.

Coventry

The A46 continues for 8 miles (13km) to **Coventry** ㉖, through whose streets (according to legend) the 11th-century Lady Godiva rode naked, with only her long tresses to protect her modesty. She was the wife of a powerful Saxon earl, Leofric, and she rode in protest against her husband's imposition of taxes.

Today, Coventry is a car-manufacturing town that was terribly bombed during World War II. The **New Cathedral** stands juxtaposed with the ruined shell of the old. By Sir Basil Spence, it was completed in 1962 and is imagi-

native with immense stained-glass windows and a richly coloured interior; Jacob Epstein's sculpture of St Michael and the Devil is among the stunning works here. Two museums are of particular note: near the cathedral is the family-friendly **Herbert Art Gallery and Museum** (Mon–Sat 10am–4pm, Sun noon–5pm; free). Permanent collections cover natural history, social history and art. On Hales Street, the **Coventry Transport Museum** (daily 10am–5pm; free) documents the development of road transport.

On the B4103 southwest of Coventry are the ruins of the medieval **Kenilworth Castle** (Apr–Oct daily 10am–5pm, Nov–Mar Sat–Sun 10am–4pm; charge), the former home of Robert Dudley, with a fine Elizabethan Garden.

Birmingham

To the west of Coventry, **Birmingham** ㉗ was a manufacturing centre long before the Industrial Revolution of the late 18th century. The canals and railways of that era confirmed its importance. In the 1960s, the construction of the Bullring Shopping Centre became

The futuristic Selfridges department store in Birmingham's Bullring.

BELOW: historic tableau inside Warwick Cathedral.

The National Sea Life Centre in Birmingham is home to over 1,000 creatures, including hundreds of species of tropical fish such as this scorpionfish.

BELOW: the water sculpture in front of Birmingham's Council House represents youth and eternity.

one of the country's most famous examples of revolutionary urban planning at the same time as the city became the focus of the national motorway network. However, by the 1990s Birmingham, affectionately known as Brum, was in dire need of a facelift.

In the last couple of decades, the city has been much improved, with the new **Bullring Shopping Centre**, where highlights include a branch of the department store **Selfridges**, in an acclaimed building by Future Systems.

In the city centre is **Victoria Square**, an enormous pedestrian esplanade dotted with contemporary sculptures and flanked by the classical **Town Hall**, and the Renaissance-style **Council House** with its mosaic and pediment relief entitled *Britannia Rewarding the Manufacturers of Birmingham*. The nearby **Museum and Art Gallery** (Mon–Thur, Sat 10am–5pm, Fri and Sun 12.30–5pm; free) is famous for its collection of Pre-Raphaelite paintings. Waterloo Street climbs to **St Philip's Cathedral**, built in 1715 and a fine example of English Baroque, with stained-glass windows by Edward Burne-Jones (1833–98).

The canalside development to the west of the city centre is the location for the Symphony Hall and the **National Sea Life Centre** (daily 10am–5pm, Sat–Sun until 6pm; charge).

Further south, on Hurst and Inge streets, the National Trust's **Back to Backs** (tel: 0121-666 7671; www.nationaltrust.org; by timed ticket and guided tour only, Feb–Dec Tue–Sat 10am–5pm, mid-Feb–mid-Dec Sun 11am–4pm; charge) is Birmingham's last surviving court of houses built literally back to back, a common feature in the industrial towns of 19th-century Britain. Visitors are taken through four of the dwellings, restored and decorated to reflect the lives of chosen inhabitants from the 1840s, 1870s, 1930s and 1970s.

Near the east gate of the University of Birmingham, at Edgbaston, is the **Barber Institute of Fine Arts** (Mon–Sat 10am–5pm, Sun noon–5pm; free), an Art Deco building housing a fine collection of works ranging from Botticelli and Rubens to Gainsborough, Turner, Monet and Magritte. ❑

RESTAURANTS, TEAROOMS AND PUBS

Restaurants

Prices for a three-course dinner per person with a half-bottle of house wine:
£ = under £25
££ = £25–50
£££ = £50–100
££££ = over £100

Arlingham
The Old Passage Inn
Tel: 01452-740 547
www.theoldpassage.com ££
Fresh seafood is a speciality at this friendly, award-winning restaurant on the banks of the River Severn. Also organic meat and vegetarian dishes and a mouthwatering selection of puddings.

Barnsley
The Village Pub
Tel: 01285-740 421
www.thevillagepub.co.uk ££
An upmarket gastropub serving European cuisine using top-quality local organic ingredients. Try the local beef-in-ale pie or quail Scotch eggs.

Bibury
Bibury Court Restaurant
Bibury Court Hotel
Tel: 01285-740 337
www.biburycourt.co.uk ££
Expect to be spoilt by this grandiose hotel's prestigious chef, Anthony Ely, who is passionate about the use of local ingredients in his inventive dishes.

The Swan
Tel: 01285-740 695
www.cotswold-inns-hotels.co.uk/property/the_swan_hotel?/swan ££
In a stunning location by the bridge over the River

Coln, this charming stone hotel puts a stylish European twist on modern British dishes. Smart dress (no jeans or trainers).

Birmingham
Loves Restaurant
The Glasshouse, Canal Square, Browning Street
Tel: 0121-454 4141
www.loves-restaurant.co.uk
££–£££
Award-winning chef Steve Love offers simple but accomplished, French-inspired dishes using the freshest ingredients at this stylish restaurant. Closed Sun.

Broadway
Tisanes
21 The Green
Tel: 01386-853 296
www.tisanes-tearooms.co.uk £
A gorgeous little tearoom in a 17th-century Cotswold-stone shop. Excellent service, delicious cakes and wonderful teas and coffees.

Cheltenham
Le Champignon Sauvage
24–26 Suffolk Road
Tel: 01242-573 449
www.lechampignonsauvage.co.uk ££–£££
Highly acclaimed, two-Michelin-starred restaurant. The modern European menu is inventive and there's a good-value three-course set menu (Tue–Fri only).

The Daffodil
18–20 Suffolk Parade
Tel: 01242-700 055
www.thedaffodil.com
££–£££
In a former 1920s Art

Deco cinema, this restaurant serves modern European and British food. Good-value fixed-price lunch and early evening menus with classics such as seared fillet of sea bass. Closed Sun.

Gloucester
Bearlands Restaurant and Wine Bar
Bearlands House, Longsmith Street
Tel: 01452-419 966 ££
In a candlelit vaulted cellar dating back to 1740, try traditional and contemporary dishes like pan-fried pigeon breast with pancetta. Closed Sun and Mon.

Great Milton
Le Manoir aux Quat'Saisons
Church Road
Tel: 01844-278 881
www.manoir.com ££££
Raymond Blanc's two-Michelin-starred French restaurant plucks organic vegetables and herbs from its own kitchen garden. Rooms available. Reserve well in advance.

Oxford
Brasserie Blanc
71–72 Walton Street
Tel: 01865-510 999
www.brasserieblanc.com ££
A link in Raymond Blanc's chain of upmarket restaurants, where you can get light but traditional French dishes in a bright and airy dining room. Children's menus available.

Gee's Restaurant
61 Banbury Road
Tel: 01865-553 540
www.gees-restaurant.co.uk
£££

One of Oxford's best and most atmospheric restaurants, serving modern British food, much of it from the owner's Oxfordshire farm. Live jazz on Sunday evenings.

Grand Café
84 High Street
Tel: 01865-204 463
www.thegrandcafe.co.uk £
Housed in an old marmalade factory, this place is a smart café by day (breakfasts, light meals and afternoon teas) and a chic cocktail bar by night.

Woodstock
The Feathers
Market Street
Tel: 01993-812 291
www.feathers.co.uk £££
A modern European award-winning menu. Sunday lunch in the 17th-century panelled dining room is a grand affair; there's also a more informal bistro for lighter meals.

Pubs

Oxford's pubs include the **Turf Tavern**, hidden down an alley almost under the Bridge of Sighs and the **Eagle and Child** on St Giles'. There are a number of country-style pubs on the city's doorstep, notably the **Trout Inn** at Godstow and **The Plough** at Wolvercote (good walks along the adjacent canal, too).

In Stratford, the **Dirty Duck** on Waterside is popular with actors; in Warwick, the **Old Fourpenny Shop** on Crompton Street has great guest beers; and in the Cotswolds, Dursley's **Old Spot Inn** is know for its real ales.

CAMBRIDGE AND EAST ANGLIA

Once cut off from the rest of England by forest and uncrossable marshland, the countryside and historic towns of East Anglia have managed to retain their otherworldliness

Edinburgh

London

East Anglia, comprising the four counties of Norfolk, Suffolk, Cambridgeshire and Essex, and bulging into the North Sea between the Thames estuary and the Wash, has the least annual rainfall in all of Britain. You would not know this, however, since it is also a region of fens and great rivers, of lakes, called meres or broads, and bird-filled coastal marshes. The beauty of East Anglia is not a typical one. Few places rise higher than 300ft (90 metres) above sea level.

The region is approached from the south by the A12 (heading northeast) from London to Colchester, famed for its oysters, and on to Ipswich before continuing north to the seaside towns of Lowestoft and Great Yarmouth. From east London the M11 runs north up to Cambridge 53 miles (85km), from where the A11 goes northeast to Norwich and the A10 continues to King's Lynn and the fenlands around the Wash. The main rail routes run from London's King's Cross and Liverpool Street stations.

A rich heritage

In the 11th century, when the area was surveyed by the compilers of the Domesday Book, the counties of East Anglia were some of the richest and most highly populated in the country. Later, the region became a sanctuary from the power struggles that racked the rest of the emerging kingdom, and it was to East Anglia that many religious orders fled for peace. They left a legacy of churches, cathedrals and abbeys; in Norfolk alone there are 600 churches.

The houses once occupied by the gentry still mark the landscape much as the churches do. **Audley End ❶** (tel: 0870-333 1181; Apr–Sept Mon, Wed–Sun, house: noon–5pm, garden: 10am–6pm, Oct house and garden close one

Main attractions
CAMBRIDGE
ELY CATHEDRAL
NORWICH
NORFOLK BROADS
HOLKHAM BEACH
SOUTHWOLD
LAVENHAM
BURY ST EDMUNDS

PRECEDING PAGES: Old Moot Hall, Aldeburgh. **LEFT:** punting on the Cam in Cambridge. **RIGHT:** waiting for the tide to come in at Wells-next-the-Sea.

The Imperial War Museum's outpost at Duxford.

hour earlier; charge) in the medieval town of **Saffron Walden**, 15 miles (24km) south of Cambridge, was built for a Lord Treasurer and said by James I to be "too large for a king". As it stands today the house is large, but it is only a fraction of the original; much of it was demolished in 1721. The interior decoration, by Robert Adam, and the immaculate gardens, landscaped by "Capability" Brown, are classics of English country design. The thriving organic kitchen garden, with its 170ft (52-metre) -long vine house, is much as it was in its Victorian heyday. Just across the road is a miniature railway (tel: 01799-541 354).

East Anglia is still a region of wealth, but what the visitor feels most in East Anglia nowadays is the sense of isolation. It has changed little for centuries. Undisturbed by both the sooty touch of the Industrial Revolution and the bombs of World War II, many villages and towns remain unspoiled, apart from noise pollution around the airforce bases at Mildenhall and Laken-

heath. The only element that destroys East Anglia is the sea, which is devouring the eastern shores. East Anglia harbours myriad landscapes that range from the flat wilds of north Norfolk to the rolling green tranquillity of south Suffolk. Gainsborough and Constable both declared that the beauty of Suffolk landscapes – the winding lanes, sloping fields and still waters – was what spurred them to paint.

Eight miles (13km) northwest of Saffron Walden is the small village of **Duxford**, which has two 12th-century churches, a 14th-century chapel, picturesque inns – and Europe's biggest air museum, **Imperial War Museum Duxford** ➋ (www.duxford.iwm.org.uk; tel: 01223-837 000; daily summer 10am–6pm, winter, 10am–4pm, last admission one hour before closing; charge). As well as a collection of classic British warplanes including a Spitfire and a Lancaster, it has a Comet and a Concorde, plus tanks, trucks, midget submarines and naval helicopters. A separate building houses the American Air Museum, with such classics as a B-17 Flying Fortress and a B-52 Stratofortress.

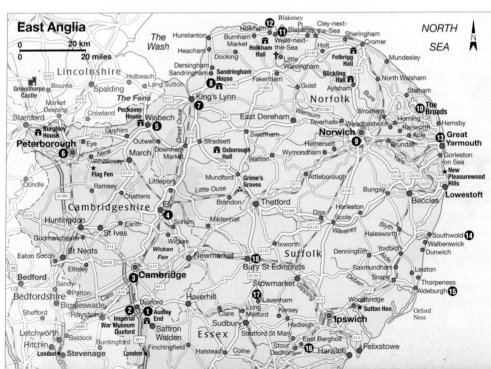

Cambridge

An Elizabethan historian once described the fen dwellers as "brutish, uncivilised and ignorant". Today's Oxford undergraduates invoke this claim when they scornfully refer to the university at **Cambridge** ❸ as the "Fenland Polytechnic", but some of the world's finest thinkers, artists and architects matured in this fenland town.

University buildings

Cambridge, which takes its name from the River Cam, was founded in the 12th century by a settlement of Franciscans, Dominicans and Carmelites. In 1209, a handful of scholars hurriedly fled Oxford after a disagreement with the town authorities and settled in Cambridge. It was this – and the founding in 1284 of the first college, Peterhouse, by Hugo de Balsham, Bishop of Ely – that established the university.

Other colleges were soon founded under the patronage of local gentry and a succession of monarchs. On King's Parade and central to the University is **King's College** ❹, founded in 1441 by Henry VI. Five years later,

King's College Chapel – considered the glory of Cambridge – began construction, which took nearly 70 years. Chapel services are open to visitors, and it is a worthwhile experience to stand in the ancient pews alongside Rubens's *Adoration of the Magi*, listening to the voices of the famous choir float up the curves of the magnificent fan-vaulted ceiling and gazing at the series of 25 16th-century stained-glass windows, which portray the story of the New Testament.

Next door is the dignified **Senate House** (closed to the public), the university parliament, built by James Gibbs between 1722 and 1730, and now used for degree ceremonies. Next door, on the corner of Trinity Street, is **Gonville and Caius College**, while behind, are the "Backs". From the top of **Great St Mary's Church** ❸, opposite Senate House, visitors can see the whole of Cambridge, including the distant gaunt tower of the **University Library**. Like the Bodleian at Oxford, the University Library at Cambridge by law receives a copy of virtually every book published in the United Kingdom.

TIP

Cambridge's Scott Polar Research Institute Museum (www.spri. cam.ac.uk/museum; Tue–Sat 10am–4pm; free), on Lensfield Road, explores the history of polar exploration.

BELOW: King's College, Cambridge.

The beauty of Cambridge is its compactness; a few steps in any direction will take you past a piece of history, whether it be the Anglo-Saxon tower of the tiny church of St Bene't's (eclipsed by the college buildings, but older by at least 250 years) or the Cavendish Laboratory, the site of the first splitting of the atom.

In the gardens of **Christ's College** a tree said to have shaded the poet John Milton (1608–74) as he worked still stands. The Great Court at **Trinity**  is the largest university quadrangle in the world, but look closely at the figure of its founder, Henry VIII, above the gateway: instead of a sceptre he holds a chair leg. Trinity's library, seen from the riverfront, was built by Sir Christopher Wren. Further north is **St John's**, founded in 1511. Its three-storey gatehouse, decorated with carvings of heraldic beasts, is magnificent. Behind it is the **Bridge of Sighs** (1831), loosely modelled on its more famous namesake in Venice. Across Bridge Street from St John's is the **Church of the Holy Sepulchre**, one of only four Norman round churches in Eng-

land. This one was founded in 1130, possibly in connection with the Crusades. The shape is based on that of the Holy Sepulchre in Jerusalem.

Queens' College, hidden behind St Catharine's, has an unusual and seemingly rickety half-timbered President's Lodge. A little beyond the town centre along Trumpington Street stands **Peterhouse**, the oldest, smallest and reputedly most conservative of the colleges. Next door is the **Fitzwilliam Museum** (Tue–Sat 10am–5pm, Sun noon–5pm; free), a spectacular collection of art, books and antiquities including works by Turner, Titian and Rembrandt, and the original manuscripts of William Blake's poems.

The best way to see many colleges is to hire a punt – either self-hire or chauffeured, gondolier-style – from Scudamore's Boatyard at the end of Mill Lane. Drift down the "Backs" from Charles Darwin's House to the Bridge of Sighs, gliding between the willows at the backs of the colleges; those in the know punt along the lower reaches of the river through the meadows to Grantchester.

Stone carving on St John's College, whose alumni include William Wilberforce, William Wordsworth and Cecil Beaton.

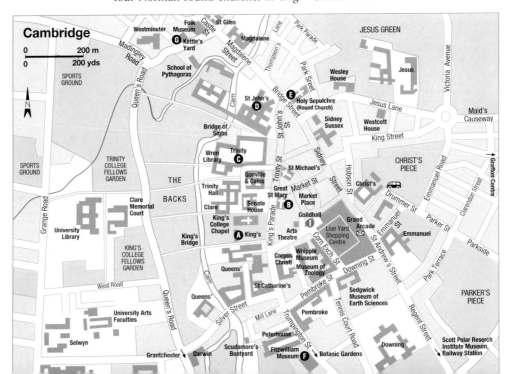

Other attractions

Beyond the Fitzwilliam the **Botanic Gardens** (Apr–Sept 10am–6pm, Feb, Mar, Oct until 5pm, Jan, Nov, Dec until 4pm; charge) make a haven for tired visitors and students alike.

On the other side of town, in Castle Street, is a delightful **Folk Museum** (Tue–Sat 10.30am–5pm, Sun 2–5pm; charge) and, adjacent, the University-owned **Kettle's Yard** G (house Tue–Sun summer 1.30–4.30pm, winter 2–4pm; gallery Tue–Sun 11.30am–5pm). The former home of Tate gallery curator Jim Ede, this charming museum in four cottages is filled with Ede's collection of modern works by artists such as Ben Nicholson and Henry Moore.

The wetlands

Flat, spongy and soppy the Yarmouth area may have seemed to Charles Dickens' young David Copperfield, but the **fenland** is flatter, spongier and soppier still. The village names – Landbeach, Waterbeach, Gedney Marsh and Dry Drayton – all tell the same story. For centuries no one tried to cross the marshes, let alone build on them, yet today the black fenland soil is some of the most productive land in the country.

The Romans were the first to try to drain the 2,000-sq-mile (5,200-sq-km) marsh that stretched from Cambridge to Lincoln, but success came only in the 17th century, when the Dutch engineer Vermuyden cut rivers through the marshes. Even he was not prepared for the dramatic land-shrinking that resulted. Today's fields are often 10ft (3 metres) below the rivers that were cut to drain them. Only one fen remains undrained; at **Wicken Fen** (signposted off the A10, 17 miles/27km north of Cambridge) the windpump keeps 600 acres (240 hectares) of marshland wet, preserved by the National Trust.

Ely

Where the A10 approaches **Ely** ❹, 16 miles (25km) north of Cambridge, the everlastingly flat skyline is broken. **Ely Cathedral** (summer daily 7am–6.30pm, winter Mon–Sat 7am–6.30pm, Sun 7am–5.30pm; charge), completed in 1351, dominates the fens from its perch on what used to be called the Isle of Eels – after the staple diet of the villagers – earning it the title of "Ship of the Fens". The Isle, a knoll of dry land, was selected as a monastery site by St Etheldreda in AD 673. Some 400 years later it made an ideal refuge for Hereward the Wake when pursued by William the Conqueror. Hereward seemed unreachable on Ely (then an island), but eventually the monks tired of the siege and showed the conqueror's men the secret pathway through the marshes, giving Hereward away.

The splendour of Ely Cathedral lies in its unusual situation and in its unique lantern. In the evening, this octagonal tower of wood and glass, built high on the back of the nave in an extraordinary feat of engineering, reflects the rays of the dying sun. By night its glass gleams with the light within.

The A1101, on the left 5 miles (8km) north of Ely, crosses the unimagina-

EAT

In between sightseeing in Cambridge, follow in the footsteps of the Granchester Group (which included the philosopher Ludwig Wittgenstein, the novelists Virginia Woolf and E.M. Forster and the artist Augustus John) and take tea at The Orchard (45–7 Mill Way, Granchester; tel: 01223-551 125), 2 miles (3km) from central Cambridge along the River Cam. The location feels wonderfully rural, and the tea garden, with deckchairs outside under the apple trees, is genteel and relaxing. Punting here makes the trip feel even more civilised.

BELOW: Ely Cathedral.

There are 119 Saxon flint round towers in Norfolk. The Normans, however, considered the local stone undramatic. So, to build Norwich Cathedral, they shipped white stone from Normandy across the Channel and up the River Wensum.

tively named Hundred Foot Drain and passes between the rows of marching crops to **Wisbech** ❺, a market town that styles itself the capital of the fens. The two imposing Georgian streets (South Brink and North Brink) illustrate the prosperity fen drainage brought. In the eccentric **Wisbech and Fenland Museum** (Museum Square; Tue–Sat 10am–4pm; free) are the complete furnishings of a Victorian post office.

West of Wisbech on the A47, **Peterborough** ❻ is worth a visit for its Norman cathedral, begun in 1118. Nearby is **Flag Fen** (tel: 01733-313 414; Sat–Sun 10am–4pm, Mar–Oct until 5pm, last entry one hour before closing), a vast archaeological centre devoted to Britain's Bronze Age.

While Wisbech has been preserved by a lack of economic development, **King's Lynn** ❼, 12 miles (20km) northeast along the coast, has marched on. Much of the town has been rebuilt since the late 1950s but it retains many fine Georgian houses, with **King Street** marking the heart of the old town. King's Lynn is unique in having two medieval guildhalls, one the largest in Britain.

Sandringham House

Eight miles (13km) northeast of King's Lynn, **Sandringham House** ❽ is still used as a royal country retreat. Edward VII, when Prince of Wales, built Sandringham in 1870, but it is decorated in styles ranging from Jacobean to Regency. The house is closed when a member of the royal family is in residence, but 600 acres (240 hectares) of parkland are kept open to visitors year round (www.sandringhamestate.co.uk; house: Easter–Oct daily 11am–4.45pm, closed last week in July; charge).

Norwich

A city that retains its sense of history alongside economic success is a rare place, yet **Norwich** ❾, the county town of Norfolk and once the third-richest town in England, manages to do both. It has a church for every week of the year and a pub for every day, they say, and every vista of this surprisingly hilly town confirms it. Within the city walls 32 medieval churches still stand, though some now have secular purposes. **St James Church** is a puppet theatre; the imaginative **Eliz-**

BELOW:
Sandringham
House's gardens.

abethan Theatre at the Maddermarket is a combination of chapel and warehouse; and **St Peter Hungate** at the top of Elm Hill is a museum of ecclesiastical treasures.

Besides the **cathedral** (www.cathedral.org.uk; daily 7.30am–6pm; donation) and its fine **cloisters**, worth seeing are the flinted-frame cottages and Georgian terraces in **Cathedral Close**, and **Pull's Ferry** (last used as a river crossing in 1939). **Norwich Castle**, imposingly set on Castle Meadow and built by the Normans as a royal palace, is now home to the city's **museum and art gallery** (Mon–Sat 10am–4.30pm, Sun 1–4.30pm, July–Sept until 5pm; charge), which showcases the work of the Norwich School of artists and Lowestoft Porcelain, and also hosts visiting exhibitions.

When the Industrial Revolution left the city behind – it had no source of fuel readily available to drive machines – retailing became the profession of the prosperous. It was a succession of wealthy grocers who, century by century, added to **Strangers' Hall**. The result today is a charming museum (Wed and Sat 10.30am–4.30pm; charge) with a series of interlinking rooms furnished in a range of styles from Tudor to Victorian.

The city is still an excellent place to shop, from Jarrold's traditional department store to the old-fashioned city-centre market adjacent and the historic Royal Arcade, home to **Colman's Mustard Shop**, where customers can still buy mustard for their foot baths. Also notable are **Elm Hill**'s antiques shops and **St Benedict's Street**, peppered with stylish independent boutiques, cafés and restaurants.

Lottery money funded the city's modern **Forum**, a striking glass-and-steel hangar located next to the huge church of **St Peter Mancroft**, and housing BBC Norfolk and the city's Millennium library and tourist information centre.

Today's wealthy grocers are no less munificent than those of yesteryear: in the 1970s the high-street supermarket family, Sainsbury, commissioned Sir

Timber-framed building in Norwich. The city's Elm Hill district has more Tudor buildings than can be found in the whole of London.

LEFT:
Norwich Cathedral.

Cathedrals of East Anglia

Three enormous Norman cathedrals, all started around 1100, grace the region. Founded in 1081, Ely *(right)* is best known for its massive, octagonal lantern, built by Alan de Walsingham to cover the crossing of the nave and transepts when the Norman tower fell down in 1322. But the whole interior, with its 250ft (76-metre)-long nave, is magnificent, reflecting many architectural styles, from Norman to early Renaissance.

Peterborough Cathedral, begun in 1118, is in part a good example of the late Norman style, though it was added to in nearly every later architectural period. The cathedral was severely damaged by Oliver Cromwell's troops in the 17th century. Visitors today, however, can still marvel at its painted wooden ceiling, dating from around 1220, though it has been repainted twice.

Norwich Cathedral was founded in 1096. The nave's original wooden roof was replaced in the 15th and 16th centuries by stone vaulting and embellished by carved and painted bosses illustrating Bible scenes. Norwich's spire, at 315ft (96 metres), is second only to that of Salisbury. A very modern take on a Norman refectory, designed by Sir Michael Hopkins, was recently incorporated into the cathedral's outer flint walls.

Boats tied up at dusk on the Norfolk Broads.

by a pastoral silence. In winter, drizzle drips into the peat-dark waters of Bure marshes, and somewhere a coot grates its voice in alarm as the white triangle of the sail of a late-season yachtsman slides slowly through the brown sedge. Heeding the alarm, a cormorant splashes across the water's surface and labours into the heavy air before watchful ornithologists.

This is the **Broads** ❿. For the birdwatcher, winter is a gripping time here, but most visitors to this chain of lakes – thought to be medieval peat-diggings which have flooded over the centuries – come with the summer sun.

Norman Foster to design the **Sainsbury Centre for Visual Arts** (www.scva. org.uk; Tue–Sun 10am–5pm; charge for special exhibitions), a short drive or bus journey west of the city centre, on the University of East Anglia campus (follow the signs to UAE, then to the Sainsbury Centre). Its broad collection of works by Francis Bacon, Giacometti and Balthus, alongside ancient artefacts, is grouped by geographical region.

The Norfolk Broads

Northeast of Norwich, the A1161 turns off to the village of **Woodbastwick**. As you approach it, the buzz of distant tractors fades, and is replaced

Hiring a boat is undoubtedly the best way of enjoying the Broads, since they are largely inaccessible by road. There are some 10,000 craft on the 200 miles (320km) of navigable waterways, though fortunately not everyone goes afloat at the same time. From the water the landscape is one of church towers, windmills, reeds and sails cutting through fields, all of which would be missed from the land. Until the early part of the 20th century, sailing wherries laden with cargo used to navigate the

BELOW: seals at Blakeney Point.

River Yare from Norwich to the sea; one such vessel is preserved at Horning.

At **Ranworth**, the home of the floating Broadland Conservation Centre, the tower of **St Helen's Church** provides a magnificent view of the network of waterways. A little further down the River Bure, on a sand-and-gravel island called Cow Holm, stand the ruins of **St Benet's Abbey**, first built in AD 870 but now oddly misshapen thanks to the stump of a windmill (now disused) that was added to the ruins 200 years ago.

In some places the Broads are tidal, and the slightly brackish water attracts coots, heron and bittern, and the nation's largest species of butterfly, the swallowtail, lives in the reeds. Plant life, however, has disappeared from the waters of all but a few Broads over the past few decades. Some blame agricultural fertilisers, others the disturbance caused by pleasure craft. The exact cause remains unknown.

North Norfolk

On the north Norfolk coast, **Cley-next-the-Sea** is now more than a mile (1.6km) from the shore, but the resulting combination of salt marshes, reedbeds and lagoons attracts a remarkable number of wading birds. Nearby **Blakeney Point** attracts a host of seabirds during the summer, and it is also home to common and grey seals that bask on the sands at low tide. **Wells-next-the-Sea** ⓫ is a working port, with coasters along the quay and fishing boats bringing in whelks, crabs and shrimps. Further west are the spectacularly broad sands of the beach at **Holkham** ⓬, featured in films such as *Shakespeare in Love*; **Holkham Hall** (Apr–Oct Sun, Mon, Thur noon–4pm; charge), the grand neoclassical stately home of the Earl of Leicester, is well worth a visit.

South of Holkham is the upmarket village of **Burnham Market**, dubbed "Chelsea-on-Sea" for the number of well-heeled Londoners who have second homes here. Its hat shop claims

the queen as one of its customers.

An alternative way of heading inland is to take the light railway from Wells to **Little Walsingham**, a place of pilgrimage once as important as Canterbury. In addition to the modern Roman Catholic shrine, the village has an attractive medieval high street and is also home to the excellent Norfolk Riddle farm shop and restaurant.

The heyday for holidaying in East Anglia was undoubtedly the Victorian era, when the Great Eastern Railway Company's network opened up a dozen resorts on the sunny coastline. Two towns that have retained that atmosphere are **Sheringham** and **Cromer** (the latter is especially famous for its crabs), in north Norfolk, a coastline lashed by winter storms. In 1855–6 there were 500 wrecks off this shore. Even today almost every village has its own lifeboat.

Holiday meccas

Midway around the coast, **Great Yarmouth** ⓭ – once the scene of great activity with the arrival of the herring catch – is today a rather tacky

BELOW: traditional Punch and Judy show, Southwold.

Southwold has what must be the cheapest passenger ferry in the country (90p per person), which plies across to Walberswick, a village frequented by painters.

BELOW: Martello tower at Aldeburgh, built as a coastal defence during the Napoleonic Wars and now rented as a holiday home by the Landmark Trust.

place, with the golden sands of the beach hidden behind the spires of the helter-skelters and the walls of the roller-coaster. So changed is Yarmouth that the 1969 film of Charles Dickens' *David Copperfield* had to be shot in the resort of **Southwold** ⑭, 20 miles (32km) south. This dignified town's manicured appearance is due partly to a fire in 1659 which destroyed much of the fishing village and allowed careful reconstruction. Its tasteful image was enhanced in 2001 with the reopening of the long-neglected pier. In the town's magnificent Perpendicular Church of St Edmunds (daily Sept–May 9am–4pm, June–Aug until 6pm), Southwold

Jack, a medieval figure in armour, rings in the services by striking a bell with his sword. Other landmarks include Southwold's lighthouse (tours May–Oct Sat–Sun 2–4pm; charge). Despite the dominance of tourism, Southwold has one of the few estuary ports still used by fishermen.

The ancient capital of **Dunwich** at one time had eight churches; now the sea has swept most of the town away, leaving only a few cottages, the remains of a monastery and a town museum.

Aldeburgh

From the Blythe estuary at Walberswick to **Aldeburgh** ⑮ is a rewarding, though long, walk. The composer Benjamin Britten (1913–76) made the fishing village (whose name means "old fort") his home and in 1948, together with the tenor Peter Pears, started the prestigious annual music festival that now runs for two weeks every June (www. aldeburgh.co.uk). Since then, Aldeburgh has become fashionable indeed.

Eighteen miles (29km) southwest of Aldeburgh, at Melton, is the National Trust site of **Sutton Hoo**, an atmospheric Anglo-Saxon royal burial site where ancient treasures were excavated in 1939. The site has been reconstructed, and there are fine country walks.

Ten miles (16km) to the southwest is the Suffolk county town of **Ipswich**. It has little to recommend it apart from an atmospheric Victorian dockland, complete with lightship and sailing barges, on the River Orwell. George Orwell, the author of *Nineteen Eighty-Four*, took his pen name from the river, but the Stour, which meets the Orwell at its mouth around the North Sea passenger and cargo ports of **Harwich** and **Felixstowe**, is the more famous of the two rivers, thanks to the work of a much-loved British artist.

Suffolk: Constable country

The Suffolk countryside alongside the Stour is called **Constable country**. John Constable (1776–1837) painted the river, the trees and the villages with a love that has made this landscape familiar even to those who have never been here. The artist was born in the grand village of **East Bergholt** ⑯ (just off the A12 between Ipswich and Colchester), where the bells of the church tower are housed in a shed in the graveyard. His father was the mill owner at **Flatford**, just down the hill. The setting had great sentiment for Constable, and he recreated it in the painting *The Hay Wain*. The water mills of nearby **Stratford St Mary** were another favourite subject. In fact, all along the River Stour is Constable's element. The National Trust arranges guided walks through "Constable scenes" from Flatford Bridge Cottage (tel: 01206-298 260).

The village of **Dedham**, only a few miles up the banks of the Stour from Flatford and best approached that way, has changed little. The row of neoclassical houses that faces the church is pristine. And yet Dedham is not entirely unmodern: inside the timeless church one of the pews is decorated with medallions from the first moon landing.

Unspoilt as Dedham may seem, the villages inland are even more so. In **Kersey**, **Hadleigh** and **Lavenham**, many of the timbered houses that lean over the streets date from the early 16th century. This is wool country, and these villages were well known and wealthy for 700 years after the Norman Conquest (Kersey cloth is mentioned by Shakespeare). The rich mill owners lived in grand halls and worshipped in magnificent churches, all built with their profits. Fine examples of both of these are at **Long Melford**, north of Sudbury. The village's Tudor houses present a pleasing visage of turrets and moats; the two best examples are Melford Hall and Kentwell Hall.

Lavenham

In the remarkably preserved medieval village of **Lavenham** ⑰, many of the houses are 400 years old. The Little Hall (Apr–Oct Mon 11am–5.30pm, Wed, Thur, Sat–Sun 2–5.30pm; charge) and the National Trust-run Guildhall (Apr–Oct daily 11am–5pm, Jan–Feb Sat–Sun 11am–4pm, Mar Wed–Sun 11am–4pm; charge) are open to the public. Telegraph poles have been removed and the

In 1923 a water tower at Thorpeness, north of Aldeburgh, was turned into a "house in the clouds", and today has five bedrooms and three bathrooms – but there are 68 steps to climb.

BELOW: Lavenham.

At Kentwell Hall, a moated Tudor manor in Long Melford, women dry wool while a man ploughs the field in a living-history reenactment.

BELOW:
the Abbey ruins, Bury St Edmunds.

wires buried underground to preserve the village's Tudor appearance.

Bury St Edmunds

Timber-framed houses give the villages their beauty, but flint and brick dominate at **Bury St Edmunds** ⑱, midway between Ipswich and Cambridge on the A14. The cathedral city is no backwater: the narrow streets around the **Buttermarket** are jammed with people, as is the **Nutshell** on The Traverse, said to be the smallest pub in Britain.

On Cornhill, the **Moyse's Hall Museum** (daily 10am–5pm, last entry 4pm; charge), built in 1180, is considered the oldest Norman house in East Anglia. It is also said to have been the house of a Jewish merchant, or even a synagogue, but with no evidence to support the claims. Inside, exhibits include Bronze Age and Saxon artefacts. At the centre of the town in Market Cross is a beautiful building by Robert Adam housing the **Smiths Row** (Tue–Sat 10.30am–5pm; free), a contemporary art gallery and craft shop.

The gems of Bury are the ancient **abbey** and **cathedral** (daily 8.30am–6pm), with beautiful walled grounds laid out as formal gardens and twice the size of the city centre. Below the 12th-century cathedral lie the remains of the abbey. Founded in the 7th century, it was an important place of pilgrimage after the body of Edmund, last king of the East Angles, who was killed by the Danes, was placed there in about 900. In 1214 a group of barons swore before the altar to raise arms against King John if he refused to set his seal to the Magna Carta. He did, unwillingly, a year later, and today Bury still celebrates this event – and Edmund's burial – in its motto: Shrine of a King, Cradle of the Law. ❑

RESTAURANTS AND PUBS

Restaurants

Prices for a three-course dinner per person with a half-bottle of house wine:
£ = under £25
££ = £25–50
£££ = £50–100
££££ = over £100

Aldeburgh

The Golden Galleon Fish and Chip Shop
137 High Street
Tel: 01728-454 685 **£**
If you can stand the queue you will be amply rewarded. Take your fish and chips down to the pebbly beach across the road, or sit upstairs in the restaurant.

The Lighthouse
77 High Street
Tel: 01728-453 377
www.lighthouserestaurant.co.uk **£–££**
Fish features heavily on the menu here and the potted Norfolk shrimps and fish soup are popular dishes. Lunch and dinner menus change daily.

Bulmer Tye, nr Sudbury

The Bulmer Fox
Tel: 01787-312 277
www.thebulmerfox.com **£–££**
On Sunday lunchtimes, the Fox's no-booking policy together with its raging popularity mean that the car park is full before the doors have even opened. Relaxed bistro-style restaurant in Edwardian country pub.

Cambridge

Alimentum
152–154 Hills Road
Tel: 0223-413 000
www.restaurantalimentum.co.uk **££**
Ethical values underpin this sleek venture, from being the first UK restaurant to serve humanely produced *foie gras* right down to the biodegradable cocktail straws. Skilfully prepared modern European dishes, impressively presented. Closed Sun.

Midsummer House
Midsummer Common
Tel: 01223-369 299
www.midsummerhouse.co.uk **£££**
Elegant, modern European cuisine served up in the stylish surroundings of a walled Victorian house on the banks of the Cam. The only two-star Michelin restaurant in East Anglia, with seasonal menus featuring dishes such as sautéed scallops, celeriac and truffle, and raspberry and tarragon roulade. Closed Sun and Mon.

Three Horseshoes
Madingley, nr Cambridge
Tel: 01954-210 221
www.threehorseshoes madingley.co.uk **££**
Stunningly presented Mediterranean, Asian-fusion and British food (including delicious puddings) is served in the airy conservatory-cum-dining-room of a thatched inn in a quaint village 2 miles (3km) from Cambridge.

Lavenham

Angel Hotel
Market Place
Tel: 01787-247 388
www.maypolehotels.com **££**
Grilled sea bass fillet with creamed spinach and spiced pork cutlet with braised endive are just two of the mains you can expect at Lavenham's oldest inn. Dating back to 1420, the Angel still retains much of its Tudor character.

Little Walsingham

The Norfolk Riddle
2 Wells Road
Tel: 01328-821 903
www.walsinghamfarmshop.co.uk **£**
It's hard to beat this place, with its wonderfully calming, minimally decorated dining room (white walls, stripped wooden floors) and its excellently executed, frequently changing menu that focuses on seasonal, local produce (meat from its own farm shop, just across the road, and lots of fish) at bargain prices. Closed Mon and Tue but it also has a top-notch fish-and-chip shop next door that is open daily.

Morston, nr Blakeney

Morston Hall
Morston, Holt
Tel: 01263-741 041
www.morstonhall.com **£££**
This 17th-century country house hotel, owned by Michelin-starred chef Galton Blackiston, has a fantastic restaurant championing local produce such as Blakeney lobster and Morston mussels.

Norwich

The Bicycle Shop
17 St Benedicts Street
Tel: 01603-625 777
This intimate little café-restaurant has the feel of a bohemian Parisian bistro with candles and flowers. The food is simple but tasty, with lots of vegetarian options. Also hosts events (music nights etc) in the evenings.

Stanton

Leaping Hare Vineyard Restaurant
Wyken Vineyards
Tel: 01359-250 287
www.wykenvineyards.co.uk **£–££**
An elegant café-restaurant set on the edge of a country estate in one of Britain's most respected vineyards. Californian-style, locally sourced (within 5 miles, where possible) cuisine accompanies its own wines.

Pubs

In Cambridge, the **Free Press** on Prospect Row is a tiny Victorian pub with imaginative, home-made food, and the **Green Dragon** on Water Street is a former coaching inn (Oliver Cromwell stayed here) with a real fire on cold days.

In Norwich, the **Coach & Horses** on Thorpe Road, an old coaching inn, has good ales and the **Fat Cat** on West End Street has its own brewery and around 30 real ales. The lofty bar at the Picturehouse Cinema City, on St Andrew's Street, is a more trendy drinking hole.

In Aldeburgh, the **Mill Inn** on Market Cross Place is situated near the beach and, appropriately, serves good fish.

THE SOUTHEAST

Kent and Sussex offer the hedonist a deckchair on a sunny beach, the delights of rolling countryside, the thrill of walking in high places, and the discovery of churches and rambling country houses

The counties of **Kent** and **Sussex** in the southeast corner of England lie south of the Thames estuary, between London and the English Channel. Any part of them can be visited on a day trip from the capital, particularly their historic centres such as Canterbury, Rye, Brighton and Chichester, which are best explored on foot. From London's orbital M25 motorway the M23 leads south to Brighton, principal resort of Sussex, while the M2 and M20 head for the Channel ports of Folkestone and Dover in Kent. Victoria, Charing Cross and London Bridge stations provide the rail links.

Lie of the land

At Dover, the Kent coast is 21 miles (34km) from France, and in 1875 the two countries were proved to be within swimming distance by Captain Matthew Webb (it took him 21 hours 45 minutes). As the nearest point to the Continent, this is the way invaders came: Romans, Angles, Saxons and Britain's last conquerors, the Normans, who scorched the date of 1066 into the history books with their triumph at the Battle of Hastings. Towers, castles and moated mansions were built to withstand later invasion attempts

by France, Spain and, in the 20th century, Germany, while cathedrals rose at Chichester and Canterbury, the church of England's spiritual home and the focus of centuries of pilgrims.

The counties have a common geology, in which all the strata run east to west. Kent's North Downs mirror the Sussex South Downs, and the filling in this cake is greensand, Weald clay and sandstone, repeated in reverse order. All contribute to a rich variety of landscape in a relatively small space. The chalky South Downs, with

Main attractions
ARUNDEL
BRIGHTON
RYE
SISSINGHURST CASTLE
HEVER CASTLE
CHARTWELL
CHATHAM
KNOLE
CANTERBURY

LEFT: Canterbury Cathedral at night.
RIGHT: Bateman's, to the south of Burwash village in East Sussex, where the writer Rudyard Kipling lived from 1902 to 1936.

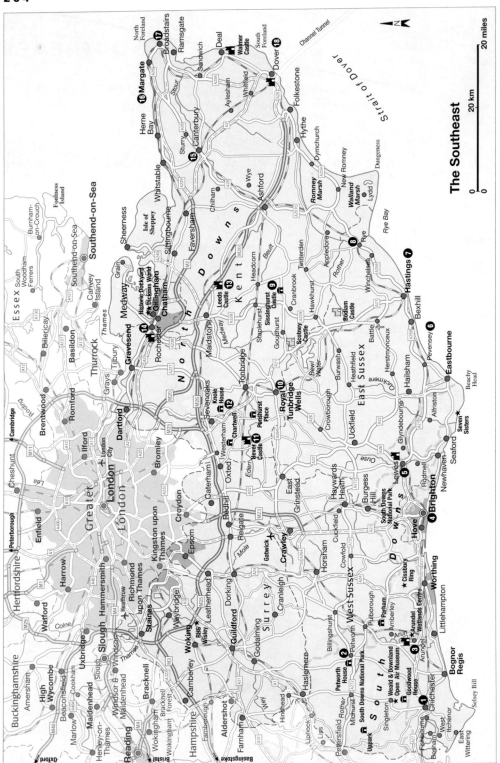

The Southeast

0 20 km

0 20 miles

a walking trail along their summit, were hailed somewhat exaggeratedly by the eminent 18th-century naturalist Gilbert White as "a chain of majestic mountains". They reach the sea at the spectacular cliffs at Beachy Head, near Eastbourne; the North Downs end at the white cliffs of Dover.

In between the North and South Downs is the Weald, an excellent area for fruit growing, particularly apples, and grapes for white English wines (the chalk Downs are the same geological strata that runs through France's Champagne region). Hops grown for beer were once picked by London's East Enders in a holiday mood, but barely 50 hop farms remain.

Chichester

To the west lies the county town of **Chichester ❶** where the spire of the **Cathedral** (www.chichestercathedral.org.uk; daily 7.15am–6pm, summer until 7pm; free 45-min tours Mon–Sat 11.15am and 2.30pm) rises like a beckoning finger above this typical English rural town of notable Georgian houses. The **South Downs** provide a backdrop,

and the creeks and marshes of its harbour nearly reach its walls.

The 270ft (82-metre) 14th-century cathedral spire, the only one in the country visible from the sea, was rebuilt in 1861 by Sir George Gilbert Scott, after a storm had brought it down. Inside, the modern altar tapestry by John Piper (1903–92) is a dramatic surprise. Among many fine carvings and relief work the most remarkable is the 12th-century *Raising of Lazarus*, which can be found in the south side of the choir. There is a stained-glass window by Marc Chagall.

Pallant House Gallery (tel: 01243-774 557; www.pallant.org.uk; Tue–Sat 10am–5pm, Thur until 8pm, Sun 11am–5pm; charge) is another attraction housing a unique collection of 20th-century British art within a Queen Anne (1712) town house and a modern extension.

The 15th-century **Market Cross** is one of the finest in the country. Good local pubs with accommodation include The Ship in North Street. To

Chichester Cathedral.

BELOW:
Goodwood, a major racecourse close to Chichester.

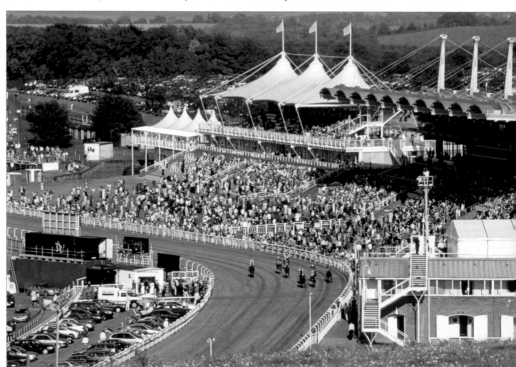

RHS Wisley (Mar–Oct 10am–6pm, Nov–Feb Mon–Fri 10am–4.30pm, with exceptions; charge), the flagship garden of the Royal Horticultural Society, is located off the A3 east of Woking.

BELOW: *Anne Carr, Countess of Bedford* by Anthony van Dyck, part of the art collection at Petworth House.

the north of the town is the **Festival Theatre** (www.cft.org.uk), a theatre-in-the-round where Laurence Olivier was the first director, from 1962 to 1965.

Little of Chichester's Roman walls remain, but at **Fishbourne** (daily Feb, Nov, Dec 10am–4pm, Mar–Oct 10am–5pm; charge), a mile to the west, Britain's largest Roman palace was uncovered in 1960. It is worth seeing for its well-preserved mosaics, including the famous *Cupid on a Dolphin*, as well as to appreciate its formidable scale and size. The estuary it stood beside has receded and Chichester's harbour now has myriad muddy inlets (harbour tours from **West Itchenor**), the most attractive being at **Bosham**.

In the South Downs behind Chichester is **Goodwood**, site of a racecourse and country house. At the summit is the hill-fort of the Trundle, giving won-

derful views before dropping down to **Singleton** and the **Weald and Downland Open Air Museum** (www.wealddown.co.uk; summer: 10.30am–6pm, winter: 10.30am–4pm, daily with exceptions; charge). For this 45-acre (18-hectare) open-air project, buildings from the 13th to the 19th centuries have been conserved and rebuilt.

Continuing north for 6 miles (9km) the A286 arrives at the market town of **Midhurst**, where a right turn on to the A272 leads another 6 miles to **Petworth** ❷. Here, narrow streets are twisted and turned by the walls of the great 17th-century **Petworth House** (Mar–Nov Sat–Wed 11am–5pm; charge), seat of the Percys, Earls of Northumberland. It has a deer park (daily year-round 8am–dusk), landscaped by "Capability" Brown, and an exceptional art collection. J.M.W. Turner painted here in 1810 and 1830. It also has astounding wood carvings by the English sculptor Grinling Gibbons.

Follow the Rother downstream to join the Arun and below is **Pulborough**. This is the fishing capital of Sussex, famed for Arundel mullet and Amberley trout. The pretty village of **Amberley**, 5 miles (8km) to the south, has archetypal English whitewashed, thatched cottages and a castle (now a luxury hotel; www.amberleycastle.co.uk).

Just to the northeast lies **Parham**, a remote, carefully restored Tudor house (Apr–July, Sept Wed–Thur, Sun and bank holiday Mon 2–5pm, Aug Wed–Fri, Sun 2–5pm; gardens: noon–5pm (May–July also open Tue and Fri); charge); it has a delightful 4-acre (1.6-hectare) walled garden with a maze and 1920s' Wendy House.

Arundel

The Arun finally emerges from the South Downs around **Arundel** ❸, which is commanded by the imposing **castle** (www.arundelcastle.org Apr–Oct Tue–Sun, Aug also Mon, noon–5pm, with last admission 4pm, with exceptions, check website; charge) of the Dukes of Norfolk, Earls Marshal of England, organisers of the pomp of state processions. More French than English, the competing views of the castle and churches (both Anglican and Catholic under one roof at St Nicholas's) dominate the skyline. Much reconstruction through the 19th century has made the castle a rather eclectic architectural mix, but it's certainly flamboyant. There are splendid views of the castle from Swanborne Lake in the grounds. Beyond the lake, about a mile from the castle through an avenue of trees, is the excellent **WWT Arundel Wetlands Centre** (daily 9.30am–5.30pm; charge).

Earlier peoples clung to the heights around here, and the Downs are littered with hill-forts, flint mines, burial mounds and tracks used 2,000 years before the Romans came. The **Amberley Working Museum**, dedicated to the industrial heritage of the area, is at Houghton Bridge, Amberley (Apr–Oct Tue–Sun 10.30am–5.30pm and throughout local school hols, last admission 4.30pm; charge), and 10 miles (16km) east are two hills worth a climb, **Cissbury** and **Chanctonbury**, which has a crown of beeches. These are all along the **South Downs Way**, an 80-mile (130km) footpath which spans the entire length of the South Downs National Park, from Petersfield, Hampshire, to the coast at Eastbourne.

Brighton

The history of **Brighton** ❹ is that of a poor fishing town that became the country's best-known seaside resort thanks to a local doctor, Richard Russell, who prescribed sea bathing for his patients. With the patronage of George IV (then Prince of Wales), he opened an establishment with attendants called "bathers" for men and "dippers" for women. London society followed. In 1785 the prince stayed in a villa on the Old Steine, later redesigned as the **Royal Pavilion** (www.brighton-hove-rpml.org.uk; daily Apr–Sept 9.30am–5.45pm, Oct–Mar 10am–5.15pm; charge) by John Nash, the architect of London's Regent Street. Indian in style outside and Oriental within, the Pavilion, which was completed in 1823, is one of the decorative wonders of the world. Highlights include the Great Kitchen – innovative in its day – and

TIP

The Lanes – the square mile of narrow alleys that make up the original village of Brighton – are peppered with antiques shops, jewellers, fashion stores, pubs, wine bars and restaurants. Another good area for shopping is the rather bohemian North Laine (www.northlaine.co.uk), around North Road, Church Street and North Street to the south of the station. It's full of the kind of hip, indie boutiques that characterise Brighton.

BELOW LEFT:
Arundel Castle.
BELOW RIGHT:
Brighton's Royal Pavilion.

Oast houses are a typical feature of the Kent countryside, and a reminder of Britain's brewing industry. They were used as kilns for drying hops.

BELOW: Brighton Pier.

a magnificent banqueting room. The Pavilion frequently hosts exhibitions and large-scale concerts. Within the Pavilion estate is the **Brighton Museum and Art Gallery** (Tue–Sun 10am–5pm; free), well worth a visit for its eclectic collections, ranging from archaeology to 20th-century art and design. The **Marina** to the east of the town groups bars, restaurants, shops and cinemas around a harbour full of smart yachts and pleasure boats.

Brighton Pier (www.brightonpier.co.uk; daily; rides 10am–8pm) has an endearing, old-fashioned amusement arcade, fish-and-chip shops and fun fair and is thronged in summer. The city's other pier, the ruined **West Pier** – ravaged by two fires – is set to be rebuilt. At its root end, a 490ft (150-metre)-tall observation tower, the **i360**, is being built by the architects who created the London Eye *(see page 135)*, hence its nickname, the "Brighton Eye".

Lewes ❺, the county town of East Sussex, lies to the northeast of Brighton. Its hills have been the scene of battles since Saxon times, and it seems almost overburdened with history. From the Barbican entrance and the Norman **castle** to the Regency **Court Hall** and Victorian **Town Hall**, the High Street drops steeply to the river. **Bull House** was the home of Thomas Paine, author of *The Rights of Man*, from 1768 to 1774. In the same High Street, 10 men and women were burned at the stake during times of religious intolerance.

From Lewes the A27 to Eastbourne passes near **Glyndebourne**, the celebrated opera house that hosts a key event of the classical music summer season *(see page 155)*. The area on the opposite, southern, side of the highway could be described as rural Bloomsbury. At **Rodmell** Leonard and Virginia Woolf lived in **Monk's House** until Leonard's death in 1969 (Apr–Oct Wed and Sat 2–5.30pm; charge).

From Berwick, the River Cuckmere runs south to **Alfriston**. Next to the church is the 14th-century thatched **Clergy House** (Mar–July Sat–Wed 10.30am–5pm, Aug Fri–Wed 10.30am–5pm, Oct–mid-Dec Sat–Wed 11am–4pm; charge), and in the village are former smugglers' inns. Chalk

cliffs, called the "Seven Sisters", lead to **Beachy Head**, at 530ft (160 metres) the highest cliff on the coast, and to the traditional resort town of **Eastbourne**, with its pier, fortress and numerous other attractions including Devonshire Park, where the famous Lawn Tennis Championships are held.

Rye

In the levels to the east, **Pevensey** ❻ has the most considerable Roman monument in Sussex, but the Roman fort was incomplete and could not withstand the landing in 1066 of William, Duke of Normandy, the last man to invade Britain. The conqueror met up with Harold of England some 10 miles (16km) inland; Senlac Field, where Harold fell, his eye famously pierced by an arrow, was marked by William, who built upon it the high altar of the abbey church at **Battle** (Apr–Sept daily 10am–6pm, Oct 10am–4pm) as a thanksgiving. An imposing 14th-century gatehouse leads to the grounds and ruins of the abbey.

The place where William prepared for battle is 6 miles (9km) southeast of Battle. The hilltop Norman castle at **Hastings** ❼, above a warren of caves where smugglers' adventures are re-enacted (Easter–Oct Mon–Fri 10am–3pm, Sat–Sun 10am–4pm; charge), is now a ruin, though a siege tent inside retells the battle story. On the Stade, the stretch of shingle beach, tall weatherboarded sheds used by the fishermen for storing nets are architectural fantasies.

To the east is **Winchelsea**, which, like the neighbouring small town of **Rye** ❽, has suffered from floods and the French and now lies high and dry. Edward III (1327–77) gave Rye its walls and gates. The **Landgate** and **Ypres Tower** survive, as well as much half-timbering. Today, tourism and crafts are the mainstay of this attractive town. There is an active artists' colony whose work can be seen at the Stormont Studio in East Street (entrance from 107 High Street; Thur–Sat 10.30am–

1.30pm, 2–5pm, Sun noon–3pm) and the Easton Rooms in the High Street (tel: 01797-222 433; Wed–Mon 10.30am–5pm, closed for lunch 1–2pm).

From Rye the land lies flat across the great expanse of **Romney Marsh**, a low-lying wetland area that is home to a special breed of sheep (named after the marsh), and wading birds such as the Kentish plover.

Tenterden and the Weald

But before continuing in this direction, a detour back up from Rye on the B2082 to the white weatherboard town of **Tenterden**, home of a small historic railway, leads towards the **High Weald**. The region to the west of here was made rich by Flemish weavers, notably around **Cranbrook**. Daniel Defoe is said to have written *Robinson Crusoe* here in 1719.

Some 50 years later, during the Seven Years War (1756–63), 23-year-old Edward Gibbon, who wrote *The Decline and Fall of the Roman Empire*, was guarding French prisoners in **Sissinghurst**

The Mermaid Inn in Rye dates from 1156 and was rebuilt in its present form in 1420.

BELOW:
Sissinghurst Castle.

BELOW: a pop concert at Leeds Castle. The name derives from an Old English spelling and has no connection with the city of Leeds in West Yorkshire.

Castle  (Mar–Oct Fri–Tue 10.30am–5pm; charge), 2 miles (3km) to the east. The 16th-century manor house was in ruins when it was bought by Vita Sackville-West (1892–1962), poet, novelist and gardener, and her politician husband Harold Nicolson in 1930. The beautiful gardens that they created, most famously the White Garden, are among the most visited in Britain.

Eight miles (13km) west is **Goudhurst**, peaceful enough now, but in 1747 the villagers locked themselves in the church while a gang of smugglers from nearby **Hawkhurst** fought the local militia in the churchyard. From this half-timbered town there are wonderful views south over hop and fruit country, and nearby are several places worth visiting. **Bodiam Castle**, to the south beyond Hawkhurst, is a classic medieval fort set within a 3-acre (1.2-hectare) moat (mid-Feb–Oct daily 10.30am–5pm; Nov–Dec Wed–Sun 11am–4pm, Jan Sat–Sun 11am–4pm; charge), while the romantic-looking **Scotney Castle**, 5 miles (8km) southwest of Hawkhurst at Lamberhurst,

has been described as one of the loveliest surviving landscapes in the 18th-century pictorial tradition; it comprises a ruined, moated medieval castle, an Elizabethan-style house built in 1837 and spectacular gardens (castle: late-Feb–Oct Wed–Sun 11am–3pm; house: late Feb–Oct 11am–5pm, early–mid-Dec Sat–Sun 11am–4pm; gardens: late Feb–Oct Wed–Sun 11am–5.30pm, Sat–Sun 11am–5pm; charge).

Tunbridge Wells

Halfway down the A21 between London and Hastings lies **Royal Tunbridge Wells**. Dudley, Lord North, a hypochondriac, brought fame and fortune to the town in 1606 when he discovered the health-giving properties of a spring on the common. Court and fashion followed, and the waters, rich in iron salts, were, and still are, taken at the Pantiles. This terraced walk, with shops behind a colonnade, is named after the original tiles laid in 1638, some of which are still there.

The former home of the novelist William Thackeray in London Road is now a restaurant and wine bar with a good reputation (see page 215). There are also good second-hand bookshops in the old part of town. **Penshurst Place** (Apr–Oct daily, house and toy museum: noon–4pm, grounds: 10.30am–6pm; charge), just to the northwest of the town, is one of Kent's finest mansions, dating from 1340. Home of the Viscount de L'Isle, it was for two centuries the seat of the Sidney family, notably Sir Philip Sidney, the Elizabethan soldier and poet. It's fun for children, with a toy museum and adventure playground.

A few miles to the west lies **Hever Castle** (Apr–Oct Wed–Sun, castle: noon–6pm, last admission 5pm; gardens: daily 10.30am–6pm, with exceptions; charge), the childhood home of Anne Boleyn, the second wife of Henry VIII. The latter first met Anne here, then seized Hever after her execution and murdered her brother. William

Waldorf Astor (1848–1919) applied his American millions to make massive, sympathetic improvements to the moated castle, 35-acre (15-hectare) lake, and gardens where flower beds are laid out just as they were in Tudor times.

Knole

Some 10 miles (16km) to the north on the B2026 is **Westerham**, a town that commemorates General James Wolfe, who decisively drove the French from Canada when he stormed Quebec in 1759. South of the village is **Chartwell**, Winston Churchill's home from 1924 until his death in 1965. The house is much as it was when he left it, and includes his studio, where many of his paintings are on display (tel: 01732-868 381; house: Mar–June, late Aug–Oct Wed–Sun 11am–5pm, July–late Aug Tue–Sun 11am–5pm, garden: daily 11am–4pm with exceptions; charge).

Sevenoaks is the town 5 miles (8km) to the east on the far side of the A21, and on its outskirts is **Knole @**, one of the largest private houses in the country (tel: 01732-450 608; house: Mar–Oct Wed–Sun noon–4pm, garden: Apr–Sept Tue 11am–4pm; charge). It was the Archbishop of Canterbury's residence until confiscated by Henry VIII, and Elizabeth I gave it to Thomas Sackville, who greatly extended it. It was the birthplace and childhood home of Vita Sackville-West and the setting for Virginia Woolf's 1928 novel *Orlando*. It has 365 rooms, 52 stairways and seven courtyards. There are fine portraits of the Sackville family by Gainsborough and Van Dyck, as well as some rare furniture, including the prototype of the Knole settee. There is a 1,000-acre (400-hectare) deer park and an Orangery.

Kent's pride and joy lies to the east, 6 miles (10km) beyond the county town of **Maidstone. Leeds Castle @**, the castle of the queens of medieval England, is a fairytale place built on two islands on the River Len. It has 500 acres (200 hectares) of parkland and is a popular day out (daily 10.30am–5.30pm, last entry 4.30pm; charge).

Maidstone lies on the River Medway which empties into the Thames estuary between **Rochester @** and **Chatham**, 10 miles (16km) to the north. A Norman **castle** stands above the river at Rochester (Apr–Sept daily 10am–6pm, Oct–Mar until 4pm; charge). Chatham grew around the Royal Navy dockyard established by Henry VIII. **The Historic Dockyard** (mid-Feb–Mar and Nov daily 10am–4pm, Apr–Oct daily 10am–6pm; charge) is now a museum where you can discover 400 years of maritime history. Nearby at Chatham Maritime is **Dickens World** (www.dickensworld.co.uk; daily 10am–4.30pm, last entry 3pm; charge), an indoor theme park based on the life of Charles Dickens; it gives you an authentic taste of Victorian England.

Canterbury

Canterbury @ is the cradle of English Christianity. Star attractions are William the Conqueror's castle, the

Chartwell, Sir Winston Churchill's old home, is run by the National Trust.

BELOW: Canterbury Cathedral, founded in AD 602.

Dover Castle, where you can visit the labyrinth of secret wartime tunnels built deep in Dover's White Cliffs.

BELOW: the beach at Botany Bay, near Broadstairs.

cathedral *(see box below)* and its Thomas Becket Shrine (a magnet for pilgrims for centuries), and in St Margaret's Street the **Canterbury Tales** (Nov–Feb daily 10am–4.30pm, Mar–Oct 10am–5pm (July–Aug from 9.30am); charge) promises a "medieval adventure" with the sights, sounds and even the smells of the journey made by several of Chaucer's characters.

Despite German aerial bomb attacks in 1942, much of Canterbury's medieval character remains, and there are a number of good pubs in its narrow streets. The town's delights include the remains of the original Roman wall that once enclosed it. Also worth visiting are the excavated ruins of **St Augustine's Abbey** (Apr–June Wed–Sun 10am–5pm, July–Aug daily 10am–6pm, Sept–Mar Sat–Sun 10am–5pm; charge). Further east along Longport

is **St Martin's Church** where Christian worship has taken place since AD 597. In the 4th century this area was selected by rich Romans for their villas, and remains can still be seen.

The **Museum of Canterbury** is located in Stour Street (daily 10am–5pm, last entry 4pm; charge) and exhibits range from pre-Roman times to the present day. For the young at heart, there's also a Rupert Bear Museum.

From Margate to Deal

Further east lies **Margate** ⓰, which the railway opened up to London's East Enders, helping to make it one of the capital's most popular seaside resorts by the late 19th century. Bathing machines were invented here by a local Quaker, and while it is still a seaside resort, even the new **Turner Contemporary** arts venue (Tue–Sun 10–7; free) cannot disguise its rather less prosperous demeanour today.

A couple of miles away is **North Foreland**, Britain's most easterly spot. Immediately below is **Broadstairs** ⓱, a more up-market resort with a sheltered sandy bay and landscaped

Canterbury Cathedral

The first church on the site was established in AD 597 by St Augustine, who had been sent by Pope Gregory the Great to convert the heathen English. In 1170, Archbishop Thomas Becket, who had been quarrelling with King Henry II, was murdered in the cathedral by four of the king's knights. In 1220, his bones were transferred to a shrine in the Trinity Chapel, a place of pilgrimage. In 1935, the shameful murder of Thomas Becket was recounted in verse by T.S. Eliot.

The nave – Europe's longest medieval nave – was rebuilt in the 14th century, and the main Bell Harry Tower was added a century later. The stunning stained glass rivals the best in France (Mon–Sat Jun–Sept 9am–5pm, Sun 12.30–2.30pm; Mon–Sat Oct–May 9am–4.30pm; charge unless you are attending a service).

cliffs, which Dickens described as being "left high and dry by the tide of years". When he knew it, the clifftop **Bleak House** was called Fort House. He spent his summer holidays there in the 1850s and 1860s; there are currently plans to turn the house into a boutique hotel. Fans of the novelist may wish to visit the small **Dickens House Museum** at 2 Victoria Parade (Mon–Sat 9am–6pm; charge), housed in the former home of Miss Mary Pearson Strong, on whom the character of Betsey Trotwood, from *David Copperfield*, was based. Just a few steps west along the parade is **Morelli's**, a wonderful Art Deco ice-cream parlour.

Sandwich lies along the River Stour, 2 miles (3km) from the sea. As long ago as the 9th century it was an important port, but by the 17th century the progressive silting up of the estuary left it high and dry, and it is now surrounded by a 500-acre (200-hectare) coastal bird sanctuary. In the 11th century, Sandwich became one of the original Cinque Ports, a string of safe harbours from here to Hastings fortified against invaders.

Walmer Castle (tel: 01304-364 388;

Easter–Sept daily 10am–6pm, Mar and Oct daily 10am–4pm; charge) in **Deal** is still the official residence of the Lord Warden of the Cinque Ports, a post held by the late Queen Mother for 24 years. On the shingle beach of this small resort Julius Caesar landed in 55 BC, and there is a plaque commemorating the event.

Dover

Sandwich, Deal and **Dover** ⑱ are now billed as "**White Cliffs Country**", and at Dover, Britain's busiest passenger port, the chalk massif of the South Downs drops dramatically into the sea. On these cliffs the Romans built a lighthouse, the Normans a **castle** (tel: 01314-211 067; Apr–July, Sept daily 10am–6pm, Aug 9.30am–6pm, Oct daily 10am–5pm, call for other opening days/times; charge), and from here Calais can be seen on a clear day. In the castle you can experience a medieval siege and visit tunnels used by the military in World War II. The excavated **Roman Painted House** (June–mid-Sept Tue–Sat 10am–5pm, Sun 2–5pm; charge) in York Street is also worth a visit. ❏

Dover is connected to France by ferries, but it is at Folkestone that the continent comes more sharply into view. The town is next to the UK entrance to the Channel Tunnel, which provides fast train and car shuttle services between England and France.

BELOW: the "Seven Sisters" cliffs.

RESTAURANTS AND PUBS

Restaurants

Prices for a three-course dinner per person with a half-bottle of house wine:
£ = under £25
££ = £25–50
£££ = £50–100
££££ = over £100

Amberley, near Arundel

Amberley Castle
On the B2139 between Storrington and Bury Hill
Tel: 01798-831 992
www.amberleycastle.co.uk
££
Evocatively restored 12th-century castle, where you can dine in splendour in the Queen's Room Restaurant with a splendid 16th-century mural. Classic cuisine is cooked and served with panache.

Brighton

Gingerman
21a Norfolk Square
Tel: 01273-326 688
http://gingermanrestaurants.com ££
Modern European cooking with imaginative touches is served in a pleasant dining space with bare wooden floors. You pay by course rather than by dishes chosen.

Terre à Terre
71 East Street
Tel: 01273-729 051
www.terreaterre.co.uk ££
A popular restaurant on a road running down to the sea, offering a brilliantly innovative vegetarian menu and organic wine.

Broadstairs

Osteria Posillipo
14 Albion Street

Tel: 01843-601 133
www.posillipo.co.uk ££
This family-friendly Italian restaurant is a little slice of Naples in Broadstairs, enjoying a great location on the seafront (there's a terrace out front with great views over the bay). The large menu includes rustic pasta dishes, classic pizzas and seafood, and salads. Posillipo is hugely popular with the local crowd, making booking essential on Fridays and weekends. It's not cheap for an Italian, but atmospheric and fun.

Canterbury

The Goods Shed
Station Road West
Tel: 01227-459 153
http://thegoodshed.co.uk
££–£££
A disused Victorian railway building now serves as a farmers' market and restaurant, with excellent fresh, seasonal (often organic) food. There's also a food hall. Closed Mon.

The Granville
Street End, Lower Hardres
Tel: 01227-700 402
www.thegranvillecanterbury.com ££
Under the same ownership as the excellent Sportsman in Seasalter (see page 215), the light, airy Granville –in a village location just south of Canterbury – uses top-quality local, seasonal produce for its modern European changing menu. Dishes might include smoked salmon tart with beetroot relish or *coq au vin*. Extra touches, such as home-

made chocolates, add to the dining experience.

Chilgrove, near Chichester

The Fish House
High Street (B2141 Chichester to Petersfield)
Tel: 01243-519 444
www.thefishhouse.co.uk ££
This is a bar and hotel in a former 18th-century coaching inn near Goodwood racecourse. The fish theme is evident in paraphernalia throughout the hotel and naturally reflected in the excellent menu. There's even an Oyster Bar.

East Grinstead

Gravetye Manor
Vowels Lane (southwest of East Grinstead)
Tel: 01342-810 567
www.gravetyemanor.co.uk
££–£££
Elizabethan manor house, with wood-panelled rooms and fine gardens. Excellent traditional and modern British cooking, and some great fixed-price menus. In summer 95 percent of the fruit and vegetables used in its dishes come from its own garden.

Dover

The Allotment
9 High Street
Tel: 01304-214 467
www.theallotmentdover.co.uk £–££
David Flynn's cosy bistro with worn wooden floors, painted wood-slatted walls and cheery stained-glass front windows is all about keeping the food-miles low, using super-fresh produce from either his own allotment or

other local ones. Gorgeous menu.

Faversham
Read's
Macknade Manor,
Canterbury Road
Tel: 01795-535 344
www.reads.com ££–£££
Located in a supremely elegant Georgian manor house, Read's has a Michelin star for the exquisite cooking of chef/owner David Pitchford. Local game, fresh fish and home-grown herbs and vegetables are used to perfection in a menu that may include Kentish lamb and locally smoked eel. Closed Sun and Mon.

Jevington
The Hungry Monk
High Street
Tel: 01323-482 178
www.hungrymonk.co.uk ££
In the Cuckmere Valley, this restaurant retains its quirky rustic character. Excellent desserts (it claims to be the birthplace of Banoffi Pie) and cheeseboard. Reservations essential.

Rye
Landgate Bistro
5–6 Landgate
Tel: 01797-222 829
www.landgatebistro.co.uk
£–££
Housed in two interconnecting Georgian cottages, the elegant Landgate Bistro has a local following for its traditional and modern British food, including bistro favourites and dishes that reflect the changing seasons. Locally caught fish and Romney Marsh lamb are highlights, as are the

homemade puddings.

Tunbridge Wells
Carluccio's Café
32 Mount Pleasant Road
Tel: 01892-614 968
www.carluccios.com ££
This branch of the Carluccio's chain brings his reliable Italian cooking and flair to Tunbridge Wells. The restaurant is light and airy, and there's a deli attached.

Thackeray's House
85 London Road
Tel: 01892-511 921
www.thackerays-restaurant.co.uk ££–£££
Occupying the pretty Grade II-listed 17th-century former home of the 19th-century novelist, this restaurant serves critically acclaimed modern French food.

Whitstable
Whitstable Oyster Company
Royal Native Oyster Stores, Horsebridge
Tel: 01227-276 856
www.whitstableoyster company.com ££–£££
Oysters and other fish are served at red-gingham-covered tables in this busy bistro right on the beach. For value for money there are other places in town that are better; it's the exceptional seafront location and appeal of the historic warehouse building that is the real draw here.

Seasalter
Sportsman
Faversham Road
Tel: 01277-273 370
www.thesportsmanseasalter.co.uk £££

Located in a remote spot on the old coastal road between Faversham and Whitstable, the Sportsman is extraordinary in that it serves Michelin-starred food in relaxed gastropub surroundings. Its daily chalkboard menu and tasting menu offer local, seasonal produce and lots of fish.

Pubs
In Brighton, the **Basketmakers Arms** on Gloucester Road is decorated with old signs and has good-value pub grub. In Lewes, the **Gardener's Arms** on Cliffe High Street has good beers.

In Chichester, the **Four Chestnuts** is noted for its beers and generous food, and has music evenings. In Tunbridge Wells, **The Hare** on Langton Green is a pleasant pub that serves large portions of mostly modern European food and excellent desserts.

In Canterbury, **The Phoenix** on Old Dover Road is a beamed tavern with lots of cricketing memorabilia (it's located by the cricket ground).

In Dover, **The White Horse** on St James Street is a tavern dating to 1365 and is about beer rather than food.

LEFT: preparing a Dover sole, named after the fishing port that landed the most sole in the 19th century.
RIGHT: fresh produce at The Goods Shed. **ABOVE:** view from the Queen's Room Restaurant, Amberly Castle.

THE ENGLISH GARDEN

England's temperate climate encourages a great diversity of gardens which blend the grand and the homely in a cosmopolitan range of styles

The formal gardens of great houses have both followed fashion and set the style for the nation's favourite hobby. In medieval times, fruit trees, roses and herbs were grown in walled enclosures. In the 16th century, aromatic plants were incorporated in "knots" (carpet-like patterns). Tudor gardens (like those at Hatfield House in Hertfordshire) were enclosed squares of flowers in geometric patterns bordered by low hedges and gravel paths.

A taste for small flowerbeds persisted through the 17th and 18th centuries when fountains and canals began to be introduced.

The Art of the landscape

In the 1740s a rich banker, Henry Hoare, inspired by Continental art during his Grand Tour, employed William Kent (1685–1748) to turn his gardens at Stourhead in Wiltshire into a series of lakes dotted with buildings in the classical style. This was the birth of the landscape garden, known as *le jardin anglais*.

"Capability" Brown *(see panel, right)* rejected formal plantings in favour of natural parkland, and restricted flowers to small kitchen gardens. But Humphry Repton (1752–1815) reintroduced the formal pleasure garden. The Victorians put the emphasis on plants and Gertrude Jekyll (1843–1932) promoted the idea of planting cycles to ensure that colour lasted through the year.

LEFT: classical statues graced many gardens in the 17th century. This one is at Belvoir Castle, Leicestershire. Until the late 18th century many statues were made of lead.

ABOVE: this Wiltshire garden at Stourhead, birthplace of England's landscape movement, is dotted with lakes and temples and has many rare trees and shrubs. The artful vistas were created in the 1740s, and their magnificence contrasts with the severe restraint of the Palladian house (1721–4).

ABOVE: the 4th Duke of Marlborough employed "Capability" Brown *(see right)* in 1764 to impose his back-to-nature philosophy on Blenheim Palace. Brown's most dramatic change was to create a large lake by damming the River Glyme.

ABOVE: a 17th-century Cotswold house at Mickleton in Gloucestershire, Hidcote Manor has one of the most beautiful English gardens, mixing different types of plot within various species of hedges. Although covering 10 acres (4 hectares), it's like a series of cottage gardens on a grand scale, prompting Vita Sackville-West to describe it as "haphazard luxuriance".

LEFT: this example at Henry VIII's Hampton Court Palace outside London shows the Tudor liking for knots – small beds of dwarf plants or sand and gravel laid out in patterns resembling embroidery. Topiary, statues and mazes provided a counterpoint to the mathematical order.

THE GREAT GARDENERS

Lancelot Brown (1715–83) was nicknamed "Capability" when he rode from one aristocratic client to the next pointing out "capabilities to improvement". His forte was presenting gardens in the "natural" state, and his lasting influence lay in his talent for combining quite simple elements to create harmonious effects.

Brown liked to create elegant lakes for his parks, as at Blenheim Palace in Oxfordshire. He was also involved with the gardens at Stowe in Buckinghamshire, which the National Trust today describes as "Britain's largest work of art", and with the gardens at Kew, Britain's main botanical establishment, just outside London.

One of the 20th century's most influential gardeners was Vita Sackville-West (1892–1962), who developed her gardens at Sissinghurst Castle in Kent. She revived the 16th-century idea of dividing a garden into separate sections, combining a formal overall style with an informal choice of flowers.

BELOW: thanks to the influence of the Gulf Stream, subtropical flora can flourish at England's southwestern tip. Tresco Abbey Gardens, on the Isles of Scilly, were laid out on the site of a Benedictine priory and contain many rare plants.

HARDY COUNTRY

Wessex, in central southern England, was immortalised by the novelist Thomas Hardy. It is especially rich in history and ancient monuments, including the magnificent stone circle at Stonehenge

Few literary works bear the impress of place as strongly as the novels of Thomas Hardy (1840–1928), and no place has had its character and the character of its people revealed as Wessex has by Dorset's most famous son. Wessex is in fact an ancient kingdom, rather larger than the one in which the novelist's trail winds. This was the kingdom of the West Saxons, who had supremacy in England from AD 802 to 1013. It extended across the modern counties of Hampshire, Wiltshire, Dorset and Somerset and even for a short while included Devon and Cornwall.

The M3 motorway southwest of London leads to the ancient capital of Winchester in little more than an hour, and beyond it to the urban sprawl of Southampton, once a transatlantic liner port. Skirting it, the A31 continues through the New Forest to the smart seaside town of Bournemouth; the A35 then heads further west to Dorchester, centre of the Hardy tours. To the north, the A303 leaves the M3 at junction 8 and heads for Salisbury Plain and Devon. Trains to London arrive at Waterloo.

Winchester

Not only the capital of Wessex, **Winchester ❶** was England's first capital too, until all decision-making was moved to London in the 17th century. Beneath the

medieval and modern city is a Roman town, and a Norman **cathedral** (Mon–Sat 9.30am–5pm, Sun 12.30–3pm; charge) replaced the Saxon one.

Older than Canterbury Cathedral and the longest in Europe, the building's Norman transepts and tower survive, but its nave and choir were modernised by William of Wykeham in Perpendicular style towards the end of the 14th century. The organ's first notes were heard at the Crystal Palace in London's Hyde Park at the Great Exhibition in 1851. The palace, clois-

LEFT AND RIGHT: North Presbytry aisle and stone carving, Winchester Cathedral.

TIP

Stretching from Winchester in Hampshire to Lewes in East Sussex and covering around 620 sq miles (1,600 sq km) is England's newest national park (established in 2011), the South Downs National Park (www. southdowns.gov.uk). The South Downs Way runs the length of the park and is a trail for walkers, cyclists and horse riders.

ters, colleges and mill are all breathtaking. The Great Hall near Westgate is all that is left of Henry III's castle – but it is one of the finest in the country. Sir Walter Raleigh was condemned to death here in 1685 and it still functions as the county court.

Salisbury

Heading west from Winchester, the A272 drops suddenly to the broad main street of **Stockbridge**, on the River Test, a delightful stop before the 15-mile (24km) haul across the rolling countryside to Salisbury. **Salisbury ②** ("Melchester" in the Hardy novels) has a cathedral built between 1220 and 1258, with "as many windows as days in the year, as many pillars as hours, and as many gates as moons". The spire took even longer to complete. **The Close**, a green space fringed with fine houses (mostly Georgian), distances the confusion of the modern city.

Stonehenge

About 8 miles (13km) north of Salisbury on the A345 is Amesbury, and from there the A303 leads west to that famous collection of standing stones, **Stonehenge ③** (daily, mid-Mar–May 9.30am–6pm, June–Aug 9am–7pm, Sept–mid-Oct 9.30am–6pm, mid-Oct–mid-Mar 9.30am–4pm; charge). On first view, it may seem disappointingly small; the American poet and essayist Ralph Waldo Emerson (1803–82) thought it "looked like a group of brown dwarfs on the wide expanse". The largest standing stone is 21ft (6 metres) high and extends more than 8ft (2.5 metres) below ground. The stones are believed to date from 2,400 BC.

Stonehenge consists of an outer ring of larger sarsen stones, brought from the Marlborough Downs, and an inner (earlier) horseshoe of smaller bluestones, from the Prescelli Hills in Pembrokeshire. Its purpose is unknown, though the tumuli around the site hint at an ancient funerary significance. Some scholars suggest a link with astronomy to mark significant prehistoric dates.

Just west of Salisbury is the great house of **Wilton** (house: Easter–early Sept Sun–Thur 11.30am–4.30pm, grounds: mid-Apr–early Sept daily 11am–5pm, with exceptions; charge), the family-run

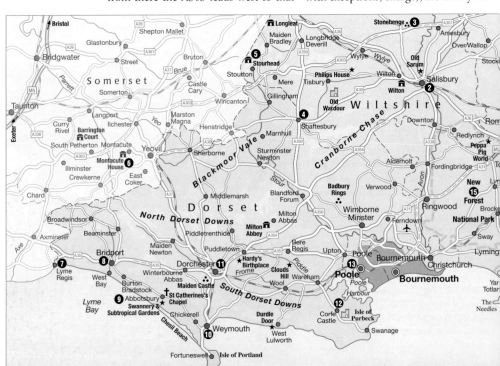

seat of the Earls of Pembroke. Treasures include a lock of Queen Elizabeth I's hair, Napoleon's despatch case and some Rembrandts and Van Dycks.

Shaftesbury

Leaving Wilton, the A30 bounds the wilderness of the old hunting forest of **Cranbourne Chase** and then climbs to one of southern England's few hill towns, **Shaftesbury ❹**. Hardy renamed it "Shaston" in his 1895 novel *Jude the Obscure*. Walk the town walls above the steep drop to the horse-and-hound country of Blackmore Vale, and put the clock back centuries with a climb up the cobbled **Gold Hill** – like pilgrims to St Edward the Martyr's resting place.

In the village of Stourton, about 10 miles (16km) north of Shaftesbury, near Mere, is the mansion at **Stourhead ❺** (tel: 01747-841 152; www.nationaltrust. org.uk; garden: daily 9am–6pm, house: Mar–early Nov Fri–Tue 11am–5pm with exceptions; charge), built for Henry Hoare, a banker, in 1720–4. The magnificent gardens are landscaped around the lake. Gothic cottages and towers are reflected in the lake's dark waters,

best seen in the half light of the flint and pebble-lined grotto *(see page 216)*. Further south, 16 miles (25km) west of Shaftesbury, is **Sherborne**. Once an important centre in Wessex and the burial place of two Saxon kings, the market town retains a medieval flavour.

At **Yeovil**, 5 miles (8km) west of Sherborne, you stray into Somerset for a visit to another National Trust property, **Montacute House ❻** (house: mid-Mar–Oct Wed–Mon 11am–5pm, garden: Jan–mid-Mar and Nov–Dec Wed–Sun 11am–4pm, mid-Mar–Oct Wed–Mon 11am–5.30pm; charge), an Elizabethan house built for Sir Edward Phelips, the opening prosecutor at the trial of Guy Fawkes. Constructed of golden Ham Hill stone, the ornamental gazebos or lookouts at the corners of the forecourt are exquisite mansions in miniature.

In the church at **East Coker**, around 3 miles (5km) to the south, are the ashes of T.S. Eliot (1888–1965). The poet's ancestors emigrated from here to America. "In my beginning is my end," he wrote in the poem named after the village.

Such is the allure of Stonehenge that here, on Midsummer Day, Druids celebrate their rites; in hooded white robes with mistletoe in hand, they sing and chant before dawn. Since the mid-1980s, however, Midsummer festivities have been subject to restrictions – and sometimes banned – to prevent damage to the site.

BELOW: Gold Hill, Shaftesbury.

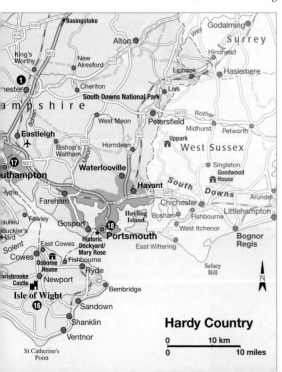

Lyme Regis

There is a warm briny wind at **Lyme Regis** ❼, just east of the Devon border, in Dorset. This old fishing town was once as fashionable a resort as Bath, and it was popular 100 years before Bournemouth was even thought of. Regency bow windows and trellised verandas on Victorian villas line the **Parade** on the way to the tiny harbour and its curved protecting arm, the **Cobb**, where the Duke of Monmouth landed in 1685, aspiring to the crown. Its sea-lashed walls had a supporting role with Meryl Streep in the 1981 movie *The French Lieutenant's Woman*.

The Cobb also features in *Persuasion*, by the novelist Jane Austen. Her house, **Bay Cottage** (now a café), where she supposedly wrote much of the novel, is near the harbour end of the parade. During a visit in 1804, she also stayed in Pyne House at 10 Broad Street. Other famous visitors include Charles II's illegitimate son, Monmouth, who stayed at the George; his blue ensign flew in the marketplace.

The road that hugs the sea to the east has a precarious footing above the landslips, descending to Charmouth and Austen's "happiest spot for watching the flow of the tide". Hereabouts, the cliffs reveal the existence of earlier residents, such as the elephant and rhinoceros, in fossil form. Ichthyosaurus was also found here in 1811. **Bridport** ❽ ("Port Bredy" to Hardy) is 2 miles (3km) from the sea, yet there is no denying its marine character. Rope and cordage, nets and tackle: this was the stuff of Bridport's prosperity.

West Bay is Bridport's improbable harbour. A narrow channel dug in the shingle bank and flanked by two high piers only feet apart offers a needle-threading operation for the small craft that lie uneasily in the little basin. In the old days, coasters had to be hauled in with Bridport ropes. Visit on a Wednesday or Saturday for the outdoor market.

Chesil Beach

The next town east, the nearby **Burton Bradstock**, is summed up in thatch and smoky stone, flowers everywhere and a stream that trickles to the sea below Burton Cliff; this turned the wheel of the flax mills until the last one closed in 1930.

Chesil Bank, which is more familiar nowadays by its alternative name of Chesil Beach, thanks to the 2007 novel *On Chesil Beach* by Booker Prize-winning author Ian McEwan, begins here, curving away eastwards to where it becomes the slender link that makes the **Isle of Portland** (*see opposite*). The pebbles of the steeply shelving bank increase in size towards Portland, and, at night, local fisherman docking at any point on the 16-mile (25km) ridge can tell exactly where they are from the size of the pebbles. The bank has no mercy – to drive a boat in here spells almost certain disaster for the uninitiated. **St Catherine's Chapel**, on a green hill above the bank at **Abbotsbury** ❾, leads a double life. A place of prayer for 500 years, it is also maintained as a mark for seamen. On the land side it overlooks the most fascinating miscel-

lany of monastic ruin, a swannery and subtropical gardens. The 15th-century abbey barn, bigger and more splendid than many a parish church, was built as a wheat store. Further along the same road, by the saltwater of Fleet, is the swan sanctuary founded in the 14th century.

Weymouth and Portland

George III did **Weymouth** ❿ a good turn when he went there in 1789 for his convalescence after a serious illness. The grateful citizens responded by erecting the brightly coloured statue that ends the half-mile esplanade.

The king bathed from his bathing machine, which was wheeled down to the shallow waters, to the music of his own anthem. Fanny Burney records the occasion in the diary she kept while Second Mistress of the Robes to Queen Charlotte. George can be seen in chalk outline on a neighbouring hillside astride a horse.

There is much of the character of the 18th-century watering place about Weymouth today. Stuccoed terraces front the esplanade, the sands are golden and the sea is blue. There are museums of sea life, diving and shipwrecks. From Weymouth's jetty, ferries maintain a regular service to the Channel Isles.

To the south of Weymouth a narrow strip of land carries the road to the **Isle of Portland**, which is in fact a peninsula. Thomas Hardy observed that the people who lived on what he called "the Gibraltar of Wessex" had manners and customs of their own. The sheer structure of Portland makes it a place apart. Everything is made of the eponymous white-grey stone, which has been quarried on the island for centuries. The lighthouse on the island's south tip (Portland Bill) overlooks the broken water of the treacherous Portland Race.

Thomas Hardy's heartlands

The green of the high hills inland of Weymouth comes as a welcome relief. Dorchester, 8 miles (13km) north, is best approached from the great hill of **Maiden Castle**, *Mai Dun* ("great

Durdle Door at Lulworth Cove, 17 miles (27km) east of Weymouth. The limestone has been eroded to form a striking arch.

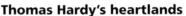

LEFT: King George III (reigned 1760–1820) in full regalia on Weymouth promenade.
BELOW: togetherness on Weymouth's beach.

During the Civil War of 1641–53, Abbotsbury's Benedictine abbey was used to store gunpowder, and the explosion that reduced most of its buildings to ruins provided the whole neighbourhood with material for new houses. The vicarage, farm and countless cottages in the village all have the telltale white stones in their walls.

hill" – probably the world's largest earthwork), just before the town on the left. Excavations have shown that the hill was occupied 4,000 years ago, and a clever maze conceals the hill fort's entrance.

Dorchester ⓫, Dorset's county town, is well aware of its past, and the pace of life here, beyond the fast motorways, is noticeably slower. Thomas Hardy, Judge Jeffries and the Tolpuddle Martyrs all try to catch the visitor's eye: Hardy's statue commands his "Casterbridge" from the top of the High Street; the courtroom in the **Shire Hall** (Mon–Fri 10am–noon and 2–4pm) looks remarkably unchanged since 1834 when the Martyrs were convicted for trying to gain better working conditions. The **Dinosaur Museum** (Icen Way; daily Jan–Mar 10am–4pm, Apr–Sept 10am–5pm, Oct–mid-Dec 10am–4pm; charge), the only one in the country dedicated solely to these great beasts, mixes fossils, skeletons, reconstructions and multimedia displays.

Hardy's is perhaps the most potent influence. He was apprenticed to an architect at 39 South Street, and after

he left the practice in 1885, he used his knowledge to design his own house, **Max Gate** (Easter–Oct Wed–Sun 11am–5pm; charge), on the Wareham Road, where he wrote some of his most famous works, including *Tess of the D'Urbervilles* and *Jude the Obscure*, and where he died, in 1928. The house is now run by the National Trust.

There is a memorial collection, entitled "A Writer's Dorset", devoted to Hardy in the **Dorset County Museum** (Apr–Oct Mon–Sat 10am–5pm, Nov–Mar Tue–Sat, Mon also in Jan 10am–4pm; charge) on High West Street, a cast-iron building of 1880, cheerfully decorated in bright primary colours. Stunning finds from **Maiden Castle** (Sept–June Mon–Sat, July–Aug daily; free) are here, too.

Hardy was actually born in the cottage (**Hardy's Birthplace**; mid-Mar–Oct Wed–Sun 11am–5pm; charge) his great-grandfather built at **Higher Bockhampton**, just northeast of Dorchester, in 1840. Also now run by the National Trust, it was where *Far From the Madding Crowd* and *Under the Greenwood Tree* were written. Heading east from

BELOW RIGHT:
Thomas Hardy's birthplace at Higher Bockhampton.

The Genius of Thomas Hardy

Film-makers today continue to be drawn to *Tess of the D'Urbervilles* and *Jude the Obscure*, finding that their strongly drawn characters and melodramatic situations translate effectively to the screen. Yet when the novels first appeared, in the 1890s, reviewers condemned them for their pessimism and immorality. Certainly, they are much darker than Hardy's early novels such as *Under the Greenwood Tree* and *Far from the Madding Crowd*, published in the 1870s, although even these more pastoral stories convey a strong sense of the utter indifference of fate towards their protagonists – a defining characteristic of Hardy's writing.

Hardy (1840–1928) was the son of a stonemason, and trained as an architect. All his major novels are set in Wessex and, despite their often bleak outlook, he draws their rustic characters (especially his female protagonists) with affection. He is also an observer of the natural surroundings, about which he writes lyrically. Hardy married twice, first (in 1874) to Emma Gifford, from whom he was later estranged, then, in 1914, to his much younger secretary. He was hugely affected by Emma's death in 1912, revisiting places of their courtship and increasingly writing poetry that reflected on her death. Romantically, his heart remained with Emma, metaphorically and physically; when he died his ashes were buried in Westminster Abbey in London, but his heart was placed in Emma's grave, in Stinsford.

here, then south along the B3390 and 1½ miles (2.5km) east of the Waddock crossroads, is the National Trust-run **Clouds Hill** (mid-Mar–Oct Wed–Sun 11am–5pm; charge), a tiny cottage that was the retreat of the explorer T.E. Lawrence, or Lawrence of Arabia as he is popularly known.

The village of **Milton Abbas**, deep in the Dorset countryside 12 miles (20km) northeast, annoyed Viscount Milton. It interfered with the view from his rebuilt mansion, **Milton Abbey** (access during daylight hours), so in 1752 he moved the village as well, half a mile away, sticking to the rustic tradition of cob and thatch. The result is a harmonious parade of thatched cottages.

The 30-mile (48km) coast from Weymouth east to Swanage, below Poole Harbour, is strictly for walking, army operations permitting, but approachable by car at **West Lulworth**, Kimmeridge and Worth Matravers.

Corfe Castle

Towards the east, the chalk hills around the **Isle of Purbeck** break at the National Trust's **Corfe Castle** ⑫ (daily Mar and Oct 10am–5pm, Apr–Sept 10am–6pm, Nov–Feb 10am–4pm; charge), a picturesque ruin haunted by treachery, cruelty and murder. Here King Edward was murdered by his stepmother in 978, French prisoners were starved to death in the dungeons by King John, and the castle was treacherously handed over to the Roundheads in 1646 who pulled a large part of it down.

In **Swanage** ("Knollsea" to Thomas Hardy) at Durlston Country Park, look out for the stone globe, 10ft (3 metres) in diameter, weighing 40 tons, and flanked by panels lettered with sobering information on the nature of the universe.

Around Poole Harbour's creeks, mud flats and islands is **Poole** ⑬ itself, most beautiful on the quay and overlooking ships and shipyards, yachts and chandler's stores. Curving steps meet under the portico of the **Custom House**

with its coat of arms representing an authority the Dorset smuggler never acknowledged. The town is famous for its pottery.

Beyond Poole are the hotels and elegant terraces of **Bournemouth**, the sedate resort built at the end of the 19th century. To the northwest lies **Wimborne Minster**, where the church has a fine 13th-century astronomical clock, and just east of Bournemouth is 100-year-odd-plus **Christchurch** on the mouth of the Avon. There is a turret at the **Priory** with an interlaced pattern of Norman arches that recalls Pisa's leaning tower.

The New Forest

Good rivers and harbours make this popular yachting country. **Lymington** is the next safe port of call, and on the River Beaulieu (pronounced *Bew-lee*) 6 miles (10km) beyond, **Buckler's Hard** was famous for shipbuilding from the mid-18th century. Many of Nelson's warships took to the water here, launched between the two rows of shipwrights' cottages. At the end of

The ruins of Corfe Castle. In the English Civil War, Parliamentary forces laid siege to the castle unsuccessfully in 1643 but captured it in 1646, using explosives to destroy its effectiveness.

BELOW: battle re-enactment at Corfe Castle.

The New Forest is a great place to holiday with children. In addition to campsites galore and ponies wandering free, it's also home to Peppa Pig World (tel: 023-8081 4442; www.peppapig world.com; Apr–Oct 10am–5.30pm with exceptions; charge) at Paultons Park. Rides, playzones and a life-sized Peppa and George from the popular pre-school cartoon make this hog heaven for toddlers. Take swimming costumes and change of clothes for the muddy puddles and wet-play area.

BELOW: riding in the New Forest.

the Napoleonic wars it all came to an abrupt end, but the **Maritime Museum** (daily Mar–June and Sept–Oct 10am–5pm, July–Aug 10am–5.30pm, Nov–Feb 10am–4.30pm; charge) captures the flavour of the past.

In **Beaulieu** ⓮ itself, the church is unique: the monks' dining room was transformed into a pulpit. Lord Montagu runs **Beaulieu National Motor Museum** (Palace House, Beaulieu; daily late May–Sept 10am–6pm, Oct–late May 10am–5pm; charge), with more than 250 vehicles, plus attractions including World of Top Gear and a James Bond Experience.

Beaulieu is in the heart of the **New Forest National Park** ⓯, which lies behind this coast. To describe this wild, dense 100-sq-mile (260-sq-km) woodland as "new" would seem to support the traditional belief that William the Conqueror had a hand in its creation. But this was always forest; William merely enforced measures to protect his deer. When driving through, remember that wild ponies have priority. Alice Hargreaves (née Lidell), the inspiration for the writer Lewis Car-

roll's Alice, lived in and is buried in **Lyndhurst**, the forest's capital, 8 miles (13km) north of Lymington.

Isle of Wight

From Lymington a regular ferry crosses to the **Isle of Wight** ⓰ in around 30 minutes (tel: 0871-376 1000; www.wight link.co.uk). The 147-sq-mile (380-sq-km) island is shaped like a kite, with the capital, **Newport**, just about where you might attach a string.

Close by is **Carisbrooke Castle** (daily Oct–Mar 10am–4pm, Apr–Sept 10am–5pm; charge), built by Elizabeth I as a defence against the Spanish Armada and remembered chiefly as the prison where Charles I was held before being tried and executed.

Cowes, at the mouth of the Medina River, is the venue in August for Cowes Week (www.aamcowesweek.co.uk), the yachtsman's Ascot.

Osborne House (tel: 0870-333 1181; daily, Apr–Sept 10am–6pm, Oct–Mar 10am–4pm, winter check times; charge) is (very) high Victorian in style – it was Queen Victoria's favourite residence – and is very much as it was

in her lifetime; highlights include the queen's bathing machine. The chalk cliffs of the island shatter spectacularly in the Needles at the eastern end. Tucked behind them is **Alum Bay**, where sands come in all the colours of the rainbow, and are carried away in bottles as souvenirs. The poet John Keats took inspiration from the woods at **Shanklin**, and countless holidaymakers take to Sandown's pier. Pretty bays, thatched villages, roses and honeysuckle – England in miniature.

Southampton and Portsmouth

One way to return from Cowes is up the long arm of Southampton Water to **Southampton ⑰**. The armies that won the battles of Crécy and Agincourt embarked from here, the tiny *Mayflower* sailed for America from here and many ocean liners have followed since.

Ferries also cross the Solent from the Isle of Wight to "Pompey", the important naval base of **Portsmouth ⑱**. This, too, was heavily bombed in the war, but the naval tradition could never be destroyed. The Royal Navy Museum is here, at the **Historic Dockyard** (daily Apr–Oct 10am–6pm, Nov–Mar 10am–5.30pm, last entry 90 mins before closing; charge), but the most popular attraction here is Admiral Lord Nelson's flagship *Victory*, on which he died at the Battle of Trafalgar in 1805, and the hulk of the *Mary Rose* (currently withdrawn from public view for restoration and set to reopen within her own museum on site in 2012; tel: 02392-728 060 or see www.historicdockyard.co.uk), Henry VIII's "favourite warship", dredged up from the Solent in 1982.

Soaring above the harbour, the 560ft (170-meter) **Spinnaker Tower** (Sept–July daily 10am–6pm, Aug Fri–Sun 10am–6pm, Sun until 7pm; charge) has great views and displays covering the area's history.

Portsmouth is also notable as the birthplace of Charles Dickens – at 393 Old Commercial Road you can visit the house in which he was born, now the **Charles Dickens Birthplace Museum** (Apr–Sept daily 10am–5.30pm; charge), which is laid out in the style of the time and displays memorabilia connected with the writer. ❑

HMS Victory, Lord Nelson's flagship, on show in Portsmouth.

RESTAURANTS AND PUBS

Restaurants

Beaulieu

Montagu Arms Hotel
Palace Lane
Tel: 01590-612 324 www.montaguarmshotel.co.uk £££
Chef Matthew Tomkinson's Michelin-starred restaurant at this opulently furnished 17th-century country-house hotel serves superb, innovative English food.

Brockenhurst

Simply at Whitley Ridge
Beaulieu Road
Tel: 01590-622 354
www.whitleyridge.co.uk £–££
It is all about first-rate, seasonal, local food served in relaxed surroundings at this historic country-house hotel.

Hordle, nr Lymington
The Mill at Gordleton
Silver Street
Tel: 01590-682 219 www.themillatgordleton.co.uk ££
Good-value home cooking; seasonal, local ingredients; a good wine list; and an attractive riverside location are the draws at this 400-year-old mill-cum-hotel.

Southampton
P.O.S.H.
1 Queensway

Prices for a three-course dinner per person with a half-bottle of house wine:
£ = under £25
££ = £25–50
£££ = £50–100
££££ = over £100

Tel: 023-8022 6377
www.posh-restaurant.com £
This Indian restaurant is decked out as an ocean liner, hence the "Port Out, Starboard Home" reference.

Stuckton
The Three Lions
Stuckton Road
Tel: 01425-652 489
www.thethreelionsrestaurant.co.uk ££–£££
Michelin-starred chef/owner Mike Womersley cooks technically outstanding modern British/French food.

Winchester
Hotel du Vin & Bistro
14 Southgate Street
Tel: 01962-841 414
www.hotelduvin.com ££

This, the original Hotel du Vin, offers an attractive menu of well-prepared modern British and French food, using local produce where possible.

Pubs

In Brockenhurst, try the unpretentious **Foresters Arms** on Brookley Road. Portsmouth has the **Hole in the Wall** on Great Southsea Street, with a remarkable range of real ale and simple food, and the landmark, waterfront **Still & West Country House** on Bath Square (with a beer garden and fine harbour views). In Southampton, Bugle Street's historic **Duke of Wellington** opened in 1494.

THE WEST COUNTRY

Lying between the Bristol and English channels,
the West Country comprises Somerset, Devon and
Cornwall: rural counties heavily influenced by the
sea but with plenty to draw the visitor inland also

The extreme southwest of England, also known to as the West Country, transcends its reputation as Britain's most popular holiday destination. It is an area steeped in legend – the land of King Arthur, Camelot and the Holy Grail; the land of Jack the Giant Killer and the myth of an ancient Druid who gave weary travellers sips of water from a golden cup. History here takes on a romantic quality, with facts obscured by time, and fictions embellished with tales of piracy, smuggling and shipwrecks.

An island mentality

West Country people have always considered themselves special, celebrating their Celtic origins and taking pride in their self-reliance. There's a certain island mentality here – in fact Cornwall itself is almost an island: the River Tamar flows along all but 5 miles (8km) of the Devon border. Old traditions flourish, like the Helston Furry Dance in early May when people fill the town with flowers and dance in the streets.

Historically, the Southwest has been cut off from the mainstream of British culture by both geography and choice. The peninsula was settled by hard-working Celts from Brittany who scraped a living off the essentials of the land. They dug tin and copper, grazed

their sheep and cattle on windswept moors, and braved treacherous currents to take fish from the sea.

The tip of the peninsula, Land's End, is 290 miles (465km) from London. The main artery into the region is the M5, which comes down from Birmingham, meeting the M4 from London at Bristol, and continuing down to Exeter. On a good day the 175-mile (282km) drive from London to Somerset will take 3 hours, although traffic jams frequently cause delays. Tourist routes are well signposted, and walkers can make the

Main attractions
BRISTOL
ROMAN BATHS, BATH
WELLS CATHEDRAL
EXMOOR NATIONAL PARK
LAND'S END
PENZANCE
THE EDEN PROJECT
PLYMOUTH
DARTMOOR NATIONAL PARK
EXETER

PRECEDING PAGES: Castle Combe.
LEFT: Somerset from Glastonbury Tor.
RIGHT: Fowey, Cornwall, is a sailing centre.

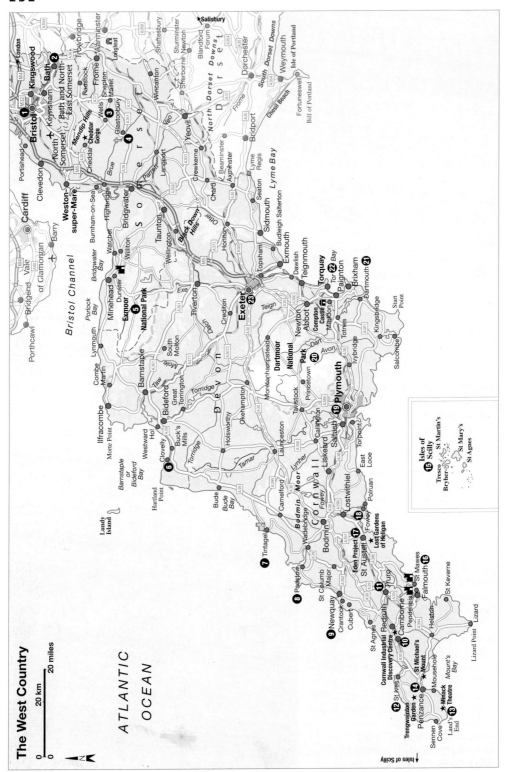

The West Country

most of the 500-mile (800km) coastal footpath that extends from Minehead in Somerset to Poole in Dorset.

The region is served by train from Paddington station in London.

Bristol

One gateway to the region is the old Atlantic port of **Bristol ❶**. John Cabot set off for Newfoundland from here in 1497; later on it was a portal to the British Empire. The excellent **British Empire and Commonwealth Museum** (daily 10am–5pm; charge), occupying Old Bristol Station, charts Britain's colonial expansion from 1500 until 1914.

Other attractions have flowered around the redeveloped docks, including the contemporary arts venue, the **Arnolfini Gallery** (tel: 0117-917 2300; www.arnolfini.org.uk; Tue–Sun 11am–6pm; free) and **At-Bristol** (tel: 0845-345 1235; www.at-bristol.org.uk; daily 10am–5pm, Sat–Sun until 6pm; charge), a complex of interactive science museums geared to children. Britain's most famous engineer, Isambard Kingdom Brunel (1806–59), was very active in Bristol, designing the world's first ocean-going propeller ship, **SS Great Britain**, which can be visited in its original dock near the **Maritime Heritage Centre** (daily 10am–4.30pm, Apr–Oct until 5.30pm; charge). Brunel was also responsible for the **Clifton Suspension Bridge**, which spans the Avon gorge at Clifton village.

Bath

Another jumping-off point for the West Country is the celebrated spa town of **Bath ❷**, 13 miles (21km) southeast of Bristol. King Offa founded **Bath Abbey** some 200 years before King Edgar was crowned King of All England there in 973. But the baths, which had been enjoyed by the Romans, were forgotten until the 18th century, when bathing became fashionable.

The city owes its good looks to Bath stone and the genius of two men, the elder and younger John Wood, who in the 18th century gave its streets, squares

and crescents an impressive harmony. Bath's architectural heritage has been wonderfully preserved with architectural masterpieces including Robert Adam's **Pulteney Bridge**, which has shops on it like the old Ponte Vecchio in Florence, and, in the Upper Town, the **Royal Crescent**, **The Circus**, the **Assembly Rooms** (daily 10.30am–5pm, Mar–Oct until 6pm; charge) and **Queen Square**.

But the steamy core of it all is the **Roman Baths** (www.romanbaths.co.uk; daily Mar–Oct 9am–5pm, July–Aug until 9pm, Nov–Feb 9.30am–4.30pm; charge), at basement level to the modern city, and its adjoining **Pump Room**, which became the hub of fashionable society in the the 18th century.

West of the Roman Baths lies the luxurious **Thermae** spa complex (tel: 0844-888 0844; www.thermaebathspa.com; charge), created from a cluster of historic baths at the top of Bath Street. Five minutes from here, at 40 Gay Street, Bath's most famous resident is celebrated at the **Jane Austen Centre** (tel: 01225-443 000; www.janeausten.co.uk; Apr–Oct daily 9.45am–5.30pm,

The crowning glory of the Thermae spa complex in Bath is its open-air rooftop pool. Submerged in the hot mineral waters, you can take in beautiful views of the Abbey and the surrounding countryside. The views are particularly evocative at twilight and after dark.

BELOW: Bath Abbey.

South of Cheddar along the A371 is the Ebbor Gorge. Formed 270 million years ago, this is the most beautiful gorge of the Mendips, a lush mix of elm, oak and ash trees, mosses, fungi and ferns. Caves here contain the remains of Stone Age pots, axes and reindeer.

BELOW: Glastonbury Tor is the mythical home of Gwyn ap Nudd, the Lord of the Underworld and King of the Fairies.

July–Aug Thur–Sat until 7pm, Nov–Mar Sun–Fri 11am–4.30pm, Sat 9.45am–5.30pm; charge), which documents the novelist's links with the city.

Americans can feel at home at Claverton Manor, which houses the **American Museum** (tel: 01225-460 503; www.americanmuseum.org; mid-Mar–Oct Tue–Sun 2–5pm with exceptions; charge), high above the Avon valley, 4 miles (6km) south of Bath. The period-furnished rooms and displays of folk art offer an absorbing picture of American domestic life between the 17th and 19th centuries.

Ten miles (16km) notheast of Bath, in the county of Wiltshire, is **Castle Combe**, one of several places claiming to be "the prettiest village in England". It has a good claim.

The Mendip Hills, just east of the coast and south of Bristol, mark an abrupt end to the flat, cultured landscape of the Avon Valley and the start of the wild expanses of the Southwest. Across the crest of the hills runs the **West Mendip Way**, a popular hiking trail that twists from Wells, 20 miles (32km) southwest of Bath, to the Bris-

tol Channel, and offers superb views of the countryside. Much of the natural scenery here is simply breathtaking; **Cheddar Gorge**, 12 miles (20km) northwest of Wells, cuts through the Mendips to the northwest of Wells. In Cheddar village itself you can visit vast caverns carved by a river that now runs underground (daily 10.30am–5pm, July–Aug until 5.30pm; charge).

On the Holy Grail trail

At the southern tip of the Mendips is the city of **Wells** ❸, centred around its **cathedral** (www.wellscathedral.org. uk; daily 7am–6pm, Apr–Sept until 7pm; charge), a massive Gothic shrine started in about 1185 and finished four centuries later. Unlike other English cathedrals, it has two main towers that were built outside the church proper, thus extending the western facade into a massive gallery for 400 individual statues. More than 25 percent of the sculpture has been destroyed (most by rampaging Puritans in the 17th century) but the remaining group is an array of bishops and kings, saints and prophets, angels and apostles. The interior is no less spectacular, especially the "hour-glass" arches at the junction of the nave and transept. These were constructed in the 14th century after the cathedral threatened to collapse under the weight of a new central tower.

Outside the cathedral, the **Vicar's Close** comprises a row of 14th-century buildings that are the only complete medieval street remaining in Britain. The exteriors have changed little from their original design. South of the cathedral, the **Bishop's Palace** (daily Apr–Oct 10.30am–6pm; charge) is outstanding. One of the oldest inhabited houses in England, the palace is home to the Bishop of Bath and Wells (a position famously mocked in Rowan Atkinson's comedy series *Blackadder*). The high wall surrounding it dates from the beginning of the 13th century. Swans glide across the broad moat and, since Victorian times, have been trained to ring a bell for their food. On the

Cathedral Green the **Wells and Mendip Museum** (Easter–Oct Mon–Sat 11am–5pm, Sun 1.30–4pm, Oct–Easter daily 11am–4pm; charge) houses plaster casts of the cathedral statues.

Glastonbury

It's a pity that the abbey at **Glastonbury ❹**, 6 miles (10km) southwest, has not been preserved in the same way, for it was once the richest and most beautiful in England. Little remains of the great complex – a few ruined pillars and walls. But these are an impressive monument to the power of the Roman Catholic church in England before Henry VIII's dissolution of the monasteries.

The origins of the abbey are shrouded in myth. One story claims that St Patrick founded the abbey and that St George killed the famous dragon nearby. The most popular legend centres on Joseph of Arimathea, the man who gave his tomb to Christ. Having sailed to Britain to convert the heathens in AD 60, he thrust his staff into the ground while he rested on Wearyall Hill, where it rooted and flowered, an omen that he should settle and found the abbey. Allegedly, Joseph brought with him the chalice from the Last Supper, the Holy Grail. In the 6th century King Arthur came to Glastonbury in search of the Holy Grail; tradition says he and Guinevere are buried under the abbey floor.

A short walk to the steep, conical hill called **Glastonbury Tor**, which rises up from the flat Somerset plain, is worthwhile for the view from the top, surmounted by the remains of the 15th-century St Michael's Church.

East of Glastonbury lie two of England's finest stately homes. The first is **Longleat** (tel: 01985-844 400; www. longleat.co.uk; mid-Feb–Nov daily 10am–4pm, later during summer, see website for seasonal details; charge), the 16th-century seat of the Marquess of Bath; its grounds are home to a safari park. The second is **Stourhead**, a Palladian mansion famous for its landscaped gardens (*see page 221*).

Exmoor National Park

The boundary between Somerset and Devon falls within the confines of **Exmoor National Park ❺**, 265 sq miles (690 sq km) evocatively depicted in Richard Doddridge Blackmore's classic novel, *Lorna Doone* (1869), the story of a 17th-century family of outlaws. The landscape of the park, dotted with pretty villages, ranges from windswept ridges covered with bracken and heather to forested ravines carved out by whitewater streams.

The undulating **Somerset and Devon Coast Path**, stretching more than 30 miles (48km) along the shore, north of the A39, is the most fascinating of Exmoor's many hiking trails. Hugging tightly to cliffs and coves, it offers splendid views of the Bristol Channel and the far-off Atlantic.

Porlock Bay, 6 miles (10km) west of Minehead, is good for birdwatching. Just east of Minehead, the village of Dunster has had a fortress since Saxon times, but the present castle dates from the 13th century. Most of the original structure was destroyed after Charles I's execution in 1649.

Nowadays, the name Glastonbury is synonymous with the outdoor music festival (www.glastonbury festivals.co.uk) held at Worthy Farm, east of the town itself, over the last weekend in June (almost every year). The first festival in 1970 had 1,500 attendees; in 2010, some 135,000 people came. Today, "Glasto" injects a staggering £100 million a year into the British economy.

BELOW: the ruins of Glastonbury Abbey, where the legendary King Arthur is said to have been buried.

*Coastal path leading
to the ruins of
Tintagel Castle.*

*Exmoor ponies, direct
descendants of the
prehistoric horse, are
the most ubiquitous
animals on the moor,
but there are also red
deer, sheep and
Devon Red cattle.*

BELOW:
Porlock Weir.

The graceful turrets and towers are 19th-century. The village itself is a perfect replica of feudal times, largely because one family, the Luttrells, owned it for 600 years until 1950.

On the northwest tip of the peninsula, **Morte Pointe** (not safe for swimming), northwest of **Barnstaple**, is also good for birdwatching.

King Arthur's country

Where Devon turns to Cornwall, a chain of fishing villages and hidden beauties lies beside the A39 running down to Tintagel. To the west along the Devon coast, **Westward Ho!**, near Bideford, is a popular seaside resort named after the novel by Charles Kingsley (1819–75); it has 3 miles (5km) of sandy beach. Next is the village of **Clovelly** ❻, where cars are banned, and donkeys (with their own website: www.clovellydonkeys.co.uk) carry visitors' luggage. The steep cobbled street descends 400ft (120 metres) to the sea in a series of steps. A romantic 2-mile

(3km) walk west from the harbour leads to a magnificent range of cliffs. Nearby **Buck's Mills** is an unspoiled village of thatched cottages.

Heading south into Cornwall, the rolling waves at **Bude** have long attracted surfers, while **Summerleaze Beach**, a sheltered, sandy expanse north of the River Neet, is better for swimmers.

The legend of King Arthur comes alive at **Tintagel Castle** ❼ (www. english-heritage.org.uk; daily Apr–Sept 10am–6pm, Oct 10am–5pm; charge), a wild and romantic spot on the north Cornwall coast about 18 miles (29km) south of Bude. Tradition claims Arthur was born or came ashore at Tintagel, where he built a castle for his Knights of the Round Table and Guinevere. All that's left is the ruins of a 6th-century Celtic monastery and a 12th-century bastion, most of it swept away by the sea.

In the town, the picture-perfect 14th-century **Old Post Office** on Fore Street is owned by the National Trust (mid–Feb–end Feb, mid-Mar–end Mar and Oct–early Nov 11am–4pm, Apr–Sept 10.30am–5.30pm; charge).

Padstow and Newquay

Some 20 miles (32km) south on the A39 and then west along the A389 is **Padstow** ❽, the only safe harbour in north Cornwall and an important port for more than 1,000 years. The town is named after St Petroc, a Celtic missionary who landed here in the 6th century to convert the heathen Cornish. Celebrity chef Rick Stein's restaurants and shops are the reason many foodies come here. Historic sights include **Prideaux Place** (tel: 01841-532 411; www.prideaux place.co.uk; Sun–Thur, house: 1.30–4pm, grounds: 12.30–5pm, with exceptions so check before visiting; charge), a richly furnished Elizabethan manor in delightful grounds that overlook the town.

Clustered around the harbour are the historic **Abbey House**, **St Petroc Church**, the **Harbour Master's Office** and **Raleigh Cottage**, where Sir Walter collected port dues as the Royal Warden of Cornwall. Every May Day, the town fills up when a bizarre Hobby Horse festival ("Obby Oss" day) creates a carnival atmosphere.

The next major coastal town heading south is **Newquay** ❾, Cornwall's Malibu – where surfers cruise the waves. It was famous in the 18th and 19th centuries as a pilchard port. It is also the setting for **Newquay Zoo** (daily Apr–Sept 9.30am–6pm, Oct–Mar 10am–5pm; charge) in Trenance Gardens.

Cornish tin-mining legacy

South of Newquay is an ancient Norman church at **Crantock**. Crantock Beach is lovely, too. Further south again is **Cubert**, which has a church tower shaped like a bishop's mitre. The interior of the church has some fine Norman and 14th-century carvings.

The corridor between the neighbouring towns of Redruth and **Camborne** ❿, 18 miles (29km) southwest and inland, was the fulcrum of Cornish tin mining for more than 200 years. Little active mining remains, but you can get some idea of what tin meant to the economy by visiting the **Cornwall Industrial Discovery Centre** (Apr–Oct Sun–Fri 11am–5pm; charge) at Pool, just outside Camborne. Outside Camborne Library stands a statue of local boy Richard Trevithick, the "Father of the Locomotive", who manu-

King Arthur's presence is strong at Tintagel, though it isn't backed by archaeological evidence. According to medieval accounts, he led the defence of Britain against the Saxon invaders in the early 6th century, but scholars can't agree on whether he really existed. The tales were given a boost in T.H. White's 1958 novel The Once and Future King *and, less reverentially, in* Monty Python and the Holy Grail.

BELOW: Clovelly, owned and preserved by an estate company.

Tate St Ives, the western outpost of the Tate group of art galleries.

factured the first high-pressure steam engine in 1797.

Truro ⓫, 10 miles (16km) east, is the cathedral city of Cornwall and the unofficial capital. In the 18th century it was both a centre for tin smelting and a society haunt that rivalled Bath. **Lemon Street**, laid out around 1795, features fine Georgian architecture. The **Royal Cornwall Museum** (www. royalcornwallmuseum.org.uk; Mon–Sat 10am–5pm; charge) has displays of antiquities as well as local artefacts.

Out to the coast again on the A390, St Agnes Beacon, outside the village of **St Agnes**, offers a view of 32 church towers and 23 miles (40km) of coast from 628ft (190 metres) above. Much of the surrounding area was once mining land. Today the scars of industry give the area a melancholy beauty.

BELOW LEFT: garden sculpture at the Barbara Hepworth Museum. **BELOW RIGHT:** surfer at St Agnes.

St Ives

One of the last ports of call on this north coast is **St Ives ⓬**, a classic Cornish fishing town popular with artists since the end of the 19th century. Among them was the sculptor Barbara Hepworth (1903–75), who lived and worked here from 1949 until her death. Her home is now the **Barbara Hepworth Museum** (Mar–Oct daily 10am–5.20pm, Nov–Feb Tue–Sun 10am–4.20pm; charge). The works of many other local artists from St Ives' heyday – including Ben Nicholson, Peter Lanyon and Naum Gabo – form a small permanent exhibition, complemented by temporary exhibitions, at **Tate St Ives** (www.tate.org.uk; Mar–Oct daily 10am–5.20pm, Nov–Feb Tue–Sun 10am–4.20pm; charge), which occupies a stunning building by Porthmeor Beach.

Land's End

Penwith is the name given to the barren and windswept piece of land that juts out into the Atlantic at the end of Cornwall. This is a land of bleak hills and wide open spaces, surrounded by

deep blue sea and sometimes thick Atlantic fog. The **Cornwall Coastal Path** traces the entire shore of Penwith, passing submerged reefs and wave-eroded cliffs, sheltered coves and weird-shaped rocks. **Land's End** ⓭, the most westerly point on mainland Britain, is an eerie but beautiful place almost constantly swept by North Atlantic storms and swirling underwater currents. The **Land's End Centre** (daily 10am–dusk; charge) has a discovery trail and exhibitions.

At **Sennen Cove** there's a tiny inn and a Royal Naval Coastguard station constantly on alert for a shipwreck or yachting disaster. Tin mines at **Geevor** (Apr–Oct Sun–Fri 9am–5pm, Nov–Mar 9am–4pm; charge) have tunnels that extend 250 fathoms below the sea floor. There's a mining museum with tours of the treatment plant, magnetic separators and tunnels.

Travelling east from the headland, Porthcurno is home to the open-air **Minack Theatre** (tel: 01736-810 181; www.minack.com), which is spectacularly set carved into the cliffs overlooking the sea. During the summer season (June–Sept) productions include everything from Shakespeare to musicals and children's shows.

Further on, two picturesque villages sit on the south shore of Penwith. **Mousehole** (pronounced *mowzel*) is as tiny as the name suggests, a cluster of granite cottages and half-timbered pubs. The village is named after an old smugglers' cave called the Mouse Hole. Nearby, Newlyn has the **Newlyn Gallery** (Mon–Sat 10am–5pm; donation), featuring work by regional artists.

Penzance

Penzance ⓮ has long been the premier town of western Cornwall thanks to its commanding site on **Mount's Bay**. It has served a number of important functions over the centuries: tin-shipping port for the Roman Empire and medieval Europe, passenger terminal for emigrants bound for the New World and, most recently, a popular holiday resort. Within the town lies the **Barbican**, an 18th-century fish market transformed

Mousehole has a safe beach, popular with families.

BELOW: Land's End, once a bleak headland, has attracted theme-park developers.

Pendennis Castle.

BELOW: St Michael's Mount resembles Mont St Michel in Normandy because French Benedictine monks were involved in both.

into a lively arts and crafts centre. The **Western Promenade** is lined with 18th- and 19th-century Regency town houses, but the heart of Penzance lies at the junction of Chapel Street and Market Jew Street, an ancient cobble-stoned quarter that retains much of the flavour of its seafaring past. There are a number of historic buildings, such as the 18th-century **Union Hotel** and the **Penlee House Gallery and Museum** (Mon–Sat Easter–Sept 10am–5pm, Oct–Easter 10.30am–4.30pm; charge), which displays works by artists of the Newlyn School. The **Morrab Gardens** cultivate a variety of exotic plants, but even better is the National Trust's **Trengwainton Garden** (www.national-trust.org.uk; mid-Feb–Oct Sun–Thur 10.30am–5pm; charge), 2 miles (3km) inland at Madron.

Islands

Offshore, 28 miles (45km) west of Land's End, are the **Isles of Scilly** (pronounced "silly") ⑮, which can be reached by ferry or helicopter from Penzance. Phoenician traders landed here before the birth of Christ in search of tin, copper and other metals. Five of the islands are inhabited and all but one, Tresco, is part of the Duchy of Cornwall, which belongs to the Prince of Wales.

Highlights on Tresco include the **Abbey Gardens** (daily 10am–4pm; charge), while the island of St Mary's is home to the **Isles of Scilly Museum** (www.iosmuseum.org; Easter–Sept Mon–Fri 10am–4.30pm, Sat 10am–noon, Oct–Easter Mon–Sat 10am–noon; charge).

Sitting in Mount's Bay is **St Michael's Mount** (www.stmichaelsmount.co.uk; Apr–Oct Sun–Fri 10.30am–5pm; charge). At low tide you can reach the island along a sandy causeway; at other times you go by ferry. According to legend, a fisherman saw St Michael standing on the granite outcrop, so a Benedictine priory was founded here in 1140. It became a grand private house in the 17th century.

Falmouth

To the east, beyond the treacherous Lizard Point and the Helford River, lies the port of **Falmouth** ⑯. A fishing centre for more than 300 years, it is one of Cornwall's most interesting towns. It was a tiny hamlet until 1699, when it became the most westerly Mail Packet station in England. Ships from America, the West Indies and the Mediterranean called here to transfer their mail to stagecoaches bound for London.

Pendennis Castle (www.english-heritage.org.uk; Apr–June 10am–5pm, July–Aug 10am–6pm, Oct 10am–4pm; charge) guarded the town for three centuries against Spanish and French raids and against Cromwell's troops during a 23-week siege in the Civil War; you can learn more about this history at the **National Maritime Museum** (www.nmmc.co.uk; daily 10am–5pm; charge) on the town's redeveloped Discovery Quay. The museum is excellent for children. Also family-friendly is the **Falmouth Art Gallery** (Mon–Sat 10am–5pm; free),

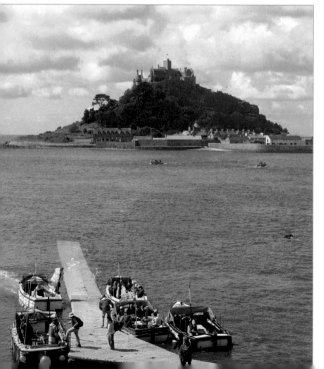

located in municipal buildings in the main square.

The Eden Project

Off the A390, at Bodelva, east of St Austell, is Cornwall's biggest attraction, the **Eden Project** ⓱ (tel: 01726-811 911; www.edenproject.com; Apr–Oct daily 9.30am–6pm, Nov–Mar 9.30am–3pm; charge). Built in a disused clay pit, this ambitious site consists of huge covered conservatories called biomes – a humid tropical one and a warm temperate zone – plus a large outdoor landscaped area, all mimicking the planet's diverse climates. There are numerous environmentally based special exhibitions, plus educational projects. The place gets very crowded, and only groups can book in advance, so be prepared for queues at busy times.

Fowey (pronounced "foy") ⓲, on the A3082 off the A390, is a pretty little town, its ancient centre still intact, with a sheltered, deep-water working port that also offers a snug harbour for pleasure craft and fishing boats. **St Catherine's Castle** (built by Henry VIII), the 18th-century Town Hall and the 14th-century **Toll Bar House** can all be visited.

The writer Daphne Du Maurier loved the town and set several of her novels in Cornwall; for more information on her, visit **the Fowey Tourist Information and Du Maurier Literary Centre** at 5 South Street (tel: 01726-833 616; www.fowey.co.uk). You can also take the very regular ferry across the harbour to the picturesque town of **Polruan**.

Plymouth

Plymouth ⓳, on the Devon–Cornwall border, is the city from which Drake, Raleigh and the Pilgrim Fathers embarked on their various adventures. It is still a thriving port, industrial centre, market town and cultural mecca, the largest city west of Bristol.

Francis Drake sailed from the port in 1577 on his renowned global circumnavigation, and upon his return the citizens of Plymouth elected him as mayor. The Pilgrims sailed from Plymouth's West Pier in 1620 aboard the fragile *Mayflower* to the New World. (They had originally launched

Detail from the Royal Navy war memorial at Plymouth Hoe containing the names of 23,000 naval personnel who died in two world wars.

BELOW: the Eden Project, built in a disused china clay pit, contains the world's biggest greenhouse.

It's illegal to feed the 5,000 ponies that roam Dartmoor. They are related to prehistoric horses that have lived on this land for millions of years. The Galloway and Highland cattle and black-faced sheep are later imports.

BELOW: Haytor Rocks, Dartmoor.

from Southampton, but bad weather damaged their ship and they called at Plymouth for repairs.)

On the Hoe, the open space above the harbour, is **Smeaton's Tower**, a red-and-white-striped lighthouse that offers excellent views of the Sound. Nearby is the 17th-century **Royal Citadel** (www.english-heritage.org.uk; May–Sept Tue, Thur, tours at 2.30pm; charge), and down by the port is the cobblestoned quarter known as the Barbican, with its pubs, cafés and art galleries. On the other side of the harbour is the **National Marine Aquarium** (www.national-aquarium.co.uk; daily Apr–Oct 10am–6pm, Nov–Mar 10am–5pm; charge).

Dartmoor

Directly inland from Plymouth is **Dartmoor National Park ⑳**, 365 sq miles (915 sqkm) of wild forest and moorland that remain very much as it has been for 1,000 years. Beneath all that heather and bracken is a solid core of stone, one of five granite masses that form the geological heart of the West Country. There are hun-

dreds of miles of public footpaths and hiking trails across the moor, walked by an estimated 8 million people each year.

Dartmouth ㉑, directly east of Plymouth, is yet another of the Southwest's famous ports. The town retains much of its seafaring heritage in the form of **Britannia Royal Naval College**, which has trained the likes of Prince Charles and the Duke of Edinburgh for the Royal Navy. Dartmouth Harbour is lined with 16th-century merchants' houses and half-timbered taverns. The historic **Pannier Market** sells fruit and vegetables on Friday mornings; the rest of the week there are art and craft stalls.

A range of boat cruises is available from the small harbour, up the River Dart to Totnes, Kingswear and Greenway (Agatha Christie's family home) or up the coast to Torquay. One of the main operators is River Link (tel: 01803-555 872; www.riverlink.co.uk).

The English Riviera

Just a stone's throw up the coast lies **Torbay ㉒**, a conurbation of Torquay, Paignton and Brixham which is

Water Sports

Spectacular scenery, a long coastline and benevolent weather make water sports a major attraction to visitors to the Southwest. You can try your hand at sailing in Portscatho, Fowey or Exeter, sail a tall ship to the Isles of Scilly (tel: 01872-580 022; www.classic-sailing.co.uk), kayak up Exeter Ship Canal or surf the Atlantic's waves. Surfing hotspots include Bude and Newquay, and the season runs from autumn to spring, when the surf can consistently hit between 4 and 12ft (1.2–3.7 metres). The best time for surfing is usually late September to mid-November, when mild air and water temperatures combine with regular swells and quieter beaches; tides can make the sea rise and fall up to 15ft (4.6 metres), making conditions variable and challenging. Swells in summer are smaller, averaging 1–4ft (0.3–1.2 metres).

known as the English Riviera because of its mild climate and long beaches. **Brixham** alone maintains something of its fishing-village ambience with a replica of the *Golden Hinde*, Sir Francis Drake's ship that circumnavigated the globe in 1577, moored in its sheltered harbour (www.goldenhind.co.uk; daily 10am–4pm; charge).

Three miles (5km) on is **Marldon**, with a lovely old church, and 1 mile further still is the National Trust's **Compton Castle** (Apr–Oct Mon, Wed and Thur 10.30am–4.30pm; charge). This manor house, still the seat of the Gilbert family, was built in 1340. Sir Humphrey Gilbert (1539–83) founded Newfoundland, the first British colony in North America, and was the half-brother of Sir Walter Raleigh.

Exeter

North of Torquay is **Exeter** ㉓, a lively university and cathedral city. The immense **cathedral** (www.exeter-cathedral.org.uk; Mon–Sat 9am–4.45pm; charge) dominating the skyline was built from the 11th to 14th centuries in Norman Gothic style and is the city's big draw. The exterior displays a remarkable collection of stone statues, the largest surviving group of 14th-century sculpture in England. The lavish interior is dominated by a striking vaulted ceiling, carved to resemble the radiating branches of a palm tree. Among the church's treasures are the 14th-century Bishop's Throne and the *Exeter Book of Old English Verse*, compiled between AD 950 and 1000.

On nearby Queen Street is the **Royal Albert Memorial Museum and Art Gallery** (tel: 01392-665 858; www.ram museum.org.uk; currently closed, due to reopen in late 2011). Just off Queen Street lies the **Phoenix** arts and media centre (www.exeterphoenix.org.uk).

The old, cobbled **Quayside** houses shops, cafés and a visitor centre in former warehouses, and there are pretty canalside walks. Bikes and canoes can be hired (tel: 01392-424 241; www.saddle paddle.co.uk), or take a cruise (contact the visitor centre; tel: 01392-271 611) down to the pretty village of **Topsham**, which has a small museum of local maritime history and wildlife (Apr–Oct Mon, Wed, Sat–Sun 2–5pm; free).   ❏

Exeter was founded as a fortress by the Romans in around AD 50–55. In medieval times the city prospered through farming and the wool trade, and it hallmarked its own silver until the early 19th century. Its growth as a trading centre was hampered by its position on the River Exe: as ships grew larger, the river's facilities became inadequate.

BELOW: a replica of Sir Francis Drake's ship in Brixham.

RESTAURANTS AND PUBS

Restaurants

Prices for a three-course dinner per person with a half-bottle of house wine:
£ = under £25
££ = £25–50
£££ = £50–100
££££ = over £100

Bath and Around

The Circus
34 Brock Street
Tel: 01225-466 020
www.thecircuscafeand
restaurant.co.uk ££
Family-run café/restaurant serving refined rustic British food between the Circus and the Royal Crescent.

The Dower House
16 Royal Crescent
Tel: 01225-823 333
www.royalcrescent.co.uk

£££
Within the walled gardens of the Royal Crescent Hotel, this place offers fine food in an elegant setting.

The Hole in the Wall
16 George Street
Tel: 01225-425 242
ww.theholeinthewall.co.uk
£££
Those in the know head for this long-established, upmarket restaurant that offers highly imaginative, finely presented modern British cuisine, using the best seasonal produce.

The Moon and Sixpence
27 Milsom Place
Tel: 01225-320 088
www.moonandsixpence.co.
uk ££
Modern British food, including old favourites

with an imaginative twist, plus a few international dishes to boot are served in an attractive location.

The Olive Tree
Queensberry Hotel,
4–7 Russel Street
Tel: 01225-447 928
www.thequeensberry.co.uk
£££
The restaurant within the chic Queensberry boutique hotel is a foodie favourite, serving tip-top modern British cooking with French, Italian and Spanish influences.

The Park
Lucknam Park, Colerne
Tel: 01225-742 777
www.lucknampark.co.uk
£££
Michelin-starred British cuisine with a serious, expensive wine list is served in the spacious, chandelier-lit dining room of this Georgian manor, some 6 miles (9.5km) from Bath.

Bristol

Bell's Diner
1–3 York Road, Montpelier
Tel: 0117-924 0357
www.bellsdiner.com ££
Bell's marries modern cooking with traditional craft and has won awards over the years for its innovative modern European food. It's a short drive out of the centre, in the bohemian Montpelier district, but worth the journey.

Bordeaux Quay
V-Shed, Canons Way
Tel: 0117-943 1200
www.bordeaux-quay.co.uk
££
In the vanguard for being eco-friendly and using

locally sourced, organic ingredients, this restaurant serves fresh, flavoursome Mediterranean-style dishes. The harbourside complex is also home to a bakery, brasserie and deli.

Culinaria
1 Chandos Road
Tel: 0117-973 7999
www.culinariabristol.co.uk
££
Bistro-style place offers comfort food with the emphasis on top-quality seasonal ingredients. You can eat in or take away.

Chagford, Dartmoor

22 Mill Street
Tel: 01647-432 244
www.22millst.com ££
This restaurant in the foothills of Dartmoor National Park, Devon, serves stylishly presented modern European food. You can also stay in one of three bedrooms.

Gidleigh Park
Tel: 01647-432 367
www.gidleigh.com ££££
Michael Caines' two-Michelin-starred restaurant at this country house hotel has won plenty of accolades. The exquisitely presented cuisine is innovative traditional with a classical French influence and uses the absolute best seasonal produce. Reservations essential.

Exeter

Abode Exeter
Cathedral Yard
Tel: 01392-223 638 ££££
Culinary star Michael Caines' restaurant in his home town of Exeter is beautifully situated on the green by the cathe-

dral. Great-value lunch and early dining (6–7pm) menus. Book ahead.

Q
28 Fore Street
Tel: 01726-833 302
www.theoldquayhouse.com
££
Set in the Old Quay House hotel, right on the waterfront, Q offers imaginative dishes, classy decor and superb estuary views.

11 The Quay
11 The Quay
Tel: 01271-868 090
www.11thequay.co.uk
££–£££
Damien Hirst's restaurant and art gallery aims to do for Ilfracombe what Rick Stein did for Padstow. The imaginative menu is strong on local seafood and West Country cheeses, as well as international dishes. Reserve.

The Angel Inn
Upton Scudamore
Tel: 01985-213 225
www.theangelinn.co.uk **££**
This country inn, about 5 miles (8km) from Longleat on the edge of Salisbury Plain, has a relaxed feel with a walled garden and a terrace for alfresco dining. The cooking is creative modern British.

The Moody Goose
The Old Priory Hotel, Church Square
Tel: 01761-416 784
www.moodygoose.co.uk **£££**
Set in a medieval priory near Bath, this restaurant offers exquisite modern British cuisine prepared with locally-sourced poultry, meat and game.

St Petroc's Bistro
4 New Street
Tel: 01841-532 700
www.rickstein.com **££–£££**
Reasonably priced option for trying Rick Stein's cutting-edge fish cuisine, but you still need to book.

The Seafood Restaurant
Riverside
Tel: 01841-532 700
www.rickstein.com **££££**
The crowing glory of west-country cuisine is fish and seafood, as championed by celebrity chef Rick Stein. Many people come to Padstow for his restaurants alone, which are among the best for seafood in Britain. His fine-dining option offers simple dishes using only the freshest ingredients cooked with minimum fuss. Booking essential.

Barbican Kitchen
Black Friars Distillery,
60 Southside Street, Plymouth
Tel: 01752-604 448
www.barbicankitchen.com
£–££
This brasserie serves food that you really want to get your teeth into, like Devon red beef burgers and smoked Dartmouth haddock. Ideal for lunch.

Alba
Wharf Road
Tel: 01736-797 222
www.thealbarestaurant.com
££
This place combines minimalist decor and harbour views from a refurbished lighthouse right on the waterfront. The set menus feature lots of fish, but there's meat too and good vegetarian

options. Strong on seasonal, local produce.

Alfresco
Wharf Road
Tel: 01736-793 737
www.stivesharbour.com **££**
Alfresco is set in a trendy harbourside spot and cooks up an inventive Mediterranean menu, with the emphasis on stylish fish dishes.

One-Eyed Cat
116 Kenwyn Street
Tel: 01872-222 122
www.oneeyedcat.co.uk **££**
The combination of an eye-popping location and some neatly executed dishes with the emphasis on seafood and fresh Australasian flavours makes this a top choice in Truro.

Pubs

In Bath, the **Old Green Tree** on Green Street is an appealing old pub but can get crowded. The **Coeur de Lion**, in North-

umberland Place off High Street, is even smaller but is charming. The **King William** on St Thomas Street has good beers and fresh food.

In Bristol, a Campaign for Real Ale favourite is the **Cornubia** in two Georgian houses on Temple Street.

In Plymouth, **China House** at Sutton Wharf is a converted warehouse with good ale and good views, while In Torquay, Park Lane's **Hole in the Wall**, near the harbour, is atmospheric and serves real ale in an even older 16th-century building.

Visitors to the quaint Cornish village of Mousehole can stop at the traditional **Ship Inn**.

On the harbour front of St Ives, the **Sloop Inn** traces its history to 1312, and on the water at Fowey, the **King of Prussia** is a family-friendly pub with a nautical theme. The **Ship Inn** on Trafalgar Square serves good meals upstairs.

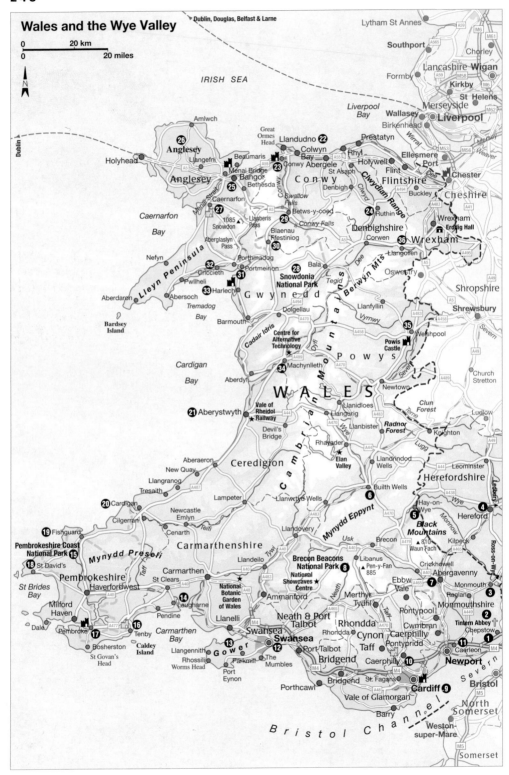

Wales and the Wye Valley

0   20 km
0   20 miles

N

Dublin, Douglas, Belfast & Larne

Lytham St Annes

Southport

Chorley

Lancashire Wigan

Formby

Merseyside
St Helens
Kirkby

IRISH SEA

Dublin

Liverpool Bay

Wallasey
Birkenhead
Wirral

Liverpool

Amlwch

Great
Ormes
Head

Llandudno **22**

Colwyn
Bay

Prestatyn

Ellesmere
Port

Chester

Cheshire

26 Anglesey

Holyhead

Llangefni

Beaumaris

Conwy **23** Abergele

Rhyl

Holywell

Flint

Flintshire

Anglesey

Menai Bridge
Bangor **25**
Bethesda

Conwy

St Asaph

Denbigh

Clwyd

Buckley

A494

Cheshire

*Caernarfon
Bay*

Caernarfon **27**

Swallow
Falls

Betws-y-coed

Conwy Falls

Ruthin **24**

Clwydian Range

Wrexham

Erddig Hall

Wrexham **36**

1085
Snowdon

Llanberis
Pass

29

Denbighshire

Corwen

Llangollen

Shropshire

Nefyn

Aberglaslyn
Pass

Porthmadog

Blaenau
Ffestiniog

30

Bala

Dee

Berwyn Mts

Oswestry

A49

Lleyn Peninsula

32
Criccieth

Portmeirion

28

Snowdonia
National Park

L
Tegid

Llanfyllin

Welshpool

Shrewsbury

Pwllheli

31

Aberdaron

Abersoch

33 Harlech

*Tremadog
Bay*

Dolgellau

A494

Gwynedd

Vyrnwy

A483

Severn

*Bardsey
Island*

Barmouth

Cadair Idris

Centre for
Alternative
Technology

Llanfair

Powis
Castle **35**

Church
Stretton

*Cardigan
Bay*

Aberdyfi

34 Machynlleth

Powys

Newtown

A489

A470

Ludlow

21 Aberystwyth

Vale of
Rheidol
Railway

W A L E S

Llanidloes

Llangurig

Clun
Forest

Terne

Devil's
Bridge

A44

A470

Llanbister

Radnor
Forest

Knighton

Lugg

Leominster

Aberaeron

Rhayader

Llandrindod
Wells

Herefordshire

New Quay

Elan
Valley

Llangranog

Tresaith

Lampeter

Llanwrtyd Wells

Builth Wells

6

Hay-on-
Wye **5**

A44

Leborn

Hereford **4**

20 Cardigan

Cilgerran

Newcastle
Emlyn

Teifi

Cenarth

Llandovery

Mynydd Eppynt

Brecon

Usk

Black
Mountains
810
Waun Fach

Kilpeck

Ross-on-Wye

19 Fishguard

Pembrokeshire Coast
National Park **15**

Carmarthenshire

Llandeilo

A40

Brecon Beacons
National Park **8**

Pen-y-Fan
885

Crickhowell

A40

Abergavenny **7**

Monmouth **3**

18 St David's

*St Brides
Bay*

Mynydd Preseli

Carmarthen

St Clears

National
Botanic
Garden
of Wales

National
Showcaves
Centre

Neath

Merthyr
Tydfil

Ebbw
Vale

A465

Raglan

Monmouthshire

A449

Pembrokeshire

Haverfordwest

14

Laugharne

Pendine

Llanelli

Ammanford

Neath & Port
Talbot

Rhondda

Pontypool

Cwmbran

Tintern Abbey **2**

Chepstow **1**

Milford
Haven

Dale

Pembroke

17

Tenby **16**

*Carmarthen
Bay*

13

Swansea

Swansea **12**

Port Talbot

Cynon
Taff

Caerphilly

Pontypridd

Caerphilly **10**

Caerleon **11**

Newport

Bosherston
St Govan's
Head

Caldey
Island

Llangennith
Rhossili
Worms Head

Gower
Parkmill
Port
Eynon

The
Mumbles

Bridgend

St Fagans

Cardiff **9**

Severn

Bristol

North
Somerset

Porthcawl

Bridgend

Vale of Glamorgan

Barry

Bristol Channel

Weston-
super-Mare

Somerset

M5

THE WYE VALLEY AND SOUTH WALES

Follow the River Wye into Wales from Chepstow, via Cardiff and Swansea and on to the beautiful Pembrokeshire coast. Along the way explore wild countryside, ancient castles and cultural attractions

Traditionally, Wales is a melodic land of green hills and welcoming valleys, of Welsh cakes, crumbling castles, poets and song. It has sweeping sandy beaches and dramatic coves and towns with an old-fashioned, retro appeal that are promoted as a welcome antidote to the frenetic pace of 21st-century, big-city life. Wales is less populous than England, though its accessibility from southern, central and northern parts of the country make it a popular holiday haunt, with Snowdonia in the north a particular magnet for visitors in search of outdoor activities.

The country is little more than 135 miles (216km) long and at one part less than 35 miles (56km) wide. The border runs from the mouth of the Dee in Liverpool Bay in the north to the mouth of the Wye on the Severn estuary in the south. It roughly follows the lines of the dyke built to contain the Celts by Offa, the powerful Anglo-Saxon king of Mercia from 757 to 796 *(see box, page 250)*.

From London and the south of England, use the M4, which skirts Bristol, crosses the Second Severn Crossing and plunges immediately into Wales, following the industrial south coast past Newport, Cardiff and Swansea to the Gower Peninsula and the cliffs and beaches of Pembrokeshire beyond.

Alternatively take the M48, which branches off the M4 just after Bristol and crosses the original Severn Bridge, taking you into Chepstow, gateway to the Wye Valley and the Vale of Usk. A toll is payable when travelling westbound on either Severn bridge (www. severnbridge.co.uk). If you're coming from the Midlands, take the M5 and exit at junction 8 (about halfway between Birmingham and Bristol), where the M50 leads west towards the pretty town of Ross-on-Wye, and meets the A40 from Gloucester, crosses the border at Mon-

Main attractions
TINTERN ABBEY
MONMOUTH
HEREFORD
BRECON BEACONS NATIONAL PARK
CARDIFF
CAERPHILLY CASTLE
SWANSEA
THE GOWER PENINSULA
THE PEMBROKESHIRE COAST

PRECEDING PAGES: Welsh rugby fans at Cardiff's Millennium Stadium.
RIGHT: the original Severn Bridge.

Prince of Wales is a title given to the heir apparent (ie the royal heir who is first in line to the throne by birth). Prior to Prince Charles (who was given the title in July 1958), the last Prince of Wales was Edward, later Edward VIII and then, following his abdication, the Duke of Windsor.

mouth and dives between the Black Mountains and Brecon Beacons before heading back down to the Pembrokeshire coast. Trains to South Wales run from London's Paddington station.

Chepstow

Commanding the mouth of the Wye, where it empties into the River Severn near the suspension bridge, is the small town of **Chepstow ❶**, unremarkable but for its impressively intact Norman fortress, set high on a rock. Two miles (3km) from the centre of Chepstow, heading north towards Monmouth on the A466, you pass **Chepstow Racecourse**, a popular venue for enthusiasts of steeplechasing. For most visitors, however, the true high spot of the Wye Valley is **Tintern Abbey ❷** (Apr–Oct daily 9am–5pm, Nov–Mar Mon–Sat 9.30am–4pm, Sun 11am–4pm; charge), 5 miles (8km) north of Chepstow, the handsomest and most complete of Britain's ruined monasteries. Lauded by Wordsworth and painted by Turner, this ancient abbey occupies an extraordinarily lovely spot by the river, framed by wooded slopes. It was founded by

Cistercian monks in 1131, though the present remains date from the late 13th century. The area around Tintern is superb walking country, with footpaths in all directions.

Monmouth

Some 10 miles (16km) further north on the A466 is **Monmouth ❸**, a market town at the confluence of the Wye and Monnow rivers. Monmouth's most famous son was Henry V, who won the battle of Agincourt and was immortalised by Shakespeare in the eponymous play. He was born in 1387 in Monmouth Castle, which was largely destroyed in the Civil War: a few walls are all that remain. Monmouth also has a **Nelson Museum** (Mar–Oct Mon–Sat 11am–1pm and 2–5pm, Sun 2–5pm, Nov–Feb 11am–1pm and 2–4pm, Sun 2–4pm; free), dedicated to the Admiral, a celebrity in his day, who visited the city.

Seven miles (11km) southwest of Monmouth on the A40 is **Raglan Castle** (Apr–Oct daily 9am–5pm, Nov–Mar Mon–Sat 9.30am–4pm, Sun 11am–4pm; charge). The late-medieval structure, which has an elegant hexagonal moated keep, was besieged during the Civil War, but the remains are impressive. On the other (eastern) side of Monmouth is the **Forest of Dean**, a 40-sq-mile (105-sq-km) former royal hunting ground criss-crossed by trails. The **Dean Heritage Centre** (www.deanheritagecentre.com; daily Mar–Oct 10am–5pm, Nov–Feb 10am–4pm; charge) is sited on the forest's northeast side at Camp Mill.

Just to the north is **Symonds Yat**, a dramatic outcrop 400ft (122 metres) over a loop in the Wye valley. The river twists along to the east of the A40 for another 8 miles (13km) to **Ross-on-Wye**, a pretty town centred on an arcaded 17th-century market hall where there's a market on Thursday and Saturday.

Hereford

Black-and-white, half-timbered Tudor buildings are a speciality of these Welsh

Offa's Dyke

Offa's Dyke, an earthen bank running the length of the England–Wales border, was built at the command of King Offa (AD 757–96) as the first official boundary between England and Wales. Its exact purpose – military or administrative – is uncertain. Compared to Hadrian's Wall, built to keep the Scots at bay, it can hardly be regarded as a serious line of defence. It was not intended to be permanently manned, nor was it a continuous structure.

The dyke ran from Prestatyn on the North Wales coast to Sedbury near Chepstow on the Severn Estuary, a distance of 142 miles (227km). But there were many breaks along the way, especially in densely wooded river valleys. The building of the dyke must, nevertheless, have represented a monumental effort. A deep ditch was dug on the Welsh side. Above this, an earthwork barrier rose up to 20ft (6 metres) high. The overall structure, ditch and earthwork, was in places over 70ft (22 metres) wide.

This 1,200-year-old barrier has vanished along some of its route, but walkers can trace its course on the long-distance **Offa's Dyke Path** (www.offas-dyke.co.uk). Hay-on-Wye, Monmouth and Knighton, 17 miles (28km) west of Ludlow, are good access points.

border towns. Above Ross are **Ledbury**, which has a renowned herring-bone patterned Market House, and **Hereford** ❹, 10 miles (16km) distant, with its **cathedral** (www.herefordcathedral. org; Mon–Sat 9.15am–5.30pm, Sun 9.15am–3.30pm; donation) founded by King Offa. Its greatest treasure is the **Mappa Mundi**, one of the first maps of the world, dating from around 1300. There's also a medieval chained library. On the pedestrianised High Street, the Jacobean **Old House** (Tue–Sat 10am–5pm, Apr–Sept also Sun 10am–4pm; free) dominates the pedestrianised High Town.

Some 8 miles (13km) southwest of Hereford off the A465 Abergavenny road, **Kilpeck** has a wonderfully ornate Norman church: **St Mary and St David**, built around 1140, has extraordinary carvings on its portal, including the Sheelah-na-gig, a Celtic fertility symbol.

Hay-on-Wye

Just off the A438, 23 miles (38km) west of Hereford, is **Hay-on-Wye** ❺. It was transformed into a "book town" in the 1960s when the eccentric Richard Booth, the self-proclaimed "King of Hay", seeing shops and cinemas close as they lost business to bigger towns nearby, converted them into bookstores in a bid to focus tourism. Other booksellers moved in, and it soon became the biggest second-hand book centre in the world. Each year (at the end of May), a high-profile literary festival (www.hayfestival.com) is held, attracting well-known authors and celebrities from around the world. Most of the town is in Wales. William de Braose, a Marcher Lord, built a castle here to replace the one burned down by King John. The Welsh ruler Owain Glyndwr destroyed it in the 15th century, though a gateway, the keep and part of the wall remain.

Heart of Wales

The next major town on the Wye is **Builth Wells** ❻, 20 miles (32km) west. This is pony-trekking, walking and fishing country. The Royal Welsh Show (www.rwas.co.uk), a huge agricultural fair featuring livestock and with

Hereford Cathedral, close to the Wye, just on the other side of the Welsh border.

BELOW: Richard Booth, who revived the economically ailing Hay-on-Wye by buying up every vacant building and turning it into a second-hand bookshop.

Pathway leading to the Elan Valley dam.

exhibitions related to country pursuits, is held here in early July. Seven miles (10km) to the north is **Llandrindod Wells**, a spa town which in its Victorian heyday attracted some 80,000 visitors a year who came here to "take the waters". The annual Victorian Festival in August returns the town to the days of hansom cabs, frock coats and mutton-chop whiskers.

To the west, near the source of the Wye, is the attractive town of **Rhayader**, where many Welsh crafts are on sale. Beyond is the **Elan Valley**, where in the late 19th century reservoirs were built to supply water to the thirsty city of Birmingham. The visitor centre (www.elanvalley.org.uk), in Elan village, gives a good introduction to the lakelands and the important wildlife habitats.

The Black Mountains

On the south side of Hay-on-Wye is the 2,220ft (677-metre) Hay Bluff that heralds the Black Mountains, which rise to 2,660ft (810 metres) at Waun Fach, 6 miles (10km) beyond. To the south, the Black Mountains are cut off from the neighbouring Brecon Beacons by

the Usk Valley, which the A40 follows between Abergavenny and Brecon (15 miles/24km southwest of Hay).

Abergavenny ❼, the area's main town, sits in a hollow surrounded by hills: **Sugar Loaf** (1,955ft/596 metres), **Skirrid Fach** and **Skirrid Fawr**, and the **Blorenge**, which has a lovely footpath running around its ridge with far-reaching views of the surrounding countryside. The town itself is a smart shopping centre, which hosts a lively annual food festival (www.abergavenny foodfestival.com) in September. Abergavenny is an ideal gateway to the 80 sq miles (207 sq km) of the Black Mountains, with their opportunities for pony-trekking, hang-gliding and good old-fashioned exploring.

Take the road to Capel Y Ffin running along the side of the mountains to connect with Hay-on-Wye, a lovely journey that takes in the romantic ruins of **Llanthony Priory**, an Augustinian monastery founded in the 12th century. Good walks lead into the hills behind the abbey, and refreshments are available in Llanthony Priory Hotel (*see page 366*) built into the abbey.

BELOW RIGHT: paragliding above Abergavenny.

Capturing the Tradition of King Coal

South Wales has long been associated with coal. At its peak, in 1921, some 271,000 men worked in the industry; in the 1920s there were 66 pits in the Rhondda Valley alone. All have closed.

The best place to get a feel for what it must have been like to work the coalface is the evocative Big Pit Mining Museum (tel: 01495-790 311; www.museumwales.ac.uk/en/bigpit; daily 9.30am–5pm; warm clothing and practical shoes recommended; children must be over 3ft 3in/1 metre tall to go underground) in Blaenafon, near Abergavenny. The mine closed in 1980 but is now a Unesco World Heritage Site. The hour-long guided tours underground are run by former miners. Donning a miner's safety helmet, you are transported down a 300ft (90-metre) shaft into the bowels of the earth, where you can get a glimpse of what life

was like for the thousands of men (and in earlier times, the women, children and pit ponies) who worked in the dank, dark tunnels.

Aboveground, there's a range of colliery buildings to visit, including the engine house, blacksmith's shop, pithead baths and pitman's cabin, with a gift shop and cafeteria in what was the miners' canteen.

Historic **Crickhowell**, 6 miles (10km) west of Abergavenny, is another good base for exploring the Black Mountains or the Brecon Beacons. Though scarcely more than a village, it has some excellent shops and good pubs.

The Brecon Beacons

Covering 529 sq miles (1,370 sq km) and stretching 20 miles (32km) south to Merthyr Tydfil is the **Brecon Beacons National Park ❽** (www.brecon beacons.org). These old red sandstone mountains are the highest in south Wales, rising to 2,906ft (885 metres) at **Pen-y-Fan** (meaning "the top of the place"); they take their name from their use as locations for signal fires. The landscape bears the marks of long glacial history: sheer precipices hang like waves about to break over huge, semicircular valleys gouged out by the ice.

Brecon itself is an old market town, at the confluence of the Usk and the Honddu rivers, and known for its jazz festival held every August. William the Conqueror's half-brother built Brecon Castle; its surviving tower and battle-mented section of wall are nearly all in the garden of the Castle Hotel. He also had a hand in the building of the nearby Brecon Cathedral (www.brecon cathedral.org.uk; daily 8.30am–6pm; donation), a largely 14th-century church, heavily restored in the 19th century. The **Brecon Beacons National Park Information Centre** (tel: 01874-623 366; www.breconbeacons.org), off the A470 at **Libanus** 4 miles (6km) south of Brecon, provides information on walking, climbing, pony-trekking, and sailing on the reservoir.

Some miles southwest of Brecon is the **National Showcaves Centre** (www.showcaves.co.uk; Apr–Oct daily 10am–3pm; charge) at Dan-yr-Ogof, said to be the largest showcave system in Western Europe. Apart from the underground spectacle of narrow passageways and limestone formations, the site also has a massive dinosaur park, an Iron Age farm, a shire-horse centre and an indoor adventure playground, making it a popular family attraction.

Just off the A465, known as the Heads of the Valleys road, travelling along Brecon Beacon National Park's

TIP

If you set off walking in the benign-looking Brecon Beacons, make sure you have a map and compass and know how to use them. The weather is highly unpredictable and the rounded shapes of the mountains are very similar, making orientation difficult.

BELOW: hiking to Pen-y-Fan, the highest peak in south Wales.

As a city, Cardiff (Caerdydd in Welsh) is a youngster, having nothing like the length of capital status enjoyed by either London or Edinburgh. It was designated as such only in 1955. It is also a comparatively anglicised city, where you are less likely to hear Welsh spoken than in, say, Swansea.

southern boundary near Merthyr Tydfil, is the narrow-gauge **Brecon Mountain Railway** (tel: 01685-722 988; www.breconmountainrailway.co.uk). It runs a scenic 7-mile (11km) round trip into the Beacons.

Cardiff

Between the mountains and the industrial south coast run the valleys whose names – Merthyr, Ebbw Vale, Rhondda, Neath – were once synonymous with mining and made **Cardiff ❾** the world's greatest coal port. Today, only a handful of deep mines remain, but Cardiff (pop. 336,200), the capital of Wales, is now a thriving centre for business, government and tourism.

Cardiff Castle (daily Mar–Oct 9am–6pm, Nov–Feb 9am–5pm; charge) brings together the strands of the city's history. The outer walls contain Roman stonework and the Norman keep, built at the end of the 11th century, still stands tall. At the height of Cardiff's prosperity in the 1860s, the Marquis of Bute (responsible for building many of the docks) added to the castle, with a clock tower and elaborate banqueting halls.

Nearby, the **National Museum and Gallery Cardiff** (www.museumwales.ac.uk; Tue–Sun 10am–5pm; free) covers science, history and archaeology, and has galleries for its collection of Impressionist, English and Welsh paintings.

But for those who really want to know about Wales, the **National History Museum** (www.museumwales.ac.uk; daily 10am–5pm; charge), just to the west of the city, is a must. Set in parkland around an Elizabethan manor house, it collects together reconstructed buildings from across the country – a toll gate, a chapel, a school room, a quarryman's cottage, a cock pit – and there are demonstrations by craftspeople.

Europe's largest urban-renewal scheme at **Cardiff Bay** is reuniting the city with its docks and coastline. The waterfront now centres on the new **Cardiff Bay Barrage**, a remarkable feat of engineering that has created a vast freshwater lake and 8 miles (13km) of coastline.

Close by there's **Techniquest** (Mon–Fri 9.30am–4.30pm, weekends 10am–5pm; charge), a science museum with hands-on exhibits that enable you to launch a hot-air balloon, fire a rocket and much more. The bay is home to the **Wales Millennium Centre**, a state-of-the-art theatre for musicals, opera and dance, in the foyer of which is the city's tourist office (tel: 029-2087 7927; www.visitcardiff.com; daily 10am–6pm, until 7.30pm on performance days). Additionally, it is the site of the new Welsh Assembly Building, the **Senedd**, built (as the Millennium Centre was) using traditional Welsh materials. Visitors can see debates from the public gallery (tel: 0845-010 5500; www.assemblywales.org; debates: Tue 2pm, Wed 12.30pm).

In a country that has long been famed for its singing tradition, it is apt that one of the highlights of Cardiff's cultural calendar is the biennial BBC-sponsored Cardiff Singer of the World. The competition (www.bbc.uk/wales/cardiffsinger), established in 1983, is now considered to be one of the main international showcases for young

BELOW:
the Millennium
Stadium in Cardiff.

opera and concert singers at the start of their careers. Around 600 singers compete for the final 20 places and the ultimate title of Singer of the World. Concerts take place in St David's Hall (on The Hayes) and the New Theatre (Park Place). In 2011 the competition was won by the Moldovan Valentina Mafornita; past winners include Karita Mattila, Dmitri Hvorostovsky and Ekaterina Scherbachenko.

Caerphilly and Carleon

Five miles (8km) north of Cardiff, guarding the southern approaches to the Valleys, is mighty **Caerphilly Castle ❿** (Apr–Oct daily 9am–5pm, Nov–Mar Mon–Sat 9.30am–4pm, Sun 11am–4pm; charge). Its presence in an otherwise ordinary town is wholly unexpected. The 13th-century fortress, with its sophisticated system of water defences, concentric fortifications and leaning tower, is Britain's biggest castle after Windsor.

East of Cardiff is **Newport**, Wales's third-largest conurbation. Like Cardiff and Swansea, this rather drab industrial city on the mouth of the River Usk is the product of rapid industrial expansion in the 19th century. Of more interest to the visitor in this area is **Caerleon ⓫** (www.museumwales.ac.uk; Mon–Sat 10am–5pm, Sun 2–5pm), one of only three Roman fortress towns in Britain (Chester and York being the other two). It was built to accommodate elite legionary troops, and you can see the impressive remains of the fortress baths, walls, amphitheatre and barracks.

Some 22 miles (35km) west of Cardiff is **Bridgend**, named after the original bridge that still crosses the River Ogmore. A former mining town, it has found readjustment difficult – it tragically hit the headlines in 2007–8 for an exceptionally large cluster of suicides. Further up the coast there are happier connections at **Port Talbot**, a tiny town with an extraordinary acting legacy – famous sons include Richard Burton, Anthony Hopkins and Michael Sheen.

Swansea

Dylan Thomas (1914–53) described his home town, **Swansea ⓬**, as "an ugly, lovely town... crawling, sprawling, slummed, unplanned, jerry villa'd and smug-suburbed by the side of a long and splendid curving shore". (The poet was born in the residential Uplands district, at No. 5 Cwmdonkin Drive). Although scarred by industrialisation and World War II bombs, Swansea is nevertheless a personable city that has been improved somewhat in the last few years. The most impressive "new" addition, opened in 2005, is **the National Waterfront Museum** (www.museumwales.ac.uk/en/swansea; daily 10am–5pm; free), set within a Victorian warehouse (built in 1902) with a swanky 21st-century extension by Stirling Prize-winning architects Wilkinson Eyre. The museum tracks the last 300 years of Welsh industry, enlivening the subject with multimedia displays.

Other sights in the city include an attractive **indoor market**, a vast glass building offering everything from ice cream to antiques and laverbread (con-

Roman re-enactment at Caerleon.

BELOW: Cardiff's church built for Norwegian seamen and its memorial to Antarctic explorer Captain Robert Scott (1868–1912).

taining seaweed) to carpets, and, in the former Guildhall on Somerset Place, the **Dylan Thomas Centre** (daily 10am–4.30pm), which celebrates the life of the city's most famous son.

To the west, a tree-lined sea wall skirts the 4-mile (6km) bay to the Victorian pier at **The Mumbles**, a popular sailing centre and small upmarket resort. It hit the headlines when Swansea's most famous daughter, Catherine Zeta-Jones, had a £2 million house built at Limeslade, on the peninsula's southern coast. Property here has clearly been given a boost – in 2010 the Mumbles was named as one of the most expensive seaside resorts in Britain in which to buy property, leading to it being dubbed the "Monaco of Wales".

Gower Peninsula

The Mumbles is the start of the **Gower Peninsula** ⑬, a small finger of land that juts out into Carmarthen Bay, designated as the first Area of Outstanding Natural Beauty in Britain. It has three National Nature Reserves and 21 Sites of Special Scientific Interest. From the Mumbles, the sheltered shoreline plunges and soars out of pine-clad limestone bays, dotted with occasional palms. **Langland Bay** is the nearest to town and popular with surfers (as is Oxwich Bay further on). At the west end of the peninsula is the gracious 3-mile (5km) sweep of beach at **Rhossilli**. The spectacular **Worms Head** promontory at one end of the beach is accessible on foot at low tide. Here there's a large seabird colony and half a dozen bed-and-breakfast establishments. The nearby **Paviland Caves** are thought to be the oldest occupied site yet excavated in Europe, dating back 100,000 years.

Llanmadoc Hill, just north of Llangennith, is topped by a hill fort – the best viewpoint at this end of the peninsula. Meanwhile, on the northern coast, the cockle women of **Penclawdd** traipse across the mudflats to collect the cockles and seaweed for laverbread, keeping alive the region's traditions.

Carmarthen

On the mainland behind the peninsula, the River Tywi forces the road inland to **Carmarthen**, a typical Welsh market town. On the south side of the river is the **National Botanic Garden of Wales** (www.gardenofwales.org.uk; daily Oct–Mar 10am–4.30pm, Apr–Sept 10am–6pm; charge), a visionary garden dedicated to conservation and education. Its centrepiece, the Great Glasshouse designed by Lord Foster, is stunning.

Southwest of Carmarthen is **Laugharne** ⑭. This tranquil town provided Dylan Thomas with inspiration for Llareggub (spell it backwards) in *Under Milk Wood*, his famous "play for voices". The picturesque boathouse where he spent the last few years of his life is now a museum (daily May–Oct 10am–5.30pm, Nov–Apr 10.30am–3.30pm; charge).

The Pembrokeshire coast

Pembrokeshire, in the extreme southwest of Wales, is renowned for its rugged

Three Cliffs Bay on the Gower Peninsula.

BELOW: the boathouse in Laugharne where Dylan Thomas spent the last 4 years of his life.

coastline. The **Pembrokeshire Coast National Park** ⓲ (www.pcnpa.org.uk) stretches from Amroth in Carmarthen Bay around St David's Head and up to Cardigan in Cardigan Bay, taking in 160 miles (260km) of spectacular coastal scenery. The only inland tracts in the park take in the **Preseli Hills**, pretty rather than dramatic, and the wooded valley of **Cwm Gaun**, which separates the Preselis from Fishguard.

Tenby ⓰ is the major resort along this golden coast. The Harbour Beach is overlooked by hilltop castle ruins and elegant pastel-shaded Georgian townhouses. Tenby has three more lovely beaches, and its 13th-century medieval walls are almost intact. From the harbour you can take a boat to **Caldey Island**, 2½ miles (4km) offshore, where Cistercian monks make perfume from the gorse and lavender that carpet the tiny island.

The coast around **St Govan's Head**, 12 miles (20km) west of Tenby, offers some spectacular scenery. Just behind the wave-battered cliffs lie the calm waters of **Bosherston**, man-made lakes covered in waterlilies in June. A few miles north in the natural harbour of **Milford Haven** (a major oil terminal) is the town of **Pembroke** ⓱. The main street of Victorian and Georgian houses leads up to **Pembroke Castle** (tel: 01646-684 585; www.pembroke-castle. co.uk; daily, Apr–Sept 9.30am–6pm, Mar and Oct 10am–5pm, Nov–Feb 10am–4pm; charge), birthplace of Henry VII, founder of the Tudor dynasty. The walls of this imposing Norman fortress are 16ft (5 metres) thick, and it is bounded on three sides by a tidal inlet of the Milford Haven Waterway. There are many boating facilities in the area, particularly around the sheltered waters of **Dale**.

St David's and Fishguard

The toll-paying Cleddau Bridge leads over Milford Haven; otherwise the road around the valley via the market town of **Haverfordwest** is circuitous. The coast west of here is drawn in to sandy **St Bride's Bay** with St Ann's Head and the bird sanctuary islands of Skomer and Skokholm in the south, and Ramsey Island and St David's Head, which is Wales's western extremity, in the north.

TIP

The best way of seeing the coast is to follow the Pembrokeshire Coast Path. It provides dramatic views of the sea cliffs and endless opportunities for watching gannets, fulmars, puffins, cormorants and other wildlife that thrives in the region.

BELOW: Tenby's colourful harbour.

It is believed that Ireland's patron saint, Patrick, was born close to where St David's Cathedral stands in Cardiff. The monastic site became a major centre of pilgrimage for kings and commoners alike. Two pilgrimages here were worth one to Rome and three were worth one to Jerusalem.

If it weren't for its majestic cathedral, dedicated to the patron saint of Wales, **St David's** ⑱ would be just a pretty village instead of Britain's smallest city. A cluster of shops and restaurants surround the main square; there are a couple of hotels, a few pubs, a few chapels (backs turned resolutely to the cathedral) and that's about it. Apart, that is, from the **Cathedral** (tel: 01437-720 202; www.stdavidscathedral.org.uk; daily 8.40am–6pm; donation). Together with the now-ruined 14th-century **Bishop's Palace** adjacent, it was built into a grassy hollow, half a mile from the sea to keep it out of sight of marauders.

Only when approaching it through the south gate does the full majesty of the purple-stoned cathedral become apparent. Fears of attack on this coast were not ill-founded: the last foreign invasion was in 1797, when the French landed at **Fishguard** ⑲, 16 miles (25km) to the north, though they were tricked into surrendering by the townswomen. Nowadays, as well as being the main shopping centre for north Pembrokeshire, the town is a Stena Lines ferry port providing the "shortest sea route

to Ireland". **Lower Fishguard**, with its pretty harbour, was the setting for the 1971 film of Dylan Thomas's *Under Milk Wood*, starring Richard Burton.

Cardigan

Eighteen miles (28km) further north on the A487 is **Cardigan** ⑳, a lively market town with agricultural and seafaring connections. Inland from Cardigan the road winds close to the Teifi River, which provides some of the best fishing in Wales. Upstream, **Cenarth** survives as a centre for coracle fishermen. Coracles are light, walnut-shaped boats, traditionally made of animal hides stretched over a wooden frame. They float down the river to catch salmon on their way upstream, and can be easily carried on the fisherman's back to the next sweep of river to be fished. Today coracle fishing is confined to the River Teifi, and to the Tywi above Carmarthen in south Wales.

From Cardigan, the A487 traces the coast north past attractive little inlets and coves such as **Tresaith** and **Llangrannog** before reaching the small seaside resort of **New Quay**, an old shipping town with a lovely quay. Just beyond, among rocky headlands, is the port of **Aberaeron**, a small, well-ordered town with a stone-walled harbour and elegant sea captains' houses built during the town's 19th-century heyday.

Aberystwyth

As well as being a commercial centre, the university town of **Aberystwyth** ㉑ is a popular holiday resort (it has a large but stony beach) and a convenient base for exploring the hinterland of sheep walks and lonely lakes. It is also the headquarters of the Welsh Language Society, founded here in 1963.

Aberystwyth's Alexandra Road Station is the sea-end terminal of the steam-operated **Vale of Rheidol Railway** (www.rheidolrailway.co.uk). The line culminates 12 miles (20km) inland at **Devil's Bridge**, actually three bridges, built one over the other, spanning the gorge of the River Mynach. ❏

BELOW: traditional coracles, used for fishing, can be carried easily, even by this 86-year-old.

RESTAURANTS AND PUBS

Restaurants

Prices for a three-course dinner per person with a half-bottle of house wine:
£ = under £25
££ = £25–50
£££ = £50–100
££££ = over £100

Abergavenny and Around

The Bell at Skenfrith
Skenfrith, northeast of Abergavenny
Tel: 01600-750 235
www.skenfrith.co.uk ££
Located in the tiny village of Skenfrith, The Bell uses locally sourced produce, from lamb and cheese to ales and ice cream, plus vegetables, herbs and fruit from its own organic kitchen garden.

The Foxhunter
Nantyderry, nr Abergavenny
Tel: 01873-881 101
www.thefoxhunter.com ££
In an old stationmaster's house, this cosy restaurant serves immaculately presented dishes made from organic produce.

The Walnut Tree
Llandewi Skirrid, east of Abergavenny
Tel: 01873-852 797
www.thewalnuttreeinn.com
£££–££££
This well-known historic inn serves prime-quality fish, local meat and game, plus vegetables from its own garden. Good-value set lunches. Closed Mon and Sun. Rooms available.

RIGHT: the Walnut Tree, near Abergavanny.

Brecon

Felin Fach Griffin
On the A470 3 miles (5km) north of Brecon
Tel: 01874 62011
www.eatdrinksleep.ltd.uk £££
Chef Ross Bruce creates well-prepared dishes using locally reared meat, vegetables from the restaurant's own garden, Welsh cheeses and local seafood. There's an informal atmosphere, with log fires in winter and garden tables in summer. You can even eat in the Library – something that should appeal to bookworms visiting from nearby Hay-on-Wye.

Cardiff

Bosphorus
31 Mermaid Quay, Cardiff Bay
Tel: 029-2048 7477
www.bosphorus.co.uk ££
Located on a small pier, this Turkish restaurant serves the freshest food with a premium on flavour.

Sir Henry Morgan
635 Newport Road, Cardiff
www.sirhenrymorgan rumney.com ££
Characterful old pub serving well-executed comfort food in the Rumney area of town.

Hay-on-Wye

The Three Tuns
Broad Street
Tel: 01497-821 855 ££
This restaurant has won rave reviews for its stylishly executed international dishes, mouth-watering desserts and friendly service.

Hereford

Stewing Pot
17 Church Street
Tel: 01432-265 233
www.stewingpot.co.uk ££
Expect mostly classic British fare using sustainable seafood and locally sourced meat, notably Hereford beef, and the occasional surprise such as Herefordshire snails in garlic butter.

Kington

The Stagg Inn
Titley, 3 miles (5km) east of Kington (B4335)
Tel: 01544-230 221
www.thestagg.co.uk £££
Critically acclaimed roadside pub in north Herefordshire that emphasises local and home-grown produce. Great-value Sunday lunches. Essential to book.

Swansea

Didier & Stéphanie
5 St Helen's Road, Uplands
Tel: 01792-655 603 ££
This gem of a French restaurant is out of town, on the way to The Mumbles, but it's worth it for the great food and intimate, romantic atmosphere.

Solva

The Old Pharmacy
5 Main Street
Tel: 01437-720 005
www.theoldpharmacy.co.uk ££
On the coast, this place serves lip-smacking fish and seafood. The house speciality is *bouillabaisse* (fish stew).

Tenby

The Blue Ball Restaurant
Upper Frog Street
Tel: 01834-843 038
www. theblueballrestaurant. co.uk ££
This informal restaurant serves good honest grub, offering local produce and smoking its own fish, meat and cheese.

Pubs

In Cardiff, the **Goat Major** on the High Street and the smattering of watering holes, including **The Borough**, on St Mary Street are reliable traditional pubs. In Swansea's pub-packed Wind (rhymes with "kind") Street, the **No Sign Bar**, founded in 1690 and patronised by Dylan Thomas, has a Dickensian feel to it and a good range of wines and beers. And in book town Hay-on-Wye, the central **Kilverts Inn** has an airy bar, outdoor seating and a landscaped garden, and its own brewery.

NORTH WALES

No visitor to North Wales can fail to be
impressed by the dramatic mountainscape
of Snowdonia or the massive, and largely
preserved, fortresses of the coast

Snowdonia's great crags and gullies have long attracted hikers, rock-climbers and mountaineers. Equally deserving, though less well publicised, is the region's glorious coastline, stretching north from the Dovey estuary round the Lleyn Peninsula and Anglesey to the River Conwy. Nowhere else in Britain are high mountains and attractive seaside resorts found in such close proximity.

From Chester – largest of the towns on the English side of the border – the Dee estuary, followed by the A548, leads out to the sandy resorts of North Wales, starting with **Prestatyn**, 28 miles (45km) west. Adjoining it is **Rhyl**, which has amusements and a 3-mile (5km) promenade, but the largest and most pleasant of these resorts is **Llandudno ㉒**, 15 miles (24km) further on, along the A55 North Wales Coast Expressway. It lives up to its reputation as one of Britain's finest Victorian seaside resorts – grand hotels fronted by a broad promenade sweep round North Shore to the splendid pier without an entertainments arcade or fast-food outlet in sight.

Behind the town on the 679ft (207-metre) summit of the Great Orme Country Park, there are spectacular views of the North Wales coast. All these resorts are within easy reach of Snowdonia National Park.

Conwy

Opposite Llandudno, on the far side of Thomas Telford's impressive **Conwy Suspension Bridge** (daily Easter–end Oct daily 11am–5pm; charge), which is now owned by the National Trust and pedestrianised, lies **Conwy ㉓**. Enclosed by battlemented walls, Conwy is one of the best-preserved medieval fortified towns in Europe. The stunning **castle** (Mar–Oct daily 9.30am–5pm, Nov–Feb Mon–Sat 10am–4pm, Sun 11am–4pm; charge) was built by Edward I as part of his

Main attractions

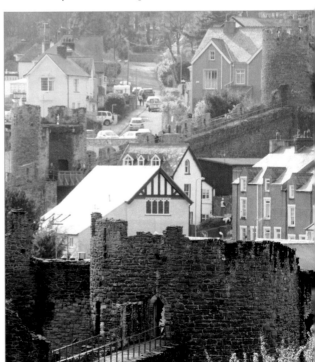

LEFT: River Llugwy, Betws-y-coed.
RIGHT: the walled town of Conwy.

The medieval walled town of Conwy sits on the mouth of the River Conwy. A suspension bridge built by Thomas Telford in 1826 spanning the river is now a National Trust site and open to visitors.

RIGHT: a tribute to lifeboat crews at Moelfre Seawatch Centre on Anglesey.

campaign to conquer Wales between 1277 and 1284. Conwy is also home to Britain's finest Elizabethan townhouse, **Plas Mawr** (www.cadw.wales.gov.uk; Tue–Sun Apr–Sept 9am–5pm, Oct 9.30am–4pm; charge), notable for its elaborate plasterwork.

St Asaph

South of Rhyl, 5 miles (8km) along the A525, is **St Asaph** in the tranquil Vale of Clwyd – a city that's the size of a village. Its small cathedral dates back to the 1st century AD and was restored in the 19th century by Gilbert Scott.

Further south is the market town of **Denbigh**, once home to Welsh princes and a centre of anti-English resistance. Denbigh's mighty castle (www.cadw.wales.gov.uk; daily 10am–4pm; charge) was built after the forces of Edward I crushed the town.

The A525 continues to **Ruthin** ㉔, a bustling town besieged by Owain Glyndwr in 1400. The town's former jail (daily mid-Feb–Oct 10am–5pm; charge) is now a visitor attraction and focuses on prison conditions in Victorian times. Ruthin Craft Centre (www.

ruthincraftcentre.org.uk), on Well Street, is the main centre for contemporary art in Wales, with craft studios, exhibition space and a café.

From Ruthin it is a 21-mile (35km) journey east to the town of **Wrexham**, near the English border. The town's most famous landmark is the 136ft (41-metre) Gothic tower of **St Giles Church**, on Church Street.

Two miles (3.2km) to the south is the National Trust's **Erddig Hall** (tel: 01978-355 314; www.nationaltrust.org.uk; house: daily mid-Mar–Oct 12.30–4.30pm, Nov, Dec 11am–3.30pm, gardens: Jan–mid-Mar 11am–4pm, with exceptions; charge), a fine 18th-century stately home with extremely well preserved servants' quarters and a walled garden with rare fruit trees.

Bangor and Anglesey

Heading back to the coast, **Bangor** ㉕, a university town, is 20 miles (32km) northwest. From here, another Telford bridge – the Menai Suspension Bridge, built in 1826 and the first of its kind, and the most difficult feat in the great Holyhead Road scheme that Telford

Castles in North Wales

There are two distinct kinds of castle in North Wales: "native" structures and those built by Edward I following his successful campaigns against the Welsh in the late 13th century.

Those in the former category, such as Powis and Criccieth, were built by Llywellyn the Great (d.1240), who as Prince of Gwynedd devoted his life to securing the territorial integrity of Wales. His grandson, Llywellyn the Last, sought to establish his own authority as Prince of Wales, but his refusal to pay homage to Edward I resulted in the invasion that put an end to any hopes of independence. The last of the Welsh castles to fall was Castell y Bere on the western flanks of Cadair Idris, in 1283.

Edward's own castles at Conwy, Beaumaris, Caernarfon and Harlech, supported by fortified town walls, are fine examples of medieval military architecture. Their theatrical siting to guard strategic points against Welsh resistance would have intimidated any enemy. Even so, all except Caernarfon were taken, if only briefly, in the Welsh rebel Owain Glyndwr's uprising at the start of the 15th century.

engineered to link Dublin to London – crosses the **Menai Strait** to reach the 276-sq mile (715-sqkm) island of **Anglesey** ㉖. This ancient Celtic island was the final stronghold of the Druids, who were massacred here by the Romans. The Romans settled the island and you can see the remains of a 1st-century farmstead, Din Lligwy, at Lligwy. Nearby is a Neolithic burial chamber. The Roman name for Anglesey was Mona, but the Welsh call it *Mon, mam Cymru* (Anglesey, mother of Wales) because this was the country's granary. Nowadays it is probably best known as being home to Prince William and his wife Catherine, Duchess of Cambridge, while William serves as a search-and-rescue helicopter pilot at RAF Valley.

Just after reaching Anglesea, the A5 passes the village of **Llanfairpwllgwyngyllgogerychwyrndrobwllllantysiliogogogoch**; its name is an accurate description of the place: "St Mary's Church in the hollow of the white hazel near the rapid whirlpool of St Tysilio close to the red cave". If you can't quite manage the full name,

do as the locals do, and call it "Llanfair PG" instead. To the east is **Beaumaris**, with its fine moated castle, while in the extreme northwest is the tiny island of **Holyhead**, from where ferries depart for Ireland.

On a clear day from the 722ft (220-metre) Holyhead Mountain there is a view of Ireland to the west, and southeast to Wales's highest mountain, Snowdon. A drive across Anglesey, along its small lanes and winding roads, can be frustrating for anyone in a hurry to catch the ferry, but it is a good way to see some of the farming way of life and the small, lime-washed cottages with slurried roofs.

Back on the mainland, **Caernarfon** ㉗, the largest town in the area, is at the opposite end of the Strait. With its city walls and towers intact, Caernarfon is a fine resort, popular with yachtsmen. Its strategic position meant it was an important settlement long before the present castle was built.

The Romans arrived in AD 78 and built a fortress, Segontium; some excavated remains can be seen. Begun in 1283, the **castle** (Mar–Oct daily

TIP

Less energetic visitors can get to the summit of Snowdon on the Snowdon Mountain Railway (www.snowdon railway.co.uk), a rack railway that starts in Llanberis.

BELOW LEFT: Beaumaris Castle.
BELOW RIGHT: the Menai Strait.

Welsh Fights Back

Revived in schools, and with its own TV channel, Welsh is alive and well, even in the anglicised valleys of the south

Driving into Wales on any major road supplies a painless and instant introduction to the Welsh language. The road signs are in Welsh as well as English, and even the weakest of linguists will likely take on board sooner or later that *milltir* means miles, *lôn* lane and *toiledau* exactly what you would expect.

Welsh is now widely in evidence all over the country, not just in more rural communities, *de rigueur* from railway stations to post offices, banks to supermarkets. Cities and towns carry their Welsh names as a matter of course: Cardiff/*Caerdydd*, Swansea/*Abertawe*, Newport/*Casnewydd*, Abergavenny/*Y Fenni*. A heavily subsidised Welsh television channel, S4C, backs up the language and creates a market for actors, writers and film producers working in Welsh. Its most popular soap opera, *Pobol y Cwm* (People of the Valleys) has been running since 1974 and is watched by half of all Welsh speakers in the country.

The Welsh equivalents of the Irish *Gaeltacht*, its language strongholds, are the north and west. Historically, in South Wales, the hold of the language was broken by the Industrial Revolution and the massive influx of immigrant workers from England and Ireland. Contemporary trends are also, it is argued, diluting the Welsh-speaking pool, as English retirees and those in search of a more peaceful way of life migrate to north and west Wales from the big cities of central and northern England.

Welsh renaissance

In the north, second homes are seen as a major threat in previously homogeneous Welsh villages, but many incomers make strenuous efforts to learn Welsh. In recent years, there has been a notable surge of interest in the language, not least in South Wales, where a significant number of parents want their children educated entirely through the medium of Welsh. The language's most remarkable quality must be its powers of survival. Living in the closest possible relationship with English, one of the most all-pervading languages on earth, the miracle is that it was not swallowed without trace centuries ago. Yet, according to the 2001 census, 594,500 people (20.5 percent) speak Welsh fluently. That's a far cry from the million who spoke it in 1900, but it's holding its own better than Scots or even Irish Gaelic.

Welsh is not easy to learn, but it holds the key to a rich literature going back through the hymns and folk ballads of the 18th century and medieval storytelling to the bards of the 6th century, and the odes and elegies of Taliesin and Aneirin. They were writing in the earliest British language – Welsh, which with Cornish belongs to the Brythonic branch of Celtic speech – and references to Catraeth (Catterick) show that their Britain went beyond present-day Wales. In a sense, therefore, Welsh is not exclusively the preserve of Wales. ❑

LEFT: a pageant at Anglesey keeps traditions alive.
TOP: road signs and markings are bilingual in Wales.

9.30am–5pm, Nov–Feb Mon–Sat 10am–4pm, Sun 11am–4pm; charge) was the largest of Edward I's network of fortifications. The exterior walls and three towers remain intact and are hugely impressive. Queen's Tower houses the **Royal Welch Fusiliers Museum** (www.rwfmuseum.org.uk; daily Mar–June and Sept–Oct 9.30am–5pm, July–Aug until 6pm; admission included in Caernarfon Castle charge). The Victoria Dock in Caernarfon is home to **Galeri Caernarfon** (tel: 01286-685 250; www.galericaernarfon.com), an excellent contemporary arts venue with a theatre, cinema and gallery.

Snowdonia

Immediately behind these coastal resorts is Eryri, the Place of Eagles, and **Snowdonia National Park ㉘**, Wales's most mountainous region, which covers much of northwest Wales, from Machynlleth in the south to Bala in the east, hugging the coast up to Porthmadog in the west and stretching almost to Llandudno in the north. The region contains 15 summits above 3,000ft (1,000 metres), and **Snowdon** itself is the highest at 3,560ft (1,085 metres). Sculpted by glacial activity, these mountains have been a playground for generations of climbers and walkers. Rolling green foothills rise into sheer crags, and stone sheepfolds cling impossibly to high slopes. Simply driving around Snowdonia is an exhilarating experience. Roads such as the A4086 through the sheer-sided Llanberis Pass to the east of Caernarfon, the A5 through the stunning **Ogwen Valley** between Capel Curig and Bethesda, and the A498 south of Capel Curig via the **Pass of Aberglaslyn** to Porthmadog on the coast, offer breathtaking views of the mountain scenery, which is studded with brilliant lakes. One mile (1.6km) north of the Pass of Aberglaslyn is **Beddgelert**, a tiny, compact village nestled in the middle of beautiful scenery.

Purists insist that, like the poet William Wordsworth, visitors should climb Snowdon in order to see the dawn. The easiest and most popular path to the summit starts on its northern side at **Llanberis** and is 5 miles (8km) long. Shorter, but more difficult, paths include the **Miners' Track** and the **Pyg Track**, both of which start at the Pen-y-Pass car park at the top of the Llanberis Pass and are 4 miles (6.4km) long. Bear in mind that the return journey doubles the length of all these walks. There is a visitor centre and café, designed to blend in with the landscape, on the summit of Snowdon.

Betws-y-coed

Betws-y-coed ㉙, situated at the junction of the A5 and the A470 and at the meeting point of three valleys, Lledr, Llugwy and Conwy, is another popular centre for outdoor enthusiasts. In the Wybrnant valley, 3½ miles (5km) southwest, is a small cottage called **Ty Mawr Wybrnant** (Thur–Sun Easter–Oct noon–5pm, Oct noon–4pm; charge), the birthplace of Bishop William Morgan (1545–1604), who first translated the Bible into Welsh, now protected by the National Trust. Two

TIP

Betws-y-coed can be reached by train on the Conwy Valley Line that runs from Llandudno Junction to Blaenau Ffestiniog. Several easy walks start from the village, particularly up to Llyn Elsi by the Jubilee Path, to forest-fringed Llyn y Parc, and along the River Llugwy to the Miners Bridge. All are clearly marked.

BELOW:
Lynnau Mymbyr, Snowdonia.

TIP

For those who love outdoor activities, the Snowdonia Rope Centre (www.ropesandladders. co.uk; tel: 01286-872 310) is an outdoor climbing centre for 4 years and up, located next to the Welsh Slate Museum.

miles (3km) west of Betws-y-Coed on the A5 towards Capel Curig are the famous **Swallow Falls**.

The legacy of slate

Snowdonia is full of stupendous natural scenery, but man has also left his mark on the area. Slate quarrying was once the most important industry of northwest Wales, and the huge heaps of slate spoil which overshadow places including Llanberis, Bethesda and, most famously, **Blaenau Ffestiniog ⑳** on the A470 to the east are its enduring legacy. Though the mountainsides are scarred, they do become eerily beautiful when wetted by the rain which falls so plentifully here.

The slate industry has also given rise to some of the region's best tourist attractions, including, at Llanberis, the **Welsh Slate Museum** (Easter–Oct daily 10am–5pm, Nov–Easter Sun–Fri 10am–4pm; charge), where the sight of workmen splitting and dressing slate will make any idle onlooker feel clumsy; and, in Blaenau Ffestiniog, the **Llechwedd Slate Caverns** (daily Apr– Sept 10am–6pm, Oct–Mar 10am–5pm;

BELOW: the Ffrestiniog Railway.

charge), where visitors can take a tour on Britain's deepest underground railway. From Blaenau Ffestiniog, slate was transported by rail to **Porthmadog**. Porthmadog was the creation of William Maddocks (1773–1828), a local mill owner and parliamentarian. He constructed the mile-long embankment, called the Cob, across the river mouth, which reclaimed 7,000 acres (2,800 hectares) and gave rise to the lovely town. In its industrial heyday, slate was shipped from the quaysides here all over the world.

The Ffestiniog Railway and Portmeirion

The steam-powered **Ffestiniog Narrow-Gauge Railway** (tel: 01766-516 000; www.festrail.co.uk; runs all year) was rescued from oblivion in 1954 and is now very popular with visitors. The 13½-mile (22km) journey from Porthmadog to Blaenau Ffestiniog up the beautiful Vale of Ffestiniog provides spectacular views of the mountains from the carriage windows. The rail link between Caernarfon and Porthmadog has been restored, making it

The Making of Portmeirion

Taking his inspiration from Portofino in Italy and buildings he had seen in Austria, Sir Clough Williams-Ellis gradually built up Portmeirion using odds and ends of houses rescued from demolition – "the home of fallen buildings," he called it. He developed "a light opera approach to architecture," aiming to produce "beauty without solemnity".

An example of this rescue process is the village's town hall. After seeing by chance that a Flintshire mansion, Emral Hall, was being torn down, Williams-Ellis bought the hall's ballroom ceiling for £13; there were no other bidders at the auction for "so awkward and speculative a lot". At vast expense, the 17th-century ceiling was brought to Portmeirion in 100 different pieces to form the centrepiece of Hercules Hall.

The village's artistic imagination has inspired many people. Noël Coward wrote his play *Blithe Spirit* while on holiday there in 1941. It also provided the surreal backdrop for Patrick McGoohan's cult TV series *The Prisoner*, filmed there in 1967 (the 2009 remake was shot in Namibia).

possible to travel from Caernarfon to Blaenau Ffestiniog.

The architect Sir Clough Williams-Ellis had an even more vivid imagination than Maddocks, when, in 1926, he decided to build an Italianate village beside Porthmadog in the Dwyryd estuary (*see box opposite*). This elaborate folly, **Portmeirion** ③ (tel: 01766-770 000; www.portmeirion-village.com; daily 9.30am–7.30pm; charge), incorporates a hotel. Portmeirion is also known internationally for its pottery.

Lleyn Peninsula

Wales is sometimes depicted as an old lady throwing a ball out to sea. Her head is Anglesey, her leg is Pembroke and the **Lleyn Peninsula** is her arm (with Porthmadog in her armpit). Caernarfon lies on her shoulder, and from **Aberdaron** (situated at the tip of the peninsula), **Bardsey Island**, her ball, can be reached. In the 7th century monks came to settle on the island, giving it the title "Island of 20,000 saints". Around the peninsula are tiny coastal harbours such as **Porth Dinllaen** and **Nefyn**. Travelling north of Nefyn on the B4417, the mountain range **Yr Eifl** ("The Forks") appears large on the left – 1,850ft (564 metres) at its highest peak. On its eastern peak is the site of **Tre'r Ceiri**, an ancient Iron Age fort.

Heading back towards Porthmadog, the pleasant resort of **Criccieth** ㉜ is dominated by its **castle** (daily Apr–Oct 10am–5pm, Nov–Mar Fri, Sat 9.30am–4pm, Sun 11am–4pm; charge), which has been a ruin since it was besieged by Owain Glyndwr in the early 15th century. Just west of Criccieth is **Llanystumdwy**, childhood home of David Lloyd George, Britain's prime minister during World War I. The **Lloyd George Museum** (May Mon–Fri, June Mon–Sat, July–Sept daily, all 10.30am–5pm; charge) is filled with memorabilia of the colourful "Welsh Wizard", who came to the village as a young boy after the death of his father and lived with his mother in Highgate Cottage opposite the Feathers Inn until 1880.

Men of Harlech

At the other side known of Tremadog Bay lies **Harlech** ㉝, the perfect place from which to view the Lleyn Penin-

Some of the eight locomotives, such as Palmerstone and Prince, powering the Ffestiniog Railway are restored from the original 1860s engines. Others have been recently constructed using old designs – David Lloyd George was built in 1992, for example, to look like an 1880s locomotive and is powerful enough to pull 12 carriages.

BELOW LEFT: Porthmadog harbour. **BELOW RIGHT:** Portmeirion.

The Llangollen Railway runs from Llangollen Station to the village of Carrog, daily in summer and on weekends during winter. Call 01978 860979 to book tickets or for more information.

BELOW: the Owain Glyndwr Centre in Machynlleth.

sula and Snowdonia in one breathtaking gaze. The **castle** (daily Apr–June and Sept–Oct 9.30am–5pm, July–Aug 9.30am–6pm; charge), perched on a promontory looking out to sea, fell to Owain Glyndwr in 1404. It was recaptured by the English within 5 years and featured in the Wars of the Roses, when the siege (and surrender) by the Lancastrian garrison inspired the marching song *Men of Harlech* (music 1794, lyrics added in 1860, and often mistaken for Wales's national anthem – which is *Hen Wlad Fy Nhadau*, meaning *Old Land of our Fathers*, set to music by James James with words by Evan James).

Eleven miles (18km) south of Harlech is the holiday resort of **Barmouth**, attractively built against towering cliffs and offering superb views of **Cadair Idris**, the mountain at the other side of the estuary. From here the road turns inland up the Mawddach Valley to **Dolgellau**, the epitome of a sturdy, close-knit Welsh community, and an excellent base for exploring Cadair Idris.

South of Dolgellau on the A487, 3 miles (5km) north of Machynlleth, is the **Centre for Alternative Technol-**

ogy (www.cat.org.uk; daily 10am–5pm, with exceptions; charge). Founded in 1973, its relevance is as strong as ever, as it demonstrates environmentally friendly approaches to energy saving and climate change.

Machynlleth

Machynlleth itself is a pleasant market town at the southern edge of Snowdonia National Park. The principal attraction here is the **Owain Glyndwr Centre** (tel: 01654-702 932; www.canol fanglyndwr.org; daily Mar–Sept 10am–5pm, Oct–Dec 11am–4pm; charge) on the site where Glyndwr established the country's first parliament in 1404.

Northeast of Dolgellau, the A494 leads to **Lake Bala** (Llyn Tegid), around 18 miles (29km) away – the largest natural expanse of water in Wales and a great centre for water sports. Just a short drive away, on the A4212, is the **National White Water Centre** (tel: 01678-521 083; www.ukrafting.co.uk), which offers canoeing, kayaking and whitewater rafting.

Heading east from Dolgellau on the A458, it's a 37-mile (60km) drive to **Welshpool** , county town of Powys. There are unexpected red-brick Georgian houses here, but there are also ancient, timbered, lopsided hotels and pubs. A mile southwest is the National Trust's **Powis Castle** (tel: 01938-551 944; www.nationaltrust.org.uk; Wed–Thur Mar, Oct 1–4pm, Apr–Sept 1–5pm, Nov–Dec noon–4pm; garden open longer, see website for details; charge), built by Welsh princes around 1300. The dramatic terraced gardens were created between 1688 and 1722.

Thirty miles (48km) to the north of Welshpool is **Llangollen** , home of the **International Musical Eisteddfod** and regarded as the centre of Welsh culture and music. Its two most famous residents, Lady Eleanor Butler and the Hon. Sarah Ponsonby, scandalised contemporary society by setting up home together in 1780 at **Plas Newydd Cottage** (www.denbighshire.gov.uk; Apr–Oct Wed–Sun 10am–5pm; charge). ❏

RESTAURANTS AND PUBS

Restaurants

Prices for a three-course dinner per person with a half-bottle of house wine:
£ = under £25
££ = £25–50
£££ = £50–100
££££ = over £100

Aberdyfi
Penhelig Arms Hotel
Tel: 01654-767 215
www.penheligarms.com **££**
Old-fashioned country cooking in an 18th-century harbour-side inn with gorgeous views. Generous portions and excellent wine list.

Abersoch
Porth Tocyn Hotel
Tel: 01758-713 303
www.porthtocynhotel.co.uk
££–£££
There's a lovely restaurant with gorgeous views in this family-friendly boutique country hotel. Menu is creative without being fussy, and changes daily.

Anglesey
The White Eagle
Tel: 01407-860 267
www.white-eagle.co.uk
£–££
A popular old pub which does favourites such as fish and chips, steaks and even a veggie Anglesey brie burger. Classic puddings too. Located on the southwest coast of the island, in Rhoscolyn, with good sea views.

Caernarfon
Castell
33 Y Maes
Tel: 01286-677 970
www.castellcaernarfon.co.uk
£–££

There's lots of fresh Welsh produce on the menu at this restaurant in the town centre. Fish features prominently – hake and chips, Menai mussels etc – and there are good vegetarian choices.

Eglwysfach, nr Machynlleth
Ynyshir Hall
Tel: 01654-781 209
www.ynyshirhall.co.uk **£–££**
Local ingredients such as Cardigan Bay seafood, wild salmon, venison, game and farmhouse cheeses will grace your dinner plate at this country-house hotel.

Gresford, nr Wrexham
Pant-yr-Ochain
Old Wrexham Road
Tel: 01978-853 525
www.pantyrochain-gresford.co.uk **££**
This 16th-century manor house offers a reasonably priced menu with options for vegetarians. The terrace overlooking pretty gardens is ideal for alfresco dining in summer.

Harlech
Castle Cottage
Y Llech
Tel: 01766-780 479
www.castlecottageharlech.co.uk **££**
Set in the centre of Harlech, this oak-beamed, modern-look restaurant (with rooms) does great, equally modern British cuisine. Lots of local, seasonal produce: fish (Barmouth lobster bisque), Welsh lamb, Brecon venison, Hereford chicken, Camarthen ham etc.

Llandrillo, nr Corwen
Tyddan Llan
Tel: 01490-440 264
www.tyddynllan.co.uk **£££**
The tasting menu at this "restaurant with rooms" enables you to sample the best of Welsh produce. The award of a Michelin star ensures that tables are reserved well in advance.

Llandudno
Osborne's Café Grill
17 North Parade
Tel: 01492-860 330
www.osbornehouse.co.uk
££
Café is hardly the word to describe this opulent hotel restaurant, which offers tasty British classics at very reasonable prices. Also a good venue for afternoon tea, with smoked salmon, traditional Welsh *bara brith* (a type of fruit loaf) and moreish scones.

Portmeirion
Portmeirion Hotel Dining Room/Castell Deudreath
Tel: 01766-772 440
www.portmeirion-village.com **££** (Castell) **£££** Dining Room
Enter fully into the Portmeirion experience by dining in the impressive curvilinear Art Deco restaurant of the historic Hotel Portmeirion, built by Sir Clough Williams-Ellis in 1931. The cuisine is fine modern European. For a more low-key meal, the Dining Room's chef, Wayne Roberts, oversees the food at the Castell Deudraeth gastropub, where the empahsis is on local produce, including

Welsh lamb that graze Portmeirion's own fields, herbs and vegetables from its own garden, and lots of local seafood.

Pwllheli
Plas Bodegroes
Nefyn Road
Tel: 01758-612 363
www.bodegroes.co.uk
£££
This award-winning, Michelin-starred restaurant with rooms in a beautiful Georgian country house is set amidst pretty gardens. Welsh produce features strongly on the modern British menu, which might include dishes such as Nefyn Bay scallops, ribeye of Welsh Black beef, a baked lemon custard for dessert and even a Welsh rarebit (a posh one, mind you) for the cheese course.

Pubs

In Llandudno, the 300-year-old **King's Head** in Old Road has an open fire in winter and a good restaurant to boot.
In Porthmadog, **Spooner's Bar** is situated in the terminus of the Ffestiniog Steam Railway and specialises in unusual beers from microbreweries.
Y Branwen Hotel, below Harlech Castle, has a popular bar with cask ales and many malt whiskies.
In Llangollen, **The Corn Mill**, on Dee Lane off Castle Street, is an old watermill with a great atmosphere and pretty decent food.

OUTDOOR ACTIVITIES

With its dramatic mountain peaks and deep valleys, Snowdonia is a magnet for hillwalkers, for whom there is an almost bewildering choice of routes

In the north the **Carneddau** offer vast grassy whaleback ridges, while the adjacent **Glyders** and **Tryfan** are strewn with frost-shattered boulders. Behind Tremadog Bay rise the **Rhinogs**, unfrequented mountains of ankle-twisting rock and deep heather.

Both the **Cadair Idris** and **Snowdon** massifs offer rugged walking, sustained gradients and wonderful views, but can be busy. By contrast, the featureless and often boggy **Migneint** between Bala and Ffestiniog is strictly for connoisseurs of solitude; the **Aran Ridge** running north from Dinas Mawddwy to Lake Bala also offers an escape from the crowds. West and north of Blaenau Ffestiniog, the **Moelwyns** are laced with slate-mining relics.

For family groups and the less mobile there are miles of gentler footpaths and bridleways. Good examples may be found in **Gwydir Forest** around Betws-y-Coed, in **Coed y Brenin Forest** near Dolgellau and around many of Snowdonia's more accessible **lakes**.

There is estuary-edge walking on the **Mawddach Trail** west of Dolgellau. Sections of the **Anglesey** shoreline possess marvellous coastal paths, notably on the island's west and north, and there are good stretches of path, too, around the tip of the **Lleyn Peninsula**. Then there are the **Precipice Walks**, principally around the Mawddach Estuary. Not as hazardous as they sound, they are well-made footpaths that traverse very steep hillsides. Waymarked long-distance trails include the 108-mile (174km) **Dyfi Valley Way**, the 60-mile (97km) **North Wales Path** between Prestatyn and Bangor, and the circular 121-mile (195km) **Anglesey Coast Path** (for information on walking trails, see http://walking.visitwales.com).

Challenging walks include the **Welsh 3000s** (www.welsh3000s.co.uk), a gruelling 30-mile (48km) tramp over all 15 of Snowdonia's 3,000ft (914-metre)-plus summits within 24 hours – not for the faint-hearted.

Hikers in need of a rest can hop on the 40-mile (25km) restored Ffestiniog Narrow-Gauge Railway, which runs from Caernarfn to Porthmadog.

ABOVE: a hiker 3,060ft (933 metres) above sea level looks across the national park to Mount Snowdon.

ABOVE: off-road 4x4 driving events, mainly using Land Rovers, are organised on private land near Lake Bala, the largest natural lake in Wales.

LEFT: Precipice Walks are not as fearsome as they sound. They usually have well-made footpaths and are of very moderate length.

THE CHOICE FOR CLIMBERS

Snowdonia's great buttresses and gullies have attracted rock climbers in ever-increasing numbers since before World War I, when Colin Kirkus and John Menlove Edwards pioneered audacious new ascents. Later, in the 1950s, the likes of Joe Brown and Don Whillans immortalised such locations as the Llanberis Pass and Snowdon's Clogwyn Du'r Arddu.

More recently, interest has spread out from the inland crags to embrace the sea cliffs of Anglesey, the Lleyn Peninsula, Llandudno's Great Orme and the cliffs north of Tremadog.

Courses in rock climbing, scrambling (requiring the use of hands as well as feet) and various types of mountaineering, as well as hill-walking, mountain biking, skiing, kayaking and more, are provided at the Welsh National Mountain Centre, Plas y Brenin, Capel Curig (tel: 01690-720 214; www.pyb.co.uk).

ABOVE: climbers on Llanberis Pass. Some of the most notable breakthroughs in British climbing took place on precipices here.

RIGHT: Snowdonia has a broad appeal for birdwatchers. The variety extends from birds of prey such as kestrels and peregrine falcons to seabirds such as the red-throated diver, from buzzards and choughs to pied flycatchers and the lesser spotted woodpecker. There are eight bird reserves in the area.

ABOVE: Snowdonia's natural forests comprise a mix of Welsh oak, birch and ash, although there are also large planted coniferous areas such as Gwydir Forest.

LEFT: a helicopter helps move heavy stones to keep pathways in Snowdonia National Park accessible.

SHROPSHIRE AND THE NORTHWEST

Highlights in this part of England include bucolic Shropshire, two of the country's most vibrant cities, and Lancastrian seaside resorts including Blackpool, the "Jewel of the Northwest"

This chapter covers the rural farming county of Shropshire and, north of it, the part of England generally classed as the Northwest, incorporating the counties of Merseyside and Lancaster. The main motorway access is the M6, which runs from Birmingham up between Liverpool and Manchester, then along the eastern side of the Lake District and on to Carlisle; and the M62, which runs between Manchester and the northeast of the country, via Bradford and on to Leeds. Manchester is around 180 miles (290km) from London. If you're heading here by train from London and the South, superfast tilting Pendolino trains take just over 2 hours to both Liverpool and Manchester, leaving from London's Euston station.

The northern identity

In Britain, the north is associated with the old heavy industries of shipbuilding, steel, coal mining and car manufacturing. These industries have long been in decline, and many of the Victorian factory towns have been plagued by unemployment. Recent decades have, however, brought regeneration, with hi-tech businesses, new universities, cultural centres and tourism in some of these historic cities. Despite post-industrial decline, for example, Liverpool remains a proud city, while the Victo-

rian city of Manchester is the capital of northern England. It was in the vanguard of the Industrial Revolution and is still a relatively prosperous city, internationally famed for the sporting prowess of its footballers. Around it is rolling green countryside, and not far away are the city's favourite holiday resorts on the Lancashire coast.

Shropshire

The county town of Shropshire is **Shrewsbury ❶**, home of the scientist Charles Darwin (1809–82) and World

LEFT: Liverpool's Liver Building clock tower.
BELOW: *B of the Bang* sculpture, Manchester.

Shropshire and the Northwest

War I poet Wilfred Owen (1893–1918). It is beautifully situated on a bend in the River Severn, crossed by the English bridge and the Welsh bridge, and has houses dating from the 15th century, plus fine parks and gardens. The pink sandstone **castle**, near the station, was converted into a house by the 18th-century engineer Thomas Telford, after whom a neighbouring town (*see below*) was named, and now incorporates the **Shropshire Regimental Museum** (June–mid-Sept Fri–Wed 10.30am–5pm, mid-Sept–mid-Dec, mid-Feb–Apr 10.30am–4pm; charge).

Shrewsbury was also the home of the poet A.E. Housman (1859–1936), who eulogised the dreamy slopes of this agricultural land in *A Shropshire Lad*, his 1896 series of 63 nostalgic verses. All along the Welsh border, the softly rolling hills can be explored by paths, bridleways and woodland trails. (For more on the Welsh borders towns, see The Wye Valley chapter; *see page 249*.)

Ludlow

Perhaps the loveliest of the border towns is **Ludlow ❷**, where Housman's ashes lie, to the south of Shrewsbury along the A49. It has recently spearheaded an English gastronomic revival with a bounty of quality local produce. The centre is remarkably consistent architecturally, with 13th-century taverns and Tudor market buildings overlooked by the impressive **Ludlow Castle** (now self-catering accommodation). The town is also known for its cultural festival in late June/July (www.ludlowfestival.co.uk).

Telford

East from Shrewsbury along the A5 is **Telford ❸**, a new town named after the 18th-century engineer Thomas Telford. Begun in the 1960s, the ambitious project takes in **Coalbrookdale**, where coke was first used to smelt iron, and **Ironbridge** on the River Severn, where the world's first iron bridge was built by Telford in 1773. The **Ironbridge Gorge Museum** (http://ironbridge.org.

uk; daily 10am–5pm; some sites closed in winter), now a Unesco World Heritage Site, has Abraham Darby's original coke furnace, and **Blists Hill Victorian Town** *(see box below)* recreates late 19th-century local life.

Chester

Heading north, the A49 and then the A41 lead to the foot of the Wirral peninsula *(see page 278)* and **Chester** ❹, the most northerly of the timbered Tudor towns of the Welsh Marches. In the centre of town, Eastgate, Watergate and Bridge streets all have their Rows – double tiers of shops and covered walkways, one on top of the other. The oldest dates from 1486, but most of them were built in the following century.

In Roman times Chester was an important stronghold, called Deva, and part of an **amphitheatre** can be seen just outside the city walls by St John's Street. This offers the best access to the 2-mile (3km) round trip of the **city walls** – Chester is one of the few British cities with its medieval walls still intact.

The **cathedral** (www.chestercathedral. com; Mon–Sat 9am–5pm, Sun 1–4pm),

off St Werburg Street, was a Benedictine Abbey until Henry VIII's dissolution of the monasteries. Unusually squat, it has a short nave and a massive south transept featuring a grand Victorian stained-glass window.

The **Grosvenor Museum** (Mon–Sat 10.30am–5pm, Sun 1–4pm; free), on Grosvenor Street, records the city's Roman legacy with models of the fortress and tombstones from the period, and has a natural history gallery named after the Victorian writer and naturalist Charles Kingsley. Under the Normans, Chester was a near-independent state governed by a succession of earls. The tidal estuary of the Dee allowed the city to flourish as a port until the 15th century, when it began to silt up and shipping was transferred to the larger natural port of Liverpool.

Attractions outside Chester include, at Upton, 2 miles (4km) north of the city, **Chester Zoo** (daily 10am–5pm, winter until 4pm; charge), the largest one outside London, set in 80 acres (32 hectares) of gardens and home to more than 7,000 animals.

Chester's Eastgate clock tower, built to commemorate Queen Victoria's Diamond Jubilee in 1897.

How Ironbridge Gorge Drove Forward the Industrial Revolution

Situated on the River Severn in the heart of Shropshire, the Ironbridge Gorge is named after the world's first-ever cast-iron bridge, constructed over the river in 1779. It was designed by Thomas Farnolls Pritchard, a Shrewsbury joiner-turned-architect. The giant ribs for the structure were cast in open sand and raised with the aid of scaffolding. Intriguingly, the joints in the ironwork are based on traditional carpentry methods, including dovetails, wedges, mortises and tenons.

The Coalbrookdale area had been a centre of mining and ironworking since the time of Henry VIII, but by the end of the 17th century, the wood used to make charcoal to fuel the furnaces was becoming scarce. The pioneering use of a furnace to smelt iron with coke made from local coal turned the area into the busiest industrial centre anywhere in the world.

There are 10 museums around Ironbridge Gorge. The most popular is the Blists Hill Victorian Town. Until the 1860s, Blists Hill was a thriving industrial site, but then decline set in, and by 1960 it was abandoned. Acquired by the Ironbridge Gorge Museum Trust, it was inaugurated as an open-air museum in 1973. The original furnaces, foundry, and brick and tile works are part of this working museum, but around them a "Victorian town" has been created.

Designed to showcase 19th-century trades, the buildings have mostly been dismantled from elsewhere and rebuilt. They are staffed by costumed demonstrators, including a tinsmith, a cobbler, a printer, a leather worker, a decorative plasterer and a candlemaker. The pub has a traditional sawdust floor, and a bakery sells fine pies and pasties. The Squatters Cottages show the effects of the Industrial Revolution on the lives of working people.

China kilns such as this one at Stoke-on-Trent were once common in the region, with products being transported on the canal system.

Eastern Cheshire and Staffordshire

It is worth making a special expedition to the extreme east of Cheshire (Chester's county) to **Little Moreton Hall** ❺ (tel: 01260-272 018; mid-Mar–Oct Wed–Sun 11.30–5pm, Nov–Dec, late-Feb–mid-Mar Sat–Sun 11.30am–4pm; charge), due east of Chester via the A54 and A34. Now owned by the National Trust, this ornately decorated, half-timbered, moated Tudor manor was built in 1450–1580 and has a delightful Knot Garden.

To the east of Cheshire is Staffordshire, classed as being in the West Midlands as opposed to the Northwest. The region's largest city, **Stoke-on-Trent** ❻, is also the main town of The Potteries, the region that has supplied Britain with its finest china since the 17th century with major maunfacturers including Royal Doulton, Royal Grafton, Coalport, Minton and Spode. Stoke was one of the towns featured in the *Five Towns* novels of Arnold Bennett (1867–1931), depicting life in the potteries during the industrial era. The industry here has all but died, leaving the former pottery towns a shadow of their former selves. Mining and steel were major industries around here, too, and these have also now died out.

Liverpool

Back on the northwest coast is the city of **Liverpool** ❼ (pop. 435,000) – a proud city, famed for its football club, its contribution to pop music, and its community solidarity. The shipping industry upon which Liverpool prospered has now all but deserted the Merseyside port, which suffered heavy unemployment throughout the 1970s and 1980s. But a great deal of rejuvenation has since taken place, and parts of the city, including much of the waterfront, were designated a Unesco World Heritage Site in July 2004. The sturdy red-brick buildings of the Albert Dock area now house a complex of small shops, bars and restaurants as well as several museums in the old warehouse buildings. Foremost among the latter is Tate Liverpool (tel: 0151-702 7400; www.tate.org.uk; Tue–Sun 10am–5.50pm, June–Aug daily, which has the largest collection of modern and contemporary art outside London.

Nearby, the Britannia Pavilion houses the **Beatles Story** (www.beatlesstory.com; daily 9am–7pm; charge), an "experience" of the city's illustrious sons that is naturally open "eight days a week" and features the Yellow Submarine and a stroll down Penny Lane. Buses for the Magical Mystery Tour (tel: 0151-709 3285; www.beatlestour.

The Beatles

Formed in Liverpool in 1960, The Beatles or "Fab Four" – John Lennon, Paul McCartney, George Harrison and Ringo Starr – became arguably the most successful pop group the world has ever seen. They are the best-selling band in history, the album cover for *Sgt. Pepper's Lonely Hearts Club Band* is widely regarded as a pop-art masterpiece, and "Beatlemania" is seen as integral to the social history of Britain in the 1960s. Liverpool's pride in its four famous sons is much in evidence.

The Beatles played many of their early gigs at the Cavern Club on Liverpool's Mathew Street. The original Cavern Club closed in 1973, but was reconstructed in 1984 and is now going strong again as a venue for local bands (tel: 0151-236 1965; www.cavernclub.org). It also stages a Beatles tribute show on Beatles Day, 10 July, each year. This was the memorable day in 1964 when the band returned to Liverpool from their US tour just in time for the premiere of their film *A Hard Day's Night*.

The Beatles broke up in 1970 to pursue individual music careers. Lennon and McCartney each chalked up several more hits of long-lasting appeal, and George Harrison brought out a successful triple album, *All Things Must Pass*. Ringo Starr achieved some success as a solo artist in the 1970s, but his post-Beatles career is now chiefly remembered for his narration of the *Thomas the Tank Engine* children's television series.

org) leave daily from the Albert Dock's tourist information centre and take in all the important landmarks, including Strawberry Field, Penny Lane, Eleanor Rigby's grave and the Cavern Club *(see box, page 276)* on Mathew Street. Most tours last 2 hours, though dedicated fans can also join a full-day tour (tel: 0844-800 4791; www.nationaltrust.org.uk; book ahead; charge), which includes visits to the National Trust-owned **Mendips**, where John Lennon grew up, as well as Paul McCartney's childhood home, **20 Forthlin Road**. Beatles groupies can also get their fix by buying memorabilia at the Beatles Shop and at From Me To You at Nos. 31 and 9 Mathew Street, respectively.

An altogether more serious story is told at the dockside **Merseyside Maritime Museum** (daily 10am–5pm; charge), which also incorporates the **International Slavery Museum**, offering a thought-provoking view of the slave trade. Also in the vicinity is the **Museum of Liverpool** (www.liverpoolmuseums.org.uk; daily 10am–5pm; free), dedicated to telling the city's history.

Liver architecture

Liverpool's architecture is on a grand scale. The docks accommodate the **Royal Liver Building** (with the mythical liver birds sitting atop the two clock towers), the **Cunard Building** and the **Port of Liverpool Building**. Collectively, they are known as "The Three Graces", and were built in the early 20th century at the height of the city's prosperity.

The city's fine churches include the Roman Catholic **Metropolitan Cathedral,** designed by Sir Frederick W. Gibberd and consecrated in 1967. Its circular structure is topped with a spire that represents the Crown of Thorns. The crypt, begun in 1930, was the work of Sir Edwin Lutyens, and was the only part of his original design to be carried out before lack of cash halted work.

The neo-Gothic **Anglican Cathedral**, Britain's largest, by Sir Giles Gilbert Scott (of Tate Modern's historic building and the red telephone box fame), was begun in 1904 and com-

Some tribute bands may not look much like the Beatles, but they can still make money in Liverpool's tourist trade. The original Fab Four got started in 1960 and learned their trade through gruelling gigs at the Cavern Club.

BELOW: Liverpool's "Three Graces" – the Royal Liver Building, the Cunard Building and the Port of Liverpool Building.

WHERE

Seven miles (4km) north of Liverpool (via the A565, or 20 minutes by train from Liverpool Central station) is Crosby, where the wide expanse of sands is peopled with 100 cast-iron naked figures, moulded by artist Antony Gormley from his own body. Called *Another Place*, this haunting installation was originally a temporary one, but has now been given a permanent home here, after a certain amount of controversy.

pleted in 1978 after two world wars delayed its construction. Its neo-Gothic style gives it the appearance of a much older building.

The city's other excellent museums and galleries include, on William Brown Street, the **World Museum** (www.liverpoolmuseums.org.uk; daily 10am–5pm; free), with collections of archaeology and ethnology as well as an aquarium. Nearby is the **Walker Art Gallery** (www.liverpoolmuseums.org.uk; daily 10am–5pm; free), which has an outstanding collection of paintings from Rembrandt to Hockney. There is also a children's gallery, with lots for small kids to do.

The Wirral Peninsula

Southwest of Liverpool is the peninsula known as the Wirral. Here is the delightful "model" village of **Port Sunlight ⑧**, built by the soap magnate William Hesketh Lever, later Lord Leverhulme (1851–1928), for his workforce. At the **Lady Lever Art Gallery** (daily 10am–5pm; free) there is a good Pre-Raphaelite collection, along with some Turners and Constables. To

reach Port Sunlight, take Queens Way across the Mersey if you are driving, and follow the signs, or use the Merseyrail Wirral Link to Port Sunlight or Bebington station.

Manchester

The Victorian city of **Manchester ⑨** is the uncrowned capital of northern England. The city came to prominence during the 19th century when it was at the forefront of the Industrial Revolution. Its "dark satanic mills" sprang up when cotton production was revolutionised by Richard Arkwright's steam-powered spinning machines in the late 18th century. When a railway line linked the city with Liverpool in 1830, and the Manchester Ship Canal was completed in 1894, Manchester's prosperity was sealed, and the huge Victorian civic buildings we can see today are evidence of a city that believed in its own destiny. The tenements in which the mill workers lived were razed by slum-clearance projects in the 1950s.

The city today

But Manchester's docks went the way of many others, and for years the city centre was drab, underused and underpopulated, before a huge revitalisation process began. Now the centre throbs with life. There's Europe's largest city-centre shopping mall (the Arndale, rebuilt after a bombing in 1996), a colourful Chinatown, a Gay Village (around the pedestrianised, waterside Canal Street), numerous excellent museums and three universities. The city and its surrounding area is also known for its music scene, earning international renown during the Hacienda heyday of the 1980s and early 1990s and spawning musicians including The Smiths, Morrissey, Joy Division and Oasis to name but a few (for music tours: tel: 07958-246 917; www.manchestermusictours.com).

Close to the city's Victoria station is the **cathedral** (www.manchestercathedral.org), set in attractive gardens on

BELOW: Manchester Town Hall.

Victoria Street. Its imposing, largely 19th-century exterior conceals some interesting medieval details within. Adjacent, in Cathedral Gardens, the towering glass **Urbis** exhibition and cultural centre is set to house the world's largest football museum, the **National Football Museum** (opening in early 2012; www.nationalfootball museum.com or tel: 0161-870 9275 for updates) – a move that is highly appropriate given this city's enduring success in the "beautiful game" (*see margin right*). Just southeast of here is the aforementioned enormous Arndale Centre.

Continuing south brings you to **Albert Square**, home to the city's neo-Gothic **Town Hall**. The Sculpture Hall is open to the public during working hours. Just east of here, Pre-Raphaelite art and 20th-century British works can be enjoyed in the **Manchester Art Gallery** (www.manchestergalleries.org; Tue–Sun 10am–5pm; free), along with an extensive collection of decorative art.

The vibrant **Chinatown** is packed with restaurants and is also home to the **Chinese Arts Centre** (tel: 0161-832 7271; www.chinese-arts-centre.org; Tue–Sat 10am–5pm; free), featuring changing exhibitions by contemporary Chinese artists. Just east of here is the coach station, then, around the canal, the Gay Village, while east again is Manchester Piccadilly railway station, the terminus for London trains.

At Castlefield, a few minutes' walk southwest of the city centre, is the **Museum of Science and Industry** (www.mosi.org.uk; daily 10am–5pm; charge). It has an impressive collection of technology from Victorian times to the Space Age, with lots to interest children. It also incorporates Liverpool Road, the world's first railway station.

On the University of Manchester campus to the south, the **Whitworth Art Gallery** (www.whitworth.manchester. ac.uk; Mon–Sat 10am–5pm, Sun 2–4pm; free) has an outstanding collection of British watercolours and a sculpture gallery that includes major works by Barbara Hepworth, Joseph Epstein and Elisabeth Frink.

At **Salford Quays**, to the west of the city centre, is the **Lowry Centre** (www.thelowry.com; Sun–Fri 11am–

TIP

Football fans can pay homage to the "beautiful game" at the Manchester United Football Club Museum and Tour Centre (www. manutd.com; daily 9am–5pm except match days; charge) at the Old Trafford ground, the "theatre of dreams", on Sir Matt Busby Way, Old Trafford, south of Salford Quays.

BELOW: Chinatown and the Museum of Science and Industry, Manchester.

EAT

If you fancy a curry while you're in Manchester, you could do worse than head for Wilmslow Road, a stretch of which is nicknamed "curry mile" for its proliferation of Indian restaurants.

5pm, Sat 10am–5pm; charge). It has the world's largest collection of work by local artist L.S. Lowry (1887–1976). This striking multimedia arts centre also houses two theatres, bars and a restaurant, and won the Building of the Year Award shortly after it opened in 2000. The stunning, asymmetrical building opposite, designed by American architect Daniel Libeskind, houses the **Imperial War Museum North** (http://north.iwm.org.uk; daily 10am–5pm; free). Also at Salford Quays are several BBC (British Broadcasting Corporation) studios, following the relocation of some BBC departments from London.

Towards Wigan

On the way from Liverpool to Wigan, take a diversion north up the A59 towards Ormskirk. On the A59 (Liverpool Road) is **Rufford Old Hall** ⓾ (tel: 01704-821 254; www.nationaltrust.org.uk; late Feb–early Mar 11am–4pm; mid-Mar–Oct Sat–Wed 11am–5pm; charge). It is one of Lancashire's finest 16th-century buildings, especially well known for the Great Hall with a hammer-beam roof and carved wooden screen. It is said that Shakespeare performed here for the owner, Sir Thomas Hesketh, whose family owned the house for 400 years. The Carolean Wing has collections of 17th-century furniture and tapestries. There are also Victorian-style gardens and a wildflower meadow, plus a restaurant serving light lunches and teas.

Heritage-mania at its worst can be found at **Wigan** ⓫, between Manchester and Liverpool, which is still trying to make up for the image George Orwell gave it in his 1937 book about tough working conditions in the north, *The Road to Wigan Pier*. Nowadays, the town trades on nostalgia, putting a romantic gloss on those hard times with a reconstructed shop, schoolroom, pub, cottage and even a coal mine. Wigan is also remembered as the birthplace of the Northern Soul music and dance movement – in the 1970s it shot to international fame for the Northern Soul all-night events at Wigan Casino. The building burned down in 1982 and was demolished in 1983.

BELOW: Blackpool's North Pier.

Blackpool

On the coast to the north of Liverpool is a cluster of traditional sandy resorts with wide, long beaches. From from south to north, they are **Southport**, **Lytham St Anne's** (good for yachting) and then **Blackpool ⓬**. Britain's most popular seaside resort, it receives some 6 million visitors each year, even though, sadly, it has lost the shine of yesteryear and retains its working-class, "kiss-me-quick" image, with fish-and-chip shops, illuminations (the town is "illuminated" from the end of August to October; a clever ploy to lengthen the summer season) and arcade penny-slot machines. The **promenade**, all 7 miles (11km) of it, is centred on the 518ft (160-metre) Eiffel-style **Blackpool Tower** and its **Golden Mile**, which the local council wants to rebrand the "Queen Elizabeth Promenade" in a bid to take the resort more upmarket.

Blackpool Pleasure Beach (www. blackpoolpleasurebeach.com) is another popular attraction, with its fairground rides for all the family. Tickets must be booked in advance, up to 12 hours before your visit. Other attractions include the **Winter Gardens** (daily 11am–4pm), a large, impressive entertainment complex housing an opera house, a ballroom and several theatres, on Church Street, set back slightly from and perpendicular to the seafront.

Preston to the Ribble Valley

East of Blackpool along the M55 is **Preston ⓭**, where attractions on the Market Square include the **Harris Museum and Art Gallery** (www.harris-museum.org.uk Wed–Mon 10am–5pm; free), with a notable collection of fine and decorative art, plus textiles and photography. Preston is England's newest city, having been granted this status in 2002 to commemorate the Queen's 50-year reign.

Further east is the former mill town of **Blackburn**, once a celebrated textiles centre but hard hit by post-industrial decline. Further east still, on the Manchester Road, is **Accrington ⓮**, home to the **Haworth Art Gallery** (Wed–Fri noon–5pm, Sat–Sun noon–4.30pm; free), home to the largest public collection of Tiffany Art Nouveau glass in Europe, attractively set within a fine historic Edwardian mansion.

Close by, there are more historic collections at the National Trust's **Gawthorpe Hall ⓯** (tel: 01282-771 004; www.nationaltrust.org.uk; Apr–Oct Tue–Thur, Sat–Sun 1–5pm, garden: all year daily 10am–6pm; charge), an Elizabethan masterpiece in Padiham, near Burnley. Located on the Burnley Road, it was restored in the 19th century by Sir Charles Barry (architect of London's Houses of Parliament), who created many of the magnificent interiors. The collection of paintings includes some on loan from the National Portrait Gallery in London, and there is a rare collection of needlework, displaying samplers and lacework. There is also a rose garden and a tea room.

South of Accrington is Helmshore, home to the **Helmshore Mills**

The main political parties take it in turns to hold their annual autumn conferences in Blackpool.

BELOW: Blackpool Tower.

As well as collections of fine and decorative art, the Harris Museum and Art Gallery is also home to the Mrs French Perfume Bottle Collection, the largest in the country.

BELOW: Morecambe bay.

Textile Museum (tel: 01706-226 459; Apr–Oct Mon–Fri noon–4pm, Sat–Sun until 5pm; charge), which documents Lancashire's textile heritage, especially wool and cotton production. The museum is housed in two original Lancashire mills.

Heading northwest from Accrington is the **Ribble Valley**; a good base is the small, pleasant town of **Clitheroe**. From the remains of its ancient castle, perched on a limestone crag, there are splendid views of the valley. Nearby stands the remains of the 13th-century Cistercian **Whalley Abbey**, and a parish church with Saxon crosses outside. To the west, **Ribchester**, a pretty village with a 17th-century bridge over the river, has the remains of a huge Roman fort, part of which has been excavated to reveal the foundations of two granaries.

Another attraction partly set within the Ribble Valley is the **Forest of Bowland** (www.forestofbowland.com), also know as the Bowland Fells. This area of outstanding natural beauty covers 321 square miles (808 sq km) of rural Lancashire and North Yorkshire and offers activities including walking, cycling, horse riding and fishing.

Lancaster

Back west along the A59, then north up the M6, is **Lancaster** ⓰, the county town of Lancashire, founded by the Romans. In 1322 Robert the Bruce razed the castle and much of the town to the ground but it was rebuilt by John of Gaunt, and his **Gateway Tower** at the castle is a fine specimen. During the 15th-century Wars of the Roses, the House of Lancaster was symbolised by the red rose, the House of York by the white. The **castle** (daily 10am–5pm; charge), on Castle Parade, and the Shire Hall can be visited, although some parts of the castle are not accessible when the Crown Court is in session. There's also an interesting church, Lancaster Priory (St Mary's), on Priory Close, with a fine Saxon doorway and beautiful choir stalls.

Morecambe Bay

Returning west to the coast takes you to **Morecambe** ⓱, a pleasant holiday resort on the bay, which claims to have originated the idea of autumn illuminations in order to lengthen the summer season.

The town is now largely known for the walk across the sands of the bay, a trip of about 8 miles (5km). The walk must only be done with a guide, as it is fraught with the twin dangers of quicksand and unusually rapid rising tides. Cedric Robinson, a former fisherman who has been leading charity walks for more than 40 years, has earned the title of Queen's Sand Pilot (contact the Tourist Information Centre on tel: 01539-534 026). The bay is also known for its shrimps, which are small, brown and tasty. ❏

RESTAURANTS AND PUBS

Restaurants

Prices for a three-course dinner per person with a half-bottle of house wine:
£ = under £25
££ = £25–50
£££ = £50–100
££££ = over £100

Blackpool

Oliver's Restaurant
Lancaster House Hotel,
272 Central Drive
Tel: 01253-341 928
www.oliversblackpool.co.uk
££
No, not Jamie Oliver, but a chef who knows what to do with good fresh ingredients, including Morecambe Bay shrimps.

Chester

Simon Radley at The Chester Grosvenor
Chester Grosvenor Hotel,
Eastgate Street
Tel: 01244-324 024
www.chestergrosvenor.co.uk
££–£££
This Michelin-starred restaurant is situated within a grand hotel in central Chester. Its British cuisine is beautifully cooked and exquisitely presented.

Liverpool

60 Hope Street
60 Hope Street
Tel: 0151-707 6060
www.60hopestreet.com
££–£££
Regional ingredients, tasteful preparation and smooth service in an airy venue. Typical dishes include roast crown of wood pigeon with herb risotto, and sea bass with clam chowder.

The Monro
92 Duke Street
Tel: 0151-707 9933
www.themonro.com **££**
This gastropub has won plaudits for its finely presented, locally sourced modern European (mostly English) dishes, which may include Goosenargh duck breasts or leek and asparagus crêpes. Serves a classic Sunday lunch

The London Carriage Works
Hope Street Hotel,
40 Hope Street
Tel: 0151-705 2222
www.thelondoncarriage
works.co.uk **££**
A boutique hotel restaurant that emphasises top-quality, locally sourced produce such as vegetables from the Wirral, and Barnston beef. Produce from within a 25-mile (40km) radius is mostly used for the excellently priced prix-fixe menu.

Yuet Ben Restaurant
1 Upper Duke Street
Tel: 0151-709 5772
www.yuetben.co.uk **£**
A Liverpool institution since 1968, it serves well-cooked authentic Northern Chinese food at very reasonable prices.

Ludlow

La Bécasse
17 Corve Street, Ludlow
Tel: 01584-872 325
www.labecasse.co.uk **£££**
This place in the foodie town of Ludlow merits its Michelin star. Head chef Will Holland uses top-quality ingredients in clever ways to create exquisite modern British cuisine. The oak-panelled dining room provides the atmospheric setting.

The Clive Bar and Restaurant
Bromfield
Tel: 01584-856 565
www.theclive.co.uk **££–£££**
Located a couple of miles north of Ludlow, this highly rated restaurant combines elegance with informality and uses produce from Ludlow, Shropshire and the surrounding area, as far as possible. Wenlock Edge ham, Woofferton beef and local cheeses are just some of the treats.

Manchester

Chaophraya Thai Restaurant
15–17 Chapel Walks
Tel: 0161-832 8342
www.chaophraya.co.uk **££**
For excellent Thai food and friendly service, this bustling restaurant is a reliable option.

Choice
Castle Quay, Castlefield
Tel: 0161-833 3400
www.choicebarand
restaurant.co.uk **££**
Choice puts an emphasis on local products such as black pudding and Cheshire ham, and a selection of Lakeland breads, in a pleasant canalside setting.

Pubs

Greater Manchester has a huge range of pubs. Those receiving honourable mentions from the Campaign for Real Ale include **Britons Protection** in Great Bridgewater Street, the waterside **Dukes 92** in Castle Street and the Victorian **Marble Arch** in Rochdale Road, Ancoats.

In Liverpool, the **Philharmonic Dining Rooms** on Hope Street is one of the most ornate Victorian pubs in the country. The **Baltic Fleet** in Wapping near the Albert Dock is a listed building with a nautical theme and the Wapping Brewery in the cellar. Other interesting Victorian pubs include **Peter Kavanagh's** in Egerton Street, the **Belvedere Arms** in Sugnall Street and the **White Star** in Rainford Gardens.

In Chester, **The Albion** on Albion Street has a restful Victorian ambience and World War I memorabilia. The **Bear & Billet** is located in a 1664 building in Lower Bridge Steet and has lots of original woodwork.

RIGHT: dynamic interior of The London Carriage Works.

THE PEAK DISTRICT AND EAST MIDLANDS

The Peak District's landscape can be dramatic, with crags and moorland or rolling green dales, with stone walls creating a chequerboard of fields. It is also dotted with some splendid stately homes

I n a region littered with the relics of ancient wars, no sign remains of some comparatively recent hand-to-hand combat. Unless, that is, you count the sign that reads: "Public access to this private land has been granted by agreement with the owners."

This access was bought through direct action when, in 1932, a group of hikers – workers from the industrial cities of Manchester and Sheffield – staged a mass trespass on Kinder Scout (*see page 287*), the district's highest peak, in pursuit of their demand to be able to walk over the land for weekend recreation. They were met by owners' gamekeepers armed with clubs and guns, arrested, and five of them imprisoned. Their action received popular support and led, eventually, to the creation in 1951 of the **Peak District National Park ❶**, the first in England (*see box page 287*).

Derby

Motorists approaching the Peak District from the south could leave the M1 motorway at junction 24 and pass through **Derby ❷**, 116 miles (187km) northwest of London (trains to most of the East Midlands leave London from St Pancras station). This ancient county town on the River Derwent has Britain's first real factory, a silk mill built in 1718. In the 19th century railway engineering became the main employer. Rolls-Royce opened a major

plant here in 1908, but the main site was in the final stages of demolition at time of printing.

City-centre highlights include the cathedral, notable for its fine "Bakewell" wrought-iron screen, and the **Derby Museum and Art Gallery** (tel: 01332-641 901; Tue–Sat 10am–5pm, Sun 1–4pm; free), home to a collection of works by 18th-century local artist Joseph Wright as well as a fine collection of Derby porcelain and more.

From Derby the A52 approaches the National Park through **Ashbourne ❸**,

Main attractions
PEAK DISTRICT NATIONAL PARK
BUXTON
CASTLETON CAVERNS
CHATSWORTH HOUSE
SHEFFIELD
BELVOIR CASTLE
LINCOLN
BURGHLEY HOUSE

LEFT AND RIGHT: hiking in the Peak District.

Fishing on the River Dove, famed for its trout.

Visiting Dovedale, Dr Samuel Johnson compared it favourably with Scotland: "He who has seen Dovedale has no need to visit the Highlands."

BELOW: rock climbing on Stanage Edge.

with exceptions; charge), find Ashbourne a handy place to stay, although there are two hotels within the theme park itself.

Buxton

From Ashbourne, take the A515 north into the National Park, taking the left turn down the quiet lane that twists through **Dovedale**. Sheep populate these dales, and sheepdog trials are popular summer distractions. A few miles further along the A515 – or, for the adventurous, after a delightful mystery tour through unclassified country lanes – is the small, attractive spa town of **Buxton ❺**, a familiar name nowadays thanks to the bottled product of its nine springs.

Between 1570 and 1583, Mary, Queen of Scots sought treatment in Buxton for her rheumatism, a complaint doubtless aggravated by her imprisonment in a succession of draughty establishments. At the end of the 18th century, the 5th Duke of Devonshire planned and built a grand crescent here, intending the town to outshine Bath. Although this aim was never achieved, the town has its fair

12 miles (20km) west. Its main thoroughfare, Church Street, contains a 16th-century school, 17th-century almshouse and, at weekends, 21st-century traffic jams. George Eliot (1819–80) described St Oswald's church as "the finest mere parish church in the kingdom". Each Shrove Tuesday, Ashbourne hosts the Royal Shrovetide football match, in which up to 300 players a side try to score goals by touching the walls of Sturston Mill and Clifton Mill, 3 miles (5km) apart.

Families visiting **Alton Towers ❹**, a huge theme park with some hairraising rides (www.altontowers.com; Easter–end Oct daily 10am–5pm, later at weekends and until 9pm in summer,

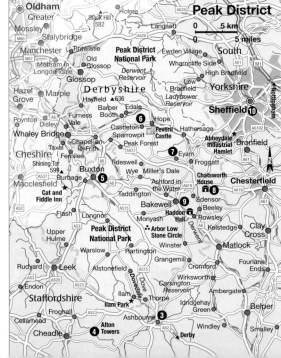

share of visitors who come to swim in the indoor spa-water pool at the Pavilion Gardens. The gardens themselves are a pleasant spot to spend some time, with a conservatory, a bandstand, a number of cafés and children's play areas.

Other attractions nearby include the ravine of the **Wye**, which provides a beautiful limestone route for walkers.

Into the Peak District

Chapel-en-le-Frith, on the A625, is a small market town. "Frith" means "forest", but little of that is left today. Located nearby, north of the A625, is **Edale**, a tidy little village huddled at the foot of the peat-covered **Kinder Scout** peak, the challenging start of the Pennine Way hiking route, which ends on the Scottish borders.

Further along the A625, **Castleton** ❻ is a centre for subterranean exploration. At the foot of **Winnats Pass**, **Speedwell Cavern** (www.speedwell cavern.co.uk; daily 10am–5pm; tours at regular intervals; charge) is so high that rockets have shot up 450ft (140 metres) without hitting its roof. The **Treak Cliff Cavern** has the most spec-tacular formations and is one of the few sources of the semiprecious Blue John stone. The mineral was much in demand in the 18th century, which meant the most substantial veins were worked out, but it is still a working mine. The blackened ceiling in the entrance to the **Peak Cavern** dates from the time when it was occupied by a community of rope-makers.

Above the village, **Peveril Castle** (summer daily 10am–5pm, winter Thur–Sun 10am–4pm; charge) was the setting for Sir Walter Scott's 1823 novel *Peveril of the Peak*. The castle was built by William Peveril after the Norman Conquest, and it is said King Malcolm of Scotland paid homage to Henry II here in 1157.

Hathersage, on the same road, is the hillside village that inspired "Morton" in Charlotte Brontë's *Jane Eyre* (1847). She also gave her heroine the surname of the local lord of the manor, Robert Eyre.

To the north of Hathersage is **Stanage Edge**, the longest and most impressive of the Peak's gritstone edges and a playground for both rock climbers and hang-gliders. The

BELOW: Treak Cliff Cavern.

Peaclond

"**P**eak District" is a misnomer. Visitors seek in vain for pointed mountaintops; in fact, the name comes from the Old English *peac*, which just meant a hill. In the 10th-century *Anglo-Saxon Chronicle*, the area was known as Peaclond: the hilly land. The park begins in Derbyshire and extends northwards 30 miles (48km) into Yorkshire, offering open-air adventures to the inhabitants of half a dozen adjacent cities. Some of the summits in the area rise to 2,000ft (600 metres), attracting hang-gliders and providing rock-climbing opportunities for novices and experts alike. Potholers, too, are drawn here. Sir Arthur Conan Doyle (1859–1930), creator of Sherlock Holmes, wrote: "All this country is hollow. Could you strike it with some gigantic hammer, it would boom like a drum or possibly cave in altogether."

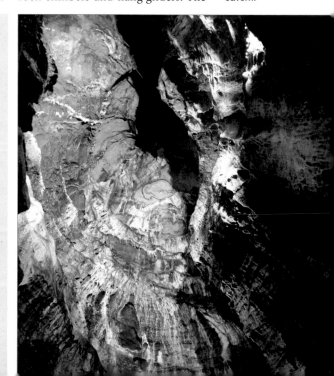

Bakewell tarts (more properly, Bakewell puddings) are widely available in the region. The jam pastry was created accidentally in 1820 when, so it's said, a cook, instead of stirring the eggs and almond paste mixture into the pastry, spread it on top of the jam. When it is topped with icing and a cherry, it is called a Bakewell cake.

highest point is at High Neb, near the north end.

A diversion south along the B6001 leads to **Eyam ❼** (pronounced "eem"), remarkable for the action of its villagers in 1665. Finding plague-infested fleas in a box of cloth sent from London to the local tailor, they sealed off the village to confine the disease; within a year, three-quarters of the 350 inhabitants were dead. The story is told in the **Eyam Museum** (Hawkshill Road; late Mar–early Nov Tue–Sun 10am–4.30pm; charge).

Chatsworth House

Near Baslow, off the A619, is **Chatsworth House ❽** (house: mid-Mar–mid-Dec daily 11am–5.30pm, park: year-round 11am–6pm; charge for the house). Known as the "Palace of the Peak", this is a vast Palladian mansion built between 1687 and 1707 and set in a spacious deer park with gardens landscaped by "Capability" Brown. The seat of the Duke and Duchess of Devonshire, it houses priceless collections of books and furniture, as well as fine paintings by Rembrandt and

Reynolds. Chatsworth boosts business by staging fairs, pop concerts and horse trials, and has been used as a location for Pemberley, Mr Darcy's home, in the 2005 film of *Pride and Prejudice* and in *The Duchess* (2008), based on the life of Georgiana, Duchess of Devonshire (1757–1806).

Heading back south, the A6 passes through **Bakewell ❾**, a stone-built town with two medieval bridges over the Wye and famed for its "puddings" *(see margin)*. The town's name, however, has nothing to do with baking. An entry in the *Domesday Book* (1086) calls the town Badequella, which means bath-well. Two of the town's iron-rich wells survive and a colourful well-dressing ceremony is held in June. Two miles (4km) southeast, **Haddon Hall** (May–Sept daily noon–5pm, Apr and Oct Sat–Mon; charge) is one of Britain's best-preserved, most atmospheric old houses, dating in parts from the 12th century. Its tapestries are especially renowned.

Sheffield

Although located in Yorkshire, and that county's largest city, **Sheffield ❿** lies just to the east of the Peak District and is ideally accessed from other major towns and areas in the region covered by this chapter. The city prospered at the foot of the Pennines, using the cascading water to drive grindstones manufactured from their millstone grit. However, its pre-eminent position as a steel town has been lost: Sheffield steel may still be best, but Korean cutlery costs less. The **Magna Science Adventure Centre** (daily 10am–5pm; charge) in **Rotherham**, set within a former steelworks, tells the story of the steel industry, and has an adventure and water park (summer only) for children.

Sheffield's shopping centre is emphatically modern, neat suburbs cling to steep gradients, and the **Crucible Theatre** has a national reputation. The **Weston Park Museum** (Mon–Fri 10am–3pm, Sat–Sun 11am–4pm,

BELOW: Chatsworth House.

daily 11am–4pm during school hols), housed in a grand neoclassical building, showcases the city's family-friendly collections of archaeology, natural history, art and social history.

The **Millennium Galleries** (daily 10am–4pm; free) at Arundel Gate comprise four galleries in one, displaying art, craft and contemporary design and including the eclectic **Ruskin Gallery**.

Out to the west on Abbeydale Road South is the **Abbeydale Industrial Hamlet** (Apr–Sept Mon–Thur 10am–4pm, Sun 11am–4.45pm; charge), a living museum of Sheffield's industrial past, where craftsmen demonstrate their traditional skills.

Nottingham

Southeast of Sheffield is **Nottingham** ⑪. The cultural and nightlife hub of the East Midlands, this attractive city is centred around a broad market square, with two large shopping centres, the original Paul Smith shop, a major arts complex and myriad restaurants. Until the 20th century, Nottingham was world-renowned for lacemaking, with the historic Lace

Market quarter the heart of production. The city's attractive Victorian buildings are now home to a growing number of upmarket restaurants, bars, shops and hotels. There's also a new art gallery, **Nottingham Contemporary** (Tue–Fri 10am–7pm, Sat 10am–6pm, Sun 11am–5pm; free), which puts on changing exhibitions and has a cool bar/restaurant downstairs.

For more classic sights, **Nottingham Castle**, actually a 17th-century mansion on the site of the original castle, is set in impressive grounds and houses the **Castle Museum and Art Gallery** (daily, Mar–Sept 10am–5pm, Oct–Feb 10am–4pm; charge), with collections of silver, glass, armour and paintings. There are also tours of the castle caves, but note that they are quite tiring.

Nottingham's most famous literary son is the writer D.H. Lawrence (1885–1930), and there are informative tours of the **D.H. Lawrence Birthplace Museum** (tel: 01773-717 353; Tue–Fri,

Battle re-enactments are a feature of August's Sheffield Fayre. It also includes flower shows, crafts tents and children's rides. For details, check www.sheffield. gov.uk.

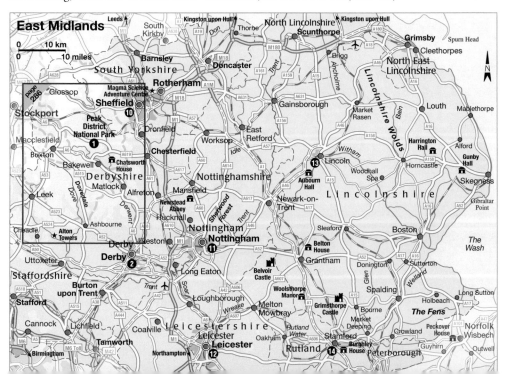

East Midlands

The mythical outlaw Robin Hood, here commemorated at Nottingham Castle, keeps the city on the tourist map.

BELOW: Lincoln Cathedral, which the art critic John Ruskin (1819–1900) called "the most precious piece of architecture in the British Isles".

Sun entry by tour only; tours daily 10am–4pm, wth exceptions Sun; charge), a modest house in the village of Eastwood (to reach it, exit the M1 at junction 26 and take the A610 to Eastwood). There is also a small museum about his work at **Nottingham University**, to the southwest of the city.

Leicestershire, Lincolnshire and Rutland

South of Nottingham is Leicestershire (pronounced "lester-shire"), whose county town is **Leicester** . Highlights include **Bosworth Battlefield** (daily 10am–4pm, Apr–Oct until 5pm; charge), site of the struggle in 1485 that ended the Wars of the Roses, resulting in Tudor rule; and the **Abbey Pumping Station**, a museum occupying a handsome Victorian building, which explores Leicester's industrial and scientific heritage (Feb–Oct 11am–4.30pm; free). The city is also known for its excellent curry houses along the "Golden Mile".

In north Leicestershire stands **Belvoir Castle** (pronounced "beaver"; tel: 01476-871 002; www.belvoircastle.com; tours May–Aug Sun, Mon with exceptions; charge), home to the Duke and Duchess of Rutland.

East of Nottingham, Lincolnshire has several important sights worth seeking out. **Lincoln** is a Roman city, with some well-preserved medieval buildings which attest to the wealth derived from a flourishing wool trade. You can get a good look at the city by taking a canal trip on the *Brayford Belle* (tel: 01522-881 200; daily in summer; charge). Lincoln's **cathedral** (www.lincolncathedral.com), with its impressive hilltop location, is a mixture of Norman and Perpendicular styles and one of the finest medieval buildings in England. One of only four surviving copies of the Magna Carta of 1215 is kept in the cathedral archives.

If you head east from Lincoln, you will reach the North Sea coast, where there are several resort towns, including **Mablethorpe**, where land yachting is popular on the long sandy beaches; and **Skegness**, a family resort for many decades.

If you are heading south, you can take the A1, A15 or A16 to reach **Stamford** , 47 miles (76km) south of Lincoln, an attractive historic town on the River Welland, with stone-built houses and a 13th-century church. There you will find one of Britain's finest Elizabethan stately homes, **Burghley House** (mid-Mar–Oct daily 11am–4.30pm; charge), built in 1560–87 by William Cecil, 1st Lord Burghley. The Gardens of Surprise incorporate mazes, fountains and a Contemporary Sculpture Garden, and the 300-acre (120-hectare) deer park was landscaped in 1756 by "Capability" Brown *(see page 217)*. Burghley's horse trials, held in September, are a major annual equestrian event.

South of Lincolnshire is Rutland, England's smallest county in terms of population. Highlights include the attractive market town of **Oakham** and **Rutland Water** nature reserve (www.rutlandwater.org.uk). ❑

RESTAURANTS AND PUBS

Restaurants

Prices for a three-course dinner per person with a half-bottle of house wine:
£ = under £25
££ = £25–50
£££ = £50–100
££££ = over £100

Ashbourne

Dog and Partridge Country Inn
Swinscoe, Ashbourne
Tel: 01335-343 183 ££
An attractive little country inn with a restaurant serving well-cooked food – trout is a speciality.

Ashford in the Water

Riverside House Hotel
Fennel Street, nr Bakewell
Tel: 01629-814 275
www.riversidehousehotel.co.uk ££
In a beautiful position overlooking the River Wye, the conservatory restaurant of this Georgian house offers high-class English cuisine, especially game and fish.

Baslow

Fischer's at Baslow Hall
Calver Road
Tel: 01246-583 259
www.fischers-baslowhall.co.uk £££
Outstanding Michelin-starred restaurant serving traditional British food. Local produce might include Derbyshire spring lamb, wild hare or Chatsworth venison.

Buxton

Columbine
7 Hall Bank
Tel: 01298-78752 ££
Small, friendly, family-run restaurant. Excellent fish soup, puddings and English cheeseboard.

Dovedale, near Ashbourne

Izaak Walton Hotel
Tel: 01335-350 555
www.izaakwaltonhotel.com ££
Occupying a 17th-century farmhouse, this hotel restaurant, overlooking Dovedale in the Peak District, specialises in Anglo-French dishes using locally sourced ingredients. Smart dress code.

Hambleton

Hambleton Hall
Near Oakham
Tel: 01572-756 991
www.hambletonhall.com £££
Elegant dining room serving modern British cuisine by Michelin-starred chef in a gorgeous country-house hotel next to Rutland Water. Reserve.

Hassop

Hassop Hall Hotel
Near Bakewell
Tel: 01629-640 488
www.george-hotel.net ££
Beautiful hotel-restaurant, set in glorious rolling parkland right in the Peak District National Park. Book ahead.

Hathersage

The George Hotel
Main Road
Tel: 01433-650 436
www.hassophallhotel.com ££
This smart hotel's award-winning restaurant, George's, offers a marriage of traditional (the setting, a 500-year-old former inn) and contemporary (the decor and elegant modern British menu).

Chequers Inn
Froggatt Edge
Tel: 01433-630 231
www.chequers-froggatt.com ££
Local produce is used in European and British dishes served up in this inn's rustic dining room. Good range of ales available too.

Leicester

MemSaab
59 Highcross Street
Tel: 0116-253 0243
www.mem-saableics.com ££
One of the best of the city's Indian restaurants. Located within the Highcross shopping centre, it has airy contemporary decor and the cooking is all about fresh ingredients, natural flavours and beautiful presentation.

Nottingham

Hart's
Standard Hill, Park Row
Tel: 0115-988 1900
www.hartnottingham.co.uk ££
Innovative modern British dishes are served in this contemporary-styled restaurant that is under the same acclaimed ownership as Hambleton Hall. There's an interesting, well-priced wine list.

Ridgeway, nr Sheffield

Old Vicarage
Tel: 0114-247 5814
www.theoldvicarage.co.uk £££
Set in beautiful gardens, this large Victorian country-house hotel has a Michelin-starred restaurant that offers an outstanding fixed-price menu, with dishes including its speciality, sage-roasted saddle of Ridgeway hare, and Chatsworth lamb.

Sheffield

Greenhead House
84 Burncross Road, Chapeltown; Tel: 0114-246 9004
www.greenheadhouse.com ££
Set in a quaint 17th-century cottage, Greenhead House offers welcoming, friendly service and excellent food. Vegetables and herbs come from their own attractive walled garden, where guests can also sit out for drinks in good weather.

Pubs

The Peak District has many unspoilt pubs that welcome walkers: try **The Barrel** at Foolow, the **Millstone Inn** at Hathersage, the **Cheshire Cheese** at Hope, the **Lathkil Hotel** at Over Haddon or **The Quiet Woman** at Earl Sterndale. South of Buxton on the A515, near Flagg, **The Bull i' th' Thorn** is an ancient coaching inn with Tudor panelling, while in Bakewell the **Castle Inn** on Bridge Street is a Georgian-fronted 17th-century pub.

Nottingham's **Ye Olde Trip to Jerusalem**, in Brewhouse Yard below the castle, is built into the castle rock and is said to date from 1189.

In Lincoln, **The Tap & Spile** in Hungate offers real ale and a live-music programme. **The Victoria** in Union Road also appeals to real-ale fans.

YORKSHIRE AND THE NORTHEAST

The moors of the northeast are untamed, wide-
open spaces, littered with evidence of a turbulent
past, but they shelter picture-book villages,
bustling towns and the historic city of York

L ong before Sunday afternoon strollers trod Pennine millstone grit and mountain limestone, this corner of England was pounded by the feet of armies. The region's history is as turbulent as the sudden storms that rage on the high moors; no other part of England has more fortifications.

In AD 122, the Roman emperor Hadrian built a fortified wall for 73 miles (117km) across the country from sea to sea to keep back "barbarian" Scots. The Wars of the Roses (1455–85) saw the Houses of Lancaster (red rose) and York (white rose) locked in a struggle to win control of the throne. The Civil War from 1641 to 1653 divided local allegiances between king and parliament.

Living traditions

Although many of the north's industries have all but died out, traditional life lives on. At **Huddersfield**, to the north of the Peak District and 15 miles (24km) southwest of Leeds, the famous choral society has performed Handel's *Messiah* in the Town Hall just before Christmas every year since 1836. On the A642, halfway between Huddersfield and Wakefield, the **National Coal Mining Museum** (www.ncm.org.uk; daily 10am–5pm; free) illustrates the industry's history with an underground tour of a former mine.

Halifax ❶, 10 miles (16km) north-west of Huddersfield, earned its wealth from textiles and has several famous sons, including the novelist and playwright J.B. Priestley, the composer Frederick Delius (1862–1934) and the writer Alan Bennett (b.1934).

A main attraction is the award-winning **Eureka! The Children's Museum** (during term-time Tue–Fri 10am–4pm, Sat–Sun 10am–5pm, during school hols daily 10am–5pm; charge), with over 400 interactive exhibits designed for children up to the age of 11.

LEFT: Haworth's Main Street.
RIGHT: traditional Morris dancers step out in Ripon, North Yorkshire.

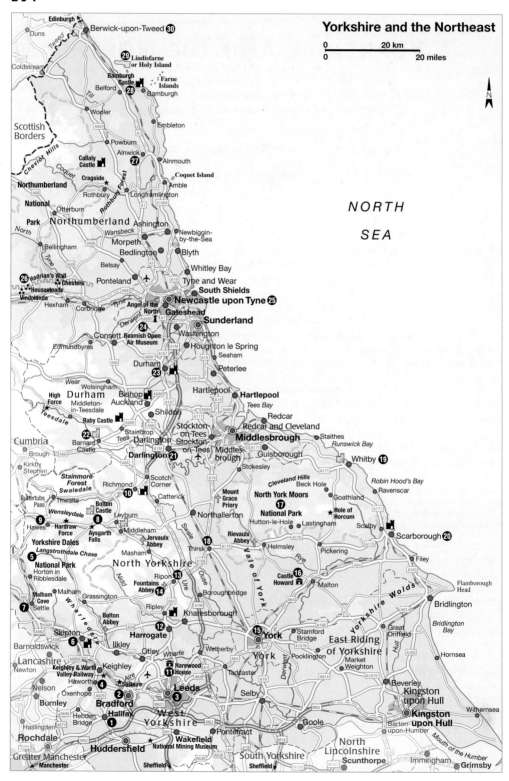

Yorkshire and the Northeast

0   20 km
0   20 miles

NORTH SEA

In nearby **Bradford** ❷, the 19th-century textile barons built solid dependability and vigour into every brick of the city's Italianate Town Hall and its Gothic Wool Exchange. One of the richest, Sir Titus Salt, enshrined his ideals in the nearby model village of **Saltaire**. In 2001 the preserved village was designated a Unesco World Heritage Site. The giant **Salt Mill** (tel: 01274-531 163; www.saltsmill.org.uk; daily 10am–5.30pm, Sat–Sun until 6pm; free), where all the residents worked, provides wonderful gallery space and has one of the largest collections of art works by David Hockney, who was born in Bradford in 1937.

The wool trade attracted many immigrants to Bradford, and it now has a multiethnic population, especially evident during the Mela festivals in Peel Park. Asians are estimated to make up around 28 percent of Bradford's old city, and Muslim influence is strong.

In the town centre is the **National Media Museum** (tel: 0844-856 3797; www.nationalmediamuseum.org.uk; Tue–Sun 10am–6pm; charge). Its three cinemas include an IMAX screen, five storeys high. The museum houses the world's first negative, the earliest television footage and what is regarded as the world's first moving pictures – Louis Le Prince's 1888 film of Leeds Bridge.

Leeds to Ilkey

Yorkshire's main city, **Leeds** ❸, is a lively university city and a world centre for the ready-made clothing industry. Its big tourist attraction is the **Royal Armouries Museum** (daily 10am–5pm; free) at Clarence Dock. It displays 3,000 years of arms, from musket-balls to parts of the late dictator Saddam Hussein's supergun. It's also an attractive shopping centre, with highlights including a branch of Harvey Nichols on Briggate, in the historic Victoria quarter.

Just a few miles to the west – though a world away – from the vast Bradford/Leeds conurbation is the hill village of **Haworth** ❹, with steep cobbled streets and grey-stone houses. Scorched in summer and lashed by rain and wind in winter, this atmospheric place

Statue in Leeds of Joseph Priestley, the 18th-century theologian often credited with the discovery of oxygen.

BELOW: fencing demonstration at the Royal Armouries Museum, Leeds.

MEN-AT-ARMS

TIP

To see production of the cheese that made Wensleydale a household name, call in at the Wensleydale Creamery Visitor Centre (www.wensleydale.co.uk) in Hawes. Wallace and Gromit heaven!

BELOW RIGHT:
Bolton Abbey was founded by the Augustinians in 1154. It ceased to be a priory in 1539 when Henry VIII dissolved the monasteries.

is home to the **Brontë Parsonage** (tel: 01535-642 323; www.bronte.org.uk; daily Apr–Sept 10am–5.30pm, Oct–Mar 11am–5pm; charge), where Charlotte, Emily, Anne and their brother Branwell grew up, and masterpieces such as *Wuthering Heights* and *Jane Eyre* were written.

Haworth station is headquarters of the **Keighley and Worth Valley Railway** (tel: 01535-645 214; www.kwvr.co.uk), which runs steam locomotives on a restored 5-mile (8km) track between **Keighley** and **Oxenhope**. Ingrow (West) station, a mile from Keighley, has a **Museum of Rail Travel**.

North of Haworth, the spa town of **Ilkley,** immortalised its rugged climate in the Yorkshire anthem, *On Ilkla Moor baht 'at*, which, translated, tells you that it is not prudent to venture forth on Ilkley Moor without a hat.

The Yorkshire Dales

To the north of Ilkley lies the expanse of the **Yorkshire Dales National Park ❺**, characterised by dry-stone walls, lively market towns, isolated farmhouses and cathedral-like caverns.

The easiest excursion takes you into surrounding **Wharfedale**, an alluring mix of water, wood, crag and castle. The ruins of the 12th-century **Bolton Abbey** (daily 9am–7pm, with exceptions; charge for parking), located 5 miles (8km) northwest of Ilkley off the A59 to the east, enjoy a stunning location by the River Wharf.

West of Ilkley is the market town of **Skipton ❻**, the "gateway to the Dales", whose position on the Leeds–Liverpool Canal brought great prosperity during the Industrial Revolution. Many of the warehouses still stand, and so does the stout and well-preserved **Skipton Castle** (daily 10am–6pm, Sun from noon, Oct–Feb until 4pm; charge), which dates from the 12th century. Nearby and to the north of Malham village is **Malham Cove**, an enormous limestone crag with the largest area of limestone pavement in Britain at its top.

Further west still is the small market town of **Settle ❼**, a logical point from which to begin a circular tour of the flat-topped **Ingleborough** hill, taking in the magnificent **Ribblehead Viaduct**, built in 1869–76 to carry the

Brontë Country

The tiny manuscripts on display at the Brontë Parsonage Museum *(see above)* in Haworth, West Yorkshire, are a reminder of the secrecy with which Charlotte *(pictured)*, Emily and Anne surrounded their work. These were middle-class female writers working in a man's world.

In the town, the church where the Brontës' father was parson was rebuilt by his successor in 1879. All the Brontës except Anne, who was buried in Scarborough, lie in the family vault near where the Brontë pew stood in the old church. Still very visible is the congestion of old tombstones in the graveyard, recalling mid-19th-century conditions here, when average life expectancy was 28 and the town was racked with typhus and cholera.

Above Haworth, the moors retain their fabled grandeur: the wild skyline setting at Top Withins may have inspired "Wuthering Heights" in Emily Brontë's novel. It is a popular destination for Brontë pilgrims today, reached in about an hour along a path starting at the Penistone Hill Country Park.

Settle–Carlisle Railway across Batty Moss. To the north, **Wensleydale**, famous for its crumbly cheese, is broad and wooded. Attractions here include the medieval **Bolton Castle** ❽ (tel: 01969-623 981; www.boltoncastle.co.uk; daily mid–Feb–Oct 11am–5pm with exceptions; charge), perched on a hillside. Tradition has it that the mortar was mixed with oxblood to strengthen the building. Inside, you can readily imagine yourself transported back to 1568, when Mary, Queen of Scots was imprisoned here. Nearby are the impressive **Aysgarth Falls**.

Situated at the heart of the Yorkshire Dales National Park and around 16 miles (25km) due west on the A684, one of the main attractions of **Hawes** ❾ is the excellent **Dales Countryside Museum** (Feb–Dec daily 10am–5pm, Jan Tue, Sat–Sun 10am–5pm; charge), housed in the former railway station. Nearby is **Hardraw Force**, England's largest single-drop waterfall, where water cascades an impressive 100ft (30 metres) over the cliff. Access is via the Green Dragon pub.

To the east is the town of **Middleham**, famous for its racehorse stables and its moated **castle** (Mar–Oct daily 10am–6pm, winter Thur–Mon 10am–4pm; charge), the childhood home of Richard III. The 12th- to 14th-century remains include the massive keep, gatehouse and three chapels.

Buttertubs Pass ("buttertubs" are deep limestone shafts) is 1,730ft (530 metres) high and links Wensleydale with **Swaledale** to the northeast. Swaledale is steep and rocky, with intricate patterns of drystone walls and field barns. Its market town, **Richmond** ❿, has a cobbled square and Norman **castle** (www.english-heritage.org.uk; Mar–Sept daily 10am–6pm, Oct Thur–Mon 10am–4pm; charge), dramatically sited above the River Swale.

Around Harrogate and Ripon

North of Leeds, just off the A61, is **Harewood House** ⓫ (www.harewood.org; mid-Apr–Oct daily noon–4pm; charge), a stately home with interiors by Robert Adam and furniture by

A sheep farmer in the Yorkshire Dales.

BELOW: the sweeping countryside of Swaledale, one of the more remote northern dales.

Thomas Chippendale. It was built in the 1760s. The landscaped gardens, featuring a remarkable bird garden, were laid out by "Capability" Brown. The 11 Harewood Penguins are a big attraction for children.

Eight miles (13km) further along the A61 is **Harrogate ⑫**, a handsome spa town. The **Royal Pump Room** (tel: 01423-556 188; www.harrogate.gov.uk; Mon–Sat 10.30am–5pm, Sun 2–5pm; charge) still serves the strongest sulphur water in Europe. The **Royal Hall**, Britain's last surviving Kursaal (Cure Hall), was built in 1903 by the theatre designer Frank Matcham.

Art-lovers should make for the **Mercer Art Gallery** (Swan Road; tel: 01423-556 188; Tue–Sat 10am–5pm, Sun 2–5pm), which has around 2,000 works of art, mainly 19th- and 20th-century paintings and prints. A changing exhibition programme features works from the permanent collection.

Around 4 miles (6.5km) north, **Ripley** is a village of cobbled squares and stone cottages conceived in the style of Alsace-Lorraine, after the French region took the fancy of the local landowner, Sir William Amcotts Ingilby, on his travels. The squire's home, **Ripley Castle** (tel: 01423-770 152; www.ripleycastle.co.uk; 90-min guided tours Apr–Sept daily, Mar and Oct–Nov Tue, Thur, Sat–Sun, Dec–Jan Sat–Sun, all 10.30am–3pm; charge) has fine collections of art and armour.

Ripon ⑬, further along the A61, developed around the Saxon **cathedral** (www.riponcathedral.or.uk) founded by St Wilfrid in the 7th century. Today's building is the fourth cathedral to stand on this site, but you can see the crypt of the first church, created by St Wilfrid in 672. The cathedral also has an Art Nouveau pulpit and 15th-century carvings in the choir – the one depicting a griffin chasing a rabbit down a hole is thought to have inspired Lewis Carroll in his *Alice's Adventures in Wonderland*. His father was one the cathedral's canons, and Carroll visted many times. The cathedral also has associations with the war poet Wilfred Owen, who visited it in 1918, before being sent back to France, where he was killed. He composed two poems to Ripon.

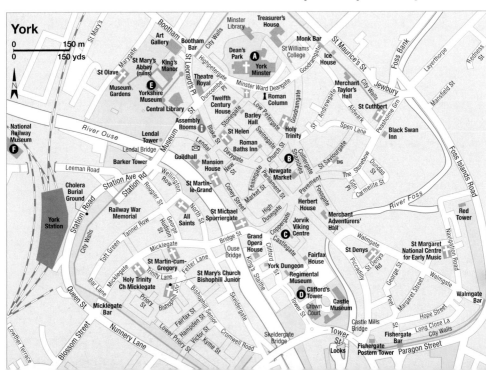

Three miles (5km) to the southwest are **Fountains Abbey**  (www.fountains abbey.org.uk; daily Apr–Sept 10am– 5pm, Oct–Mar 10am–4pm; charge). A Unesco World Heritage Site, the Abbey was part of what was once Britain's richest Cistercian monastery, and the atmospheric remains are the largest monastic ruins in the country. Kitchens and dormitories survive, a tribute to old craftsmanship, giving today's visitor an unusually clear idea of medieval monastic life. The water garden has a mill and a deer park. Adjacent to the abbey grounds is **Studley Royal**, an estate with Georgian water gardens and a deer park. Also close to the Abbey are **Brimham Rocks**, strangely shaped sculpted sandstone dumped here during the Ice Age.

York

The Yorkshire Dales are separated from the North York Moors by the broad Vale of York. At its centre is **York** ⓯, an attractive city of partly Roman but mainly medieval walls and streets, centred around England's largest cathedral.

York Minster Ⓐ (tel: 0844-939 0011; www.yorkminster.org; Mon–Sat 9am– 5pm, Sun noon–3.45pm; charge) is a fusion of classical, Norman, Saxon and English influences. Constantine the Great was declared Roman Emperor here, providing an improbable link between Yorkshire and the founding of Constantinople.

In the shelter of the cathedral, to the south, is a maze of medieval streets and alleys, including **the Shambles** Ⓑ, the former butchers' quarter. Some alleys are so narrow that overhanging upper storeys of timber-framed buildings almost touch across the street. Surrounding the old centre are the **city**

Viking life displayed at the Jorvik Viking Centre through sights, sounds and, very convincingly, smells.

BELOW: York Minster.

Mouseman Carvings

Sharp young eyes will love searching for the carved wooden mouse on the wooden stalls in the Lady Chapel of York Minster. The carved creature was the trademark of Robert Thompson (1876–1955), popularly known as the "Mouseman". The self-taught craftsman came from nearby Kilburn and was known for his use of traditional techniques and top-quality, naturally seasoned English oak, which followed on from the belief in hand-worked craftsmanship promoted by disciples of the Arts and Crafts movement. The mouse logo is still used by craftsmen at the Mouseman Centre, where there's also a museum that documents the Mouseman tradition (www. robertthompsons.co.uk; daily Easter–Sept 10am–5pm, Oct Tue–Sun 10am–5pm, Nov, Dec Wed–Sun 11am–4pm; charge).

Clifford's Tower in York was built to replace a wooden keep that had burned down in 1190 when around 150 Jewish people who had taken refuge there were attacked. Fostered by the Crusades, anti-Jewish sentiment spread throughout England during the reign of Henry II.

BELOW: National Railway Museum, York.

walls, though it can take 2 hours to complete the circuit on foot.

Eight centuries after the Romans arrived in York, the Vikings came, renaming the settlement Jorvik. A routine archaeological dig in 1976 turned up a treasure chest of 15,000 artefacts, now the core of the **Jorvik Viking Centre**  (www.jorvik-viking-centre. co.uk; daily Easter–Oct 10am–5pm, Nov–Easter 10am–4pm; charge). Visitors ride in electric buggies down a "time tunnel" into a reconstructed 10th-century Viking village. The buggies then pass through the actual excavation site.

Other historic sights of note include **Clifford's Tower** , to the south of the Jorvik Centre. It was hurriedly thrown up by William the Conqueror after the Battle of Hastings (1066) to keep the north country under control. In 1684 a fire – some say started deliberately – set off the powder magazine and blew off the roof, leaving the structure as it is today. It is thought to take its name either from the powerful Clifford family, hereditary constables in the area, or from Sir Richard Clifford, who

was hanged there in 1322 after a failed rebellion. Beyond the tower mound is the **Castle Museum** (www.yorkcastlemuseum.org.uk; daily 9.30am–5pm; charge), named after the castle that once stood on this site, whose focus is documenting York life over the centuries.

History is at the heart of the **Yorkshire Museum**  (www.yorkshire museum.org.uk; daily 10am–5pm; charge), too. Situated near the railway station to the north of the old town, the museum's Roman, Anglo-Saxon and Viking treasures include the Middleham Jewel. You can picnic in the botanical museum gardens, where peacocks roam.

West of here, just south of the River Ouse, is the **National Railway Museum**  (www.nrm.org.uk; daily 10am–6pm; free). This is the world's largest such museum, and includes the famous *Flying Scotsman* as well as Queen Victoria's luxurious carriage.

Around York

Among maritime attractions in the Museum Quarter at **Kingston upon Hull**, 43 miles (69km) southeast of

York Minster's Glorious Glass

As the masons worked, and the Minster slowly took its present form, artistry of a different kind was flourishing in small studios all over York. As a result, the whole history of English stained glass ranging from the 12th century to the present day can be seen in the Minster.

The Great East Window contains the world's largest area of medieval stained glass in a single window. It was completed in 1407 by Coventry glazier John Thornton. The window's theme is the beginning and the end of the world, using scenes from the Bible. The West Window, painted in 1338, is known as the Heart of Yorkshire because of the heart shape in the ornate tracery of the window arch. The north transept is dominated by the stunning Five Sisters Window, the oldest complete window in the Minster, made of green and grey Grisaille glass set in geometric patterns.

During the two world wars all 100,000 pieces of glass were taken out and buried for safety. In the south transept, the Rose Window narrowly escaped total destruction when lightning struck the Minster in 1984.

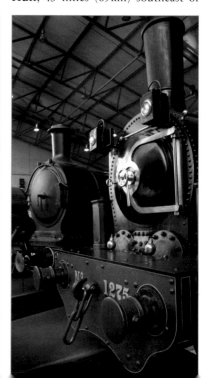

York, is **The Deep** (daily 10am–6pm; charge), the world's only "submarium", where you can admire sharks and other sea creatures, both living and extinct.

Some 15 miles (24km) northeast from York on the A64 is **Castle Howard** ⓰ (www.castlehoward.co.uk; Apr–Oct daily 11am–4pm; charge), one of the grandest Baroque stately homes in Britain. It is also famous since it featured heavily in the television adaptation of Evelyn Waugh's *Brideshead Revisited*.

North York Moors

Further north lies the **North York Moors National Park** ⓱. Stretching from the Vale of York to the east coast, the park embraces the largest expanse of heather moorland in England and Wales. Approaching from the west or the south, many visitors arrive in the quaint market town of Helmsley. And just to the east of the A1 is the thriving market town of **Thirsk** ⓲, famous as the "Darrowby" of the vet books by James Herriot (real name Alf Wight, 1916–95), which were translated into a 1980s TV series, *All Creatures Great and Small*. Wight's former surgery is now **The World of James Herriot** (23 Kirkgate; daily, Apr–Oct 10am–5pm, Nov–Mar 11am–4pm; charge), devoted to the author and a fun place to take children for its focus on animals,

Nearby, deep in the Rye Valley, are the romantic ruins of **Rievaulx Abbey** (www.english-heritage.org.uk; Apr–Sept daily 10am–6pm, Oct Thur–Mon 10am–4pm; charge), another of Yorkshire's great medieval monasteries.

The great dome of the park's moorland heather is penetrated by dales of lush pasture. In some places they create dramatic natural features, such as the **Hole of Horcum** above the Vale of Pickering; elsewhere they enfold villages and farmhouses built mainly of warm, honey-coloured sandstone. The prettiest villages include **Hutton-le-Hole** in Farndale, with a broad green, and nearby **Lastingham**, with a splendid Norman crypt.

On the northern flanks, above Eskdale, are **Goathland** and **Beck Hole**, the latter a delightful hamlet with an arc of cottages facing a green. Across it all, for 18 miles (29km) from Pickering to Whitby, runs the steam-powered **North Yorkshire Moors Railway** (see www.nymr.co.uk for timetable). For the more energetic, there is the **Lyke Wake Walk** (www.lykewake.org), which traverses the Moors for 42 miles (68km) between Osmotherley and Ravenscar.

Whitby to Filey

The Moors end at the east coast, where breaks in the precipitous cliffs provide space for pretty villages and the occasional town. **Whitby** ⓳ is a picturesque fishing port with a jumble of pantiled cottages climbing from the harbour. On **East Cliff** are the remains of the 13th-century **Whitby Abbey** (www.english-heritage.org.uk; Apr–Sept daily 10am–6pm, Oct Thur–Mon 10am–4pm; charge), on which site

Castle Howard was the location for the lavish TV and film versions of Evelyn Waugh's classic 1949 novel Brideshead Revisited. *Today, the Howard family helps to finance the estate by staging concerts and allowing camping in the extensive grounds.*

BELOW: the Shambles, York.

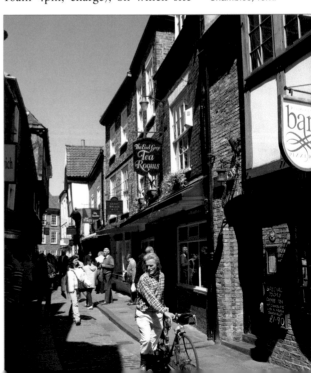

a 7th-century monk wrote the *Song of Creation*, considered as the start of English literature. The abbey is also believed to have inspired Bram Stoker's *Dracula*.

The Pacific explorer Captain James Cook (1728–79) lived in this former whaling port. The **Captain Cook Memorial Museum** (daily Apr–Oct 9.45am–5pm, Mar 11am–3pm; charge) in Grape Street is the focal point of a Cook heritage trail.

To the north of Whitby, steep roads lead down to **Runswick Bay**, a self-consciously pretty assortment of fishermen's cottages, and **Staithes**, where the young Cook was briefly and unhappily apprenticed to a grocer.

To the south, seekers of solitude can detour from the coastal road to find **Ravenscar**, which has fine walks *(see page 301)*, but little else except one imposing clifftop hotel. Nearby **Robin Hood's Bay** is said to have once offered sanctuary to the outlaw after whom it is named, and was a smugglers' haunt. Today its cobbled streets and beautiful, unspoilt sandy beaches are popular with families.

Further south lies **Scarborough** , a posh watering hole whose **Grand Hotel** was the handsomest in Europe when it opened in 1863. The 12th-century **castle** (Apr–Sept daily 10am–6pm, Oct–Mar Mon and Thur–Sun 10am–4pm; charge) is worth seeing, and Anne Brontë – who, like so many invalids, came for the bracing air – is buried in the graveyard of **St Mary's Church**. The town has long enjoyed a connection with Alan Ayckbourn, the local-born playwright who has premiered most of his prolific output at the **Stephen Joseph Theatre** (www.sjt.uk.com). Ayckbourn was artistic director at this theatre-in-the-round until 2009.

Filey offers unpretentious delights to day-trippers, including amusement arcades, a splendid beach and **Filey Brigg**, the breakwater at the northern end of the bay. Off the dramatic 400ft (130-metre) cliff at nearby **Flamborough Head**, the American squadron of John Paul Jones won a sea battle with two British men-of-war in 1779.

Teesside

Heading north from Whitby now and leaving Yorkshire behind, the lively, sandy-beached resort of **Redcar** is a playground for the former Teesside industrial centres of **Middlesbrough**, **Stockton-on-Tees** and **Darlington**. The region boomed in the 19th century as coal and iron were discovered and the railways were built, but is less prosperous nowadays. George Stephenson's *Locomotion No. 1* (1825) is displayed at Darlington's railway museum, **Head of Steam** (www.darlington.gov.uk; Apr–Sept Tue–Sun 10am–4pm, Oct–Mar Wed–Sun 11am–3.30pm; charge), near where it once ran on the world's first railway line, between Stockton and Darlington.

Sixteen miles (25km) to the west, on the River Tees, is the the old market town of **Barnard Castle**. Here the impressive, palatial **Bowes Museum** (daily 10am–5pm; charge) has a superb collection of exhibits, notably a won-

BELOW: Whitby and its abbey.

derful 1773 clockwork silver swan. The museum is renowned for its connections with the late Queen Mother, whose maiden name was Bowes Lyon.

Near **Staindrop**, on the A688 to the northeast, is the nine-towered **Raby Castle** (tel: 01833-660 202; www.raby castle.com; park and gardens: 11am–5.30pm, castle: 1–4.30pm, May, June, Sept Sun–Wed, Mon–Wed by guided tour only, July–Aug Sun–Fri; charge), set in a 250-acre (100-hectare) deer park.

To the northwest, off the B6277 near **Middleton-in-Teesdale**, one of England's most impressive waterfalls, **High Force**, crashes down 70ft (21 metres).

Durham

Northeast is the historic university city of **Durham** ㉓. Until 1836 the prince-bishops of the County Palatine of Durham were granted complete sovereignty within their diocese, holding their own parliaments and minting their own coins. The spectacular Romanesque **cathedral** (tel: 0191-386 4266; www.durhamcathedral.co.uk; Mon–Sat 7.30am–6pm, Sun 7.45am–5.30pm; donations), dramatically sited

above a meander in the River Wear, is one of Europe's finest. Its Chapel of the Nine Altars is the final resting place of St Cuthbert, who evangelised from Lindisfarne Abbey.

The city's splendid **castle** (for guided tours, tel: 0191-334 3800) was the only northern stronghold not to fall to the marauding Scots, and is now occupied by University College.

Many American visitors head north of Durham for the town of **Washington** and the 17th-century **Old Hall** (www.nationaltrust.org.uk; mid-Mar–Oct Sun–Wed 11am–5pm; charge). The handsome stone manor house is the ancestral home of the USA's first president.

The Bowes Museum was built by John and Joséphine Bowes (a Parisian actress), who assembled 15,000 paintings, ceramics, furniture and textiles between 1862 and 1874, when Joséphine died. Sadly, John did not live to see the museum open in 1892.

BELOW LEFT: Scarborough. **BELOW RIGHT:** Temple of the Four Winds, Castle Howard.

A section of the 73-mile (117km) Hadrian's Wall, begun in AD 122 to secure the northern boundary of Roman rule in Britain.

BELOW: the Tyne Bridge and the Sage concert hall and, in the background, the Gateshead Millennium Bridge and the Baltic Centre.

Newcastle upon Tyne

Continuing north up the A1, a 20-metre (66ft) -tall steel giant marks the entry into Tyneside. The **Angel of the North** stands on the site of a former coal mine and was created by artist Antony Gormley.

For a realistic look at how life used to be in the northeast, visit the **Beamish Open Air Museum ㉔** (www.beamish.org.uk; Apr–Oct daily 10am–5pm, Nov–mid March Tue–Thur and Sat–Sun 10am–4pm; charge), 8 miles (13km) southwest of Newcastle. It has a working 1913 village with buildings and artefacts collected from all over the region.

Next stop is is **Newcastle upon Tyne ㉕**, a sprawling former shipbuilding city celebrated for its resilient natives ("Geordies"), whose dialect borders on impenetrability, and for its potent brew, Newcastle Brown (pronounced *broon*) Ale. Newcastle has a large university and a thriving arts and folk music scene.

In the city itself, the striking **Gateshead Millennium Bridge** links Newcastle Quayside with the new developments on Gateshead Quays. These include the **Baltic Centre for Contemporary Art** (tel: 0191-478 1810; www.balticmill.com; Mon–Sat 9am–6pm; free) and the **Sage** concert hall and music education centre (www.thesagegateshead.org). The latter's shimmering, shell-like form was designed by Norman Foster.

Roman northeast

The strategic importance of the site of Newcastle was first recognised by the Romans, who founded the city as a minor fort and bridge on **Hadrian's Wall ㉖** (www.hadrians-wall.org) almost 2,000 years ago. Begun during the reign of Emperor Hadrian in AD 122, Hadrian's Wall runs 73 miles (117km) across the north of England.

At nearby South Shields, archaeologists have excavated the **Arbeia Roman Fort** (www.twmuseums.org.uk; Easter–Sept Mon–Sat 10am–3pm, Sun 1–5pm, Oct–Easter 10am–3.30pm, closed Sun; charge). To the west, near Hexham, **Housesteads Roman Fort** (www.english-heritage.org.uk; daily Apr–Sept 10am–6pm, Oct until 4pm; charge) is the best preserved of the 16 forts along the wall, and nearby is the major site of **Vindolanda** and the **Roman Army Museum** (www.vindolanda.com; daily Apr–Nov 10am–6pm, Oct until 5pm; charge).

Just above Hexham the wall crosses the River North Tyne at **Chesters** (www.english-heritage.org.uk; daily Apr–Oct 10am–6pm, winter until 4pm; charge), site of a Roman cavalry fort with a remarkably well-preserved military bathhouse.

Alnwick to the Farne Islands

Around 34 miles (54km) north of Newcastle is the fortified town of **Alnwick** ㉗, home to one of Britain's best examples of a medieval fortress on a large scale. The **castle** (www.alnwickcastle.com; Apr–Oct daily 11am–5pm; charge), home of the Dukes of Northumberland (the Percy family), and a backdrop to Harry Potter and many other films, is the second-largest residential castle in Britain, after Windsor Castle. The grounds are fun for children, with the Poison Garden, Serpent Garden, Bamboo Labyrinth and a Tree House complex linked by walkways.

There are more fine fortresses along the coast, including the romantic ruins of **Dunstanburgh** (www.nationaltrust.org.uk; Jan–Mar and Nov–Dec Thur–Mon 10am–4pm, Apr–Sept daily 10am–5pm, Oct daily 10am–4pm; charge) and the giant keep of **Warkworth** (www.english-heritage.org.uk; daily Apr–Sept 10am–5pm, Oct–Mar 10am–4pm; charge). The most stunning is **Bamburgh Castle** ㉘ (www.bamburghcastle.com; mid-Feb–Oct daily 10am–5pm, Nov–mid-Feb Sat–Sun 11am–4.30pm; charge), 16 miles (25km) north. From here, on a clear day, you can see the **Farne Islands**. Boats for this former saints' sanctuary now colonised by seabirds and grey seals leave from Seahouses harbour (tel: 01665-720 308; www.farne-islands.com; daily, every hour 10am–3pm; charge).

Lindisfarne

Further north still is **Lindisfarne** ㉙ (or Holy Island), which can be reached only at low tide via a causeway. Monks from the Scottish Isle of Iona, led by St Columbine, settled here in the 7th century and founded a **priory** (www.english-heritage.org.uk; daily Apr–Sept 9.30am–5pm, Oct until 4pm; charge) that achieved renown as a centre of scholarship. The illuminated *Lindisfarne Gospels*, now in the British Museum, were produced here. Birdwatchers also flock to the island's breeding grounds.

On the border with Scotland is the port of **Berwick-upon-Tweed** ㉚, England's most northerly town. Walk along the well-preserved Elizabethan ramparts to gaze down on its cobbled streets and out towards the shoreline. ❏

Hadrian's Wall is 15ft high and 7½ft thick (5 by 2.5 metres) and snakes across the Borders for 73 miles (117km). It has several easy points of access from the A69, but the best section is the 4 miles (7km) between the Twice Brewed Inn and Sewingshields Crag (the site of a former castle under which, legend says, King Arthur sleeps).

BELOW:
Alnwick Castle.

RESTAURANTS, TEAROOMS AND PUBS

Restaurants

Prices for a three-course dinner per person with a half-bottle of house wine:
£ = under £25
££ = £25–50
£££ = £50–100
££££ = over £100

Bolton Abbey

Devonshire Arms Country House Hotel
Tel: 01756-710 441
www.thedevonshirearms.co.uk £££
The Michelin-starred restaurant in this lovely former coaching inn is furnished with antiques from Chatsworth. The cooking is as elegant as the surroundings, with classic dishes using seasonal, local produce, given a modern touch.

Bradford

Nawaab
32 Manor Road
Tel: 01274-730 371
www.nawaabs.net £–££
With the scores of curry houses in Bradford, you couldn't do better than start at this city-centre evergreen. Diana, Princess of Wales, Imran Khan and Frank Bruno have all eaten here.

Chester-le-Street

Black Knight Restaurant
Lumley Castle Hotel
Tel: 0191-389 1111
www.lumleycastle.com £££
This restaurant, in the town of Chester-le-Street, 7 miles (11km) from Durham, is in the 14th-century ancestral home if the Earl of Scarborough. Dress up for an excellent meal.

Durham

Bistro 21
Aykley Heads House,
Aykley Heads
Tel: 0191-384 4354
www.bistrotwentyone.co.uk ££
Robust classic French country cooking in a 16th-century farmhouse with an informal atmosphere, on the edge of the city.

Helmsley

Feversham Arms
Tel: 01439-770 766
www.fevershamarmshotel.com £–££
The restaurant in this former coaching inn (now a four-star hotel and spa) offers local produce such as slow-cooked pork belly with red cabbage and lemon sole with crayfish mousse. Tasty desserts, including a dark chocolate tart with clotted cream, add to the enjoyment.

Harrogate

Van Zeller
8 Montpellier Street
Tel: 01423-508 762
www.vanzellerrestaurants.co.uk ££–£££
If you're not heading for Bettys, like everyone else, a good option is this restaurant in Harrogate's chic Montpellier district. It offers fine food in minimalist surroundings with main courses such as venison served with a beetroot fondant, and wild turbot with leeks. And for dessert, there's a chocolate delice and lemon iced parfait.

Ilkley

Box Tree
35–37 Church Street
Tel: 01943-608 484
www.theboxtree.co.uk ££
Young Marco Pierre White cut his culinary teeth in this intimate 18th-century stone farmhouse that serves modern French classics.

Leeds

Brasserie Forty 4
44 The Calls
Tel: 0113-234 3232
www.brasserie44.com ££
Located in a converted grainhouse, this bright, modern brasserie is always lively, and the food (classic British comfort food, with lots of meaty dishes and old-school puddings) provides good value for money. You might spot a well-known face here, too.

Malham

The Buck Inn
Tel: 01729-830 317
www.buckinnmalham.co.uk ££
Built in 1874 overlooking the village green, this historic inn offers home-cooked traditional fare in the bar, including its speciality, Malham and Masham pie, à la carte in the candlelit restaurant.

Moulton

Black Bull Inn
Tel: 01325-377 289
www.blackbullmoulton.com ££
This upmarket white-washed inn has several dining spaces with nooks and corners, plus a conservatory, Fish Bar and "Hazel", a 1932 First Class Pullman dining car. Modern British food with ingredients including Yorkshire venison and foraged wild mushrooms.

Blackfriars Restaurant

Friars Street

Tel: 0191-261 2945

www.blackfriarsrestaurant.
co.uk **££**

Reputedly the oldest purpose-built restaurant in Britain, with a medieval banqueting hall. The actor Kevin Spacey declared it served "the best roast dinners in England".

Café 21

19–21 Queen Street

Tel: 0191-222 0755

www.cafetwentyone.co.uk
££–£££

Upmarket contemporary bistro on the Quayside with a handsome interior and an appetising modern European menu. Good lunch and early evening deals, too.

Seaham Hall Hotel

Lord Byron's Walk

Tel: 0191-516 1400

www.seaham-hall.co.uk **£££**

An award-winning restaurant in a spa hotel 20 minutes from Newcastle. In 1815 Lord Byron was married in the Byron Room.

Winteringham Fields

Tel: 01724-733 096

www.winteringhamfields.
co.uk **££–£££**

Just south of the Humber Bridge, this is a 16th-century manor bursting with character. This restaurant (with rooms) has an extensive menu, including a tasting menu featuring mainly local ingredients and large cheeseboard.

Greens

13 Bridge Street

Tel: 01947-600 284

www.greensofwhitby.com **££**

There's lots of good seafood, including Whitby squid and scallops, at this informal bistro.

The Magpie Café

14 Pier Road

Tel: 01947-602 058

www.magpiecafe.co.uk **££**

This is a legendary harbour-side restaurant known for its superb fish and chips.

Café Concerto

21 High Petergate

Tel: 01904-610 478

www.cafeconcerto.biz **££**

Very popular with the locals, this café near the Minster becomes a bistro in the evenings, with dishes including grilled sea bass and comforting sausage and mash.

Gray's Court

Chapter House Street

Tel: 01904-612 613

www.grayscourtyork.com **££**

Sit in squashy sofas in the stunning oak-panelled gallery of this historic house and enjoy lovingly prepared modern British cuisine. In summer, you can sit in the beautiful garden.

Tearooms

**Bettys & Taylors
of Harrogate**

1 Parliament Street,
Harrogate

Tel: 01423-814 070

www.bettys.co.uk

Founded in 1919, Bettys' family-run business is an institution, with the original Tea Room in York. Now it is teamed with tea and coffee merchant Taylors of Harrogate, founded in 1886. Bettys' elegant Tea Rooms serve wonderful cakes and pastries and are also at:

Harlow Carr: RHS Gardens

Ilkley: 32 The Grove

Northallerton: High Street

York: 6–8 St Helen's Square (the original Bettys) and 46 Stonegate.

Pubs

In Bradford, **Sir Titus Salt** is a Wetherspoon conversion of the old swimming baths and is handy for the National Media Museum (the outside is admittedly far more impressive than the inside).

Among the ornate Victorian pubs in Leeds are **The Scarborough** in Bishopsgate Street and **The Victoria** in Great George Street.

In Harrogate, **Hales Bar** in Crescent Road has good beers and retains some original gaslight fittings.

In York, **Maltings** in Tanners Moat promotes good beers and is handy for the Railway Museum.

The Blue Bell in Fossgate is a small place with well-preserved Edwardian decor.

In Whitby, **The Duke of York** has fine views over the harbour.

In Durham, **The Victoria** in Hallgarth Street lives up to its name with tributes to the queen and Victorian decor. **The Dun Cow** in Old Elvet, parts of it 16th-century, dispenses the locally popular Castle Eden ale.

In Newcastle upon Tyne, **The Cluny** in Lime Street is a converted whisky-bottling plant that also serves as an art gallery, artists' studio and music venue. For ornate architecture, try **Crown Posada** in The Side, off Dean Street; the famous art historian Nikolaus Pevsner admired its Pre-Raphaelite stained-glass windows. The **Centurion Bar**, a former first-class waiting room at the central railway station, has amazing tiles.

LEFT: Bettys Tea Rooms in Harrogate. **RIGHT:** the Tan Hill Inn on Swaledale, Britain's highest pub *(see page 10)*.

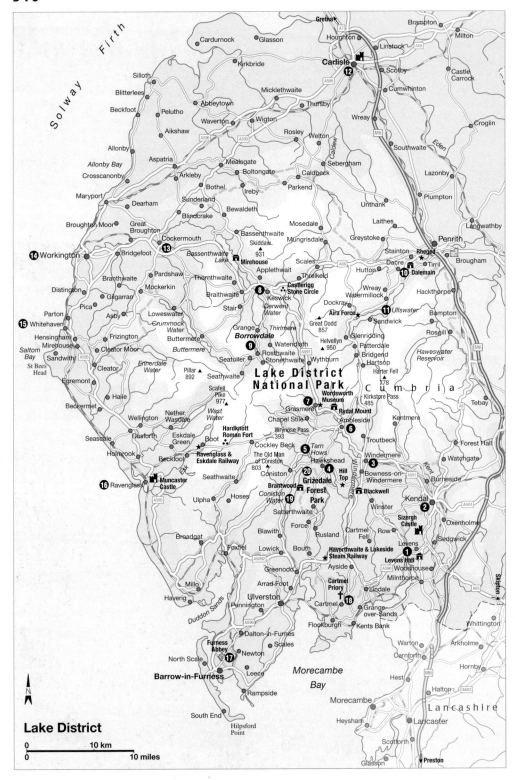

Lake District

Solway Firth

Cardurnock
Glasson
Gretna
Houghton
Brampton
Milton
Kirkbride
Linstock
Scoby
Carlisle
⓬
Castle Carrock
Silloth
Micklethwaite
Cumwhinton
Blitterlees
Thursby
Croglin
Beckfoot
Abbeytown
Wigton
Wreay
Southwaite
Pelutho
Waverton
Rosley
Welton
Lazonby
Allonby
Aikshaw
Caldew
Eden
Aspatria
Mealsgate
Boltongate
Sebergham
Plumpton
Allonby Bay
Arkleby
Caldbeck
Langwathby
Crosscanonby
Bothel
Ireby
Parkend
Unthank
Brougham
Maryport
Dearham
Sunderland
Bewaldeth
Laithes
Plumpton
Broughton Moor
Blindcrake
Mosedale
Greystoke
Stainton
Penrith
Great Broughton
Bassenthwaite
Skiddaw 931
Mungrisdale
Rheged
Workington ⓮
Cockermouth
⓭
Bassenthwaite Lake
Mirehouse
Scales
Dacre ⓾ Dalemain
Tirril
Bridgefoot
Applethwaite
Threlkeld
Hutton
Pardshaw
Thornthwaite
Castlerigg Stone Circle
Wreay
Hackthorpe
Branthwaite
Mockerkin
Braithwaite
Keswick
Watermillock
Distington
Gilgarran
Stair
⓼
Derwent Water
Dockray
Ullswater ⓫
Bampton
Pica
Asby
Loweswater
Grange
Aira Force
Great Dodd 857
Sandwick
Parton
Frizington
Crummock Water
Thirlmere
Glenridding
Rosgill
Whitehaven ⓯
Buttermere
Watendlath
Helvellyn 950
Patterdale
Haweswater Reservoir
Hensingham
Mirehouse
Cleator Moor
Buttermere
Borrowdale
Rosthwaite
Bridgend
Hartsop
Saltom Bay
Sandwith
Cleator
⓽
Seatoller
Stonethwaite
Wythburn
Harter Fell 778
St Bees Head
Ennerdale Water
Pillar 892
Seathwaite
Kirkstone Pass 485
Egremont
Haile
Scafell Pike 977
Lake District National Park
Wordsworth Museum
Cumbria
Tebay
Beckermet
Wast Water
Grasmere ⓻
Rydal Mount
Kentmere
Wellington
Nether Wasdale
Hardknott Roman Fort 393
Chapel Stile
Ambleside ⓺
Forest Hall
Seascale
Eskdale Green
Boot
Wrynose Pass
Troutbeck
Watchgate
Gosforth
Ravenglass & Eskdale Railway
Cockley Beck
⓹ Tarn Hows
Windermere
Burneside
Holmrook
Beckfoot
The Old Man of Coniston 803
Hawkshead
⓷
Bowness-on-Windermere
Ravenglass ⓰
Muncaster Castle
Coniston
⓴
⓸ Hill Top
Kendal ⓶
Seathwaite
Grizedale Forest Park
Blackwell
Sizergh Castle
Ulpha
Hoses
Brantwood
⓳
Winster
Oxenholme
Satterthwaite
Coniston Water
Levens
Sedgwick
Blawith
Force
Rusland
Cartmel Fell
Row
Levens Hall ⓵
Broadgat
Foxfiel
Lowick
Bouth
Haverthwaite & Lakeside Steam Railway
Woodhouse
Millo
Greenodd
Ayside
Milnthorpe
Haverig
Arrad Foot
Cartmel Priory
Lindale
Duddon Sands
Ulverston
⓲
Grange-over-Sands
Pennington
Cartmel
Dalton-in-Furness
Flookburgh
Kents Bank
Whittington
Furness Abbey
Newton
Scales
Warton
Arkholme
Barrow-in-Furness
⓱
Leece
Morecambe Bay
Hest
Carnforth
Hornby
Rampside
Halton
South End
Heysham
Lancashire
Hilpsford Point
Morecambe
Lancaster
Scotforth
Glasson
Preston

N

0   10 km
0   10 miles

THE LAKE DISTRICT

From the time of the first guidebook to the area,
Thomas West's 1778 *Guide to the Lakes*,
its pleasures have remained those of the eye;
the landscape is what matters most

The Lake District in northwest England covers a small area (although the National Park that protects it is England's largest, at 885 sq miles/2,290 sq km), measuring 40 miles (64km) from north to south and 33 miles (53km) east to west. But, as the poet William Wordsworth, who was born here at Cockermouth in 1770 and spent most of his life in the region, rightly remarked: "I do not know any tract of country in which, within so narrow a compass, may be found an equal variety in the influences of light and shadow upon the sublime or beautiful features of landscape."

The Lake District is 250 miles (400km) from London and 75 miles (120km) north of Manchester, and it is one of the most frequently visited regions of outstanding natural beauty in the country. Generally, it has proved remarkably able to cope with the vast numbers of visitors, but traffic congestion can be a big problem in summer.

The two routes that were popularised by the first tourists in the 1760s still carry the greatest share of summer traffic. One is from Penrith to Ambleside by the west shore of Ullswater (scene of Wordsworth's poem *The Daffodils*) and over the Kirkstone Pass, now the A592; the other is from Keswick to Windermere by the side of Thirlmere,

Grasmere, Rydal Water and Windermere, now the A591.

The draw of the Lakes

The central area of mountains was never much affected by industry or quarrying, and the 19th-century developments in shipbuilding, iron manufacturing, coal mining and lesser trades that once flourished by the Cumbrian coast have now almost entirely disappeared. Sheep farming was the traditional way of life of the hill folk, and it continues today throughout the area

Main attractions
KENDAL
BOWNESS-ON-WINDERMERE
BEATRIX POTTER'S HILL TOP
BEATRIX POTTER GALLERY
TARN HOWS
DOVE COTTAGE
CASTLERIGG STONE CIRCLE
DERWENT WATER
CARLISLE
WORDSWORTH HOUSE
FURNESS ABBEY
CONISTON WATER'S *GONDOLA*

PRECEDING PAGES: the rolling hills near Elterwater. **BELOW:** cycling is suited to the Lake District.

Beatrix Potter (1866–1943) spent her life surrounded by plants and animals, and she was involved in preserving Herdwick sheep. Her two pet rabbits, Benjamin and Peter, star in her books. She became an authority on mycology (lichens and fungi), illustrating her work with beautiful paintings. Illustrations were an essential part of her later books that told stories about animals, set in the countryside around Hawkshead.

BELOW: sheep can create a traffic jam as they are moved between fields.

covered by the Lake District National Park, often on farms owned and leased by the National Trust.

In the early 19th century, visitors began to walk the high paths over the fells, and after about 1860 they started to climb the more difficult rock faces. Climbers still congregate in **Great Langdale**, **Borrowdale** and **Wasdale** to tackle the central heights of the **Langdales**, **Scafell Crags**, **Great Gable**, **Steeple** and **Pillar**. There are hundreds of miles of paths to tempt the walker. Paths over the high fells must be tackled with respect for the region's notoriously rapid changes of weather, and with the proper equipment, but there are innumerable easy walks by the lakesides or along the streams that anyone can enjoy.

Around Levens

Approaching the Lake District from the south along the M6, a turn-off at junction 36 leads to the town of **Levens** ❶. **Levens Hall and Gardens** (www.levenshall.co.uk; Apr–mid-Oct Sun–Thur, house: noon–4.30pm, last admission 4pm, gardens: 10am–5pm;

charge) is a largely 16th-century house built around a 13th-century pele tower, with a famous topiary garden that has changed little since its trees were first shaped in the 17th century.

Nearby, the National Trust's **Sizergh Castle** (mid-Mar–Oct Sun–Thur noon–5pm, garden: daily mid-Mar–Oct 11am–5pm, Nov–Dec 11am–4pm; charge), near Kendal, shows its origins as a medieval defensive structure even more clearly.

Kendal

Kendal ❷, a good gateway for the Lakes, is a just northeast of Levens. It is still a working town, not just a holiday centre, all the more fascinating for carrying on in the midst of fine 17th- and 18th-century buildings. Among these are old coaching inns, and a shop specialising in items made out of horn. The church is a fine, unusually broad Perpendicular building. Beside it stands **Abbot Hall Art Gallery** (Mon–Sat Apr–Oct 10.30am–4pm, Nov–Mar 10.30am–4pm; charge), a mid-17th-century house that now displays a collection of furniture, china

Wainright's Way

St Bees Head is Cumbria's most westerly point and the starting point of the legendary fellwaker and guidebook author Alfred Wainwright's 190-mile (305km) Coast to Coast Walk across northern England, from St Bees to Robin Hood's Bay. Wainwright (1907–91) was born in Lancashire and was 23 when he first saw the Lake District and fell under its spell. He is most famous for his seven-volume handwritten and beautifully illustrated *Pictorial Guide to the Lakeland Fells*, which he compiled between 1952 and 1966, and which people continue to use as their bible for hiking the Lake District's fells.

There is a Wainwright memorial in the church at Buttermere. His ashes were scattered on nearby Haystacks, his favourite mountain.

and paintings by local artists, in particular the portrait painter George Romney. There are also watercolours by John Ruskin. Beside the gallery is the **Museum of Lakeland Life** (times as for the gallery), which has two rooms devoted to the *Swallows and Amazons* author Arthur Ransome (1884–1967).

Potter and the Wordsworths

The A591 runs from Kendal to **Windermere ❸**, a Victorian town that owes its growth to the visitors who arrived here by train on their way to **Bowness-on-Windermere**, just below. In Bowness, **The World of Beatrix Potter** (www.hop-skip-jump.com; daily summer 10am–5.30pm, winter 10am–4.30pm; charge) takes you on a tour through the children's author's life and books. There is also a family-friendly Potter-themed tearoom with tables indoors and a re-creation of the kitchen garden from the Peter Rabbit tales.

Also at Bowness is the car ferry to Far Sawrey and **Hill Top**, Beatrix Potter's house (tel: 01539-436 269; www.nationaltrust.org.uk; mid-Feb–Apr and Sept–Oct Sat–Thur 10.30am–3.30pm with exceptions, Apr–Aug 10am–5pm; garden open daily; charge for timed ticket entry), a fine example of a traditional Lakeland farmhouse. Note that the house is small and you may have to queue to get in, but the archetypal English cottage garden is a good place to wait.

To the south of Bowness just off the A5074 is **Blackwell** (daily, Apr–Oct 10.30am–5pm, Nov–Mar 10.30am–4pm; charge), the Arts and Crafts house designed by M.H. Baillie Scott for a wealthy Manchester brewery owner.

In nearby **Hawkshead ❹**, in a characterful 17th-century building on Main Street, is the National Trust's **Beatrix Potter Gallery** (tel: 01539-436 355; www.nationaltrust.org.uk; mid-Feb–Mar 11.30am–3.30pm, Apr, May and Sept, Oct 11am–5pm, Apr–Aug 10.30am–5pm; charge for timed ticket entry) in the office of her solicitor husband William Heelis. It has displays of many of the original sketches and watercolour paintings from Potter's famous children's books.

Other notable buildings in Hawkshead include the **Old Grammar School** (Apr–Sept Mon–Sat 10am–1pm and 2–5pm, Sun 1–5pm, Oct Mon–Sat 10am–1pm and 2–3.30pm, Sun 1–3.30pm; free), established in 1585. The school now houses a small museum on the history of the building. Downstairs, it suggests little of the excellence of its teaching in the 1780s when the Wordsworth brothers studied there – William was a pupil here for 7 years, carving his initials into his desk – but upstairs is a superb library.

Also of note in the village is the large, handsome **St Michael's Church**. Its inner walls are adorned with murals and painted texts dating from the 17th century. The church holds concerts on Sundays in summer.

West of Hawkshead, near the junction with the Ambleside road, stands the 15th-century arched **courthouse** (Apr–Oct daily 11am–4pm; access only with the key from the National Trust shop, The Square, Hawkshead),

Kendal, a town whose prosperity was based on wool, is now perhaps most famous for Kendal Mint Cake, a slabby, sweet confection, which continues to be an essential part of many outdoor survival kits, whether in the Lake District or in the Himalayas.

BELOW:
the lakes are replenished by generous rainfall.

Castlerigg Stone Circle, probably built around 3000 BC, may have had astronomical significance.

TIP

Tarn Hows provides some of the most spellbinding views of the Lakeland fells. The best vantage point is the southern side of the lake, where the path takes to higher ground.

BELOW: the Old Mill at Ambleside.

a relic of times when the Cistercian monks from Cartmel ruled much of the southern part of the area. Further west, on the B5285, is **Tarn Hows ❺**, considered by many to be the prettiest lake in the Lake District. Only a half-mile (800 metres) long, it was originally three smaller lakes but joined after a dam was built.

Whether you continue towards the head of Lake Windermere on this west side, or take the A591 northwest from Windermere, you will eventually reach **Ambleside ❻**, and just beyond it **Rydal Water**, a reedy lake with several islands. At the head of the village, near the start of a footpath leading to Grasmere, is **Rydal Mount and Gardens** (tel: 01539-433 002; www.rydalmount.co.uk; Mar–Oct daily 9.30am–5pm, Nov–Dec, Feb Wed–Sun 11am–4pm; charge), home of the Wordsworths from 1813 until William died in 1850. The house contains portraits and family mementos; the grounds are laid out in their original form and afford fine views. Vistors can also book exclusive 90-minute evening tours (charge).

Grasmere

Two miles (3km) north lies **Grasmere ❼**. The southernmost part of the village, **Town End,** is where Wordsworth and his sister Dorothy first settled in 1799. The white cottage is movingly simple in its furnishings, but it takes the display of manuscripts and portraits of the poet's family and friends in the nearby **Grasmere Wordsworth Museum** (tel: 01539-435 544; www.wordsworth.org.uk; daily 9.30am–4pm, Mar–Oct until 5.30pm; charge for combined ticket with Dove Cottage, *see below*) to bring home the magnitude of the poetry that was written here and the significance of Wordsworth (and his fellow Romantic poet Samuel Coleridge – also covered) in the cultural life of their day.

St Oswald's Church is a plain, roughly built structure with a remarkable and much-altered ancient timber roof. The Wordsworth family graves, and that of Coleridge's son Hartley, lie behind it. All about are the paths,

streams and hills that Dorothy Wordsworth described along with the daily life of **Dove Cottage** in her 1800–2 *Journal*. Wordsworth lived at the whitewashed cottage from 1799 to 1808. Its rooms are rather cramped, and it's hard to imagine how the poet, Dorothy, his wife Mary (a childhood friend he married in 1802) and other friends all fitted in.

The 17-mile (28km) journey northwest to Keswick on the A591 passes **Thirlmere**, a reservoir created out of two smaller lakes in 1890 to supply the water needs of Manchester. **Helvellyn**, the third-highest mountain in England (3,120ft/950 metres), rises steeply to the right.

Close to Keswick you may turn off to **Castlerigg Stone Circle**, an ancient monument of 48 large stones commanding tremendous views. Early tourists associated it with the Druids. Recent scholars think the stones may have been intended as a giant calendar to show by its shadows the turn of the seasons for planting and reaping.

Pencils for poets

Keswick ❽ (whose name is Old English for "cheese farm"), a Victorian town with an older centre, has been popular with visitors since the 1760s, when the poet Thomas Gray stayed there to explore its lake, **Derwent Water**. With fear and trembling, Gray ventured to the mouth of mountain-surrounded **Borrowdale** ❾, just past the southern end of the lake, which early visitors associated with the sublimity and terror of the Italian Salvator Rosa's Baroque paintings. Even today one might fear that the tottering pinnacles will detach themselves and fall upon one's head. A favourite excursion since Gray's time is the **Bowder Stone**, balanced on the side of the hill a little way up the valley. Another attraction is the waterfall at **Lodore**, near the head of Derwent Water.

Borrowdale was famed among the early tourists for the "wad" or black lead mine that enabled the manufacture of pencils in Keswick, which is

now home to the family-friendly **Cumberland Pencil Museum** (daily 9.30am–5pm, last admission 4pm; charge).

Keswick's **Museum and Art Gallery** (Tue–Sun 10am–4pm; free), in Fitz Park, documents the town and its surroundings and has letters by Wordsworth and his fellow "Lakeland Poet" Robert Southey, and manuscripts from Hugh Walpole, who lived nearby and whose "Rogue Herries" novels are set in and around the area.

Another local, the poet Samuel Taylor Coleridge, settled at **Greta Hall** on the outskirts of Keswick in 1800 and persuaded Southey (his brother-in-law) to join him there. **Crosthwaite Church**, which stands about half a mile beyond Greta Hall, has memorials to Southey and members of his family.

Northwards, the churchyard looks towards **Bassenthwaite Lake**, the eastern side of which is dominated by Skiddaw (3,050ft/931 metres). Below the mountain lies **Mirehouse** (www.mirehouse.com; Apr–Oct Sun and Wed, Aug Sun, Wed and Fri, 2–5, last entry

Crosthwaite Church. The poet Thomas Gray (1716–71) described the view as one which, if it could be captured "in all the softness of its living colours, would fairly sell for a thousand pounds".

BELOW: Wordsworth memorabilia at Dove Cottage.

The poet William Wordsworth spent much of the last 50 years of his life in Grasmere and was buried in the cemetery there. He was loyally supported by his sister Dorothy (1771–1855), whose Grasmere Journal *sheds light on both her and their life and work.*

BELOW: boating on Ullswater.

at 4.30pm, grounds and teashop daily 10am–5pm; charge), the 18th-century home of the Spedding family.

A 15-mile (24km) drive eastwards from Keswick on the A66 to the old town of **Penrith** can include a visit to **Dacre** ⑩, a few miles before the town on the right. It has a largely Norman church, even earlier carvings and views of 14th-century **Dacre Castle** (closed to the public). A short detour leads to **Rheged – The Village in the Hill** (www.rheged.com), just off the M6. Housed in Europe's largest grass-covered building, named after Cumbria's Celtic Kingdom, the centre is home to a cinema, indoor and outdoor children's play areas, exhibitions that take the visitor through 2,000 years of Cumbria's history, shops and places to eat.

Nearby is **Dalemain** (tel: 017684-86450; www.dalemain.com; Apr–Sept Sun–Thur 11.15am–1pm, 1.30–4pm, Oct until 3pm; charge), an old house last altered in 1750 that offers fine interiors (including a Chinese drawing room with mid-18th-century wallpaper), paintings and a pleasant garden. The Medi-

eval Hall is now an impressive tearoom, serving good cakes and lunches.

Dalemain lies just off the A592, which leads past **Ullswater** ⑪ and over the Kirkstone Pass to Ambleside. Ullswater is the second-largest lake in the district after Windermere. There arconise steamers on the lake from which one can enjoy excellent views of Helvellyn and other surrounding mountains, and **Aira Force** – on the north shore beneath Gowbarrow Fell – is one of the most impressive waterfalls in the Lake District.

Back closer to Penrith, just to the town's southeast, is **Brougham Castle**, a Norman castle built on the foundations of a Roman fort.c

Carlisle

Carlisle ⑫, just 21 miles (34km) north of Penrith on the M6, also deserves an excursion, although it takes you outside the borders of the Lake District National Park. The **Castle** here obtained its unusual outline when its roof was strengthened to carry early cannons. It is linked by a pedestrian subway to the **Tullie House Museum and Art Gallery** (Apr–Oct Mon–Sat 10am–5pm, Sun 11am–5pm, Nov–Mar galleries close at 4pm; charge), which houses a collection of Roman materials and Pre-Raphaelite paintings.

The western Lakes

To get back to the Lake District, the A595 from Carlisle runs southwest to **Cockermouth** ⑬, an old-fashioned stone-built town stretching along a lengthy main street. The National Trust's restored **Wordsworth House** (www.wordsworthhouse.org.uk; Mar–Oct Sat–Thur 11am–5pm, last admission 4pm; charge) is where William and Dorothy spent their earliest years. Actors in period costume play the parts of the servants, cooking, cleaning and working in the garden.

Adjacent to the remains of **Cockermouth Castle** (privately owned and only occasionally open to the public) is **Jennings Brewery** (tel: 0845-129

7190; www.jenningsbrewery.co.uk; guided tours, check website or call for times; charge). Established over 150 years ago, the company moved to Cockermouth in 1874. The tour includes a sample of their real ales.

Heading west leads towards the Solway Firth and **Workington** ⓱, a town at the mouth of the River Derwent. On the outskirts, on the A66 at the junction of Stainburn and Park End roads, is the **Helena Thompson Museum** (Tue–Sun 1.30–4.30pm; free), set in an elegant Georgian mansion and charting the maritime and social history of the town. **Workington Hall** in Curwen Park – refuge for Mary, Queen of Scots during her last night of freedom in May 1568 – is a ruin, but plaques give visitors a flavour of the hall's long history, dating from the 14th century.

South along the coast, **Whitehaven** ⓯ is a lively town with a redstone promontory. The port's role in the rum trade unfolds at **The Rum Story** (tel: 01946-592 933; www.rumstory.co.uk; daily 10am–4.30pm; charge), set in the Jefferson family's 18th-century premises on Lowther Street. Delve further into the area's history at **The Beacon** (www.thebeacon-whitehaven.co.uk; daily 10am–4.30pm; charge) with its five floors of interactive exhibits and galleries. A footpath leads from behind the Beacon to the **Haig Colliery Mining Museum** (tel: 01946-599 949; www.haigpit.com; daily 9am–4.30pm; charge) on the former site of the Haig Pit. The pit's mighty steam winding engine is operated on most days, and guided walks may be arranged.

Roman hairpins

Southwest Lakeland is rich in interest. One of the most dramatic sites of all is best approached on the Windermere-based "Mountain Goat" mini-coach service (tel: 01539-445 161; www.mountain-goat.com) by anyone lacking both an extremely agile car and nerves of steel. The road over the Wrynose and Hardknott passes, 10 miles (16km) west of Ambleside, was improved by

the Romans, but they probably intended their narrow road, with its hairpin bends and sheer drops, for pedestrians only. But the situation of **Hardknott Roman Fort** high above **Eskdale**, with its view of the highest peaks and the distant sea, is unforgettable.

Eskdale's mines and quarries were the reason for the construction of the **Ravenglass and Eskdale Railway** (www.ravenglass-railway.co.uk), known locally as the "Ratty", a narrow-gauge line that delights summer visitors with its miniature steam engines. The line runs for 7 miles (11km) from the visitor centre at Dalegarth down to Ravenglass harbour.

From **Eskdale Green**, a road runs over Birker Fell to the **Duddon Valley**, an area of great natural beauty.

Ravenglass ⓰, on the coast, lies close to **Muncaster Castle** (www.muncaster.co.uk; Mar–Oct Sun–Fri, castle: noon–4.30pm, gardens: 10.30am–6pm; charge), home of the Pennington family since 1325, when a new tower was built on the foundations of a Roman watchtower commanding

In the village of Lowther is the Lakeland Bird of Prey Centre, which offers daily falconry displays. Visitors who wander around may see hawks, eagles and owls.

BELOW: Coniston.

Before the arrival of the railway in 1847, Windermere was the hamlet of Birthwaite, situated a mile (2km) from the lake anciently known as Vinard's Mere. It owes its expansion to the visitors who arrived by train and who had to pass through it to reach the lakeside at Bowness, just below the town.

BELOW: rowing on Lake Windermere.

extensive views of the fells and Eskdale. Henry VI sought refuge here and is said to have given his drinking bowl, the "Luck of Muncaster", to his host. The bowl is still in the house, which, in the course of 18th- and 19th-century alterations, has grown from a medieval tower into an attractive mansion. An Owl Centre and children's indoor MeadowVole Maze have the same opening times as the gardens.

Abbey lands

The southern tip of Lakeland was in medieval days the heart of the great Cistercian estate farmed by the monks of **Furness Abbey** (www.english-heritage.org.uk; Oct–Mar Sat–Sun 10am–4pm, Apr–June, Sept Thur–Mon 10am–5pm, July–Aug daily 10am–5pm; charge). The impressive ruins, which English Heritage is attempting to stop from sinking, are set in the pretty Vale of Deadly Nightshade, on the north side of the shipbuilding town, **Barrow-in-Furness**.

The abbey was the second-richest Cistercian establishment in England prior to its suppression in 1537 during Henry VIII's dissolution of the monasteries. Its buildings date from the 12th and 15th centuries.

To the east is **Cartmel Priory** (daily, Apr–Sept 9am–5.30pm, Oct–Mar 9am–3.30pm; free), near the resort of Grange-over-Sands on a finger of land pointing down into Morecambe Bay. It was founded in 1188 by the Baron of Cartmel and saved from destruction by the quick-wittedness of local people who claimed that it was, in fact, their parish church.

Returning northward, the visitor approaches the foot of **Windermere**, from where the **Haverthwaite and Lakeside Steam Railway** (www.lakesiderailway.co.uk) runs from April to October. To the west is **Coniston Water**, the third-largest of the lakes. Between these lies **Grizedale Forest Park**, a large tract of land the Forestry Commission has given over to nature trails, interesting modern sculptures and a 23-seat theatre. Coniston was famous for the residence of John Ruskin (1819–1900), the great Victorian art historian and writer on social and economic themes, and later by the world water speed record attempts of Donald Campbell, who died in the last attempt here in 1967.

The best way to cross the lake is on the Victorian steam yacht *Gondola* (tel: 01539-432 733; www.nationaltrust.org.uk; Apr–Oct daily, see web or call for times; charge), which runs a regular timetable travelling from Coniston Pier, with a full head of steam. The design for the boat was approved by Ruskin, a man with discerning tastes. He lived at **Brantwood** (www.brantwood.org.uk; daily mid-Mar–Oct 11am–5.30pm, Nov–mid-Mar 11am–4.30pm; charge), on the northeast shore, and those on the *Gondola* can disembark here. The house remains much as he left it, and nowadays there's a restaurant, where you can take lunch on an attractive terrace. ❏

RESTAURANTS AND PUBS

Restaurants

Prices for a three-course dinner per person with a half-bottle of house wine:
£ = under £25
££ = £25–50
£££ = £50–100
££££ = over £100

Ambleside

The Glass House Restaurant
Rydal Road
Tel: 01539-432 137
www.theglasshouse
restaurant.co.uk **££**
This attractive restaurant does good modern British and European dishes such as fish pie, and braised lamb and duck confit with Cumberland stuffing.

Lucy's on a Plate
Church Street
Tel: 01539-432288
www.lucysofambleside.co.uk
£–££
A very popular local deli and restaurant with a wide range of dishes with fresh, local produce, including a good selection for vegetarians.

Zeffirellis
Compston Road
Tel: 01539-433845
www.zeffirellis.com **£–££**
Stylish vegetarian pizzeria with a pleasant buzz. In the complex, there's also a café, jazz bar and cinema.

Carlisle

Garden Restaurant
Tullie House Museum and Art Gallery, Castle Street
Tel: 01228-618 718
www.tulliehouse.co.uk **£–££**
The restaurant of the Tul-

lie House Museum offers reliable daily specials, a salad bar and home-baked treats in an elegant setting.

Cartmel, nr Grange-Over-Sands

L'Enclume
Cavendish Street
Tel: 01539-536 362
www.lenclume.co.uk **£££**
Run by chef Simon Rogan, this Michelin-starred restaurant is certainly the most creative, if not the best, in the Lakes. The food is a combination of traditional and modern, using many ingredients foraged from the wild.

Coniston

Jumping Jenny
Brantwood
Tel: 01539-441 715 **£**
(lunch)
In the grounds of Ruskin's house, this restaurant, open during the day only, serves homemade soups, savoury tarts and pasta dishes as well as a great afternoon tea.

Eskdale

The Woolpack Inn
Holmrook
Tel: 01946-723 230
www.woolpack.co.uk **£–££**
This boutique hotel set within a traditional hostelry in the western Lake District serves reliably good comfort food (Herdwick Lamb Tatie pot, local steak-and-kidney pies, home-roasted ham etc), alongside a selection of real ales.

Grasmere

The Jumble Room
Langdale Road

Tel: 01539-435 188
www.thejumbleroom.co.uk
££
A highly recommended eatery, serving up great food from cullen skink to sweet-potato ravioli, using local, organic produce wherever possible. Also does great desserts. Colourful decor.

Kendal

Tapestry Tearoom
Friends Meeting House, Stramongate
Tel: 01539-722 975 **£–££**
This is one of the best places for vegetarian food in the Lakes, with mains made with fresh local produce, and fabulous cakes and puds. In warm weather, you can order a picnic to eat in the lawned garden.

Keswick

Highfield Restaurant
Highfield Hotel, The Heads
Tel: 01768-772 508
www.highfieldkeswick.co.uk
££
This award-winning restaurant is one of the best in the area. It does very good modern British food – think spiced crabmeat and celeriac coleslaw or escalope of Cumbrian veal – using local ingredients.

Whitehaven

Zest
Low Road
Tel: 01946-692 848
www.zestwhitehaven.com **££**
Grilled meats, particularly steak, feature heavily among the modern British dishes served at this contemporary restaurant. The stress is also on locally sourced produce.

Also has a more low-key sister restaurant, The Harbourside, at 8 West Strand.

Windermere

Miller Howe
Rayrigg Road
Tel: 01539-442 536
www.millerhowe.com **££**
With offerings such as Lancashire cheese, Cumbrian ham and Herdwick mutton, this restaurant within a country-house hotel is a great place to try some well-cooked, imaginative local food from a head chef who used to work at Raymond Blanc's esteemed Manoir aux Quat'Saisons (see page 185). Romantic views over Lake Windermere.

Pubs

At Ambleside, **Kirkstone Pass Inn**, Lakeland's highest pub, is hiker-friendly. All-day food.

In Kendal, **Burgundy's Wine Bar** in Lowther Street also has a good range of bottled beers.

In Hawkshead, the oak-beamed **Queen's Head Hotel** on Main Street does freshly cooked fare to go with its real ales and relaxed environment.

In Coniston, the **Sun Hotel**, dating to the 16th century, has a warm bar in winter and a pleasant beer garden in summer. The historic **Black Bull** coaching inn has an outdoor seating area.

At Windermere, **The Queen's Head**, Troutbeck, is cosy, with oak beams, flag floor and a log fire. There's a terrace out the front, too.

Scotland

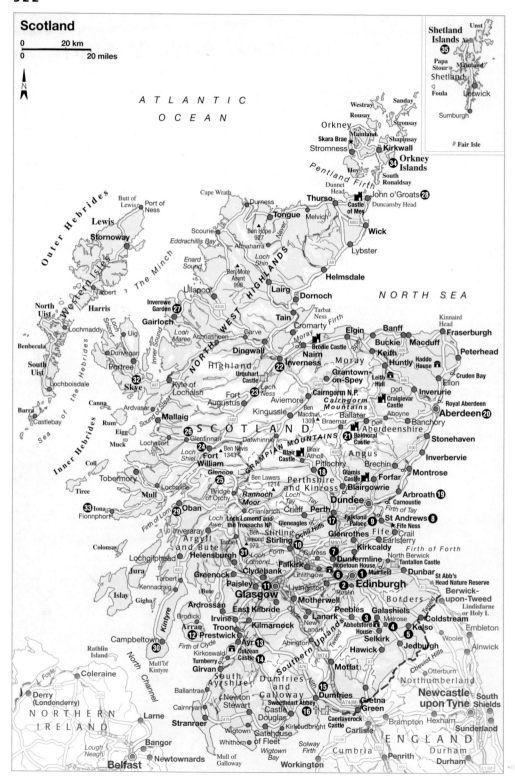

0   20 km
0   20 miles

N

ATLANTIC OCEAN

Shetland Islands ㉟
Unst
Yell
Papa Stour
Foula
Mainland
Shetland
Lerwick
Sumburgh

Fair Isle

Westray
Rousay
Sanday
Stronsay
Shapinsay
Orkney
Mainland
Skara Brae
Stromness
Kirkwall
Orkney ㉞ Islands
Hoy
South Ronaldsay

Pentland Firth

Dunnet Head
Castle of Mey
John o'Groats ㉘
Duncansby Head

Cape Wrath
Butt of Lewis
Port of Ness
Lewis
Stornoway

Outer Hebrides

Durness
Thurso
Tongue
Melvich
Wick
Lybster

Ben Hope 927
Altnaharra
Scourie
Eddrachillis Bay
Loch Shin
Helmsdale

Enard Sound
Ben More Assynt 998
Ullapool
Lairg
Dornoch

NORTH SEA

North Uist
Lochmaddy
Benbecula
South Uist
Lochboisdale
Barra
Castlebay

Harris
Tarbert
The Minch

Western Isles

Inverewe Garden ㉗
Gairloch
Loch Maree
Achnasheen
Garve
Dingwall
Tarbat Ness
Tain
Cromarty Firth
Moray Firth
Elgin
Banff
Buckie
Macduff
Fraserburgh
Kinnaird Head
Peterhead
Cruden Bay

Uig
Dunvegan
Portree
Skye ㉜
Kyle of Lochalsh
Loch Ness
Inverness ㉒
Urquhart Castle
Nairn
Brodie Castle
Keith
Huntly
Haddo House
Ellon
Inverurie
Royal Aberdeen
Aberdeen ⑳

Canna
Ardvasar
Sound of Sleat
Fort Augustus
㉓
Highland
Grantown-on-Spey
Cairngorm N.P.
Leith Hall
Don

Rum
Eigg
Muck
Lochailort
Mallaig
Glenfinnan ㉖
SCOTLAND
Aviemore
Kingussie
Ben Macdhui 1309
Cairngorm Mountains
Ballater
Braemar
Aberdeenshire
Dee
Aboyne
Banchory
Craigievar Castle
Stonehaven

Inner Hebrides

Coll
Tiree
Tobermory
Mull
Lochaline
Iona ㉝
Fionnphort
Oban ㉙

Argyll and Bute

Loch Shiel
Fort William ㉔
Ben Nevis 1343
Glencoe
㉕
Bridge of Orchy
Rannoch Moor
Ben Lawers 1214
Loch Tay
Crianlarich
Crieff
Perthshire and Kinross
Blair Castle
Blair Atholl
Pitlochry
Balmoral Castle ㉑
Angus
Brechin
Forfar
Montrose
Inverbervie
Arbroath ⑲

Colonsay
Inveraray
Loch Awe
Firth of Lorn
Loch Lomond and the Trossachs NP
Gleneagles
㉘
Glamis Castle
Blairgowrie
Dundee
Carnoustie
Firth of Tay
St Andrews ⑧
Fife Ness

Jura
Lochgilphead
Tarbert
Helensburgh
Loch Lomond
Ben Lomond 973
㉛
Stirling ⑩
Ochil Hills
Perth ⑰
Falkland Palace
Fife
Glenrothes ⑨
Crail
Earlsferry
Firth of Forth

Islay
Gigha
Kennacraig
Greenock
Clydebank
Paisley
Glasgow ⑪
Motherwell
Culross
Dunfermline ⑦
Kirkcaldy
Hopetoun House ①
Muirfield
North Berwick
Tantallon Castle
Dunbar

Kintyre
Campbeltown
Mull of Kintyre
Ardrossan
East Kilbride
Irvine
Troon ⑫
Prestwick
Kilmarnock
Ayr ⑬
New Lanark
Lanark
Peebles
Abbotsford House ③
Galashiels
Melrose
Selkirk
④
Kelso ⑤
Jedburgh
Coldstream
Embleton
Wooler
Alnwick

Rathlin Island
Coleraine
Derry (Londonderry)

NORTHERN IRELAND
Larne
Bangor
Newtownards
Belfast
Lough Neagh

Ballantrae
Cairnryan
Newton Stewart
Stranraer
Wigtown
Whithorn
Mull of Galloway

South Ayrshire
Girvan
Culzean Castle ⑭
Kirkoswald
Turnberry
Dumfries and Galloway
Sweetheart Abbey
Castle Douglas
Kirkcudbright
Gatehouse of Fleet
Wigtown Bay
Solway Firth

Hawick
Moffat
Dumfries ⑮
㉚
Gretna Green
⑯
Caerlaverock Castle
Carlisle
Cumbria

Borders
Berwick-upon-Tweed
Lindisfarne or Holy I.
St Abb's Head Nature Reserve
Cheviot Hills
Otterburn
Northumberland
Newcastle upon Tyne
South Shields
Sunderland
Hexham
Brampton
Penrith

ENGLAND
Durham
Workington

Firth of Clyde
Abington
Livingston
Linlithgow ⑥
Edinburgh ②
Roslin
Stirling
Clyde
Bute
Arran ㉚
Brodick

THE SCOTTISH LOWLANDS

Scotland is a place of endless variety: in the Lowlands there are hills and seascapes, impressive stately homes and the historic Burns country, and the vibrant cities of Edinburgh and Glasgow

Scotland is a separate experience. The Scots themselves have a keen sense of identity, of different values and of their own history and traditions unparalleled in Great Britain. Things might have been different if two Roman emperors had not built walls (Hadrian's Wall, *see page 304*, and the Antonine wall) across the north of Britain to keep in place the region's painted Celtic warriors, the Picts and the Scots.

The Scots joined England in the Union of the Crowns in 1603 – James VI of Scotland became James I of England, the first "British" monarch – and in 1701 joined England in the Union of the Parliaments, whereby the two parliaments met jointly at Westminster. Scotland regained its own independent parliament in 1999. Throughout, the Scots maintained their own legal and educational systems and continued to print their own design of banknotes – often the first clue to visitors that they are in a different country.

Scotland's 30,400 sq miles (78,740 sq km) cover one-third of Britain, yet its population, of which more than 30 percent live in or around the three most populous cities, Edinburgh, Glasgow and Aberdeen, is less than one-tenth of the whole. Aberdeen, on the northeast coast, boomed in the 1970s with the discovery of North Sea oil.

Glasgow and Edinburgh, stimulating but quite different cities, lie only 43 miles (69km) apart at opposite sides of the Lowlands, hidden from England by the rolling Southern Uplands, and a breather before the dramatic hurdles of the Highlands. Both cities are about 380 miles (610km) from London.

Scotland's capital

Between the Pentland Hills and the Firth (estuary) of Forth is **Edinburgh ❶**. On the south side of its main thoroughfare

Main attractions
EDINBURGH
ABBOTSFORD HOUSE
MELROSE ABBEY
HOPETOUN HOUSE
ST ANDREWS
GLASGOW
CULZEAN CASTLE
DUMFRIES

PRECEDING PAGES: Edinburgh Castle.
RIGHT: Royal Mile piper, Edinburgh.

The One O'Clock Gun is fired at Edinburgh Castle.

TIP

At Edinburgh Castle don't miss the display of the Scottish crown, sceptre and sword of state, known as the "Honours of Scotland". They form the oldest royal regalia in Europe.

of **Princes Street**, beyond sunken gardens, rises the basal ridge on which medieval Edinburgh is built. The **castle** Ⓐ (daily Apr–Sept 9.30am–6pm, Oct–Mar 9.30am–5pm; charge) dominates the horizon.

In the castle complex is the 12th-century **St Margaret's Chapel**, built for the wife of King Malcolm Canmore by her son, David I; the **Great Hall**, which is still used for banquets and has a magnificent hammerbeam ceiling; the tiny room where in 1566 Mary, Queen of Scots gave birth to the future James VI of Scotland (James I of England); and the **National War Memorial**. Also to be seen are the crown jewels and the Stone of Destiny, or Stone of Scone, the coronation seat of Scottish kings.

The Royal Mile

Four streets – **Castlehill**, **Lawnmarket**, **High Street** and **Canongate** –

make up the **Royal Mile** Ⓑ, which descends from the esplanade in front of the castle (where the Tattoo is held in August) and ends at the Palace of Holyroodhouse. This, the centre of Edinburgh life until the end of the 18th century, is still lively. Along its route are some of the best examples of 16th- and 17th-century domestic architecture in Britain.

At the top is the **Scotch Whisky Experience** (daily 10am–6pm; charge), which gives visitors an overview of the Scottish national drink. Nearby is the **Camera Obscura** (July–Oct 9.30am–7.30pm, Apr–June 9.30am–6pm, Nov–Mar 10am–5pm; charge), where an extraordinary contraption projects live images of the surrounding city.

Further along stands **Parliament House**, now the law courts; and the **High Kirk of St Giles** Ⓒ (May–Sept Mon–Fri 9am–7pm, Sat 9am–5pm, Sun 1–5pm, Oct–Apr Mon–Sat 9am–5pm, Sun 1–5pm; charge) with the magnificent **Thistle Chapel**. There is also the **John Knox House Museum** (Mon–Sat 10am–6pm, July–Aug also Sun noon–6pm; charge), from whose

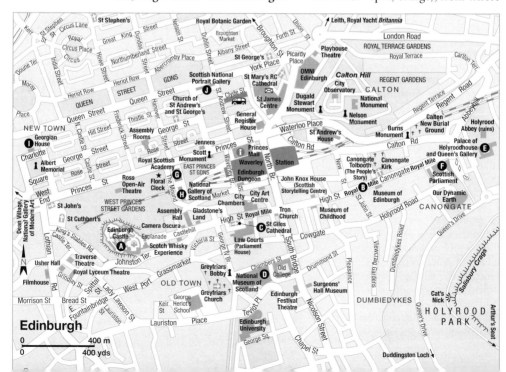

windows the Protestant reformer once preached; the 16th-century **Canongate Tolbooth** (housing the **People's Story**; Mon–Sat 10am–5pm, Sun noon–5pm; free); and the Dutch-looking 17th-century **Canongate Kirk**.

On the High Street, the **Museum of Childhood** (Mon–Sat 10am–5pm, Sun noon–5pm; free) has displays of historical toys and runs activities for children.

For local history, the **Royal Museum** and **National Museum of Scotland** **D** (both www.nms.ac.uk; daily 10am–5pm; free), both in Chambers Street, are worth a visit.

The **Palace of Holyroodhouse** **E** (daily, Apr–Oct 9.30am–5pm, Nov–Mar until 3.30pm; charge) is the official residence of the queen when she visits Scotland. The palace was begun in 1498 by James IV, enlarged by James V and later by Charles II, and has close associations with Mary, Queen of Scots. The last of the Stuarts to live here was Charles Edward Stuart (1720–88), remembered as Bonnie Prince Charlie.

The **Queen's Gallery** (opening times as above; joint ticket available), in front

of the palace, has changing exhibits of artworks from the Royal Collection.

Across the road is the controversial **Scottish Parliament** **F** (tel: 0131-348 5200; www.scottish.parliament.uk; Mon–Sat, see website for times; free), completed in 2004 after exceeding its £40 million building budget more than 10 times over.

Princes Street and the New Town

Edinburgh's main shopping street is **Princes Street**, which runs roughly parallel with the Royal Mile on the far side of the gardens below the castle. Its most conspicuous landmark is

The Royal Mile, outside the High Kirk of St Giles. The route is a mix of tourist shops, pubs and eateries; it is also home to Scotland's main legal institutions.

BELOW: Edinburgh Castle is a rich architectural mix of palace, fortress, barracks, chapel and war memorial.

A statue to Greyfriars Bobby remembers the faithful Skye terrier who kept watch for 14 years, from 1858 to 1872, over his master's grave.

RIGHT: the former royal yacht *Britannia.*

the huge **Gothic monument to Sir Walter Scott** opposite Jenners department store. To the west is the turning for The Mound, which harbours the **Royal Scottish Academy** ❼ (www.royalscottishacademy.org; Mon–Sat 10am–5pm, Sun noon–5pm; charge) and the **National Gallery of Scotland** ❽ (www.nationalgalleries.org; daily 10am–5pm, Thur until 7pm; free).

On the north side of Princes Street is the New Town, a splendid example of 18th-century town planning, in marked contrast to the chaotic street plan of the medieval Old Town. (Both the Old and the New Town are Unesco World Heritage Sites.) Visitors can learn more about the building of the New Town and its residents at the **Georgian House** ❶ (tel: 0844-493 2117; www.nts.org.uk; Mar–Nov daily, see website for times; charge) at 7 Charlotte Square. At the eastern end of Queen's Street is the **Scottish National Portrait Gallery** ❿ (details as for National Gallery).

To the east of Princes Street is **Calton Hill,** a volcanic outcrop that offers stunning views of the city. Crowning

the hill are the old **City Observatory**, with a Grecian-style dome; the **National Monument**, an unfinished copy of the Parthenon in Athens; and the **Nelson Monument** (Apr–Sept Mon–Sat 10am–6pm, Oct–Mar 10am–3pm; charge).

On the hill's lower slopes are the **Burns Monument** and the **Old Calton Burial Ground**, where many of the great names of Scotland's 18th-century Enlightenment are interred.

Beyond the New Town

North of the New Town is the **Royal Botanic Garden** (daily 10am–4pm, Feb–Oct until 6pm; charge for glasshouses), at 70 acres (28 hectares). Following the Water of Leith northeast leads to the old docklands of **Leith**, where the decommissioned royal yacht *Britannia* (daily 10am–3.30pm, summer until 4.30pm; charge) is moored at the **Ocean Terminal**. In recent decades, the district around has been given a considerable makeover and is now home to many of the city's most fashionable bars and restaurants.

Back upstream to the west of the New Town lies the picturesque **Dean**

The Royal Yacht *Britannia*

There have been 83 royal yachts since the restoration of King Charles II in 1660, and this was the very last. The present queen launched *Britannia* in 1953, and witnessed her decommissioning in 1997. She has not been replaced owing to budgetary constraints. During her working life as the royal yacht, *Britannia* undertook almost 700 official foreign visits, hosted several US presidents, and took Prince Charles and Diana on their honeymoon. Her last foreign trip was from Hong Kong, conveying the colony's last governor and Prince Charles away after the handover to China on 1 July 1997.

Today, *Britannia* is moored at Ocean Terminal in Leith, near Edinburgh, and is open to the public daily *(see above).* As well as the queen's bedroom – and Prince Philip's separate, and rather spartan, bedroom – highlights include the State Dining Room and an old Rolls-Royce in its own on-board garage. Visitors can now also enjoy refreshments in the recently opened Royal Deck. Another new attraction is the 1936 racing yacht *Bloodhound*, which was owned by the queen in the 1960s and is now moored alongside *Britannia*. Both the Prince of Wales and Anne, the Princess Royal, learned to sail in her, and she is still used for day-long yachting trips by private charter along the west coast in July and August each year (tel: 0131-555 8800).

Village. On Belford Street are the **Scottish National Gallery of Modern Art** and its sister museum, the **Dean Gallery** (details as for National Gallery).

South to the Borders

Beyond the hills ringing Edinburgh to the south lie the **Borders**: the part of Scotland along the frontier with England and the first part of Scotland to encounter the Romans, the Angles and the English in their fruitless thrusts northwards. Today, it is pastoral country, where farming, knitwear and tweed remain the principal industries, and the passions are for trout and salmon fishing and rugby, of which the Border towns are the great Scottish stronghold.

Leaving Edinburgh by the A703 the village of **Roslin** ❷ is soon reached. The interior of the 15th-century **Rosslyn Chapel** (Mon–Sat 9.30am–6pm, Sun noon–4.45pm; charge) is covered with fascinating stone carvings, which has earned it the nickname "a Bible in stone". It gained added renown when the novel *The Da Vinci Code* reiterated the long-held belief that within the chapel lies the Holy Grail.

Further south, 36 miles (44km) from Edinburgh, overlooking the River Tweed outside **Galashiels** ❸, is **Abbotsford House** (www.scottsabbotsford.co.uk; mid-Mar–Oct daily 9.30am–5pm with exceptions; charge), which was the home of the historical novelist Sir Walter Scott (1771–1832). His family were Border people, and his romantic imagination was first stirred by the derring-do of his ancestors defending their land against England.

Historic reminders

Sitting beneath the triple mounds of the **Eildon Hills**, Melrose ❹, 2 miles (3km) east of Abbotsford, was the haunt of poet and seer Thomas de Rhymer (*c*.1220–97). From the highest hill, views of the Cheviots and the hills running westwards towards Galloway can be enjoyed. In the town stand the ruins of 12th-century **Melrose Abbey** (Apr–Sept daily 9.30am–5.30pm, Oct–Mar 9.30am–4.30pm; charge), which despite its sacking by the English in 1544 is an architectural poem in red sandstone. Melrose is an agreeable base from which to walk the Eildon Hills, fish, or explore the Borders.

Nearby are other glorious medieval abbeys: at **Dryburgh**, 4 miles (6km) beyond Melrose, where Scott is buried; at Kelso, 10 miles (16km) east on the A699; and at **Jedburgh**, 8 miles (13km) south of Dryburgh on the A68. (All three abbeys: daily, with exceptions, 9.30–4.30, summer until 5.30pm; charge).

Just outside **Kelso** ❺ there are several impressive stately homes. **Floors Castle** (late Apr–Oct daily 11am–5pm; charge) is the largest inhabited castle in Scotland and seat of the Duke of Roxburgh. Also worth visiting are the Duke of Buccleuch's house, **Bowhill**, near **Selkirk** (daily July and Aug 1–4.30pm; charge), and **Mellerstain** (July–Aug Sun, Mon, Wed, Thur 12.30–5pm, May–June and Sept Sun, Wed 12.30–5pm, Oct Sun 12.30–5pm; charge), one of the finest Adam houses in Scotland, on the A6089 Kelso to Gordon road.

Abbotsford's collection of historical relics, armour and weapons includes Rob Roy's gun, Montrose's sword and a quaich (drinking bowl) that belonged to Bonnie Prince Charlie.

BELOW:
Abbotsford House and gardens.

The approach to Linlithgow Palace, where most of the Stuart kings lived.

BELOW: the annual Loony Dook swim on New Year's Day attracts hardy participants, many in fancy dress.

The Firth of Forth

East Lothian, to the east of Edinburgh, is dotted with golf courses, castles and nature reserves and, beyond the Lammermuir Hills, a hinterland of lush farmland. Some of the best golf courses are Muirfield, North Berwick, Longniddry, Luffness and Dunbar.

Dirleton Castle (Apr–Sept daily 9.30am–5.30pm, Oct–Mar 9.30am–4.30pm; charge) stands in the centre of a gorgeous eponymous village on the A198 between Gullane and North Berwick, while **Tantallon Castle** (Apr–Sept daily 9.30am–5.30pm, Oct–Mar 9.30am–4.30pm; charge) is an imposing ruin on a headland above the North Sea off the A198 between North Berwick and Dunbar.

Colonies of gannets and other sea birds populate **Bass Rock**, standing 2 miles (3km) offshore from **North Berwick**; boat excursions are available between May and September (tel: 01620-890 202; www.seabird.org). Alternatively, state-of-the-art technology in the **Scottish Seabird Centre** shows all that is happening on Bass Rock

on video screens (10am–6pm, shorter hours in winter). More birds can be seen further south at **St Abb's Head Nature Reserve**.

Closer to Edinburgh is **Aberlady Bay**, whose dune-backed beach has been designated a nature reserve (tel: 01620-827 847; www.aberlady.org). Near **Haddington**, a town of 17th- and 18th-century houses 6 miles (10km) inland from here, stands **Lennoxlove House**, seat of the Dukes of Hamilton and now a smart hotel.

Ancient and modern

On Edinburgh's western fringe is **South Queensferry**, the location of **Hopetoun House** ❻ (late Apr–Oct daily 10.30am–5pm; charge), a glorious, massive Georgian pile belonging to the Marquess of Linlithgow. The work of several great Scottish architects, including the Adam family, it has a sumptuous interior and vast grounds. The observatory affords a splendid view of the Forth Bridge.

From here the M9 leads to **Linlithgow**, where, above a loch and park, stands the roofless red sandstone shell of **Linlithgow Palace** (tel: 01506-842 896; www.historic-scotland.gov.uk; daily Apr–Sept 9.30am–5.30pm, Oct–Mar 9.30am–4.30pm; charge), home of the Stuart kings, where Mary, Queen of Scots was born. The adjacent **Church of St Michael** is the largest Pre-Reformation church in Scotland. Here, James IV saw the ghost that warned him of his defeat at Flodden Field.

A further 10 miles (16km) leads to **Falkirk** and the **Falkirk Wheel**, the world's first rotating boat-lift. Converging moribund canals at different levels are linked, not by customary locks but by a 135ft (35-metre) -high rotating wheel, which lifts boats in gondolas between the two canals. Visitors can enjoy the ride, too.

Fife

Across the wide estuary of the Firth of Forth is **Fife**, or "the Kingdom of Fife", as it is still known from its days

of insistent independence. Coal mines and industry were ubiquitous here and although the countryside is not dramatic it has some surprises. On its western fringes, along the north bank of the Forth and upriver towards Stirling, is **Culross**. This was once one of Scotland's major ports, trading in coal, salt and griddle pans for making scones. Visitors can go inside the **Palace, Study and Town House** (Apr–May and Sept Thur–Mon noon–5pm, June–Aug daily noon–5pm, Oct Fri–Mon noon–4pm; charge).

To the east is **Dunfermline ❼**, the ancient Scottish capital, with a 12th-century **Abbey** (Apr–Sept daily 9.30am–5.30pm, Oct until 4.30pm, Nov–Mar Sat–Wed 9.30am–4.30pm; charge), where Scotland's liberator Robert the Bruce was buried in 1329. Dunfermline is also the location of the **Andrew Carnegie Birthplace Museum** (Mar–Nov Mon–Sat 10am–5pm, Sun 2–5pm; free), commemorating the weaver's son who went on to become America's greatest steel baron.

On the coast of the easternmost promontory of the Neuk are the pretty fishing ports of **Earlsferry**, **St Monans**, **Pittenweem**, **Anstruther** and **Crail**. A few miles northwest is **St Andrews ❽**, with a plethora of golf courses, including the Old Course where the game has been played for 600 years, and the **British Golf Museum** (Apr–Oct Mon–Sat 9.30am–5pm, Nov–Mar 10am–4pm; charge). Other sights in the town are one of Britain's oldest universities (founded in 1412 and recently most renowned as the place where Prince William and Kate Middleton met when they both studied there), ecclesiastical ruins and remains of a castle with a grisly history of murders, perched on the sea's edge.

Inland from St Andrews is **Falkland Palace ❾** (Mar–Oct Mon–Sat 11am–5pm, Sun 1–5pm; charge), hunting lodge of the Stuarts from James IV to Mary, Queen of Scots, where a "real" (or "royal") tennis court is still in use. Near **Cupar** is the elegant Edwardian mansion known as the **Hill of Tarvit** (Apr–Oct Thur–Mon 1–5pm, grounds: daily until dusk; charge), with a splendid selection of furniture, tapestries and paintings.

The Wallace Monument above Stirling, celebrating the 13th-century patriot whose exploits were recounted in the 1995 film Braveheart.

BELOW: the Falkirk Wheel that links two canals at different levels between Edinburgh and Glasgow.

Glasgow's Scottish Exhibition and Conference Centre, on the River Clyde, is popularly known as "the Armadillo".

BELOW RIGHT:
Glasgow's George Square by night.

Stirling

Equidistant between Edinburgh and Glasgow is the city of **Stirling** , with its winding streets and medieval cobblestones. **Stirling Castle** (daily Apr–Sept 9.30am–6pm, Oct–Mar 9.30am–5pm; charge) featured prominently in the Scottish wars of succession in the Middle Ages, passing between English and Scots until the Scots finally won it for keeps in 1342. It was the home of the Stuart kings from 1370 to 1603. Today it contains the regimental museum of the Argyll and Sutherland Highlanders.

At the foot of the castle is the oldest part of Stirling, which includes historic buildings such as **Argyll's Lodging** (daily Apr–Sept 9.30am–5.30pm, Oct–Mar 9.30am–4.30pm; charge), a fine 17th-century town house, and Cowane's Hospital, once the Guildhall and now a public venue.

Also worth visiting are two religious sites: the **Church of the Holy Rude** (tel: 01786 475 275; www.holyrude.org) and the **Cambuskenneth Abbey** (www.historic-scotland.gov.uk; both attractions daily Apr–Sept; donations). As a child, Mary, Queen of Scots was crowned in the former, and following her abdication it was the scene of the coronation of her son James. The abbey, by the River Forth east of the town, was the site of Robert the Bruce's first Scottish Parliament in 1326.

Glasgow

The major city on the western side of Scotland is **Glasgow** , straddling the River Clyde 14 miles (23km) from the estuary. It grew rich on shipbuilding and engineering and by the end of the 19th century was Britain's second-largest city. However, the solid manufacturing base on which the city was founded was whipped from under it during the recession of the 1970s. Although unemployment rose distressingly, and the population has declined to around 593,000, an extraordinary renaissance has occurred since the 1990s, when Glasgow was nominated European City of Culture. Glasgow now has a respected arts scene and lively nightlife. It is also home to Scotland's national football stadium, at **Hampden Park**, and one of the venues for the 2012 Olympics.

A Tale of Two Cities

The Scottish Lowlands are divided into west and east, by character as much as by geography. Easterners regard themselves as people of taste and refinement, reflected in the ordered glory of Georgian Edinburgh. They approve of the city's sobriquet, "Athens of the North". Just 43 miles (69km) away, the westerners of industrial Glasgow consider themselves warm-hearted, less pretentious and more down-to-earth than the scions of the Scottish capital. Glasgow's ambience is closer to that of a US city than any other metropolis in Britain ("If you've got it, flaunt it!").

It's true that there is something austere in Edinburgh's beauty and this, at times, is reflected in the reserved nature of its citizens. Glaswegians, by contrast, are ebullient and demonstrative, with a black, sardonic humour nurtured by the hard times they endured when the city's industrial base, which helped power the British Empire, weakened in the 20th century.

Culturally, Edinburgh flaunts its annual arts festival, the world's biggest. But Glaswegians point out that they don't need this annual binge – *their* culture is vibrant for 12 months of the year. There's truth in this too.

Glasgow's culture is not all new. Its 12th-century **cathedral** (Apr–Sept Mon–Sat 9.30am–5.30pm, Sun 1–5.30pm, Oct–Mar daily until 4pm; free) was the only Scottish medieval cathedral to escape the destruction of the Reformation. Adjacent to it is the **St Mungo Museum of Religious Life & Art** (tel: 0141-276 1625), which faces the **Provand's Lordship**, the city's oldest house (1471), now a museum (both: daily 10am–5pm, Fri and Sun from 11am; free).

In the city centre is the seminal Art Nouveau **School of Art** (tel: 0141-353 4500; www.gsa.ac.uk; guided tours Apr–Sept 10am–5pm; charge) designed by Charles Rennie Mackintosh. On nearby Sauchiehall Street stands the **Willow Tea Rooms** *(see page 335).* More Mackintosh can be seen in the Glasgow University area, where a reconstruction of his home is an integral part of the **Hunterian Art Gallery** (Mon–Sat 9.30am–5pm; free). Also in this part of town is the **Kelvingrove Art Gallery and Museum** (daily 10am–5pm, Fri and Sun from 11am; free), which houses an impressive collection of paintings including works from the *fin-de-siècle* Glasgow Boys, the post-war Scottish Colourists and today's Glasgow Boys. There's more art to be seen on Queen Street, at the **Gallery of Modern Art** (Mon–Sat 10am–5pm, Thur until 8pm, Sun 11am–5pm; free).

On the south bank of the River Clyde stand the futuristic buildings of the **Science Centre** (daily 10am–5pm; charge), together with the 423ft (127-metre), 360-degree revolving **Glasgow Tower**, which, to minimise wind resistance, can turn along its entire height into the wind. A viewing platform is at 345ft (105 metres) and the complex contains an IMAX cinema. To the west, beyond Stobcross Quay and adjacent to Glasgow Harbour, are the £74 million, futuristic **Riverside Museum** (Mon–Thur, Sat 10am–5pm, Fri, Sun 11am–5pm; free), dedicated to transport, and The Tall Ship *Glenlee*'s new home, opened in June 2011.

Much further to the south is **Pollok Country Park** (accessible by train from Central station). As well as wildlife gardens, a mountain-bike

TIP

One translation of the original Celtic is that the city's name, Glasgow, means "dear green place". Other translations include "dear stream" and "greyhound" (which some say was the nickname of St Mungo), but the green reference is most apt, for Glasgow has over 70 parks – more green space per head of population than any other city in Europe.

BELOW LEFT: Charles Rennie Mackintosh's House for an Art Lover. **BELOW RIGHT:** Kelvingrove Art Gallery.

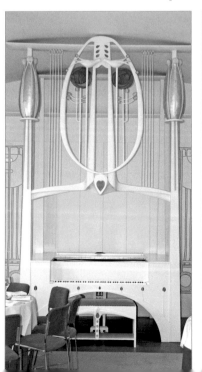

A Night with Robert Burns

Nearly a quarter of a million people around the world belong to Burns clubs – the Scottish poet's popularity has never waned

Few English people know the day on which William Shakespeare was born (23 April), but every Scot is aware that 25 January is the birthday of their country's most celebrated poet, Robert Burns. Indeed, a surprising number of people around the world suddenly recall the few drops of Scottish blood lurking in their veins.

Babbity Bowster's, a pub and hotel in a Robert Adam house in Blackfriars Street, Glasgow, has a reputation for its Burns Nights. Throughout the year its upstairs restaurant serves Scottish fare such as cullen skink (smoked haddock and potato soup), stovies (potatos cooked with onion), Loch Etive mussels and hot goat's cheese on wholemeal toast. On Burns Night it is equally traditional. Just after 7.30pm, a kilted bagpiper pipes in the first course of haggis (made with sheep's or calf's offal, oatmeal, suet, onions and seasoning boiled in the skin of an animal's stomach), bashed neeps (mashed turnips) and tatties (potatoes). Next

comes a main course of perhaps venison in port, or beef marinated in whisky. A chocolate pudding may round off the meal. And all this, of course, is washed down with *usquebaugh*, the water of life. In this case the whisky will be single-malt (unblended and the product of one distillery). Meanwhile, guests read poems from Burns's works, starting with *Address to the Haggis*, and the evening ends after midnight as everyone crosses arms, holds hands and sings a rousing chorus of *Auld Lang Syne*.

This song was one of many traditional Scottish ones that Burns collected or re-cast. "It has never been in print nor even in manuscript until I took it down from an old man singing," said Burns, though the tune may have been added later.

Burns's background

Burns, the "heaven-taught ploughman", was a well-educated farmer's son, born in 1759 in Alloway in Ayrshire, south of Glasgow (see opposite page). The inevitable Burns heritage trail takes in most of the two dozen museums, inns and houses associated with the 37 years of his life, as well as the mausoleum where his remains lie. He was 26 when *Poems, Chiefly in the Scottish Dialect* first won over Edinburgh's literary society.

Burns could write perfectly good English, and the fact that some of his Scottish dialect was just as unintelligible to its audience then as it is to us now didn't matter. It was Scottish, and something of which to be proud. Burns supported the French Revolution, and his lines on liberty and justice have touched a chord in peoples in many nations. But most of all Burns is celebrated for his carousing, his love of drink and good company and his lack of domestic responsiblity.

No wonder women were, for so long, excluded from Burns Nights. Even today they are liable to be a minority of the 200,000 who belong to Burns clubs in about 20 countries, from the Pacific Rim to Russia, where the "Ploughman Poet", champion of the workers, is particularly revered. ❏

ABOVE: Burns's birthplace at Alloway in Ayrshire.
LEFT: the mature poet had many casual love affairs.

circuit and play areas, the park accommodates two important museums. **The Burrell Collection** (daily 10am–5pm, Fri and Sun from 11am; free) displays the extraordinary bequest of shipowner Sir William Burrell (1861–1958), and includes everything from ancient artefacts to Impressionist paintings. **Pollok House** (daily 10am–5pm; charge) contains paintings by masters from El Greco to William Blake.

A short taxi ride away is the beautiful **House for an Art Lover** (www.houseforanartlover.co.uk; tel: 0141-353 4770; times vary; charge), designed by Mackintosh in 1901 but not built until 1994.

Robert Burns country

From Glasgow, the M8 motorway runs through the city centre to link with the M77, which leads south to Ayrshire, the land of Robert Burns and of the seaside resorts of **Troon**, **Prestwick**, **Ayr** and **Girvan**. Before taking this route, make a detour down the M70 to **New Lanark**, home to the social visionary Robert Owen (1771–1858). New Lanark was a model community based around water-powered cotton mills. At this Unesco World Heritage Site (Apr–Sept 10am–5pm, Oct–Mar 11am–5pm; charge) the visitor can see the village as it was, including working textile machinery.

North of Troon is **Adrossan**, the departure point for ferries to the **Isle of Arran** ⓬. Apart from knitwear, Arran is best known as the location of **Brodick Castle** (Apr–Sept daily 11am–4pm, Oct 11am–3pm, grounds: daily 9.30am–sunset; charge), parts of which date from the 14th century and have associations with Robert the Bruce.

Further up the mainland coast are **Largs** and **Wemyss Bay**, from where ferries sail to the islands of **Great Cumbrae** and **Bute**.

The Ayrshire coast opposite the island of Arran has some of the best golf courses in Scotland, including two Open Championship venues – Royal Troon (www.royaltroon.com) and Turnberry (www.turnberryresort.co.uk). To the south of Ardrossan is **Ayr** ⓭, 35 miles (56km) southwest of Glasgow. On the edge of the town is **Alloway** and the **Burns National Heritage**

TIP

The coastal town of Irvine is the home of the Scottish Maritime Museum (Apr–Oct daily 10am–5pm; charge). Visitors can board various lovingly restored vessels, including the steam yacht *Carola*, tour a shipyard worker's tenement flat restored to its 1920s appearance, peruse the exhibition and have a coffee in the Puffer Coffee Shop.

BELOW: this area of Scotland has some of the country's best golf courses.

Caerlaverock Castle, originally built between 1280 and 1300 and rebuilt in the 17th century.

Park, where the centre-piece is **Burns Cottage** (daily, Apr–Sept 10am–5.30pm, Oct–Mar 10am–5pm; charge), the "auld clay biggin" where the poet was born. At **Kirkoswald**, 12 miles (20km) south on the A77, is **Souter Johnnie's Cottage** (Apr–Sept Fri–Tue 11.30m–5pm; charge), home of the "ancient, trusty, druthy crony" featured in Burns' poem *Tam O'Shanter*, and now a museum.

On the coast close to Kirkoswald stands **Culzean Castle** (Apr–Oct daily 10.30am–5pm; charge), one of the greatest achievements of the 18th-century Scottish architect Robert Adam. General Dwight Eisenhower was given life tenure of a suite on the top floor. In addition to paintings, weapons and porcelain, a museum commemorates the US president's achievements.

Moving south

In the southwesternmost corner of Scotland lies Dumfries and Galloway, a region with pretty towns along the **Solway Firth** and wild moorlands inland. It culminates in the west in the **Mull of Galloway**, a hammerhead peninsula with sandy beaches, cliffs and hills. The northern inlet is **Loch Ryan**, famous for oysters, on whose east shore is **Cairnryan**, the principal departure port from Scotland to the Irish coast. **Wigtown**, on the neighbouring promontory, is Scotland's "book town", south of which is **Whithorn**, site of the first known Christian church in Britain.

The A75 runs eastwards, passing close to **Kirkcudbright** (pronounced "care-**coo**-bree"), formerly an artists' colony, the essence of which is distilled in **Broughton House** (Apr–Oct daily noon–5pm; charge), home of artist E.A. Hornel (1864–1933), one of the "Glasgow Boys".

Dumfries

And so to **Dumfries** , the largest town in southwest Scotland. Robert Burns, the national poet, spent the last years of his life here, and the house where he died in 1796 is now a museum, the **Burns House** (Apr–Sept Mon–Sat 10am–5pm, Oct–Mar Tue–Sat 10am–1pm, 2–5pm; free). You can also visit the stone mill on the River Nith, home to the **Robert Burns Centre** (Apr–Sept Mon–Sat 10am–1pm, 2–5pm, Sun 2–5pm, Oct–Mar Tue–Sat 2–5pm), which incorporates an art-house cinema,

South of Dumfries, on the banks of the Neith where it debouches into the Solway Firth, are the red sandstone ruins of **Sweetheart Abbey** (Apr–Sept daily 9.30am–5.30pm, Oct daily 9.30am–4.30pm, Nov–Mar Mon–Wed and Sat–Sun 9.30am–4.30pm; charge), founded in the 14th century by Devorgilla, Lady of Galloway, in memory of her husband John Balliol, founder of Balliol College, Oxford. Also here are the dramatic, romantic ruins of moated **Caerlaverock Castle** (Apr–Sept daily 9.30–5.30, Oct–Mar until 4.30pm; charge). ❑

RESTAURANTS

Restaurants

Prices for a three-course dinner per person with a half-bottle of house wine:
£ = under £25
££ = £25–50
£££ = £50–100
££££ = over £100

Anstruther
Cellar
24 East Green
Tel: 01333-310 378 **££**
Just off the harbour, a walled courtyard leads to an atmospheric restaurant serving splendid seafood, with an excellent wine list.

Cupar
The Peat Inn
Tel: 01334-840 206 **££**
This 18th-century village inn, 6 miles (10km) from St Andrews, serves the best of imaginatively cooked Scottish produce in beautiful dining rooms.

Edinburgh
The Lot
4 Grassmarket
Tel: 0131-225 9924 **£**
An arts venue as well as a bistro, this is located in a converted church near the castle. Good-value, wholesome food and a pleasant meeting place.

Oloroso
33 Castle Street
Tel: 0131-226 7614 **££–£££**
An office block foyer and lift lead to this fashionable restaurant with two sides made entirely of glass and where innovative dishes are cooked to precision. There are splendid views from the outdoor terrace.

Restaurant Martin Wishart
54 The Shore, Leith
Tel: 0131-553 3557
www.martin-wishart.co.uk
£££–££££
Historic Leith is home to one of the best restaurants in the city, complete with Michelin star, and an imaginative menu that changes daily. Closed Sun, Mon.

The Witchery by the Castle
352 Castlehill, Royal Mile
Tel: 0131-225 5613 **££–£££**
The upstairs restaurant is dark and Gothic, while downstairs is bright with greenery and a small terrace. The house classics include hot smoked salmon with hollandaise and Angus beef with smoked garlic broth.

Scottish Borders
Cringletie House Hotel
Edinburgh Road, Peebles
Tel: 01721-725 750
www.cringletie.com
££–££££
The restaurant of this elegant country-house hotel has maintained a high reputation over many years with its French-inspired cuisine. The seven-course tasting menu gives an excellent overview of its offerings.

Stirling
Ziggy Forelles
52 Port Street
Tel: 01786-463 222
www.ziggyforelles.com **££**
A sleek, modern bar/restaurant in the city centre, offering a range of stalwarts from ribs and steaks to pastas and pizzas using local produce.

Glasgow
The Arches Café Bar
253 Argyle Street
Tel: 0141-565 1035 **£**
The Arches is an arts venue under the main railway bridge at Central station. This café-bar is in the cellar underneath and it has been set up like a minimalist jazz bar. Small, good-value menu using locally sourced products.

Brian Maule at Chardon D'Or
176 West Regent Street
Tel: 0141-248 3801
www.brianmaule.com
£££–££££
Brian Maule used to be head chef at the renowned Le Gavroche restaurant in London. Here he produces a refined marriage of Auld Alliance (Scottish and French) cuisine served in a dining room decorated with Post-Impressionist art.

Mother India
8 Westminster Terrace
Tel: 0141-221 1663
www.motherindiaglasgow.co.uk **£–££**
This is Glagow's – and possibly Scotland's – best curry house, known for its legendary home-cooked food. It is licensed but you can also bring your own bottle.

Rogano
11 Exchange Place
Tel: 0141-248 4055
www.roganoglasgow.com
££–£££
A chic Art Deco institution where oysters and fish soup are specialities. The downstairs Café Rogano is more affordable.

The Ubiquitous Chip
12 Ashton Lane
Tel: 0141-334 5007
www.ubiquitouschip.co.uk
£–££
This long-established (it celebrated its 40th anniversary in 2011), engagingly named place is set in a verdant courtyard off a cobbled street, and serves fine traditional and modern Scottish cuisine. The wine list includes a large selection of malt whiskies.

Willow Tea Rooms
217 Sauchiehall Street
Tel: 0141-332 0521
www.willowtearooms.co.uk
£
Charles Rennie Mackintosh designed the interior for tearoom baroness Kate Cranston, and it's still possible to take lunch here or enjoy afternoon tea. Closed Sun.

Linlithgow
Champany Inn
Tel: 01506-834 532 **££–£££**
Located 17 miles (25km) from Edinburgh, this peaceful, atmospheric restaurant has a reputation as "best steakhouse in Britain". The seafood is also excellent. Good wine list with a fine selection of South African wines.

Troon
MacCallums' Oyster Bar
The Harbour
Tel: 01292-319 339 **££**
An unpretentious high-ceilinged stone shed right next to the fish market on the harbour, with has a great, buzzing atmosphere. Tasty grilled lobster and chips.

HISTORIC CASTLES AND ABBEYS

An Englishman's home may be his castle, but for centuries and, in some instances, even today, a Scotsman's castle has been his home

Dotted throughout the Scottish landscape are more than 2,000 castles, many in ruins but others in splendid condition. The latter, still occupied, do not fulfil the primary definition of "castle" – a fortified building – but rather meet the secondary definition: a magnificent house, such as Fyvie.

Either way, all are not merely part of Scottish history: they are its essence. Many carry grim and grisly tales. Thus, Hugh Macdonald was imprisoned in the bowels of Duntulm Castle and fed generous portions of salted beef, but he was denied anything – even whisky – to drink.

In 1746 Blair Castle was, on the occasion of the Jacobite uprising, the last castle in the British Isles to be fired upon in anger. Today, the Duke of Atholl, the owner of Blair Castle, is the only British subject permitted to maintain a private army, the Atholl Highlanders. Prior to the siege, Bonnie Prince Charlie slept here (visitors might be excused for believing there are few castles in Scotland where the Bonnie Prince and Mary, Queen of Scots did not sleep). You, too, can sleep in Scottish castles. Culzean, Dalhousie (both Queen Victoria and Sir Walter Scott visited here) and Inverlochy all have rooms to let. And, for those eager to become a laird, don the kilt and own a castle, several are invariably on the market.

ABOVE: this tranquil view of 15th-century Blackness Castle belies its formidable past. Garrison fortress and former state prison, it served to protect the port and Royal Burgh of Linlithgow.

BELOW: completed in 1511, the Great Hall of Edinburgh Castle was designed for ceremonial use but was relegated to a barracks after Oliver Cromwell's invasion of 1650. It was finally restored in 1880.

LEFT: stained glass at Stirling Castle, once called "the key to Scotland" because of its strategic position between the Lowlands and Highlands. It became a favourite residence of Stuart monarchs. Nowadays it is also the home of the regimental museum of the Argyll and Sutherland Highlanders.

SCOTTISH BORDER ABBEYS

Scotland, especially the Borders, is full of abbeys that now lie ruined but were once powerful institutions with impressive buildings. During the reign of David I (1124–53), who revitalised and transformed the Scottish Church, more than 20 religious houses were founded. Outstanding among these is a quartet of Border abbeys – Dryburgh (Premonstratensian), Jedburgh (Augustinian), Kelso (Tironensian) and Melrose (Cistercian). All have evocative ruins, though perhaps it is Jedburgh *(above and below)*, with its tower and remarkable rose window still intact, that is Scotland's classic abbey.

It was not the Reformation (1560) that caused damage to these abbeys but rather the selfishness of pre-Reformation clergy, raids in the 14th–16th centuries by both English and Scots, the ravages of weather and activities of 19th-century restorers. The concern of the Reformation, spearheaded by firebrand John Knox, was to preserve, not to destroy, the churches they needed.

Monasteries continued to exist as landed corporations after the Reformation. Why upset a system that suited so many interests? After all, the Pope, at the king's request, had provided priories and abbeys for five of James V's bastards while they were still infants.

ABOVE: nestling in the beautiful Perthshire countryside, Blair Castle is the ancient seat of the Dukes and Earls of Atholl. Now a top visitor attraction, its long history stretches back to the 13th century.

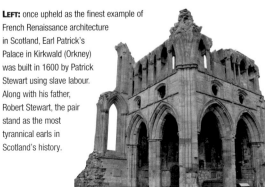

LEFT: once upheld as the finest example of French Renaissance architecture in Scotland, Earl Patrick's Palace in Kirkwald (Orkney) was built in 1600 by Patrick Stewart using slave labour. Along with his father, Robert Stewart, the pair stand as the most tyrannical earls in Scotland's history.

SCOTTISH HIGHLANDS AND ISLANDS

The Highlands and islands of Scotland form one of the last great wildernesses of Europe – endless stretches of wild country, mountains, glens and moorlands probed by the long fingers of sea lochs

The southern edge of the Highland line runs across the country diagonally from the Mull of Kintyre, the long spit of land stretching southwards from Argyll on the western edge of the Firth of Clyde, right up to a point southwest of Aberdeen near Stonehaven. More than half of Scotland lies to the north of this line, most of it mountainous, with just a few fertile glens where crops can be grown and cattle reared. The population is sparse in the northwest – in Sutherland it is fewer than 6 people per sq mile (2.6 people per sq km), compared to the national average of 955 per sq mile (369 per sq km). Just south of this line, though, is Perth, generally considered to be the gateway to the Highlands.

Tayside and the Grampians

The historic regions of Tayside and Grampian occupy the northeast section of Scotland between the Firth of Tay in the south and the Firth of Moray to the north. The Tay, which flows through the cities of Perth and Dundee, offers excellent salmon and trout fishing, while the Grampian region boasts many of Scotland's greatest castles.

On the way to Perth, up the A9, is **Gleneagles** *(see page 371)*, probably Scotland's grandest hotel, with its own championship golf courses. **Perth** ⓱ is notable for its fine Georgian terraces; for

Balhousie Castle, on Hay Street, which houses a museum (Apr–Oct Mon–Sat 9.30am–5pm, Sun 10am–3.30pm, Nov–Mar Mon–Sat 9.30am–5pm; charge) showcasing treasures relating to the Black Watch, a military regiment that now has its headquarters here; and for the Branklyn Gardens, on the Dundee Road to the southeast of the city.

Perth's road connections make it an excellent base for exploring the surrounding area, where sights include the historic **Scone Palace** (Apr–Oct Sun–Fri 9.30am–5pm, Sat 9.30am–4pm;

Main attractions
ABERDEEN
BALMORAL
INVERNESS
LOCH NESS
GLENCOE
ISLE OF SKYE
ORKNEY ISLAND
SHETLAND
IONA

LEFT: Balloch Castle and Loch Lomond.
BELOW: Highland steer.

Marischal College is the second-largest granite building in the world – the biggest is El Escorial monastery and palace complex near Madrid.

charge), once the crowning site of the kings of Scots including Macbeth and Robert the Bruce. Set in attractive grounds, it now houses a fine collection of paintings and antiques.

Continuing north on the A9, there is the pretty town of **Dunkeld**, with its ruined abbey, and a little further north still, the Victorian resort of **Pitlochry** . The latter hosts Highland Games in September (www.pitlochryhighlandgames. co.uk), and is also noted for the Pitlochry Festival Theatre.

North Sea ports

The Tay river drains into the North Sea at **Dundee**, a port known for its jam, jute and journalism industries. Its harbour is the mooring-place of Captain Scott's Antarctic ship *Discovery*, and the *Unicorn*, a 24-cannon frigate launched in 1824.

From Dundee, the A92 coast road goes through the historic ports of Montrose and Arbroath on the way to Aberdeen. At **Arbroath** ⓳ are the ruins of a 12th-century **abbey** (daily Apr–Sept 9.30am–5.30pm, Oct–Mar 9.30am–4.30pm; charge) where Scot-

land declared its independence in 1320. Inland, 12 miles (19km) north of Dundee, is **Glamis Castle** (Apr–Oct 10am–6pm, Nov–Dec 10.30am–4.30pm, last entry 90 min before closing; charge), the childhood home of the late Queen Mother.

Further up the coast is **Aberdeen** ⓴, the greatest of the North Sea ports. The granite city is the oil capital of Britain, set between the rivers Don and Dee. It has a prestigious university, of which the finest buildings belong to the 16th-century King's College, which was begun in 1500 and hailed as an outstanding example of Scottish Gothic style.

Marischal College on Broad Street, which was founded in 1593 but rebuilt in the 19th century, has the distinction of being the second-largest granite building in the world after El Escorial near Madrid. Nearby is the 14th-century **St Machar's Cathedral** (daily Apr–Oct 9am–5pm, Nov–Mar 10am–4pm). The **Art Gallery** (Tue–Sat 10am–5pm, Sun 2–5pm; free), on Schoolhill, contains a fine collection of English, French and Scottish paintings.

Castle country

The A93 runs some 50 miles (80km) inland from Aberdeen up Royal Deeside to **Balmoral Castle** ㉑, where the Queen and royal family spend much of the summer, when tourists are traipsing round her London home. Balmoral was bought by Prince Albert in 1848, though the 50,000-acre (20,000-hectare) estate dates back to the 15th century. In the castle, only the ballroom is open to the public, though the grounds can also be visited (www.balmoralcastle.com; Apr–July daily 10am–5pm; charge).

Near to Balmoral are a number of other fine castles. Just off the A944 is **Castle Fraser** (Apr–June Wed–Sun noon–5pm, Aug daily 11am–5pm, Sept–Oct Wed–Sun noon–5pm; charge), while on the A93 is **Crathes Castle** (Nov–Mar Sat–Sun 10.30am–3.45pm, Apr–Oct daily 10.30am–4.45pm; charge). **Craigievar Castle** (May–June and Sept Fri–Tue 11am–5pm, July–Aug daily 11am–5pm; charge), by the A980, is also impressive, as is the 12th-century **Blair Castle** (Apr–Oct daily 9.30am–5.30pm, Nov–Mar Tue and Sat 9.30am–2.30pm; charge), between Perth and Inverness.

This is the seat of the Duke of Atholl, the last noble in Britain licensed to have a private army.

Inverness and environs

Inverness ㉒ is the vibrant "Capital of the Highlands". For long seen as a dull backwater of Presbyterianism, the city has become a major shopping centre with good nightlife, especially at weekends, and is now the fastest-growing city in UK. With the mouth of Loch Ness only 5 miles (8km) from the town, Inverness is also a good base for monster-spotting.

Shakespeare sadly maligned the man who was the city's king for 17 years, Macbeth. His castle has disappeared, but from **Castlehill** a successor dating from the 1830s dominates the city: a pink cardboard cut-out, like a Victorian doll's house. It is now the setting of the Castle Garrison Encounter (tel: 01463-243 363), a costume re-enactment of the life of an 18th-century soldier.

In the nearby **Inverness Museum and Art Gallery** (tel: 01463-237 114; http://inverness.highland.museum; Mon–Sat 10am–5pm; free), an eclectic collection

TIP

Discovery, the ship Captain Scott took to the Antarctic in 1910, was built in Dundee and has returned. The ship and the Discovery Point exhibition are open daily 10am–5pm, summer until 6pm; tel: 01382-309 060; charge.

BELOW LEFT: Balmoral Castle and garden.
BELOW RIGHT: show of strength at a Highland gathering.

BELOW:
Loch Ness and
Urquhart Castle.

sees the death mask of Bonnie Prince Charlie share a case with Mr Punch in his "red Garibaldi coat", local showman Duncan Morrison's puppet figure that once delighted local children. Traditions are strongly represented in silversmithing, taxidermy, bagpipes and fiddles, and even a 7th-century Pictish stone depicting a wolf.

In front of the **Town House** pub on busy High Street, uphill from the river, is the **Clach-na-Cuddain**, a stone on which women used to rest their tubs of washing and have a gossip. **Abertarff House**, on Church Street, is the city's oldest secular building, dating from 1593. It has one of the few remaining examples of the old turnpike stair and is home these days to small art galleries.

A few miles east of Inverness, the B9006 runs across **Culloden Moor** where Jacobite forces under Bonnie Prince Charlie were routed in 1746. The defeat of his men by the Hanoverian army represented the end of the struggle for power by the Stuart line. On either side of the road are scattered stones marking the graves of the Highlanders. The **Culloden Moor Visi-**

tor Centre (Apr–Sept 9am–6pm, Oct 9am–5pm, Nov–Dec and Feb–Mar 10am–4pm; charge) has many artefacts of the period on display.

To the south of Inverness are the rich farmlands of the **Laigh of Moray**, along the River Spey. This is distillery country, where many of the famous malt whiskies are made. Follow the signs marked "Whisky Trail" (www.scotchwhisky.net) from Keith along the A95.

Continuing southwest, the A95 joins the A9 and leads through impressive scenery in the high glens of the Grampians, with the massive summits of the Cairngorms towering over the ski resort of **Aviemore** (www.visitaviemore.co.uk). At its centre is the impressive **Macdonald Aviemore Highland Resort**, complete with golf course and spa (www.macdonald hotels.co.uk/aviemore).

To Fort William

Heading southwest from Inverness, the A82 skirts the edge of **Loch Ness** ㉓, the second-largest loch in Scotland after Loch Lomond and famous for its elusive monster, known affectionately as "Nessie". Despite many claims of

sightings, numerous blurred photographs and even some film footage, the evidence remains inconclusive about the existence of this prehistoric survivor, despite the presence of researchers from the Academy of Applied Science in Massachusetts, who maintain a year-round vigil with state-of-the-art equipment. In summer, visitors can take boat cruises across Loch Ness from Fort Augustus and Inverness. In the nearby Drumnadrochit is the **Loch Ness Exhibition Centre** (tel: 01456-450-573; www.lochness.com), which features a scale replica of Nessie, as well as the sonar research vessel *John Murray*.

On the way, though, it's worth making a stop at the ruins of **Urquhart Castle** (daily Apr–Sept 9.30am–6pm, Oct–Mar until 4.30pm; charge), which was one of the largest in Scotland until 1692 when it was blown up to prevent the Jacobites from using it. Most photos of the Loch Ness monster have been taken from this spot.

As the A82 nears Fort William at the head of Loch Linnhe, Britain's highest mountain, **Ben Nevis**, looms above at 4,406ft (1,343 metres). There are numerous routes to the top for both walkers and climbers.

The fortification of **Fort William** ㉔ itself was constructed in the 17th century to keep out "savage clans" and sundry other undesirables. Nothing of the fort remains today: it was demolished in the late 19th century to make way for the railway, which led to rapid expansion of the town and its environs. In the town centre, near the tourist information centre, is the **West Highland Museum** (June–Sept Mon–Sat 10am–5pm, July–Aug also Sun 10am–4pm, Oct–May Mon–Sat 10am–4pm; free), which has a number of Jacobite relics including a "secret portrait" of Bonnie Prince Charlie.

Glencoe

Just southeast of Fort William is **Glencoe** ㉕, a deep mountain valley that stretches more than 7 miles (11km) from Loch Leven to Rannoch Moor through magnificent scenery. The name of Glencoe is also widely associated with a notorious massacre that occurred here in February 1692 of the MacDonald clan, by troops commanded by Robert

The Old Course in St Andrews is a public golf course held in trust under an act of Parliament. The Royal and Ancient Golf Club of St Andrews club house is located next to the first tee – one of many clubs that have access to the course, along with the general public.

BELOW: Glenfinnan, with its monument to Bonnie Prince Charlie.

Surf and Turf

Scotland's physical geography makes it one of the best places in Europe for outdoor sports. The rivers and lochs are famous for their salmon and trout fishing (salmon Jan–October; trout mid-Mar–early Oct; local permits required). Sea fishing is found around the entire coast; for more details visit www.fishing-scotland.net.

Scotland is golf's spiritual home. The Old Course (www.standrews.org.uk) is the oldest in the world, while the Royal Dornoch Golf Club (www.royaldornoch.com), 64km (40 miles) north of Inverness, is where the game was first played by monks in 1614. Carnoustie (www.carnoustiegolflinks.co.uk) is home to one of the toughest links courses in the world, while Gleneagles (www.gleneagles.com) has three 18-hole golf courses, one of which will host the 2014 Ryder Cup.

Mallaig harbour, Skye.

BELOW RIGHT: climbing Ben Nevis, Britain's highest mountain.

Campbell of Glenlyon as a punishment for the tardiness of their chief in giving allegiance to the English king. The **Glencoe Visitors' Centre** (tel: 0844-493 2222; www.glencoe-nts.org.uk; Apr–Oct 9.30am–5.30pm, Nov–Mar 10am–4pm; charge) provides further details of this notorious episode.

Bonnie Prince Charlie country

From Fort William, a spectacular train journey runs west to the small port of **Mallaig** (from where ferries leave for the Isle of Skye). The A830 road follows the same route. This is Bonnie Prince Charlie country, and begins with the stunning view from the viaduct at **Glenfinnan** ㉖, down Loch Shiel and over to the monument on the shore that marks the spot where the Young Pretender himself raised the Stuart standard (visitor centre: tel: 0844-493 2221; www.nts.org.uk; daily Apr–June and Sept–Oct 10am–5pm, July–Aug 9.30am–5.30pm; charge). Here the clans gathered to begin the Jacobite Rebellion of 1745. It was in this area, too, that the Prince hid with a price of £30,000 on his head after

his defeat at Culloden.

Beyond Lochailort there is a view seawards over the bright water and rocky islets of **Loch nan Uamh**, where the Bonnie Prince landed in 1745 and from where he left 14 months later, despite all the pleadings of the haunting Jacobite songs, never to return. The pebbly beaches of Loch nan Uamh give way to the silver sands of Morar and Arisaig.

The North

Further up the west coast is the **Kyle of Lochalsh**, which is linked to the Isle of Skye by a road bridge. Heading north from here is the A890 through Glen Carron and then the A896 via Shieldaig. These roads intersect with the A832, which returns west down Glen Docherty to **Loch Maree**, one of the prettiest lochs in Scotland, and beyond to **Loch Ewe** and the exotic **Inverewe Garden** ㉗ (daily Apr–Sept 10am–5pm, June–Aug until 6pm, May 10am–5.30pm, Oct 10am–4pm, Nov–Mar 10am–3pm; donations).

From Inverewe the road heads north and then winds back to the east, providing many wonderful vistas along

The Munros of Scotland

A "Munro" is a Scottish mountain over 3,000ft (914 metres). The name comes from Sir Hugh Munro, who produced the first list of such mountains in 1891. There are 283 Munros, and a further 227 Munro "tops" (subsidiary peaks on Munros). Perhaps the most famous Munros are Ben Nevis, the highest mountain in Great Britain at 4,409ft (1,344 metres); Ben Macdui (4,295ft/1,309 metres) in the Cairngorms; and Buachaille Etive Mòr (3,353ft/1,022 metres) at the entrance to Glencoe. Other Scottish mountains are categorised as Corbetts, which are between 2,500 and 3,000ft (760–910 metres) in height, and Grahams, which are between 2,000 and 2,500ft (610–760 metres).

A popular practice amongst hillwalkers is "Munro Bagging", the aim being to climb all of the listed Munros. Having climbed all of them, a walker is entitled to be called a Munroist. As of 2009 more than 4,000 have reported completing the full list. The first continuous round of the Munros was completed in 1974, whilst the current record for the fastest continuous round is 39 days, 9 hours. One person has completed the full list 13 times. Winter ascents of certain Munros provide challenging ice climbs. Walkers need to be well prepared for the often extreme weather conditions; there are numerous fatalities every year.

the way. It eventually arrives at the A835, which runs north to **Ullapool**, a fishing village on Loch Broom.

The further north you go past Ullapool towards Scotland's "scalp" on the north coast between Durness and John o' Groats, the longer the days are in summer, and the more the landscape takes on the eerie beauty that is strictly for wilderness lovers. **John o' Groats** ㉘ is popularly referred to as the northernmost tip of the British mainland. In actual fact, Dunnet Head, to the west, is further north by a few miles. Just 6 miles (9.5km) west of John o'Groats on the A836 is the **Castle of Mey** (www.castleofmey.org.uk; May–Sept 9.20am–4pm; charge), the summer home of the late Queen Mother. It remains just as she left it, with her coat and wellington boots left just inside the door.

Argyll

Stretching south of Fort William is the scenic region of **Argyll**. Heading down the coast, the first major town is **Oban** ㉙, a faded Victorian resort, but still important as a departure point for ferries to the Hebridean islands. Continuing southwards, the A816 leads to Lochgilphead, and below that, via the A83, to the picturesque region of Knapdale and the Crinan Canal, which connects Loch Fyne with the Atlantic Ocean. Beyond the pretty fishing village of **Tarbert**, the road enters the Kintyre Peninsula.

Eventually you come to the ferry port of Tayinloan, from where, in summer, there are hourly crossings to the pretty island of **Gigha**. The main attraction here is the **Achamore House Gardens** (daily 9am–dusk; charge), created by the late Sir James Horlick, one of the world's great horticulturalists.

Back in Kintyre, the A83 keeps on going to the fishing port of **Campbeltown** ㉚. A local museum, the **Cambeltown Museum** (Mon–Fri, 9am–5pm; free) tells the history of the region, and exhibits a fine collection of Scottish paintings. Heading south once more, the road finally runs out at the **Mull of Kintyre**, made famous in a song by

one-time local resident Paul McCartney. The area is now a bird reserve.

Returning north, this time up the east side of the peninsula, you eventually rejoin the A83 and follow the road up to **Inveraray**. To one side of the pretty white town is **Inveraray Castle** (Apr–Oct daily 10am–5.45pm; charge), for centuries the seat of the Dukes of Argyll (the fierce Clan Campbell). The present Gothic Revival building, famous for its magnificent interiors and art collection, was started in 1743.

From Inveraray, the A83 continues east towards **Loch Lomond** ㉛, the largest freshwater lake in Britain, 23 miles (37km) long and 5 miles (8km) across at its widest point. All around is the Loch Lomond and the Trossachs

A steam train crosses the Glenfinnan viaduct, completed in 1901, which made a magic appearance in several Harry Potter films.

BELOW: Inverewe Garden.

TIP

At many of the island ports, smaller boats offer round trips to spot wildlife. From Elgol on the Isle of Skye, try Bella Jane Boat Trips (tel: 01471-866 244; www.bellajane.co.uk). Sea Life Surveys (tel: 01688-302 916; www.sealifesurveys.com) depart from Tobermory on the Isle of Mull for all-day whale-watching cruises. Remember to take several layers of clothes and warm wet-weather gear.

BELOW: the Isle of Skye.

National Park (tel: 01389-722 600; www.lochlomond-trossachs.org), encompassing 720 sq miles (1,865 sq km) of wonderful scenery.

THE ISLANDS

Off the west coast of Scotland lie several hundred islands. making up the **Inner** and **Outer Hebrides**. The southernmost group comprises Gigha, Islay, Jura and Colonsay. Further north there are the large islands of Mull and Skye and the smaller islands of Iona, Staffa, Tiree, Coll, Muck, Eigg, Rum and Canna. The Outer Hebrides are made up of Lewis, Harris, North Uist, Benbecula, South Uist, Eriskay and Barra. Most of these can be reached by ferry (tel: 0800-066 5000; www.calmac.co.uk).

Off the north coast of Scotland are the Orkney Islands and the Shetlands. They are serviced by ferries departing from Aberdeen and Scrabster (tel: 0845-6000 449; www.northlinkferries.co.uk).

The Isle of Skye

Perhaps the most impressive of the Hebrides – and certainly the most accessible – is the **Isle of Skye ❷**. The busy

fishing port of Mallaig is one of the ferry departure points for Skye, while the principal crossing is over the bridge at Kyle of Lochalsh, further north.

From the fjord-like sea lochs of the west, across to the sheer Cuillin Mountains in the south, to the craggy northern tip of the Trotternish Peninsula, Skye epitomises Scotland's wild Celtic appeal. A day's hike or cycle ride around the 50-mile (80km) -long island will still set you squarely in the wilderness.

The Cuillin Mountains are a 6-mile (10km) arc of peaks, 15 of which exceed the 3,000ft (900 metres) needed to make them "Munros" *(see page 344)*. If the summits seem forbidding, take the walk down Glen Sligachan into the heart of the mountains and through to the other side, 8 miles (13km) due south to the beach of Camasunary in Loch Scavaig. In the Sleat area, on the southern tip of Skye, is **Armadale Castle Gardens and Museum of the Isles** (castle: daily Apr–Oct 9.30am–5.30pm, gardens: year round; charge).

The main attraction of northwestern Skye is **Dunvegan Castle** (Apr–mid-Oct daily 10am–5.30pm; charge), which

captures the clan spirit of Scotland in its paintings and Macleod relics.

On the west side of the Trotternish Peninsula, **Uig** is an attractive village that encircles a bay from where ferries depart for the outer isles. This northern arm of Skye has been less altered by tourism than any part of the island.

Iona

One of the most extraordinary islands in the Hebrides is **Iona** ㉝, accessible by ferry from Mull. Its major attractions are the Benedictine **Iona Abbey** (Apr–Sept 9.30am–5.30pm, Oct–Mar 9.30am–4.30pm; charge) and the relics of the settlement founded here by St Columba in AD 563. Celtic Christianity endured here throughout the Dark Ages before spreading out through Scotland and to Europe beyond.

The Orkney Islands

The 70 **Orkney Islands** ㉞ were invaded by Norsemen in the 11th century, and did not pass into British hands until late in the 16th century. Ruins from the Norse era are all around. The "ey" in the name is Old Norse for islands, so to be grammatically correct, one should refer to Orkney and not "the Orkneys" or "the Orkney Islands".

Everywhere in Orkney there is the feeling of being wide open to the sky, of great cliffs and rocky sea pinnacles. Seals (both common and grey) are abundant in the waters here. North of Stromness on **Mainland** (the largest island), the coast offers one of the most dramatic cliff walks in Britain, from Black Craig north to the Bay of Skaill. Another excursion for wilderness lovers is the ferry to Moaness Pier on the **Isle of Hoy**.

Kirkwall, 10 miles (16km) east of Stromness, is the largest town in Orkney. It is largely uninspiring except for the **Bishop's Palace**, a 12th-century ruin with a round tower added in the 16th century, and the **Earl's Palace**, one of the finest examples of Renaissance architecture in Scotland (both palaces: daily summer 9.30am–5.30pm, winter 9.30am–4.30pm; charge). **St Magnus Cathedral**, built in 1137, is dedicated to Magnus Erlendsson, martyred 1st Earl of Orkney.

Places of antiquity grace the countryside under the banner of the Heart of

Dunvegan Castle claims to be the oldest continuously inhabited castle in Scotland; it has been the seat of the chiefs of Clan Macleod for more than 700 years.

BELOW:
Lerwick, in the Shetland Islands.

Shetland Statistics

Sheep outnumber people on Shetland by more than 10 to 1. "They eat everything," says one islander. Shetland ponies are more loved. They were carefully bred to keep their legs short so that they could pull carts through Britain's coal mines, but these days they graze freely. However, it's birds that dominate Shetland.

Because of the lack of woodlands there are fewer than 50 breeding species, but no lack of numbers. Filling the sky and cliff ledges are around 30,000 gannets, 140,000 guillemots and 300,000 fulmars. Shetland supports more than 50 percent of the world's population of great skuas (bonxies). Puffins begin to arrive in May, and before long there are 250,000 of them. Take a small boat round the islands and, as well as the birds, you can find seal colonies, porpoises and dolphins.

*Dragon's head on
the prow of a replica
Viking ship in
Orkney.*

Neolithic Orkney Unesco World Heritage Site. Best known are the wonderfully preserved settlement at **Skara Brae** (www.historic-scotland.gov.uk; daily Apr–Sept 5.30pm, Oct–Mar 9.30am–4.30pm; charge), dating back to *c.*3000 BC, and **Maeshowe** (tel: 01856-761 606; www.historic-scotland.gov.uk; daily Apr–Sept 5pm, Oct–Mar 9.30am–4.30pm, book in advance; charge), a huge, chambered megalithic tomb from 2700 BC with fine runic graffiti left by 12th-century Norse plunderers. On **Papa Westray**, one of the smaller Orkney islands, is the oldest extant house in Europe.

The Shetland Islands

Britain's most northerly archipelago is the **Shetland Islands** ㊉, just 48 miles (78km) north of the Orkney Islands. The 15 inhabited islands – 85 or so more are uninhabited – are dotted over 70 miles (112km) of swelling seas and scarcely seem part of Britain at all. The tiny population of less than 22,000 doesn't regard itself as British, or even as Scottish, but as Norse: one of the nearest mainland towns is Bergen in Norway, Norwegian is taught in the schools and the heroes of myths have names like Harald Hardrada.

Lerwick is the capital, and there is a small airport on the main island served from most Scottish airports, a frequency maintained because of Shetland's significant oil installations – it has the largest gas and oil terminal in Europe. On the last Tuesday in January, the spectacular fire ceremony of Up-Helly-Aa involves the burning of a replica Viking longship and much revelry.

The tiny island of **Mousa**, off the east coast of the Shetlands, is the site of the world's best-preserved Iron-Age *broch* tower, a fortress that has remained intact after more than 1,000 years of battering from Arctic storms. **Unst** is the most northerly of the dozen inhabited islands, and **Muness Castle** and the ruins of **Scalloway Castle**, 6 miles (10km) to the west of Lerwick, are also worth visiting (apply to local shops for keys). At the southern tip of the mainland is **Jarlshof** (daily 9.30am–5.30pm; charge), a remarkable "layer-cake" of an archaeological site. Bronze Age dune dwellers, *broch* builders, Vikings and medieval inhabitants all left their marks. ❑

RESTAURANTS

Prices for a three-course dinner per person with a half-bottle of house wine:
£ = under £25
££ = £25–50
£££ = £50–100
££££ = over £100

Fife, Tayside, Aberdeen and the Grampians

Aberdeen

The Beautiful Mountain
11–13 Belmont Street
Tel: 01224-645 353 **£**
Tuck into a wholesome breakfast, enjoy coffee and cakes or a first-rate light lunch with delicious soups, salads and sandwiches. One of the best cafés in town (open until 4.30pm only).

Foyer Restaurant & Gallery
82a Crown Street
Tel: 01224-582 277
www.foyerrestaurant.com
£–££
Enjoy good contemporary British cuisine, often using locally sourced produce, in the former Trinity Church, which also houses an art gallery. Child-friendly. Closed Mon and Sun.

Arbroath

Old Boatyard
Fishmarket Quay
Tel: 01241-879 995
www.oldboatyard.co.uk **£–££**
Located in Arbroath's newly developed harbour, this attractive modern building retains a traditional feel within. Great choice of fish and seafood dishes, but plenty of other options and some delicious desserts, including home-made ice cream.

Dundee

Rama Thai
32 Dock Street
Tel: 01382-223 366 **£**
The packed tables of people feasting on steamed king prawns and excellent green curry tell you this is where to spice up your Dundee dining. The service can be a little hurried.

Pitlochry

Victoria's
45 Atholl Road
Tel: 01796-472 670
www.victorias-pitlochry.co.uk
£
Whether for breakfast, lunch, high tea or pre-theatre dinners, the food at Victoria's is comforting and scrumptious, and the service always friendly. Children are welcome too.

St Andrew's

The Seafood Restaurant
Bruce Embankment
Tel: 01334-479 475
www.theseafoodrestaurant.com **££–£££**
A classy place right beside the sea that offers evening diners plates of succulent lobster, prawns, halibut and scallops while they gaze out over the waves.

The West Coast & the Northwest Highlands

Inverness

Abstract
Glenmoriston Town House Hotel, 20 Ness Bank
Tel: 01463-220 220 www.abstractrestaurant.com **£££**
This stylish contemporary hotel restaurant serves excellent seasonal, Scottish food, plus a wide range of whiskies in the Piano Bar.

Chez Roux
Rocpool Reserve.
Culduthel Road
Tel: 01463-240 089
www.rocpool.com/restaurant.html **££–£££**
In the centre of town, this elegant hotel restaurant is part of the Roux brothers' empire and offers superb Scottish produce presented with a French twist. Excellent wine list.

Inverlochy Castle

Inverlochy Castle Hotel
Torlundy, near Fort William
Tel: 01397-702 177
www.inverlochycastlehotel.com **£££**
Expect full silver service with the creative modern and award-winning British cuisine in the three dining rooms of this luxury lochside hotel.

Lochinver

Achin's Bookshop
Inverkirkaig
Tel: 01571-844 262 **£**
Simple, excellent home-cooking in Scotland's most remote northerly bookshop. Hearty soups and toasties. Books (of course!) and quality craft goods also on sale (Apr–Oct 10am–5pm).

The Islands

Orkney

The Creel
Front Road, St Margaret's Hope, Orkney
Tel: 01856-831 311
www.thecreel.co.uk **££**
Friendly fish restaurant (often judged Scotland's best) serving hand-dived scallops, local mussels, organic salmon and fish, (wolf-fish, torsk, sea-witch etc) that you may not even have heard of. Also has meat (Orkney beef and lamb), and local ales and whiskies.

Shetland

Hay's Dock Café Restaurant
Hay's Dock, Lerwick
Tel: 01595-741 569
www.haysdock.co.uk **£**
In the Shetland Museum and with great views, this café/restaurant offers light meals, coffee and afternoon tea as well as first-class evening meals (not Sun–Mon) featuring local produce.

Skye

The Three Chimneys
Colbost, Dunvegan
Tel: 01470-511 258
www.threechimneys.co.uk **££**
Set in a remote old crofter's cottage, this restaurant with rooms has won a string of awards for its seasonal dishes using local ingredients such as Skye lamb, Highland beef, fish, and handmade cheese and chocolates.

RIGHT: St Andrew's stylish Seafood Restaurant.

✕ INSIGHT GUIDE — TRAVEL TIPS

GREAT BRITAIN

T RANSPORT

GETTING THERE
AND GETTING AROUND

GETTING THERE

By Air

Britain's two major international airports are Heathrow (mainly scheduled flights), which is 15 miles (24km) to the west of London, and Gatwick (scheduled and charter flights), which is 24 miles (40km) south of the capital. An increasing number of international flights now arrive at the regional airports of Birmingham, Manchester, Liverpool, Glasgow, Prestwick and Cardiff, and London's other airports, Stansted and Luton. The small London City Airport, a few miles from London's financial heart, is used by smaller aircraft to fly to European capitals. Departure taxes are included in the price of the flight at the point of purchase.

Getting to/from London Airports

Heathrow Airport, with five terminals, is sprawling – it can be a long walk to the central building.

There is a fast rail link, the Heathrow Express, between Heathrow and Paddington station. It runs every 15 minutes from 5am to midnight and takes about 20 minutes. Fares are around £14.50 single and £28 return. Prices are lowest when buying online, increasing if you purchase from a machine or on board (www.heathrow express.com). Paddington is on the District, Circle, Bakerloo and Hammersmith and City Underground train lines.

The cheapest way into central London is by the Underground (also known as the Tube), which takes about 45 minutes to the West End.

The Piccadilly line goes from Heathrow directly to central areas such as Kensington, Piccadilly and Covent Garden. The single fare is £5. Keep your ticket. You'll need it to exit the Underground system. For all London Transport enquiries: tel: 020-7222 1234; www.tfl.gov.uk.

Heathrow is also well served by taxis. A ride into town by taxi will cost £40–80, depending on your destination, size of the taxi and whether you have booked a minicab (usually cheaper) or simply hailed a black cab.

Gatwick Airport isn't on the Underground network, but has train and coach services into London and to other large cities. Gatwick Express trains leave every 15 minutes from 5am until 12.35am, and take 30 minutes to London's Victoria station. For information, see www.gatwickexpress.com. The First Capital train service between Gatwick and Victoria, and Southern Trains service to London Bridge station, are much cheaper and take only a little longer, but can be very crowded at peak hours with general commuter traffic.

A black cab taxi from Gatwick into central London costs around £80.

Luton Airport has a regular express train service from Luton Airport Parkway (take the shuttle bus) to St Pancras, City Thameslink, Blackfriars and London Bridge stations, taking 25 minutes minimum. Alternatively, Green Line 757 coaches to London's Victoria station take about an hour (tel: 0844-801 7261), or easyBus coaches (up to 1 hour 40 mins during peak times; www.easybus.co.uk).

Stansted Airport has the Stansted Express train service to London's Liverpool Street station. A frequent service operates 5.30am–12.30am and takes about 45 minutes (www. stanstedexpress.com). A non-stop coach service to London Victoria is run by Terravision (www.terravision.eu), and National Express has services to Stratford (east London) and Victoria.

London City Airport's major strength is its proximity to the West End (10 miles/16km; www.londoncityairport.com). There is a London City Airport DLR station (about 50 metres from the airport terminal), and the service from here connects with the Jubilee line (at Canning Town) and Northern, Central, Circle and Waterloo and City lines (at Bank). The Transport for London website (www.tfl.gov.uk) can be used to help plan your journey.

By Coach

The Airport Travel Line, tel: 08705-747 777, gives information on coaches into central London and between Heathrow, Gatwick and Stansted airports. Sky Shuttle runs a door-to-door coach service from Heathrow and Gatwick airports to hotels in central areas of London. Booking is essential, tel: 0845-481 0960; www.skyshuttle.co.uk.

National Express also runs coach services connecting Heathrow, Gatwick, Stansted and Luton airports, and connecting the first three airports with Victoria coach station in central London. For enquiries, tel: 08717-818 181; www.nationalexpress.com.

English Regional Airports

Birmingham International Airport is 8 miles (13km) southeast of Birmingham. The free Air-Rail Link shuttle connects the airport with Birmingham International station, from where trains run every 10–15

minutes to New Street station in the city centre (about 15 minutes).
Kent International Airport. A 30-minute drive from Dover. Rail services from London Charing Cross and Victoria to Ramsgate from where there is an Eastonways bus to the airport (www.eastonways.co.uk). Also rail links to Ashford International from rail station Ramsgate.
Liverpool John Lennon Airport is 9 miles (15km) southeast of the city centre. The Airport Airlink 500 bus runs to the city centre every 20 mins Mon–Fri and 30 mins Sat–Sun and evenings. Taxis charge about £15 for the 20-minute journey.
Manchester Airport is 10 miles (16km) south of the city. Frequent rail services run to Piccadilly station (20 minutes) in central Manchester. Or take a local bus or a taxi (about £25).
Newcastle Airport is 6 miles (9km) northwest of Newcastle city centre on the A696 at Woolsington. The airport is a main station for the Metro underground system, which takes 23 minutes to Central station.

Scottish Airports

Edinburgh Airport (8 miles/13km west of Edinburgh). The Airlink bus (www.flybybus.com) to the city centre, which runs every 10 minutes from early morning until after midnight, takes roughly 25 minutes.
Glasgow Airport (8 miles/13km west of Glasgow) has bus services every 7 minutes at peak times to the city centre, which take about 25 minutes. These also stop at Glasgow's two rail stations, Central and Queen Street.
Prestwick Airport is 30 miles (48km)

Flight Information

Birmingham Airport
www.birminghamairport.co.uk
Cardiff Airport
www.tbicardiffairport.com
Edinburgh Airport
www.edinburghairport.com
Gatwick Airport
www.gatwickairport.com
Glasgow Airport
www.glasgowairport.com
Heathrow Airport
www.heathrowairport.com
London City Airport
www.londoncityairport.com
Luton Airport www.london-luton.co.uk
Manchester Airport
www.manchesterairport.co.uk
Prestwick (Glasgow)
www.glasgowprestwick.com
Stansted Airport
www.stanstedairport.com

Coach and Train Passes

Coach: National Express, tel: 08717-818 181, www.nationalexpress.com, offers a Brit Xplorer pass, for unlimited travel on their coaches for specified periods.
Train: The BritRail ticket (from European travel agents, and online in US at www.britrail.com) gives you unlimited travel in Great Britain for specified periods. There are several passes offering discounts for both UK residents and foreign visitors, including Family, Senior Citizen and Young Person's railcards, valid for one year. They cost a fraction of a long-distance InterCity trip and allow you a third off the full journey fare on off-peak trains.

south of Glasgow on the west coast. Trains take 50 minutes to Glasgow's Central station. There are airport express buses to Glasgow and Edinburgh for people arriving outside public transport times.

Welsh Airports

Cardiff Airport (12 miles/19km east) is used mainly by charter operators. There is a bus link (www.cardiffbus.com) to Cardiff Central station in the city centre.

By Car

"Le Shuttle" trains travel through the Channel Tunnel from Nord-Pas de Calais in France to Folkestone in Kent, with at least two departures every hour during the day and a reduced service overnight (journey time 35 minutes). Booking is not essential – just turn up and take the next service. Crossings are priced on a single-leg basis and prices vary according to the level of demand; the further ahead you book, the cheaper the ticket. For UK reservations and information, tel: 08705-353 535; www.eurotunnel.com.

By Coach

"Le Shuttle" trains also take coach services from continental Europe to London's Victoria coach station. Services are run from major cities all over Europe via Eurolines (www.eurolines.co.uk), a network of cooperating national bus companies offering integrated ticketing and extensive connections. For more information on national bus travel contact National Express, tel: 08717-818 181; www.nationalexpress.com.

ABOVE: approaching London Heathrow.

By Rail

Eurostar's regular passenger trains link France and Brussels with Britain via the Channel Tunnel. Services run from Paris Gare du Nord (2 hours 15 mins) and Brussels Midi (1 hour 50 mins) to London's St Pancras International; most trains stop in Ashford, Kent. Booking is not essential, but there are offers on tickets bought in advance, and at weekends and in holidays season it is advisable to book as far ahead as possible. For UK bookings, tel: 08705-186 186. From outside the UK, tel: +44 1233-617 575, or visit www.eurostar.com.

By Sea

Sea services operate from 12 British ports to more than 20 Continental ones. Major ferries have full eating, sleeping and entertainment facilities. The shortest crossing is from Calais in France to Dover in Britain, which takes about 90 minutes by ferry. Major operators include:
Brittany Ferries (tel: 08709-076 103; www.brittany-ferries.co.uk) sails from St. Malo, Caen and Cherbourg to Portsmouth; from Cherbourg to Poole; from Roscoff to Plymouth; and from Santander to Plymouth.
P&O Ferries (tel: 08716-645 645; www.poferries.com) runs from Calais to Dover, from Bilbao to Portsmouth and from Rotterdam and Zeebruge across the North Sea to Hull.
Stena Line (tel: 08705-707 070; www.stenaline.co.uk) sails from Hook of Holland to Harwich.
Norfolkline (tel: 0870-870 1020; www.norfolkline.com) operates between Dover and Dunkerque.

If you plan to bring a vehicle over by ferry it is advisable to book, particularly during peak holiday periods. If travelling by night on a long journey it is also recommended that you book a sleeping cabin.

From the US you could arrive in style on Cunard's *Queen Mary 2*. Operating between April and December, it takes 6 nights to cross the Atlantic (to Southampton). For information in the UK, tel: 0845-678 0013; from the US call 1-800 223 0764; www.cunard.com.

GETTING AROUND

Despite perennial complaints about trains not running on time, Britain's transport network has very good coverage and generally works efficiently. The rail service extends over most of the country, and where it fails to penetrate (into parts of the Scottish Highlands, for example), there are remarkably good roads to compensate.

Driving

In Britain you must drive on the left-hand side of the road and observe speed limits. It is illegal to use a mobile phone when driving. Penalties for drink driving are severe. Drivers and passengers, in both front and back seats, must wear seat belts where fitted; failure to do so can result in a fine. For further information, consult a copy of the *Highway Code* published by the DSA and widely available in bookshops. Prepare in advance by visiting www.direct.gov.uk.

If you are bringing your own car

into Britain you will need a valid driving licence or International Driving Permit; insurance coverage; and documents proving the vehicle is licensed and registered in your country and that you are resident outside the UK.

Breakdown

The following motoring organisations operate 24-hour breakdown assistance. They have reciprocal arrangements with other national motoring clubs. All calls to these numbers are free from UK phones.
AA 0800-887 766, www.theaa.com
Britannia Rescue 0800-591 563, www.britanniarescue.com
Green Flag 0800-051 0636, www.greenflag.co.uk
RAC 0800-828 282, www.rac.co.uk

Car Hire/Rental

To hire a car in Britain you must be over 21 years old (over 23 for most companies) and have held a valid full driving licence for more than one year. The cost of hiring a car usually includes third-party insurance, mileage and road tax. Depending on the company, it might also incorporate insurance cover for accidental damage to the car's interior, wheels and tyres. However, it does not include insurance for other drivers without prior arrangement.

Some companies offer special weekend and holiday rates, so shop around. International companies (such as those listed below) are keen to encourage visitors to book in advance before they leave home and may offer holiday packages with discounts of up to 40 percent on advance bookings through travel agents or branches in your own country. Many firms provide

child seats and luggage racks for a small charge.
Avis tel: 0844-581 0147, www.avis.co.uk
Hertz tel: 08708-448 844, www.hertz.co.uk
Budget tel: 0844-544 3470, www.budget.co.uk
Europcar tel: 08713-849 847, www.europcar.co.uk

Parking

Road congestion is a problem in most town and city centres, and parking is often restricted. Never leave your car parked on a double yellow or double red line, in a place marked *permit holders only*, within a white zig-zag line close to a pedestrian crossing, or in a control zone. Also, don't park on a single yellow line when restrictions are in force, usually 8.30am–6.30pm Mon–Fri (but always consult signs on the kerb); if no days are shown, restrictions are in force daily. These are offences for which you can face a fine. Either use a meter or a car park (look for a white P on a blue background).

Pay particular attention if leaving your car in central London. In many areas illegal parking may result in wheel clamping. This means your car is immobilised with a clamp until you pay (£70) to have it released – a process that can take several hours. Alternatively, your vehicle may be towed away to a car pound. Either way, retrieving your car will cost more than £200, plus a £40 parking fine. To ascertain whether your car has been towed away or not, tel: 020-7747 4747.

Domestic Flights

From the major international airports there are frequent shuttle services to Britain's many domestic airports, giving quick and easy access to many cities and offshore islands. Airlines providing domestic services include: **British Airways** (the country's largest airline), www.britishairways.com

Speed Limits

Unless otherwise stated on signs,
• **30mph (50kph)** in built-up areas.
• **60mph (100kph)** on single-lane roads away from built-up areas.
• **70mph (112kph)** on motorways and dual carriageways (divided highways).
• **Camping vans** or **cars towing a caravan** are restricted to 50mph, (80kph) on normal roads and 60 mph (96kph) on dual carriageways.

Driving in London

If you're only in London for a short time, and are unfamiliar with the geography of the capital, don't hire a car. Central London is more than ever a nightmare to drive in, with its web of one-way streets, bad signposting, congestion charge and impatient drivers. Use public transport or taxis instead.

Parking is also a major problem. Meters are slightly cheaper than NCP car parks, but usually allow parking for a maximum of 2 or 4 hours. If parking at a meter, do not leave your car a moment longer than your time allows or insert more money once your time has run out. For either infringement you can be fined up to

£80. Some meter parking is free after 6.30pm and all day Sunday, but check the details on the meter.

In central London, drivers must pay a congestion charge. The boundaries of the Congestion Charge Zone – which extends from Park Lane in the west to the City in the east – are clearly indicated with signs and road markings. Cars driving into this zone between 7am and 6pm from Monday to Friday are filmed and their drivers are fined if a payment of £10 has not been made by midnight the same day (or £12 the following day). You can pay at many newsagents and by phone or online (tel: 0845-900 1234; www.cclondon.com).

bmi, www.flybmi.com
Easyjet, www.easyjet.com
Ryanair, www.ryanair.com

Major Domestic Airports

Aberdeen www.aberdeenairport.com
Bristol www.bristolairport.co.uk
East Midlands www.eastmidlandsairport.com
Leeds-Bradford www.leedsbradfordairport.co.uk
Liverpool John Lennon www.liverpoolairport.com
Newcastle upon Tyne www.newcastleairport.com
Newquay www.newquaycornwallairport.com
Norwich www.norwichairport.co.uk
Southampton www.southamptonairport.com

Public Transport

In London

If you are staying in London for a while it is worth buying an A–Z street map, which also gives detailed information on the capital's confusing streets and postcodes. Walking in central London is usually very managable and distances between places of interest less far than you may think.

The **Underground** (Tube) is the quickest way to get across town. It is one of the most comprehensive networks of its kind in the world. It's also the oldest, and there are constant works to redevelop its stations and for planned maintenance. Service starts at 5.30am and runs until around midnight. It gets packed in the rush hours (7–10am and 4–7pm). Make sure that you have a valid ticket as it is illegal to travel without one and you may be fined. Smoking is prohibited.

Fares are based on a zone system (1–6) with a flat fare in central London, zone 1.

London buses provide a comprehensive service throughout Greater London and have their route and number clearly displayed on the front. Some buses run hourly throughout the night, with services to many parts of London departing from Trafalgar Square. In central London you must have a ticket before boarding; most stops have machines but there are some that still do not.

Call Transport for London on 020-7222 1234 or visit www.tfl.gov.uk. Note: smoking is prohibited anywhere on the Transport for London network and children under 10 travel for free if travelling with an adult.

Coaches and Local Buses

National Express operates an extensive network of long-distance coach services with comfortable coaches running on long journeys, equipped with washrooms and disabled facilities. Fares are (usually) considerably cheaper than the equivalent journey by train, although you must book your seat in advance. Children under 2 travel free on your knee, those aged 3–15 pay about half-price. For enquiries and bookings, tel: 08717-818 181; www.nationalexpress.com.

National Express also runs scheduled day-return trips to cities of interest such as Bath and Stratford-upon-Avon, as well as transport to music festivals and Wembley and Twickenham stadiums. **Green Line**, tel: 0844-801 7261; www.greenline.co.uk, has some similar services such as to Whipsnade Animal Park.

Towns are generally well-served by buses, often owned by private companies; rural communities often have very inadequate services.

Taxis

Outside London and large cities and away from taxi ranks at stations, ports and airports you will usually have to telephone for a taxi rather than expect to be able to hail one in the street. By law cabs must be licensed and display charges on a meter. Add about 10 percent for a tip.

London "black cab" drivers are famous for their extensive knowledge of the city's streets, but they aren't cheap, especially at night. Minicabs (unlicensed taxis, which look like private cars but have a blue on white "private hire" symbol displayed) are not allowed to compete with black cabs on the street and have to be hired by telephone or from a kiosk. If hiring a minicab, confirm the fee beforehand and don't expect drivers to know precise destinations. Never pick up an unsolicited minicab in the street.

If you have a complaint, make a note of the driver's licence number and contact the Public Carriage Office, tel: 0845-300 7000.

Trains

Railways are run by about two dozen private regional operating companies. They are not known for punctuality, so if your arrival time is critical allow for possible delays. Avoid rush-hour travel in and out of big cities.

There are many money-saving deals, such as cheap day-returns, available. It can be difficult to find out about special offers, so, if in doubt, ask again. Generally, tickets bought at least 2 weeks in advance are vastly cheaper than standard rates, but they sell out fast. Some saver tickets are available only if purchased abroad before arriving. Sometimes it is cheaper to buy two singles rather than a return ticket, so be sure to ask. Children under 5 travel free on your knee, those aged 5–15 pay half-price for most tickets.

It is not usually necessary to buy tickets until the day you travel (except to get these special offers), or to make seat reservations, except over the Christmas period when InterCity trains are fully booked well in advance.

Many trains have first-class carriages with tickets up to twice the price of standard seats. It is sometimes possible to upgrade to first class at weekends for an extra payment once you board.

On long distances overnight, it may be worth having a sleeping

London Travel Tickets and Passes

• **Single tickets** on London Transport are expensive: a single journey on the tube within zones 1–6 costs £5. A journey excluding zone 1 costs £3.40. There is a flat fare of £1.20 for any bus journey but it is cheaper if you use Oyster Pay As You Go or a travelcard.
• **Off-Peak One Day Travelcard:** a one-day pass that allows unlimited travel on the Tube, buses, Docklands Light Railway and rail services within Greater London. The card also gives a third off the cost of travel on scheduled Riverboat services. It can be used after 9.30am on a weekday or all day on Saturdays, Sundays or bank holidays (until 4.30am the following day), and is available from all Tube and some mainline stations.

• **Other Travelcards** are valid for 3 days, a week or a month and can be used at any time of day. To buy one you will need to supply a passport-sized photograph. Family travelcards are also available.
• **Pay As You Go Oyster Card:** valid on the tube, buses and some overland trains service. Visitor Oyster cards cost £3 plus an initial amount, eg £10 or £15. They can then be topped up with additional credit. Buy or top up at Tube stations, London Overground stations, and online at www.tfl.gov.uk, or tel: 0845-330 9876. You can also top up at newsagents and convenience stores displaying the Oyster sign.
• A **bus pass** (valid in all zones) costs £3.50 for one day or £14 for 7 days.

Train Enquiries

• **National Rail Enquiry Service**
For train times, cancellations and
advance bookings by credit card,
tel: 08457-484 950 or visit www.
nationalrail.co.uk.
• **Rail Europe** For services from
Britain, tel: 08448-484 064; www.
raileurope.co.uk, but if you are in
London is it often best to go in
person to 1 Regent Street, SW1.

compartment. Available on InterCity
trains, these have basic but
comfortable sleeping arrangements
and must be booked in advance.
Information is available by calling
08457-484 950, or +44 020-7278
5240 from abroad; National Rail
Enquiries can then give you the phone
number to book with the relevant train
operator. Tickets can also be booked
online at www.thetrainline.com or via www.
nationalrail.co.uk.
The journey between London
(Euston or King's Cross station) and
Edinburgh or Glasgow varies from 4½
to 6 hours. For travel in Scotland you
can buy a Freedom of Scotland
Travelpass giving unlimited travel
throughout Scotland and the English
Borders on the ScotRail network. The
Travelpass also includes some coach
travel and scheduled Caledonian
MacBrayne ferries to the islands off
the west coast. There are two options:
4 days' travel in an 8-day period, or 8
days' travel over 15 consecutive days.
Call national rail enquiries or see www.
scotrail.co.uk.
For a real luxury, take a trip (2–7
nights) on the famous Royal
Scotsman (Apr–Oct). For further
information contact the Orient
Express, tel: 0845-077 2222 (within
UK), +44 20 7960 0500 (outside UK);
www.royalscotsman.com.

River Travel and Tours

London
Riverboats are an excellent way to see
many major London sights whose
history is intertwined with the river.
During the summer these are
plentiful, but there are limited winter
services. Some of London Transport's
travel passes allow a third off the cost
of travel on scheduled riverboat
services. Boats can be booked at:
Richmond, Kew, Waterloo, London
Bridge, Embankment, Westminster,
the Tower of London and Greenwich
piers.
Circular cruises between St
Katharine's and Westminster Pier are

available from **Crown River Cruises**,
Blackfriars Pier, tel: 020-7936 2033;
www.crownriver.com.
Scheduled services are run by:
Thames River Services, Westminster
Pier to Thames Barrier and Green-
wich. Mar–Nov, tel: 020-7930 4097;
www.westminsterpier.co.uk.
City Cruises Departures from
Westminster, Waterloo, Tower and
Greenwich piers, tel: 020-7740 0400;
www.citycruises.com.
London Duck Tours Guided tour of
Westminster by road and river in
amphibious vehicles used in the
D-Day landings during World War II.
Depart from Waterloo; tel: 020-7928
3132; www.londonducktours.co.uk.

Scotland
Ferry services between the mainland
and 22 islands off the west coast of
Scotland have been monopolised by
Caledonian MacBrayne. Tickets are
cheaper if you book in advance,
although it is possible to just turn up
and go. Island Rover tickets allow you
to visit as many islands as you wish
over 8 or 15 days. Hopscotch tickets
are available for a range of pre-
planned routes, taking in just two or
three islands each. Ferries to Orkney
and Shetland are operated by
Northlink.
It is advisable to make reservations
on most services and they are strongly
recommended if you wish to take a

British Waterways

Britain has over 2,000 miles
(3,200km) of rivers and canals, the
latter a legacy of the Industrial
Revolution and now extensively
restored.
There is a wide choice of
vessels to hire. Possibilities include
exploring the canals, from the
Grand Union in the Midlands to the
Caledonian, which stretches from
coast to coast in Scotland, or
taking a pleasure cruiser along
major rivers such as the Thames,
Avon or Severn, or around the
Norfolk Broads.
For information, contact
Waterscape (part of British
Waterways), tel: 01923-201 120;
www.waterscape.com.

car. In bad weather, services may be
delayed or cancelled; a less frequent
service is generally offered in winter in
any case. The ferry to the Isle of Skye
from the Kyle of Lochalsh has been
replaced by a toll bridge.
For details contact:
Caledonian MacBrayne
Tel: 0800-066 5000
www.calmac.co.uk
**Northlink Orkney and Shetland
Ferries**
Tel: 0845-600 0449
www.northlinkferries.co.uk

Steam Railways

Many steam rail lines have been
restored by enthusiasts (www.ukhrail.
uel.ac.uk). Among the most notable
are:
• **Bluebell Railway**, Sheffield Park
Station, nr Uckfield, E. Sussex TN22
3QL; tel: 01825-720 800; www.
bluebell-railway.co.uk. Britain's most
famous line.
• **Watercress Line**, Alresford,
Hampshire SO24 9JG; tel: 01962-
733 810; www.watercressline.co.uk.
Runs through beautiful country over
steeply graded track.
• **Severn Valley Railway**, Bewdley,
Worcestershire DY12 1BG; tel:
01299-403 816; www.svr.co.uk.
Spectacular views.
• **Great Central Railway**,
Loughborough, Leics LE11 1RW; tel:
01509-230 726; www.gcrailway.co.uk.
One of the most evocative
restorations of the steam age.
• **Lakeside and Haverthwaite
Railway**, nr Ulverston, Cumbria
LA12 8AL; tel: 01539-531 594; www.
lakesiderailway.co.uk. Steep ride, with

connections to boats on the lake.
• **Ffestiniog Railway**, Harbour
Station, Porthmadog, Gwynedd LL49
9NF; tel: 01766-516 000; www.fest
rail.co.uk. Scenic ride through
Snowdonia National Park.
• **North Yorkshire Moors Railway**,
Pickering Station, YO18 7AJ; tel:
01751-472 508; www.nymr.co.uk. An
18-mile (30km) line through
picturesque moorland.
• **Isle of Man Transport**, Douglas,
Isle of Man, IM1 5PT; tel: 01624-
663 366; www.iombusandrail.info. Part
of the UK's largest vintage network
remains; 15 miles (24km) of track.
• **Paignton and Dartmouth Steam
Railway**, Queen's Park Station,
Torbay Road, Paignton, Devon TQ4
6AF; tel: 01803-555 872; www.
dartmouthrailriver.co.uk. Beautiful
coastal line, with superb views.
• **Gloucestershire–Warwickshire
Railway**, Toddington, Glos GL54
5DT; tel: 01242-621 405; www.gwsr.
com. A 20-mile (32km) round trip
through the Cotswolds.

A CCOMMODATION

HOTELS, INNS, BED & BREAKFASTS

Choosing a Hotel

A variety of accommodation exists in every part of Britain, from smart luxury hotels in stately homes and castles, to bed-and-breakfast (B&B) accommodation in private family homes or country farmhouses.

By international standards, hotels in Britain are expensive, so if you are holidaying on a tight budget you should consider staying in bed-and-breakfast accommodation. Alternatively there are plenty of youth hostels, which take people of all ages. Wherever you go, always be sure to look at a room before accepting it.

Not all hotels include breakfast in their rates and they may occasionally add a service charge of 10–15 percent. However, all charges should be clearly displayed on the tariff.

Booking a Hotel

It is advisable to book in advance, particularly at Christmas, Easter and throughout the summer. During the rest of the year there is generally little difficulty in finding somewhere to stay. You can book a room through a travel agent, directly with a hotel or via hotel aggregator websites such as www.booking.com or www.hotels.com.

Most Tourist Information Centres or TICs *(see page 388)* will also book local accommodation (free or for a small fee) for personal callers, whereas those involved in the Book-A-Bed-Ahead scheme will reserve you somewhere to stay in any area where there is another TIC involved in the scheme. A small fee is required, deducted from the hotel bill. Some TICs (www.enjoyengland.com) allow you to book online directly, whilst some of

Hotel Awards

The Enjoy England Quality Rose is the mark of England's nationwide quality assessment scheme, whose ratings (1–5 stars) assess accommodation standards in different categories (for example, hotels are in a separate category to B&Bs which come under Guest Accommodation), informing you what each category has to offer.

Visit Scotland (the national tourism organsiation) and Wales both have a single Quality Assurance Scheme for which star gradings are given by inspectors, again ranging from one to five stars, reflecting facilities and quality, whilst also using accommodation categories. All

the larger ones can book you accommodation if you visit the centre in person and use the accommodation in the next 24 hours. All TICs supply free lists of local accommodation.

The **Britain and London Visitor Centre** at 1 Regent Street, London, www.visitbritain.com, provides general information as does **Visit Britain** (tel: 020-8846 9000; www.visitbritain.com), which produces a series of useful annual Official Tourist Board guides dealing with every type of accommodation in Britain, from farms, B&Bs and pet-friendly accommodation to camping and self-catering boating holidays. To be listed, an establishment first has to pay to be inspected and then pay to be given an enhanced listing – so the guides are not totally impartial.

VisitScotland publishes Where To Stay guides featuring Scottish self-catering and B&Bs. **Visit Wales** also

these national bodies assess accommodation using the same criteria.

The Green Tourism Business Scheme has vetted more than 1,400 tourism businesses in England and Scotland since 1999, awarding bronze, silver or gold awards based on an accommodation's eco-credentials (www.green-business.co.uk).

A Michelin award is the accolade for which the most notable of hoteliers strive.

The AA (Automobile Association) provides a simple scheme awarding between one star (good, but basic) to five stars (luxury). See www.theaa.co.uk.

publishes an annual Where To Stay guide covering all accommodation types in one book. Contact local Tourist Information Centres or the Visit Britain office in your own country for a list.

Many hotels offer special weekend and low-season breaks between October and April. Details can be obtained from individual hotels, chains of hotels or from Enjoy England, whose website (www.enjoy england.com) lists accomodation discounts and deals.

B&Bs and Guesthouses

These are generally private homes with a few rooms for rent. Standards vary, but you can usually expect friendly hospitality, a hearty breakfast of eggs and bacon with all the trimmings, and helpful advice on where to visit and eat in the area.

Usually identified by a B&B sign placed outside, they are most abundant on the edge of towns, at the coast and in other prime tourist spots in rural areas. B&B accommodation is also available in many farmhouses, which provide rural accommodation with an insight into British farm life. Contact local tourist offices for lists of recommended accommodation.

B&Bs tend to be good value, and it is always advisable to book in advance during the peak seasons.

Somewhere between a hotel and a B&B in terms of size, price and facilities, guesthouses are generally small, family-run businesses where breakfast is usually included.

Companies that specialise in B&Bs include:

Bed & Breakfast Nationwide
Tel: 01255-831 235
www.bedandbreakfastnationwide.com
London Bed & Breakfast Agency
Tel: 020-7586 2768
www.londonbb.com
Farm Stay UK
Tel: 024-7669 6909; www.farmstay.co.uk
Produces the annual Farm Stay UK guide, covering over 1,200 rural options for Farm B&B and self-catering.

The AA publishes an annual *Bed & Breakfast Guide* to more than 4,000 inspected B&Bs. See also www.theaa.com.

Hotels

Hotels belonging to big chains such as Holiday Inn, Marriott and Hilton tend to offer a reliable, if at times impersonal, service. The following groups have hotels in most parts of the country:

Premier Travel Inn tel: 0870-242 8000 in the UK; +44 1582-567 890 outside the UK; www.premierinn.com. Simple but smart budget hotels in cities and towns.

Travelodge tel: 0871-559 1839; www.travelodge.co.uk. Budget hotels, often located on the outskirts of town near major roads.

Intercontinental Hotels and Resorts tel: +44 0800-405 060; www.ichotelsgroup.com.
Hilton International tel: 0870-590 9090; www.hilton.co.uk.
Accor Hotels tel: 0870-609 0961; www.accorhotels.com.

Britain also has many grand stately homes and castles that have been converted into country-house hotels. This growing trend in luxury accommodation has saved many a historic building from dereliction. Most provide an extremely high standard of traditional accommodation and service, often with superb restaurants. They are often the choice for romantic breaks: many such hotels have four-poster beds and offer special packages for those seeking a romantic weekend or honeymoon. From champagne, chocolates and flowers awaiting in your room, to a candlelit dinner or a balloon flight, hotels will arrange just about anything you ask for. Book well in advance for Valentine's Day (14 February), Britain's day for lovers.

The business traveller on an expense account is increasingly well catered for, in both urban and country areas, where there are many hotels offering large conference rooms and health and leisure facilities in addition to IT and communications services. In addition there is a whole host of private hotels.

Inns and Pubs

Inns are a great British institution that have become increasingly popular for accommodation. They are cheaper and smaller than hotels and offer character and the opportunity of meeting local people.

There are many historic taverns, particularly in rural towns and villages. Many are along roads where travelling pilgrims may have rested in the Middle Ages or stagecoaches stopped in the 17th century. Often they retain an old-world character with open fires, low beams, ale on tap and a warm ambience. Standards and food vary from basic to sophisticated. In urban areas pubs may have more of an institutional feel.

CAMRA (Campaign for Real Ale), 230 Hatfield Road, St Albans AL1 4LW; tel: 01727-867 201; www.camra.org.uk, publishes a guide, *Beer, Bed & Breakfast*, listing the best accommodation.

On a Budget

Camping

Despite Britain's reputation for rainy weather, camping is very much on the up. Facilities have been improved at campsites, the retro image of camping is appealing to many, and the development of "glamping" (glamorous camping) is convincing others that it can be a comfortable experience after all.

There are hundreds of campsites across the country, ranging from camping resorts with excellent facilities (swimming pools, children's clubs etc) to a small field behind a country pub. Websites such as www.ukcampsite.co.uk and www.campinguk.com provide listings. The Forestry Commission also runs a large number of campsites around Britain, some with rustic cabins. See www.forestholidays.co.uk for details.

The fashionable concept of glamping involves staying in yurts, cabins, tipis or bell tents in picturesque locations. Your accommodation usually has standing room, a proper bed, a stove and maybe even a sofa. Best of all, it's pre-erected so you do not need any special equipment, and the bed is made up for you when you arrive. Sites tend to be smaller and have good facilities. See http://goglamping.net for a wide selection of quirky places to stay.

Self-Catering Agencies

Blakes Country Cottages
Tel: 08700-781 300 (UK only); +44 1282-846 145 (overseas); www.blakes-cottages.co.uk.
Cornish Traditional Cottages
Tel: 01208-821 666; www.corncott.com.
English Country Cottages
Tel: 08700-781 100 (UK only); +44 1282-846 137 (overseas); www.english-country-cottages.co.uk.

Tips on Reserving and Booking Rooms

• When you book a hotel room, ensure that the price quoted is inclusive, and isn't going to be bumped up by a mysterious "travellers' charge" or other extras. Service is usually included in hotel bills.
• If you reserve in advance, you may be asked for a deposit. Reservations made, whether in writing or by phone, can be regarded as binding contracts, and you could lose your deposit or be charged a percentage of the cost if you fail to turn up.

• If you have reserved a room, the hotel will usually keep it for you until early evening, unless you agree otherwise. Rooms must usually be vacated by midday on the day of departure.
• Some hotels and most self-catering cottages do not allow single-night stays over the weekend.
• Most hotels offer better rates if you stay for several nights, or opt for dinner, bed and breakfast. It can be worth your while to bargain. You can also save money by booking online.

Hiring History

It is possible to stay in restored old buildings, from a medieval castle to a lighthouse. Many such properties have been beautifully restored and are maintained by the Landmark Trust and the National Trust.

The Landmark Trust is a private charity, set up in 1965 to rescue historic buildings. It now has more than 180 properties to let, ranging from castles and manor houses to mills, lighthouses, forts and follies, all restored and furnished in keeping with their original character. Detailed information can be found in a handbook available by post. The book's price is refunded against bookings. Tel: 01628-825 925; www. landmarktrust.org.uk.

The National Trust and National Trust for Scotland have more than 400 cottages and smaller houses of historical interest to let, from a romantic cabin hideaway overlooking a Cornish creek to an apartment in York with clear views of the Minster. Contact: The National Trust, tel: 0844-800 2070; www.nationaltrust cottages.co.uk and The National Trust for Scotland, tel: 0844-493 2108 within UK; +44 131-243 9331 outside UK; www.ntsholidays.com.

University Digs

In some cities, you may find that universities rent out their student accommodation to visitors during the long summer holidays. This can be an inexpensive option, and some places even offer full board. See www. university-rooms.com for universities that participate in such schemes.

Youth Hostels

There are more than 200 youth hostels in England and Wales, ranging from town houses to beach chalets. Facilities and accommodation are basic but cheap. Shared dormitories of bunk beds are the norm, but as they also appeal to families and older people, many now offer private rooms, including family rooms, with and without private bathrooms.

Some hostels provide a full meals service while others have self-catering kitchens, but hostels are only for those who don't mind mucking-in, communal living and a shortage of creature comforts. The maximum length of stay is 10–14 days. You must be a national or international member to stay at a hostel, although anyone of any age can join the association, overseas or in the UK. Contact the **Youth Hostel Association** (YHA), tel: 01629-592 700, www.yha.org.uk, or the **Scottish Youth Hostels Association** (SYHA), tel: 08701-553 255, www.syha.org.uk. London Hostels include:
38 Bolton Gardens, Earl's Court SW5 0AQ, tel: 0845-371 9114; 186 beds. Holland House, Holland Walk, Kensington W8 7QU; tel: 0845-371 9122; 200 beds.
36–8 Carter Lane, St Paul's, EC4V 5AB; tel: 0845-371 9012; 190 beds. 20 Salter Road, Thameside SE16 5PR; tel: 0845-371 9756; 320 beds.

Hotel Listings

The suggestions in this book are for hotels in places that will serve as good bases for exploring the regions covered in the guide. Unless otherwise stated, all the rooms have private bathroom facilities.

ACCOMMODATION LISTINGS

LONDON

Prices of hotel rooms in London are generally higher than in other capital cities in Europe. However, cost does not always mean quality, so try to view a room before accepting it. In Apr–Sept, it is advisable to book before you arrive as hotels fill up fast. You can book online at visitlondon.com, whilst www.just calllondon.co.uk (tel: 0870-471 8411) allows you to book online or call their hotel reservations centre.

The hotels listed below are located centrally and have been chosen either for their excellent position or for providing welcoming English hospitality in characterful surroundings.

Many moderately priced hotels are small and don't have restaurants, although they may provide room service. Some hotels offer babysitting and booking services for theatres and restaurants, while smarter establishments are geared up for business travellers.

Numerous hotels, including the Ritz and the Athenaeum, offer special weekend rates depending on the season. These are well worth checking out and may include incentives such as guided tours and champagne dinners. It's always worth checking directly with the hotel.

Hotel Areas

Central isn't necessarily best. Prices are high and hotels can be less characterful and sometimes more seedy than in areas a 20-minute Tube ride from the West End.
SW1 Traditionally the hotel district.
Victoria There are many delightfully old-fashioned hotels in Victoria, in most price brackets, and the streets close to Victoria station are full of terraced bed-and-breakfasts.
SW5 and **SW7** Around Kensington High Street, Earl's Court and Gloucester Road is a major centre for medium-range hotels.
West End More expensive than elsewhere in London. Bloomsbury (WC1) is central yet has reasonable prices; its hotels have a certain dignity and provide personal touches that you won't find in the Oxford Street area.

The best areas for moderately priced B&B accommodation are

Victoria, Knightsbridge, Earl's Court, Bayswater and Bloomsbury.

PRICE CATEGORIES

Price categories are for a double room including breakfast and VAT (value added tax) at high season:
£ = under £80
££ = £80–150
£££ = £150–250
££££ = over £250

Top Class

Athenaeum Hotel
116 Piccadilly
Tel: 020-7499 3464
www.athenaeumhotel.com
Smart 123-room hotel in the
heart of London with views
over Green Park. A very
English, "gentleman's club"
kind of hotel with, of course,
excellent service. **£££**

The Berkeley
Wilton Place, Knightsbridge
Tel: 020-7235 6000
www.the-berkeley.co.uk
Many consider the Berkeley
to be the best hotel in town.
It's low-key and has a
comfortable country-house
atmosphere. Facilities
include a pool. **££££**

Claridge's
Brook Street, Mayfair
Tel: 020-7629 8860
www.claridges.co.uk
Has long had a reputation
for service and style.
Includes one of Gordon
Ramsay's celebrated
restaurants. **££££**

The Connaught
Carlos Place, Mayfair
Tel: 020-7499 7070
www.the-connaught.co.uk
One of the best hotels in
London. Superb decor,
immaculate service and a
Michelin-starred restaurant.
££££

The Dorchester
Park Lane, Mayfair
Tel: 020-7629 8888
www.thedorchester.com
One of the most expensive
hotels in London, if not the
most characterful. Views
over Hyde Park. **££££**

Durley House
115 Sloane Street
Tel: 020-7235 5537
www.durleyhouse.com
Seriously luxurious suites,
with a period feel. All mod
cons and private gardens.
££££

The Four Seasons Hotel
Park Lane, Mayfair
Tel: 020-7499 0888
www.fourseasons.com
A temple of modern
opulence opposite Hyde
Park. **££££**

Metropolitan
Old Park Lane, Mayfair
Tel: 020-7447 1000
Modern, minimalist and very

chic. Home to the Michelin-
starred Nobu restaurant.
££££

The Sanderson
50 Berners Street
Tel: 020-7300 1400
www.sandersonlondon.com
Ultra-stylish hotel behind a
plain exterior. Philippe
Starck-designed interior.
££££

The Savoy
Strand
Tel: 020-7836 4343
www.fairmont.com/savoy
One of London's
institutions, with a
reputation for comfort and
personal service. It's
conveniently situated for
Theatreland and Covent
Garden. **££££**

W Hotel
10 Wardour Street, Leicester Square
Tel: 020-7758 1000
www.starwoodhotels.com
The extraordinary design of
the building and its
prominent position have
already made this
newcomer a well-known
London landmark. The ultra-
sleek interior has made it a
fashionable place to be
seen. **££££**

Luxury

Blakes Hotel
33 Roland Gardens, South
Kensington
Tel: 020-7370 6701
www.blakeshotels.com
Trendy and up-to-the-minute
hotel, popular with theatrical
and media folk. It's
cosmopolitan, tolerant and
laid-back in style. **£££–££££**

Brown's Hotel
Albemarle/Dover Street, Mayfair
Tel: 020-7493 6020
www.brownshotel.com
A distinguished, very British
hotel, founded by Lord
Byron's valet in 1837.
Smart location. **££££**

Cadogan Hotel
75 Sloane Street
Tel: 020-7235 7141
www.cadogan.com
This 19th-century institution
is well positioned between
Chelsea and Knightsbridge.
Actress Lily Langtry lived in
what is now the bar, and
Oscar Wilde was arrested in
room 118. **£££–££££**

Capital Hotel
22 Basil Street, Knightsbridge
Tel: 020-7589 5171
www.capitalhotel.co.uk
Luxurious hotel, with
tasteful decor, friendly
service and a fine
restaurant. 49 rooms.
£££–££££

Covent Garden Hotel
10 Monmouth Street,
Covent Garden
Tel: 020-7806 1000
www.firmdale.com
Understatedly chic boutique
hotel, popular with visiting
film stars. As well as its 58
rooms styled with a
contemporary English
aesthetic, the hotel also
offers a luxurious film
screening room, a DVD
library, a gym and a beauty
salon. **£££**

Duke's Hotel
35 St James's Place, St James
Tel: 020-7491 4840
www.dukeshotel.com
Traditional hotel with gas-
lamps lighting the courtyard,
and an intimate
atmosphere. The
comfortable rooms are
decorated in a classic,
understated style. **£££**

Goring Hotel
15 Beeston Place,
Grosvenor Gardens, Victoria
Tel: 020-7396 9000
www.goringhotel.co.uk
Where Kate Middleton
stayed the night before her
wedding to Prince William.
The family-owned,
delightfully traditional hotel
has a relaxed, old-world
atmosphere. **££££**

The Halkin
5 Halkin Street, Belgravia
Tel: 020-7333 1000
www.halkin.como.bz
The Halkin offers sleek
design in a Georgian town
house. It also has the only
Michelin-starred Thai
restaurant in Europe. **££££**

Hazlitt's
6 Frith Street, Soho
Tel: 020-7434 1771
www.hazlittshotel.com
Named after the great
English literary critic,
Hazlitt's occupies one of
London's oldest houses
(built in 1718), in the heart
of Soho. The 23 rooms are
all furnished with antiques.

£££–££££

Landmark London
222 Marylebone Road, Marylebone
Tel: 020-7631 8000
www.landmarklondon.co.uk
This eight-storey building
with glass domed atrium
offers good-sized rooms and
all the facilities you could
want. **£££**

The Ritz
150 Piccadilly
Tel: 020-7493 8181
www.theritzlondon.com
World-famous hotel that still
requires jackets and ties.
Rooms are rather
overblown. Tea at the Ritz is
a decadent (and expensive)
treat. **££££**

St Martin's Lane
45 St Martin's Lane
Tel: 020-7300 5500
www.stmartinslane.com
Phillipe Starck-designed,
fashionable spot in Covent
Garden. It has outlandish
lighting, good if expensive
food and 204 blindingly
white bedrooms. **£££**

The Tower Hotel
St Katharine's Way
Tel: 0871-376 9036
www.guoman.com/the-tower
This large (800+ rooms),
modern hotel is located in
the docklands near the City,
and offers breathtaking
views of Tower Bridge and
the river. **£££**

Moderate

Academy Town House
17–21 Gower Street, Bloomsbury
Tel: 020-7631 4115
www.theetoncollection.com
Small, welcoming boutique
hotel, offering a stylish bar
and smart rooms, two of
which have even have
private gardens. **£££**

Elizabeth Hotel
37 Eccleston Square
Tel: 020-7828 6812
www.elizabethhotel.com
This friendly hotel is

PRICE CATEGORIES

Price categories are for a
double room including
breakfast and VAT (value
added tax) at high season:
£ = under £80
££ = £80–150
£££ = £150–250
££££ = over £250

situated in an elegant period square, 2 minutes' walk from Victoria station. 42 classy rooms, almost all with an ensuite. **££**

The Rubens at the Palace
39 Buckingham Palace Road, Victoria
Tel: 020-7834 6600
www.rubenshotel.com
Large traditional hotel with a smart location opposite Royal Mews. **£££**

Tophams
24-32 Ebury Street
Tel: 020-7730 3313
www.tophamshotellondon.co.uk
This luxury boutique hotel in Belgravia occupies five period houses; friendly and welcoming. **£££**

Inexpensive

Airways Hotel
29 St George's Drive

Tel: 020-7834 0205
www.airways-hotel.com
Pleasant 37-room hotel (19 of which have a bath) close to Buckingham Place, Westminster Abbey and Harrods. Friendly service. **££**

Base2Stay
25 Courtfield Gardens, Kensington
Tel: 0845-262 8000
www.base2stay.com
Taking the principles and style of boutique hotels to the budget market, this hotel innovator offers "studios", with their own fridges, microwaves and media facilities, to provide the freedom of a flat with the ease of a hotel. **£–££**

County Hall Premier Inn
Belvedere Road, South Bank
Tel: 0870-238 3300
www.premierinn.com

Occupying the old County Hall across the river from the Houses of Parliament, this hotel is an excellent choice for those on a tight budget. Advance booking is essential to procure one of the 314 rooms. **£–££**

Curzon House Hotel
58 Courtfield Gardens
Tel: 020-7581 2116
www.curzonhousehotel.co.uk
Economical but comfortable small hotel close to Gloucester Road Underground station. Rooms vary from singles, twins and doubles to three-, four- and five-bed rooms to eight-bedded dormitories. **£**

easyHotel
14 Lexham Gardens, Kensington
www.easyhotel.com
While this hotel is certainly

a no-frills experience (some rooms don't even have a window), it is nevertheless ideal for budget travellers. This chain also has other branches in London. Internet bookings only. **£**

Lonsdale Hotel
9–10 Bedford Place
Tel: 020-7636 1812
www.lonsdalehotellondon.com
For a modest price, you get real character in the heart of Bloomsbury in this well-established 40-room bed-and-breakfast hotel with some ensuite rooms. **£–££**

Vicarage Private Hotel
10 Vicarage Gate, Notting Hill Gate
Tel: 020-7229 4030
www.londonvicaragehotel.com
Friendly place, with clean, simple rooms and good English breakfasts. **£–££**

THAMES VALLEY

Aylesbury

Hartwell House and Spa
Oxford Road, nr Aylesbury
Tel: 01296-747 444
www.hartwell-house.com
A delightful country-house hotel in large grounds. The rooms are furnished with antiques, and there are excellent leisure facilities in the 46 rooms. No children under 6. **£££**

Henley-on-Thames

Red Lion
Hart Street
Tel: 01491-572 161

www.redlionhenley.co.uk
Just right for the annual regatta in early July, this comfortable, family-owned 39-room hotel close to a 1786 bridge overlooks the finishing post on the River Thames. **£££**

Hotel du Vin
New Street, Henley-on-Thames
Tel: 01491-848 400
www.hotelduvin.com
Occupying an old brewery close to the river, this luxury boutique hotel has 43 well-turned-out rooms and a highly recommended bistro. **££–£££**

Taplow

Cliveden
Taplow, Berkshire
Tel: 01628-668 561
www.clivedenhouse.co.uk
One of the most beautiful and luxurious hotels in Britain is surrounded by 376 acres (152 hectares) of National Trust parkland. Convenient for Heathrow. **££££**

Windsor

Oakley Court
Windsor Road, Water Oakley
Tel: 01753-609 988

www.principal-hayley.com
Very picturesque Victorian house with extensive grounds running down to the Thames. 118 rooms. **£££**

OXFORD TO BIRMINGHAM

Ampney Crucis

Crown of Crucis
Ampney Crucis, nr Cirencester
Tel: 01285-851 806
www.thecrownofcrucis.co.uk
A 16th-century inn overlooking the village cricket green. Many of the tasteful rooms overlook a river. Some family rooms. Good food. **££**

Bibury

Bibury Court
Cirencester
Tel: 01285-740 337
http://biburycourt.co.uk
A glorious Jacobean house fulfilling everyone's idea of a Cotswold manor. Rarely does such a sense of history come with so low a price tag. The gardens are stunning. **£££**

Birmingham

Hotel du Vin
25 Church Street
Tel: 0121-200 0600
www.hotelduvin.com
Occupying a red-brick Victorian hospital, this boutique hotel is considered Birmingham's best. Lots of amenities including a popular bistro and bar. **££**

Broadway, Cotswolds

The Lygon Arms
High Street
Tel: 01386-852 255
www.barcelo-hotels.co.uk
Magnificent 16th-century
coaching inn with antique
furnishings, log fires and
old-fashioned good service.
£££

Buckland

Buckland Manor
Nr Broadway
Tel: 01386-852 626
www.bucklandmanor.co.uk
13th-century manor in
extensive 10-acre
(4-hectare) gardens. **££££**

Cheltenham

The Greenway Spa Hotel
Shurdington, nr Cheltenham
GL51 4UG
Tel: 01242-862 352
www.thegreenway.co.uk
Peaceful Elizabethan
mansion covered in Virginia
creeper. Comfortable rooms
offer a luxurious country
house feel. **£££**

Great Milton, nr Oxford

**Le Manoir aux
Quat'Saisons**
Church Road, Great Milton
Tel: 01844-278 881
www.manoir.com
Raymond Blanc's manor
house offers the ultimate

hotel experience, with
elegant, stylish bedrooms,
beauty therapies and, of
course, his two-Michelin-
starred restaurant. **£££**

Lower Slaughter

Lower Slaughter Manor
Nr Bourton-on-the-Water,
Gloucestershire
Tel: 01451-820 456
www.lowerslaughter.co.uk
Luxurious 17th-century
manor in its own grounds,
with panelled private dining
room and galleried landing.
Meticulous service. Stay in
the manor or adjoining
coach house, both
magnificent with antiques,
chintzy fabrics and
bathrooms with twin
washbasins. Superb
breakfast. **££££**

Oxford

Bath Place Hotel
4–5 Bath Place
Tel: 01865-791 812
www.bathplace.co.uk
Family-run 15-room hotel in
the heart of Oxford
occupying a cluster of
restored 17th-century
homes. A backwater oasis
with a lovely cottagey feel.
££

Eastgate Hotel
73 High Street
Tel: 01865-248 332
www.mercure.com
Traditional hotel in a central
location, adjacent to the site
of Oxford's old East Gate,

opposite the Examination
Schools. **£££**

Malmaison
3 Oxford Castle
Tel: 01865-268 400
www.malmaison-oxford.com
Occupying the former prison
– with each room consisting
of three cells knocked into
one – this stylish boutique
hotel offers luxuries its one-
time residents could only
have dreamed of. The
brasserie is one of Oxford's
best restaurants. **££**

Old Bank Hotel
92–4 High Street
Tel: 01865-799 599
www.oldbank-hotel.co.uk
One of the city's most stylish
hotels, housed in an elegant
Georgian former bank.
Rooms are contemporary in
style and the fashionable
Quod Brasserie is
downstairs. **£££**

Old Parsonage Hotel
1 Banbury Road
Tel: 01865-310 210
www.oldparsonage-hotel.co.uk
A fine hotel in a renovated
old parsonage with 30
deluxe en-suite bedrooms.
The restaurant is open to
non-residents. **£££**

Randolph Hotel
Beaumont Street
Tel: 0844-879 9132
www.randolph-hotel.com
Grand Victorian 151-room
hotel in central Oxford
offering traditional service
with all the trimmings. **£££**

The Tower House
15 Ship Street
Tel: 01865-246 828

www.towerhouseoxford.co.uk
Located centrally, just off
Cornmarket, this friendly,
family-run guesthouse
dates from the 17th century.
The seven bedrooms are
furnished with antiques and
are decorated to a high
standard. **£–££**

Stow-on-the-Wold

Grapevine Hotel
Sheep Street, Stow-on-the-Wold
Tel: 01451-830 344
www.vines.co.uk
Welcoming hotel in a 17th-
century stone building,
named after the old vine
that shades the
conservatory restaurant. **££**

Stratford-upon-Avon

Alveston Manor
Clopton Bridge,
Stratford-upon-Avon
Tel: 0844-879 9138
www.macdonaldhotels.co.uk
A charming half-timbered
16th-century manor,
thought to have been the
location of the first
performance of A
Midsummer Night's Dream.
£££

Tetbury

The Snooty Fox
Market Place
Tel: 01666-502 436
www.snooty-fox.co.uk
An old Cotswold stone
coaching inn on the market
square of this historic town.
Oak panelling, log fires,
antique furniture. Fine
restaurant; 12 rooms, some
with four-poster beds and
ensuite whirlpool
bathrooms. **££**

Upper Slaughter

Lords of the Manor
Upper Slaughter, near Bourton-on-
the-Water
Tel: 01451-820 243
www.lordsofthemanor.com
This 16th-century former
rectory is set in the rolling
Cotswold countryside. Many
rooms have parkland and
lake views. Michelin-starred
restaurant. **£££–££££**

BELOW: the sleek interior of the Varsity Hotel and Spa, Cambridge.

CAMBRIDGE AND EAST ANGLIA

Burnham Market

The Hoste Arms
The Green
Tel: 01328-738 777
www.hostearms.co.uk
Characterful 17th-century inn on the green of this fashionable village near where Admiral Nelson was born and close to Sandringham's royal estate. Good restaurant. **££**

Cambridge

The Varsity Hotel and Spa
Thompson's Lane, off Bridge Street
Tel: 01223-306 030
www.thevarsityhotel.co.uk
This attractive contemporary hotel is by far the most stylish place to lay your head while you're in Cambridge. Add the rooftop garden with views over the colleges, the impressive restaurant, a beautifully designed spa and gym, and even complimentary guided walking tours and punting on the river, and you've got a compelling first choice. **£££**

Hotel du Vin and Bistro
15–19 Trumpington Street
Tel: 01223-227 330

www.hotelduvin.com
Located in the heart of town, just opposite the Fitzwilliam Museum, this elegant boutique hotel occupies a fine historic town house. The bistro is one of the best restaurants in Cambridge. **££–£££**

Ely

Lamb Hotel
2 Lynn Road
Tel: 01353-663 574
www.thelamb-ely.com
This is a former coaching house with a history that can be traced back to 1416. Occupying a city-centre location in the shadow of Ely's magnificent cathedral, the rooms here include an impressive four-poster suite. **£**

Lavenham

The Angel
Market Place
Tel: 01787-247 388
www.maypolehotels.com/angelhotel
A 15th-century inn overlooking this old wool town's market place, with an excellent restaurant and exposed beams in most of the bedrooms. **££**

Morston, nr Holt

Morston Hall
Morston, nr Holt
Tel: 01263-741 041
www.morstonhall.com
For a comfortable stay and Michelin-starred cuisine, you can't do better than this flint manor house on the Norfolk coast. **£££**

Norwich

Dunston Hall
Ipswich Road
Tel: 01508-470 444
www.devere.co.uk
This grand Elizabethan-style country house offers every facility you could wish for: spa, swimming pool, gym, golf course, bars and restaurants. What's more, the prices are reasonable and children are welcome. **££**

Southwold

The Crown
High Street
Tel: 01502-722 275
www.adnams.co.uk
This old inn is owned by Adnams Brewery so you know the beer will be good. The rooms are comfortable

and the restaurant has a considerable reputation locally. **££**

The Randolph Hotel
Wangford Road, Reydon, near Southwold
Tel: 01502-723 603
www.therandolph.co.uk
A 15-minute walk from Southwold, this is a good base for exploring the Suffolk Heritage Coast, with a choice of 10 modern, comfortable rooms. **££**

Wells-next-the-Sea

The Crown Hotel
The Buttlands
Tel: 01328-710 209
www.thecrownhotelwells.co.uk
A fine old coaching inn in a pretty port on the north Norfolk coast. Popular bar and restaurant. **££**

THE SOUTHEAST

Alfriston

The George Inn
High Street
Tel: 01323-870 319
www.thegeorge-alfriston.com
This beautiful half-timbered 14th-century pub/hotel is in the middle of a pretty village. It has oak-beamed rooms, and local fish is a speciality in the restaurant. **££**

Arundel

Amberley Castle
Near Arundel
Tel: 01798-831 992
www.amberleycastle.co.uk
This 12th-century castle has been opulently revamped

with antique furniture and Jacuzzis in every bathroom. **£££**

Brighton

The Ambassador Hotel
22–23 New Steine, Marine Parade
Tel: 01273-676 869
www.ambassadorbrighton.co.uk
Traditional and cheerful seaside hotel with a difference – the vegetarian and vegan-friendly menu. **££**

The Grand
97–99 King's Road
Tel: 01273-224 300
www.devere.co.uk
Victorian grandeur and friendly service. Overlooks the beach; indoor pool, gym and spa. **££–£££**

Hotel du Vin
Ship Street
Tel: 01273-718 588
www.hotelduvin.com
A plum location near the seafront combined with the building's historic character make this hotel a top choice for Brighton. The stunning suites are ideal for romantic getaways. **££–£££**

Hotel Pelirocco
10 Regency Square
Tel: 01273-327 055
www.hotelpelirocco.co.uk
All rooms are playfully designed – and have their own playstations – in this chic hotel in the best-preserved Regency square in town. **££**

PRICE CATEGORIES

Price categories are for a double room including breakfast and VAT (value added tax) at high season:
£ = under £80
££ = £80–150
£££ = £150–250
££££ = over £250

Canterbury

Falstaff
8–10 St Dunstan's Street
Tel: 01227-462 138
www.thefalstaffincanterbury.com
Historic 15th-century coaching inn within easy reach of Canterbury cathedral and shops.
££

Chichester

The Millstream Hotel
Bosham,
nr Chichester
Tel: 01243-573 234
www.millstream-hotel.co.uk
Quiet country hotel near Bosham harbour. Good food. Enjoy afternoon tea in the beautiful gardens.
££

Suffolk House Hotel
3 East Row
Tel: 01243-778 899
www.suffolkhousehotel.co.uk
Private hotel in a fine Georgian building with restaurant and garden. **£**

Eastbourne

The Grand Hotel
King Edward's Parade
Tel: 01323-412 345
www.grandeastbourne.com
Built in 1875, with comfortable rooms and splendid service. Formal restaurant. **£££**

New Romney

Romney Bay House
Coast Road, Littlestone
Tel: 01797-364 747
www.romneybayhousehotel.co.uk
Next to the sea, with stunning views and 10 individually decorated rooms. Good food; excellent cream teas. **££**

Rye

The Mermaid Inn
Mermaid Street
Tel: 01797-223 065
www.mermaidinn.com
Timbered 15th-century inn in this ancient coastal port. Excellent restaurant. There are 31 rooms (8 with four-poster beds). **£–££**

Tunbridge Wells

Hotel du Vin and Bistro
Crescent Road
Tel: 01892-526 455
www.hotelduvin.com
A central location, individually decorated rooms, friendly staff, great breakfasts and a superb bistro are among the many reasons for staying here.
££

HARDY COUNTRY

Brockenhurst

Balmer Lawn Hotel
Lyndhurst Road
Tel: 01590-623 116
www.balmerlawnhotel.com
Former hunting lodge in the heart of the New Forest with superb views. Has a pool, sauna and gym. **£££**

Careys Manor
Lyndhurst Road
Tel: 01590-623 551
www.careysmanor.com
An environmentally-friendly 1888 mansion complete with Thai spa and pool. Rooms in garden wing have balconies overlooking walled garden. Choice of three restaurants. **££–£££**

New Park Manor
Lyndhurst Road
Tel: 01590-623 467
www.newparkmanorhotel.co.uk
Excellent 24-room retreat, in landscaped grounds in the New Forest. Once the hunting lodge of Charles II. Excellent restaurant; croquet lawn, heated pool, spa. **££**

Evershot

Summer Lodge
Summer Lane
Tel: 01935-482 000
www.summerlodgehotel.co.uk
This Georgian dower house set in mature gardens is luxuriously furnished and noted for its high standards of service. **££**

Lyme Regis

The Alexandra
Pound Street
Tel: 01297 442 010
www.hotelalexandra.co.uk
Large 18th-century house with 25 rooms set in fine grounds overlooking the bay. Comfortable and welcoming. **££**

New Milton

Chewton Glen
Christchurch Road
Tel: 01425-275 341
www.chewtonglen.com
One of England's best-known country-house hotels, in an elegant 18th-century mansion on the edge of the New Forest National Park. The swimming pool is modelled on the bathhouses of ancient Rome. Majority of rooms have private gardens or balconies. **££££**

Salisbury

White Hart
1 St John Street
Tel: 1722-327 476
www.mercure.com
This elegant Georgian establishment combines old-world comforts with modern conveniences.
££

THE WEST COUNTRY

Bath

Bath Paradise House Hotel
86–8 Holloway
Tel: 01225-317 723
www.paradise-house.co.uk
Less than 10 minutes' walk from the city centre, this hotel's rooms have a country-house feel and lovely bathrooms. Three of the 11 rooms have four-poster beds. Town garden rooms are in an attractive annexe. **£££**

The Bath Priory
Weston Road
Tel: 01225-331 922
www.thebathpriory.co.uk
Gothic-style 19th-century house in beautiful gardens. Michelin-starred restaurant.
££££

Bath Spa Hotel
Sydney Road
Tel: 0844-879 9106
www.macdonaldhotels.co.uk/bathspa
Near Sydney Gardens and set in its own extensive grounds. All comforts, including spa and excellent restaurant. **£££**

Bloomfield House
146 Bloomfield Road
Tel: 01225-420 105
www.ecobloomfield.com
Upmarket B&B in large 18th-century house. Some four-

poster beds. No smoking. **££**
Combe Grove Manor Hotel
Brassknocker Hill, Monkton Combe
Tel: 01225-834 644
www.barcelo-hotels.co.uk
Luxurious 18th-century
house and garden lodge.
Pools, gym, tennis, golf and
driving range. **£££**
Dorian House
1 Upper Oldfield Park
Tel: 01225-426 336
www.dorianhouse.co.uk
Smart accommodation in an
elegant Victorian town house
run by a London Symphony
Orchestra cellist. The rooms
are named after famous
classical musicians. **££**
The Hollies
Hatfield Road
Tel: 01225-313 366
www.theholliesbath.co.uk
Grade II-listed Victorian
B&B. Three attractive rooms
and pretty garden. No
children under 16. **£**
The Manor House
Monkton Combe
Tel: 01225-723 128
www.manorhousebath.co.uk
Attractive medieval manor
offering very reasonably
priced accommodation. Fig
Tree Restaurant open Fri–
Sat evening. **££**
Royal Crescent Hotel
16 Royal Crescent
Tel: 01225-823 333
www.royalcrescent.co.uk
The ultimate address in
Bath, with a central location.
Antiques, paintings,
individually decorated
rooms, a noted restaurant
and secluded garden at the
back. With 45 rooms. **££££**
The Queensberry Hotel
Russel Street
Tel: 01225-447 928
www.thequeensberry.co.uk
This smart boutique hotel
occupying three Georgian
houses knocked together
offers comfort, character
and the esteemed Olive Tree
Restaurant. **££–£££**

Bigbury-on-Sea

Burgh Island Hotel
South Devon
Tel: 01548-810 514
www.burghisland.com
This Art Deco hotel is closely
associated with Agatha
Christie, who wrote two of

her books here. The hotel is
on an island, so access is by
sea tractor. **££££**

Bradford-on-Avon

Bradford Old Windmill
4 Masons Lane
Tel: 01225-866 842
www.bradfordoldwindmill.co.uk
Hidden-away converted
windmill offering bed and
breakfast. No smoking. Only
three rooms **££**

Bristol

Hotel du Vin
The Sugar House, Narrow
Lewins Mead
Tel: 0117-925 5577
www.hotelduvin.com
Located within a beautifully
restored 18th-century
warehouse, this chic hotel
includes several luxurious
loft-suites, as well as some
40 stylish standard rooms.
There's also a buzzing
bistro. **££–£££**

Castle Combe

Manor House Hotel
Castle Combe, nr Bath
Tel: 01249-782 206
www.manorhouse.co.uk
Parts of this manor house
are 14th-century. Best
rooms have beams,
exposed stone walls and
quality furnishings. Golf-
break packages include
unlimited access to the
championship green,
although a handicap
certificate is a must. **£££**

Chagford, Devon

Gidleigh Park
Chagford
Tel: 01647-432 367
www.gidleigh.com
Quintessentially English, a
huge, half-timbered house
in expansive grounds within
Dartmoor National Park;
babbling brook, log fires and
impeccable service.
Excellent restaurant, with
two Michelin stars. **££££**
Mill End Hotel
Dartmoor National Park
Tel: 01647-432 282
www.millendhotel.com
Pretty old mill, complete

ABOVE: one of the cosy suites at Fowey Hall, in Cornwall.

with wheel, in peaceful
setting on River Teign.
Excellent for families;
seasonal gourmet events by
award-winning chef. **££**

Colerne, nr Bath

Lucknam Park
Colerne, nr Bath
Tel: 01225-742 777
Luxurious manor with
equestrian centre and spa.
££££

Dartmouth

The Royal Castle
11 The Quay
Tel: 01803-833 033
www.royalcastle.co.uk
On Dartmouth's quayside,
this 17th-century coaching
inn serves good Devon
cuisine. 25 rooms, some
with river views). **££–£££**

Fowey

Fowey Hall
Hanson Drive
Tel: 01726-833 866
www.foweyhallhotel.co.uk
Imposing turrets outside,
sumptuous decor inside, but
relaxed atmosphere and
kids are well catered for.
On-site spa. **££**
Old Quay House
28 Fore Street
Tel: 01726-833 302
www.theoldquayhouse.com
Right on the quayside, a
traditional exterior conceals
sleek modern decor. The
views are stupendous and
the Q Restaurant is highly
recommended. **££–£££**

Freshford

Homewood Park
Abbey Lane, Hinton Charterhouse
Tel: 01225-723 731
www.homewoodpark.co.uk
South of Bath, this Victorian
country-house hotel has an

outdoor swimming pool,
beautiful gardens and a
cosy bar. Some rooms have
Victorian free-standing
baths; 19 rooms. **£££**

Isles of Scilly

St Mary's Hall Hotel
Church Street, St Mary's
Tel: 01720-422 316
www.stmaryshallhotel.co.uk
On the edge of Hugh Town
close to the beaches, this
hotel has a longstanding
reputation for good food.
Price includes dinner. **££**
Island Hotel
Tresco
Tel: 01720-422 883
www.tresco.co.uk
This fine hotel has
everything you could wish
for: a fine location in subtropical gardens, a private
beach, a pool, a tennis court
– even its own sailing
school. The restaurant is
renowned for its fine
modern British cuisine. **£££**
Hell Bay
Bryer
Tel: 01720-422 947
www.hellbay.co.uk
This stylish new hotel offers
25 spacious rooms that
make the most of the
spectacular views and
bright light of the Scilly
Isles. The restaurant is
renowned, and other
facilities include a
swimming pool, sauna and
gym. The hotel also boasts
an impressive collection of
paintings by artists with
local connections. **£££**

PRICE CATEGORIES

Price categories are for a
double room including
breakfast and VAT (value
added tax) at high season:
£ = under £80
££ = £80–150
£££ = £150–250
££££ = over £250

Marazion/ St Michael's Mount

Mount Haven Hotel
Turnpike Road, Marazion, Penzance
Tel: 01736-710 249
www.mounthaven.co.uk
A pretty, modern hotel with light, airy rooms, some with balconies and private terraces, overlooking St Michael's Mount. Restaurant serves delicious fish. **££**

Penzance

Abbey Hotel
Abbey Street
Tel: 01736-366 906
www.theabbeyonline.co.uk
Owned by 1960s supermodel Jean Shrimpton, this delightful blue-stuccoed hotel is renowned for its warmth of atmosphere. It also offers

period features, views over the harbour and a Michelin-starred restaurant. **££**

St Ives

Carbis Bay Hotel
Carbis Bay
Tel: 01736-795 311
www.carbisbayhotel.co.uk
Good restaurant, splendid views of one of Britain's most beautiful bays, private beach. **£–££**

Ston Easton

Ston Easton Park
Nr Bath
Tel: 01761-241 631
www.stoneaston.co.uk
Notable for its Humphrey Repton gardens, with grotto, bridges over River Norr and 18th-century ice house, this fine Palladian manor

provides country-house splendour in the Mendip Hills. Some rooms with Chippendale four-posters. Restaurant's organic produce comes from the Victorian kitchen garden. **££££**

Tintagel

Michael House
Trelake Lane, Treknow
Tel: 01840-770 592
www.michael-house.co.uk
Among the benefits of staying at this vegetarian and vegan guesthouse are its wonderful location, seaviews and reasonable tarriffs. **£**

Truro

The Lugger Hotel
Portloe, Truro

Tel: 01872-501 322
www.luggerhotel.com
An idyllic stay at the Lugger involves a perfect setting in a tiny Cornish fishing village, luxurious rooms with seaviews, and a wonderful restaurant serving up local seafood and produce with style and panache. **££**

Woolacombe

Woolacombe Bay Hotel
Tel: 01271-870 388
www.woolacombe-bay-hotel.co.uk
Built in the late 1880s and set in 6 acres (2.5 hectares) of grounds by the sea. Pools, fitness classes, squash, tennis, nine-hole pitch-and-putt golf course, diving, yacht charter, snooker, table tennis, gym and spa. Local surfing school. **££**

WYE VALLEY AND SOUTH WALES

Abergavenny

Llanthony Priory Hotel
Llanthony, Abergavenny,
Monmouthshire
Tel: 01873 89048
www.llanthonyprioryhotel.co.uk
This small country inn is part of an Augustinian priory and the four rooms in the tower are furnished in a fittingly historic style. **££**

Aberystwyth

Conrah Hotel
Chancery, Ceredigion
Tel: 01970-617 941
www.conrah.co.uk
Expect some traditional country comfort at this peaceful hotel located a few miles south of Aberystwyth. Good touring centre. Has 17 rooms. **££**

Brecon

Peterstone Court
Llanhamlach, Powys
Tel: 01874-665 387
www.peterstone-court.com
Comfortable 18th-century manor with a prime location in the Brecon Beacons National Park; 12 rooms. **££**

Cardiff

St David's Hotel and Spa
Havannah Street
Tel: 02920-454 045
www.principal-hayley.com
Spectacular views over Cardiff Bay, luxurious rooms and an excellent restaurant make this a strong choice. **£££**

Crickhowell

Bear Hotel
Crickhowell, Powys
Tel: 01873-810 408
www.bearhotel.co.uk
Famous inn on old stagecoach route. Atmospheric bar popular with locals and visitors. Good food and wine; comfortable rooms. **££**

Gower Peninsula

Fairyhill
Reynoldston
Tel: 01792-390 139
www.fairyhill.net
Situated near stunning beaches, this 18th-century house set in parkland has one of the best restaurants locally. **££–£££**

Hereford

Castle House
Castle Street
Tel: 01432-356 321
www.castlehse.co.uk
Former home of the Bishop of Hereford, in the centre of town, close to the cathedral, this 15-room boutique hotel provides an excellent base. Renowned for its restaurant. **£££**

Llangammarch Wells

Lake Country House and Spa
Llangammarch Wells, Powys
Tel: 01591-620 202
www.lakecountryhouse.co.uk
Mock-Tudor mansion set in grounds that slope down to the lake. Wonderful views from individually-designed bedrooms. Offers fishing breaks. **££**

Llyswen

Llangoed Hall
Llyswen, Powys
Tel: 01874-754 525
www.llangoedhall.com
Luxurious 17th-century

manor house on the banks of the River Wye, with Black Mountain views. Brimming with antique furniture and Elanbach fabrics. Parts date from 1632, but the Edwardian architect Sir Clough Williams-Ellis rebuilt it in 1919. Excellent breakfasts. **£££**

Newport

Celtic Manor
Coldra Woods, Usk Valley
Tel: 01633-413 000
www.celtic-manor.com
This 19th-century manor offers landscaped gardens, three golf courses (it was a venue for the 2010 Ryder Cup), an indoor pool, tennis and shooting. **£££–££££**

ABOVE: the eccentric Portmeirion Hotel in the fantasy model village where *The Prisoner* TV series was filmed in the 1960s.

NORTH WALES

Betws-y-Coed

Tan-y-Foel Country House
Capel Garmon, nr Betws-y-Coed
Tel: 01690-710 507
www.tyfhotel.co.uk
An award-winning stone manor turned country guest house with stunning views and good food. Modern and informal. No children under 12. **££**

Isle of Anglesey

Ye Olde Bull's Head Inn
Castle Street, Beaumaris
Tel: 01248-810 329
www.bullsheadinn.co.uk
Historic 13-room coaching inn on the route to the Irish ferry. Comfortable oak-beamed rooms, fine restaurant and old-world charm. **££**

Llandrillo, nr Corwen

Tyddyn Llan
Denbighshire
Tel: 01490-440 264
www.tyddynllan.co.uk
Excellent base for walking, this grey stone Georgian house in the Vale of Edeyrnion has 4 miles (6km) of fishing on the River Dee. Elegant, antique-furnished

rooms. Large gardens. Award-winning restaurant. **£–££**

Llandudno

Bodysgallen Hall
Llandudno
Tel: 01492-584 466
www.bodysgallen.com
Stunning sandstone manor house with superb gardens and woodland walks. Country-house feel. Spa. Children under 6 not permitted. **££**

Empire Hotel
Church Walks
Tel: 01492-860 555
www.empirehotel.co.uk
The third generation of the Maddock family run this elegant Victorian hotel. Quality fittings and marble bathrooms. Indoor and outdoor heated pools. **££**

Llansanffraid Glan Conwy

The Old Rectory
Llanrwst Road
Tel: 01492-580 611
www.oldrectorycountryhouse.co.uk
Awarded five stars by the AA, this Georgian guest house has fine views from Conwy Castle to Snowdonia and an informal

atmosphere. Six rooms with antique furnishings. Overlooks Conwy RSPB bird reserve. **££**

Eglwysfach, nr Machynlleth

Ynyshir Hall
Eglwysfach, Powys
Tel: 01654-781 209
www.ynyshirhall.co.uk
Attractive 15th-century country house hotel with nine bedrooms. It was one of Queen Victoria's hunting lodges but now has an exuberant Mediterranean feel, with rooms painted in bright yellows and deep blues and the boldly coloured paintings of the owner, artist Rob Reen, on most walls. Warm service and excellent food. Nature reserve on the doorstep. **£££**

Portmeirion

Hotel Portmeirion
Tel: 01766-770 000
www.portmeirion-village.com
This eccentric 14-room hotel is central to architect Sir Clough Williams-Ellis's model fantasy village on the coast above Tremadog Bay. The interior is simple and

contemporary; many rooms have direct views of the estuary. **£££**

Harlech

Maes-y-Neuadd
Talsarnau, nr Harlech, Gwynedd
Tel: 01766-780 200
Excellent views, bar with inglenook fireplace and a friendly welcome are some of the charms of this manor-house hotel, some of which dates from the 14th century. Rooms are variable, the

PRICE CATEGORIES

Price categories are for a double room including breakfast and VAT (value added tax) at high season:
£ = under £80
££ = £80–150
£££ = £150–250
££££ = over £250

SHROPSHIRE AND THE NORTHWEST

Chester

Chester Grosvenor Hotel
Eastgate Street
Tel: 01244-324 024
www.chestergrosvenor.co.uk
Grand hotel in central
Chester, with a Michelin-
starred restaurant. **£££**

Liverpool

Britannia Adelphi Hotel
Ranelagh Place
Tel: 0151-709 7200
www.adelphi-hotel.co.uk
Grand neoclassical stone
block; one of Liverpool's

major landmarks, next to
Lime Street station. **££**

Hope Street Hotel
40 Hope Street
Tel: 0151-709 3000
www.hopestreethotel.co.uk
Boutique hotel with large,
light rooms, wood floors,
friendly staff and excellent
restaurant. **££–£££**

Manchester

Malmaison Manchester
1–3 Piccadilly
Tel: 0161-2781 000
www.malmaison-manchester.com
Occupying an old

warehouse, this boutique
hotel is decidedly luxurious.
££

Tulip Inn
Old Park Lane
Tel: 0161-755 3355
www.goldentulip.com
Opposite the 280-shop
Trafford Centre, overlooking
Salford Quays; 161 rooms;
under-16s stay free. **£**

Shrewsbury

The Lion
Wyle Cop
Tel: 01743-353 107
www.thelionhotelshrewsbury.co.uk

This beamed 16th-century
inn in the centre of medieval
Shrewsbury has bags of
character and a top-notch
restaurant. **££**

PEAK DISTRICT AND EAST MIDLANDS

Ashford in the Water

Riverside House Hotel
Bakewell
Tel: 01629-814 275
www.riversidehousehotel.co.uk
Small 18th-century house
on the Wye with some four-
poster beds, river views, log
fires and antiques, and
plenty of tasteful ruffles and
chintz; 15 rooms. Good
restaurant. **££**

Bakewell

Rutland Arms Hotel
The Square
Tel: 01629-812 812
www.rutlandarmsbakewell.co.uk
Jane Austen is said to have
stayed at this grand
Derbyshire hotel while
working on *Pride and
Prejudice*. Its 54 antique
clocks in public areas hint
at its traditional flavour.
££

Belton

Belton Woods Hotel
Nr Grantham
Tel: 01476-593 200
www.devere-hotels.com
Lakeside hotel with two
championship-standard
18-hole golf courses and
one 9-hole course. 136
rooms, plus lodges in the
grounds. **££**

Buxton

Buckingham Hotel
1–2 Burlington Road
Tel: 01298-70481
www.buckinghamhotel.co.uk
Old and sometimes creaky
building but welcoming,
informal atmosphere.
Bar is known for its range
of real ales. 37 rooms.
££

Old Hall Hotel
The Square
Tel: 01298-22841
www.oldhallhotelbuxton.co.uk
A landmark since the 16th
century, this dignified hotel
is the top choice for Buxton.
Rooms overlook Pavilion
Gardens and the Opera
House is nearby. **££**

Dovedale

Izaak Walton Hotel
Nr Ashbourne
Tel: 01335-350 555
www.izaakwaltonhotel.com
Named after the 17th-
century author of *The
Compleat Angler*, who
fished in the area. In the
jaws of Dovedale beneath
Thorpe Cloud; 35 simple
but comfortable rooms.
££

Hassop

Hassop Hall Hotel
Nr Bakewell

Tel: 01629-640 488
www.hassophallhotel.co.uk
A classical Georgian
house set in spacious
parkland not far from
Bakewell. Choose from 13
elegant rooms; it is worth
getting one at the front to
wake up to the view.
££–£££

Hathersage

George Hotel
Main Road
Tel: 01433-650 436
www.george-hotel.net
Former 16th-century
coaching inn; lovely
courtyard and a fine
restaurant. **££**

Millstone Country Inn
Sheffield Road
Tel: 01433-650 258
www.millstoneinn.co.uk
Above the village with fine
views down the Hope Valley
to Kinder Scout. **££**

Matlock Bath

Temple Hotel
Temple Walk
Tel: 01629-583 911
www.templehotel.co.uk
On a hilltop with splendid
views, this 14-room hotel,
in a gorgeous Georgian
building, is central and
has a bar serving real
ale by an open fire.
£

Melton Mowbray

Stapleford Park
Stapleford, nr Melton Mowbray
Tel: 01572-787 000
www.staplefordpark.com
Sumptuous 17th-century
country-house hotel with 55
rooms and 500 acres (200
hectares) designed by
"Capability" Brown.
Designers of the deluxe
rooms include Mulberry.
Facilities include a spa,
pool, golf course, tennis
courts and field sports such
as shooting and falconry.
££££

Nottingham

Hart's Hotel
Standard Hill, Park Row
Tel: 0115-988 1900
www.hartsnottingham.co.uk
The clean, modern styling
of this smart hotel gives it
a light and calm
atmosphere. In addition to

the gym and chic bar, it also has what is probably Nottingham's finest restaurant. **££–£££**

Oakham

Hambleton Hall
Hambleton, Near Oakham, Leicestershire
Tel: 01572-756 991
www.hambletonhall.com
Elegant country-house hotel on the edge of Rutland Water. Famed for its dining

room serving modern British cuisine by Michelin-starred chef Aaron Patterson. **£££**

Rowsley

East Lodge Country House Hotel
Matlock
Tel: 01629-734 474
www.eastlodge.com
A pretty, tastefully furnished country house located in 10 acres (4 hectares) of grounds, just off the A6. The

restaurant has a fine reputation. **£££**

Stamford

The George
71 St Martins, Stamford, Lincolnshire
Tel: 01780-750 750
www.georgehotelofstamford.com
This old coaching inn is something of an institution in Stamford. It offers homely comforts and hearty food. **££**

YORKSHIRE AND THE NORTHEAST

Belford

The Blue Bell Hotel
Market Place
Tel: 01668-213 543
www.bluebellhotel.com
Located on the coast near Lindisfarne, this charmingly old-fashioned 17th-century coaching inn is furnished in period style with en-suite bathrooms and some four-poster beds. **£–££**

Bolton Abbey

Devonshire Arms Country House Hotel
Skipton
Tel: 01756-710 441
www.thedevonshirearms.co.uk
This hotel has 40 rooms, open fires, and lounges furnished with antiques from Chatsworth, home of the Duke and Duchess of Devonshire. **£££**

Durham

Farnley Tower Hotel
The Avenue
Tel: 0191-375 0011
www.farnley-tower.co.uk
Renovated Victorian house with guesthouse feel situated in a quiet residential street within walking distance of the city centre. Cathedral and castle views. 13 rooms. **££**

Three Tuns Hotel
New Elvet
Tel: 0191-386 4326
www.swallow-hotels.com
With its wood-panelled

restaurant and old-fashioned service, this is a grand place to stay. **££**

Harrogate

The Boar's Head
Ripley Castle Estate, nr Harrogate
Tel: 01423-771 888
www.boarsheadripley.co.uk
Located 10 minutes from Ripley. Expect antiques and comfy chairs; good, plentiful food; 25 rooms. **££**

The Ruskin Hotel
1 Swan Road
Tel: 01423-502 045
www.ruskinhotel.co.uk
Small, old-fashioned hotel in centre. Good service and food; beautiful gardens. **££**

Haydon Bridge

Langley Castle
Langley-on-Tyne
Tel: 01434-688 888
www.langleycastle.com
A medieval fortified castle-turned-hotel with individual rooms and luxury facilities. Outdoor activities plus hot-air ballooning/off-road driving. **££–£££**

Helmsley

Black Swan Hotel
Market Place
Tel: 01439-770 466
www.blackswan-helmsley.co.uk
Comfortable boutique-style hotel in the centre of town at the foot of the North York Moors. 45 rooms, plus restaurant and tearoom. **££**

Hexham

County Hotel
Hexham
Tel: 01434-603 601
www.thecountyhexham.co.uk
Excellent hospitality in a market town. Handy for exploring the Pennines, Hadrian's Wall. 8 rooms. **£**

Wensleydale

The Wheatsheaf
Carperby, nr Leyburn
Tel: 01969-663 216
www.wheatsheafinwensleydale.co.uk
Where the author James Herriot and his wife spent their honeymoon. Pretty country inn. 13 rooms. **£–££**

York

Dean Court
Duncombe Place
Tel: 01904-625 082
www.deancourt-york.co.uk
Comfortable 37-room traditional hotel close to the Minster. Part of the Best Western chain. **£££**

Elmbank
The Mount
Tel: 01904-610 653
www.elmbankhotel.com
A city hotel with a country-house atmosphere. Full of Victorian Art Nouveau features. **££**

The Groves
15 St Peter's Grove
Tel: 01904-559 777
www.thegroveshotelyork.co.uk

Victorian town house within easy walking distance of the city centre, with pleasant accommodations. **££**

Middlethorpe Hall and Spa
Bishopthorpe Road
Tel: 01904-641 241
www.middlethorpe.com
Elegant country hotel, run with style in a 17th-century house; 29 rooms. **£££**

Minster Hotel
60 Bootham
Tel: 01904-621 267
www.yorkminsterhotel.co.uk
A skilful conversion of two Victorian houses, 4 minutes' walk from the Minster, has created a stylish hotel with a rooftop garden and superb views. **££**

PRICE CATEGORIES

Price categories are for a double room including breakfast and VAT (value added tax) at high season:
£ = under £80
££ = £80–150
£££ = £150–250
££££ = over £250

THE LAKE DISTRICT

Ambleside

Rothay Manor
Rothay Bridge
Tel: 01539-433 605
www.rothaymanor.co.uk
Quintessential country-house hotel with gardens and warm and friendly service. **££–£££**
Wateredge Inn
Borrans Road, Waterhead
Tel: 01539-432 332
www.wateredgeinn.co.uk
Family-run hotel with views over Lake Windermere from most rooms. Lakeshore garden. Restaurant. **££**

Cartmel, nr Grange-over-Sands

Aynsome Manor Hotel
Aynsome Lane
Tel: 01539-536 653
www.aynsomemanorhotel.co.uk
16th-century house and cottage in a picturesque village, off the tourist track. Dinner included. **££–£££**

Easedale

Lancrigg Vegetarian Country House Hotel
Grasmere, Cumbria
Tel: 01539-435 317

www.lancrigg.co.uk
Beautiful country house and separate cottage set in fine gardens. Chintzy decor. **££**

Kendal District

Heaves Hotel
Heaves
Tel: 01539-560 396
www.heaveshotel.com
Well-preserved Georgian mansion with large rooms, a library and fine views. **££**

Keswick District

Armathwaite Hall Country House
Bassenthwaite Lake
Tel: 01768-776 551
www.armathwaite-hall.com
Castellated mansion with plenty of facilities and activities, including pool and falconry. **££–£££**
The Borrowdale Gates
Grange-in-Borrowdale
Tel: 01768-777 204
www.borrowdale-gates.com
Large Victorian lakeland house with sweeping views and good food. **££**
The Cottage in the Wood
Whinlatter Forest, Braithwaite
Tel: 01768-778 409

www.thecottageinthewood.co.uk
This former coaching house has been turned into chic accommodation with designer bathrooms. **££–£££**
The Lodore Falls Hotel
Lodore Falls, Borrowdale
Tel: 01768-777 285
www.lakedistricthotels.net
Luxury hotel in 40 acres (16 hectares) with excellent facilities. Some rooms overlook Derwent Water. **£££**
The Pheasant
Bassenthwaite Lake, nr Cockermouth
Tel: 01768-776 234
www.the-pheasant.co.uk
Former coaching inn in a beautifully peaceful setting. Atmospheric bar. **££**

Ullswater District

Netherdene Country House B&B
Troutbeck
Tel: 07933-826 325
www.netherdene.co.uk
Small, comfortable country house set in landscaped gardens. **£**
Sharrow Bay
Sharrow Bay, Ullswater
Tel: 01768-486 301
www.sharrowbay.co.uk

Italianate luxury hotel set in formal gardens overlooking Ullswater. Michelin-starred restaurant. **£££**

Windermere

Fayrer Garden House Hotel
Lyth Valley Road, Bowness-on-Windermere
Tel: 01539-488 195
www.fayrergarden.com
For comfort and service, this hotel cannot be bettered. Good restaurant. **££–£££**
Miller Howe Hotel
Rayrigg Road
Tel: 01539-442 536
www.millerhowe.com
Prestigious luxury hotel with stunning views and fine cuisine. Rates include dinner, breakfast. **£££**

THE SCOTTISH LOWLANDS

Edinburgh

Channings
12–16 South Learmonth Gardens
Tel: 0131-315 2226
www.channings.co.uk
Five adjoining Edwardian houses (including Ernest Shackleton's former home) fronting onto a quiet cobbled street close to the city centre. **££–£££**
Salisbury Hotel
45 Salisbury Road
Tel: 0131-667 1264
www.the-salisbury.co.uk
Georgian listed building with walled garden, impressive restaurant, 18 rooms and private parking. **££**
The Scotsman
20 North Bridge
Tel: 0131-556 5565

www.thescotsmanhotel.co.uk
This highly successful make-over of a newspaper office offers five-star accommodation and great amenities, including a spa and state-of-the art cinema. **££££**
Six Mary's Place
Raeburn Place, Stockbridge
Tel: 0131-332 8965
www.sixmarysplace.co.uk
Highly-rated guesthouse, with a breakfast menu that even includes vegetarian haggis. **££**

Glasgow

Malmaison
278 West George Street
Tel: 0141-572 1000
www.malmaison-glasgow.com

This stylish hotel occupies a former church in the centre of town. Recommended brasserie serves British cuisine. **£££**
One Devonshire Gardens
1 Devonshire Gardens
Tel: 0141-339 2001
www.hotelduvin.com
Head and shoulders above any other Glasgow hotel, with excellent service, plush rooms and an oak-panelled bistro restaurant. **£££**
The Town House
4 Hughenden Terrace
Tel: 0141-357 0862
www.thetownhouseglasgow.com
Elegantly furnished guesthouse in restored Victorian terrace in West End; 10 spacious rooms, ample parking. **£**

Kelso

Roxburghe Hotel
Heiton by Kelso
Tel: 01573-450 w331
www.roxburghe.net
An 18th-century country-house hotel in riverside surroundings. Facilities include world-class fishing

and a golf course. **£££**

Peebles

Cringletie House Hotel
Edinburgh Road
Tel: 01721-725 750
www.cringletie.com
Set in a large estate, this

turreted mansion set in 28 acres has fine food and great atmosphere; 12 rooms. **£££**

Troon

Troon Marine Hotel
8 Crosbie Road

Tel: 01292-314 444
www.barcelo-hotels.co.uk
Traditional, 89-room luxury hotel in the heart of Burns country, overlooking the 18th hole of Royal Troon golf course. Close to the sea with a health club and restaurant. **££**

Turnberry, nr Ayr

Westin Turnberry Resort
Maidens Road
Tel: 01655-331 000
www.turnberry.co.uk
Luxury country club/spa has two golf courses and its own loch. **££££**

THE SCOTTISH HIGHLANDS

Auchterarder

Gleneagles Hotel
Tel: 0800 389 3737 (UK);
(01764) 662 231 (international)
www.gleneagles.com
Famous for its sports facilities, this is a magnificent hotel on a massive scale. Expect to see more than a few famous faces. **££££**

Crieff

Knock Castle Hotel
Drummond Terrace
Tel: 01764-650 088
www.knockcastle.com
The former home of a shipping magnate, this Victorian mansion is now a hotel and spa complex. Luxurious rooms, impressive facilities and a no-children policy. **££–£££**

Dunkeld

Royal Dunkeld Hotel
Atholl Street
Tel: 01350-727 322
www.royaldunkeld.co.uk
The staff at this 19th-century coaching inn are unfailingly helpful; rooms are simple, food is hearty and delicious, bar is well stocked. **£–££**

Fort William

Barcaldine House
Barcaldine, between Oban and Fort William
Tel: 01631-720 219
www.barcaldinehouse.co.uk
This country house retains an old-world feel with antique furnishings and excellent service. The restaurant is also something to write home about. **££–£££**
Holly Tree Hotel
Kentallen Pier, Glencoe

Tel: 01631-740 292
www.hollytreehotel.co.uk
The Holly Tree makes an excellent base for a family holiday. Facilities include the award-winning Seafood Restaurant and a large indoor swimming pool. **££**
Inverlochy Castle
Torlundy
Tel: 01397-702 177
www.inverlochycastlehotel.com
A majestic castle in 500 acres (200 hectares) of grounds at the foot of Ben Nevis. Everything is on a grand scale, from the frescoed Great Hall and crystal chandeliers to the individually decorated bedrooms. **££££**

Glenlivet

Minmore House
Glenlivet Crown Estate
Tel: 01807-590 378
www.minmorehousehotel.com
Small (nine-room) Victorian hotel in fine grounds with scenic views. Bar has over 100 malt whiskies. **££**

Inverness

Dunain Park
Tel: 01463-230 512
www.lochnesscountryhousehotel.co.uk
Georgian mansion with gardens and woodland, and stunning views. Traditional country-house feel with congenial service. More than 200 malt whiskies. Six suites, five rooms and two cottages. **£££**
Loch Ness Lodge
Brachla, on the A82, Loch Ness-side, nr Inverness
Tel: 01456-459 469
www.loch-ness-lodge.com
This is the finest luxury hotel in the area – ideal for a

romantic getaway or a weekend of relaxation. Guests enjoy glorious views over Loch Ness, an award-winning restaurant and a spa suite. **££££**

Isle of Skye

Duisdale Hotel
Isle Ornsay, Sleat
Tel: 01471-833 202
www.duisdale.com
The No. 1 hotel choice on Skye, with 18 smart guest rooms looking out over the sea or the extensive gardens. Guests also benefit from day trips on the hotel owner's luxury yacht. **£££**
Toravaig Hotel
Sleat
Tel: 01471-820 200
www.skyehotel.co.uk
Rooms offer fine coastal views. The in-house restaurant offers sumptuous cuisine – probably the best on Skye. **££–£££**

Kintyre Peninsula

Cairnbaan Hotel
Cairnbaan, near Lochgilphead, Argyll
Tel: 01546-603 668
www.cairnbaan.com
A historic hotel in an idyllic spot on the Crinan Canal, this country inn is renowned locally for the welcoming atmosphere of its bar and the scrumptious food served in its restaurant. **£–££**

Orkney Islands

Foveran Hotel
St Ola, Kirkwall
Tel: 01856-872 389
www.foveranhotel.co.uk
This family-run hotel is set in 35 acres (14 hectares) overlooking Scapa Flow. **££**

Pitlochry

Craigmhor Lodge
27 West Moulin Road
Tel: 01796-472 123
www.craigmhorlodge.co.uk
Bedrooms in the original Victorian house are complemented by a further 12 designer rooms in a smart courtyard building. An excellent family option. **£–££**
East Haugh House
Old Perth Road, East Haugh
Tel: 01796-473 121
www.easthaugh.co.uk
Family-run hotel offering a warm ambience and excellent food. It is a popular with fly fishermen, as the hotel even has its own fishing beat on the Tay. **££**
Grand Hotel
Commercial Street, Lerwick
Tel: 01595-692 826
www.kgqhotels.com
The oldest purpose-built hotel in Shetland is conveniently located near the town centre. **££**

PRICE CATEGORIES

Price categories are for a double room including breakfast and VAT (value added tax) at high season:
£ = under £80
££ = £80–150
£££ = £150–250
££££ = over £250

A CTIVITIES

CALENDAR OF EVENTS, THE ARTS, SHOPPING, SPORTS, OUTDOOR ACTIVITIES AND TOURS

CALENDAR OF EVENTS

For details of regional events, contact tourist boards (see page 388).

January

Burns Night (25 January). Scots celebrate birth of Robert Burns, often with a haggis supper and a wee dram.

February

Chinese New Year. London and Manchester. Chinatowns host colourful street celebrations.
Jorvik Viking Festival, York. A week-long programme of battle re-enactments, talks, themed walks and exhibitions coincides with schools' half-term holidays.
London Fashion Week. The fashion world descends on the capital to see what the next seasons have in store.

March

Oxford and Cambridge Boat Race (last Sat of March/first Sat of Apri), the university rowing teams battle it out between Putney and Mortlake.

April

London Marathon. One of the world's biggest runs starts in Blackheath and ends up at Buckingham Palace.
Queen's Birthday (21st). Gun salute in Hyde Park and Tower of London.

May

Bath International Music Festival. Prestigious festival of chamber and orchestral music, opera and some jazz.
Brighton Festival. One of Britain's biggest and most varied arts festivals also offers events for children.
Chelsea Flower Show. The Queen usually opens this week-long and oversubscribed show at the Royal Hospital, Chelsea.
Hay-on-Wye Festival of Literature and the Arts. High-profile literary festival attracts well-known authors and celebrities from around the world.

June

Aldeburgh Festival. Composer Benjamin Britten inaugurated this classical music festival in 1948 and it still runs for 2 weeks every June.

Arts Festivals Around Britain

There are hundreds of arts festivals for literature, music, dance and theatre held throughout Britain each year and the number is increasing.
Edinburgh The most famous of Britain's arts festivals (actually two simultaneous festivals, the official one and the "fringe"), this takes place for about a month in August and September. The city also hosts jazz, folk, and film and TV festivals at other times during the year. See www. eif.co.uk; www.edfringe.com; www. edinburghfestivals.co.uk.
Glasgow hosts Celtic Connections in January, as well as holding its own International Jazz and International Piping festivals.
Wales The Royal National Eisteddfod of Wales (www.eisteddfod. org.uk) dates back to 1176 and is the most important of the hundreds of eisteddfodau which take place in Wales annually. It is a festival devoted to music and literature in the Welsh language and is held for a week in August in a different venue each year.

The **Llangollen International Musical Eisteddfod** (www. international-eisteddfod.co.uk), which takes place in the picturesque town of Llangollen in north Wales each July, was established after World War II to bring nations together in a festival of song, dance and music.
Countrywide Other notable arts festivals are held at Chichester, Brighton, Salisbury, Harrogate and York. In addition to Proms festivals in London, Glasgow and Cardiff, music festivals are held in Aldeburgh, Buxton and Bath (for dates, see above and page 375).

Dickens Festival, Kent Literary types converge on Rochester, Kent, for the annual Charles Dickens jamboree.
Royal Academy of Arts Summer Exhibition, London. Large exhibition of work (until Aug). All works for sale.
Trooping the Colour Horse Guards Parade, London. The Queen's official birthday celebrations.

July

Cardiff Festival. Events in July and August include the Welsh Proms and the Lord Mayor's Parade.
Great Yorkshire Show. Three-day agricultural show in Harrogate features livestock competitions, show jumping, food tastings and hot-air balloon rides.

Henley Royal Regatta. Five days of rowing races on the Thames draw a crowd of well-dressed champagne quaffers.

International Musical Eisteddfod. Over 4,000 performers attend this festival of music and dance in Llangollen, in northeast Wales.

August

Cowes Week. More than a thousand yachts compete in dozens of races each day on the Solent. The festivities conclude with a fireworks display.

Edinburgh International Festival, Fringe Festival, Book Festival, Jazz and Blues Festival, Military Tattoo. It packs the city.

Notting Hill Carnival (bank holiday weekend), London. Colourful West Indian street carnival with floats, steel bands and reggae music.

September

Abergavenny Food Festival. The largest food festival in Wales features cooking demonstrations, tastings and exhibitions of artisanal fare.

London Open House Weekend. Historic and architecturally interesting buildings all over London open their doors to a curious public. www. londonopenhouse.org

October

London Film Festival. The country's largest celebration of cinema takes place at BFI Southbank and some West End venues. www.bfi.org.uk/lff/

Manchester Comedy Festival. Manchester welcomes old hands from the circuit and exciting new talent at a variety of venues across town.

November

Guy Fawkes Day (5th). Fireworks displays and bonfires countrywide to celebrate the foiled Catholic plot against the Crown in 1605.

London to Brighton Veteran Car Run (first Sun). Hundreds of immaculately preserved cars and their proud owners start out from Hyde Park and make their sedate way to Brighton.

State Opening of Parliament. The Queen in full regalia travels by horse-drawn coach from Buckingham Palace to Westminster.

December

Hogmanay New Year's Eve revels, 4 days at the end of December, best celebrated in Edinburgh.

THE ARTS

Theatre

Britain's rich dramatic tradition is reflected in the quality of its theatre. Most towns and cities have at least one theatre that hosts productions from their own company or from touring companies that may include the Royal Shakespeare Company (RSC) and the National Theatre (NT). Many of these theatres are part-funded by the Arts Council, the government body for arts funding. Recent cuts in grants have meant that the future of some theatres is precarious; many are now trying to balance the books by staging more commercial shows such as comedy and touring musicals. For detailed information, go to www.theatresonline. com. It is advisable to book tickets in advance, from the box office or through commercial ticket agents in major cities.

London

Several dozen of London's theatres – which total over 140, including fringe and suburban – are in the West End's Theatreland, centred around Covent Garden and Shaftesbury Avenue.

Tickets West End shows are popular so good tickets can be hard to obtain and are expensive. If you cannot book a seat through the theatre box office, try Ticketmaster, tel: 0870 534 4444 (UK); +44 161 385 3211 (overseas); www.ticketmaster.co.uk.The "tkts" booth at Leicester Square has unsold tickets available at bargain prices on the day of the performance. It's located in the Clock Tower building and open Mon–Sat 10am–7pm, Sun noon–3pm. Payment is by cash or card and there

Comedy

There is a well-established circuit for stand-up comedy in Britain. Many hold amateur "open-mic" events, and have warm-up acts by new talent before the main attraction of a well-known comedian. Notable venues around the country include the branches of The Comedy Store (tel: 0844-871 7699; www.thecomedystore.co.uk) in London and Manchester, and Jongleurs (tel: 08700 111 960; www.jongleurs.com), which runs venues in many towns, including Bristol, Nottingham, Leeds and Glasgow. Big-name comedy acts (Bill Bailey, Eddie Izzard, Michael Mcintyre etc) often play big venues. Manchester and Glasgow have their own annual comedy festivals (www.manchestercomedyfestival.co.uk; www.glasgowcomedyfestival.com), while the Edinburgh Fringe Festival showcases an impressive range of comedy talent, from unknowns to big names.

may be long queues (www.tkts.co.uk). Some theatres, such as the National, keep back some tickets to sell at the box office from 9.30am on the day. Avoid ticket touts unless you're prepared to pay several times a ticket's face value for a sold-out show.

There is usually no problem buying a ticket for a fringe show on the door. Consult listings in London's weekly *Time Out* magazine, newspapers or www.theatreguidelondon.co.uk.

Open-air plays On summer afternoons and evenings Shakespeare's plays are performed (weather permitting) at the open-air theatre in Regent's Park. Check www. openairtheatre.org for listings.

ABOVE: the reconstructed Shakespeare's Globe in London.

Barbican Arts Centre, Silk Street, London, tel: 020-7638 8891; www. barbican.org.uk. Purpose-built arts complex containing the Barbican Theatre, Concert Hall and The Pit, which are comfortable, with good acoustics, although somewhat sterile. Not easy to find your way around. Tube: Barbican.

National Theatre, South Bank, tel: 020-7452 3000; www.nationaltheatre.org. uk. A wide range of modern and classical plays staged in three theatres in this concrete structure beside the Thames: the Olivier, the Lyttelton and the Cottesloe. Tube: Waterloo.

Royal Court Theatre, Sloane Square, tel: 020-7565 5000; www.royalcourt theatre.com. Home to the English Stage Company, which produces plays by contemporary playwrights. Tube: Sloane Square.

Shakespeare's Globe, 21 New Globe Walk, Bankside, is a reconstruction of Shakespeare's original open-to-the-elements Elizabethan theatre. It hosts summer seasons of plays, recreating the atmosphere of the 16th-century performances. There is a choice of (recommended) bench seating or standing, and actors are encouraged to interact with the audience; amplification and artificial lighting are not used. An engaging and authentic experience. The Globe Exhibition uses touch-screens and includes a guided tour of the theatre (tel: 020-7902 1500; www.shakespeares-globe.org; Apr–Oct Mon–Sat 9am–12.30pm and 1–5pm, Sun 9–11.30am and 12–5pm, tours every 15–30 mins).

Liverpool

Liverpool's **Playhouse**, Williamson Square, tel: 0151-709 4776, www. everymanplayhouse.com, and the related **Everyman**, Hope Street, tel: 0151-709 4776 both stage excellent and sometimes innovative works. The **Empire**, Lime Street, tel: 0844-847 2525, www.liverpoolempire.org.uk, concentrates on light entertainment and musicals.

Manchester

Manchester has several theatres, including the **Royal Exchange Theatre**, St Ann's Square, tel: 0161-833 9833, www.royalexchange.org.uk. This extraordinary glass-walled theatre-in-the-round is situated within the historic Victorian Cotton Exchange Buildings. To the west of the city centre is the **Lowry Centre**, Pier 8, Salford Quays, tel: 0870-787 5780, www.thelowry.com, where two theatres stage high-quality theatre and musical performances.

Newcastle upon Tyne

Theatre Royal, 100 Grey Street, tel: 08448-112 121; www.theatreroyal.co.uk. This beautiful Edwardian theatre presents drama, opera and dance. It is also the winter home of the RSC. **Northern Stage**, Barras Bridge, tel: 0191-230 5151; www.northernstage. co.uk, has three stages and is the home of Newcastle's Northern Stage company; it co-hosts the RSC season.

Stratford-upon-Avon

The Royal Shakespeare Company actually has three theatres in Stratford. Apart from the newly revamped Royal Shakespeare, there is the **Swan Theatre,** an Elizabethan-style theatre-in-the-round on Waterside, and the **Courtyard Theatre** on Southern Lane.

The RSC season at Stratford runs from April to October. Box office tel: 0844 800 1110; www.rsc.org.uk.

Scotland

Scotland's theatres include:
Royal Lyceum, Grindlay Street, Edinburgh, tel: 0131-248 4848, www. lyceum.org.uk. The Sept–May season produces high-quality drama productions. **The Traverse**, Cambridge Street, Edinburgh, tel: 0131-228 1404, www.traverse.co.uk offers quality contemporary productions, commissions and supports writers and hosts numerous workshops. **Festival Theatre**, 13–29 Nicholson Street, Edinburgh, tel: 0131-529 6000, www.festivaltheatre.org. uk, Edinburgh's showcase theatre with huge glass frontage; major opera, ballet, variety productions. **The Tron Theatre**, 63 Trongate, Glasgow, tel: 0141-552 4267, www. tron.co.uk, a stylish venue featuring contemporary innovative programmes of drama and dance. **Citizens' Theatre**, 119 Gorbals Street, Glasgow, tel: 0141-429 0022, www.citz.co.uk, a repertory company renowned for adventurous productions.

Wales

There are a number of art centres and theatres that attract leading companies. Swansea has six theatres, including the **Swansea Grand Theatre**, Singleton Street, tel: 01792-475 715, www.swanseagrand. co.uk, while Cardiff Bay's **Wales Millennium Centre**, tel: 08700-402 000, www.wmc.org.uk, hosts international theatre, musicals, contemporary dance, comedy, ballet and opera.

Classical Music

Many British cities have their own professional orchestras and promote seasons of concerts. These include the Royal Liverpool Philharmonic, The Hallé in Manchester, and the City of Birmingham Symphony Orchestra. In London there are the London Philharmonic and the LSO (London Symphony Orchestra).

In the summer the Scottish National Orchestra (SNO) presents a short Promenade season in Glasgow, while in London the BBC sponsors the Proms at the Royal Albert Hall. The BBC also funds several of its own orchestras, the BBC Symphony and the BBC Scottish Symphony Orchestra.

Chamber music has considerable support in Britain and there are professional string and chamber orchestras such as the English Chamber Orchestra and The Academy of Ancient Music.

London Venues

Barbican Hall, Silk Street, tel: 020-7638 8891, www.barbican.org.uk, is home to the London Symphony Orchestra.

Royal Festival Hall, Belvedere Road, tel: 0871-663 2500, www.southbank centre.co.uk, is the premier classical music venue. Free Friday lunchtime classical, jazz and folk performances in the foyer. Also in the South Bank complex are the Queen Elizabeth Hall (chamber concerts and solos) and the small Purcell Room.

Wigmore Hall, 36 Wigmore Street, tel: 020-7935 2141, www.wigmore-hall. org.uk, is an intimate hall renowned for its lunchtime and Sunday morning chamber recitals. There are evening peformances, too.

Royal Albert Hall, Kensington Gore, tel: 020-7589 8212, www.royalalberthall.

Glyndebourne

For classical music lovers Glyndebourne is a highlight. Off the beaten track in Sussex, it is not the most obvious site for a major international opera festival. But ever since an ex-Eton schoolmaster inherited a mansion there and built an opera house, it has attracted top artists from around the world and become a major event. Performances are in the evening (bring your own Champagne and picnic hampers) from May until August. Tel: 01273-815 000. www.glyndebourne.com.

Welsh Choirs

The Welsh are renowned for their fine voices. Most places in Wales have a choir. The Wales Tourist Board (tel: 08708-300 306; www.visitwales.com) has details. If you can't get there, there's always the London Welsh Male Voice Choir (www.londonwelshmvc.org).

com, comes alive in summer for the BBC-sponsored Promenade Concerts. **Open-air concerts** Summer evening concerts are performed at the Kenwood Lakeside Theatre, Kenwood House, Hampstead Lane, tel: 0870-333 1181, www.picnicconcerts.com.

Outside London

Major venues attracting world-class performers include:
Bridgewater Hall, Manchester, tel: 0161-907 9000, www.bridgewater-hall.co.uk
Birmingham Symphony Hall, NEC, tel: 0121-780 3333, www.thsh.co.uk
City Hall, Northumberland Road, Newcastle, tel: 0191-261 2606, www.newcastlecityhall.org
The Sage, Gateshead Quays, tel: 0191-443 4666, www.thesagegateshead.org
Philharmonic Hall, Hope Street, Liverpool, tel: 0151-210 2895, www.liverpoolphil.com
The Royal Concert Hall, 2 Sauchiehall Street, Glasgow, tel: 0141-353 8000, www.glasgowconcerthalls.com
St David's Hall, The Hayes, Cardiff, tel: 02920-878 444, www.stdavidshallcardiff.co.uk
Wales Millennium Centre, Cardiff Bay, tel: 08700-402 000, www.wmc.org.uk

Opera

The Royal Opera and the English National Opera perform regular seasons in London.
Royal Opera House, Bow Street, tel: 020-7304 4000, www.roh.org.uk. Home to the Royal Ballet and the Royal Opera, this is a magnificent theatre with a worldwide reputation for lavish performances in their original language. Dress is more formal and tickets expensive unless you are prepared to stand or accept a very distant view.
London Coliseum, St Martin's Lane, tel: 0871 911 0200, www.eno.org. This elegant Edwardian theatre is where the English National Opera (ENO) stages performances in English; ticket prices are lower than at the Opera House.

ABOVE: for full coverage of current dance events, check www.ballet.co.uk.

Welsh National Opera has a new home at the Wales Millennium Centre in Cardiff Bay, tel: 08700-402 000, www.wno.org.uk. Performances are also staged at theatres and concert halls throughout Wales.
Scottish Opera Scotland has its own opera company (www.scottishopera.org.uk), based at the Theatre Royal, 282 Hope Street, Glasgow, tel: 0870-060 6647, www.ambassadortickets.com. It tours Scotland and northern England, performing short seasons in Edinburgh.
Opera North Regional opera companies include Opera North (www.operanorth.co.uk), which is based in Leeds at the Grand Theatre, 46 New Briggate, tel: 0870-121 4901, www.leedsgrandtheatre.com, and tours the north of England.
Buxton The Opera House, Water Street, Buxton, Derbyshire, tel: 0845-127 2190, www.buxtonoperahouse.org.uk, hosts a major opera, theatre and music festival (3 weeks in July).

Ballet and Dance

Major venues are the Royal Opera House and the London Coliseum, home to the Royal Ballet and English National Ballet, respectively.
Sadler's Wells, Rosebery Avenue, London, tel: 0844-412 4300, www.sadlerswells.com, is a flexible state-of-the-art performance venue with an innovative programme of modern and classical dance. Other performances are held at the Peacock Theatre, Kingsway, in London's Holborn (same phone number for bookings).
Birmingham Royal Ballet, based at the Hippodrome, tel: 0121-245 3500, www.brb.org.uk, tours nationwide.
Northern Ballet School Based at the Dancehouse Theatre, 10 Oxford Road, Manchester, tel: 0161-237 9753, www.northernballetschool.co.uk. Tours all around the UK.

Wales Leading ballet companies perform at the Wales Millennium Centre in Cardiff and the Grand Theatre in Swansea (see above).
The Scottish Ballet, based in Glasgow, tel: 0141-331 2931, www.scottishballet.co.uk, tours the UK.

Live Music and Jazz

Over the last 50 years, Britain has made a major contribution to new music in all genres and the situation doesn't look like changing any time soon. A visit to Camden in North London is a great place get your finger on the pulse with clubs, bars and other venues, but major cities around Britain are also active on the music scene.

Nationwide, there are pubs and clubs that host live jazz, but aficionados will find most clubs of note in London and Edinburgh.

What's on Where

To find out what's on in London, in print there is the long-established weekly *Time Out* (out on Wednesdays, the Londoner's bible); Saturday's *The Guardian* free supplement previewing the week ahead; and daily listings in the free *Evening Standard*.

For details of events elsewhere, the quality daily newspapers have limited listings sections, but your best port of call is the local Tourist Information Centre (see www.visitbritain.com). Many local papers have a weekly section on Fridays with details of places to visit and things to do in their area. Websites worth consulting include: www.timeout.com and www.bbc.co.uk for a wide variety of listings, www.bachtrack.com for classical music and opera and www.britinfo.net for cinema.

Ronnie Scott's, 47 Frith Street, tel: 020-7439 0747, www.ronniescotts.co.uk, in London's Soho, is Britain's best-known jazz venue, showcasing top international artists.

For listings of gigs and concerts nationwide, consult www.gigsandtours.com; in London, see also the pages of *Time Out* magazine (www.timeout.com).

SHOPPING

What to Buy

If you are looking for something typically British to take back home, there's a remarkably wide choice.

Textiles Probably Britain's most famous speciality, top-quality wools and clothes worth seeking out include the wonderful hand-knitted woollens from the Scottish islands of Shetland, Arran and Fair Isle, and the Guernsey and Jersey sweaters of the Channel Islands. There is fine Harris Tweed cloth from Lewis. You can even have a kilt made in your own clan tartan. The scenic Ochil Hills north of Edinburgh have a long tradition of woollen production where visitors can take the Scottish Mill Trail.

Another important centre for the cloth and wool industry is Bradford, through which 90 percent of the wool trade passed in the 19th century. The area's many remaining mill shops are a bargain-hunter's paradise where lengths of fabric, fine yarns and fleeces can be bought. Some mills give guided tours.

The Lakeland Sheep and Wool Centre in Cockermouth, Cumbria, hosts excellent daily sheep shows and sells high-quality goods.

Wales, too, has many mills that produce colourful tapestry cloth in striking traditional Celtic designs.

Suits If you want a finished project, the flagship of Britain's bespoke tailoring industry is Savile Row in London, where gentlemen come from all over to have their suits crafted. Other outlets for traditional British attire are Burberry's (for raincoats and more), Aquascutum and Austin Reed, which have branches in Oxford Street and Regent Street in London and in many department stores in other cities.

Fashion Britain has a thriving fashion industry, with its heart in London. Its top designers (including Caroline Charles, Jasper Conran, Katharine Hamnett, Bruce Oldfield, Stella McCartney, Paul Smith and Vivienne Westwood) are the height of *haute couture*, and world-famous. Many top international designers can also be found in London's Knightsbridge and Mayfair, and to a lesser extent in department stores nationwide. For quality everyday clothing, Marks & Spencer's stores retain their popularity. Mulberry is famous for its leather accessories, from personal organisers to weekend bags, all embossed with the classic tree logo.

China and porcelain Top-price china, glass and silver items can be found in Regent Street and Mayfair in London at exclusive shops such as Waterford, Wedgwood, Thomas Goode, Asprey and Garrard. Stoke-on-Trent (in The Potteries, Staffordshire) is the home of the great china and porcelain houses, including Wedgwood and Royal Doulton, Minton, Spode and Royal Stafford (www.thepotteries.org). All these have visitor centres where you can often pick up some real bargains. You can also visit Portmeirion in North Wales, the Caithness Glass factory at Crieff in Scotland and Dartington Crystal at Great Torrington in Devon.

Jewellery The centre for British jewellery production is in Hockley, Birmingham, an industry that developed here in the 18th century along with other forms of metalworking such as brass-founding and gunsmithing. Today more than 200 jewellery manufacturers and 50 silversmiths are based here. London's jewellery quarter can be found at Hatton Gardens on the edge of the City. But all over the country are artisan jewellers making one-off and affordable pieces.

Perfumes English flower perfumes make a delightful gift. The most exclusive of these come from Floris in Jermyn Street, and Penhaligons in Covent Garden, London. The Cotswold Perfumery in the picturesque village of Bourton-on-the-Water, Gloucestershire, makes its own perfumes.

Antiques If you are coming to Britain to look for antiques it is worth getting in touch with the London and Provincial Antique Dealers' Association (LAPADA), 535 King's Road, London, tel: 020-7823 3511, www.lapada.org. A number of antiques fairs are held nationwide throughout the year and many towns such as Bath, Harrogate and Brighton have antique centres and markets. Good places to start are the market and stalls around Portobello Road in London's Notting Hill (main market day is Saturday) and the indoor Alfie's Antiques Market on Church Street, Marylebone (Tue–Sat).

Food and Drink British delights that are easy to transport include Twinings or Jacksons tea, shortbread and handmade fudge. Charbonnel et Walker (www.charbonnel.co.uk) is a famous British chocolatier, established in 1875, but there are other modern producers such as Paul A. Young (www.paulayoung.co.uk) and William Curley, who also teaches the art (www.williamcurley.co.uk)

Britain is particularly proud of its conserves, jams, honeys, pickles and mustards (not least the famous anchovy spread, Gentleman's Relish). Local delis and farm shops around the country are often worth exploring for edible gifts. Regional specialities to look out for include Cornish pasties, Bakewell tarts, Eccles cakes and Kendal Mint Cake.

For Britain's groceries at their finest, visit Fortnum & Mason, 181 Piccadilly, London, an Aladdin's cave of mouth-watering goodies.

Scotch whisky is also popular; if you can't visit a distillery yourself, upmarket wine merchants usually stock a fair selection, or for unusual single malts try The Whisky Shop (www.whiskyshop.com), which has several branches; the one at 28 Victoria Street in Edinburgh's Old Town is easy to find.

Crafts There are many workshops in rural areas, where potters, wood-turners, leather workers, candle-makers and other craftspeople can be seen producing their wares. London has many craft boutiques and stalls, for example at Covent Garden market. A free map can be obtained from the Crafts Council, 44a Pentonville Road, London, tel: 020-7806 2500, www.craftscouncil.org.uk. For information on

BELOW: Britain has over 270,000 shops.

Welsh crafts, contact the Wales Craft Council, tel: 01938-555 313; www.walescraftcouncil.co.uk). In Scotland, contact Craftscotland, tel: 0131-466 3870 www.craftscotland.org.

Books London's Charing Cross Road has long been the centre for second-hand and specialist bookshops, though there are fewer these days than there used to be. Cecil Court, just off Charing Cross Road, remains a haven for antiquarian dealers. Waterstones branches nationwide are popular, and Foyles in London has five crammed floors. Outside London, university towns are the best places for books. Blackwells in Oxford and Heffers in Cambridge are equally good for publications in English and most prominent foreign languages. Serious book-lovers should head for Hay-on-Wye, on the border of England and Wales *(see page 251)*; it has more than 30 bookshops and also hosts a lively literary festival, with top-notch guests, in late May (www.hayfestival.com).

Gifts Some of the best places to seek out tasteful presents to take home are museum gift shops (especially the ones at London's British Museum and the Victoria and Albert Museum) and the shops at National Trust properties.

Export Procedures

VAT (value-added tax) is a sales tax of 20 percent that is added to nearly all

ABOVE: Camden Passage in London's Islington mixes bric-a-brac and antiques.

goods except food (excluding that in restaurants), books and children's clothes. It is generally included in the price marked on the item. Most large department stores and smaller gift shops operate a scheme to refund this tax to non-European visitors (Retail Export Scheme), but often require that more than a minimum amount (usually £50) is spent. For a refund you need to fill in a form from the store, have it stamped by Customs on leaving the country and either post it back to the store or hand it in to a cash refund booth at the airport. If you leave the country with the goods within 3 months of purchase you will be refunded the tax minus an administration fee.

Markets and Boot Sales

Many towns have regular open-air farmers' markets (see www.farmers markets.net); some also have French markets when French traders cross the Channel to sell their produce.

London has several traditional markets which have become tourist attractions over the years:

• **Camden Market**, NW1. Hugely popular at the weekends, this sprawling market near Camden Lock sells clothes, jewellery, arts and crafts, food and antiques.

• **Columbia Road Flower Market**, E2. Cut flowers and houseplants are sold here at wholesale prices on Sundays, 8am–2pm. Other specialist shops on Columbia Road open to coincide with the market.

• **Petticoat Lane**, Middlesex Street, E1. London's oldest market is named for the undergarmets and lace once sold here by French Huguenots. Cheap clothes, fabrics and leather goods are still sold here in some of the 1,000 stalls.

• **Portobello Road**, W11. Renowned for its antiques, this is also a good place to pick up fashionable and vintage clothing, art and general bric-a-brac. It gets very crowded on Saturdays, but has a buzzing atmosphere.

• **Spitalfields**, Commercial Street, E1. This historic covered market has been gentrified with cafés and boutiques, but remains a great place to spot new talent, as many young fashion and jewellery designers sell their wares here. Music, vintage clothing, organic food and childrenswear are sold too.

A phenomenon all over Britain is the weekend **boot sale**, held in out-of-town fields or in school playgrounds in town. Participants sell all kinds of household goods – and junk – from the boot (trunk) of their car. In America, it would be known as a massive tag sale, and has the same friendly atmosphere. Some venues have hundreds of pitches.

SPORT

Tickets

Tickets for major sporting events can be purchased from agents such as Ticketmaster, tel: 0870-534 4444, www.ticketmaster.co.uk; and Keith Prowse, tel: 0870-840 1111, www.keithprowse.com.

Participant Sports

For information on sports and leisure facilities in each area you can contact the local council's leisure services department. Alternatively, get in touch with Sport England, tel: 020-7273 1551; www.sportengland.org.

The English Federation of Disability Sport promotes and develops sport for people with disabilities. For further information, contact EFDS, tel: 0161-247 5294; www.efds.co.uk.

Golf

The game we recognise as golf originated in Scotland, where the first written record (1457) is of James II banning the game because it distracted people from the more useful pursuit of archery. Even the most famous clubs are open to the public. St Andrew's, however, is so much in demand that games are subject to a lottery. Courses close to London are generally heavily booked. To find a local course, visit www.uk-golf guide.com. You can book a session, often at a discount, at almost 250 clubs around the UK through www.teeoff times.co.uk.

Tennis

There are tennis courts in some of Britain's public parks that anyone can use for a small fee. Contact the Lawn

Tennis Association for regional offices and information on clubs and courts: tel: 020-8487 7000; www.lta.org.uk.

Spectator Sports

Athletics

Athletics are governed by the Amateur Athletics Association (AAA), with the main national sports centre for athletics at Crystal Palace, south London, tel: 020-8778 0131; www. englandathletics.org.

Highland Games are held in Scotland (May–Sept) and coincide with the annual gatherings of clans. Activities include such distinctive events as tossing the caber (basically an 18ft/5.5-metre tree trunk) and throwing the hammer as well as dancing and piping competitions. The best-known games are at Braemar, near Balmoral, on the first Saturday in September (www.braemargathering.org); these are sometimes attended by the Royal Family. There are also gatherings at Aboyne, Oban and Cowal. See www.visitscotland.com.

Cricket

Quintessentially English, cricket can be seen on village greens up and down the country throughout the summer. Usually a light-hearted performance, it is played by very amateurish amateurs, with a visit to the pub a ritual at the close of play.

England's professional teams compete in a national championship, with 4-day matches taking place all summer. But one of the most entertaining ways to be initiated into the intricacies of the game is to go along to a pacier, less serious 1-day match or Twenty20 game.

On an international level, every season England plays 5-day Test matches against one or two touring teams from Australia, India, New Zealand, Pakistan, Sri Lanka or the West Indies. These take place at half a dozen grounds in Britain including Lord's and the Oval in London, Edgbaston in Birmingham, Trent Bridge in Nottingham and Headingly in Leeds. Test match tickets are sought-after and sell out well in advance, but there's generally less competition for seats for 1-day internationals.

The governing body of the world game is Marylebone Cricket Club (MCC), based at Lord's Cricket Ground in London's St John's Wood, tel: 020-7616 8500; www.lords.org. Cricket can also be seen at the Oval, Kennington, in south London, tel: Surrey County Cricket Club, 08712-

The Sporting Calendar

February
Rugby Six Nations Championship.

March
Football Carling Cup Final, Wembley Stadium.
Racing Cheltenham Gold Cup, Cheltenham, Gloucestershire.
University Boat Race Oxford and Cambridge, on the Thames between Putney and Mortlake, London.

April
Horse Racing Grand National Race Meeting, Aintree, Liverpool.
London Marathon Finishes on the Mall, in front of Buckingham Palace.
Rugby Union County Championship Final, Twickenham. Six Nations Cup.
Snooker World Championship, The Crucible Theatre, Sheffield.

May
Football FA Cup Final, Wembley Stadium.
Golf PGA Championship, Wentworth Club, Surrey.
Horse Trials Badminton, Gloucestershire.
Horse Racing 1,000 and 2,000 Guineas Stakes, Newmarket, Suffolk.
Horse Show Royal Windsor, Home Park, Windsor.
Cricket Test matches.

June
Cycling London to Brighton bike ride.
Horse Racing Royal Ascot, Ascot, Berkshire. The Derby, Epsom, Surrey. The Oaks, Epsom, Surrey.
Tennis British Tennis Championships, Queen's Club, London. Wimbledon Lawn Tennis Championships, All England Lawn Tennis and Croquet Club: the world's most famous tennis tournament, held in southwest London suburb.
Cricket Test matches.
Highland Games Aberdeen.

461 100; www.surreycricket.com. For venues outside London, see www.play-cricket.com.

Equestrian Sports

Flat racing takes place between March and early November. The most important races are the Derby and Oaks at Epsom, the St Leger at Doncaster and the 1,000 and 2,000 Guineas at Newmarket. The Royal Ascot meeting is a major social event where racegoers dress in their finest.

July
Show Jumping Royal International Horse Show, Hickstead.
Motor Racing British Grand Prix, Silverstone, Northamptonshire.
Rowing Henley Royal Regatta Week, Henley-on-Thames.
Golf Open Championship, venue varies.
Cricket Test matches.
Polo Cartier International, Guards Polo Club, Surrey.

August
Highland Games Cowal, Perth and Aboyne, Scotland.
Horse Racing Glorious Goodwood
Polo Cheltenham Cup
Sailing Cowes Week Regatta, Isle of Wight.
Cricket Test matches.
Rugby League Carnegie Challenge Cup Final.

September
Braemar Royal Highland Games Memorial Park, Scotland.
Cycling The Tour of Britain 8-day road race.
British Superbike Championship Silverstone.
Golf: World Matchplay, Wentworth, Surrey. British Masters, the Belfry, West Midlands.

October
Great North Run Newcastle. The world's largest half-marathon.
Show Jumping Horse of the Year Show, NEC, Birmingham.

November
RAC London–Brighton Veteran Car Run is a 60-mile (100km) race for 500 cars built before 1905.

December
Wales Rally of Great Britain Cardiff.
Olympia, The London International Horse Show Olympia, London.

Steeplechasing and **hurdle racing** take place from September to early June. The National Hunt Festival meeting at Cheltenham in March is the most important event; the highlight is the Gold Cup. The most famous steeplechase, watched avidly and gambled on by millions in Britain, is the Grand National held at Aintree in Liverpool.

Show jumping is the equestrian sport every young rider aspires to. Major events are the Royal

International Horse Show and the British Jumping Derby at Hickstead, West Sussex, the Horse of the Year Show at the NEC, Birmingham, and the Olympia International Horse Show in London.

Polo matches take place at Windsor Great Park or Cowdray Park, Midhurst, West Sussex on summer weekends. The governing body is the Hurlingham Polo Association, tel: 01367-242 828; www.hpa-polo.co.uk.

Horse trials are held in spring and autumn nationwide. The major 3-day events (cross-country, show jumping and dressage) are held at Badminton, Bramham, Burghley, Chatsworth and Gatcombe.

The main equestrian body in Britain is **The British Horse Society**, which governs the Pony Club and Riding Club. It also runs the British Equestrian Centre at Stoneleigh in Warwickshire, where it is based. For further information, contact The British Horse Society, tel: 0844-848 1666; www.bhs.org.uk.

Football (Soccer)

This is the country's most popular spectator sport and participant team sport. The professional season is August–May. England and Scotland have separate football associations (FAs), with four divisions in England (top of which is the Premier League) and four in Scotland.

Most **Premier League** matches can be watched only on satellite TV. Many pubs have large screens, and are popular places for watching big games. The climax of the English season is the FA Cup, played at the new Wembley Stadium. Scotland's highlight is the **Scottish FA Cup** at Hampden Park near Glasgow.

League matches usually start Sat or Sun at 3pm, midweek 7pm. Results are aired on Saturday at 4.45pm on the main terrestrial channels (BBC and ITV). Radio 5 Live (693 or 909 AM) and talkSPORT (1053 or 1089 AM) broadcast matches and discuss the sport at length with experts and listeners. For details of Premier League fixtures, check www.premier league.com for club contact details; for other English fixtures, www.football-league.co.uk. For Scottish fixtures, see www.scottishfootballleague.com.

Golf

The most important national golfing event is the Open Championship, which takes place every July. Other prestigious competitions include the **Ryder Cup** for professionals and the

ABOVE: Wimbledon Lawn Tennis Championships begin in the last week of June.

Walker Cup for amateurs. Both of these are played between Britain and the USA every other year. Another prestigious tournament is the **World Match Play Championship** at Wentworth, Surrey, in September.

For information on dates and venues of tournaments, contact the Professional Golfers' Association (PGA), tel: 01675-470 333.

Motor Racing

The heart of motor racing worldwide, Britain has produced a number of World Champions, from Mike Hawthorn and Jim Clark to James Hunt, Nigel Mansell and Damon Hill. The British Grand Prix, the highlight of the British motor-racing calendar, is traditionally held at **Silverstone** on the second weekend in July (tel: 0844-3750 740; www.silverstone.co.uk). But Britain's race tracks (including **Brands Hatch** and **Donington**) also host a range of race meetings from touring cars to powerful single seaters. Rallying is also very popular.

Details of races from the Motor Sports Association, tel: 01753-765 000 or visit www.msauk.org. See also www.brdc.co.uk.

Rugby

Rugby is said to have been invented when one of the pupils of Rugby public school picked up the ball and ran in a game of football early in the 19th century. It is a national institution today, with two types, Union (played in Scotland, Wales and predominantly the south of England) and League (the north of England game).

Rugby Union, formerly for amateurs only, is now professional. The season runs from September to May, with matches played at Twickenham, Murrayfield and the Millennium Stadium. One of the highlights of the season is the Six Nations Championship, a knock-out between England, Ireland, Scotland, Wales, France and Italy.

Rugby League culminates in the Super League final at Old Trafford in September.

For details of Rugby Union fixtures, tel: 0871-222 2120; www.rfu.com. For Rugby League, tel: 0871-226 1313; www.rfl.uk.com.

OUTDOOR ACTIVITIES

National Parks

Brecon Beacons National Park (South Wales) is made up of red sandstone mountains (including South Wales's highest peak, Pen-y-Fan: 2,907ft/886 metres), and picturesque lowland areas of woodland, meandering rivers and rolling farmland. Attracts walkers, cyclists, sailors, canoeists, cavers and rock climbers. **The Broads** Britain's largest protected wetland is situated in Norfolk and Suffolk. Rare plants and animals abound and the ideal way to explore is by water, with 125 miles (200km) of boating on lock-free tidal rivers. **Cairngorms National Park** Taking in much of the subarctic plateau of the Cairngorm Mountains, the park

Wimbledon Lawn Tennis Championships

The Wimbledon fortnight is one of Britain's best-loved sporting highlights, attracting nearly 400,000 spectators in person and millions of television viewers worldwide. It takes place in June/July on the immaculate grass courts at the All England Club in Wimbledon, southwest London.

Most tickets are allocated by public ballot (obtain an application form by sending a stamped SAE to the Ticket Office, AELTC, PO Box 98, Wimbledon, London SW19 5AE by the end of the previous year). For details, tel: 020-8971 2473; www.wimbledon.org. Around 1,500 tickets are kept back for some courts if you are prepared to camp out the night before, and spare seats are always to be had in late afternoon. Expect to pay more than 22p per strawberry if you want to try the traditional strawberries and cream.

includes large remnants of the ancient Great Caledonian Forest. Dissected by the valley of the River Spey, home to abundant wildlife, including the rare capercaillie, largest of the grouse family.

Dartmoor Ponies roam across this expanse of Devon moorland, with granite tors, heath and peaty bogs. Highest point is High Willhays (2,039ft/621 metres). Home of Dartmoor prison and setting for the 1901 Sherlock Holmes mystery *The Hound of the Baskervilles.*

Exmoor Straddling the border between Somerset and Devon, with heathery moorland and breathtaking coastline. Home to Exmoor ponies, sheep, red deer and cattle.

Lake District Stunningly beautiful countryside in Cumbria: 16 lakes are interspersed with high fells, the highest being Scafell Pike (3,210ft/ 978 metres). A haven for fishing, boating, climbing and walking.

Loch Lomond and the Trossachs Centred on Loch Lomond, it includes the haunts of Scottish folk hero Rob Roy MacGregor. The Trossachs, with picturesque villages, offer breathtaking views on quieter minor routes into the Highlands.

New Forest Running from the Solent coast to the Wiltshire chalk downs and lying mainly in southwest Hampshire, this landscape combines woodland, heath, farmland and coastal saltmarsh. Originally used for hunting by William the Conqueror, the forest is home to native ponies and birds of prey.

Northumberland 405 sq miles (1,048 sq km) in the far northeast characterised by rugged moorland, wooded valleys and huge unspoilt views. The Pennine Way marches through it, from Hadrian's Wall to the Cheviot Hills on the Scottish border.

Private Gardens

Under the National Gardens Scheme (tel: 01483-211 535; www. ngs.org.uk) the gardens of Britain's many horticultural enthusiasts are open to the public. For a small fee visitors can explore nearly 3,500 gardens, the majority of which open in spring and summer. The *Yellow Book* (from larger bookshops) lists all gardens open each year and is published annually.

Flanked on the east by spectacular coastline, Northumberland has more castles than any other British county.

North York Moors A coastline of rugged cliffs, expanses of low moorland, deep valleys and heathered uplands, this national park covers 554 sq miles (1,436 sq km), including the 110-mile (177km) -long Cleveland Way.

Peak District This well-preserved area of natural beauty at the tip of the Pennines was England's first national park. Characterised by high, bleak moors and low, gentle limestone countryside with dramatic wooded valleys and rivers.

Pembrokeshire Coast Remote and rugged park taking up most of the coast of Pembrokeshire, southwest Wales. A coastal path stretches 186 miles (299km), from Amroth beach to Teifi near Cardigan. Popular with surfers and rock climbers.

Snowdonia A diverse area of stunning beauty covering 823 sq miles (2,130 sq km) in the northwest of Wales. Encompassing forests, lakes and torrential streams, and craggy high peaks, with Mount Snowdon the highest point south of the Scottish border. Mountaineering, walking, pony trekking, canoeing, fishing, sailing.

Yorkshire Dales This wild expanse, of great natural beauty, covers 680 sq miles (1,760 sq km) in the Pennine Hills, featuring deep dales, waterfalls, caves and quarries. Made famous in fiction by vet James Herriot in books such as *All Creatures Great and Small.*

Adventure Sports

Scotland

Despite erratic snowfall in recent years, Scotland's five ski centres – Cairngorm, The Lecht, Glenshee, Glencoe and Nevis Range – continue in business, though they have diversified into activities such as mountain biking to balance the books. However, when snow does fall (the main season is Jan–Apr), groomed pistes and challenging off-piste terrain become the playground for skiers, boarders and ski-mountaineers. Consult www.ski-scotland.com for details of resorts and activities.

Another way to enjoy the Scottish mountains is by hiking and climbing them. Companies such as Mountain Innovations (tel: 01479-831 331; www.scotmountain.co.uk) offer holidays and "skills" courses on navigation or tackling the mountains in the snow.

Wilderness Scotland (tel: 0131-625 6635; www.wildernessscotland.com) organizes walking holidays for all levels of ability as well as mountain-biking and skiing breaks.

Wales

For a different white-knuckle experience, try whitewater rafting. The Canolfan Tryweryn National White Water Centre, at Frongoch near Bala in Snowdonia (tel: 01678-521 083; www.ukrafting.co.uk), organises trips down the rapids of the River Tryweryn.

Birdwatching

Birdwatching is a popular pastime in Britain. There are hundreds of bird reserves all over the country, many owned and run by the **Royal Society for the Protection of Birds** (www.rspb.

Walking Tours

There are designated, well-marked walking paths all over Britain: around the coasts, across the Pennines, over the South Downs, along Hadrian's Wall and many other places. Local tourist offices will supply information and sell detailed walkers' maps, many giving distances, estimated times and levels of difficulty.

BELOW: canoeing down the River Tryweryn, Snowdonia.

org.uk). You can visit many of them free of charge; others have a modest entrance fee. Other important conservation bodies which maintain reserves include the Wildfowl & Wetlands Trust (www.wwt.org.uk) and the Scottish Wildlife Trust (www.swt.org.uk).

Good places to see rare birds include the north Norfolk coast, especially at Titchwell, Holkham and Cley, the Suffolk coast at Dunwich and Minsmere, the west coast of Scotland and the Hebrides, and the national parks (see above).

Cycling

The **National Cycle Network** (www.sustrans.org.uk) comprises 12,600 miles (20,300km) of cycle paths. The routes aim to minimise contact with motor traffic, and although some are on minor roads, many others are on disused railway lines, canal towpaths and bridleways. The network is signposted using a white bicycle symbol on a blue background, with a white route number in an inset box. In addition, there is the **National Byway** (www.thenationalbyway.org), a 4,000-mile (6,400km) cycling route that runs along quiet roads around England and parts of Scotland and Wales. It includes a number of loops so that cyclists can start and finish in the same place. These circular routes range in length from 16 miles (26km) to 50 miles (80km). Signposts have white writing on a brown background.

There are many opportunities to hire bikes in the UK. There is no national coordination or chain of outlets, but each region will have a number of shops and cycle centres that rent out a variety of models, from mountain bikes to tandems. Ask for the nearest outlet at the local Tourist Information Centre.

Fishing

Fishing is Britain's top participant sport, attracting 8 million people. A useful website is www.anglingnews.net/bodies.asp, which lists many British angling clubs. For angling clubs and organisations in Scotland go to www.fishing-uk-scotland.com.

Horse Riding

There are plenty of public riding stables in rural areas, but most do not let riders out unaccompanied. Pony-trekking is particularly popular on Dartmoor and Exmoor, in the New Forest and in Wales.

For further information and a list of approved riding stables, contact **The British Horse Society**, tel: 08701-202 244; www.bhs.org.uk.

Water Sports

Britain offers plenty of opportunities to those interested in sailing, particularly on the south coast and around Pembrokeshire, southwest Wales, but also on the lakes and lochs of the north of England and Scotland; Kielder Water, situated in northwest Northumberland, is the largest man-made reservoir in northern Europe, with a shoreline of more than 27 miles (43km). The lake offers the opportunity to take part in a variety of water sports (www.kielderwatersc.org). There are excellent facilities for canoeing, windsurfing, jet-skiing and boating, too, on Britain's many inland waters. Cornwall is a popular surfing centre.

Superb windsurfing conditions can be found on the Scottish island of Tiree, and around John o'Groats on the north coast of Scotland.

There are National Water Sports Centres at Isle of Cumbrae, Ayrshire, Scotland (tel: 01475-530 757; www.nationalcentrecumbrae.org.uk) and Holme Pierrepont, Nottinghamshire (tel: 0115-982 1212; www.nwscnotts.com).

Heritage Sites

There are a number of organisations that look after Britain's old buildings, gardens and countryside. Government-funded heritage organisations run key historic sites, while the National Trust, a charity, maintains stately homes and areas of coast and countryside.

English Heritage manages more than 400 properties, including Stonehenge and Dover Castle. Annual membership entitles you to free entry to all sites, plus discounts for events held at them throughout the year. A 1- or 2-week Overseas Visitor Pass is also available. Contact: English Heritage, tel: 0870-333 1181; www.english-heritage.org.uk.

Historic Scotland (tel: 0131-668 8831; www.historic-scotland.gov.uk) maintains more than 300 properties including Glasgow Cathedral and Edinburgh Castle. Annual membership allows free access to all. Offers 3-, 7- and 10-day Explorer passes to visitors.

Cadw (Welsh Heritage; tel: 01443-336 000; www.cadw.wales.gov.uk) has some 100 properties, from prehistoric sites to Caernarfon Castle and Tintern Abbey. Offers 3- or 7-day Explorer Pass.

The National Trust was founded in 1895 as an independent charity for the conservation of places of historic interest and natural beauty. It has more than 300 properties open to the public, from large country houses and abbeys to lighthouses and industrial monuments. It also maintains more than 200 gardens and protects 612,000 acres (248,000 hectares) of countryside, including over 700 miles (1,100km) of shoreline and woodland. The majority of its funding comes from its members.

Membership entitles you to free entry to properties and a copy of The National Trust Handbook. Tel: 0844-800 1895; www.nationaltrust.org.uk.

The National Trust for Scotland is a separate body with more than 120 properties covering 187,000 acres (76,000 hectares). Sites in its care include castles, battlefields, islands, countryside and the birthplaces of famous Scots. Tel: 0844-493 2100; www.nts.org.uk.

All these heritage groups have reciprocal arrangements, and the NT also has reciprocal arrangements with trusts overseas, including in Australia, Italy, New Zealand, Canada, the Bahamas, Malta, Jersey and Guernsey.

The Great British Heritage Pass, which allows unlimited access to 580 historic buildings, is a bargain for visitors interested in history. It is available exclusively for overseas visitors, can be bought online (www.britishheritagepass.com), then sent to a home address or collected at certain visitor centres around Britain.

SIGHTSEEING TOURS AND EXCURSIONS

All British cities of historical interest have special double-decker buses that tour the sites. Some are open-topped and many have a commentary in several languages.

The Original Tour was the first and is the biggest London sightseeing operator. Hop on and hop off at over 90 different stops. With commentary in several languages and a Kids' Club for 5–15-year-olds. Buy tickets on bus or in advance. Operates year-round. Tel: 020-8877 1722; www.theoriginaltour.com.

The Big Bus Company operates two routes of hop-on-hop-off services. Tel: 020-7233 9533; www.bigbustours.com.
Duck Tours uses World War II amphibious vehicles which drive past famous London landmarks before taking to the water. Departure from Chicheley Street, Waterloo. Tel: 020-7928 3132; www.londonducktours.co.uk.
Golden Tours offers a wide choice of day trips for London and sites and cities all over Britain. Contact: tel: 020-7233 7030, or within USA tel: 1-800 548 7083; www.goldentours.co.uk.

Literary Pilgrimages

Ayrshire: Robert Burns (1759–96). Scotland's literary hero. The original copy of his *Auld Lang Syne* is in the Burns National Heritage Park museum, tel: 0844-493 2601, www.burnsmuseum.org.uk, next to the cottage where he was born in Alloway, near Ayr. During the last years of his life, he lived in a small house in a backstreet of Dumfries – now a museum. The Bachelors' Club in Tarbolton, a 17th-century thatched cottage where Burns and his friends formed a debating club in 1780, is now run by the National Trust for Scotland.
Dorset: Thomas Hardy (1840–1928). Hardy was born in Higher Bockhampton where he wrote *Far from the Madding Crowd* and *Under the Greenwood Tree*. He later lived in Dorchester after studying architecture, designing his own house at Max Gate on the Wareham Road. Dorset County Museum, tel: 01305-

262 735; www.dorsetcountymuseum.org, in Dorchester has a Hardy memorial collection. Hardy used the 18th-century King's Arms, High Street, Dorchester, as a setting for *The Mayor of Casterbridge*, and also wrote *Tess of the d'Urbervilles* and *Jude the Obscure* there.
Hampshire: Jane Austen (1775–1817). The daughter of a Hampshire clergyman, Austen grew up in the village of Steventon. From 1809 to 1817 she lived with her mother and sister in a house in Chawton, Hampshire, where she wrote *Mansfield Park*, *Emma* and *Persuasion*. Now a museum (tel: 01420-83262; www.jane-austens-house-museum.org.uk), it contains personal effects, letters and manuscripts. She spent time in Bath where the Jane Austen Centre (tel: 01225-443 000; www.janeausten.co.uk) can be visited; and Lyme Regis, where she wrote much of *Persuasion* from Bay Cottage on The Parade. She is buried in Winchester Cathedral.
Kent: Charles Dickens (1812–70). Most of his life was spent in Kent and London. He grew up at 11 Ordnance Terrace, Chatham, Kent. From 1837 to 1839 he lived with his wife and son at 48 Doughty Street, London, now owned by the Dickens Fellowship and housing a wide range of personal belongings, manuscripts and books (tel: 020-7405 2127; www.dickensmuseum.com). In 1856 he moved to Gad's Hill Place near Rochester (now a school), where he died. Dickens was fond of the seaside town of Broadstairs and lived there in Bleak

House, where he wrote part of *David Copperfield*.
The Lake District: William Wordsworth (1770–1850). In Main Street, Cockermouth (tel: 01900-820 884; www.nationaltrust.org.uk) you can visit Wordsworth's birthplace and childhood home. Dove Cottage, now a museum and art gallery, is in Town End, Grasmere, where he lived with his sister Dorothy during the most creative years of his life (tel: 01539-435 544; www.wordsworth.org.uk). Rydal Mount, his family house and garden near Ambleside, is also open to visitors (tel: 01539-433 002; www.rydalmount.co.uk).
Nottingham: D.H. Lawrence (1885–1930). The son of a miner, Lawrence grew up in Victoria Street, Eastwood, which has been restored to give an insight into his working-class childhood (Lawrence Birthplace Museum, tel: 01773-763 312, www.broxtowe.gov.uk). Nearby at 28 Garden Road is Breach House, where the Lawrence family lived from 1887 to 1891, the setting of the Morels' house in *Sons and Lovers*.
South Wales: Dylan Thomas (1914–53). Thomas was born in the industrial town of Swansea in Wales, growing up in 5 Cwmdonkin Drive in the Uplands district. Follow the Dylan Thomas Uplands Trail and visit the boathouse where he lived and worked in Laugharne (tel: 01994-427 420; www.dylanthomasboathouse.com). The annual Dylan Thomas Festival takes place at the end of October (www.dylanthomas.org).
Warwickshire: William Shakespeare (1564–1616). Stratford-upon-Avon is synonymous with Britain's greatest playwright. The Shakespeare Birthplace Trust (tel: 01789-204 016; www.shakespeare.org.uk) administers the following Tudor properties (combined ticket available): Shakespeare's Birthplace, Henley Street; Anne Hathaway's Cottage, Shottery; Hall's Croft, Old Town; New Place/Nash's House, Chapel Street; Mary Arden's Farm, Wilmcote, where his mother grew up (and now a museum of rural life).
Yorkshire: The Brontë Sisters: Anne (1820–49), **Charlotte** (1816–55), **Emily** (1818–48). All were born in Thornton, West Yorkshire, but the family home was the Parsonage in Haworth. Now a museum run by the Brontë Society, it has been restored as it was when the family lived here (1820–61) and contains some of their furniture, manuscripts and personal belongings (tel: 01535-642 323; www.bronte.org.uk).

BELOW: Dove Cottage, Grasmere, Wordsworth's childhood home.

A HANDY SUMMARY OF PRACTICAL INFORMATION, ARRANGED ALPHABETICALLY

Admission Charges

The major national museums and galleries, such as the British Museum, National Gallery, Imperial War Museum and the various Tate galleries, are free. Some municipal museums are free but donations are always welcome; others make a charge. A comprehensive website is www.culture24.org.uk.

The Great British Heritage Pass (www.britishheritagepass.com), which can be bought only outside the UK, gives entry to nearly 600 attractions; the cost of a 15-day pass would work out at about £6 a day. This includes stately homes and gardens run by the National Trust, English Heritage and their Scottish and Welsh equivalents. Passes to cover only the properties of one of these bodies can be bought through www.visitbritaindirect.com.

If you're planning to visit a lot of attractions in the capital, it's worth looking at www.londonpass.com; prices start at £44 (adult) or £29 (child) for 1 day, but 6-day passes are better value. Note that they don't cover some of the more expensive

attractions such as Madame Tussauds and the London Dungeon.

Budgeting for Your Trip

Prices for many goods and services can seem expensive to visitors, though much does of course depend on exchange rates. Public transport is very expensive compared to most countries, though admission to museums and galleries is either free or at least reasonably priced.

Central London is, unsurprisingly, likely to have the highest prices, but even there, items such as restaurant meals are kept at moderate levels by the pressure of competition. Be aware that hotels and restaurants in more far-flung places, such as the Scottish Highlands or Cornwall, can sometimes be surprisingly expensive, as overheads have to be covered during a relatively short tourist season. Average costs guide:
Pint of beer: £3
Glass of house wine: £3.50
Main course at a budget restaurant: £8
Main course at a moderately priced restaurant: £14

Main course at an expensive restaurant: £25
Bed and breakfast at a cheap hotel: £70
Bed and breakfast at a moderately priced hotel: £130
Bed and breakfast at a deluxe hotel: £250
Taxi from Heathrow to central London: £40 pre-booked, otherwise £80

Children

For ideas on museums and other attractions suitable for children of various ages, see *Top Attractions for Families* on page 8. Discounts for children are usually available for admission charges to museums and other visitor attractions.
Accommodation. Some hotels do not accept children under a certain age, so be sure to check when you book. Many of the more upmarket hotels in Britain provide travel cots for no extra charge, though they will charge for babysitting services.
Restaurants. Most accept well-behaved children, but only those that want to encourage families have

children's menus, high-chairs and nappy-changing facilities. Only pubs with a Children's Certificate can admit children, and even these will usually restrict the hours and areas open to them. Publicans, like restaurateurs, reserve the right to refuse entry.

Public transport. Up to four children aged 11 or under can travel free on London's Underground if accompanied by a ticket-holding adult. Children aged 11–15 can get unlimited off-peak travel for £1 per day or "Kids for a Quid" single fares if travelling with an adult holding an electronic Oyster card. Children aged 11–15 will, however, need a photo Oyster card (this can take up to 2 weeks to obtain and you need to be an EU national).

Buses are free for all children under 16, but 11–15-year-olds will need a 11–15 Oyster photocard. Buses can take up to two unfolded pushchairs (buggies) at one time (they must be parked in a special area halfway down the bus). Any further pushchairs must be folded. Either way, it is up to the driver's discretion.

Climate

In a word, unpredictable. In a few words, temperate and generally mild. It is unusual for any area in the British Isles to have a dry spell for more than 3 weeks, even in the summer months from June to September. However, it rains most frequently in the mountainous areas of north and west Britain where temperatures are also cooler than in the south.

In summer, the average maximum temperature in the south of England is in the 70s Fahrenheit (23–25°C), although over 80°F (27°C) is not unusual. In Scotland temperatures tend to stay within the mid-60s

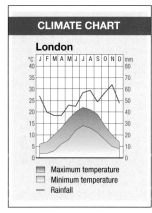

CLIMATE CHART

London

- Maximum temperature
- Minimum temperature
- Rainfall

Fahrenheit (17–19°C). During the winter (November to February), the majority of Britain, with the exception of mountainous regions in the North, tends to be cold and damp rather than snowy.

For recorded weather information, tel: 0871-200 3985 or visit www.met office.org.

When to Visit

The peak holiday season in Britain is July and August. While these months generally have the greatest number of hours of sunshine, they do also coincide with the school holidays and are very busy. Visiting in May, June or September is therefore preferable. During the winter, attractions such as stately homes are generally closed. Likewise, in more remote regions such as the Scottish Highlands, some hotels and many attractions close over the winter period when the weather is poor.

What to Wear

Due to the unpredictability of the weather, be prepared. Bring suitable warm- and wet-weather clothing whatever the season. Generally, short sleeves and a jacket are fine for summer but a warm coat and woollens are recommended for winter.

On the whole the British tend to dress casually and with a few exceptions formal dress is not essential, although a jacket and tie on men is required by smart hotels and restaurants.

Crime and Safety

Serious crime is low, but in big cities the Dickensian tradition of pick-pocketing is alive and well. Hold on tightly to purses, do not put wallets in back pockets, and do not place handbags on the ground in busy restaurants. Gangs of professional thieves target the Tube in London.

In a genuine emergency, dial 999 from any telephone (no cash required). Report routine thefts to a police station (address under Police in a telephone directory or call tel: 101). The threat of terrorism has led to an increase in police patrols, so don't hesitate to report any suspicious packages.

Customs Regulations

If you enter the UK directly from another European Union (EU) country, you no longer need to exit Customs through a red or green channel – use the special EU blue channel, as you

Electricity

230 volts, 50 Hertz. Square, three-pin plugs are used, and virtually all visitors will need adaptors if planning to plug in their own equipment.

are not required to declare any goods you have brought in for personal use. However, if you bring in large amounts of goods such as alcohol, tobacco or perfume you may be asked to verify that they are not intended for resale.

Visitors entering the UK from non-EU countries should use the green Customs channel if they do not exceed the following allowances for goods obtained outside the EU, or purchased duty-free in the EU, or on board ship or aircraft:
- **Tobacco** 200 cigarettes or 100 cigarillos or 50 cigars or 250g of tobacco
- **Alcohol** 2 litres still table wine plus 1 litre spirits (over 22 percent by volume) or 2 litres fortified wine, sparkling wine or other liqueurs
- **Perfume** 60ml of perfume plus 250ml of toilet water
- **Gifts** £145 worth of gifts, souvenirs or other goods.

It is illegal to bring animals, certain drugs, firearms, obscene material and anything likely to threaten health or the environment without prior arrangement. Any amount of currency can be brought in. Consult the HM Revenue and Customs website for further details: www.hmrc.gov.uk.

Disabled Travellers

Details of transport access for disabled people can be found on a government website, www.dft.gov.uk/transportforyou/access. www.artsline.org.uk is a disability access website providing searchable information on over 1,000 arts venues across London.

Toilets: Britain has a system of keys to open many of the public toilets available for disabled people. To obtain a key, contact RADAR on tel: 020-7250 3222. There is a charge of £4.20 for the key and £16.99 for the guidebook detailing their locations. Both prices include UK postal delivery.

Embassies and Consulates

Most countries have diplomatic representation in London (a selection is given below). Others can be found through the Yellow Pages or by calling Directory Enquiries. Many also have consulates in Edinburgh and Cardiff.

Australia, Australia House, Strand, London WC2 4LA, tel: 020-7379 4334; www.australia.org.uk.
Canada, 1 Grosvenor Square, London W1K 4AB, tel: 020-7258 6600; www.dfait-maeci.gc.ca/canadaeuropa.
New Zealand, 80 Haymarket, London SW1Y 4TQ, tel: 020-7930 8422; www.nzembassy.com.
South Africa, South Africa House, Trafalgar Square, London WC2N 5DP, tel: 020-7451 7299; www.southafricahouse.com.
USA, 24 Grosvenor Square, London W1A 1AF, tel: 020-7499 9000; www.usembassy.org.uk.

Emergencies

Only in an absolute emergency call tel: 999 for fire, ambulance or police. In the case of a minor accident or illness, take a taxi to the nearest casualty department of a hospital. For non-urgent calls to the police in London, dial tel: 0300-123 1212; outside the capital, ask Directory Enquiries *(see Telephones, below)* for the number of the nearest police station. They will also be able to give you the telephone number of your country's embassy or consulate if needed.

Etiquette

There are relatively few matters of etiquette that visitors need be concerned about. The most important principles to bear in mind are that the British expect politeness in even the most trivial everyday encounters, and also that gender equality is taken very seriously. Otherwise, common sense and a little caution will see you through almost any situation. Visitors should dress modestly when entering religious buildings. Queue-jumping is not viewed favourably. When using the escalator in the London Underground stand on the right unless you want to keep moving; then walk down or up on the left-hand side.

G ay and Lesbian Travellers

With Europe's largest gay and lesbian population, London has an abundance of bars, restaurants and clubs to cater for any taste. Many of them make space for one or more of London's free gay weekly magazines, *Boyz*, the *Pink Paper* and *QX*. Monthly magazines on sale at newsstands include *Gay Times*, *Diva* and *Attitude*.

Two established websites for meeting other gay people in London are www.gaydar.co.uk and the female version, www.gaydargirls.com. Other websites reflecting Britain's gay scene include www.gaydarnation.com and www. outuk.com; Manchester and Brighton have proportionately large gay communities.

Useful telephone contacts for advice and counselling include **London Lesbian and Gay Switchboard** (tel: 7837 7324) and **London Friend** (7.30–10pm, tel: 020-7837 3337).

H ealth and Medical Care

If you fall ill and are a national of the EU, you are entitled to free medical treatment in most cases. Most other visitors have to pay for medical and dental treatment and should ensure they have adequate health insurance.

In the case of minor accidents, your hotel will know the location of the nearest hospital with a casualty department. Self-catering accommodation should have this information, plus the number of the local GP, on a notice in the house.

Treatment: Seriously ill visitors are eligible for free emergency treatment in the Accident and Emergency departments of National Health Service hospitals. However, if they are admitted to hospital as an in-patient, even from the Accident and Emergency department, or referred to an out-patient clinic, they will be asked to pay unless they fall into the above exempted categories.

Walk-in clinics: There are more than 90 National Health Service walk-in centres across the country, usually open 7 days a week from early morning to late evening, 365 days a year. A charge may be made to non-EU nationals.

Pharmacies: Boots is the largest chain of chemists, with many branches around the country. As well as selling over-the-counter medicines, they make up prescriptions. If you need medications outside normal business hours in London, visit Zafash 24-hour Pharmacy (233–5 Old Brompton Road; tel: 020-3489 0555).

Supplies for children: Infant formula and nappies (diapers) can be purchased from pharmacies and supermarkets.

L ost Property

If you have lost your passport, you must get in touch with your embassy as quickly as possible.

For possessions lost on trains you must contact the station where the train on which you were travelling ended its journey. The same applies if you leave something on a coach. For anything lost on public transport in London, contact Transport for London, tel: 020-7486 2496, www.tfl.gov.uk.

For possessions lost in the street, contact the police to report the loss. You will need this if you are intending to claim on your travel insurance.

M aps

Insight Guides' best-selling FlexiMaps are laminated for durability and easy folding and contain clear cartography as well as practical information. British titles include London, Cornwall, the Cotswolds, Edinburgh and the Lake District.

In London, map lovers should head for Stanford's (12–14 Long Acre, in the Covent Garden area), one of the world's top map and guidebook stores.

Tourist Information Centres can often provide visitors with a free basic map of the area in which they are situated. A–Z maps of London are sold in most newsagents and book shops.

Media

Newspapers

With more than 100 daily and Sunday newspapers published nationwide, there's no lack of choice in Britain. Although free from state control and financially independent of political parties, many nationals do have pronounced political leanings. Of the quality dailies *The Times* and *The Daily Telegraph* are on the right, *The Guardian* and *The Independent* in the middle. On Sunday *The Observer* leans slightly left of centre, while the *Independent on Sunday* stands in the

BELOW: the weather – a very British preoccupation.

ABOVE: the big cities have newsstands – and sometimes free newspapers.

middle and the *Sunday Times* and *Sunday Telegraph* are on the right.

The Financial Times is renowned for the clearest, most unbiased headlines in its general news pages, plus exhaustive financial coverage.

The mass-market papers are a less formal, easy read. *The Sun* and *The Star* are on the right and obsessed with the Royal Family, soap operas and sex. *The Mirror, Sunday Mirror* and *Sunday People* are slightly to the left. In the mid-market sector, the *Daily Mail* and *Mail on Sunday* are slightly more upscale equivalents of the *Express* and *Sunday Express*.

Scotland's quality dailies are *The Scotsman*, based in Edinburgh, and *The Herald*, based in Glasgow; the *Daily Record* is the most popular Scottish tabloid. Wales has the *Western Mail* and the *Daily Post*.

Some cities have free newspapers, paid for by advertising and often handed out at railway stations. Foreign newspapers can usually be found in large newsagents and railway stations nationwide. Branches of W.H. Smith, in larger towns, usually have a reasonable selection.

Television

Britain has a somewhat outdated reputation for broadcasting some of the finest television in the world. There are five national terrestial channels: BBC1, BBC2, ITV, Channel 4 (C4) and Five. Both the BBC (British Broadcasting Corporation) and ITV (Independent Television) have regional stations that broadcast local news and varying programme schedules in between links with the national networks based in London (see local newspapers for listings). They also broadcast some programmes in the local language (Gaelic, Welsh). The BBC is financed by compulsory annual television licence fees and

therefore does not rely on advertising for funding. The independent channels, ITV, C4 and Five, are funded entirely by commercials.

BBC1, ITV and Five broadcast programmes aimed at mainstream audiences, while BBC2 and C4 cater more for cultural and minority interests. However, the advent of cable and satellite channels has forced terrestrial stations to fight for audiences with a higher incidence of programmes such as soap operas and game shows. Both the BBC and ITV also have satellite channels.

There are hundreds of cable and satellite channels on offer, ranging from sport and films to cartoons and music. Pricier hotel rooms often offer a choice of cable stations, including CNN and BBC News Channel.

Radio Stations

In addition to the national services listed below, there are many local radio stations which can be useful for traffic reports. Note that the frequencies indicated below may vary in different parts of the country.

BBC Radio 1 98.8FM
Britain's most popular radio station, which broadcasts mainstream pop.

BBC Radio 2 89.2FM
Easy-listening music and chat shows.

BBC Radio 3 91.3FM
24-hour classical music, plus some drama.

BBC Radio 4 93.5FM
News, current affairs, plays.

BBC Radio Five Live 909MW
Rolling news and sport.

BBC World Service 198LW/648kHz
International news and reports.

Classic FM 100.9 FM
24-hour classical and movie music, unpompously presented.

While BBC Radio 1 is the main station for the latest pop releases, music fans might also tune into

Absolute Radio (105.8FM) for middle-of-the-road rock music, Kiss (100FM) for 24-hour dance tracks, and the digital-only radio station, BBC Radio 6 (DAB: 12B), for "alternative" music, including indie, punk, funk, soul and hip-hop.

Money

Pound Sterling. Pounds are divided into 100 pence. Scotland issues its own notes, which are not technically legal tender in England and Wales, but banks and most shops accept them. Exchange rates against the US dollar and the euro can fluctuate significantly.

Euros. A few shops, services, attractions and hotels accept euro notes, but give change in sterling. Most will charge a commission.

ATMs. The majority of bank branches have automatic teller machines (ATMs) where international credit or cashpoint cards can be used, in conjunction with a personal number, to withdraw cash. ATMs can also be found at many supermarkets, in shopping centres and petrol stations.

Credit cards. International credit cards are accepted in most shops, hotels and restaurants.

Exchanging money. The major banks offer similar exchange rates, so it's worth shopping around only if you have large amounts of money to change. Banks charge no commission on travellers' cheques presented in sterling. If a bank is affiliated to your own bank at home, it will make no charge for cheques in other currencies either. But there is a charge for changing cash into British currency. Some high-street travel agents, such as Thomas Cook,

Public Holidays

Compared to most of Europe, the UK has few public holidays:

January New Year's Day (1)

March/April Good Friday, Easter Monday

May May Day (first Monday of the month), Spring Bank Holiday (last Monday)

August Summer Bank Holiday (last Monday)

December Christmas Day (25), Boxing Day (26).

On public holidays, banks and offices are closed, though some supermarkets and newsagents are open. Roads can be heavily congested as people head for the coast or the countryside or to see relatives.

operate bureaux de change at comparable rates. There are also many privately-run bureaux de change (some of which are open 24 hours a day) where exchange rates can be low but commissions high.

O pening Hours

Town-centre shops generally open 9am–5.30pm Mon–Sat, although a few smaller shops may close for lunch in rural areas. Many small towns and villages have a half-day closing one day in the week and shopping centres in towns and cities are likely to have at least one evening of late-night shopping (often on Thursday). Increasing numbers of shops are open on Sunday, usually 10am–4pm.

Supermarkets tend to be open 8 or 8.30am to 8 to 10pm Mon–Sat and 10 or 11am to 4pm on Sunday, and some branches of the larger stores are open all night on certain days of the week (often Thursday or Friday night). Some local corner shops and off-licences (shops licensed to sell alcohol to be consumed off the premises) stay open until 10pm or even later.

Most banks open 9.30am–4.30pm Mon–Fri, with Saturday morning banking common in shopping areas. Most post offices are open 9am–5.30pm Mon–Fri with an hour for lunch.

British pubs' opening hours vary due to flexible closing times. Some have a 24-hour opening licence. Some may close for periods during the day, while others may just apply for the extended opening hours licence for special events such as New Year's Eve.

P ostal Services

Post offices are open 9am–5.30pm Monday–Friday, and 9am–12.30pm on Saturday. London's main post office is in Trafalgar Square, behind the church of St Martin-in-the-Fields, It is open Monday–Friday until 6.30pm, until 5.30 pm on Saturday.

Stamps are sold at post offices, selected shops and newsagents, some supermarkets and from machines outside larger post offices. There is a two-tier service for mail within the UK: first class should reach its destination the next day, and second class will take a day longer. The rate to Europe for standard letters is the same as first-class post within Britain.

R eligious Services

Although Christians, according to the last census for which there are figures,

constitute about 71 percent of the population, half never attend church, so visitors will have no trouble finding a place in a pew. All the major varieties of Christianity are represented, but the predominant one is Church of England. Britain is a multifaith society and other main religions, including Buddhism, Hinduism, Judaism, Islam and Sikhism, are freely practised. About 23 percent of Britons follow no particular religion.

S moking

Smoking is banned in all enclosed public spaces, including pubs, clubs and bars (though not in outside beer gardens) and also on train platforms.

Student Travellers

International students can obtain various discounts at attractions, on travel services (including Eurostar) and in some shops by showing a valid ISIC card (www.isiccard.com).

T elephones

It is usually cheaper to use public phones or even your own mobile (cell-) phone than those in hotel rooms, as hotels make high profits out of this service.

British Telecom (BT) is the main telephone operating company for landlines and provides an ever-diminishing number of public telephone kiosks; nowadays so many people have mobile phones it is not worth their while. Stations, shopping centres and pubs (especially in country areas) are good places to look for a public phone booth.

Only a few take coins; most take plastic phone cards and/or credit cards. Phonecards can be bought from post offices and newsagents in varying amounts between £1 and £20.

The most expensive time to use the telephone is 8am–6pm weekdays, while the cheapest is after 6pm on weekdays and all weekend. Call charges are related to distance, so a long-distance conversation on a weekday morning can eat up coins or card units in a phone box.

Numbers beginning with the prefixes 0800, 0500, 0321 or 0808 are freephone lines. Those prefixed by 0345, 0645 or 0845 are charged at local rates irrespective of distance. Those starting with 0891, 0839, 0640, 0660 and 0898 are costly premium-rate numbers.

The Directory Enquiries service, once exclusively a BT money-earner,

was opened up to competition from other companies and the result was a confusing variety of expensive numbers such as 118 500. A better bet is to use British Telecom's online service, www.192.com.

Mobile phones: you can buy pay-as-you-go SIM cards from most mobile-phone retailers and many newsagents. If your mobile phone accepts SIM cards from companies other than the one you usually use it with, you should be able to register the SIM and use it during your trip. Cheap handsets cost around £10 if you want to buy one for your visit.

Useful Numbers

Operator 100
Directory Enquiries (UK) 118 500, 118 888 or 118 811
International Directory Enquiries 118 505, 118 866 or 118 899
International Operator 155
International dialling code for the UK +44

City dialling codes
Edinburgh 0131
Cardiff 029
Bristol 0117
Manchester 0161
Newcastle 0191

International dialling codes
Australia +61
Canada +1
New Zealand +64
South Africa +27
USA +001

Time Zone

Greenwich Mean Time (GMT) is 1 hour behind Continental European Time, 5 hours ahead of Eastern Seaboard Time, and 9 hours behind Sydney, Australia. British Summer Time (GMT + one hour) runs from late March to late October.

Tipping

The culture of tipping is much less defined in the UK than, say, in the US. However, it does exist. Most hotels and restaurants automatically add a 10–15 percent service charge to your meal bill. It's your right to deduct this amount if you're not happy with the service. Sometimes, when service has been added, the final total on a credit card slip is still left blank, the implication being that a further tip is expected: most people do not pay this unless the service has been exceptional. Be sure that you do not pay for this if you don't want to. You

Weights and Measures

Our system of unitary measurement is a bit of a mess, and reflects Britain's ambivalence about whether it prefers its Imperial past or its European, metric present. So you will fill up a car with litres of fuel (which may be as well since, confusingly, an Imperial gallon is larger than a US gallon) but roadsigns will direct you to your destination in miles. You buy beer by the pint in a pub. A supermarket will sell you a pint of milk, but most other drinks are packaged as litres.

In a few controversial cases, greengrocers have been fined for selling vegetables by the pound instead of by the kilo.
The main conversions are:
Kilometres and miles
1 mile = 1.609 kilometres
1 kilometre = 0.621 miles
Litres and gallons
1 gallon = 4.546 litres
1 litre = 0.220 gallons
Kilos and pounds
1 pound = 0.453 kilos
1 kilo = 2.204 pounds

Tourist Information

Tourist Offices Abroad

The official tourist authority, Visit Britain (www.visitbritain.com), has offices worldwide:
Australia
Level 16, Gateway, 1 Macquarie Place, Sydney, NSW 2000, tel: 02-9377 4400
Canada
5915 Airport Road, Suite 120, Mississauga, Ontario, L4V 1T1, tel: 1888 VISITUK
New Zealand
17th Floor, NZI House, 151 Queen Street, Auckland 1, tel: 9-303 1446
South Africa
PO Box 41896, Craighall 2024, tel: 11-325 0343
USA – Chicago
625 N. Michigan Avenue, Suite 1001,

don't tip in pubs, cinemas or theatres, but it is customary to give hairdressers, sightseeing guides and cab drivers a tip of around 10 percent.

Chicago, IL 60611, tel: 1-800 462 2748
USA – New York
7th Floor, 551 Fifth Avenue, New York, NY 10176, tel: 1-800 GO 2 BRIT or 212-986 2266.

Tourist Offices in London
Visit Scotland
19 Cockspur Street, London SW1Y 5BL, tel: 0845-225 5121; www.visit scotland.com.
Visit Wales Centre
Telephone line for ordering brochures, accommodation, booking and all general tourist information, tel: 08701-211 251; www.visitwales.com.
British Travel Centre
Britain and London Visitor Centre, 1 Regent Street, Piccadilly Circus, London SW1Y 4NS; www.visitbritain.com. Tickets for rail, air and sea travel and sightseeing tours can be bought from the travel-agency desk. The centre also has an internet lounge and a currency-exchange bureau. The centre is open 9.30am–6.30pm Mon,

9am–6.30pm Tue–Fri and 10am–4pm weekends (during summer it is open 9am–5pm Sat).

Regional Tourist Offices
There are more than 800 Tourist Information Centres (TICs) throughout Britain, which provide free information and advice on local sights, activities and accommodation. Most are open office hours, which are extended to include weekends and evenings in high season or in areas where there is a high volume of visitors all year round. Some close from October to March. TICs are generally well-signposted and denoted by a distinctive "i" symbol. The website www.visitbritain.com can be used to access information from regional tourist boards; just click on the relevant area of the map.

Visas and Passports

To enter the UK you need a valid passport (or any form of official identification if you are an EU citizen). Visas are not needed if you are an American, Commonwealth citizen or EU national (or come from most other European or South American countries). Health certificates are not required unless you have arrived from Asia, Africa or South America.

Send Us Your Thoughts

We do our best to ensure the information in our books is as accurate and up-to-date as possible. The books are updated on a regular basis using local contacts, who painstakingly add, amend and correct as required. However, some details (such as telephone numbers and opening times) are liable to change, and we are ultimately reliant on our readers to put us in the picture.
   We welcome your feedback, especially your experience of using the book "on the road". Maybe we recommended a hotel that you liked (or another that you didn't), or you came across a great bar or new attraction we missed.
   We will acknowledge all contributions, and we'll offer an Insight Guide to the best letters received.

Please write to us at:
   Insight Guides
   PO Box 7910
   London SE1 1WE
Or email us at:
   insight@apaguide.co.uk

BELOW: beer is still dispensed in pints, though wine measures are metric.

FURTHER READING

History

The Concise Pepys by Samuel Pepys. A first-hand account of the Great Fire of London and daily life in 17th-century England.
A History of Britain by Simon Schama. Enjoyable and richly illustrated romp through British history.
Living Back to Back by Chris Upton. An extraordinarily absorbing portrait of domestic life in the working-class districts of the industrial Midlands.
London: The Biography by Peter Ackroyd. Mammoth work on the great city, seen as a living organism.
Scotland: A Very Short Introduction by Rab Houston. An hugely readable and intelligent account of Scottish political, social and economic history.
Woodlands by Oliver Rackham. A fascinating history of Britain's landscape, focusing on its woodlands and forests.

Literature

The Adventures of Sherlock Holmes by Sir Arthur Conan Doyle. The Sherlock Holmes stories are wonderfully evocative of the London of the late 19th century.
Canterbury Tales by Geoffrey Chaucer. Written at the end of the 14th century, these stories provide a warm yet penetrating portrait of English society at the time.
Cider with Rosie by Laurie Lee. Spellbinding memoir of an idyllic youth in rural Gloucestershire in the 1920s.
How Green was My Valley by Richard Llewellyn. Story of a Welsh mining community, and a slice of social history.
Lorna Doone by R.D. Blackmore. The story of a tragic heroine and her lawless family on Exmoor.
The Mabinogion by Gywn Jones and Thomas Jones (translators). Eleven medieval stories from Wales.
The Mayor of Casterbridge by Thomas Hardy. Rural life and tragedy in the Wessex countryside.
Mrs Dalloway by Virginia Woolf. A day-in-the-life of an Edwardian matron in London.
Oliver Twist by Charles Dickens. The classic tale of Victorian pickpockets in London's East End.
On the Black Hill by Bruce Chatwin. Story of a family on a Welsh hill farm against the backdrop of 20th century history.
Pride and Prejudice by Jane Austen. Genteel society at the turn of the 19th century provided wonderful material for the wit and psychological insight of Jane Austen.
The Prime of Miss Jean Brodie by Muriel Spark. The story of a strong-willed Edinburgh schoolmistress.
A Shropshire Lad by A.E. Housman. Poems on the themes of Shropshire country life, and the life of a soldier.
Waverley by Sir Walter Scott. A gripping tale of Highland clans at the time of the Jacobite rising of 1745.
Westward Ho! by Charles Kingsley. Heroic tale of West Country seafarers.
Wuthering Heights by Emily Brontë. Passion and repression on the brooding Yorkshire Moors.
Under Milkwood by Dylan Thomas. Dreamlike "play for voices" set in an imaginary Welsh village.

Travel Writing

The Literary Guide to London by Ed Glinert. A detailed, street-by-street guide to the literary lives of London.
Vanishing Cornwall by Daphne du Maurier. A perceptive view of the changing face of Cornwall.
Waterlog: A Swimmer's Journey Through Britain by Roger Deakin. An eccentric travelogue, written with wit, style and humanity.
The Scottish Islands by Hamish Haswell-Smith. An encyclopedic guide to the geography, geology, wildlife and history of every Scottish Island.
Rodinsky's Room by Rachel Lichtenstein and Iain Sinclair. Psychogeography is at its very best in this narrative of a mysterious episode in London's East End.

Images of Britain

Derelict London by Paul Talling. The nostalgic snapshots in this original little book focus on the side of London few tourists see.
The Hebrideans by Gus Wylie. These photographs of the people of the Hebrides offer wit, warmth, narrative intrigue and great beauty.
In England by Don McCullin. An absolutely compelling portrait in pictures of the British people, from high society to low life.
The Last Resort by Martin Parr. A Magnum photographer presents a poignant and at times edgy view of the British themselves on holiday.
Once Upon a Time in Wales by Robert Haines. Only recently rediscovered pictures that bring back to life the forgotten world of industrial Wales in the 1970s.

Art and Architecture

Blimey! From Bohemia to Britpop by Matthew Collings. Funny, readable and copiously illustrated account of the London art world of the last few decades.
Charles Rennie Mackintosh by James Macaulay. Magisterial biography of the Scottish architect, designer and artist who was responsible for Glasgow School of Art and many other wonderful buildings.
The History of British Art: 1870–Now by David Bindman. Authoritative account of artists and movements, trends and themes in the art of the last 150 years.
The Regency Country House by John Martin Robinson. Beautiful photographs and lively text bring to life the world of the Prince Regent and his architects.

Other Insight Guides

The **Insight Guides** series includes books on *England, Scotland, Ireland* and *Oxford*, as well as *Best Hotels: Great Britain and Ireland*.
Insight Great Breaks series includes guides to every major holiday area in the UK, including *Cornwall, Cotswolds, Edinburgh, Glasgow, Oxford, York* and *Bath and Surroundings*, as well as popular national park titles such as *Devon and Exmoor, Lake District* and *Snowdonia*.
Insight Step by Step *London*, written by local experts, has 20 self-guided walks and tours, and includes a useful full-size fold-out map.

ART AND PHOTO CREDITS

INDEX

Main references are in bold type

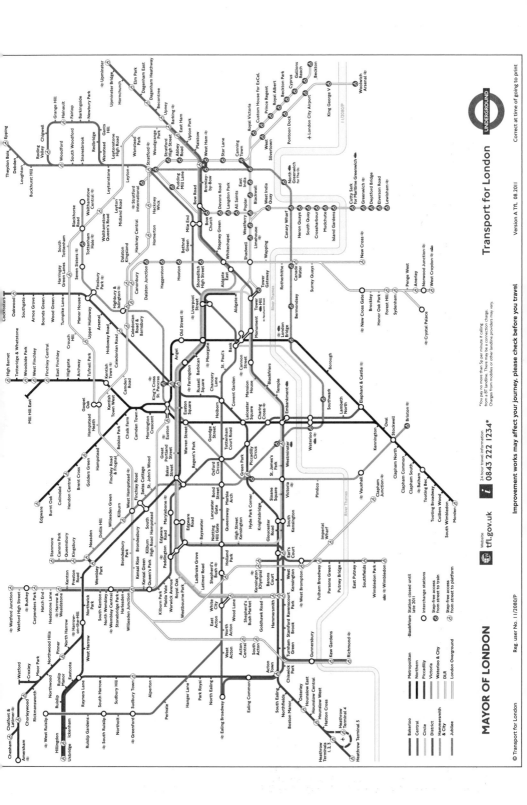